PLATO AND ARISTOTLE IN AGREEMENT?

OXFORD PHILOSOPHICAL MONOGRAPHS

OTHER TITLES IN THE SERIES INCLUDE

Kant's Empirical Realism
Paul Abela
Against Equality of Opportunity
Matt Cavanagh
Causality, Interpretation, and the Mind
William Child
Metaphor and Moral Experience
A. E. Denham
Semantic Powers
Meaning and the Means of Knowing in Classical Indian Philosophy
Jonardon Ganeri
Kant's Theory of Imagination
Bridging Gaps in Judgement and Experience
Sarah L. Gibbons
Of Liberty and Necessity
James A. Harris
The Grounds of Ethical Judgement
New Transcendental Arguments in Moral Philosophy
Christian Illies
Projective Probability
James Logue
Understanding Pictures
Dominic Lopes
Wittgenstein, Finitism, and the Foundations of Mathematics
Mathieu Marion
Truth and the End of Inquiry
A Peircean Account of Truth
C. J. Misak
The Good and the True
Michael Morris
Hegel's Idea of Freedom
Alan Patten
Nietzsche and Metaphysics
Peter Poellner
The Ontology of Mind
Events, Processes, and States
Helen Steward
Things that Happen Because They Should
A Teleological Approach to Action
Rowland Stout

Plato and Aristotle in Agreement?

Platonists on Aristotle from Antiochus to Porphyry

GEORGE E. KARAMANOLIS

CLARENDON PRESS · OXFORD

KH

OXFORD
UNIVERSITY PRESS

Great Clarendon Street, Oxford OX2 6DP

Oxford University Press is a department of the University of Oxford. It furthers the University's objective of excellence in research, scholarship, and education by publishing worldwide in

Oxford New York

Auckland Cape Town Dar es Salaam Hong Kong Karachi Kuala Lumpur Madrid Melbourne Mexico City Nairobi New Delhi Shanghai Taipei Toronto

With offices in

Argentina Austria Brazil Chile Czech Republic France Greece Guatemala Hungary Italy Japan Poland Portugal Singapore South Korea Switzerland Thailand Turkey Ukraine Vietnam

Oxford is a registered trade mark of Oxford University Press in the UK and in certain other countries

Published in the United States by Oxford University Press Inc., New York

First published 2006

British Library Cataloguing in Publication Data

Data available

Library of Congress Cataloguing in Publication Data

Data available

Typeset by SPI Publisher Services, Pondicherry, India
Printed in Great Britain
on acid-free paper by
Biddles Ltd., King's Lynn, Norfolk

ISBN 0–19–926456–2 978–0–19–926456–8

To my mother Anna
and
in memory of my father Emmanouil Karamanolis

Acknowledgements

This book is the revised version of my D.Phil. thesis which I submitted to the Faculty of Literae Humaniores of the University of Oxford in June 2001. During my graduate studies in Oxford, I was fortunate enough to be guided by Michael Frede, who went beyond his ordinary duties as a supervisor in order to teach me how to achieve clarity, precision, and philosophical sensitivity. Over the years he spared no time and energy in discussing various points of this project with me. Had he not done this much, I certainly would not have gone far with a topic which in retrospect I find tremendously difficult and complex. I would not have studied in Oxford, had I not had the good fortune to meet Averil Cameron who suggested that I should continue with my studies after I had finished a master's degree at King's College, London. As my tutor in Keble College, she encouraged and advised but also taught me how to be cautious in historical matters. The Greek State Foundation of Scholarships (IKY) funded me generously for three and a half years. Keble College, Oxford, provided a friendly ambience and helped financially and bibliographically.

Voula Kotzia suggested the topic, offered insights, and imparted faith that this may be a useful book. Richard Sorabji gave me the opportunity to present much of my work in his graduate seminars, and I benefited greatly from his knowledge and philosophical acumen. John Dillon and Mark Edwards examined the thesis and offered constructive criticism and encouragement to publish it as a monograph. The comments from two anonymous reviewers appointed by the Press have been extremely helpful. For further comments on parts of this book, I am indebted to Riccardo Chiaradonna, Eyjólfur Emillson, Pavlos Kalligas, Jan Opsomer, Bob Sharples, Anne Sheppard. James Ponczoch improved the style of several chapters. Chris Deliso undertook the burden of checking the style of my penultimate draft, helping me to be more succinct. I am particularly grateful to the philosophy editor, Peter Momtchiloff, and the staff of the OUP for their expert guidance and constant help at all stages of the preparation of this book. Finally, my parents have supported me in all possible ways. My mother has been caring, loving, and supportive, despite her wonder at how after so many years of study there still exist books which

I have not read. My father trusted that there certainly are. Unfortunately, he did not live to see this book finished. To my parents this book is dedicated.

Contents

Abbreviations

In the following I list the abbreviations of names, works, and editions which are most often referred to. The rest of my abbreviations for the most part follow the conventions of H. Liddell, R. Scott, and H. Jones, *A Greek–English Lexicon* (Oxford, 1940; 9th edn).

AGP	*Archiv für die Geschichte der Philosophie*
AJP	*American Journal of Philology*
ANRW	*Aufstieg und Niedergang der römischen Welt*
CAG	Commentaria in Aristotelem Graeca
CQ	*Classical Quarterly*
DG	H. Diels, *Doxographi Graeci* (Berlin, 1879).
DK	H. Diels and W. Kranz, *Die Fragmente der Vorsokratiker* (Berlin, 1934–7; 5th edn)
DL	Diogenes Laertius
E-K	I. Edelstein and I. G. Kidd (eds.), *Posidonius*, i–iii (Cambridge, 1972–99).
fr., frs.	fragment, fragments
GRBS	*Greek, Roman, and Byzantine Studies*
HSCPh	*Harvard Studies in Classical Philology*
JHS	*Journal of Hellenic Studies*
Index Acad.	Philodemus, *Index Academicorum*, ed. T. Dorandi, *Filodemo: Storia dei filosofi. Platone e l' Academia* (*PHerc.*1021 e 164). (Naples, 1991).
LSJ	H. Liddell, R. Scott, and H. Jones, *A Greek-English Lexicon* (Oxford, 1940; 9th edn).
OCT	Oxford Classical Texts
OLD	P. G. W. Glare, *Oxford Latin Dictionary* (Oxford, 1982).
OSAP	*Oxford Studies in Ancient Philosophy*
PE	Eusebius, *Praeparatio Evangelica*
PHP	Galen, *De placitis Hippocratis et Platonis*
RE	Pauly-Wissowa, *Real-Enzyclopädie der klassischen Altertumswissenschaft* (Stuttgart and Munich, 1894–1980).
SVF	H. von Arnim, *Stoicorum Veterum Fragmenta*, i–iii (Leipzig, 1903–5; vol. iv, index, compiled by M. Adler, 1924).
V. Plot.	Porphyry, *Vita Plotini*
Sent.	Porphyry, *Sententiae*
W	F. Wehrli, *Die Schule des Aristoteles*, i–x (Basel and Stuttgart, 1944–62).

Introduction

1. THE STUDY OF ARISTOTLE'S PHILOSOPHY BY PLATONISTS IN LATE ANTIQUITY

Anyone who begins to study the philosophy of late antiquity must find striking the fact that the known commentaries on Aristotle's works after AD 300 are written exclusively by Platonists.[1] Two important features make this fact particularly conspicuous. The first is that the practice of writing extensive commentaries on Aristotle's works had started, as we would expect, with the Peripatetics, and for a long time had remained their undisputed domain. The Peripatetics had been commenting on several Aristotelian works, especially the *Categories*, since the days of Andronicus, Boethus, and Aristo of Alexandria in the first century BC, but their exegetical activity culminated in the second century AD with Adrastus, Herminus, Aspasius, and especially with Alexander of Aphrodisias (*c.* AD 200). The three centuries following Alexander, however, were utterly bereft of Peripatetic commentators of any significance,[2] while many important Platonists devoted much of their time to writing commentaries on Aristotle.

Secondly, a telling indication of the Platonist preoccupation with commenting on Aristotle is the fact that the written work of several Platonists of this era (third–sixth centuries AD), such as Ammonius Hermeiou (435/45–517/26) and Simplicius (6th century),[3] consists largely of commentaries on Aristotle. What is remarkable here is not that these Platonists were engaged in writing commentaries. For

[1] For some basic information about the Greek commentators see Praechter (1909, 1910), whose views have been modified by I. Hadot (1978, 1991); see also Sorabji (1990: 1–30).

[2] With the possible exception of Themistius (*c.* 317–88); on him see Blumenthal (1990).

[3] On the commentaries of Ammonius and Simplicius and their attitude to Aristotle see Westerink (1990), I. Hadot (1978: 20–32) and Hoffmann (1987).

philosophers of late antiquity, commenting on ancient authorities both orally and in writing was the main way of doing philosophy. What is remarkable rather is that Platonists, who had been commenting on Plato since at least the time of Crantor (late fourth–early third century BC),[4] began around AD 300 to write commentaries on Aristotle quite systematically. And for some of them this became their main literary activity.

How and why did Aristotle become so important to the Platonists as to be considered an authority deserving extensive commentary? One may be tempted to think that Aristotle became a useful guide to Platonists in areas which Plato had insufficiently explored, such as biology, or, more generally, science and especially logic. This is true, at least so far as logic is concerned. A large number of Platonist commentaries are on the *Categories*, the *De interpretatione*, and the *Analytics*. Such a strong interest in logic is understandable in view of the fact that in late antiquity logic acquired educational value and became part of the syllabus.[5] However, the story here is more complex. Aristotle's logic, as expounded in one of his most popular works in late antiquity, the *Categories*, involves, as we know, metaphysical views quite different from those Plato had presented in his dialogues. Yet, judging by the activity of Platonist commentators, if there was one work which every Platonist in late antiquity had to study, it was the *Categories*. How, we wonder, did the *Categories* become such a basic text for Platonists to study, given its non-Platonic metaphysics?

Platonists also studied Aristotle's major works on the soul and on the universe, such as the *De anima* and the *De Caelo*, and wrote long commentaries on them.[6] In these works, however, Aristotle rejects several views which were subsequently regarded as the core of Plato's philosophy, most famously the view that the soul is immortal, and the idea that the universe had been created by a divine craftsman. How,

[4] Crantor commented on the *Timaeus* (Proclus, *In Tim.* 1. 76. 1–2), yet it is unclear in what form he did so, and we should not assume that he wrote a commentary like the late antique ones. See Ch. 7, pp. 324–5.

[5] See Clarke (1971: 2–7, 126) and Sandy (1997: 29–34). The Christian Origen included dialectic in his course of studies (Eusebius *Hist. Eccl.* 6. 18. 3), while both Gellius and Apuleius seem to have learnt logic (Gellius, *NA.* 15. 26, 16. 8, Apuleius, *Florida* 20).

[6] One must bear in mind that several commentaries have been lost. Like Simplicius, Syrianus also wrote commentaries on the *De caelo* and the *De anima*, yet they do not survive; see Praechter (1926); Cardullo (1986).

then, did Platonists committed to Plato's philosophy come to find Aristotle's views worthy of study?

The question becomes more pressing given that, for Platonists of all ages, and especially for those of late antiquity, nothing which was considered to be systematically contradictory to, or critical of, Plato could be acceptable, let alone philosophically important and beneficial, precisely because Plato enjoyed an enormous authority and his philosophy was taken for truth. Any philosophical activity aiming to refute or to criticize Plato was assumed a priori to be mistaken or not even worthy of the name of philosophy. Apparently the Platonists who did study Aristotle regarded him as being neither systematically nor radically in conflict with Plato.

In fact, it turns out that the majority of Platonists in this era shared the view that Aristotle's philosophy, when understood in the right spirit, is essentially compatible with Plato's doctrine, as they interpreted it. Platonists actually maintained that the core of Aristotle's philosophy both supports and complements Plato's philosophy, and this, they argued, was not accidental. If it were, it could neither be helpful in the study of philosophy nor of particular importance, and thus hardly worthy of systematic study. When confronted with contradictions between Aristotle and Plato, Platonists argued that such contradictions were only apparent, the results of uncritical focus on the letter and not the real spirit of the texts.[7] And they explicitly stated that Aristotle's works were both useful and philosophically important for a Platonist.[8] For this reason, such a study, they believed, had to be done in a systematic and proper way.

This means at least two things. First, Aristotle's work was assigned a definite place in the Platonist philosophical curriculum. Platonists wrote introductions (*Prolegomena*) in which they gave an overview of Aristotle's philosophical work and explained how his philosophy is to be studied. Thus Aristotle's treatises were integrated in the context of such a curriculum.[9] What is more, the study of Aristotle was a requirement which had to be fulfilled early, because it was considered preparatory for

[7] See Simplicius, *In Cat.* 6. 7–18, 7. 23–32, *In De caelo* 454. 23–4, 640. 27–8, Philoponus, *In de anima* 10. 8–12. 12, Olympiodorus, *Proleg.* 4. 3–15, *In Met.* 7. 21–30. See Blumenthal (1986: 92–7).

[8] See Ammonius, *In Cat.* 6. 9–16, Simplicius, *In Cat.* 6. 6–15, 13. 27–8. Olympiodorus, *Proleg.* 9. 14–30, 22. 3–12 Elias, *In Cat.* 132. 5–21.

[9] See e.g. Ammonius, *In Cat.* 7. 15–13. 11, Simplicius, *In Cat.* 3. 18–6. 18. See Westerink (1990: 341–7) and esp. Plezia (1949: 70–81), who lists all the relevant references.

the study of Plato's philosophy,[10] the final aim for any serious Platonist. Second, students were guided and assisted in their study of Aristotle. This was done in two main ways. First, as was the case with Plato's dialogues, Platonist teachers suggested a certain order in which their students should read Aristotle's works so that they could make progress. As their divisions of Aristotle's works suggest, they considered his philosophy to form a system (e.g. Simplicius, *In Cat.* 4. 10–5. 2). But unlike Andronicus' systematization of Aristotle's writings, this system was devised specifically for Platonists.[11] Second, Platonists assisted their students by either lecturing or writing commentaries on Aristotle. Often we find that these merely reproduce their oral teaching in their schools in Athens or Alexandria.[12] It thus becomes clear that the existence of so many commentaries by Platonists is to meet a perceived need in the envisioned philosophical curriculum, which was the study of Aristotle.

It is not, then, the case that some Platonists from the third to sixth century AD studied Aristotle's philosophy for its own sake. Rather, Aristotle was appropriated by Platonists because they found his philosophy, if properly studied, a prerequisite for, and conducive to, an understanding of Plato's thought. And as I. Hadot has argued convincingly, amending Praechter's earlier view, Alexandrian Platonists (Ammonius, Philoponus, Olympiodorus, David, Elias) also approached Aristotle in the same way as did Athenian Platonists (e.g. Simplicius).[13] The extant commentaries on Aristotle, then, are merely the tip of an iceberg. They testify to a systematic study of Aristotle and also to the existence of a certain prevailing ideology concerning his philosophy, namely that it is essentially in accord with that of Plato. Of course this ideology, however dominant, was discussed and challenged among Platonists. Syrianus, Proclus, and Philoponus are examples of Platonists who questioned aspects of it and criticized several Aristotelian doctrines in their work. But they were also thoroughly familiar with Aristotle's work, and showed considerable respect for it.[14] From what we know,

[10] Syrianus, we are told (Marinus, *V. Procli* 13), guided Proclus to read within two years the entire work of Aristotle, and thus introduced him through it to Plato's metaphysics. See Saffrey (1990: 176–9); I. Hadot (1991: 176–87).

[11] Cf. Ammonius, *In Cat.* 4. 28–5. 30; Olympiodorus *In Cat.* 7. 24–9. 13; Philoponus, *In Cat.* 7. 1–8. 22; Elias, *In Cat.* 113. 17–119. 25. See I. Hadot (1987*b*).

[12] See Richard (1950: 191–222); cf. Clarke (1971: 106–7).

[13] I. Hadot (1991: 176–8). See also Westerink (1990).

[14] Syrianus finds it crucial to make clear that, despite his argument against some of Aristotle's metaphysical views, especially his criticism of the Pythagorean metaphysics, he admires his logic, ethics, and physics (*In Met.* 80. 4–81. 14). Proclus studied Aristotle extensively along with Plato, as his biographer Marinus tells us (*V. Procli* 9. 12–14); see Saffrey (1990). For Philoponus' attitude to Aristotle see Verrycken (1990).

almost all Platonists agreed that Aristotle's logic, which included his theory of the categories, does not contradict Plato's ontology and is philosophically valuable. Yet for most Platonists Aristotle was important in several other areas. So the Platonists of that time quite generally acknowledged Aristotle as another, albeit limited, authority next to Plato. In their view, Aristotle is an authority in a weak sense; they tend to give credit to some of his doctrines after examining its merits, while Plato comes out as the stronger authority. For dyed-in-the-wool Platonists, all he says is true, and their interpretations of his doctrines strive to prove exactly that.

Our initial questions now become more pressing and well defined. First, how did Aristotle become such an authority for the Platonists, given their commitment to Plato's philosophy? Second, what precisely did the study of Aristotle offer to them?

In order to answer these questions, we have to go back to the period from Antiochus to Porphyry. It was at this time that Aristotle started to be treated as an authority next to Plato. This tendency on the part of some Platonists triggered a heated discussion among them about the value of Aristotle's philosophy, which lasted for four centuries (first century BC–third century AD). Given that for them Plato's philosophy was the measure against which everything was judged, they had to discuss Aristotle's philosophy in the context of its agreement or non-agreement with that of Plato. It is this discussion on which my book focuses. In order to understand how it arose, we first have to address the question of what Aristotle had to offer to Platonists.

2. WHY ARISTOTLE? THE PROBLEM OF RECONSTRUCTING PLATO'S PHILOSOPHY

Ancient Platonism is characterized by one crucial feature: the paradoxical tension between Plato's way of philosophizing, and the way Platonists tended to consider the man and his work. And since this is a book about ancient Platonism we should be clear from the start about the distinction between *Platonic* (i.e. Plato's) philosophy and *Platonist* interpretations of it. Plato, as we know, deliberately chose a special way of writing philosophy, through dialogues, which precluded making authoritative statements. Nowhere does Plato profess to tell us his own specific view on any given topic—in fact, he never appears as an interlocutor in his dialogues. He rather presents arguments which are discussed, challenged, refuted, or revised either in the same or in a subsequent dialogue. Even if one believes that this or the other view is right, or the one that Plato actually believed, yet the reader is continuously reminded of problems and complications concerning such a view, and is thus invited to continue the inquiry.

Apart from their very form, Platonic dialogues also contain some other indications to the effect that neither the theories nor the views put forward in them should be taken as authoritative. To take the example of Plato's most popular dialogue in late antiquity, the *Timaeus*, the speaker, Timaeus, warns the audience that he will offer only a 'likely account' (*Timaeus* 29d2), not secure knowledge.[15] To take another example from a dialogue that was intently studied in late antiquity, in the first part of the *Parmenides*, the speaker, Parmenides, is presented as a severe critic of the theory of Forms, as we know it from the *Phaedo* and the *Republic*. Objections against the same theory are raised also in the *Sophist* (248a–251c). Such evidence suggests that if there was one thing that Plato wanted to deter by all means, it was the reading of his dialogues as authoritative documents in which specific doctrines are defended. Rather, he wanted to make people think about the problems examined in the dialogues and the arguments presented in them.[16]

Platonists, however, invested Plato and his work with an enormous authority immediately after his death. And as is usually the case, the need for authority goes along with requirements for commitment. This is commitment in a strict and rather technical sense. Ancient philosophers had a strong notion of allegiance to their philosophical schools, something that would become even stronger in the Hellenistic period.[17] Their membership in such a school carried with it a special sense of commitment to the thought of their school authority or authorities: doing philosophy largely amounted to elaborating on the thought of these authorities. But given Plato's way of philosophizing, one wonders

[15] Scholars have been divided on the question of whether *Timaeus*'s account is fiction or not. Vlastos (1975: 95–6), for instance, wonders: 'once you renounce hope of attaining knowledge in your theories about the natural universe, would you still have good reason to engage in such theorizing?' Why not?

[16] In Philodemus' *Index Acad.* Plato is presented as an architect of problems . . . *καὶ τῶν μα|θημάτων ἐπίδοσις πολλὴ κατ' ἐκεῖ|ν[ον] τὸν χρόνον, ἀρχιτεκτονοῦντο[ς]|| μ[ὲ]ν καὶ προβλήματ[α] διδόντος τοῦ | Π[λ]άτωνος* . . . (col. Y Dorandi). The source of this passage may well be Dicaearchus. See Appendix I, p. 335 n. 28. See Frede (1992) for a similar interpretation of Plato's arguments and the dialogue form.

[17] On this matter see Sedley (1989).

what the Platonists were committed to, and what they considered Plato to be authoritative about.

For all we know, Platonists attributed to Plato specific views from a very early stage, that is from his first successors in the Academy, Speusippus and Xenocrates. Although the evidence about them is limited and second-hand, it quite clearly emerges that they first set out to clarify and develop Plato's thought as reflected in the dialogues, and this process involved attempts to specify what Plato's views on certain issues were. One reason for such attempts was the fact that Plato was criticized, most notably by Aristotle, for views he had argued for in his dialogues. The Academics, being motivated by a sense of loyalty to Plato, engaged themselves in defending the views presented in his dialogues, which Aristotle criticized, by showing what these views actually amounted to and how they should be understood. But they did so exactly because they assumed that some of the views discussed in Plato's dialogues are Plato's own doctrines[18] and, as a result, they treated Aristotle's criticisms of them as a threat.

This seems to be the case especially with Xenocrates, whose opinions seem to have often been shaped in response to Aristotle.[19] His interpretation of Forms, for instance, is likely to have been provoked by the wish to defend Plato against the attacks of Aristotle (fr. 30 Heinze). Yet Xenocrates also assumed the existence of aether like Aristotle did (fr. 53 Heinze). This should not necessarily be taken as an agreement with Aristotle, since Plato himself refers to aether,[20] but it is reasonable to assume that Xenocrates considered Aristotle's relevant doctrine for his interpretation of Plato. Such evidence suggests some tension between the early Academy and Aristotle, and perhaps even some rivalry. It may have something to do with their different attitudes to Plato's philosophy. Presumably Aristotle was not motivated by a similar sense of loyalty to Plato as Xenocrates, but rather considered his criticism of Plato's views as a means of continuing Plato's spirit of philosophical inquiry.[21] The

[18] The dogmatic character of the philosophy of the early Academics is suggested by their treatment by Antiochus who, as I will argue in Ch. 1, tried to reconstruct Plato's doctrines relying partly on them. See Dillon (1977: 11–39) for an overview of the evidence about their philosophy and now Dillon (2003).

[19] Xenocrates is attested to have divided philosophy in three parts (Sextus, *Adv. Math.* 7. 16), which is indicative of a certain attempt to credit Plato with a system of philosophy; see Dillon (2003: 98–155) and below p. 14 n. 40.

[20] *Timaeus* 58d1–2; *Phaedo* 109b9. On the Platonic credentials of aether see further Ch. 2, p. 104.

[21] On this see my discussion in Appendix I.

tension between the early Academy and Aristotle seems to be resolved, at least partly, in the work of Xenocrates' successor, Polemo, who appears to have absorbed much from Aristotle.[22] Yet in general the concern of the early Academics to advocate Plato's views by fending off Aristotle's criticisms led them to treat Aristotle's philosophy in ways which ranged from suspicion to caution.

Things changed quite dramatically three centuries later. Antiochus of Ascalon (*c.*130–68 BC) was also concerned with defending Plato's views, but did not hesitate to approve openly of Aristotle's philosophy, notably being the first Platonist to do so. He argued that Aristotle had basically followed Plato's philosophy, as he understood it (Cicero, *Acad.* 1. 17–18, 2. 15, *De fin.* 5. 7). This was an amazing claim for a Platonist to make. One wonders how Antiochus came to make such a claim, how he understood Plato's thought, and why his interest in Aristotle's philosophy arose at all. These are crucial questions. To answer them, we need some background information.

With the succession of Arcesilaus around 273 BC the philosophical viewpoint of the Academy changed radically. According to Arcesilaus, Plato did not commit himself to any definite views which should be then defended by his successors. In his view, Plato was a sceptic, which means that Plato's philosophy essentially consisted in examining philosophical questions dialectically without ever reaching final conclusions. For Arcesilaus the only correct appreciation of Plato's thought was to retain his sceptical spirit and to apply it to all philosophical questions.[23] Arcesilaus' successors consolidated the sceptical interpretation of Plato which became canonical in the Academy until the time of Philo of Larissa (scholarch, 110 to *c.* 87/6 BC). Presumably even in this period there were Platonists who rejected scepticism and preferred a dogmatic Plato instead, but they were rather marginalized and remained an anonymous minority. This minority is likely to have found expression in the Pythagorean treatises of the Hellenistic period, which have strong Platonist content and in a sense continue the Pythagorean interpretation of Plato initiated by Speusippus and Xenocrates.[24]

[22] Polemo's testimonies have been collected by M. Gigante, *Polemonis Academici Fragmenta* (Naples, 1977). For a discussion of his ethics, see Ch. 1, pp. 73, 77.

[23] Reports of Arcesilaus' position include Cicero *Acad.* 1. 43–6, 2. 66–7, 2. 76–7 Plutarch *Adv. Col.* 1120C, 1121E–1122A, DL 4. 28–43, Sextus, *PH* 1. 232–4. See Long-Sedley (1987: i. 438–60). On the sceptical interpretation of Plato there is a rich literature. I single out Long (1986: 88–106) and Annas (1992).

[24] See Burkert (1962: 83–4).

The dogmatic interpretation of Plato returns visibly with Antiochus. For some time a disciple of Philo, Antiochus originally espoused Philo's sceptical Platonism. Around 95 BC Philo came to maintain a weak scepticism allowing for the adherence to beliefs concerning not only practical issues but also philosophical questions. His position, however, satisfied neither sceptical nor dogmatic Platonists. Members of both camps reacted against him and left the Academy.[25] Antiochus in particular seceded and returned to the dogmatic interpretation of Plato's philosophy. His secession marked the end of a long argument with Philo, which I outline briefly in Chapter 1. The crucial point to stress here is the one which Antiochus felt strongly about, namely that the sceptical interpretation of Plato's philosophy, which dominated the Academy for two centuries, rested on the mistake of taking Plato's non-dogmatic way of writing philosophy as suggesting a sceptic philosophical profile. Antiochus rather argues that Plato had specific doctrines and his philosophy indeed constitutes a dogmatic system to which the early Academics and Peripatetics were loyal (*Acad.* 2. 15). But if Plato had doctrines, what were they?

As I have already alluded to, Plato's thought is elusive, if one confines oneself to the dialogues, since they do not offer us direct expression of his views. Rather, they are sophisticated literary monuments in which Plato raises basic philosophical problems and shows ways to argue about them. Yet they hardly contain clear solutions to these problems, let alone offer doctrines. Many dialogues investigating questions such as what is x (e.g. justice, virtue), how we know anything, and what counts as knowledge, end in *aporia*, in puzzlement. Besides, several arguments in them are clearly not endorsed, they are purely dialectical. What is more, in every dialogue Plato reveals his thought only partially, and his approach to a problem differs from one dialogue to another. If one confines oneself to the *Theaetetus*, for instance, one never learns what Plato's position about knowledge is, as all three suggestions offered in the *Theaetetus* are refuted by Socrates. If Plato's view is to be sought in another dialogue, like the *Sophist* or the *Philebus*, how can one justify that this dialogue rather than any other preserves it?

The question of how Plato's thought developed is a complicated matter which has puzzled ancient and modern Platonic scholarship.[26] Clearly, though, Plato tries different approaches revising his point of

[25] From the sceptical camp, it was Aenesidemus who left the Academy. See Ch. 1, pp. 49–50.

[26] For a brief survey see Kraut (1992: 9–20).

view, sometimes going against positions which he seems to have adopted in earlier dialogues. I have already referred to the theory of Forms as presented in the *Phaedo* and the *Republic* against Plato's arguments in the *Parmenides* and the *Sophist.* Another example is the question of the first principle. Here one is confronted with several possibilities for elucidating what Plato believes about it; the Form of the Good in *Republic* 6, the One in the first hypothesis of the *Parmenides*, the demiurge in the *Timaeus*. Platonists in late antiquity devoted much of their attention to this question and disagreed with each other about which one is the first principle and how it relates to the others. As regards the theory of knowledge, Plato in the *Meno* presents us with an apparently successful account of knowledge as a species of correct belief (*doxa*), the result of recollection and guidance by a teacher like Socrates, in the *Republic* he makes no reference to recollection and seems to highlight the gap between knowledge and belief, while in the *Theaetetus*, we are confronted with an acknowledged failure to find out what knowledge truly is.

Plato's approaches to questions about the soul also seem to elicit considerably different answers. In the *Republic* (439d–443b) we are told that the soul consists of three parts, the rational, the spirited, and the appetitive, in the *Phaedrus* (246a–247c) it is implied that the soul has four parts, the charioteer, the good horse, the bad horse, and the chariot, while in the *Politicus* 309c and in the *Timaeus* (65a, 69c–e) the soul is divided in two parts or genres, one immortal and another mortal.

This material gives rise to two related questions. The first is whether the intellect is part of the soul, as *Republic* 4 suggests, an instrument of the soul ('the eye of the soul; *Republic* 533d2), or distinct from it, as the *Phaedrus* (247b–c) and the *Sophist* (249a) appear to suggest. The second, related to the previous one, is whether the entire soul is immortal or only the intellect. As has been noted, even within the *Phaedo* there is support for both answers,[27] so the question would vex Platonists in late antiquity. Confronted with such diversity of views, even the assumption that Platonists in late antiquity often made, that Plato reveals his views through specific speakers,[28] does not help much, since in other dialogues, or even within the same one, one of these

[27] In *Phaedo* 81c8–e3 the immortality seems to extend to all conscious activities of the soul, while in 65a8–d3, 81b1–8, 83b3–c2 it applies only to the intellect. See Bostock (1986: 22–35). The latter view is also found in *Timaeus* 41c6–7, and is implied in *Republic* 611b–e and in *Sophist* 249a–b.

[28] See DL 3. 52; cf. Sextus *PH* 1. 221.

speakers appears to take a different position on a certain issue, and also because clearly Plato often takes some distance from the views of his characters, however much he likes them (e.g. Socrates). Because of this richness and diversity of positions, Plato's philosophical work as a whole strongly resists systematization, however much interpreters, from antiquity to the present, try to impose it.[29]

Antiochus is the first of a series of Platonists who undertook the tantalizing task of constructing a philosophical system from Plato's works, and he seems well aware of the difficulties inherent in it. He hints at this when claiming that Plato 'was a thinker of variety, complexity and fertility' (*Acad.* 1. 17).[30] In his view, though, the variety, diversity, and richness of views expressed in the dialogues do not suggest that Plato had resisted committing himself to doctrines, as the sceptic Academics thought, but rather reflect Plato's resourcefulness. However difficult this feature makes the reconstruction of Plato's doctrines, yet Antiochus is convinced that such doctrines exist and do form a system, and that the dialogue form is just a literary device by means of which Plato conceals them.[31]

But why was he, let alone later Platonists, convinced that such a doctrinal system existed at all? The reason for this is an assumption which is very pronounced in Antiochus' mind, that any philosopher worthy of the name,

[29] See, for instance, the modern attempts by Irwin (1995) and Annas (1999). Both make quite strong assumptions about the sources through which Plato's doctrine can be reconstructed. See below nn. 50, 77.

[30] Other Platonists talk similarly. In a passage which may reflect Taurus, Aulus Gellius argues about Plato's discussion of pleasure as follows: *Plato ante hos omnis ita varie et multiformiter de voluptate disseruit, ut cunctae istae sententiae, quas supra posui, videantur ex sermonum eius fontibus profluxuisse* (*NA* 9. 5. 7; Taurus fr. 18 Gioè). (Before all these Plato talked about pleasure in so many and varied ways that all those opinions I have presented above [of Epicurus, Zeno, Antisthenes, Speussipus, Critolaus], seem to have flowed from the founts of his discourses.)

[31] The view of Antiochus and later dogmatic Platonists has been maintained by a part of modern Platonic scholarship, pre-eminently by the partisans of an esoteric Plato. H. Krämer, for instance, writes about Plato's dialogues: 'Was dort an Lehren vorgetragen wird, erscheint in dialogischer Verkleidung und wird außerdem eingeschränkt und oft wieder aufgehoben durch die Aporien der Schlüsse, die Ironie und Distanzierung des Gesprächführers und dergleichen.' (What is introduced as doctrines appears in dialogue cloth, and on the top of that the doctrinal account is restrained and often demolished again through the aporetic conclusions, the irony, the distance of the main speakers and other features of the same kind.) H. Krämer, 'Die Platonische Akademie und das Problem einer systematischen Interpretation der Philosophie Platons', in K. Gaiser (ed.), *Das Platonbild* (Darmstadt 1969), 198. This interpretation of Plato's philosophy was already espoused by Leibniz, Kantian philosophers like G. Tennemann, and Hegel. On this interpretation of Plato see Tigerstedt (1974: 64–8).

let alone one of Plato's calibre, must have a system (cf. *Acad.* 2. 27–9). How did Antiochus come to make such an assumption?

We first must remember that the two most popular schools on the philosophical scene at his time were Stoicism and Epicureanism. Unlike their contemporary Academy, these schools considered philosophy to be a system of doctrines. This belief has much to do with their conception of philosophy as, above all, an art of living. This means that for them ethics was the most crucial part of philosophy to which all others were subordinate, in the sense that any philosophical consideration should bear on the question of how we should live.[32] This attitude was rooted first in the conviction that the principal use of all knowledge is to be applied to, and make a difference in, practical life, secondly in the belief that man needs to have secure knowledge of many things in order to be able to live a good life, and third in the view that man has the potential to acquire such knowledge. Man must be able, for instance, to know with certainty what is good or right in order to pursue it systematically, because, they claimed, otherwise one cannot achieve a good life. But this is a rather advanced kind of knowledge which presupposes the knowledge of more basic things, such as what are the things that we perceive. On this view, philosophy as an art of living must have its own doctrines like all theoretical or theoretically based arts, such as geometry, astronomy, and medicine.[33]

In Stoicism, which had a particularly strong impact on Antiochus, the rationale behind such an idea seems to be roughly the following. The universe is permeated by concrete rational laws which God, being identical with reason, had established. These laws also concern humans who are part of the universe. Since humans are rational, they, by using

[32] Seneca argues that *Philosophia studium virtutis est, sed per ipsam virtutem; nec virtus autem esse sine studio sui potest nec virtutis studium sine ipsa... cohaerent inter se philosophia virtusque.* (Philosophy is the study of virtue, by means, however, of virtue itself; but neither can virtue exist without the study of itself, nor can the study of virtue exist without virtue itself... philosophy and virtue cling closely together; *Epist.* 89. 8; tr. Gummere). Cf. Cicero, *Nat. D.* 1. 7.

[33] *nulla ars contemplativa sine decretis suis est, quae Graeci vocant dogmata, nobis vel decreta licet appelare vel scita vel placita, quae et in geometria et in astronomia invenies. Philosophia autem et contemplativa est et activa; spectat simul agitque* (no art that concerns itself with theories can exist without its own doctrines; the Greeks call them *dogmas,* while we Romans may use the term 'doctrines' or 'tenets', or 'adopted principles', such as you will find in geometry or astronomy. But philosophy is both theoretic and practical; it contemplates and at the same time acts; Seneca, *Epist.* 95. 10; tr. Gummere). Philosophy is described as *vitae dux* (*Tusc. Disp.* 5. 5), *lex vitae* (2. 11), *ars vitae* (2. 12; *De fin.* 3. 4), *vivendi ars* (*De fin.* 5. 16; *Acad.* 2. 23).

their reason, must discover these laws and comply with them, if they want to live a happy or good life (*eudaimonia*). For the Stoics such life is nothing more than compliance with universal laws—or as they put it 'accordance with nature'. And philosophy is viewed as the business of working out these laws. The philosopher is the person whose understanding of how things are in the world brings him to achieve knowledge of them (*sciens*); he knows why he must conform to them, and he actually does so, thus reaching the stage of wisdom (*sapiens*) towards which all philosophy allegedly aims (*Tusc. Disp.* 2. 11–12, *Acad.* 2. 30–1).

The Greek and Latin terms for 'doctrine' are indicative of this background. The Greek *dogma* suggests that something has been settled by rational decision,[34] and like the Latin *decretum* has connotations of legislation.[35] The *decreta* or *dogmata* are rules imposed by an authority, a legislator, or an assembly, having the right and the ability to legislate. The philosopher is like the legislator; he sets laws crucial for leading a good life, that is, he creates a system of doctrines which enable the attainment of good life.[36] This conception of philosophy as a doctrinal system also entailed a definite idea as to what the teaching of philosophy was about. According to this idea, it amounts to imparting to students the tenets of the school authority, which would help them to make sense of reality and, most especially, in the light of this, to lead good lives.[37]

It is this largely Stoic view about the nature and the teaching of philosophy that Antiochus shared. This should not surprise us. Aside from Epicureanism, Stoicism was the modern philosophy of the time. Academics in particular had been well acquainted with it, and despite having a long rivalry with Stoicism, they were indeed much influenced by it, availing themselves of Stoic terms and concepts, and to some extent tried to accommodate themselves to Stoic views. Such a tendency is visible in Antiochus' teacher, Philo, who, as is known, was greatly indebted to Stoic ethics (see Ch.1, p. 50). This development is actually quite understandable. At the time of Philo, Academics were concerned with the consistency of the sceptical stance in practice and with the

[34] See e.g. *Laws* 926d2; cf. LSJ, s.v.

[35] See *Acad.* 2. 27, 29, Seneca *Epist.* 95. 60–1; cf. *OLD* s.v. (meaning 3).

[36] *αὐτὸ τοίνυν τὸ δογματίζειν ἐστὶ δόγματα τιθέναι ὡς τὸ νομοθετεῖν νόμους τιθέναι* (to be a dogmatist in philosophy is to lay down positive dogmas, as to be a legislator is to lay down laws; tr. by Hicks; DL 3. 51). Atticus argues that Aristotle is not a philosopher, but a scientist, and thus it is not his business to determine the universal laws (*νομοθετεῖν*; fr. 5. 13–15 Des Places); see Ch. 4, pp. 174–7.

[37] For the implications of this idea on the teaching of philosophy in late antiquity see Donini (1994).

possibility of holding opinions on philosophical issues, and several views were in circulation. Antiochus came to argue that Philo was as inconsistent as the Stoics; the former mixed scepticism with Plato's doctrines, while the latter created a doctrinal system adapting that of Plato, but on several important points they deviated from Plato.[38] For Antiochus both Philo and the Stoics had betrayed Plato's philosophy, that is, Plato's actual doctrines, as he understood them.

Nevertheless, Antiochus' understanding of Platonic philosophy was inspired by the Stoic conception of philosophy as a system comprising three parts, ethics, physics, and logic, and he divided Plato's philosophy accordingly.[39] Antiochus may have argued that already the early Academics applied this division to Plato's philosophy. We do not know with certainty whether Antiochus was right about this.[40] What we do know is that in the subsequent centuries the majority of Platonists, starting with Eudorus, follow Antiochus in considering Plato's philosophy as such a system of doctrines covering all major philosophical issues.[41] And like Antiochus, later Platonists, for the most part, appear to maintain that, despite the diversity of views represented in Plato's work, Plato held certain doctrines on any given issue, which they set out to specify.[42] These Platonists show little interest in *how* Plato argues but rather in *what* he argues for. The thesis of Owen, shared by many scholars today,

[38] *Acad.* 1. 43, 2. 15; *De fin.* 4. 60, 5. 22; cf. Ch. 1, pp. 51–9.

[39] *Fuit ergo iam accepta a Platone philosophandi ratio triplex, una de vita et moribus, altera de natura et rebus occultis, tertia de disserendo et quid verum, quid falsum, quid rectum in oratione pravumve, quid consentiens, quid repugnans esset iudicando* (There already existed, then, a threefold scheme of philosophy inherited from Plato: one division dealt with conduct and morals, the second with the secrets of nature, the third with dialectic and with the judgement of truth and falsehood, correctness and incorrectness, consistency and inconsistency in rhetorical discourse; tr. Rackham; *Acad.* 1. 19). In *De fin.* 5. 9–11, though, the order is 'physics, logic, ethics'. This order is that of the Peripatetic system, as is also that of Philo, as Boyance (1971: 130) argued, while in his view the order in *Acad.* 1. 19 and *De leg.* 1. 58–62 is Antiochean.

[40] Sextus reports that Xenocrates, the Peripatetics, and the Stoics adopted the threefold division of philosophy which they inherited from Plato (*Adv. Math.* 7. 16; *SVF* ii. 38); see Dillon (2003: 98–9). Plutarch reports that Crysippus admitted that the threefold division of philosophy goes back to the 'ancients' (*De Stoic. Rep.* 1035A; *SVF* ii. 42). Diogenes Laertius 7. 39 (*SVF* ii. 37), on the other hand, argues that Zeno was the first to divide philosophy in three parts, but it is ambiguous whether he means the first philosopher or the first Stoic. See also the remarks by Boyance (1971: 137–44).

[41] Eudorus in Stobaeus 2. 42. 7–13 (fr. 1 Mazzarelli); Atticus fr. 1 Des Places; Apuleius, *De Platone et eius dogmate* 1. 3, 187–8 Beaujeu; Alcinous, *Didascalicos*, ch. 3, 153. 25–154. 9 Hermann, DL 3. 56, Aristocles fr. 1. 17–53 Heiland (cf. also *Suda*, s.v. Plato; see below pp. 37–8). See Dörrie–Baltes (1996), Bausteine 101. 1–101. 5, pp. 205–30.

[42] Plato was considered to be *polyphonos* but not *polydoxos* (Stobaeus 2. 49. 25–50. 1, 2. 55. 5–7). On the meaning and the implications of this statement see Annas (1999: 14–15).

according to which Plato's main goal was to find ways to tackle philosophical problems rather than to come to finalized views, was rarely upheld in late antiquity.[43]

Given their conception of Plato's philosophy, the task that Platonists set themselves was to reconstruct and systematize Plato's doctrines. Indeed, Antiochus seems to consider this as the very task of a Platonist (*Acad.* 1. 19–33) and plenty of evidence shows that the late antique teaching of Plato's philosophy involved training in working out Plato's doctrines. Diogenes Laertius 3. 66 and a papyrus dated to the second century AD (PSI 1488) lay out specific signs that the student of Plato should use for indicating the doctrines of Plato (*diplê*) and the agreement of his doctrines (the asterisk).[44] Such teaching of Plato was assisted by writing summaries of Plato's doctrines, like Alcinous' *Didascalicos* or Apuleius' *De Platone et eius dogmate.* Nevertheless Platonists are aware of the severe difficulties that the reconstruction of Plato's doctrine presents. Like Antiochus (*Acad.* 1. 17), probably also Taurus (in Gellius, *NA* 9. 5. 7) stressed Plato's diversity, while Plutarch, Ammonius Saccas (as I will argue), Plotinus, and Porphyry highlighted Plato's obscure or enigmatic thought and expression.[45]

One way in which Platonists tried to overcome such difficulties was by relying on the statements of philosophers who were indebted to Plato's thought. For Platonists of this stripe the statements of authors contemporaneous with the master were as valuable to knowledge of Plato's philosophy as were the dialogues, if not more so, since they solve the mystery of what Plato really believed. Authors of such statements were thought to be part of the 'Platonist tradition', which helps to understand Plato, as, in a similar sense, the Apostolic tradition sheds light on Jesus' teaching.

But who qualifies to be considered as part of the 'Platonist tradition'? Platonists disagreed on who is part of this tradition and who falls

[43] See mainly Owen (1986) and his 'Notes on Ryle's Plato' in his *Logic, Science and Dialectic* (London, 1986), 84–103. Even the Anonymous, *In Theaetetus* 59. 8–17, who is closer to a sceptical interpretation of Plato, claims that Plato shows through his criticisms the view he prefers: τοῖς μέντοι ἐμπείροις[τῆς] μεθόδου λεληθό[τως] δεικνύει τὸ ἑαυτῷ [ἀ]ρέσκον. Sceptical Platonism did not altogether disappear in this period. But as the example of the Anonymous suggests, it was quite a mitigated sceptical Platonism, much softer than the Academic one. See Opsomer (1999) for a good discussion of the varieties of sceptical Platonism in late antiquity.

[44] See M. Gigante 'Un papiro attribuibile ad Antigono di Caristo? PSI 1488, *Vite dei Filosofi*', *Papiri Filosofici Miscellanea di Studi II* (Florence, 1998), 111–14.

[45] They argued that Plato speaks with riddles. See Ch. 5, p. 204 nn 31–2 for references.

outside it, exactly because they did not agree on what precisely it meant to be a Platonist. There was some basic agreement that the early Academics who were directly associated with Plato and who first tried to make Plato's philosophy comprehensible in terms of specific doctrines qualify, even if they were not always correct. But who else qualifies? Antiochus argued that membership in the Academy should hardly be a criterion. Numenius (mid second century AD) takes the same view in his work *On the Dissension of the Academy from Plato*, though he reaches it from a different standpoint. Given that Plato had a strong impact on many philosophers, Platonists could champion anyone whom they felt to be fundamentally indebted to Plato and capable of illuminating Plato's real beliefs.

In this light, Aristotle appeared as a particularly good candidate for two main reasons. As a long-time student of Plato and indeed, as it was widely accepted, a particularly gifted one (e.g. Cicero, *De div.* 1. 53), Aristotle was well acquainted with Plato's views. His comprehension of them is made manifest in his numerous reports about them.[46] As is well known, Aristotle frequently refers to Plato and credits him with specific views, sometimes approving of them and some other times criticizing them. He reports on Plato's views on the soul, the first principle, the Forms, the role of pleasure, or the creation of the world.[47] What is more, Aristotle distinguishes within Plato's dialogues between the views of Socrates and those of Plato, and discusses the merits of both. He criticizes Socrates, for instance, for identifying virtue with knowledge[48] and for denying the possibility of incontinence.[49] His implication clearly is that this was not Plato's position. Platonists and others who regarded Plato's philosophy as a doctrinal system, not only saw in such reports confirmations of their belief that Plato espoused set

[46] It is still a matter of debate how Aristotle came to attribute views to Plato and how these are to be valued. It is difficult to believe that Aristotle was so often confused or not interested in the accurate presentation of Plato's philosophy, as Cherniss (1945: esp. 72–82) has argued, but it is true that his accounts are given from a certain point of view and often are polemical. Against Cherniss argues Sayre (1983: 75–117).

[47] Cf. *Met.* 987^{a}29–988^{a}17, 992^{a}20–2, 1028^{b}18–21, 1070^{a}18–19, 1073^{a}3–5, 13–21, 1083^{a}31–6; *De anima* 404^{b}16–27, 429^{a}27–9; *Physics* 202^{b}34–203^{a}16, 206^{b}16–33, 209^{b}11–17; *NE* 1172^{b}28–31; *De caelo* 280^{a}28–30, 300^{b}16–19; *De gen. et. corr.* 325^{b}24–33, 330^{b}15–17, 332^{a}27–30; *Pr. An.* 67^{a}22–7; *Post. An.* 71^{a}29–^{b}8.

[48] *NE* 1144^{b}17–30; *EE* 1246^{b}32–7; esp. about courage cf. *NE* 1116^{b}3–26; *EE* 1229^{a}14–16, 1230^{a}6–8. For a short discussion see Irwin (1995: 8–10).

[49] *NE* 1145^{b}21–31, 1147^{b}13–17.

doctrines, but considered them as illuminating of these doctrines.[50] They also appear to take the evidence of Aristotle as suggesting that Plato put forward his views in the middle and late dialogues, so they assume a distinction between 'Socratic' and 'Platonic' dialogues (e.g. Antiochus, *Acad.* 1. 17–18). Besides, Aristotle was familiar with the doctrines of early Academics like Speusippus and Xenocrates, which largely were meant to be interpretations and elaborations of Plato's alleged doctrines.[51]

Secondly, Aristotle qualifies because he expounds positions which are ostensibly maintained in Plato's dialogues and which sometimes prevail therein. It has been widely maintained by both ancient and modern interpreters of Plato that Aristotle sides with what he perceived as Plato's ethical tenets against those of Socrates. Such a belief has constituted the basis for some attempts of reconstruction of Plato's ethics in antiquity as well as in modern times. It is this belief which guides the reconstruction of Plato's ethics by Platonists like Antiochus and Plutarch but also, fairly recently, by scholars like Terence Irwin.[52]

Aristotle's writings were potentially valuable for Platonists who were interested in what Plato meant not only because Aristotle was assumed to be indebted to Plato's doctrines but also because Aristotle was expounding his views in a systematic way. This was further highlighted when Aristotle's works were at some point arranged in a way meant to suggest that they constitute a system (for instance, in Andronicus' edition in the first century BC). Several Platonists as well as Peripatetics (as we will see below in section 4) held then that this system to some extent reflects Plato's hidden system of doctrines, given Aristotle's profound intellectual debt to Plato.

50 A late source which argues this is Philoponus, *De aet. mundi* 211. 18–24. Modern scholars often follow a similar practice. F. P. Hager, for instance, rests his argument about Plato's first principle on Aristotle's report in *Met.* 1091^{b}13–15, according to which the Form of the Good is identical with the One; Hager, 'Zum Problem der Originalität Plotins', *Archiv fur die Geschichte der Philosophie*, 58 (1976), 10–22; cf. idem, *Der Geist und das Eine* (Berne, 1970). See also J. N. Findlay, *Plato: The Written and Unwritten Doctrines* (London, 1974) for a reconstruction of Plato's philosophy based largely on Aristotle's statements. Cf. Cherniss (1944: pp. ix–xxiv).

51 Aristotle's reports about early Academic views include *Top.* 141^{a}5–8, 152^{a}5–10, 25–30; *Met.* 987^{b}20–4, 991^{b}27–30, 1028^{b}21–32, 1075^{b}37–1076^{a}4, 1080^{b}21–30, 1090^{b}13–29; *Post. An.* 97^{a}6–22; *NE* 1096^{b}5–8, 1173^{a}15–17; *De caelo* 279^{b}32–280^{a}5; *De anima* 404^{b}27–30.

52 Antiochus reportedly admits it (*Acad.* 1. 15–18; *De fin.* 5. 12), while Plutarch argues this in *De virt. mor.* 442B–C (see Chs. 1 and 2, pp. 51–2, 115–23. Similarly Irwin (1995: 8) argues that 'it would not be a gross exaggeration to describe Aristotle's ethical theory as a systematic defense of the theory that Plato develops in opposition to Socrates'.

The problem, however, lay in adducing to what extent this was so. As is known, some of Aristotle's reports of Platonic and Academic views involve severe criticism.[53] Of course, they may still be useful for those who want to figure out what Plato meant, but such a critical attitude should have suggested to Platonists that Aristotle was not like the members of their school who claimed loyalty to all of Plato's doctrines. At most, Aristotle could be regarded as Platonist in some sense, that is, as a member of the 'Platonist tradition' or Plato's 'school of thought'. The Greek term for this is *αἵρεσις*, and the Latin equivalent of the term is *disciplina*.[54] This notion plays a crucial role in Antiochus' argument that Aristotle is as valuable as the Old Academics for reconstructing Plato's system,[55] and is used later by Porphyry when he examines the question of how Platonic and Aristotelian philosophy compare.[56]

Antiochus' view had antecedents in developments in Hellenistic philosophy. Early Epicureans and Stoics often regarded Plato and Aristotle as sharing the same view, and therefore attacked them jointly.[57] Panaetius and Posidonius, unlike earlier Stoics but like many others at the time, came to respect Plato and Aristotle as ancient authorities (*οἱ ἀρχαίοι*, *veteres*),[58] and also assumed their basic agreement. Posidonius in particular reacted against the Stoic doctrine of the soul as solely reason, in favour of the alleged doctrine of Plato and Aristotle, a move that implies the belief that Aristotle preserves Plato's position.[59] Such views have found their way to doxography[60] and must have played a role in the formation of Antiochus' conviction that Aristotle largely resumes Plato's doctrines and belongs to his *αἵρεσις*.

[53] Cf. e.g. *Pr. An.* 67a22–7; *Post. An.* 71a29–b8; *Met.* 997b3–4, 1072b30–4, 1090b13–29; *De caelo* 279b4–283b22; *NE* 1096b5–8; *De gen. et. cor.* 315a14–33; 329a13–14, 335b10–11; *Top.* 152a25–30; *De part. anim.* 642b5–20. See Cherniss (1944) and Jaeger (1948: 171–93).

[54] See Ch. 1, pp. 52–4, ch 7, pp. 249–52.

[55] See *Acad.* 1. 17–18; cf. Ch. 1, ss. 2, 3.

[56] Cf. the title of Porphyry's work *Περὶ τοῦ μίαν εἶναι τὴν Πλάτωνος καὶ Ἀριστοτέλους αἵρεσιν* (*Suda*, s.v. Porphyry).

[57] Cf. Plutarch, *Adv. Col.* 1115A–C, Seneca, *Ep.* 65. 4–14. For further references see Ch. 2, p. 88 n. 73.

[58] Panaetius: Cicero, *Tusc. Disp.* 1. 79; *De fin.* 4. 79; Philodemus, *Stoic. Hist.* col. 61, 2–7 Dorandi; Posidonius: Galen, *PHP* 4. 7. 39; Strabo 2. 3. 8. There was a revival of interest in Plato and Aristotle at the time. Their works were studied by people of different backgrounds (e.g. Asclepiades of Bithynia) and regardless of schools. Yet the term 'ancients' can cover several other thinkers; it can include also Theophrastus and Zeno (Porphyry in Stob. 1. 49. 25a; fr. 253 Smith), Pythagoras and Empedocles (Porphyry, *De abstinentia* 3. 6. 5).

[59] Galen, *PHP* 4. 7. 39, 5. 7. 10. See Vander Waerdt (1985*b*).

[60] See ps-Plutarch 1. 9. 10 (*DG*, p. 308; on matter), Stobaeus 1. 13. 1 (*DG*, pp. 309–10; on causes), 1. 21. 6 (*DG*, p. 327; one world), 1. 1. 29 (*DG*, p. 305; on God); disagreement is

But the problem is that, as in *Meno's* paradox, in order to claim that Aristotle recasts Plato's views and to rely on him for reconstructing them, one first has to know, or at least must be inclined to assume, that certain views are Plato's, given that various parts of Plato's work suggest different views. As I have mentioned, Antiochus argued that, apart from Aristotle, the Stoics too partly followed Plato's doctrines. This to some extent is true and has not been sufficiently appreciated in scholarship. The Stoics follow views expounded in Plato's work which in their opinion reflect those of Socrates. Aristotle mostly rejects them in favour of others. The problem is that one cannot justify one's preference for the Platonic views that Aristotle preserves against those that the Stoics maintain unless one first assumes that the former are closer to Plato's actual views.

Let me give some examples. If we wonder what Plato's views on moral psychology and ethics are, we are confronted with different pictures. In the *Gorgias* (493b), the *Republic*, and other dialogues the soul is presented as consisting of a rational and an irrational part.[61] In *Republic* 4 in particular, the soul is said to consist of an appetitive, a spirited, and a rational part, each of which has beliefs and desires that motivate us differently. Emotions and non-rational desires stem from the two non-rational parts, and have to be informed by reason so that one acts virtuously. Aristotle's moral psychology is largely built on this conception. By contrast, in the *Protagoras* the soul appears to be identical with reason, and emotions are mere mistakes of reason. This part of Plato's work inspired the Stoic view of the soul and also their ethical theory.

If we look further on in Plato, his actual position on moral psychology and more specifically on emotions does not become any clearer. Nor is it the case that in the so-called 'Platonic' dialogues one view prevails; the monistic view of the soul can be detected also in the *Phaedo* (80a–e), for instance. Regarding love, the *Republic* (581c) posits different kinds of it as motivators of human action, including the love of the rational part of the soul for certain activities. In the *Symposium* love is considered to have both rational and irrational aspects (210c–211e) and is both praised and criticized. In Socrates' first speech in the *Phaedrus* love is altogether dismissed as irrational (238b–c), while in his second

recorded about the Forms ps-Plutarch 1. 10.11 (*DG*, p. 309), or the nature of the soul Hippolytus, *Elenchus* 1. 20: *καὶ σχεδὸν τὰ πλεῖστα τῷ Πλάτωνι σύμφωνός ἐστιν* [sc. Aristotle] *πλὴν τοῦ περὶ ψυχῆς δόγματος* (*DG*, p. 570). See Mansfeld (1992: 58–9). Doxographers often set Aristotle also in accord with Pythagoras. Cf. Ch. 3, pp. 133–5.

[61] Cf. *Politicus* 301c; *Timaeus* 41c, 69c; *Laws* 904b–c.

speech love is treated as a kind of madness which pertains also to the rational part of the soul (249c–e). The dialogue's main thesis about emotions and love, most especially, seems to be that these are excessive states and as such mistaken, as is illustrated by the image of the unruly horse (253b–256e); this is the view with which the Stoics sympathized.

As regards pleasure, which was considered an emotion (*pathos*), different theories prevail in different dialogues. Is pleasure our goal, as the *Protagoras* suggests, or only a constituent of happy life together with virtue, as we are told in the *Philebus* (20c–22b)? Or, perhaps, should we educate our drive for pleasure, as is recommended in the *Republic* and the *Laws*? Plato's theories inspired different doctrines in later philosophers, like Peripatetics and Stoics, and this was acknowledged already in antiquity. Aulus Gellius argues to this effect, probably reflecting Taurus (*NA* 9. 5. 7 cited above p. 11 n. 30).

Plato's different views on the emotions shape different views on what virtue is and how it can be acquired. If emotions are conducive to virtue when guided by reason, as the *Republic* suggests, then a certain amount of emotion is required in order to attain it. Aristotle agreed with this view. However, if the emotions are altogether mistaken, virtue cannot be attained unless emotions are completely eradicated, as the *Phaedrus* and also the *Phaedo* (64a–67e) suggest. This view was adopted by the Stoics. Different conceptions of virtue bear on different conceptions of happiness or good life (*eudaimonia*). Certain parts of the *Republic* (e.g. 586d–587a) and the *Philebus* (21d–e, 63e) suggest that a good life is that of virtue but also of pleasure, health, and so on; these are the parts with which Aristotle sympathized. The *Gorgias* (474c–475b, 507c), the *Timaeus* (87c–d), and the *Laws* (660e2–5), on the other hand, suggest that virtue is the sole good thing and as such is sufficient for a good life, a position which we find amplified in the *Phaedo* (64b–65d, 82c–83b) and the *Theaetetus* (176a–b). These parts of Plato must have inspired the Stoic doctrine of the self-sufficiency of virtue.

Being divided by their own philosophical preferences for this or the other Platonic view, the Platonists inevitably disagree as to whether Aristotle or the Stoics properly transmit Plato's real doctrine. For those who thought that according to Plato only virtue is good (e.g. Atticus), Plato's view was represented by the Stoic position on the matter. For those who highlighted the parts of Plato's work which suggest that there also are other goods, like health, essential for a good life (e.g. Antiochus, Plutarch, Taurus), Plato's real view is the one articulated by Aristotle.

A similar approach is adopted in other philosophical areas and questions. Much of Stoic metaphysics, I take it, is inspired by Plato's late dialogues; for instance, their view on the world-soul (DL 7. 143) is largely inspired by the *Timaeus* and *Laws* 10, while their belief in cosmic reason is probably inspired by *Philebus* (22c, 28e–31b). Yet other aspects of Plato's metaphysical thought found their way into Aristotle's work, for instance the idea that God is an intellect beneficent to man, the source of intelligibility and order which accounts for the existence of everything.[62] Depending, then, on which part of Plato a Platonist sympathized with, one would take either the Aristotelian or the Stoic view as representative of his thought.

If Platonists appreciate Aristotle differently and disagree about his adherence to the Platonist tradition, it is because they are making different assumptions about what in fact Plato's actual doctrine is. And depending on which views they take to be Plato's among those suggested in the dialogues, they accordingly choose the instrument by which Plato's doctrines are to be reconstructed, that is, either Aristotle or the Stoics. This does not mean that Platonists in general have to side either with Aristotle or the Stoics. On many issues, such as the nature of the soul, or the first principle, they simply reject both Aristotelian and Stoic views and rely on parts of Plato which they construe in different ways. It is only when they need to reinforce their defence of their reconstruction of Plato's doctrines that they resort to Aristotle or the Stoics. If they find either party to be in accord with Plato's doctrines, it is only in the sense that Aristotle or the Stoics follow them. Admittedly those who took Aristotle as representing Plato's views often argued that Aristotle is a Platonist in a relatively strong sense, that is, a member of Plato's school of thought because of Aristotle's close relation with Plato, whereas those who found Plato's views preserved by the Stoics never argued along the same lines. The crucial point, however, is that both Aristotelian and Stoic philosophy were merely instrumental for Platonists who felt that in the Aristotelian or the Stoic writings they read nothing but Plato in a more dogmatic form.

This may explain why Platonists like the author of the pseudo-Plutarchean *De Fato* profess to give Plato's definition of chance but in fact give Aristotle's (572A–B; *Physics* 197^{a}5–6); or why Apuleius juxtaposes Aristotelian with Platonic definitions of justice in his account of

[62] On the question how Plato inspired the Stoic and Aristotelian theology, see Solmsen (1942: 131–48).

Plato's doctrines (*De Platone* 2. 229 referring to *NE* 1130^{a}9–10), or why he presents as Platonic doctrine the mixed constitution which goes back to Aristotle (*De Platone* 2. 260–1; cf. *Politics* 1265^{b}33–1266^{a}30);[63] or why Alcinous ascribes to Plato Chrysippus' definition of time,[64] or why anonymous Platonists, on the assumption that Aristotle follows Plato's method of division, ascribe to Plato the so-called *Divisiones Aristoteleae.* In the same spirit Platonists like Plutarch (*De virt. mor.* 443C–E), Alcinous (*Didascalicos* 184. 14–36), or Porphyry (*On what is up to us*; in Stob. 2. 168. 10–11; 271F. 1–2 Smith) maintain explicitly or implicitly that Aristotle's view of virtue as a mean between extreme emotions is actually Plato's because they find it outlined in several Platonic passages.[65] Because all these Platonists are convinced of the Platonic origin of such Aristotelian or Stoic views they show hardly any loyalty to Aristotelian or Stoic philosophy as a whole. Alcinous, for instance, presents as Plato's definition of virtue Aristotle's doctrine of the mean (*Didasc.* 186. 14–36), and yet he thinks that Plato also maintained the self-sufficiency of virtue, which the Stoics developed as one of their doctrines.[66] And Antiochus relies on Aristotle for reconstructing Plato's ethics, but finds Stoic epistemology closer to Plato's spirit, as I show in detail in Chapter 1.

Platonists were actually prepared to argue at length that Aristotelian and Stoic writings contain Plato's views in disguise, on the grounds that Aristotle and the Stoics had drawn their doctrines from Plato, and in this sense their work somehow also was the intellectual property of the Platonists. Clement (writing *c.* AD 200) reports that Platonists used to write entire books to show that the Stoics and Aristotle had stolen their doctrines from Plato.[67] In this way Platonists apparently tried to justify their dependence on Aristotle and the Stoics in their attempt to reconstruct Plato.

63 See Beaujeu edn. (1973: 270–1, 306–7), Dillon (1977: 336).

64 *Didasc.* 170. 24–5; cf. *SVF* ii. 509–10 and Dillon (1993: 129).

65 Cf. *Republic* 431c, 619a–b; *Philebus* 64d–e; *Politicus* 284d–285a; *Laws* 728e, 792c–d. Aristotle's report in *NE* 1153^{b}1–6 about Speusippus suggests that this view was known in the Academy. See Dillon (1977: 19).

66 *Didasc.* 180. 39–41, *SVF* iii. 29–37; cf. Apuleius, *De Plat.* 2. 225, 252. Similar is the position of Plutarch. See Ch. 2, pp. 115–23.

67 *πολλοί τε τῶν ἀπὸ Πλάτωνος συγγραφὰς πεποίηνται, καθ' ἃς ἀποδεικνύουσι τούς τε Στωϊκούς, ὡς ἐν ἀρχῇ εἰρήκαμεν, τόν τε Ἀριστοτέλη τὰ πλεῖστα καὶ κυριώτατα τῶν δογμάτων παρὰ Πλάτωνος εἰληφέναι. ἀλλὰ καὶ Ἐπίκουρος παρὰ Δημοκρίτου τὰ προηγούμενα ἐσκευώρηται δόγματα* (Many Platonists write works in which they demonstrate that the Stoics, as I have already mentioned, but also Aristotle had taken over most of their principal doctrines from Plato. Also Epicurus had built his doctrines after those of Democritus); *Stromata* 6. 2. 27. 3–4. Cf. ibid. 2. 19. 100–101. 1, 5. 14. 95. 1–3, where it is argued that the Stoics derived their ethics from Plato.

At the heart of this Platonist attitude lies their belief that Plato's philosophy is perfect, that is, a doctrinal system both true and complete, on which several later philosophers draw.[68] This belief motivated Platonists to appropriate Aristotle's developments in logic and natural philosophy, claiming that they have Platonic origins too. They argued that Aristotle's categories are outlined in Plato's dialogues, like the *Parmenides* (Alcinous, *Didasc.* 159. 43–4), the *Theaetetus* (Anon., *In Theaet.* 68. 7–22), or the *Timaeus* (Plutarch, *De an. procr.* 1023E), or that Aristotle's account of language is prefigured in the *Cratylus* (*Didasc.* 159. 44–5). Furthermore, some Platonists were attracted by Aristotle's suggestion that the soul has faculties (*dynameis*) by means of which it operates within the body (*De anima* 414^a29–34, 433^a31–b3) assuming that this also was Plato's view, though they rejected Aristotle's argument about the ontological status of the soul.[69] Still others adopted Aristotle's theory of scientific demonstration as is outlined in *Posterior Analytics*, but they combined it with Platonic recollection rather than Aristotelian induction, which originally meant to support it.[70] For Platonists, all these Aristotelian theories were essentially Platonic, and as such they felt entitled to use and study them.[71] And apparently they could go so far as to consider an entire Aristotelian work essentially Platonic. This is presumably why Plutarch, for instance, wrote on both the *Topics* and the *Categories*.[72]

The answer, then, to the question of what Aristotle had to offer to Platonists was a recapitulation of the doctrines of Plato harmonious with their own thinking. And thus Aristotle offered to them an instrument in the reconstruction of Plato's alleged philosophical system.

If this is so, then the situation is misrepresented when scholars argue that Platonists mix Aristotelian or Stoic views with Platonic ones, or

68 Cf. Atticus fr. 1. 17–18 Des Places; Albinus, *Isagogê* 149. 18–19, DL 3. 56.

69 This is the view of the author of Tyrwitt's fragments pp. 60–71 Sandbach, presumably Plutarch (see Ch. 2, pp. 112–13), Severus (Ch. 4, p. 188), and Porphyry (Ch. 7, pp. 299–301). Such a view could be justified by the evidence of Plato who sometimes talks in terms of faculties of the soul (*Republic* 532a2; *Sophist* 227b7; *Laws* 899a3). Platonists use the term ὑπογραφή in order to indicate that Plato outlines in his dialogues theories expounded by later philosophers. See Plutarch, *De an. procr.* 1023E; Alcinous, *Didasc.* 159. 39; Porphyry, *In Cat.* 111. 28–9.

70 Alcinous, *Didasc.* ch. 5, 156. 24–158. 4, ch. 25, esp. 177. 45–178. 12. See the analysis by Schrenk (1993).

71 Also the Peripatetics argued similarly, though to a much lesser degree. Adrastus in his commentary on the *Timaeus* argued that the theory of epicycles, discovered by Hipparchus (2nd c. BC), was already outlined in Aristotle. See Moraux (1984: 306, 310–1).

72 Lamprias nrs. 56 and 192. I list their titles in Appendix II.

when they speak of their contaminated or syncretistic Platonism.[73] Nor is there any point in distinguishing between eclectic Platonists of Aristotelizing or Stoicizing tendency on the one hand and orthodox ones on the other, as is the current scholarly practice,[74] since all of them were after Plato's actual doctrines, but given their disagreement about which these were, they chose different means of reconstructing them, that is via Aristotle or the Stoics. Clearly, however, no one was willing to leave Plato for either Aristotle or the Stoics.

One may perhaps object that this nevertheless happened, despite what Platonists thought, and to the extent that it happened, they did inevitably become eclectics or syncretists. This in some sense is true, though it depends on how one understands the term 'eclecticism'. The fact that Platonists were often influenced by Aristotle and the Stoics in their interpretation of Plato, despite their claims of loyalty to the thought of the master is not sufficient to qualify them as eclectics in the usual sense of the term, which is largely pejorative, because these Platonists operate eclectically *within* Plato's own work. They do so in two ways. First, they have views about the parts of Plato which are more important for a given domain, such as ethics. Secondly, they construct Plato's doctrines focusing on some parts of Plato, which they interpret in a certain way. Platonists use Aristotle or the Stoics only as a backup to their overriding argument that Plato's doctrines must be identified with certain views held in his dialogues.[75] Naturally Platonists take into account the advances in philosophy made by Peripatetics and Stoics as well as their objections to Plato. Such an attitude is characteristic of the life of philosophy in general. Yet the fact that Platonists often operate with Aristotelian or Stoic terminology, or with Aristotelian and Stoic conceptions and theories, such as the Stoic theory of living in conformity with nature (*oikeiôsis*), the Stoic theory of cognition, or the

[73] Thus it does not do justice to the situation to say that 'Middle Platonists oscillated between two poles of attraction . . . Peripateticism and Stoicism', or that they 'accepted the Stoic ideal of *apatheia*' (Dillon 1977: 51, 195), to speak of syncretism of Aristotelian and Platonic doctrines (cf. Donini 1974: 53), about contamination of Plato's philosophy with Aristotelian and Stoic components or about reconciliation of Platonism with Aristotle and the Stoics (Whittaker 1987: 110–17; Zambon 2002: 29, 317). Similarly scholars miss the point when they speak of 'stoicizing or Aristotelizing Platonism' (e.g. Graeser 1972: 3).

[74] This distinction was introduced by Praechter (1910), (1922 = 1973: 137) and is still very prominent. See Dillon (1988*a*). Antiochus, for instance, is considered eclectic (e.g. by Annas 1993: 180–1), while Atticus 'orthodox' (e.g. Zambon 2002: 129, 133–4).

[75] This is why Moraux's distinction (1984: p. xxii) between intended and actual orthodoxy does not apply either, as it is still not clear what Plato's actual views were.

Aristotelian doctrine of homonymy or potentiality and actuality, should not confuse us in this regard. All this merely represents a modernization of the language of philosophy; it does not imply anything about the philosophical loyalties of the Platonists.[76] What is important is how they understand such theories. And as we will see, their understanding is often considerably different from that of their inventors. So these often amount to considerably different theories. Antiochus' use of *oikeiôsis* is a characteristic example in this regard (see Ch. 1, s. 5, pp. 72–80). Even when Platonists espouse the Aristotelian or the Stoic viewpoint at all, this is only because they actually take it to be Plato's own viewpoint, never for its own sake.

This is manifested by two facts. The first is that those Platonists who draw on Aristotle, such as Antiochus, Plutarch, Taurus, or Severus, also criticize him for abandoning some Platonic doctrines, or at least appear to disapprove of some of his doctrines. Plutarch, for instance, explicitly criticizes Aristotle in his *Adversus Colotem*, and yet relies heavily on his ethical doctrine in the *De virtute morali*. Such evidence suggests that Platonists are quite aware of Aristotle's departures from Plato and draw from him only what they consider to be Plato's doctrine. This is even more the case with the Stoics. Platonists like Antiochus criticize them, and still draw from them what they regard as essentially Platonic doctrine.

Secondly, Platonists frequently make arguments that indicate their reliance on Aristotle or are conditional on their perceived function as sources of Platonic doctrine. For example, Antiochus argues that Aristotle was a Platonist (*Acad.* 1. 17) and that he preserved Plato's ethical doctrines (*De fin.* 5. 12), as he also argued that Stoic epistemology is close to Plato's spirit (*Acad.* 1. 35); and Plutarch argues that Aristotle adhered to Plato's ethical principles (*De virt. mor.* 442B-C). Such arguments aim to justify a certain reconstruction of Plato's doctrine from sources indebted to Plato, such as Aristotle or the Stoics, but at best only show that these sources are indebted to Plato. Nothing in them indicates that these sources actually express Plato's mind on a given issue. But at any rate the crucial point is that they were used only because they were regarded thus.

[76] E.g. the Stoic theory of *oikeiôsis* is adopted by many Platonists and Peripatetics (see Ch. 1, s. 5), there were Platonists who read the Stoic theory of 'criterion' into *Theaetetus* (Anon. *In Theaet.*, fr. D, Sedley 1997*b*), while Plotinus speaks in terms of potentiality and actuality. Graeser (1972: 2–3) is wrong to claim that this feature shows that Platonism lost 'awareness of its own generic roots', just because Plotinus adapts Aristotle's conceptions to fit his Platonist framework. See my analysis in Ch. 6.

Admittedly some of the Platonists who sympathized with a Platonic view which they found in Aristotle were also sympathetic towards him, and they sometimes refrained from criticizing him. But this is not always the case. The same Platonists often accused Aristotle, as well as the Stoics, of stealing or distorting Plato's doctrine.

Apart from Antiochus who accused the Stoics of stealing Plato's doctrines and the Platonists referred to in Clement's testimony (see n. 67) we must consider the Pythagorean Platonist Moderatus (first century AD). He argues that Plato and Aristotle, among others, did not do other than simply adapt Pythagorean doctrines (Porphyry, *V. Pyth.* 53). For Moderatus and other Platonists of Pythagorean conviction, or for Pythagorean authors such as those of the pseudo-Pythagorean ethical treatises, Platonic and Aristotelian philosophy were merely instrumental for reconstructing the philosophy of Pythagoras. There are variations of this tendency. Some use Aristotle for reconstructing Pythagorean philosophy,[77] either relying on Aristotle's numerous reports about the Pythagoreans or assuming that Aristotle's doctrines are Pythagorean. This is the case with Plutarch (see Ch. 2, p. 87), and with many Pythagoreans.[78] For some other Pythagorean Platonists, though, Aristotle's philosophy was instrumental for reconstructing Plato's philosophy, and the latter was in turn instrumental for reconstructing that of Pythagoras. This is the case with Eudorus (first century BC), who despite his overall critical attitude to Aristotle's philosophy, reconstructs Plato's doctrine about the first principles relying on Aristotle's reports in *Metaphysics* (986^{a}22–3, 988^{a}8–17). In Eudorus' conception, Plato maintains Pythagoras' metaphysical monism.[79]

The discussion about how Plato's doctrines are to be reconstructed, which started with Antiochus, lasted for almost four centuries, until Porphyry. During this period so many alternative interpretations of Plato opposed each other and claimed loyalty to Plato's thought that the term 'Platonist' philosophically appears to be almost empty.[80] The

[77] See Plutarch fr. 202 Sandbach; Porphyry, *V. Pyth.* 41.

[78] See Ch. 3, pp. 133–5 and Mansfeld (1992: 50–3, 178–83, and *passim*).

[79] Instead of Aristotle's *τὰ γὰρ εἴδη τοῦ τί ἐστιν αἴτια τοῖς ἄλλοις, τοῖς δὲ εἴδεσιν τὸ ἕν* (*Met.* 988^{a}10–11), Eudorus reads... *τοῖς δὲ εἰδόσι τὸ ἓν καὶ τῇ ὕλῃ* (Aspasius in Alexander *In Met.* 58. 31–59. 8; fr. 2 Mazzarelli (1985: 200–1); cf. Simplicius, *In Phys.* 181. 7–30 (frs. 3–5 Mazzarelli). See Dodds (1928: 139) and below, Ch. 1, pp. 81–2.

[80] The attempt to distinguish between canonical and marginal interpretations at this time, as Annas (1999: 94, 163) implies, does not do justice to the situation. Annas (1999) appears to be treating Alcinous as representing the canonical 'unitarian' thesis, according to which Plato's ethical doctrine is that virtue is sufficient for happiness, while she treats Antiochus, Plutarch, and Taurus as exceptions (pp. 32–4, 50–1) without much justification. See my criticism in Karamanolis (2004*a*) and her reply in *Rhizai*, 2 (2005), pp. 121–5.

disparity of Platonist interpretations is indicative of the considerably different philosophical profiles of Platonists, and this is why I proceed by examining them individually in this book. Antiochus and Numenius, for instance, have very little in common, apart from the claim that they adhere to Plato's doctrines. Since so many different doctrines had Platonic credentials, Platonists were concerned to make a convincing argument that their individual view, rather than any other, was right. And since Plato's views were regarded as the right ones, the implication was that the view they were defending was necessarily Plato's. Platonists typically tried to discredit other interpretations of Plato before establishing their own, arguing that these express someone's personal views not Plato's mind (Plutarch, *De an. procr.* 1013B; Porphyry, In Philop. *De aet. mundi* 522. 2–9). Quite crucial in this situation was the fact that the Academy as an institution endowed with Plato's authority ceased to exist after Philo.[81] Since Antiochus, Platonists were teaching their own circles of students whom they had to convince of their Platonist orthodoxy; and they did this in different cities, such as Athens, Alexandria, or Rome, in private or public places, which as such did not mark them as faithful followers of Plato.[82]

This period of competing interpretations of Plato is often called 'Middle Platonism'. The term may convey the sense of transition from the Academic phase of a single interpretation to the pluralism of the imperial centuries. Yet for the same reason is misleading, as it suggests a doctrinal or ideological unity which, as I argued, is hardly present.[83] For my part, I will altogether avoid this term as much as the term 'Neoplatonism'. There is one sense, however, in which the transitional character of the period seriously affects the present study. With the exception of Plutarch, the *Didascalicos* of Alcinous, and Apuleius' derivative works, for all other Platonists of this era only fragments have survived until Plotinus. Our evidence about Lucius, Nicostratus, Numenius, Atticus, Taurus, and Severus consists in excerpts preserved by later sources. And for Antiochus we rely on Cicero's reports and hardly ever can we be sure

[81] This was first suggested by Lynch (1972: 179–82) and was proved and amplified by Glucker (1978: esp. 121–58). But there still remains some doubt about the status of Antiochus; see Ch. 1, pp. 44–5.

[82] On the localization of the various Platonists see Göransson (1995: 38–41); Gioè (2002: 18–20). The circle of which we are best informed is that of Plotinus. For other circles, like the one of Plutarch's teacher, Ammonius, or that of Numenius, much speculation has arisen due to the lack of evidence. See Fowden (1977); Glucker (1978: 256–74), Edwards (1991*a*).

[83] Recent scholarship has started to acknowledge this. See e.g. Zambon (2002: 23–8).

about Antiochus' own formulations. Hence, and this is a warning to the reader, I often have to venture to reconstruct their views, regarding Aristotle's philosophy in particular, which can only be at best probable.

3. THE PLATONIST DISCUSSION OF ARISTOTLE'S PHILOSOPHY

We have seen that Platonists used Aristotle as a means of accessing Plato's thought, and that they did so in three main ways: (*a*) Aristotle's reports on Plato's views were taken as preserving Plato's teaching; (*b*) those views of Aristotle which were found also in Platonic dialogues were taken as recasting doctrines of Plato in a more systematic form; (*c*) Aristotle's developments, mainly in logic, were often thought to be prefigured in Plato. Platonists thus tended to read Aristotle's logical works as essentially Platonic accounts.

It was the second such way which Antiochus appears to have stressed, arguing that Aristotle had followed Plato in all major philosophical matters. Antiochus' argument gave rise to a heated debate on Aristotle's credentials as a Platonist. This debate runs parallel to that regarding which of Plato's doctrines are his by right, and how they should be understood, clearly because one's conceptions of what constitutes Plato's doctrines would determine one's estimation of Aristotle as a means for reconstructing them. Eudorus was the first to react to Antiochus, disputing the value of Aristotle's philosophy (see Ch. 1, pp. 82–4). Plutarch came to affirm Antiochus' position that Aristotle often preserves Plato's doctrine, but his view as to how Aristotle's philosophy compares with that of Plato is more sophisticated; he makes clearer their differences and shows more care than Antiochus in specifying that he follows Aristotle only when he represents Plato (see Ch. 2).

In the second century the discussion on how Aristotle's philosophy compares with that of Plato takes on striking dimensions. Almost all Platonists we know of take a position on this, for example, Lucius, Nicostratus, Numenius, Atticus, Taurus, Severus. Christian Platonists, like Clement or Origen, also have views on the issue.[84] Lucius and Nicostratus[85] criticize Aristotle's *Categories* for supporting an ontology

[84] On the attitude of early Christians to Aristotle's philosophy see Runia (1989).

[85] Their chronology is far from certain. Lucius may well belong to the 1st century AD, as Sedley (1997: 117 n. 26) has suggested. See the seminal article by Praechter (1922) and now also Gioè (2002: 131–2, 181–2).

incompatible with that of Plato.[86] Atticus and Taurus write special treatises on the subject. Atticus addresses those who promise the doctrines of Plato through those of Aristotle,[87] arguing that Aristotle's philosophy systematically contradicts that of Plato, and hence is altogether useless for the Platonist. Taurus on the other hand sets out to discuss the differences between Platonic and Aristotelian doctrines,[88] but, as I argue in Chapter 4, the evidence about him suggests that his attitude to Aristotle was not hostile. Works like those of Atticus and Taurus show how strong the tendency of contemporary Platonists was to rely on Aristotle for understanding Plato.

There are two key factors which determine the formation of views of Platonists as to how close to Plato is the philosophy of Aristotle. The first is how Platonists construe Plato's views but also those of Aristotle, on crucial philosophical matters. Let me here outline the range of positions on some important philosophical questions which played a crucial role in the whole discussion, since in the following chapters I am concerned to discuss the viewpoint of individual philosophers.

One crucial issue was how the world came into being. Plato's account of cosmogony in the *Timaeus* had been a subject of discussion from very early on. Aristotle, as we know, interpreted it literally, assuming that it was describing an actual cosmogony.[89] Based on *Timaeus* 30a, where matter is presented as pre-existing, he argued that such a world cannot last eternally, as was argued in the *Timaeus* (31b2, 32c1–3), since generated entities necessarily perish.[90] In Aristotle's view, the world has never had a beginning and thus it will never perish.[91] Aristotle's argument is obscure and of dubious value; it disregards the role of the demiurge in the *Timaeus*, arguing that the world came into being from disordered matter as a result of natural processes, when in fact it did not.[92] Yet it had a strong impact on generations of Platonists. The early Academics responded to Aristotle's criticism arguing that the cosmogony

[86] Simplicius, *In Cat.* 1. 18–22; see Ch. 6, pp. 234–6 and Appendix II, p. 338.

[87] *Πρὸς τοὺς διὰ τῶν Ἀριστοτέλους τὰ Πλάτωνος ὑπισχνουμένους* (frs. 1–9 Des Places).

[88] *Περὶ τῆς τῶν δογμάτων διαφορᾶς Πλάτωνος καὶ Ἀριστοτέλους* (*Suda*, s.v. Taurus).

[89] *De caelo* 280^a28–32, 283^a4–284^a2, 300^b16–18; *Met.* 1071^b37–72^a2. Aristotle's criticism is discussed by Cherniss (1944: 415–17); Baltes (1976: 5–18), Sorabji (1983: 276–82); Judson (1983: 228–42).

[90] *De caelo* 279^b17–283^b22; cf. *De philosophia* frs. 19a–c Ross.

[91] *De caelo* 283^b26–284^b5; cf. *De philosophia* fr. 18 Ross.

[92] See Judson (1983: 235–42).

of the *Timaeus* is fictional, made up by Plato only for the sake of instruction and for clarity.[93] But for the Academics, apart from the question regarding the truth of Plato's account, there was also a question as to how the 'creation' of the world is to be interpreted, since the world is perishable (*Timaeus* 41a8–9), and yet does not actually perish, but is destined to last (ibid. 41b2).

Plato's γέγονεν,[94] given its perfect tense, refers to a perfective state; it suggests that the world has come about. It is open to interpretation whether this state is a result of a certain process or not. One may take the verb in a resultative sense, according to which a cosmogonical process took place in the past and its final result is the present world (i.e. as synonymous with γεννᾶσθαι).[95] But one may also think that the verb does not have any implications about the past. On the first construal the world has an ἀρχή (cf. *Timaeus* 28b6–7, 36e4) both in the sense of 'origin' and of a principle, which according to the *Timaeus* is the divine creator, while on the second construal the world has one only in the sense of a principle, an ultimate explanation. The partisans of the first, more literal interpretation (Plutarch, Atticus) argued that the corruption of the world is prevented by God's will (*Timaeus* 41a–b), while the followers of the second, non-literal one (Severus, Taurus, Alcinous, Plotinus, Porphyry) accepted Aristotle's argument as valid, but maintained that the world was never actually created; rather, God is the principle accounting for its existence, and hence nothing in the world's nature necessitates its corruption. On this construal there was no point to ask, as Aristotle did, why the world did not come about earlier (*De caelo* 279b21–4, 283a11–24). On either interpretation, however, a range of different evaluations of Aristotle is available. Among the supporters of the literal one, Atticus regarded Aristotle as opposing to Plato, while Plutarch did not express a view in the surviving evidence, but he was never very critical of Aristotle and he may have held instead that Aristotle had simply missed Plato's point. Those in favour of the non-literal interpretation on the other hand considered Aristotle as misunderstanding Plato, but in doing so they also took a range of different positions.

[93] Speusippus frs. 54a–b Lang (61a-b Tarán); Xenocrates fr. 54 Heinze; cf. Baltes (1976: 18–22). Theophrastus seems to have agreed with the early Academics on this (in Philoponus, *De aet. mundi* 145. 20–4, 188. 9–13; *DG*, pp. 485–6).

[94] *Timaeus* 27c5, 28b7, 38b6; from γίγνεσθαι = 'come into being'.

[95] This is how Aristotle understands Plato's text (οἱ γεννῶντες τὸν κόσμον; *De caelo* 283^b31). It is noticeable that Aristotle interchanges γίγνεσθαι and γενέσθαι in describing the *Timaeus*' creation (*De caelo* 280^a19–31, 280^b7–20).

Crucial for the development of the discussion was the equation of Plato's γέγονεν with the adjective γενητός, a term which never occurs in the *Timaeus* but can be formed in analogy with adjectives like ὁρατός, ἁπτός, which do occur.[96] This was a crucial step because γενητός, due to its grammatical form, admits of several possible meanings (at least three) and even more interpretations, which amplified the whole discussion (see Ch. 4, pp. 180–6).

The question of Plato's God was among the most controversial ones for Platonists. Atticus, but presumably also Ammonius Saccas and the pagan Origen maintained that God must be identified with the demiurge of the *Timaeus*. Others, notably Moderatus, Numenius, Alcinous, Plotinus, and perhaps also Celsus, being inspired by the One of the *Parmenides*, postulated an intellect above the demiurgic intellect of the *Timaeus* which they identified with the Form of the Good of the *Republic* (508e), which is said to be beyond being.[97] One reason which accounts for the latter view is that the demiurge of the *Timaeus* creates under some constraints (e.g. matter) and brings about the best possible world, rather than simply the best one. The implication is that the demiurge is not absolutely free. Nor is he absolutely simple, given that he, as an intellect, thinks. Those who considered the demiurge as Plato's God disagreed as to how Aristotle's God is to be considered. Atticus regards Aristotle as diverging from Plato's position since Aristotle rejected Plato's Form of the Good (fr. 9 Des Places), while Ammonius is likely to have found Aristotle to be essentially in accord with Plato, if, as I argue in Chapter 5, he maintained that Aristotle's God, like Plato's, thinks of the Forms, and thus comprises the entire intelligible realm. Those who identified Plato's God with the One disagreed whether Aristotle abandoned the most important item of Plato's ontology, namely the One, as Numenius and Plotinus seem to think, or Aristotle rather omitted it, as Porphyry probably thought. It is, however, pertinent to note that Numenius and Plotinus, despite their critical attitude to Aristotle's theology, were much influenced by it, which is quite indicative of Aristotle's impact on Platonists of that age (see Ch. 6, pp. 236–7).

[96] As Baltes (1976: 2–3) argues, already Aristotle (*De caelo* 279^{b}5) talks about the world as γενητός.

[97] The controversial status of the question emerges in the statement of the Christian Origen that 'God is either an intellect or beyond intellect and being' (*C. Celsum* 7. 38. 1–2, cf. 6. 64; *De Principiis* 1. 1. 6). On this matter see Dodds's classic (1928).

Regarding Plato's Forms, there is room for several positions, since there is a variety of Platonist interpretations of them. Depending on the interpretation, Aristotle's rejection of the transcendent Forms could be seen as: (*a*) leaving them out, (*b*) contradicting them, or as (*c*) implicitly accepting them.

Platonists construed the Forms as (1) basically immanent (Antiochus), (2) both immanent and transcendent (Plutarch, Alcinous, Porphyry), (3) basically transcendent (Numenius, Atticus, Plotinus). Platonists who construed the Forms as basically immanent (Antiochus) admitted that Aristotle had abandoned an aspect of Plato's doctrine, namely the transcendent character of the Forms, but maintained that he was essentially in agreement with Plato's overall doctrine. As regards those who construed the Forms as basically transcendent (Numenius, Atticus, Plotinus), they surely accepted the existence of immanent Forms, but maintained that these are entities derivative from the transcendent ones. For them Aristotle diverged seriously from Plato's metaphysics in the following sense. They believed that only the transcendent intelligible entities have natures or essences, while sensible entities belong to the realm of becoming and thus do not qualify as beings strictly speaking. In their view, Aristotle was wrong about what being and essence is, and he was more so in rejecting what is being *par excellence*, Plato's God, the Form of Good. Those who took construal (2) considered the immanent Forms as a version of the transcendent ones, but some (Alcinous, Porphyry) believed that the latter are part of God's essence, existing in God's mind as divine thoughts. These Platonists paid attention to Aristotle's remark in *De anima* 429^{a}27–9 that the Forms exist in the part of the soul which thinks and to his argument in *Metaphysics* 6 and 12 that there are immaterial separate substances, though these are not the Forms but rather intellects. This Aristotelian view had quite some impact on later Platonists.[98] Crucial in this respect was the mediation of Alexander of Aphrodisias who upheld the identity of the divine intellect with its thoughts (e.g. *Mantissa* 108. 7–9, 16–19). Numenius (frs. 15, 16 Des Places) and especially Plotinus come to maintain that Forms do not exist outside the divine intellect (*Enn.* 5. 5). This interpretation was meant to be a solution to the problem that God is not mentioned among the principles in *Timaeus* 52 a–c, while Being is, so the assumption is that Being amounts to God plus the Forms, which is supported by *Timaeus* 30c–d. Porphyry and subsequent generations of Platonists take a further step.

[98] See Armstrong (1960: 398–413).

They argue that Aristotle implicitly accepts Plato's Forms since his God also is a thinking intellect and as such must have thoughts, like Plato's God. This view, I will argue in Chapter 5, may go back to Ammonius Saccas.

On another topic, the interpretation of Aristotle's God regarding the issue of providence was open to question. The disagreement is evident in the fact that one stream of the doxographic tradition maintains that Aristotle's God is not at all provident, while another holds that his God is provident but his providence is confined to the celestial realm.[99] The Platonist author of the *De Fato* and the Peripatetic author of the *De mundo* (first century AD?) consider Aristotle's God, though transcendent, to be also as provident as Plato's God. Plutarch and Atticus disagree with this; they accept the strong sense of divine providence found in *Laws* 10, yet they differ considerably in their assessment of Aristotle's doctrine.[100] The former is much less critical than the latter.

There also was a question as to how to understand and evaluate Aristotle's traces of dualism which occur in his early works such as the *Eudemus*, the *Protrepticus*, the *De Philosophia*, or in *NE* 10 and the *De anima* 3. 5, especially against the background of his controversial doctrine of the nature of the soul as the actuality (*entelecheia*) of the body. There were Platonists who argued that Aristotle was wrong to define the soul as the actuality of the body, but they also maintained that he was close to Plato in accepting the immortality of the intellect, a view they traced both in *De anima* 3. 5 and in his early works. Some Platonists including Plutarch seem to adhere to this view,[101] while others, like Numenius, Atticus, and Plotinus, strongly deny it. This is because they maintain that, according to Plato, the soul essentially is the principle in virtue of which we think, the intellect, not the one in virtue of which we are alive, as Aristotle argued. For them the soul is essentially rational and transcendent, which is to be identified with the immortal soul of the *Timaeus* 69d, while the irrational soul of the biological functions is an acquired one (see Ch. 3, pp. 145–8, Ch. 4, pp. 171–14).

Yet this very Platonist distinction is largely due to Aristotle's influence. Aristotle's argument that the soul is the actuality (*entelecheia*) of the living body seems to have set the agenda for the Platonist discussion

[99] The first stream is represented by ps-Plutarch 2. 3. 3, Stobaeus 1. 21. 6 (*DG* p. 330), ps-Galen, *Phil. Hist.* 46 (*DG*, p. 621), while the second by Clement, *Stromata* 5. 13. 90. 3; DL 5. 32; Aetius 2. 4. 12 (*DG*. pp. 332–3); Tatian, *Orat. Ad Graec.* 2. 2 Whittaker.

[100] See Chs. 2 and 4, pp. 105–9, 160–7.

[101] See Ch. 2, pp. 111–15 Cf. Clement, *Stromata* 5. 13. 88. 1–2; Origen, *C. Celsum* 3. 80. 15–17.

of the sense in which the soul is separable from the body and immortal. Platonists came to realize that the soul cannot be separable from the body as a capacity of movement, perception, or digestion, since, as Aristotle had stressed, it needs specific organs to carry out such functions. One sense in which the soul is separable from the body and thus immortal is by being an intellect, because for the Platonists thinking does not need special organs, as in their view the case of the divine intellect shows. First Plutarch comes close to this view, which is then further developed by Numenius and Atticus. The latter accuses Aristotle of confusing the soul, that is the intellect, with the life functions (see Ch. 4, pp. 171–4), but this very distinction was encouraged by Aristotle's psychology. This is another example of the impact Aristotle had on Platonists, no matter whether they agreed with his views.

Such an impact becomes even clearer in the case of Plotinus. He does accuse Aristotle of abandoning Plato's doctrine of the soul as a transcendent and rational entity, but his discussion of how, according to Plato, the soul relates to, and operates within, the body is plainly inspired by Aristotle's relevant views (see Ch. 6, s. 2, pp. 218–29). Finally, Porphyry goes further than Plotinus to argue that Aristotle is in accord with Plato not only in this respect, but more essentially, he argues, Aristotle follows Plato in considering the soul a transcendent and rational entity, which is how Porphyry understands the intellect of *De anima* 3. 5 (see Ch. 7, s. 6. 2, pp. 287–98).

The second element which plays a crucial role in the formation of the positions of Platonists about how close Aristotle's philosophy is to the one of Plato, lies in their tendency to have not only views about what Plato's doctrines actually are, but also a general conception of Plato's philosophy and what is important in it. Antiochus, for instance, believes that at the heart of Plato's philosophy is ethics and that the rest of it is a means to support Plato's ethics. Since he takes Aristotle to represent Plato's ethical doctrine, in his eyes Aristotle remains essentially loyal to Plato's philosophy. Thus Aristotle's rejection of the transcendent Forms (*Acad.* 1. 33) does not really diminish his high esteem of Aristotle, especially since it might not have been clear to him whether Plato did not himself have doubts about the transcendent Forms. For Numenius, however, Aristotle's rejection of transcendent Forms amounts to a complete contradiction of Plato's philosophy, as the essence of it for him is the belief in the existence of an intelligible realm structured in a hierarchy of intelligible entities in which the highest God is identified with the Form of the Good. Plutarch on the other hand considers as an essential aspect of Plato's philosophy its aporetic character. For him Aristotle's philosophy is close to Plato's, because it shares Plato's dialectical methodology.[102] For Atticus again, Plato's principal philosophical doctrine which shapes Plato's metaphysics, psychology, and ethics is that of the transcendent Forms, and since Aristotle rejects it, his philosophy is taken to be opposite to that of Plato (fr. 9 Des Places), while he also highlights the doctrine of the immortality of the soul (fr. 7. 102 Des Places). Ammonius also has a certain view about what Plato's philosophy is all about. It is, I will argue, a metaphysical monism which he probably considered compatible with Aristotle's theology (Ch. 5, s. 5).

The evidence of this discussion shows that Platonists of this period had an impressive knowledge of Aristotle's works. These were available already to Cicero,[103] but a new edition by Andronicus presumably made them even more widely accessible.[104] Nicostratus knows Aristotle's work well enough to be able to criticize Aristotle for a discrepancy between the accounts of movement given in the *Categories* and the *Physics* (Simplicius, *In Phys.* 428. 3–13).[105] Taurus not only had a good knowledge of Aristotle's works, but had them read in his seminars (*N.A.* 19. 6), anticipating what Plotinus would do later (*V. Plot.* 14. 4–14). Finally, Porphyry was teaching Aristotle to fellow Platonists through his commentaries, becoming, as I will argue, the first Platonist commentator of Aristotle. Porphyry does not have deeper knowledge of Aristotle than his predecessors but rather a different conception of Aristotle's philosophy. This will be the argument of my long Chapter 7.

Some not strictly philosophical reasons stir the Platonist discussion. Philosophy had become a profession in the first two centuries of our era, and the foundation of chairs in AD 179 by Marcus Aurelius confirms this. An essential part of professionalism is competition. Platonists and Peripatetics compete with each other and with themselves, and the debate about how Platonic and Aristotelian philosophy compare is part of the battle of professional philosophers for orthodoxy and fame for good philosophical sense. Thus they hoped to become well known and attract students. This tendency must be linked to the fact that there

[102] Similar is Cicero's attitude (cf. *Tusc. Disp.* 2. 9; *Acad.* 2. 7–9, 112–13).

[103] Cf. *De fin.* 1. 7; *Top.* 1. 1–3; *Ad fam.* 7. 19. Cicero knows many of Aristotle's dialogues—*Ad Att.* 4. 16. 2; *De fin.* 1. 14; *Orat.* 62—and refers to Aristotle's exoteric and esoteric works (*De fin.* 3. 10, 5. 12). On his knowledge of Aristotle see Long (1995) and Barnes (1997: 44–59).

[104] On the availability of Aristotle's works and Andronicus' role, see Barnes (1997).

[105] Cf. *Categories* 15^a13–34 and *Physics* 225^a25–225^b9. See Gottschalk (1990: 81) and Gioè (2002: 216–17).

was a general appreciation of philosophy in the second century AD, part of the widespread classicism of the era. Rhetoricians, poets, and scientists were interested in philosophy,[106] although their motivation was not always purely philosophical. They respected the 'ancients' for their style but also for their achievement in logic, or in science. Platonists like Taurus and Apuleius provided education on these aspects, often through Aristotle's works.[107] It is reasonable to assume that their use of Aristotle may have raised the question in their students of how his philosophy compares with that of Plato.

4. THE PERIPATETICS ON HOW ARISTOTLE'S PHILOSOPHY COMPARES WITH PLATO'S

The discussion of how Aristotle's philosophy compares with Plato's may have been particularly vivid in the Platonist camp, but was not exclusively confined to it. There is much evidence to suggest that the Peripatetics in late antiquity also discussed this issue, though to a lesser degree.[108] In the present study I confine myself to Platonists, yet in the following I briefly review the evidence regarding the Peripatetic positions on the issue. The main reason why I do this is because, as will be seen, the Platonist and Peripatetic debates run parallel and inform one another, so we cannot fully appreciate the arguments of some Platonists without knowledge of their contemporary Peripatetics.

While for Platonists Aristotle's philosophical works were mainly instrumental to understanding Plato's philosophy, for Peripatetics some knowledge of Plato's work was essential for two main reasons. First, they considered Plato the starting point of the Peripatetic tradition and, like other philosophers in late antiquity, they highly valued their origins. Secondly, they realized, as we do nowadays, that one cannot understand Aristotle's thought properly without some knowledge of Plato, since Aristotle had been in one or another way greatly indebted to Plato for the development of his thought. For these reasons Peripatetics throughout antiquity studied Plato's work with various degrees of

[106] See Bowersock (1969: 66–8).

[107] For the teaching of science Taurus used [Aristotle's] *Problemata* (*N.A.* 19. 6); cf. Apuleius, *Apologia* 36. 5, 41. 67. For Taurus' teaching of logic see *N.A.* 16. 8. The rise of interest in science is manifest at the multiplication of scientific *compendia* like Aelian's. See Sandy (1997: 27–37).

[108] For a review of the Peripatetic philosophy at the time see Gottschalk (1987).

interest. Like the Platonists, they too assumed that Plato's philosophy constitutes a doctrinal system like Aristotle's philosophy, and were also tempted to reconstruct Plato's doctrines through Aristotle's work. Peripatetics like Boethus, Aspasius, or Adrastus were eager to show the Platonic ancestry of Aristotle's views, and often went out of their way in order to do so.[109] Their difference with Platonists is that the Peripatetics often maintain that Aristotle's doctrines constitute progress over those of Plato. Yet, like Platonists, such as Antiochus and Plutarch, Peripatetics often appear to assume that Aristotle shares a Platonic doctrine, which they oppose to the relevant doctrine of the Stoics (not to mention the Epicureans). And like some Platonists, they often go as far as to consider Plato and Aristotle as forming one sound philosophical tradition, which they contrast with the other philosophical schools.

This clearly is the case with Aristocles of Messene.[110] His dating still remains uncertain; presumably he lived in the late first century BC or the early first century AD.[111] Aristocles appears to have particularly favoured Plato's philosophy and to have explicitly praised it in his writings. This he must have done in his lost work *Whether Homer or Plato was Better.*[112] But the main bulk of the evidence for his favorable attitude to Plato comes from the fragments of his treatise *On Philosophy* (*Περὶ φιλοσοφίας*), which originally covered ten books. In this work Aristocles traces the development of Greek philosophy from its early stages to Plato, Aristotle, and the Stoics. The advent of philosophy is situated in the context of a general cultural evolution in which human

109 Boethus apparently tried to set Aristotle's *Categories* in the context of the Academic–Peripatetic tradition, arguing that Plato anticipated some aspects of Aristotle's work, such as the category of relation (Simplicius, *In Cat.* 159. 12–15, 163. 6–9). See Moraux (1973: 148, 157), and Gottschalk (1990: 74). On Aspasius, Adrastus, and Alexander see below.

110 The old collection of Aristocles' fragments by H. Heiland, *Aristoclis Messeni Reliquiae* (Giessen, 1925) has been replaced by the collection with English tr. and commentary by Chiesara (2001). Yet Chiesara considers Aristocles more as a source of Pyrrhonian scepticism and less as a Peripatetic philosopher (see my review in *CQ* 54/1 (2004), 57–9). Moraux (1984: 83–207) is still indispensable for understanding Aristocles' philosophical profile.

111 The *terminus ante quem* is Eusebius (born *c.* AD 260/4) and the *terminus post quem* Aenesidemus whom Aristocles refers to (fr. 6. 205 Heiland/4. 16 Ch) as ἐχθὲς καὶ πρώην, but the date of Aenesidemus also is controversial (early 1st c. BC?; see Ch. 1, p. 49 n. 13). Moraux (1984: 86–9) argues for a dating in the second half of the 1st c. BC or the first half of the 1st c. AD; Gottschalk (1987: 1163) dates him in the second half of the 1st c. AD or early in the 2nd c. AD. See the review of the discussion in Chiesara (2001: pp. xvi–xix).

112 *Πότερον σπουδαιότερος Ὅμηρος ἢ Πλάτων* (*Suda*, s.v. Aristocles). But better in what (e.g. in style, ethics, philosophy)? At any rate, Aristocles discusses which author is more beneficial to the reader.

progress corresponds to degrees of increasing wisdom.[113] The majority of Aristocles' preserved fragments, however, are critical of the philosophies of the Eleatics, the Sceptics, the Epicureans, and the Cyrenaics. But because we know this work almost exclusively through its critical parts which Eusebius excerpted to advance his apologetic polemics, we do not have a clear picture as to what it was all about.

Aristocles argues that Greek philosophy before Plato was primitive and only in him acquired its true nature. While this veneration says much about Plato's authoritative status in Aristocles' mind, it probably was a fairly widespread view among intellectuals in late antiquity, regardless of philosophical affiliations. Yet Aristocles goes further in elaborating about the value of Plato's philosophy. In a quotation from the seventh book of his work (*PE* 11. 3; fr. 1 Heiland/Chiesara), Aristocles argues that Plato philosophized correctly and perfectly.[114] Aristocles appears to suggest that Plato's achievement was twofold. Plato was the first to cover all three parts of philosophy (fr. 1. 23–7, 39–41 H/Ch), and Plato realized the true nature of philosophy, which essentially is the science of divine and human matters (fr. 1. 38–9 H/Ch). This nature accounts for the unity of its parts in the following sense. All parts of philosophy make a whole in terms of its objective, which is man's attainment of good life, in the same sense that the parts of medicine make a whole in terms of its objective, that is, to serve man's health. While in the case of medicine knowledge of man's nature is required, in the case of philosophy some knowledge of the nature of the universe, of which man is part, is required (fr. 1. 42–8 H/Ch). Aristocles thus approves of Plato's idea for establishing the pre-eminence of theology and for founding his ethics on theology (fr. 1. 42–3, 52–3 H/Ch, vest. 1. 62–5 H; test. 5, 4 Chiesara). We should notice here that Aristocles strongly resembles those Platonists who consider Plato's philosophy as a doctrinal system aiming at good life, and Antiochus in particular.[115]

Aristocles' conception of Plato's philosophy may be indicative also of his understanding of Aristotle's philosophy, but Eusebius does not

[113] In Philoponus, *In Nicom. Isag. Arithm.* p. 1 Hoche (vestigium 1 Heiland, test. 5 Chiesara).

[114] Fr. 1. 17–18 H/Ch; cf. DL 3. 56; Atticus fr. 1. 22, 34–5 Des Places.

[115] Cf. Albinus, *Isag.* 150. 6–12; Alcinous, *Didasc.* 162. 25–8 with *Timaeus* 27a. There are some further similarities between Aristocles and Antiochus, which have not been sufficiently appreciated by Chiesara (2001). See below.

preserve anything relevant.[116] Yet much as he praises Plato, Aristocles, as a genuine Peripatetic, must have included an account of Aristotle's contribution to the development of Greek philosophy. The excerpts from the critical part of his treatise actually seem to rely on a more constructive part of his work. Indeed, it can be inferred that the constructive part contained an account of Aristotle's philosophy, and also that Aristocles regarded it is as being essentially in accord with Plato's philosophy.

Aristocles criticizes several philosophical schools of thought for deviating from what he calls the 'sound way of philosophizing' (ὀρθῶς φιλοσοφεῖν; fr. 5. 63 H; fr. 7. 9 Ch). This involves the acceptance of certain basic principles in philosophy (fr. 6. 214 H; fr. 4. 30 Ch), which, as it turns out, mainly concern epistemology and ethics. For Aristocles, violation of these basic principles amounts to annihilation (ἀναίρεσις) of the entire philosophical enterprise (fr. 6. 209–13 H; fr. 4. 30 Ch). As an example of such violation, he considers the Sceptics' distrust of the senses and their suspension of judgement. But he also targets the epistemological views of the Cyrenaics (fr. 7 H; 5 Ch), of Protagoras and Metrodorus (fr. 4 H; 6 Ch), of Xenophanes and Parmenides (fr. 5 H; 7 Ch), and of Epicurus (fr. 8 H/Ch). A close examination of Aristocles' criticisms strongly suggests that he considered the philosophies of Plato and Aristotle as the measure of sound philosophy on the basis of which quite generally philosophical views should be judged.

To begin with, it is telling that all his criticisms come after his exposition on Plato, Aristotle, and the Stoics.[117] It also is quite noticeable that he takes Plato's philosophy as a criterion for judging the Stoic philosophy (fr. 3 H/Ch), which appears to have exercised some influence on him. Further, Aristocles refers to the *Theaetetus* (fr. 4 H; 6. 3 Ch) as a source of refutation of Protagoras' theory of knowledge. Indeed, most of his criticisms in this regard are inspired by this dialogue. On the other hand, Aristocles relies much on Aristotle's *Metaphysics* (fr. 6 H; 4 Ch) and *De anima* (fr. 8 H/Ch). This evidence, which can be amplified, shows that probably Aristocles first set out to outline the sound principles of philosophy as exemplified by Plato and Aristotle, before moving to criticize those who deviated from them. These principles concern metaphysics, epistemology, and also ethics.

[116] Aristocles' view that philosophy is the philosophical inquiry into eternal and unchanged beings (vestigium 1a Heiland) reminds us of Aristotle's notion of first philosophy which corresponds to theology.

[117] For the order of the fragments see Chiesara (2001: pp. xxxi–xxxv).

More specifically, Aristocles appears to find Aristotle in accord with Plato in accepting two ontological principles, God and matter (fr. 3 H/Ch), and, unlike the Stoics,[118] in maintaining that God is incorporeal (fr. 3. 9–13 H/Ch). But it was their accord in epistemology that Aristocles seems to have highlighted. In Aristocles' view, we naturally are enabled to know (fr. 6. 12 H; 4. 1 Ch) and to understand (fr. 6. 166 H; 4. 24 Ch) and, given man's nature, this happens in a certain way. For Aristocles the two main principles of knowledge are the senses and reason (fr. 5. 63–5 H; 7. 9 Ch; fr. 8. 27–42 H; 8. 6–7 Ch). He argues that reason plays the major role in the process of knowing, as it, unlike sense perceptions, never deceives us (fr. 4. 69–70 H; 6. 11 Ch), and in this sense it is the most divine judge (*θειότατος κριτής*; fr. 8. 49 H; 8. 7 Ch).[119] The question now is how reason operates according to Aristocles. He appears to speak of common concepts (fr. 6. 164–6 H; 4. 24 Ch) by means of which we cognize. Presumably Aristocles maintained that our mind represents reality by means of concepts, and he may have identified these with the immanent Forms. If this is so, Aristocles' thesis appears to be very similar to that of Antiochus, which I will examine in Chapter 1.

Aristocles probably tried to argue for the accord between Plato and Aristotle also in a special sense. He was concerned to discredit some invectives against Aristotle, and he singles out two as the most obnoxious and widespread of them, one pertaining to Aristotle's personal life and also the claim that Aristotle was ungrateful to Plato (*PE* 15. 2. 12). The latter criticism was voiced by various people in antiquity, most famously by Aristoxenus, the music theorist and one of Aristotle's pupils (*P.E.* 15. 2. 3; fr. 2. 20–6 H; 2. 3 Ch). With this claim Aristoxenus meant to praise Aristotle and vilify Plato. For Aristocles, though, who had a great admiration for Plato, such a view was hardly a praise for Aristotle, and so he was concerned to restore the truth. Eusebius, however, who claims that he quotes from Aristocles in order to outline Aristotle's philosophy in an objective way (*PE* 15. 1. 13), did not like this part of Aristocles' defence, as he himself subscribed to the view that

[118] Doxographers often acknowledge that Plato accepted three principles, matter, God, and the Forms; e.g. Aetius 1. 3. 21 (*DG*, pp. 287–8); Alcinous, *Didasc.* 162. 24–166. 13; Hippolytus, *Elenchus* 19 (*DG*, p. 567). Two principles are acknowledged in *Acad.* 2. 118; DL 3. 69; Irenaeus, *Adv. haer.* 2. 14. 2; cf. Aristotle, *Met.* 988^{a}7–10. For a contrast between the view of Plato and Aristotle that God is immaterial and the Stoic view see Stobaeus 1. 1. 29 (*DG*, pp. 305–6); ps-Galen, *Phil. Hist.* 16 (*DG*, pp. 608–9).

[119] cf. Plato, *Philebus* 33a–b; Aristotle, *De anima* 408^{b}18–29; *NE* 1177^{b}30; *Protrepticus* fr. 6 Ross.

Aristotle deliberately had opposed Plato's doctrines (*PE* 15. 3). Thus his quotation breaks before Aristocles turns to this matter. Yet we can be fairly sure that Aristocles addressed this claim, as he clearly had announced that he would deal with it.[120]

Aristocles was not an exception, but rather a typical Peripatetic of late antiquity as regards the issue of how Aristotelian and Platonic philosophy compare. Alexander of Damascus (second century AD) is another Peripatetic who probably took a position similar to that of Aristocles. According to Galen, Alexander was 'familiar with the doctrines of Plato but was more attached to the doctrines of Aristotle' (*De praenot.* 5, 14. 627. 1–5 Kühn).[121] More important in this century are Aspasius, Adrastus, and the Anonymous commentator on the *Nicomachean Ethics.* Like Aristocles, who wrote eight books on ethics (*Suda*, s.v. Aristocles), they are much interested in ethics and show much respect for Plato's philosophy.

To take the case of Aspasius, in his commentary he often refers with approval to Plato's work in connection with Aristotle's doctrines,[122] as he wants to show their background.[123] He appears to assume that Aristotle followed Plato on how virtue comes about and on virtue being the mean between two extreme psychological states (cf. *In NE* 53. 1–5). A similar assumption must lie behind his view that virtue is divine in the sense that through virtue man becomes similar to God (ibid. 99. 4–5), a belief which for many Platonists in late antiquity represented Plato's doctrine of the highest good (*Theaetetus* 176a–b). Further, Aspasius sees Plato and Aristotle as being in accord on the nature of emotions against the relevant Stoic doctrine (*In NE* 42. 13–47. 2). This is also

[120] ἕτερον δέ ὅτι ἠχαρίστησε Πλάτωνι; *PE* 15. 2. 12; fr. 2. 80 Heiland. Eusebius quotes next from Atticus who argues that Aristotle deliberately opposed Plato (e.g. *PE* 15. 4; Atticus fr. 2 Des Places). Immisch (1906) conjectured that in this part Aristocles cited Aristotle's elegy for Plato (in Olympiodorus, *In Gorgiam*, p. 215 Norvin; Ross, *Arist. Fragm. Sel.*, p. 146). Immisch's hypothesis is attractive, but remains highly speculative. Heiland prints the elegy as vestigium II; Chiesara (2001: p. xxv) rightly leaves it out. Moraux (1984: 145–7) finds the conjecture likely; F. Jacoby, *F. Hist. Gr.* iii/B/2, p. 482, finds it 'incredible'.

[121] On him see R. B. Todd, *Alexander of Aphrodisias on Stoic Physics* (Leiden, 1976), 4–11.

[122] On Aspasius see Moraux (1984: 226–93); Gottschalk (1987: 1156–8); Mercken (1990: 438–41); Barnes (1999). Aspasius refers to Plato's *Apology*, the *Laches*, the *Republic*, the *Theaetetus*, the *Laws*.

[123] See Aspasius on the affections of the soul and the irrational desires *In NE* 46. 5–10, on the opposite of magnanimity 117. 4–6, on *praotês* 119. 3–8. See Donini (1974: 98–125) and Becchi (1984: 63–81) on the parallels between Aspasius and the Platonist ethical views.

held by the Anonymous commentator on books 2–4 of the *Nicomachean Ethics*, who often cites Plato in support of Aristotle's doctrines.[124] The Anonymous also highlights the fact that Aristotle mentions Plato with approval in his ethics, argues that Aristotle follows Plato's views on moral virtue, and criticizes Platonists, like Atticus for example, who identified Plato's doctrine on moral virtue with the ideal of extirpation of emotions (*apatheia*).[125]

Two other Peripatetics, the author of *De mundo* and Adrastus, also regarded Aristotle's philosophy as being in accord with that of Plato in some crucial respects. The former tries to reconcile what he considers as Plato's tenet of divine providence with Aristotle's relevant doctrine.[126] His basic idea is that Aristotle's God, though transcendent in its substance, organizes the world through his power (*dynamis*) and thus is the 'saviour and creator of the world' (397^{b}20–1). This in practice means that God imparts movement from one sphere to the next, and thus sets the world in motion without direct intervention.[127] The Peripatetic interest in the *Timaeus* is undeniable. There is some evidence to suggest that Aristocles wrote on the *Timaeus*,[128] which is possible for a philosopher interested in theology (fr. 1 H/Ch) and in physics (fr. 3 H/Ch). Indicative of the Peripatetic evaluation of this dialogue is their tendency to maintain that Aristotle continued rather than contradicted Plato's cosmological doctrines exposed in it. This seems to be the case with Adrastus. In his commentary on the *Timaeus* he looked at the dialogue from a retrospective point of view, trying to explain and perhaps also to

124 See Anon. *In NE* 127. 1–9, 136. 27–137. 8, 146. 6–10, 169. 22–3, 254. 22–8. On this commentary see Mercken (1990: 419–29).

125 Anon. *In NE* 127. 3–8 (comment on *NE* 1104^{b}11–12); cf. ibid. 248. 15–29 (Atticus fr. 43 Des Places).

126 Ed. D. Furley, *[Aristotle] On the Cosmos* (Cambridge, Mass. and London, 1955, Loeb); on the date, author, and doctrine of the work see Furley's introduction, pp. 333–43; Moraux (1984: 37–48); Gottschalk (1987: 1132–39).

127 Roughly the same idea, which is recognizably of Stoic origin, occurs also in Antiochus (*Acad.* 1. 24, 28–9) and Atticus (fr. 8. 17–20 Des Places). The difference is that the author of *De mundo* and Antiochus ascribes it to both Plato and Aristotle, while Atticus to Plato only, and argues instead that Aristotle contradicts it.

128 Proclus, *In Tim.* 1. 202–3. Views are divided as to whether Proclus refers to Aristocles of Messene in this passage. H. Usener, *Rh. Mus.* 25 (1870), 614–15, and A. Festugiere, *Proclus Commentarium sur le Timée* (Paris, 1966), 48 n. 2, suggested that the author was Aristocles of Rhodes, a grammarian attested in Proclus' commentary (*In Tim.* 1. 85. 26). H. Gercke, 'Aristokles', *RE* ii (1896), 934, Heiland (1925: 89 n. 113), and Chiesara (2001: 52–23) supposed that Proclus refers to our Aristocles.

justify doctrines assumed by Plato and Aristotle by showing how these correspond to later discoveries.[129]

Unlike those Peripatetics, Alexander of Aphrodisias (appointed to the chair of Peripatetic philosophy between AD 198 and 209) considers Plato's work to be of relatively little value.[130] He does acknowledge Aristotle's debt to Plato's philosophy, often approves of Plato's arguments,[131] and contrasts Plato and Aristotle with the Stoics,[132] yet he maintains that Aristotle surpassed Plato's work so much that the latter is of only historical importance.[133] Indeed, Alexander often criticizes Plato and emphasizes the differences between Plato and Aristotle. He is, for instance, particularly critical of the idea presented in the *Timaeus* that the world had a temporal beginning,[134] and criticizes the interpretation taken by some Platonists (e.g. Atticus) that God's will would prevent the world from perishing, arguing that such an interpretation goes against logical necessity (*Quaestio* 1. 18, 1. 23).[135] But all this precisely suggests that Alexander has a polemical agenda, which is understandable given the polemics against Aristotle by Platonists like Atticus. It seems to me that Alexander's underrating of Plato is mainly motivated by his wish to respond to Platonist attacks and to safeguard Peripatetic philosophy, rather than by genuine low esteem of Plato.

129 On Adrastus' commentary on the *Timaeus* see Moraux (1984: 296–313); Gottschalk (1987: 1155–6).

130 Alexander's stance to Plato cannot be done justice here; for a brief account see Sharples (1990: 90–2).

131 e.g. on justice in *Republic* 384c–d. (*In Topica* 166. 24–7); cf. *Quaestio* 1. 1, 4. 9–13, Bruns.

132 Simplicius, *In Phys.* 420. 13–421. 2 and Vitelli (1992), fr. 2, on which more in Ch. 4, s. 2.

133 Cf. e.g. *In Top.* 540. 17–541. 6; in Simplicius, *In Phys.* 355. 13–18.

134 Simplicius, *In Phys.* 1121. 28–1122. 3; *In de caelo* 276. 14–29. See Baltes (1976: 71–81).

135 After Alexander there is little evidence of active Peripatetics. We hear of two Peripatetics contemporary with Plotinus, namely Ammonius and Ptolemy (*V. Plot.* 20. 49), but we know nothing about their views.

1

Antiochus of Ascalon

1. ANTIOCHUS' DEBATE WITH PHILO OF LARISSA

In many ways Antiochus (*c.*130–68 BC) marks the end of one era and the beginning of another. Most importantly, he puts an end to the sceptical interpretation of Plato, which was initiated by Arcesilaus and cultivated in the Academy for two centuries, until the time of Philo of Larissa (scholarch from 110 to *c.*83 BC). Antiochus considers scepticism an aberration from Plato's philosophy, one which broke the original Academic tradition so significantly that it should be marked as a 'New' Academy, as opposed to the 'Ancient' one from which it had digressed (*Acad.* 1. 46, 2. 15).[1] Antiochus secedes from Philo's sceptical Academy with the aim of restoring this ancient Academic tradition.[2] He actually sees himself as representing the original Academy (*Acad.* 2. 136).

It is a historical paradox that with Antiochus the Academy as an institution comes to an end. There has been a scholarly debate on the question regarding whether Antiochus ever actually became scholarch of the Academy. Glucker has argued against this possibility on the basis of

[1] The literature on Antiochus is rich. See mainly Lueder (1940); Luck (1953); Hunt (1954; 16–40, 89–98); Dillon (1977: 52–106); Glucker (1978: 15–120); Barnes (1989); Görler (1994: 938–80); and more recently Fladerer (1996). Antiochus' testimonies have been collected by Luck (1953: 73–94) and by Mette (1986/7). Giusta (1990: 29–33) has reviewed the two collections. The two editors were confronted with the difficulty pertaining to the evidence about Antiochus, namely that we basically rely on Cicero's reports. Antiochus' views are represented with certainty in *Acad.* 1. 15–42, *Acad.* 2. (= *Lucullus*) 19–61, and *De finibus* 5. 9–74, on which I will mainly rely in the following. Antiochus' views are probably reflected also in the anti-Stoic criticism in *De fin.* 4 and in parts of *Tusc. Disp.* 5. Cicero admits that he relied on Greek sources (*Ad Att.* 12. 52. 3), which possibly include Antiochus' originals. Excellent work on the *Quellenforschung* has been done by Glucker (1978: esp. 415–17), who has tried to trace parts of *Academica* 2 to different works of Antiochus. For a review of the *Quellenforschung* see Barnes (1989: 64–8).

[2] *vetus Academia revocata est* (*Acad.* 2. 70); cf. ibid. 1. 13, 2. 69, and Augustine, *De Civ. Dei* 19. 1.

Cicero's testimony, which implies that Antiochus lectured in a school of his own, probably located in a gymnasium in Athens, not in the Academy.[3] Yet the testimony of Philodemus' *Index Academicorum* rather suggests that Antiochus did take over from Philo as head of the Academy,[4] though it remains unclear for how long he served in this post. Almost certainly, though, the Academy as an institution ceased to exist after Antiochus (see s. 7 below).

In two other ways Antiochus marks the end and the beginning of an era. First, he is the last Platonist of any prominence to share his main philosophical concerns with those of the Hellenistic philosophers, that is to say, epistemology and ethics. And second, he is the first to draw attention to the value of Aristotle's philosophy as a means for accessing that of Plato. The evidence about Antiochus, which, we must remember, is second-hand, suggests that he was chiefly interested in arguing how secure knowledge is attainable and in showing what constitutes a good life (*Acad.* 2. 29). Regarding the first issue, he basically adopted the Stoic position, believing it to be much closer in spirit to Plato's own view. While his position on the second issue is more complex, I shall argue that to a large extent Antiochus adopted Aristotle's doctrines, which he considered to be representative of Plato's (see s. 5). This position goes along with an explicit praise for Aristotle's philosophical merit (*Acad.* 1. 18; *De fin.* 5. 7), while he remains critical of the Stoics. Antiochus' interest in Aristotle will be my primary concern in this chapter.

If we want to understand how Antiochus developed this interest we must first try to understand how he developed his conception of Plato's philosophy. As I have said, Antiochus was originally a sceptic, and he remained a member of Philo's Academy for many years (*Acad.* 2. 11,

[3] See Glucker (1978: 98–108). Cicero implies that Antiochus never took over from Philo, but rather had an audience of his own (*Acad.* 2. 69), and specifically says that he attended a lecture by Antiochus 'in eo gymnasium quod Ptolemaeum vocatur' (*De fin.* 5. 1). Before Antiochus, Clitomachus and Metrodorus of Stratonicea were also lecturing in local *gymnasia*; see von Arnim (1921: 656–9); Glucker (1978: 106–8).

[4] The reading διεδέξατο in the *Index Acad.* col. XXXV. 2–3 Dorandi (subject of the verb is 'Antiochus') suggests Antiochus' succession in the Academy, as Barnes (1989: 58) rightly claims. See Dorandi (1986: 113–18; 1991: 82 n. 305). Antiochus' succession seems to be confirmed by PDuke inv. G. 178, a list of leading philosophers ([φιλοσό]φων ἀρ[χηγέται?]). The term ἀρχηγέτης must mean 'scholarch' in this context; in col. II the ἀρχηγέται of the Academy are its scholarchs. The papyrus has been published by William Willis and Tiziano Dorandi in the *Corpus dei Papiri Filosofici Greci e Latini*, i. (Florence, 1989), 81–4.

63, 69).[5] His career as a sceptic was finished by 86 BC, when he published the *Sosus* to criticize Philo's so-called *Roman Books* (*Acad.* 1. 13, 2. 12). What prompted Antiochus to alter his philosophical standpoint so completely?

Cicero seems to imply that Antiochus changed suddenly (*subito*; *Acad.* 2. 70init.). Yet he himself gives evidence to the effect that there was an ongoing argument between Antiochus and Philo, conducted within the confines of the Academy. We know that Philo changed his views twice, both times probably because he was challenged by Academics including Antiochus. Philo's final position against which Antiochus reacted was expounded in his *Roman Books* (*Acad.* 2. 11–12). But Cicero refers to Antiochus' argument with Philo also without mentioning the *Roman Books* (*Acad.* 2. 69, 111). He offers ambition as a possible motive for Antiochus' argument with Philo: the former wanted to have his own circle of students (*Acad.* 2. 69).

However, at the time Antiochus first learnt about Philo's *Roman Books* in Alexandria, he already had such a circle (*Acad.* 2. 12). Most probably, then, Antiochus had been engaged in a long-term argument with Philo. During this period, the mature philosophical point of the former was crystallizing progressively, until he finally seceded from his teacher. The story of their argument is complicated and our knowledge of it incomplete, especially regarding the early period, but the basic outline must be roughly the following.[6]

At the time of his election in 110 BC, Philo adhered to Clitomachus' interpretation of Carneades' scepticism, according to which the Stoic apprehension (*katalêpsis*) is rejected as impossible (*akatalêpsia*) and suspension of judgement (*epochê*) is maintained (*Acad.* 2. 66–8, 108). According to this interpretation, which Antiochus initially shared (*Acad.* 2. 11), some views are more probable than others in the sense that they have greater plausibility. However, regardless of any particular view's relative plausibility, true or even proximate truth cannot be ascertained from it (Philo I).

At some point around 95 BC, Philo changed his interpretation of Carneades' scepticism. From this point on he interpreted Carneades' probable (*pithanon*) in the sense 'likely to be true', and argued that some beliefs are more likely to be true than others and that the wise man can have

[5] We know little about Antiochus' early career. See Dillon (1977: 53–5); Barnes (1989: 52–7).

[6] I am indebted to Brittain's reconstruction (2001), as far as Philo is concerned. As regards Antiochus' reaction see Glucker (1978: 13–31).

such beliefs on various theoretical issues (*Acad.* 2. 78, 148). So Philo still maintained *akatalêpsia*, but rejected complete *epochê* (Philo II).[7]

We do not know whether Antiochus challenged Philo's original Clitomachean view. However, it seems unlikely, first because Cicero neither mentions nor implies anything of the sort, and secondly because Antiochus would not have joined Philo's Academy in the first place had he disagreed with this view.[8] Clearly, though, Antiochus did criticize Philo's amended interpretation. Presumably he argued that one cannot know what is likely to be true if one does not know what truth itself is, and that Philo thus cannot possibly assert that some impressions were true and others false unless he knows how to distinguish them (*Acad.* 2. 111; cf. 2. 33–8). Antiochus may also have objected that since Philonians cannot affirm the truth of any of their premises, all their arguments are inconclusive, including the one about the indiscernibility of impressions and probable truth (*Acad.* 2. 43–4).[9]

In reaction to Antiochus' criticisms, Philo tried to demonstrate how his view that some beliefs are more likely to be true and that the wise man can have such beliefs must be understood. He did so in his *Roman Books*, published around 88/87 in Rome, the city to which Philo had fled during Mithridates' siege of Athens (Plutarch, *Brutus* 306). In this work Philo argued that the wise man can attain knowledge (*katalêpsis*), though not the infallible knowledge as defined by the Stoics.[10] In his view we can apprehend how things are in some areas of our experience and thus attain a certain degree of knowledge, but there is no criterion to guarantee that what we have in a particular impression amounts to secure or infallible knowledge of the Stoic kind. This was Philo's final position (Philo III).

Antiochus in turn criticized Philo for contradicting himself because on the one hand he held that perception could provide knowledge, but on the other he denied that it could offer secure knowledge (*Acad.* 2. 18). This criticism manifests Antiochus' assumption that knowledge must be secure, and that a mark or sign (*signum*) of truth like the Stoic criterion is required (*Acad.* 2. 34init.). Apparently

[7] See Frede (1987*e*: 213–22) and more fully Brittain (2001: 73–128). Yet Glucker (2004: esp. 118–33) has doubted that this evidence compellingly supports the epistemological position of Philo II, especially as far as Metrodorus is concerned.

[8] We do not know, however, when exactly Antiochus joined Philo's Academy; see Barnes (1989: 53).

[9] See Brittain (2001: 129–32). Note the similar criticism on the part of Aenesidemus in Photius, *Bibl.* cod. 212, 170a26–31.

[10] *Acad.* 2. 18, 32; Sextus, *PH* 1. 235; Numenius fr. 28. 6–12 Des Places.

Antiochus continued to accept the Stoic definition of knowledge (*katalêpsis*) which Philo had rejected in his *Roman Books*, and it is this that shaped his criticism of Philo's position in the *Sosus*, which he published a year after the circulation of Philo's *Roman Books* (*c.* 87/86). The appearance of this text marked Antiochus' definite break with Philo.

The debate between Antiochus and Philo had another important dimension. Philo tried to justify his final epistemological thesis (Philo III) by arguing that the Academy had in fact been unanimous and undivided all along due to its wholesale rejection of the Stoic criterion, but the Academics had never denounced knowledge in the non-Stoic sense.[11] He also argued that this Academic view was also shared by Aristotle and the Peripatos (*Acad.* 2. 112–13). This position particularly upset Antiochus, because he considered it to be merely a lie (*mentitur*; *Acad.* 2. 12fin), and he must have responded to this in his *Sosus*. But the fact that Philo backed up his final thesis (Philo III) with such a historical claim suggests that he responded to Antiochus' earlier objections to the historical legitimacy of his earlier position (Philo II). Philo must have justified also his first modification of viewpoint (Philo II) with some reference to the practice of the Academy. Presumably he argued that the Academy as well as Aristotle's Peripatos had rejected the Stoic *katalêpsis* all along, and that they had shared the dialectical methodology of arguing from both sides (*De fin.* 5. 10; *Acad.* 2. 7–9). We can be fairly confident that Philo argued along these lines, because Cicero, who never espoused Philo III, clearly takes this view.[12]

This evidence shows that the unity of the Academy was a central issue in the argument between Antiochus and Philo. It also shows that the position of Aristotle was also discussed in this connection, that Aristotle came up in this argument early on, and, most importantly, that it was Philo himself who brought up Aristotle.

One question which arises from the above story is why Antiochus did not criticize Philo's interpretation of Carneades (Philo II) from the Clitomachian standpoint, which he originally shared. The answer seems to be that this standpoint was altogether abandoned in the

[11] No passage indicates precisely this, but it is to be inferred from *Acad.* 1. 13, 2. 11–12, 18; Sextus, *PH* 1. 235. Cicero diverts the discussion in *Acad.* 2. 12 from Philo's innovations to early Academic scepticism.

[12] Cicero often argues for the unity of the Academic and Peripatetic tradition in this sense (*Tusc. Disp.* 2. 9, 4. 6; *De off.* 1. 2). Already Carneades regarded Peripatetics as sharing with the Academy a common dialectical spirit (*Acad.* 2. 112–13). See Glucker (1978: 63) and Long (1995: 52–9).

Academy. Different Academics found the Clitomachean interpretation of Carneadean scepticism unsatisfactory, each for different reasons which are reflected in their subsequent reactions. Philo wanted to defend an epistemology which was neither Carneadean nor dogmatic, and shifted to his revised position along with Metrodorus (*Acad.* 2. 78; Philo II); Aenesidemus espoused a radical scepticism and defected from Philo's Academy to re-establish Pyrrhonean scepticism,[13] while Antiochus became dogmatic. So both Aenesidemus and Antiochus rejected Philo's revised scepticism (Philo II), the former because he found it very dogmatic, the latter because he found it not dogmatic enough. But now we come to the question of when Antiochus started to become dogmatic and why.

The existing evidence does not offer a clear answer. We do know though that Antiochus associated with Stoic philosophers like Mnesarchus, Dardanus (*Acad.* 2. 69), and Sosus, after whom Antiochus named his book. They probably influenced him in thinking as follows.[14] All philosophical schools other than the Academy agreed on the possibility of attaining knowledge (*concursus omnium philosophorum*; *Acad.* 2. 70). The standard sceptical reply to this claim was that the dogmatists disagree among themselves on most issues (*Acad.* 2. 115), and hence their knowledge is questionable.[15] However, Antiochus progressively realized first that the Academic sceptics were no less dogmatic than the other dogmatics, since they had raised *akatalêpsia* to a dogma (*Acad.* 2. 28–9, 109), and also that the early Academics, the Peripatetics, and the Stoics, despite their disagreements, agreed on two crucial issues, that secure knowledge is attainable and that virtue is the essence of a good life; what is more, their agreement on these matters could be explained in terms of their common reliance on Plato. As a support for this Antiochus could take the fact that early Academics,

[13] The date of Aenesidemus' defection is controversial. I agree with Brittain (2001: 6) that he must have defected from Philo's Academy in the 90s, as his claim that the Academics are merely 'Stoics, fighting with Stoics' (Photius, *Bibl.* cod. 212, 170a16–17) must refer to Philo II or III. The view of Decleva-Caizzi (1992) that the defection occurred in 60s–50s is unlikely, because at the time there was no Academy to defect from and because Aenesidemus does not seem to know Philo's *Roman Books*.

[14] Numenius fr. 28 Des Places and Augustine, *Contra Acad.* 3. 41 suggest that Antiochus had studied with the Stoic Mnesarchus, a view which Barnes (1987: 53–4) accepts. For my part I remain sceptical whether this is so or a later fabrication to explain Antiochus' Stoicism. Cf. Glucker (1978: 28).

[15] This was a typical criticism levied by the sceptics against the dogmatists (Aenesidemus in Photius, *Bibl.* cod. 212, 170a24–33). Aenesidemus also argued that the Academics dogmatize over many things (ibid. 170a17–22).

Aristotle and other Peripatetics, as well as the Stoics, used to attribute to Plato views outlined in his dialogues. The Stoics Posidonius and Panaetius, in particular, spoke favourably of specific Platonic doctrines and even asserted that Aristotle also followed them.[16] It was presumably such evidence that suggested to Antiochus the idea of a dogmatic Plato.

One may come to wonder here why Antiochus was not satisfied with the concession to dogmatism that Philo made in his *Roman Books*. Glucker has argued that Antiochus probably rejected it because he found Philo's position to be an incomplete and inconsistent version of Stoicism.[17] This seems to me to be correct. In Antiochus' view, Philo kept up only sceptical appearances by denying the Stoic criterion, while he basically accepted Stoic dogmatism. And this was not unreasonable of Antiochus to maintain. Indeed, Philo's ethics is very much Stoic (Stob. 2. 39. 20–42. 6), and this must be the position he held at the time of the *Roman Books*.[18]

While Aenesidemus considered Philo's ethics dogmatic (*Bibl.* cod. 212, 170a17–19), Antiochus perhaps regarded it as not dogmatic enough. He presumably believed that ethics needs to be systematic in order to guide one towards a good life, and that ethics cannot be systematic unless it is underpinned by metaphysical postulates about both human nature and the world, which entail what is good and why. In Antiochus' view, one's life cannot be fully good unless one first knows with certainty what good is. This in turn requires secure knowledge of the principles that determine a good life, in a way similar to that of rationalist doctors who argued that in order to produce a healthy state in the body one has to know the nature of body and what health is.[19] Since Philo denied that such knowledge is possible, his ethics could not satisfy Antiochus. This is, I think, the crux of his disagreement with Philo, which will be substantiated below. Antiochus' stance reflects the impact of Stoicism, which maintains that secure knowledge is possible and crucial for achieving a good life. Accordingly, the importance of Stoicism for him is that it offers a theory of how such knowledge can be achieved which, in his view, supports what he takes to be Plato's ethics. We can better understand Antiochus' rationale for his dogmatic

[16] See Introduction p. 18.

[17] Glucker (1978: 83).

[18] On Philo's ethics see Brittain (2001: 255–95, esp. 273–95).

[19] It is noticeable that Philo parallels ethics with medical therapy (Stob. 2. 40. 1–4), but as Brittain (2001: 273–95) argues, his method is that of the empiricist doctor. That of Antiochus, I think, resembles the one of the rationalist doctor.

construal of Plato's philosophy if we look on the way in which he reconstructs it. To this I now pass.

2. ANTIOCHUS' THESIS ON THE PHILOSOPHIES OF PLATO, ARISTOTLE, AND THE STOICS

Antiochus' concept of Plato's philosophy seems to be the following. Plato, Antiochus argues, was a philosopher of stunning originality who brought philosophy to an altogether higher level than all his predecessors, including Socrates. According to Antiochus, Plato had views which amounted to a coherent system, but given the literary form of his works, it was not always clear what these views were. If we want to reconstruct Plato's philosophy, Antiochus argues, we need to discover Plato's views and order them into a system. This enterprise of recovering Plato's doctrines and structuring them into a system was originally undertaken by his disciples, the early Academics, Aristotle, and the early Peripatetics. Varro outlines Antiochus' view first regarding Socrates (*Acad.* 1. 15–16) and then about Plato and his students (*Acad.* 1. 17–18). I quote the latter part.

> Yet originating with Plato, a thinker of variety, complexity, and fertility, there was established a philosophy which, though it had two names, the one of the Academics and the other of the Peripatetics, nonetheless was a uniform system, as the two schools differed only in name but agreed in doctrine. Plato left his sister's son, Speusippus, as heir, as it were, of his philosophy, but Xenocrates of Chalcedon and Aristotle of Stagira excelled in zeal and learning. The followers of Aristotle were called Peripatetics, because they used to debate while walking in the Lyceum, while the others were called Academics because they used to meet and have discussions in Plato's own institute, i.e. Academy, which is another gymnasium; so they were named from the place. Yet, both schools drew from Plato's abundance and both composed a certain doctrinal system (*formulam disciplinae*), and this was fully and copiously set forth, whereas they abandoned the famous Socratic practice of discussing everything and leaving it in doubt without affirming anything. Hence has come about something of which Socrates hardly approved, a certain discipline of philosophy (*ars quaedam philosophiae*) with a regular arrangement of subjects and a system of doctrines (*descriptio disciplinae*). At first, as I said, there was a single system though it had two names, since there was no difference between the Peripatetics and the original Old Academy. In my view, Aristotle excelled in intellectual ingenuity,

but both schools drew from the same source, and both made the same classification of things to be desired and to be avoided. (*Acad.* 1. 17–18)

We see that Varro contrasts Plato's philosophy with that of Socrates, which he discussed first (ibid. 15–16), arguing for the superiority of the former.[20] Yet Varro neither ignores nor repudiates Plato's debt to Socrates. Rather, he admits that Plato's philosophy had its roots in Socrates' thought and acknowledges that Plato's early dialogues preserve the spirit of Socrates, since they enquire into virtue in a dialectical manner.[21] The contrast between Socratic and Platonic philosophy involves then a contrast between a Socratic and a more mature period of Plato, which is similar to our modern distinction of an early Socratic phase of Plato and a later more Platonic one.[22] Quite remarkably Varro's criticism of Socrates does not concern only his aporetic spirit (*Acad.* 1. 16–17), to which the sceptic Academics famously appealed, but also Socrates' one-sided concern with ethics (ibid. 1. 16fin). In Varro's view, Plato went far beyond Socrates in his mature and late dialogues in methodology as well as in content: first he presented doctrines instead of dialectical arguments and secondly these doctrines covered a wide range of philosophical issues and also were connected in such a way that they constituted a doctrinal system.[23] For the Antiochean Varro, Plato's merit lies precisely in these dialogues, and it is on them that Plato's students, mainly Xenocrates and Aristotle, relied in order to formulate a system based on their teacher's doctrine (ibid. 1. 17).

Two difficulties arise here. The first concerns what, according to Antiochus, Plato's students actually did. The second is how their achievement precisely relates to Plato's philosophy.

The first question involves an understanding of the term *disciplina*, which Lucullus uses in *Academica* 2. 15 to characterize Plato's philosophical heritage; he argues that Plato left behind him a *perfectissimam*

[20] Cf. *De orat.* 3. 60–2.

[21] *omnis eius* [sc. Socrates] *oratio tamen in virtute laudanda et in hominibus ad virtutis studium cohortandis consumebatur, ut e Socraticorum libris maximeque Platonis intellegi potest.* (All of Socrates' discourses were concerned with the praise of virtue and with urging men to pursuing virtue, as it becomes plain in the books of his pupils, especially those of Plato); *Acad.* 1. 16fin. Cf. *Acad.* 1. 16init. *De orat.* 3. 60. Antiochus apparently relies largely on Plato's early dialogues for his picture of Socrates.

[22] This refutes the claim of Annas (1999: 32) that ancient Platonists did not distinguish between a 'Socratic' and a 'Platonic' period of Plato but took for granted that Plato had one ethical position, and more specifically that the argument of the *Republic* 'was seen as being essentially the same with that of the Socratic dialogues' (p. 94). Quite clearly Antiochus did not believe this. See also below s. 5 on Antiochus' ethics.

[23] Cf. *Acad.* 2. 15; *De orat.* 3. 60–1.

disciplinam, the Peripatos and the Academy.[24] The term admits several meanings among which the two most relevant are the following: (*a*) a 'philosophical school' in the institutional sense (cf. e.g. *Acad.* 1. 34), and (*b*) a 'school of thought' or a 'philosophical system' (cf. e.g. *Acad.* 1. 43, *De fin.* 5. 9, 74). Clearly the first meaning does not suit our passage, as we are presented with two distinct institutions, the Academy and the Peripatos, which shared Plato's philosophy. So the term must have the meaning (*b*). The question now becomes one of locating a more specific meaning. What is that that the Academy and the Peripatos shared? Antiochus' spokesmen refer to the Peripatetic philosophy as a distinct philosophical system (*De fin.* 5. 9, 74, *Acad.* 1. 33), and as we will see they are aware of the differences between the Peripatetic and the Academic system, and also of the Peripatetic divergences from Plato (*Acad.* 1. 33–4). But such divergences cannot be asserted unless one assumes a Platonic doctrinal system. It is unclear, then, whether Lucullus suggests that Plato had had a doctrinal system, which Academics and Peripatetics developed in different ways, or whether he ascribes to Plato a school of thought rather than a fixed doctrinal system.

The latter option gains some support from Varro's claim in *Academica* 1. 17. He argues that Academics and Peripatetics constructed a *formulam disciplinae* drawing from Plato, who is presented as having a very fertile philosophical mind but no clearly articulated philosophical system.[25] Yet this passage sharpens rather than solves the question as to how, according to Antiochus, the philosophy of Academics and Peripatetics relate to that of Plato.

There are two issues here. The first concerns Antiochus' beliefs regarding Plato's identity as a systematic philosopher. Did he believe that Plato had espoused a doctrinal philosophical system, which, owing to the latter's famously obscure style of writing had required reassembly by the early Academics and Peripatetics? Or did he believe that such a system was solely the creation of the early Academics and Peripatetics, who sought to give doctrinal and systematic status to ideas Plato had only hinted at? The second issue is whether this system, be it Plato's or a later construction, was a complete one.

[24] *Plato . . . reliquit perfectissimam disciplinam, Peripateticos et Academicos* (*Acad.* 2. 15). See *OLD*, s.v. *disciplina* and Glucker (1978: 198–203), who discusses the relevant references in some detail.

[25] *Sed utrisque Platonis ubertate completi certam quandam disciplinae formulam composuerunt et eam quidem plenam ac refertam . . .* (But both [the Academy and the Peripatos] drew much from Plato's abundance and both formed a certain doctrinal system, which was elaborate and copious); *Acad.* 1. 17.

As far as the first issue is concerned, most probably Antiochus did not see much difference between the two possibilities. His view presumably was that Plato did have a philosophical system, as Varro maintains in *Academica* 1. 19, 33–4,[26] but that this system existed in disguise in his dialogues and was in need of articulation and reconstruction, which the Academics and the Peripatetics were happy to provide.[27] What matters for Antiochus is that the system which emerged from this reconstruction in a very strong sense is Plato's (*Platonis auctoritate*).[28] It is probably this belief which explains why Antiochus, at least as we know him through his spokesmen in Cicero's works, very rarely refers to Plato's texts for the reconstruction of his doctrines.[29] However, to pass to the second issue, Varro's formulations in *Academica* 1. 17 and 1. 33 clearly suggest that this system was not complete but rather a first draft (*quandam formulam disciplinae, prima forma*), that could be further elaborated and perfected. This is an important point to which I will return later on.

What also becomes clear in *Academica* 1. 17 is that Antiochus sees neither conflict nor competition between the Academy and the Peripatos, or between their respective heads, Xenocrates and Aristotle. Rather, they are considered as one in their respect for Plato and in their effort to articulate and systematize Plato's views, differing only in name not in substance.[30] Indeed, Antiochus speaks interchangeably of the 'ancient Academy' (*vetus Academia*), which comprises the Academics from Speusippus to Crantor, and of the 'ancients' (*veteres*), a term which comprises the early Academics and the Peripatetics up to Strato, that is, basically Aristotle and Theophrastus.[31]

However, Antiochus' view on the matter, as reported by Cicero, appears in a range of variations. In some passages the 'ancients' are seen as forming a union and no difference among them is

[26] On these passages see Fladerer (1996: 38–40).

[27] Cf. *De fin.* 4. 3. This is also what Sextus suggests in *Adv. Math.* 7. 16. See Introduction p. 14, n. 40.

[28] The term *auctoritas* can mean both 'origination', 'production', and 'authority' (cf. *OLD*, s.v.); in *Acad.* 1. 17 it is used in the first sense, while in *Acad.* 1. 34 in the second one.

[29] We do find a quotation from the *Laws* in *De fin.* 5. 59 and a reference to Plato's *Seventh Letter* in *Tusc. Disp.* 5. 100, but we cannot be sure that this evidence reflects Antiochus' knowledge of Plato.

[30] *Acad.* 1. 17–18, 2. 15. This is the first occurrence of the legend of the division of Plato's school in two branches and of the aetiology of their names after the meeting-places, which will be popular in doxography and in the *Prolegomena* to Aristotelian commentaries. See Düring (1957: 406–7).

[31] Important for Antiochus' view of the 'ancients' is Görler (1990).

acknowledged.[32] In other passages, though, Academics and Peripatetics appear to differ at least in terminology (*De fin.* 4. 5; cf. *De orat.* 3. 67), while elsewhere minor doctrinal differences between the two schools are acknowledged (*De leg.* 1. 37–8). These variations are easily explicable. Varro in his speech wants to emphasize the common heritage of early Academics and Peripatetics in order to contrast them with the 'New Academy'. But when he then passes on to the Peripatetics he does not hesitate to argue that they abandoned some originally Platonic doctrines (*Acad.* 1. 33–4). One of them was Plato's theory of Forms from which first Aristotle departed (ibid. 1. 33; more below, in s. 3). Theophrastus' divergence in ethics is presented as more serious (ibid.), and cautious use of his work *On Happiness* is recommended.[33]

Some other indications also suggest that Antiochus was aware that the 'ancients' in general differed among themselves, though his spokesmen do not make this explicit, as they are mainly concerned with promoting the idea of their unity. To begin with, each of the 'ancients' is depicted according to his own strengths, and some are presented as being more important than others. Most conspicuously, Antiochus does not seem to hold Speusippus in the same rank as Xenocrates and Aristotle, although he acknowledges that he was Plato's appointed successor and alleged heir (*quasi heredem*; *Acad.* 1. 17). We do not know why Antiochus was reserved against Speusippus. One possibility is that he disapproved of Speusippus' condemnation of pleasure.[34] This is possible in view of the fact that, as will be seen below in section 5, Antiochus considered bodily goods as also contributing to happiness. If Antiochus was able to discern differences between Aristotelian and Theophrastean ethics (*De fin.* 5. 12), he must have been able to see differences between Speusippean and Aristotelian ethics too.

Antiochus must have discerned differences in ethics also between individual Academics. This is suggested by the fact that he prefers

[32] *'Existimo igitur,' inquam, 'Cato, veteres illos Platonis auditores, Speusippum, Aristotelem, Xenocratem, deinde eorum Polemonem, Theophrastum, satis et copiose, et eleganter habuisse disciplinam* (I believe then, Cato, I said, that those old pupils of Plato, Speusippus, Aristotle and Xenocrates, and afterwards their pupils, Polemo and Theophrastus, had developed a philosophical system in a complete, copious and elaborate way; *De fin.* 4. 3). Cf. *Acad.* 1. 17–18, 2. 15; *De fin.* 4. 72, 5. 7, 21; *De leg.* 1. 55.

[33] *De fin.* 5. 12; cf. *Tusc. Disp.* 5. 24, 85. Theophrastus' place among the *veteres* sometimes appears doubtful (*Acad.* 1. 33, 35). His epistemology, though, is close to Antiochus' own. See below pp. 68, 76.

[34] Tarán (1981: 212–13) does not offer any insight on this; on Speusippus' ethics see Tarán (1981: 78–85) and Dillon (2003: 64–77).

Aristotle and Polemo not only to Speusippus but also to Xenocrates and Crantor. The fact he passes over their differences in silence does not mean that he was not aware of them, as Cicero argues (*Acad.* 2. 135–6). Some other differences are also ignored, namely those between Aristotle's doctrines and those of early Peripatetics, like Dicaearchus. Cicero is critical of Dicaearchus' those (*Acad.* 2. 124), and Antiochus must have been as well. However, Antiochus' spokesmen make explicit reference to Strato's severe divergence from Plato and from the other Peripatetics (*Acad.* 1. 34; *De fin.* 5. 13). On the whole Antiochus seems to be aware that the 'ancients' differed, and sometimes their differences were sometimes considerable. Where, then, does Antiochus find them to be in accord?

The prime example of the unity of the 'ancients' for Antiochus is their unanimous construal of Plato's philosophy as being doctrinal in nature. The second aspect of their philosophical concord lay in their shared commitment to articulating and arranging Plato's doctrines into a systematic philosophy. Thirdly, the harmony of the 'ancients' is also proven by their agreement on certain crucial doctrines (*re congruentes*; *Acad.* 2. 15), such as the view that man is naturally able to attain secure knowledge and that virtue is the essence of a good life but that, given man's nature, life cannot be perfectly happy unless some other goods are also obtained. Indeed, Varro highlights the latter aspect when he mentions as an indication of the common debt of the early Academics and Peripatetics to Plato's doctrine their agreement in the classification of objects to be desired and to be avoided (*Acad.* 1. 18).

The view which emerges from this evidence about the accord of the 'ancients' is confirmed if we look at Antiochus' criticism of those who broke it. On the one hand, Antiochus argues, the tradition was broken by the sceptical Academy,[35] and on the other it was broken in the Peripatos by Theophrastus' successor, Strato. While sceptical Academics altogether rejected the doctrinal nature of Plato's philosophy and the possibility of attaining secure knowledge, with Strato, Antiochus argues, the Peripatos abandoned epistemology and especially ethics, the area in

[35] Characteristic are the verbs *perturbare, everteret* (*Acad.* 2. 14–15) which Lucullus uses to describe the effect of the sceptical Academy on the philosophical heritage of the 'ancients'; cf. Numenius fr. 25. 4–101 Des Places. Numenius extends the argument about the distortion of Plato's heritage also to the early Academics (fr. 24. 10–14). See Ch. 3, s. 1, pp. 127–32.

which Peripatetics until then had specialized, to turn to natural philosophy (*Acad.* 1. 34; *De fin.* 5. 13).[36]

Antiochus then seems to believe that this process of arranging Plato's views into a system of doctrines came to an abrupt end. But as I have argued above, Antiochus' spokesmen also seem to suggest that the Platonic system of doctrines was neither perfect nor complete in their reconstruction by the early Academics and Peripatetics, but there was still room for articulating those views which had not been worked out. The thrust of Antiochus' argument against Philo's final thesis on the unity of the Academy (Philo III) lies in the claim that such a contribution took place with the Stoics. Antiochus argues that Zeno, who was, together with Arcesilaus, a student of Polemo, continued and indeed reformed (*corrigere*) the Platonist tradition.[37]

This was an amazing claim for an Academic. In what sense did the Stoics continue the Platonist tradition? In Antiochus' view, the Stoics followed the 'ancients' in an oblique way; they did not preserve their system intact but rather tried to reform it in various respects. Some of their doctrinal reformations were for the better, some for the worse, and some were mere changes in vocabulary.[38] As regards the improvements, Antiochus argues that the Stoics expounded epistemology in a way that no Platonist had done previously. In his opinion, Stoic epistemology was not one of the doctrines of the 'ancients' but nevertheless was a well-justified development (*Acad.* 1. 42). Antiochus thus admits that Stoic epistemology was not strictly speaking a reconstruction of Plato's views, but rather a genuinely Stoic theory, which, however, did justice to Plato's spirit. Below (s. 4) I will try to explain in what sense Antiochus maintained this. Regarding ethics, however, Antiochus considers the Stoic

[36] Later Peripatetics are excluded for similar reasons; cf. *De fin.* 5. 13 regarding Lyco. Different is the case of Hieronymus (*c.* 290–30) who deserted the Peripatos under Lyco and held as *summum bonum* the freedom of pain (*De fin.* 2. 8, 19, 5. 14, 73; *Acad.* 2. 131, *Tusc. D.* 5. 84) As will be seen in the next chapter, Plutarch also considers Strato as diverging from Platonic and Aristotelian philosophy (pp. 97, 110).

[37] *Zeno... corrigere conatus est disciplinam. Eam quoque, si videtur, correctionem explicabo, sicut solebat Antiochus.* (Zeno... tried to reform the doctrinal system [of Plato]. In the following I will expound this reformed discipline, as it used to be expounded by Antiochus); *Acad.* 1. 35. Cf. ibid. 1. 43.

[38] Görler (1990: 136–7) is wrong to claim that Antiochus has only praise for the Stoics because he saw in them only an improvement of the ancient system. The analysis below (ss. 4–5) proves that this was hardly the case. Antiochus' view can be found in modern scholarship. Paul Shorey argued that 'Stoicism... even more than Aristotelianism, is an episode in the history of Platonism' and that 'Stoicism differs only in terminology in which it clothed ideas borrowed from Plato and Aristotle' (*Platonism Ancient and Modern* (Berkeley, Calif., 1938). 19, 21–2).

innovations to be completely unjustified.[39] Their main innovation, he argues, was their denial of any good other than virtue on the grounds that man essentially is reason[40] and thus they postulated that virtue, as the excellence of man's essential feature, is incomparable with non-rational goods (*Acad.* 1. 38).

Antiochus' criticism of Stoic ethics will be outlined below (in s. 5). Here I want to stress that his chief criticism of the Stoics was not that they sometimes diverged from Plato's view, but rather that they did so *because* they were driven by the selfish concern to justify their novel school, a criticism which concerns primarily the Stoic divergence in ethics (*De fin.* 4. 19–68). This means that for Antiochus, the Stoics were Platonists in disguise. This actually explains why he was so seriously concerned with the value of Stoic tenets, because he thought that the Stoics systematically had drawn on, or, as Antiochus puts it, had stolen Plato's doctrines to varying extents, though they concealed this behind their sophisticated philosophical jargon (*De fin.* 4. 60, 5. 22). Once we dispense with this, or interpret this rightly, Antiochus maintained, we simply obtain Plato's views (*De fin.* 5. 88–9).

Antiochus' consideration of the Stoics shows two things. First, it seems to confirm that Antiochus did not think of Plato's philosophy as constituting a closed and fixed system, as later Platonists do,[41] but rather as a project amenable to further development. And for Antiochus, such a development was Stoic epistemology. Second, it emerges that Antiochus was concerned with the unity of the Platonist tradition as a whole, not just of the Academy. This was an important new step, whose origins, I suggested, probably go back to Philo. The replacement of the term 'Academic' with that of 'Platonist', which, as Glucker rightly argued, occurs only in the second century AD,[42] must have its roots in Antiochus' conception that being a follower of Plato amounts to adhering to Plato's doctrines rather than being a member of the Academy. In this sense Aristotle and also Zeno essentially are Platonists while Arcesilaus and Philo are not.

The question which arises now is why in Antiochus' view Aristotle and Zeno qualify to be Platonists at all. This is a complex matter. What

39 *Acad.* 1. 37–40. Notice the expressions meaning 'change': [Zeno] *commutaverat* (1. 37); *discrepabat* (ibid. 1. 39), *mutavit*: (1. 40; concerning Zeno's innovations in physics).

40 *Acad.* 2. 135; *De fin.* 4. 43–5, 5. 78.

41 See Numenius fr. 24 Des Places and more explicitly Atticus fr. 1 Des Places. See Chs. 3 and 4, pp. 127–31, 158, 174–5.

42 Glucker (1978: 206–25).

we must ask is why Antiochus believes that Aristotle conveys Platonic ethics, and why he considers Zeno's epistemology to be compatible with that of Plato. This is tantamount to asking what Antiochus considers Plato's doctrines themselves to be, a question that he never answers directly, at least in the existing evidence. I will try to reconstruct Antiochus' conception of Plato's doctrines in sections 4 and 5. Yet one answer about Antiochus' conception of Platonist identity seems to be quite straightforward. He considered agreement in ethics which united early Platonists more important than accord in epistemology. Antiochus actually emphasized that a difference in ethics amounts to a difference in one's total philosophical standpoint.[43] Accordingly, he excluded from the Platonist tradition Peripatetics like Strato and Lyco because they abandoned ethics (*Acad.* 1. 34; *De fin.* 5. 13), while Theophrastus has a rather ambiguous place in it, because his ethical views are not judged to be sound enough (*De fin.* 5. 12, *Acad.* 1. 33). On the same grounds, the Stoics' deviation in ethics from what Antiochus considered to be Platonic outweighs his approval of their epistemology and this is why he eventually excludes them from the Platonist tradition, whereas regarding Aristotle, Antiochus holds him in esteem as an important Platonist on the grounds that his ethics, together with that of Polemo, represent Plato's (*De fin.* 5. 12, 14). This shows that for Antiochus the essential criterion for judging one's Platonist identity is not dogmatism but a certain kind of dogmatism which essentially concerns ethics. It is on such grounds that Antiochus singled out Aristotle for his philosophical merit among all of Plato's pupils, and held him to be second only to Plato.[44]

3. THE EXTENT OF ARISTOTLE'S AGREEMENT WITH PLATO

Cicero offers evidence to the effect that Antiochus' respect for Aristotle and approval of his ethics, in particular, was founded on first-hand knowledge of Aristotle's work. First, Antiochus' spokesman, Piso, makes reference to the *Nicomachean Ethics* at the beginning of his

[43] *qui de summo bono dissentit, de tota philosophiae ratione dissentit* (*De fin.* 5. 14). Cf. *Acad.* 2. 132; *De fin.* 4.14.

[44] *princeps philosophorum,* Plato excepted (*De fin.* 5. 7); *abundantia quaedam ingenii praestabat Aristoteles (Acad.* 1. 18).

exposition of the ethics of the 'ancients' (*De fin.* 5. 12fin). Piso is presented as having good knowledge of Aristotle's work as a whole. He refers to Aristotle's two classes of treatises, the esoteric and the exoteric ones, to reassure us that there is no difference between them as regards his main ethical doctrine (*De fin.* 5. 12init.).[45] Secondly, Cicero expects Piso to be well versed in both Academic and Peripatetic philosophy, since he was taught by Antiochus and Staseas of Naples (*De fin.* 5. 8). Staseas' profession was the teaching of Aristotle's philosophy (*De fin.* 5. 75),[46] but Piso takes Antiochus to be a far better exponent of the Peripatetic views than Staseas himself (ibid.).[47]

Antiochus' knowledge of Aristotle is confirmed by his awareness of Aristotle's departure from some doctrines which Antiochus regards as Platonic. In the *Academica* Antiochus highlights one of Aristotle's most important points of divergence from Plato, though he seems to be aware of some further minor ones, such as Aristotle's doctrine of aether.[48] For Antiochus, Aristotle's main doctrinal departure from Plato was his abandonment of Plato's theory of Forms. The formulation of Varro's remark is quite important. I quote the relevant passage:

> Aristoteles primus species quas paulo ante dixi labefectavit, quas mirifice Plato erat amplexatus, ut in iis *quiddam* divinum esse diceret. Theophrastus autem ... vehementius etiam fregit quodam modo auctoritatem veteris disciplinae; spoliavit enim virtutem suo decore imbecillamque reddidit quod negavit in ea sola positum esse beate vivere. (*Acad.* 1. 33)

> Aristotle was the first to overthrow the Forms of which I spoke a little while before [*Acad.* 1. 30], which Plato had valued so much as to attribute to them an element of divinity. Theophrastus also ... in a way broke the authority of the old doctrine even more violently; for he robbed virtue of her sublimity and weakened her power by denying that the good life is placed in virtue alone.

The tone and substance of Varro's remark have been debated in scholarship. Reid,[49] Merlan,[50] and Görler[51] have detected strong criticism of Aristotle here. Reid even takes this criticism to be incompatible with

[45] For a commentary on this passage see Düring (1957: 265).

[46] On Staseas see Lynch (1972: 137); Moraux (1973: 217–21); Rawson (1985: 9, 22, 81).

[47] Cicero (*De fin.* 5. 75) remains sceptical as to whether Antiochus or Staseas construed more charitably Aristotle's views. Staseas emphasized bodily goods more than Antiochus. On this see below, s. 5.

[48] Antiochus appears to withhold judgement on how close Aristotle is to Plato's doctrine in this regard (cf. *Acad.* 1. 26, 39; *De fin.* 4. 12). Cf. Ch. 2, pp. 104–5.

[49] Reid (1885: 141).

[50] Merlan (1967: 53).

[51] Görler (1990: 133 n. 27).

Antiochus' general approval of Aristotle, and on these grounds he disputes that this passage reflects Antiochus. I find this hardly convincing. Barnes on the other hand seems to accept that the remark has a critical tone but he argues that there is no hostility here, because Antiochus' interest in the Forms was purely historical.[52] This does not seem to me quite right either. I agree that Antiochus is not hostile here but the fact that the passage has a historical character does not necessarily mean that Antiochus had only a historical interest in the Forms, and the following hopefully proves this.[53]

To begin with, the formulation of the passage clearly shows, I think, that Varro's remark is definitely meant to be critical. The fact that Aristotle is presented as disputing a doctrine which Plato 'valued so much' suggests that Aristotle's divergence from it is criticized. The cases of Theophrastus and Strato which follow also show that Antiochus is generally critical of the Peripatetic alterations (*immutationes*; *Acad.* 1. 33init.) of Plato's doctrine. But it also becomes clear that Antiochus' disapproval of doctrinal innovations varies depending on how serious, in his view, the break with the old doctrine was.

Two facts immediately suggest that Aristotle's divergence from Plato is regarded as much less serious than any other mentioned. First, Varro appears to mention them in ascending degree of seriousness, starting with Aristotle and ending with Strato. Secondly, Varro had first established that Aristotle on the whole preserves Plato's doctrine (*Acad.* 1. 17–18, 33). But let us first see what doctrine is exactly that Aristotle is accused of having abandoned.

Antiochus' spokesman, Varro, must be referring to Aristotle's criticism of Plato's transcendent Forms.[54] This is supported by Varro's reference to the divine aspect of the Forms. He probably refers to the Form of Good in *Republic* 6 (508e), which was often taken to be Plato's God. Also elsewhere in Plato's work the Forms are said to be divine and discernible only by the philosopher (e.g. *Sophist* 254a). Yet earlier in his account Varro, speaking of the doctrine of Forms, argues that the 'ancients' (including Aristotle), shared the view that the Forms are those immutable entities which exist in the mind. The passage is further illuminating about Antiochus' view on the Forms. I quote it below.

Quamquam oriretur a sensibus, tamen non esse iudicium veritatis in sensibus: mentem volebant rerum esse iudicem; solam censebant idoneam cui credetur,

[52] Barnes (1989: 95). [53] This has been argued by Dillon (1977: 92).

[54] As already Zeller (1923: iii. 604) argued.

quia sola cerneret id quod semper esset simplex et unius modi et tale quale esset. Hanc illi ἰδέα appellant, iam a Platone ita nominatam, nos recte speciem possumus dicere. (*Acad.* 1. 30)

To judge the truth is not a matter for the senses, although it originates in the senses. According to the 'ancients', the judge of things is the mind. They maintained that the mind alone is to be trusted, because it alone perceives that which is eternally simple, stable, the same and true to its quality. They called this thing *idea*, a name which Plato already had given to it, but we can call it appropriately form (*species*).

This account of the Forms as immutable entities is certainly Platonic in origin. Plato often argues that the Forms, being always stable and simple, qualify as true being—as opposed to the material entities which belong to the realm of becoming.[55] The passage refers to two important aspects of the Forms: (*a*) the mind perceives by capturing them, and (*b*) they are immanent in material entities and account for the way these entities are, i.e. they are their essences.[56] The latter aspect in particular turns out to be quite crucial in this context. Varro argues in what follows that the senses are fallible; either they do not notice certain things at all, or they see things as they appear to them, namely in continuous motion and change, and thus the senses only allow for opinion. The mind, on the other hand, it is argued, can achieve knowledge because it can perceive what is stable and unchanging in the objects, that is, the Forms (*Acad.* 1. 31–2). I will try to explain how this is supposed to work in section 4.

Yet we should not rush to conclude that in this passage Antiochus' spokesman considers the Forms only as immanent. The expression '*id quod semper esset simplex* ...' can be understood as either 'what eternally is simple ...', or as 'what exists eternally, simple ...'. In either case, though, it refers to the eternal existence, simplicity, and stability of the Forms. But eternal existence in particular is a feature of the transcendent Forms. Nor does the passage suggest that the Forms exist only in the mind. Quite the opposite is the case. The mind, we are told, perceives what exists outside it, but, unlike the senses, the mind perceives the Forms, which are such (stable, simple) that they can convey

[55] See Dillon (1977: 92–3) and Görler (1990: 129), who refer us to *Phaedo* 78d and *Timaeus* 28a, 35a Cf. *Philebus* 61d–e; *Sophist* 251d–252a.

[56] Fladerer (1996: 112–14) takes the *hanc* of the passage cited to refer to *mentem*, and argues that the mind is the Form, 'das objectiv Erkennende'. But this is a mistake (which vitiates his entire epistemological section); *hanc* stands for *hoc* by attraction to ἰδέαν, as Reid (1885: 136) explains. See also Görler (1990: 129).

accurate knowledge. This undermines the famous scholarly hypothesis that Antiochus regarded the Forms as thoughts in a divine mind, which, at any rate, is not supported by any evidence.[57]

The above quoted passage, and also the rest of the relevant evidence about Antiochus, strongly suggest that he considered the Forms to be both transcendent and immanent but he was much more interested in the immanent aspect of the Forms, as he was concerned with perceptual knowledge and their role in it, and was much less interested in their transcendent aspect. Besides, the fact that Eudorus, who appears to have opposed Antiochus' reconstruction of Plato's system, highlighted precisely this aspect of the Forms,[58] strengthens the belief that Antiochus did not consider them primarily as transcendent.[59]

The conclusion that emerges from the above discussion is that the Antiochean Varro does criticize Aristotle's rejection of the transcendent aspect of the Forms, which he considers as constituting part of Plato's original doctrine, but that this criticism is mild because Aristotle adheres to Plato's belief in the unchanging sameness of the Forms, which Antiochus takes to be the principal aspect of Plato's doctrine of the Forms. For this reason Antiochus appears to believe that Aristotle's difference from Plato is practically minimal in this respect. Antiochus' thesis will be strongly rejected by later Platonists like Atticus and Plotinus, who will argue (with good reason) that the difference between Plato and Aristotle in this matter is enormous. This does not mean, though, that Antiochus makes a concession to Aristotle, while later Platonists do not. Antiochus does not share the strong metaphysical concerns of later Platonists, concerns which will give rise to objections of a different order. For Antiochus the most important aspect of the

[57] This idea, which occurs in later texts, was first argued by Theiler in 1930 (I use his 2nd edn, 1964: 40–3). He was followed by Luck (1953: 28–30); Loenen (1957: 44–5); Armstrong (1960: 401–2); Dillon (1977: 93–6); Lilla (1990). But neither the texts mentioned above, nor any other text I know of compellingly shows that Antiochus held such a view. Scholars have suggested this largely because they believe that such an idea would help Antiochus square Platonism with Stoic theology. But, as I argue, Antiochus did not mean to square Platonism with Stoicism, and what is more, he was not interested in theology. For a review of the relevant literature see Fladerer (1996: 101–5).

[58] See Simplicius, *In Phys.* 181. 7–30; Alexander, *In Met.* 58. 31–59. 8 (frs. 2–5 Mazzarelli). I discuss Eudorus below at s. 7, pp. 81–2.

[59] Antiochus' acceptance of two principles matter and God, who acts on matter and permeates everything (*Acad.* 1. 24, 28, 2. 118–19), should not be taken as evidence about his position on transcendent Forms. This is a view which already Theophrastus (*DG*, p. 485) ascribes to Plato (cf. DL 3. 69; Aristocles fr. 3 Heiland/Chiesara). Antiochus relies on the *Timaeus* and *Laws* 10 from which the Stoics were inspired.

Forms is their role in attaining knowledge, and in this he argues (with some reason) that Aristotle follows Plato. The question which now arises is what precisely this role is.

4. EPISTEMOLOGY

As I already alluded to, for Antiochus the Forms have both a metaphysical and an epistemological aspect: they correspond to the essence of a thing, which is crucial for recognizing things as such. Already in Plato's middle dialogues the object of knowledge is the Forms (e.g. *Republic* 475e–480a), which are immutable and represent real beings. Plato appears to think that there must be such Forms if there is to be secure knowledge or satisfactory explanation. In his later dialogues, like the *Theaetetus* or the *Sophist*, the attainment of knowledge, including perceptual knowledge, may be considered as involving reference to the intelligible Form of an object, which is its essence.[60] In *Theaetetus* 186c–d we are told that no one can have knowledge unless he grasps being (*ousia*). And in both the *Theaetetus* (187a–b) and the *Sophist* (264b) perception involves judgement of what is true or false.

Antiochus finds in Stoicism such an essentialist or judgemental construal of knowledge. He appears to consider Forms as being primarily concepts, which enable us to perceive things as they are. This is suggested by the following evidence. After his reference to Forms in *Academica* 1. 30, Varro contends that 'knowledge exists only in the notions (*notiones*) and the reasonings (*rationes*) of the mind' (ibid. 1. 32). The discussion here (ibid. 1. 30–1) remains one over that which is stable (the Forms) and that which admits of change (material objects), and Varro continues to expound that the 'ancients' define something in terms of what is stable in it. Lucullus, who also discusses how the mind forms *notiones* from sense impressions, remarks that the Greek term for *notiones* is *ennoiai* or *prolêpseis*, which in the Stoic system amount to concepts that the human mind develops (*Acad.* 2. 30). And the Antiochean Piso refers to mental contents in similar terms;

[60] See Frede, 'Perception in Plato's Later Dialogues', in *Essays in Ancient Philosophy* (Oxford, 1987), 3–8, and esp. Burnyeat (1976: 43–9). Cf. Parmenides' response to Socrates' criticism of the Forms. Parmenides argues that if there are no Forms, there will be nothing to turn one's thought towards and no possibility of conversation (*Parmenides* 135b–c).

he talks about *notiones* with which we are endowed by nature and which reason later develops (*De fin.* 5. 59).

These passages strongly suggest that Antiochus equated the Stoic concepts (*ennoiai*) with the Platonic/Aristotelian immanent Forms. This becomes particularly clear in *De finibus* 5. 59, where Antiochus tries to reconcile the Stoic view that the mind, being at birth a *tabula rasa*, develops concepts from repeated sensations,[61] with the Platonic belief outlined in the *Meno* that our souls possess innate concepts prior to experience.[62] In the other passages I referred to above, however, Antiochus appears to remain faithful to the Stoic view of mental concepts.[63] This suggests to me that Antiochus did not see much difference between the Platonic and the Stoic view in metaphysical terms. Yet their views not only are substantially different in such terms, they are incompatible, since Plato's suggestion, as outlined in the *Meno* for instance, that we are endowed with Forms before our birth contradicts the Stoic view according to which the mind is at birth a *tabula rasa*. Antiochus does not seem to have paid attention to such differences, presumably because what was of importance for him was that the Stoic concepts and the Platonic/Aristotelian Forms have the same function in perception.

Antiochus follows the Stoics in reserving perceptual knowledge essentially for the mind by modelling it on thinking, in a way reminiscent of Descartes. This is why he argues, like the Stoics that it is not the senses but the mind *through* the senses that accounts for perception.[64]

[61] *Etsi dedit [sc. natura] talem mentem quae omnem virtutem accipere posset, ingenuitque sine doctrina notitias parvas rerum maximarum et quasi instituit docere, et induxit in ea quae inerant tamquam elementa virtutis.* (But the nature bestowed an intellect capable of attaining every virtue and implanted in it at birth and without instruction embryonic notions of the most important things, laying the foundation of its education and introducing among its endowments the elements of virtue); *De fin.* 5. 59, Rackham's tr. modified. Cf. Aetius 4. 11. 1 (=*SVF* ii. 83).

[62] See Theiler (1964: 41) on this.

[63] Reid (1885: 213) wrongly insists in his discussion of *Acad.* 2. 30 that Madvig was mistaken to believe that Antiochus had ever reconciled the Stoic teaching with the Platonic theory of recollection. The evidence supports the opposite conclusion. Alcinous, *Didasc.* 154. 10–156. 23 outlines an epistemology similar to that of Antiochus, as he also seems to assume that the natural concepts amount to Forms (ibid. 155. 24–8).

[64] *Atqui qualia sunt haec quae sensibus percipi dicimus, talia secuntur ea quae non sensibus ipsis percipi dicuntur sed quodam modo sensibus, ut haec: 'Illud est album, hoc dulce, canorum illud, hoc bene olens, hoc asperum'. Animo iam haec tenemus comprehensa, non sensibus. 'Ille' deinceps 'equus est, ille canis.'* (But then whatever character belongs to these objects which we say are perceived by the senses must belong to that following set of objects which are said to be perceived not by actual sensation but by a sort of sensation, as for example: this thing is white, this thing is sweet, that one is melodious, this fragrant,

The Stoics and Antiochus maintain, like Kant, that our perceptual knowledge is judgemental or propositional. That is to say that when we perceive a horse, we do so by thinking 'this is a horse'. Our sense impressions may be true or false, depending on whether their propositional content is true or false. The impression that this is a horse is true, because the proposition 'this is a horse' at the time is true (*Acad.* 2. 21).[65]

In Antiochus' view, in order to reach perceptual knowledge two kinds of conditions must be met; first, conditions concerning the sense impressions of the objects we perceive, and secondly conditions concerning the cognitive constitution of the perceiving subject.[66] Within the first kind fall conditions that involve sufficient light, the right distance from the object, absence of obstacles, and so on. According to the Stoic view, to which Antiochus adheres, such conditions guarantee that the impression is precise and accurate (*Acad.* 2. 20), so that the object is represented with evidence (*perspicuitas*; Greek: *enargeia*) which false impressions lack (ibid. 2. 45–6, 51). Indeed, he thinks that such impressions have a distinctive feature of truth (ibid. 2. 34).[67] There is a question as to what this mark amounts to. According to one interpretation, which can be termed 'internalist', it is a particular feature to the impression,[68] while according to an alternative, 'externalist', interpretation, it is rather the way our mind perceives such an impression, that is, as true (cf. *Acad.* 1. 40).[69] However this may be, these impressions are distinct and clear because the object is represented in a distinct and clear way, and as such they potentially convey knowledge (this is what the term *katalêptikai phantasiai* suggests).

The second kind of condition is more complicated. Not only do we need to be in a 'normal' mental state (awake, sober, etc.), but Antiochus, like Kant, maintains that in order to acquire perceptual knowledge we

this rough. We grasp this class of percepts by mind, not by the senses. Then 'this object is a horse, this one a dog'. Rackham's tr. modified; *Acad.* 2. 21); cf. ibid. 2. 27, 30–1. See also Antiochus' criticism of Asclepiades of Cos for holding that 'sensations are really perceptions and we apprehend nothing by reason' (Sextus, *Adv. Math.* 7. 201). For a commentary on basic passages on Stoic cognition, see Long and Sedley (1987: i. 241–59, texts 40A–T, 41A–I).

[65] See the text in n. 64.

[66] Cf. Sextus, *Adv. Math.* 7. 253–6 (Long and Sedley 40K), 7. 247–52 (*SVF* ii. 265; Long and Sedley 40E).

[67] Striker (1997: 262–5) has argued that this claim was not part of the original Stoic theory but Antiochus' own. Frede (1987*b*) takes this to represent the orthodox Stoic view.

[68] Striker (1997: 263–4).

[69] Frede (1987*b*: 160–3); cf. Long and Sedley (1987: i. 250).

also need to have certain concepts (*Acad.* 1. 30–2, 2. 21, 30). While the Kantian view is that we have empirical concepts like those of trees and horses and non-empirical ones like substance and causality, for the Stoics all concepts are originally empirical, though some concepts may be formed on the basis of antecedent concepts. If we lack the concept 'horse', we cannot represent the proposition 'this is a horse'. As a result, for the Stoics and Antiochus we cannot perceive a horse. If the sense impression of a horse becomes evident to our mind, this is partly because we already have the concept of a 'horse' so that we can represent it propositionally. That is to say that some sense impressions are evident to us because we have the appropriate sensory and conceptual apparatus to perceive them in such a way. It turns out then that for the Stoics and Antiochus both sense impressions and concepts are necessary for perception. It is for this reason that Chrysippus argued that the criterion of truth consists in both perception (*aesthêsis*) and concepts (*prolêpseis*).[70]

One crucial question in this regard is how we know that our concepts correspond to what we perceive, so that, when we perceive something, we perceive it as it is in reality. The Stoic and also Antiochean answer is that nature constructs us in such a way that sense impressions give rise to concepts which all humans share, and in this way our reason develops. We thus can have further cognitive impressions, this time not only of white and sweet but also of a horse and a tree, while later on in life we can come to conceive of abstract ideas.[71] According to this view, there is a tight relation between our mind and the objects in the world, such that our mind has the ability to acquire knowledge of the things in the world (*Acad.* 2. 31). If we perceive objects such as trees, this is because, by repeatedly having impressions of trees, we have come to form a concept of a 'tree'. This concerns the primary or essential qualities of a 'tree', not accidental ones like colour and size; whatever shape or form a tree may have, it primarily has the form of a tree, which remains the same despite the changes that it undergoes. And the suggestion is that the mind has the ability to perceive a tree because it is equipped with the relevant concept. If one perceives under normal conditions, one can be fairly certain that the perceived object is a tree. This certainty comes from the mind, not the senses. For Antiochus it is in this sense that secure knowledge can be attained. This human ability for secure knowledge is not accidental, because on this view there is an ineluctable foundation

[70] DL 7. 54; cf. *SVF* ii. 473 (Long and Sedley 40A).
[71] DL 7. 53; cf. *Acad.* 2. 21, 2. 30–1; *De fin.* 5. 59.

for human knowledge, which lies in the existence of a close relation between the external world and the human mind. It is such a strong connection between the mind and the external objects that underlies the Stoic cognition (*katalêpsis*) to which Antiochus adheres.

The question, of course, is how Antiochus could have justified his position as a Platonic one. He may have argued that Plato himself was particularly interested in the question what is knowledge and was much worried about the possibility of true knowledge (e.g. in *Meno*, *Republic*, *Theaetetus*, *Philebus*). Indeed, Plato was quite concerned to distinguish opinion from knowledge, and often he appears to suggest that secure knowledge (*epistêmê*) is possible and that it involves knowledge of the Forms.[72] Plato's theory of recollection, for instance, was devised to show precisely this. But Plato did not provide any insight as to how this is supposed to work. Plato, however, did stress in the *Theaetetus* and the *Sophist* that perception presupposes judgement and this is done by the soul or mind. Although Plato and also Aristotle had largely worked out the way in which the human mind achieves knowledge and even anticipated the view that sensations give rise to memory, and this in turn to concepts,[73] for Antiochus it was the Stoics who had actually developed a coherent theory of cognition. For him the main Stoic contribution consisted in their work on cognition and cognitive impressions, and especially on the criterion for judging what qualifies as such. Antiochus considered this crucial, because one is thus given a method by means of which one can decide when secure perceptual knowledge is attained. Yet even as regards cognition, Antiochus could have argued that the Stoics developed a line which was implied in the Platonic/Peripatetic tradition. Already Theophrastus, for instance, had talked about evident impressions which guarantee their truth and deserve assent.[74]

One can object, however, as Cicero did (*Acad.* 2. 112–13), that Academics and Peripatetics invariably had rejected the Stoic view that

[72] Cf. e.g. *Meno* 85c–d, 86a; *Eythydemus* 293b–294b; *Republic* 478a–d; *Phaedo* 99e; *Theaetetus* 186c–187a.

[73] In *Theaetetus* 155e–160e Plato talks about how the percipient is affected by sense impressions and similarly does Aristotle, *De anima* 424^{b}4–19. Plato seems to refer to concepts in *Phaedo* 96b. More clearly, Aristotle does this in *Post. An.* 2. 19; cf. *Acad.* 2. 30–1. Later, Plotinus will talk about the Forms as objects of perception: *Enn.* 3. 6. 18. 21–8, 4. 4. 21. 21. See Emilsson (1988: 74–7, 162).

[74] Sextus, *Adv. Math.* 7. 217–25. Besides, Antiochus would be able to find the term 'criterion' already in Plato (*Theaetetus* 178b6, c1, *Laws* 767b5). A similar epistemology to that of Antiochus is outlined in the Anon. *In Theaet.* 8. 11–38, and esp. fr. D where it is argued that *Theaetetus* is about the criterion. See Sedley (1997).

secure perceptual knowledge is possible, and since Antiochus accepts this part of the Stoic thesis, he is in respect to epistemology a Stoic rather than an Academic or Peripatetic. This criticism, which may reflect that of Philo, seems to me to be fair. It does not really matter how much of the Stoic theory of perceptual knowledge is close to Platonic and Aristotelian views, once Antiochus espouses the part which is absent in Plato and Aristotle, that is their theory of the criterion of truth, he is committed to the Stoic thesis. Aristotle, for instance, differs much from it. He does maintain that the senses are generally reliable and that perception of the proper objects of a sense admits of little falsehood (*De anima* 428^b^18–20; cf. 427^b^11–12), but he never postulates any means of definitely judging the truth of sense impressions.[75]

As has been seen, however, Antiochus did not argue that the Stoic thesis was the view of the 'ancients', but rather argued that it was an improvement (*correctio*) on their view. This suggests that Antiochus accepted the novelty of the Stoic position but maintained that it nevertheless was close to the spirit of the 'ancients'. The rationale behind the latter claim must be along the following lines. Plato and also Aristotle are not only worried about the possibility of attaining secure perceptual knowledge, but they also appear to assume that this is quite basic. Plato and Aristotle consider man to be able to attain knowledge much more advanced than the perceptual, for example, artistic, scientific, and practical knowledge. Against these varieties, perceptual knowledge is in many ways the most basic knowledge man can achieve. It is most basic first because it does not require special intelligence from a man to attain, but rather, as shown above, is in man's nature to do so, and secondly because it is required for advancing to more demanding kinds of knowledge. In logical proof, for instance, argues Lucullus, we attain knowledge by moving through a process of reasoning from things perceived to something not previously perceived.[76]

Yet there is a particular form of knowledge which played a crucial role in convincing Antiochus that secure perceptual knowledge is possible, namely practical knowledge. There is plenty of evidence for this. The Antiochean Lucullus argues that the greatest proof of our capacity to have secure knowledge is afforded by the study of ethics (*Acad.* 2. 23). The fact, he argues, that one accepts rules and repeatedly does the good

[75] For a discussion of perceptual error in Aristotle see Everson (1997: 190–1, 206–18).

[76] *Argumenti conclusio, quae est Graece ἀπόδειξις, ita definitur: 'ratio quae ex rebus perceptis ad id quod non percipiebatur adducit* (*Acad.* 2. 26).

presupposes certainty about some basic observable facts. Perceptual knowledge, he argues, is the beginning of our rational development, while the end is ethical virtue (*Acad.* 2. 29, 31).[77] Piso argues similarly. Virtue, he says, by definition is the excellence of reason (*De fin.* 5. 38), and this consists in the ability to distinguish right from wrong. In order to be able to distinguish right from wrong, let alone to do so systematically, we have to grow in reason so that we can have concepts, like good and justice, and also to have certain training, to become habituated and so on (*De fin.* 5. 59–60). All this is possible, Piso argues, because man has a natural drive and the ability to achieve knowledge (ibid. 5. 48–57) and can grow in reason to its summit, which is virtue (ibid. 5. 60; partly quoted in n. 61). But if we manage to go all the way to virtue and indeed become virtuous, as Plato and Aristotle had maintained, how can one, Antiochus wonders, question an ability as basic as that of reaching secure perceptual knowledge, which is present at the beginning of our rational development (*De fin.* 5. 42–3, *Acad.* 2. 31). For Antiochus man's ability to distinguish right from wrong with certainty presupposes the ability to distinguish true from false sense impression with equal certainty.[78]

At the basis of this belief lies Antiochus' assumption that secure knowledge is essential for attaining moral virtue. Philo, I have argued earlier, disputed this. The question for us is why Antiochus assumes it. First, Antiochus could find support for his view in Plato and Aristotle. In many parts of Plato's work, as in the *Meno*, or in *Republic* 4, Socrates suggests that knowledge is necessary for virtue or that virtue requires wisdom (*phronêsis*). In the early dialogues, in particular, Socrates appears to regard virtue as being inextricably connected with knowledge. For Aristotle, on the other hand, the person who has practical knowledge (*phronimos*) is not susceptible to mistakes; however different

[77] The mind, Lucullus argues, uses the senses to arrive at scientific knowledge of various kinds, and then through them to virtue, which is the end of philosophy as it orders the whole of life (*Acad.* 2. 31).

[78] *Quae ista regula est veri et falsi, si notionem veri et falsi, propterea quod ea non possunt internosci, nullam habemus? Nam si habemus, interesse oportet ut inter rectum et parvum sic inter verum et falsum: si nihil interest, nulla regula est, nec potest is cui est visio falsique communis ullum habere iudicium aut ullam omnino veritatis notam* (What is this canon of truth and falsehood, if we have no notion of truth and falsehood, for the reason that they are indistinguishable? For if we have a notion of them, there must be a difference between truth and falsehood, just as there is one between right and wrong. If there is none, there is no rule and the man who has a presentation of the true and the false that is common to both cannot have any criterion or any mark of truth at all); *Acad.* 2. 33, Rackham's tr. modified.

the situation, the *phronimos* will always respond in the right way. Such a consistency arguably presupposes secure knowledge.

One other reason which may lie behind Antiochus' belief that secure knowledge is essential for achieving a good life is the view that without such knowledge there would always be the fear that one may be wrong, and this fear would undermine one's good life. People must be able to know with certainty that what they are doing is good and beneficial (cf. *Charmides* 164b–c) if they are to lead a fully good life. Further, Antiochus presumably also assumed that no action can count as really virtuous unless it is acted for a reason which stems from a certain disposition which involves secure knowledge of what is right or wrong. This is the view which both Aristotle and the Stoics maintain, and which Antiochus probably regarded as representing Plato's doctrine. This is actually a view which can be detected in Platonic dialogues, for instance, in the *Euthyphro* or the *Meno*.

It emerges then that for Antiochus any argument for distinguishing right from wrong should entail the knowledge of ultimate firm principles of universal value, on which one can rely for guiding one's life. And since Antiochus believes that for the 'ancients' good life is essentially a life of virtue and that the value of philosophy lies precisely in helping us achieve it (*Acad.* 2. 31), such knowledge turns out to be crucial.

This confirms my initial suggestion that Antiochus' main reason for his conversion to dogmatism was his assumption that ethics must rest on incontrovertible theoretical foundations, and also suggests some reasons why Antiochus made this assumption, which I outlined above. We can see now in which sense Antiochus found the Stoic epistemological thesis compatible with the philosophy of the 'ancients'. He probably thought that the Stoic theory of cognition complements the accounts of the 'ancients' concerning knowledge of other kinds, logical, scientific, and, above all, practical, and, what is more, that it supports the ethics of the 'ancients', which the sceptical stance seriously undermined (*Acad.* 2. 39).

If we now return to my question about the sense in which Antiochus considers Aristotle and the Stoics to be Platonists, we can say that, in his view, the Stoics follow the spirit of the 'ancients' to the extent that their epistemology advances the most basic doctrine of the 'ancients', namely their doctrine concerning good life. And they are rated lower than the 'ancients' because of their deviation on this very doctrine, to which I now pass.

5. ETHICS

Antiochus' spokesmen appear to maintain that Plato's ethical views had been articulated well by Aristotle and Polemo.[79] These two authorities are presented as being essentially in agreement,[80] despite some minor differences (*Acad.* 2. 131). In Piso's speech in *De finibus* 5. 7–74, which in its substance must reflect Antiochus' position (cf. *De fin.* 5. 8, 75),[81] Piso acknowledges his special debt to Aristotle's ethical works, and the *Nicomachean Ethics* in particular (ibid. 5. 12), and speaks of constant use of Aristotle's work.[82] So we should expect the account which follows to be Aristotelian to some extent. The slight evidence that we have about Polemo's ethics on the other hand makes it difficult to see how much of Piso's account goes back to Polemo.[83] Some further questions arise. Where does the agreement between Aristotle and Polemo lie? And which are their differences? And why does Antiochus rely on them for ethics?

To begin with, Antiochus' claim that Aristotle and Polemo are the ones among the 'ancients' who offer the best exposition of ethics must mean first that they expound views which, according to Antiochus, represent Plato's doctrine more accurately, and secondly that their presentation is articulate and convincing. If this is so, then their agreement must mean that their ethical views are complementary, being part of the same ethical doctrine. Let us see how this may be so.

Antiochus appears to maintain that one cannot determine what a good life is unless one first has a clear conception of man's nature. In his view, man's nature is twofold, consisting of body and soul, or mind

[79] *Antiquorum... sententiam Antiochus noster mihi videtur persequi diligentissime, quam eandem Aristoteli fuisse et Polemonis docet.* (Our master Antiochus seems to me to adhere most scrupulously to the doctrine of the ancients, which according to this teaching was common to Aristotle and to Polemo); *De fin.* 5. 14; tr. Rackham. On Antiochus' ethics see Dillon (1977: 67–78); Annas (1993: 180–7, 419–25); Fladerer (1996: 137–83); and Prost (2001).

[80] Cf. also *De fin.* 2. 34; *Tusc. Disp.* 5. 30, 39, 87.

[81] Giusta (1990: 34–6) argues against Glucker (1978: 52–62) that Piso's speech, especially its doxographical part (*De fin.* 5. 16–23) does not go back to Antiochus but reflects Peripatetic ethics because Antiochus is not attested to have written a treatise on the final end. This is not convincing. See the discussion and refutation of Giusta's argument by Fladerer (1996: 139–41).

[82] *teneamus Aristotelem* ...—as opposed to Theophrastus who is used cautiously—*Theophrastum tamen adhibeamus ad pleraque*... (*De fin.* 5. 12).

[83] The evidence has been collected by M. Gigante, *Polemonis Academici Fragmenta* (Naples, 1977). Polemo's ethics has been well discussed by Dillon (2003: 159–68).

(*De fin.* 5. 34). The soul, Piso argues, is much more important than the body, and thus the excellences of the soul, such as its virtues, are much more important than those of the body, yet the latter also is part of our nature and we naturally strive towards its excellence (ibid. 5. 35). Thus, he argues, the ultimate good (*summum bonum*) must be the perfection of the whole of our nature, that is of mind and body, according to their relative importance (ibid. 5. 44). We should strive primarily towards moral virtue (*honestas*) but we should also seek the primary objects of nature (*prima naturae*), such as friendship, health, beauty, honour (ibid. 5. 21; cf. 2. 34). For the Antiochean Piso such a life would be good in that it conforms with nature (ibid. 5. 24).

Antiochus apparently espoused the Stoic theory of *oikeiôsis*,[84] according to which man should live in harmony with his nature (*De fin.* 5. 24–33). This, however, does not necessarily mean that Antiochus imports a piece of Stoic theory in ethics, as has often been suggested.[85] Nor should it mean that Antiochus reconciles Platonic and Peripatetic ethics with that of the Stoics.[86] This is first because Antiochus' argument that the Stoic theory originated with Polemo (*De fin.* 4. 14; cf. 5. 23) deserves some credit. We have Cicero's clear testimony for that (*De fin.* 2. 33–4), while Clement (*Strom.* 7. 6. 32. 9) mentions Polemo's treatise *On the life according to Nature*; (*Περὶ τοῦ κατὰ φύσιν βίου συντάγματα*), where Polemo presumably outlined his doctrine.[87] But the most important element for deciding the degree to which Antiochus' doctrine was Stoic is his understanding of human nature.

Antiochus differs considerably from the Stoics in this. He rejects the Stoic view that life according to nature amounts solely to a life of virtue. In Antiochus' view, human nature is not only our rationality, but also our animal nature. The fact, he argues, that man's indifference to things pertaining to our well-being can be fatal suggests that these things qualify as 'goods' (*De fin.* 5. 30). So some care for them must go along with our concern for virtue. Antiochus presents the Stoics with the following dilemma. Either they actually accept the ancient view but clothe it in novel terminology when talking of 'preferred indifferents' instead of 'goods' (*De fin.* 4. 58, 72, 5. 88–90), or if they do diverge

[84] See *De fin.* 3. 16–22, 62–8.

[85] e.g. Dillon (1977: 72, 74).

[86] Thus Annas (1993: 181). Cf. Fladerer (1996: 173).

[87] Cf. *De fin.* 4. 61, 5. 23; *Acad.* 2. 132; *De leg.* 1. 37. See Dillon (2003: 160–5) who reviews all the relevant evidence. Moraux (1973: 339–50) examines the possible Peripatetic origins of this doctrine.

from the 'ancients', they contradict themselves; because on the one hand they acknowledge that man's ultimate good lies in conformity with nature, accept that we are naturally inclined towards self-preservation, having friendships, and towards health, but on the other hand they deny the classification of these as goods (ibid. 4. 42, 5. 72, 89). For Antiochus, the Stoic concept of final end amounts to going against nature (*natura discedere*), because it neglects an essential part of our nature (ibid. 4. 41, 5. 89).[88] In his view, a life solely according to virtue amounts only to a good life (*vita beata*), but not to the best life (*vita beatissima*), which is the ideal for Aristotle and, especially, for Plato.[89]

Little effort has been made to sympathize with Antiochus' position; rather, it has been criticized from antiquity right through to the modern day. From the Stoic point of view, it has been criticized (with reason) for confusing differences in kind with differences in degree (*De nat. deor.* 1. 16). As is well known, for the Stoics virtue is incommensurable with all other non-rational goods, so depending on one's point of view, one can argue either that Antiochus failed to appreciate this, or that he did but found it untenable. We do not know what the case may have been, but we should remember that Plutarch will follow Antiochus in criticizing the Stoic position in a similar way.

Antiochus' view has also been criticized as a hybrid position, which does not do justice to Aristotle's position either.[90] Julia Annas has argued that Antiochus was consciously eclectic in his ethics, intending 'to mediate between Stoics and Peripatetics',[91] as he 'combines the Stoic thesis that virtue suffices for happiness with the common sense point that ... bodily and external goods make you happier than you would be without them'.[92] Yet Antiochus' aim could not possibly have been to mediate between Stoics and Peripatetics. His aim rather was: (*a*) to show that the Stoics took over most of their ethics from the 'ancients'; (*b*) to argue that to the extent the Stoic ethics diverges from that of the

[88] On Antiochus' criticism of the Stoic *telos* see Prost (2001: 262–7). Antiochus appears to repeat the relevant criticism of Carneades in *Acad.* 2. 131.

[89] *Itaque omnis illa antiqua philosophia sensit in una virtute esse positam beatam vitam, nec tamen beatissimam nisi adiungeretur et corporis et cetera quae supra dicta sunt ad virtutis usum idonea.* (Thus the whole ancient philosophy held that good life lies in virtue alone and that life cannot become best without the addition of the goods of the body and also those mentioned above which are suitable for the employment of virtue); *Acad.* 1. 22. See also *De fin.* 5. 71, 81; *Acad.* 2. 134; *Tusc. D.* 5. 22, Augustine, *De civ. Dei* 19. 3.

[90] Dillon (1977: 76–7); Barnes (1989: 87–8); Annas (1993: 180).

[91] Annas (1990: 80; 1993: 181, 419–20). Cf. Dillon (1977: 74), who claims that Antiochus is behaving more like an arbitrator in an industrial dispute than a true philosopher.

[92] Annas (1993: 183, 420).

'ancients' it contradicts itself; and (*c*) to do justice to Aristotle's ethical doctrine, which he considered as representative of Plato. The latter is supported from the explicit references of the Antiochean spokesmen to Aristotle and his *Nicomachean Ethics*. It remains to be seen, though, whether Antiochus succeeded in this.

Antiochus plainly holds:

(1) x is *beatus* iff x is virtuous

(2) x is *beatissimus* iff x is both virtuous and also rich, healthy, handsome, a *pater familias*, etc.

This is not actually present in Aristotle but derived from his distinction between happy (*eudaimōn*) and blissful (*makarios*). Aristotle's idea is that misfortunes can impede many of the activities of anybody who lives a life of virtue (*NE* 1100^{b}28–30); as a result, such a person may still be *eudaimōn* but not *makarios* (*NE* 1108^{a}6–8). This suggests that some advantages, such as health, do not supplement but rather facilitate or advance virtuous life (cf. *EE* 1214^{b}26–7). In this sense these advantages qualify as 'goods other than virtue', or 'external goods'.[93] They can actually be divided into two categories. In Cooper's formulation these are 'external goods that provide the normal contexts for the exercise of virtues [i.e. health] and those which are used instrumentally as means to the ends aimed at in virtuous activities [i.e. money]'.[94]

Cicero's accounts include evidence that Antiochus adopted a similar view. Antiochus divides Aristotle's 'external' goods into two categories, external and bodily goods. In his view external goods strictly speaking are only those external to the person, such as one's friends, parents, country, since the goods of the body, like the goods of the soul, concern one's human nature (*De fin.* 5. 68, 81; cf. *NE* 1098^{b}12–14). In this context the Antiochean Piso makes quite clear the difference between virtue and other goods. Virtue, he argues, has incomparable value, it is *the* good, while other advantages are merely goods (cf. *De fin.* 5. 90–1). The question now is in which sense these advantages count as goods according to Antiochus.

As regards bodily goods, Piso argues that they are of slight importance for a good life (*vita beata*), but that their role is to complete such a life so that it becomes best (*beatissimam vitam*), and he calls them 'supplementary

[93] *NE* 1098^{b}12–16, 1099^{a}31–3, 1153^{b}16–19.

[94] Cooper (1985: 300).

goods' (*accesiones bonorum*).[95] This seems to suggest that these advantages count as goods not only because they enable or advance a life of virtue but also independent of such a connection with virtue.

It is important to specify this further. As has been seen above (p. 55, 72 n. 82), both of Antiochus' spokesmen, Piso and Varro, criticize Theophrastus' view that goods of fortune play an important role, arguing that such a view diminishes the force and dignity of virtue (*De fin.* 5. 12). Varro in particular argues that the view of the 'ancients' was that 'good life (*beate vivere*) is placed solely in virtue' (*Acad.* 1. 33).[96] The formulation here is cautious. Good life is placed solely in virtue, yet it does not depend only on virtue but also on some bodily advantages. Cicero himself agreed with that.[97] Piso in his own speech, however, does not exclude that such advantages also count as goods independent of their connection with virtue and in this sense make a life best, though he still considers virtue as outweighing all such goods (*De fin.* 5. 90–1). In fact, Piso now turns out to be closer to the view of Theophrastus (ibid. 5. 86), which he criticized earlier on in his speech (5. 12).

As regards the external goods now, it also becomes clear that these may make a life best and maximize our happiness also independent of their connection with virtue. The Antiochean Piso argues that not all external goods are included in the ultimate good, but some of them can lead us to it by enabling us to perform acts of duty (*De fin.* 5. 68–9). Having children or friends, for instance, enables us to exercise our appropriate behaviour towards them, that is, enables the practice of virtue. But Piso also argues that relationships with other people, such as kinships, are desirable not only in connection with virtue but also as such (*propter se expetendi sint*; ibid. 5. 67fin). It emerges then that for Antiochus both bodily and external goods can make you happier not only because they

[95] *Illa enim quae sunt a nobis bona corporis numerata complent ea quidem beatissimam vitam, sed ita ut sine illis possit beata vita exsistere. Ita enim parvae et exiguae sunt istae accessiones bonorum ut, quemadmodum stellae in radiis solis, sic istae in virtutum splendore ne cernantur quidem.* (Indeed, the things we reckon as bodily goods contribute to best life, but good life is possible also without them. Because these supplementary goods are so small and slight that against the radiance of virtues they become as invisible as the stars in the sunlight); *De fin.* 5. 71.

[96] *spoliavit* [sc. Theophrastus] . . . *virtutem suo decore* . . . *quod negavit in ea sola positum esse beate vivere* (*Acad.* 1. 33).

[97] Cicero argues that the mind may desire virtue, but freedom from pain is a necessary condition for exercising it (*De fin.* 4. 36). The idea that certain things are good because they constitute conditions for practising a virtuous life is also expressed in *De finibus* 4. 41, where it is argued that 'virtue cannot be realized, unless it first obtains the primary wants of nature which are strongly relevant to the ultimate good' (*nam constitui virtus nullo modo potest nisi ea quae sunt prima naturae ut ad summam pertinentia tenebit*).

are instrumental to exercising virtue but also because they make life easier or more enjoyable. That is, such goods supplement good life so that it becomes best or blissful (*vita beatissima*).[98]

Antiochus' position results from an interpretation of Aristotle but is also inspired by Polemo. The little evidence we have about Polemo suggests that, while he insisted on the primacy of virtue to good life, he also believed in the importance of external goods.[99] There is a question whether Antiochus' position does justice to Aristotle. Discussion still goes on as to whether in Aristotle's view *eudaimonia* is a state admitting of degrees. Several passages in the *Nicomachean Ethics* seem to suggest that for Aristotle *eudaimonia* can be improved in two main ways.[100] First, the form of good life which consists in virtuous actions can be improved if we have more opportunities to engage in such actions. Second, *eudaimonia* can be improved independently of virtuous activity (*NE* $1100^{b}22$–30), when some goods, especially important ones, such as health, children, or friends, are obtained. On the other hand, Aristotle appears to believe that the *eudaimonia* of the *phronimos* is perfect, and I take this to be his own view. But from the above it emerges that Antiochus was not entirely unjustified in believing that the Aristotelian *eudaimonia* admits of degrees. Already Aristotle's distinction between good and blessed life would suffice to inspire Antiochus' position.

On the whole, though, Piso's account of good life in *De finibus* 5 and his distinction between good life and best life, in particular, not only intends to do justice to Plato's ethics but to do so while criticizing the Stoics for disregarding man's nature as a whole, despite their ideal of living a life in conformity with nature (*oikeiôsis*). Later Platonists like Plutarch and Taurus, who also speak in terms of *oikeiôsis*, do not miss the opportunity to criticize Stoic ethics either. The same view about good life occurs in Peripatetics, like Boethus and Xenarchus. And because this ethical ideal is so distinct from the Stoic one and closer to that of Aristotle and to Plato as interpreted by Polemo, these Platonists and Peripatetics are not entirely unjustified in ascribing this theory back

[98] Moraux (1973: 335–7) compares Antiochus' account with that of Arius Didymus (in Stob. 2. 126. 12–127. 2), both of which are partly inspired by Aristotle. Cf. Annas (1993: 415–21)

[99] Polemo's view is recorded by Clement, *Stromata* 2. 22. 133. 4–7 (fr. 123 Gigante) and especially by Cicero *De fin.* 2. 33–5 (fr. 127 Gigante). Cicero's formulation of the final end according to Polemo is very close to that of Antiochus—*honestas cum aliqua accessione* (ibid. 2. 35; cf. *De fin.* 5. 71). See Dillon (2003: 161–3).

[100] See Heinaman (2002: 99–145). See also Gerson (2004: 236–45) on how Aristotle's ethics can be read in line with that of Plato.

to Aristotle[101] or to Plato and Polemo.[102] Antiochus paved the way for such claims, being the first to reconstruct such an ethical ideal and argue for its Platonist credentials. And he may also be the first Platonist who set out different levels of good life, a doctrine developed later by Plutarch and Plotinus. Even if Antiochus made a concession to Stoic terminology, his doctrine is so different from the Stoic one that he cannot be accused of compromising his Platonism.

This is confirmed by Antiochus' psychology. His position on what amounts to a good life presupposes a view about human nature according to which the human soul has also an irrational part. This is the view that Plato takes in several parts of his work (e.g. *Republic* 4) and which Aristotle follows. Yet Cicero accuses Antiochus of having abandoned the view of the Academic/Peripatetic tradition, which postulates that virtuous action involves a certain amount of emotion, for the Stoic conception of virtuous action according to which, in order to attain virtue, one must eliminate emotions (*Acad.* 2. 135–6). Such a criticism has been taken as suggesting that Antiochus maintained the Stoic view of the soul as being reason only.[103] But this is quite unlikely. Piso talks about 'the dominant part of the mind' (*quae princeps animi partis*; *De fin.* 5. 36), and his formulations presuppose a partite soul (*summa omnis animi et in animo rationis*; ibid. 5. 38). Besides, he talks of moderate emotions as being natural (5. 31). Most notably, Varro explicitly criticizes Zeno for departing from the view of the 'ancients' by placing all virtue in reason (*Acad.* 1. 38) and by ruling out all emotions (ibid. 1. 39). Finally, we must remember that Antiochus' contemporary Stoics, notably Posidonius, admitted that the soul has an irrational part, and this was acknowledged as a concession to the common view of Plato and Aristotle.[104] So

[101] See Alexander, *Mantissa*. 151. 3–13. Cf. Moraux (1973: 178–9, 208–10). Boethus and Xenarchus appealed to Aristotle's *NE* 1155^b17–27, 1168a28–b10. Striker (1983) discusses well the different understandings of nature and of the theory of *oikeiôsis* among Stoics and Peripatetics.

[102] Plutarch, like Antiochus, also traces this doctrine back to Polemo (*De comm. not.* 1069E; 1070B; fr. 124 Gigante). Taurus takes issue with the Stoics on this matter, as if the theory were a Platonist one (Aulus Gellius, *NA* 12. 5. 7–9). And Longinus is attested to have written a treatise with a title similar to that of Polemo. (*Περὶ τοῦ κατὰ φύσιν βίου*; *Suda*, s.v. Longinus). Cf. Plutarch, *De sollertia anim.* 962A–E, and Porphyry, *De abstinentia* 3. 19, where he draws on Plutarch.

[103] See Görler (1994: 960); Dillon (1977: 77–8; 1983) argued that Antiochus probably equated the Stoic *eupatheiai* with the Peripatetic mean, but, as he himself admits, no evidence suggests this. Lilla (1971: 100–1) and Fladerer (1996: 178–81) rightly argue that Antiochus adheres to the partite soul.

[104] See Galen, *PHP* 4. 7. 39, 5. 7. 3, 5. 7. 10; cf. frs. 160, 163, 166E–K.

it would be strange if Antiochus ascribed to Plato the view that the soul is reason only.

One wonders, then, how the acceptance of a partite soul can be squared with the view that virtue lies in the extirpation of all emotions, which Cicero attributes to Antiochus. I think that Cicero misunderstood Antiochus in this. Antiochus appears to consider emotions not only as natural but also conducive to virtue (*De fin.* 5. 31) and seems to suggest that the moderation of emotions was a doctrine of the 'ancients' (*Acad.* 1. 39).

How, then, did Cicero come to make such a claim? The answer probably is that Antiochus adopted a view about emotions close to the Stoic one. He considered an emotion to be a sort of irrational force, not in the Stoic sense of being a mistaken belief opposite to reason, but in the sense that it is generated in the non-rational part of the soul and is powerful and intense, as is suggested in *Phaedrus* 253b–256e.[105] This is why he argued that we fail to achieve virtue when we assent to an emotion (*Acad.* 2. 39, *Tusc. D.* 5. 39). This is a view which also Boethus and Andronicus shared.[106] The difference from the Stoic position is that for Antiochus and the Peripatetics emotions can guide us to virtue if they are put in the service of reason, i.e. if they are moderated.[107] Antiochus probably considered this view, which Aristotle maintains in the *Nicomachean Ethics*, as representative of Plato's position.

Finally, there is some evidence to suggest that Antiochus found Aristotle's views useful for reconstructing Plato's ethical doctrine not only regarding the practical life but also the theoretical one. Some of the remarks ascribed to Antiochus' spokesmen suggest that Aristotle is the probable source of inspiration. Piso argues that the life of contemplation represents the highest ideal, and he refers us to descriptions of it by Aristotle and Theophrastus (*De fin.* 5. 11–12). Later on Piso argues that our mind has an innate disposition for inquiry (ibid. 5. 48), and an even more sublime one for contemplation (5. 49; cf. 4. 11–12), something which is carried out by the most divine element in us (5. 57). Theiler has argued that Antiochus was inspired by Aristotle's *Protrepticus* in this

105 This is the original sense of *pathos*, as Democritus' fr. B31 DK suggests. See Frede (1986: 96).

106 See Aspasius, *In NE* 44. 20–5, 44. 33–45. 16. Cf. Alcinous, *Didasc.* 185. 26–31. See Moraux (1973: 135–6, 178).

107 Cf. *De fin.* 5. 31. Antiochus may be the author of the term *metriopatheia*, which he may have coined in order to contradistinguish the position of the 'ancients' from the divergent Stoic view of *apatheia*. The term is found in later authors, like Alcinous, *Didasc.* 184. 24 and Porphyry, *Sententia* 32, p. 25. 7 Lamberz.

regard.[108] This is possible, but he is more likely to have been inspired by *Nicomachean Ethics* 10, since this treatise is mentioned as the foundation of Piso's ethical account (*De fin.* 5. 12). Unfortunately we lack further evidence which would allow us to better understand this aspect of Antiochus' thought.

6. CONCLUSIONS

From the foregoing discussion some conclusions can be reached. According to Antiochus, the most essential part of philosophy, and of Plato's philosophy in particular, is ethics, and his most crucial doctrine is about how we can achieve a good life. Antiochus shares the Stoic view that virtue requires secure knowledge and without such knowledge no ethical system can exist, and he is convinced that Plato has coherent and systematic ethics, which he reconstructs from that of Aristotle and Polemo. Antiochus endorses the Stoic conception of final end as a life in conformity with nature, but his understanding of this is considerably different from that of the Stoics. Being inspired by Aristotle's and Polemo's shared understanding of man's nature, Antiochus defines good life as a life of virtue accompanied by bodily and external goods. Given the special weight that these doctrines carry for Antiochus, he maintains that Aristotle's philosophy is essentially in accord with that of Plato.

Antiochus wants to back up ethics with a rigorous epistemology. Hence he espouses the Stoic theory of cognition because it provides a criterion for determining secure perceptual knowledge, which is basic for attaining higher knowledge such as the practical. Antiochus regards Stoic epistemology as an improvement on and systematization of that of Plato and Aristotle. He probably held that the Stoic view that we need to have concepts by means of which the mind represents objects of perception, is a development of the position of Plato and Aristotle that our mind perceives by identifying the immutable Forms of objects. Antiochus is critical of Aristotle's rejection of transcendent Forms, but he appears to think that Aristotle adheres to the basic aspect of Plato's doctrine, which is that the Forms are essences, and this is why he only mildly criticizes Aristotle.

[108] Theiler (1964: 52–3). Cicero himself is acquainted with this early Aristotelian work (cf. frs. 10c, 19 Ross). The place of *vita contemplativa* in Antiochus' ethics is discussed by Fladerer (1996: 166–9).

From the above it emerges that Antiochus is neither an eclectic nor a syncretist, as has often been claimed. Antiochus did not muddle various doctrines from Plato and Platonists, Aristotle, and the Stoics. Rather, he had a certain conception of Plato's philosophy which he tried to reconstruct as faithfully as he could through the testimonies of the early Academics, Aristotle, and the Stoics, according to the degree in which they were indebted to Plato.

7. APPENDIX: REACTIONS TO ANTIOCHUS: ARISTO, CRATIPPUS, EUDORUS

By maintaining that Aristotle's philosophy preserves Plato's doctrine, Antiochus triggered various responses, some of which are of significance and which I will briefly review below. Antiochus was succeeded by his brother Aristus, who must have been a much less able philosopher. This is attested by Plutarch[109] and is suggested also by the fact that two of Antiochus' pupils, Aristo of Alexandria and Cratippus of Pergamon, left Antiochus' school, probably when Aristus was its head, and became Peripatetics.[110] Cratippus in particular became an eminent Peripatetic, to whom Cicero entrusted the philosophical education of his own son (*De off.* 1. 1, 3. 5–6).[111] We do not know why the two philosophers converted to the Peripatos. One possibility is that in their view Aristotle's philosophy, unlike that of Plato, offered specific doctrines, which

[109] Plutarch, *Brutus* 2. 3 points out that Aristus was a friend of Brutus but on the whole inferior to many other philosophers of the time (*τῇ μὲν ἐν λόγοις ἕξει πολλῶν φιλοσόφων λειπόμενον*). On Aristo see Moraux (1973: 181–93). His fragments are collected by I. Mariotti, *Aristone d'Alessandria* (Bologna, 1966).

[110] ... *τὴν δὲ δι<α>|τριβὴν αὐτοῦ διεδέξατο|ἀδελφὸς ὢν[κ]αὶ μα[θ]ητὴς| Ἀρίστος, ἀκουσ[τ]ὰς δὲ καίπερ |ἀσχολούμενος ἔσχε πλεί| ους καὶ δὴ καὶ συνήθεις ἡ|μῶν Ἀρίστωνά τε καὶ Δίωνα Ἀλεξανδρεῖς καὶ Κρά|τιππον Περγαμηνόν, ὧ[ν]|Ἀρίστων [μὲν] καὶ Κράτ[ιπ]πος ΕΠ[...]ΝΑ[... ἤ]κουσα[ν ...]ΗΛΟΙC[...]| ἐγένον[το]Περιπα[τητι]κοὶ ἀ[ποστα]τήσα[ντες τῆς]Ἀ|καδημείας* (*Index Acad.*, col. 35. 2–17 Dorandi). For the text see Dorandi (1991: 252). Puglia (1998: 146) has rightly pointed out (after Bücheler) that after the name of Cratippus and before *ἤ]κουσα[ν* there should be the name of a philosopher, possibly a Peripatetic, who then must have played a crucial role in the apostasy of the two Platonists. Puglia has suggested that this philosopher may be Xenarchus and supplements as follows: *καὶ Κράτ[ιπ]πος, ἐπ[εὶ Ξε]νά[ρχου δια]|κούσα[ν]τες ζῆλον ἔ[σχον], ἐγένον[το] Περιπα[τητι]κοὶ* ... Most scholars maintain that the apostasy took place after Antiochus' death. This seems possible and even plausible, but it is not certain. See Luck (1953: 16); Mariotti (1966: 24 n. 12); Glucker (1978: 115).

[111] On Cratippus see Lynch (1972: 204–5); Moraux (1973: 223–56); and Glucker (1978: 112–20).

Antiochus had taken over in order to reconstruct Plato's philosophy. As has been demonstrated above, Antiochus' ethics and moral psychology is very similar to that of Andronicus and Boethus, and his epistemology is close to that of Boethus and Aristocles. Perhaps, then, Antiochus' students found Aristotelianism to be the best interpretation or development of Plato's philosophy in the sense that it offered a complete and systematic dogmatic philosophy—a story similar to that of the defection of Antiochus from Philo's Academy.

However the defection of Aristo and Cratippus may be explained, it shows that they had become quite familiar with Aristotle's philosophy in Antiochus' school and that they shared his high esteem of it. The limited evidence about them suggests that their philosophical interests were inspired much more by the Peripatetic tradition than by Antiochus' teaching. Aristo was interested in logic,[112] while Cratippus was interested in divination, psychological phenomena, and moral psychology.[113]

A strong reaction to Antiochus' interpretation of the philosophies of Plato and Aristotle must have come from Eudorus.[114] The existing evidence about him suggests that he inherited Antiochus' dogmatic interpretation of Plato's philosophy but he differed substantially from Antiochus' reconstruction of it. His position appears to have been close to what Numenius would maintain later, namely that Plato's philosophy essentially was Pythagorean and at odds with that of Aristotle. Eudorus focused on the *Timaeus*[115] and was particularly concerned with Plato's doctrine of the first principles,[116] but also with other issues suggested by the dialogue, such as how the coming into being of the world and

[112] Aristo wrote on the *Categories* (Simpl. *In Cat.* 159. 31–3) and the *Prior Analytics* (Apuleius, *De interpretatione* 193. 16–17 Thomas). Aristo was also concerned with epistemology and psychology, assuming two parts of the soul, if he is the one meant by Porphyry in his *On the faculties of the soul* (Stob. 1. 49. 24; fr. 251 Smith). The Stoic Aristo is unlikely to be meant here, because he was not interested in epistemology.

[113] Cf. *De divin.* 1. 70–1, 2.100–10. Varro appears through his work to be distant from Antiochus' philosophical concerns; closer to Antiochus is Brutus (*De fin.* 5. 8, *Tusc. Disp.* 5. 21, 39); see Rawson (1985: 282–9). For a good review of the evidence about Antiochus' pupils see Görler (1994: 967–75).

[114] Eudorus is often said to be Antiochus' pupil (e.g. Boyance 1971: 131), but this is neither attested nor implied in the evidence. The available evidence on Eudorus has been conveniently collected by Mazzarelli (1985). On the philosophy of Eudorus see Theiler (1965*a*: 488–98); Dörrie (1976*b*: 297–309); Dillon (1977: 117–35).

[115] Cf. Plutarch, *De an. procr.* 1012D–1013B, 1019E–1020C.

[116] See Alexander, *In Met.* 58. 31–59. 8; Simplicius, *In Phys.* 181. 7–19, 181. 22–30 (frs. 2–6 Mazzarelli).

the soul should be interpreted.[117] Eudorus appears to have postulated that according to Plato there is only one transcendent principle, the One, from which everything derives, including matter and the Forms, and he rejected the view that the Forms are a principle of the being of things.[118] Eudorus relied on Aristotle's reports on Plato's principles but he rejected Aristotle's interpretation of them. Being convinced that Plato represents the monism of Pythagoras, Eudorus construed Aristotle's reports to this effect. This suggests that Eudorus regarded Aristotle's reports about Plato as being partly misleading. Presumably he thought that Aristotle had failed to understand that Plato does not initiate a new philosophy but represents the one of Pythagoras, as Numenius will argue later.[119]

We know that Eudorus criticized Aristotle's *Categories*, becoming perhaps the first Platonist to do so. His criticism focused primarily on the number and order of the ten categories.[120] Yet Eudorus went also into some more detail regarding Aristotle's theory; he argued that the categories of quality and quantity, and also of time and place, should not be separated from that of sensible substance because they are implied in it (Simplicius, *In Cat.* 206. 10–15; fr. 17 Mazzarelli). Eudorus seems to have held that Aristotle had failed to distinguish between sensible and intelligible substance, which he considered as the most important ontological division, and in the same context he asserted his preference to the Platonic ontological categories of *per se* (*pros hauton*) and relative (*pros ti*; Simplicius, *In Cat.* 174. 14–27; fr. 15 Mazzarelli). Presumably the thrust of his criticism was that Aristotle's theory of categories fail to apply to the intelligible world, which is the realm of real beings, and thus Aristotle's categories, especially that of substance, are seriously defective. Eudorus' criticisms must have had an impact on later generations, since we find his points about the order of the categories and the category of substance developed by Lucius and Nicostratus and later by Plotinus.[121]

To pass to ethics, Eudorus returns to a view on ethics similar to that of Philo, which is close to Stoic ethics (Stobaeus 2. 42. 7–45. 6; fr. 1

[117] Plutarch, *De an. procr.* 1012D–1013B, 1019E–1020C; Achilles, *Isag.* 30. 20–25, 40. 25–30, 96. 24–34 (frs. 6–11 Mazzarelli).

[118] Alexander, *In Met.* 58. 31–59. 8; Simplicius, *In Phys.* 181. 7–30 (frs. 2–5 Mazzarelli).

[119] See further Ch. 3, s. 1.

[120] See Moraux (1984: 519–27).

[121] See e.g. Simplicius, *In Cat.* 62. 27–30, 73. 15–28, 76. 13–17. Lucius appears to have followed Eudorus in accepting as Platonic the ontological categories of *per se* and relative; see Simplicius, *In Cat.* 156. 14–23, with Gioè (2002: 151).

Mazzarelli). He presumably also argued that only virtue is the good (Stobaeus 2. 55. 22–3; fr. 31 Mazzarelli), but this, like other doctrines attested by Stobaeus and claimed by several scholars for Eudorus, is uncertain, because it is unclear how much of Stobaeus' testimony concerns him.[122] On the basis of the secure evidence alone, though, one can reasonably infer that Eudorus disregarded Aristotle's ethics as a source for understanding Plato's ethics and he possibly argued against its use.

Although our evidence is limited and second-hand, the conclusion which emerges is that Eudorus resisted Antiochus' tendency in considering Aristotle either as reporting accurately Plato's doctrines or as recasting Platonic doctrines in his own works. Eudorus' criticisms of Aristotle's philosophy rather suggest a reaction to Antiochus. Eudorus' contribution is significant because he gave voice to Pythagorean Platonism, suggesting an alternative way of reconstructing Plato's philosophy based on Pythagorean philosophy rather than on Aristotle, as Antiochus had done, and also because he drew Platonists' attention away from the standard domains of Hellenistic philosophy, epistemology, and ethics, to metaphysics. It is Antiochus and Eudorus who set the question of Aristotle's philosophy for the subsequent generations of Platonists to discuss. The first significant Platonist to address this question was Plutarch.

[122] Dörrie (1976*b*: 303–4) and Dillon (1977: 122–3) have argued that Eudorus held that the human end is assimilation to God (Stob. 2. 50. 6–10), but this is not certain and Mazzarelli (1985: 537) has rightly classified this evidence as uncertain testimony on Eudorus (fr. 25).

2
Plutarch

1. PLUTARCH'S PLATONISM

The Platonism of Plutarch (*c.* AD 45–120) is in some respects similar to that of Antiochus, but also differs from it to such an extent that he can be seen as reacting to Antiochus.[1] Plutarch is similar to Antiochus in that he considers Aristotle as a part of the Platonist philosophical tradition, despite some divergences, but he has a different conception of Plato's philosophy. He values Plato's doctrines, as Antiochus did, but he also emphasizes Plato's aporetic spirit, which he regards as integral to Plato's philosophical thought and method.[2] Plutarch forcefully argues that the sceptical interpretation of Plato, far from being a distortion of Plato's philosophy, as Antiochus had maintained, does justice to the aporetic spirit of this philosophy.[3] For Plutarch, though, this aporetic spirit remains compatible with Plato's doctrinal aspect. This is because for him scepticism amounts to a way of searching out the truth, that is, the dialectical methodology of arguing on either side of a question in order to adduce without prejudices where the truth lies. This neither amounts to a dogmatic denial of the possibility to know, nor does it mean that no conclusion can be reached in this process. Rather, Plutarch believed that Plato had often reached such conclusions and held specific doctrines. Plutarch's view becomes clear in his defence of Academic

[1] Plutarch's philosophy is a vast territory and is still being explored. See mainly Jones (1916); Babut (1969*a*); Dillon (1977: 184–230; 1986; 1988*b*); Deuse (1983: 12–47); Schoppe (1994); and most recently Opsomer (1999: 127–212). Plutarch's philosophical education and the actual conditions of his philosophical activity in the era of non-institutional Platonism are a matter of debate. See Glucker (1978: 257–80); Donini (1986*a*); Dillon (1988*b*: 358); and Opsomer (1999: 21–6).

[2] For Plutarch's defence of Socrates' spirit as it appears in the early dialogues and even in mature ones like the *Theaetetus* see Opsomer (1999: 127–62).

[3] Plutarch refers critically to Antiochus in *Cic.* 4. 1–3 and possibly also in *Adv. Col.* 1122A8–10. On two other occasions Plutarch refers to the Antiochean point of view (*Luc.* 42. 3, *Brut.* 2. 3), but there Plutarch reports the views of the Antiochean Brutus and Lucullus, as Opsomer (1999: 172) rightly observes.

scepticism, a project to which he devoted considerable energy.[4] In this Plutarch tried to disengage the term 'Academic' from implying exclusive commitment to the sceptical construal of Plato, suggesting that one can appreciate the sceptical character of Plato's philosophy and also value Plato's doctrines.

Given his conception of Plato's philosophy, Plutarch does not see Aristotle's philosophy as being in agreement with that of Plato in opposition to Academic scepticism, as Antiochus maintained. Quite the contrary. There is evidence to suggest that Plutarch perceived Aristotle's accord with Plato's philosophy partially through Aristotle's adherence to his aporetic spirit. We have seen that Cicero, like Philo before 88/87 BC, considered Aristotle to be favouring the dialectical methodology of arguing on either side of a question (*in utramque partem disserere*), and in this practice to be following the Socratic aporetic disposition.[5] Plutarch's position appears to be similar. This is suggested by the fact that he, like Cicero, was a student of Aristotle's *Topics*; he is attested to have written eight books on them.[6] Although we do not know what the form of Plutarch's work was, it is quite remarkable that, as far as we know, neither he nor any other Platonist write so extensively on any other Aristotelian work. It is a matter of speculation why Plutarch showed such a strong interest in this work, but one possibility is that he believed that this reflects dialectic as practised at the Academy under Plato, a view which may well be right.

Some further evidence corroborates the belief that Plutarch valued Aristotle's dialectical methodology. We know that Favorinus was an ardent defender of Academic scepticism and that he also favoured Aristotle,[7] and we know further that Plutarch was on friendly terms with Favorinus, to whom he addresses his work *De primo frigido*. In this Plutarch professes loyalty to Academic scepticism but also draws much

[4] See *Adv. Col.* 1121F–1122E and *Plat. Q.* 1. Note the following titles of lost treatises in the Lamprias catalogue: *Περὶ τοῦ μίαν εἶναι ἀπὸ τοῦ Πλάτωνος Ἀκαδημείαν* (no. 63), *Περὶ τῆς διαφορᾶς τῶν Πυρρωνείων καὶ Ἀκαδημαϊκῶν* (no. 64). On Plutarch's thesis on the unity of the Academy see Donini (1986*a*); Opsomer (1999: 127–212); Brittain (2001: 225–36).

[5] Cf. *Tusc. D.* 2. 9, 4. 6; *De off.* 1. 2; *De fin.* 5. 10; see Ch. 1, p. 48.

[6] *Τῶν Ἀριστοτελους Τοπικῶν βιβλία ή* (no. 56 in Lamprias catalogue); Plutarch shows his interest in this work also elsewhere (*Quaest. Conv.* 616D); see Babut (1996: 8–9).

[7] *Quaest. Conv.* 734F. On Favorinus see Glucker (1978: 280–92), and Holford-Stevens (1988: 72–92).

from Aristotle's scientific writings.[8] This is presumably to be seen as an indication of Plutarch's approval of Favorinus' attitude toward Aristotle and also as an indication that both Plutarch and Favorinus considered Aristotle's philosophy to be largely compatible with that of Plato, especially as far as natural science is concerned. Yet Aristotle's natural philosophy is dogmatic. If Plutarch and Favorinus accepted it as compatible with Platonism, this would suggest that they did not regard the doctrinal aspect as compromising the aporetic character of Plato's philosophy, and also that they considered Aristotle to be in a way a preserver of Platonic doctrines.

In this latter aspect Plutarch is very much like Antiochus. That is, Plutarch also considers Aristotle to be espousing several crucial Platonic doctrines and to be recasting them in a more systematic form. On this basis, Plutarch often used Aristotle's work either to express, or to confirm Platonic doctrines, as Antiochus had done. One important use of Aristotle's work in this regard common to both Antiochus and Plutarch is resorting to Aristotle in order to defend Plato's doctrines against critics such as the Stoics, and in the case of Plutarch also against the Epicureans. Plutarch, however, differs from Antiochus in three important ways. First, unlike Antiochus, who was driven primarily by epistemological and ethical concerns, Plutarch shows a strong interest in metaphysics, which was revived by Eudorus, and he finds Aristotle useful for clarifying Plato's doctrine on questions such as that of the relation between soul and body (s. 4). Second, Plutarch seeks in Aristotle not only Platonic but also Pythagorean doctrines, which in his view had inspired Plato.[9] Third, given his belief that Plato's philosophy is essentially aporetic, Plutarch finds Stoic epistemology, which Antiochus espoused, to be quite incompatible with Plato's thought. As a result, Plutarch is much more critical of Stoicism than Antiochus;[10] he actually

[8] The strong presence of Aristotle in this treatise has been found disconcerting. Glucker (1978: 287–9) argues that it should not be taken very seriously. But I do not see why not. Favorinus was an Academic sceptic who allowed himself to have views, and there is nothing strange in the fact that he preferred some Aristotelian scientific explanations. This appears to be the case also with Plutarch. See Opsomer (1999: 213–21).

[9] See *De Iside* 370D–F with reference to *Met.* 1. 5, 9, 985b23–987a28, 990a33–993a10. See also the report of Aulus Gellius *NA* 4. 11, according to which Plutarch found Pythagorean doctrines in Aristotle. On this see Donini (1999). Plutarch's attitude, however, can be seen as a reaction to Eudorus and perhaps was targeted later by Numenius. (See Ch. 3, s. 1)

[10] On Plutarch's epistemology see Brittain (2001: 225–36 and Opsomer (1999: 190–212). Plutarch defends the Academic suspension of judgement in *Adv. Col.* 1122A–1124B, *De primo frig.* 955C. Cf. *Plat. Q.* 1000C–D and his lost essay *Eἰ ἄπρακτος ὁ περὶ πάντων ἐπέχων* (Lamprias no. 210), but rejects universal suspension of judgement advocating the possibility of holding probable philosophical views.

maintains that the Stoics contradict Plato's philosophy as thoroughly as the Epicureans.[11] Apart from their epistemology, Plutarch also finds the materialism of Stoic metaphysics highly objectionable (*De comm. not.* 1073D–1074D), but he reserves most of his criticism for the Stoics' ethics.[12] As will be seen below, in all these areas Plutarch draws often on Aristotle's work to the extent that he perceives it as preserving Platonic doctrines, which he aims to defend.

Nonetheless, Plutarch's defence of Plato's philosophy against Stoic and Epicurean attacks sometimes gets him involved in asserting Aristotle's departures from Plato's doctrine. Plutarch does this because Stoics and Epicureans alike, in their attempt to establish their own philosophies in reaction to Platonic and Aristotelian philosophy, often disregarded the differences between the two and criticized them jointly.[13] In order to show that Stoics and Epicureans are mistaken in their assumptions about the extent of the philosophical agreement between Plato and Aristotle, Plutarch does not hesitate to discuss Aristotle's differences from Plato. He does this most clearly in his *Adversus Colotem* (see s. 3). There, however, Plutarch is not hostile to Aristotle. Quite the

[11] Plutarch often parallels Stoic views to those of the Epicureans to indicate that, despite their differences, Stoics and Epicureans equally contradict Plato's philosophy; e.g. *De comm. not.* 1082E; *De Stoic. rep.* 1052B. One of Plutarch's lost works treated Stoics and Epicureans jointly (Lamprias no. 148). See below for further examples of this Plutarchean attitude.

[12] *De Stoic. rep.* 1041E–1043A; *De comm. not.* 1060B–1073D; *De virtute morali.* Plutarch's attitude toward Stoicism is discussed fully by Babut (1969*a*). On Plutarch's criticism of Stoic ethics, see s. 5.

[13] Cf. e.g. *Non posse suav. vivi* 1086E–F, *Adv. Col.* 1114F–1115C; *De Stoic. rep.* 1040D–E, 1041A. The Stoics criticized Platonic and Aristotelian causes jointly (Seneca, *Ep.* 65. 4–14). Epicurus notoriously was very critical of Aristotle (Athenaeus 8, 354B, DL 10. 8; Aristocles apud Eusebium *PE* 15. 2. 1; Cicero, *Nat. deor.* 1. 93), and was accused of ignorance in his attack against Plato and Aristotle (Sextus, *Adv. Math.* 1. 1). Epicureans like Colotes (on whom see below s. 3), Hermarchus, and Metrodorus continued this tradition (Cicero, *Nat. deor.* 1. 93). Hermarchus wrote treatises against Plato and Aristotle (DL 10. 25), Metrodorus wrote a work against Plato's *Eythyphro* (Philodemus, *On Piety*, col. 25, 702–5, col. 34, 959–60 Obbink) and Plato's *Gorgias* (in two books; Philodemus, *Πρὸς τούς* [ ]: *PHerc.* 1005, col. XI, 14–15 Angeli), and presumably criticized Aristotle in his *On Wealth* (*PHerc.* 200; cf. Philodemus, *Oeconomicus*, col. XXI, 28–35 Jensen). Crönert (1906: 24 no. 136) has argued that Metrodorus also wrote a special treatise against Aristotle (attested in *PHerc.* 1111), but this is a conjecture; cf. Gigante (1999: 18). Also Polyaenus wrote a work against Aristotle's *Περὶ Φιλοσοφίας* (*On Piety*, *PHerc.* 1077, col. 38, 1092–5 Obbink), addressing the arguments of Aristotle's *On Philosophy*. Similar treatises were written by Polystratus (*PHerc.* 1520; see Crönert 1906: 356) and Metrodorus (*Adv. Col.* 1127B). On Epicurean polemics against Plato see D. Obbink, *Philodemus On Piety* (Oxford, 1996), 380–7 and below p. 93 n. 28, and against Aristotle Obbink ibid. 478–9, Düring (1957: 385–6) and Gigante (1999: 18–19, 33–50).

contrary. In fact, he generally appears to refrain from criticizing Aristotle's views, or else criticizes them mildly and implicitly, that is, without naming Aristotle. This suggests that Plutarch considers Aristotle as somehow belonging to the Platonist tradition. The fact, though, that he asserts Aristotle's differences from Plato's philosophy as part of his defence of the latter clearly shows that he was not prepared to accept Aristotle's views when these conflict with what he considered to be Plato's doctrine. This means that whenever he uses them, he does so because he considers them as representative of Plato's own doctrines.

2. PLUTARCH'S KNOWLEDGE OF ARISTOTLE'S WORK

The way Plutarch uses Aristotle's work confirms the belief that he often treated Aristotle as a communicator of Platonic views. The available evidence not only shows that Plutarch had a particularly good knowledge of Aristotle's work, but strongly suggests that he drew much from Aristotle's work without always acknowledging this, because he considered it hardly necessary to constantly refer to Aristotle, in the same way that he found it unnecessary to constantly name Plato. This Plutarchean tendency, however, has led some scholars to argue that, with the exception of a few, mostly exoteric works, Plutarch derived his knowledge of Aristotle from intermediate sources.[14] This was argued mainly on the grounds that Plutarch very rarely quotes from Aristotle's work. On the same grounds, the mere existence of any works by Plutarch on Aristotle's philosophy was disputed.[15] The arguments advanced for this thesis, though, not only fail to do justice to the overwhelming evidence to the opposite, but also miss what I take to be the character of Plutarch's treatment of Aristotle.

As already mentioned, Plutarch wrote entire works on Aristotelian treatises, such as the *Topics* (Lamprias no. 56) and the *Categories* (Lamprias no. 192), as well as on specific aspects of Aristotle's philosophy,

[14] Thus have argued Düring (1957: 354–5); Sandbach (1982); Donini (1974: 64–80; 1986*a*: 214–16).

[15] F. Sandbach, *Plutarch's Moralia*, 15, p. 6–12 (Cambridge Mass. 1969: Loeb) has questioned the existence of Plutarch's works *On fifth element* 5 and also *On Aristotle's Topics* 8, the latter on the grounds that Plutarch does not show much interest in the *Topics* elsewhere. But Plutarch must have in mind passages from the *Topics* when he talks about Aristotle's tripartition of the soul in the *De virtute morali* 442B; see pp. 117–8. Plutarch's interest in the fifth element is also well attested (see pp. 104–5).

such as the fifth element (Lamprias no. 44).[16] There is no evidence to cast doubts on the existence of such works. And there is much that shows that Plutarch was often inspired by Aristotle's work and did not hesitate to draw from it.[17] This is particularly prominent in several of Plutarch's scientific works like the *De primo frigido* or *De sollertia animalium*. The absence of Aristotelian quotations in these or other Plutarchean writings does not suggest lack of access to Aristotle's works, but, as Daniel Babut has argued,[18] rather reflects Plutarch's different attitude to Aristotle compared to his attitude to the Stoics and the Epicureans. Plutarch quotes much from Stoic and Epicurean sources, but this practice serves polemic purposes, that is, to expose through them his adversaries' contradictions. We encounter this practice in other polemical treatises such as Origen's work against Celsus. The fact that Plutarch quotes in order to criticize suggests that his tendency to quote rarely from Aristotle testifies to a much more favourable attitude to his philosophy than to those of the Stoics and Epicureans, rather than to his unfamiliarity with Aristotle's work.[19]

Let me give an example of Plutarch's use of Aristotle's work, which shows that familiarity with it does not necessarily entail abundance of quotations or even references. In *De sollertia animalium* Plutarch argues that animals are rational and criticizes the Stoics who denied this, making heavy use of Aristotle's biological works.[20] This becomes plain when Autobulus, who responds to the Stoic objections, flatters Optatus by saying that his expertise may save them from having to look at Aristotle's volumes.[21] This suggests that Aristotle's volumes were available to them, that probably much had been drawn from them already, and that they were constantly employed in this Plutarchean argument against the Stoic position. The treatise as a whole contains seven references to Aristotle but

16 All of them are lost today. I list these works of Plutarch in Appendix II.

17 There are about 260 references to Aristotle in Plutarch's work, according to the list of W. C. Helmbold and E. W. O'Neil, *Plutarch's Quotations* (London, 1959), 8–12; it includes citations from the *Physics*, the *Topics*, the *Metaphysics*, the *De caelo*, the *De anima*, the *Nicomachean Ethics*, the *Politics*.

18 Babut (1996: 6–7). This is clear in the *De virtute morali* where citations from the Stoics abound, while references to Aristotle are often vague (e.g. *φασίν*; 443D, referring to *NE* 1105^{b}20).

19 Teodorsson (1999) has argued that Plutarch not only draws on Aristotle's scientific works but is also inspired by the critical mind of Aristotle, as is evidenced in his disbelief to certain scientific opinions. Yet this is what one would expect from a Platonist of sceptical orientation like Plutarch anyway.

20 On this anti-Stoic work see Babut (1969*a*: 54–62).

21 *De sollertia anim.* 965D–E; Aristotle is invoked as a 'witness' at 973A–B, 979E5, 981B5, 981F2.

no quotations from his texts. A similar strategy has been detected also in other parts of Plutarch's work. His fragmentary work *On the soul* contains reminiscences of, and strong verbal similarities with Aristotle's *Protrepticus*, but again no quotations occur.[22]

Plutarch himself stresses his acquaintance with Aristotle's work also in a straightforward way. Addressing the claim of the Epicurean Colotes that Aristotle had espoused Plato's theory of Forms, Plutarch criticizes him for 'never looking at Aristotle's writings like the *De caelo* and the *De anima* or taking them into his hands' (*Adv. Col.* 1115A). Plutarch means to make a strong contrast between Colotes' ignorance and his own practice, which, as he elsewhere emphasizes, was to study Aristotle by 'taking Aristotle's works into his hands'.[23] This reference to specific Aristotelian works is part of an argument which aims to manifest not only Plutarch's first-hand knowledge of them, but also his awareness of Aristotle's work as a whole and his understanding of Aristotle's philosophical outlook. This is his argument about Aristotle's stance to Plato's doctrines, which I will discuss in detail in the next section. Plutarch refers to the *De anima* and *De caelo* as examples of Aristotle's opposition to Plato's theory of Forms, and he qualifies his claim by comparing these treatises with Aristotle's work as a whole. He argues that such an opposition is to be found also in the rest of Aristotle's work, in his treatises on ethics and natural philosophy and in his exoteric writings (*Adv. Col.* 1115B–C).[24] In the same context Plutarch also appears to know, quite generally, on which issues Aristotle followed Plato and on which he did not. His reference to Aristotle's 'Platonic works' (ἐν τοῖς Πλατωνικοῖς; *Adv. Col.* 1118C), most probably to Aristotle's dialogues, which perhaps were written while Plato was still alive, testifies to his wide knowledge of Aristotle's work.[25]

22 See Santaniello (1999: 635–8) who detected close parallels between Plutarch's fr. 178 Sandbach (*On the Soul*) and Aristotle's *Protrepticus*. See also below s. 4.

23 ἀναλαβεῖν εἰς χεῖρας (*Quaest. conv.* 616D, concerning Aristotle's *Topics*); cf. the expressions διὰ χειρῶν ἔχοντες, προχείρους ἔχειν (ibid.), ὡς δῆλόν ἐστιν ἐξ ὧν ἔγραψεν (*De virt. mor.* 442B); Plutarch argues that Colotes lacks the acquaintance with the 'ancients' that he professes to have had (*Adv. Col.* 1108D, 1109A). See Babut (1996: 10–16).

24 Plutarch's distinction between esoteric and exoteric works (cf. *Vita Alexandri* 6), or his use of works like the *Metaphysics* (ibid.) does not necessarily suggest use of Andronicus' edn., as Düring (1957: 286) maintains, but it does testify to his knowledge of Aristotle's work as a whole.

25 This is traditionally connected with Aristotle's *On Philosophy* (test. 1 Ross); cf. Jaeger (1948: 130). Plutarch is one of our best sources for Aristotle's lost dialogues; he knows and refers to Aristotle's *On Nobility* (fr. 3 Ross), *Eudemus* (frs. 1, 6, 9 Ross), *On Philosophy* (test. 1, fr. 6 Ross), *Symposium* (frs. 3, 11, 12 Ross), *On Wealth* (fr. 1 Ross), *Erotikos* (frs. 2–3 Ross), *On Justice* (fr. 4 Ross).

Plutarch's broad and first-hand knowledge of Aristotle's work is also suggested by the following evidence. Plutarch expresses a judgement about the genuineness of Aristotle's work *On nobility* (*Aristid.* 27. 2; fr. 3 Ross), compares Chrysippus' treatment of justice with that of Aristotle (*De Stoic. Rep.* 1040E; *On Justice* fr. 4 Ross), and is trusted about his first-hand knowledge of Aristotle by later authors such as Aulus Gellius (*NA* 4. 11; fr. 122 Sandbach, *On Justice* fr. 4 Ross). Most important in this regard is Plutarch's reference to Aristotle's philosophical development. In the *De virtute morali* (442B–C) he argues that Aristotle at first followed Plato's model of a tripartite soul, adopting the bipartition of the soul later on. The substance of this remark, which has been much discussed, will be examined below (s. 5), but for the moment it suffices to emphasize that such a remark would hardly be possible had Plutarch not been directly acquainted with both early and late Aristotelian treatises, such as the *Topics*, the *De anima*, and the *Nicomachean Ethics* respectively.[26]

In view of this evidence, Plutarch's familiarity with Aristotle's work must be beyond doubt. If Plutarch does not always refer to Aristotle's work and rarely quotes from it, this is because he often perceives Aristotle as representative of Plato's own views. That is, he treats Aristotle's work like Plato's, as a source on which he, as a Platonist, constantly draws without always acknowledging his debt.[27] The fact that many of Plutarch's references to Aristotle's work occur in his anti-Stoic and anti-Epicurean writings indicates his eagerness to show a firm knowledge of it, compared to his opponents' ignorant or prejudiced approach to Aristotle. Let me now pass to the most important of these references, the one we find in the *Adversus Colotem*.

3. PLUTARCH ON HOW ARISTOTLE'S PHILOSOPHY COMPARES WITH THAT OF PLATO (*ADV. COLOTEM* 1114F–1115C)

This work contains Plutarch's most substantial discussion of how Aristotle's philosophy compares with that of Plato. In it Plutarch criticizes

[26] This point is argued by S. G. Etheridge, 'Plutarch's *De Virtute Morali*: A Study in Extra-Peripatetic Aristotelianism' (Ph.D. thesis, Harvard, 1961); I have consulted only the abstract published in *HSCPh* 66 (1962), 252–7. Verbeke (1960: 246–7) and Babut (1969*b*: 45–8, 67–79) share his view.

[27] Plutarch's references to Plato are collected by Jones (1916: 109–53).

Colotes, one of Epicurus' early students who wrote (after 268 BC) a polemical treatise against all other philosophical doctrines entitled Περὶ τοῦ ὅτι κατὰ τὰ τῶν ἄλλων φιλοσόφων δόγματα οὐδὲ ζῆν ἐστιν (*Adv. Col.* 1107E), but also wrote works specifically against Plato, such as *Against Plato's Lysis* and *Against Plato's Euthydemus*.[28] Plutarch wants to show that Colotes exhibits faulty philosophical judgement and ignorance of basic facts as regards the history of philosophy. One instance which Plutarch highlights as indicative of Colotes' ignorance was the latter's claim that Aristotle, along with Xenocrates, Theophrastus, and all Peripatetics, had espoused Plato's theory of Forms. The passage needs to be discussed in some detail. I quote it below:

I intend to deal next with the attack on Plato. And first let us consider the diligence and learning of our philosopher, who says that these doctrines of Plato [i.e. the theory of Forms] were followed by Aristotle, Xenocrates, Theophrastus, and all the Peripatetics. In what wilderness did you write your book, that when you framed these charges you failed to look at their writings or take into your hands Aristotle's works *On the Heavens* and *On the soul*, Theophrastus' *Reply to the Natural Philosophers*, Heraclides' *Zoroaster*, *On the Underworld* and *Disputed Questions in Natural Philosophy*, and Dicaearchus' *On the Soul*, in which they constantly differ with Plato, contradicting him about the most fundamental and far-reaching questions of natural philosophy? Strato indeed, foremost of the other Peripatetics, on many points is not in accord with Aristotle, and has adopted views the reverse of Plato's about motion and intelligence, soul, and generation. In the end he says that the universe itself is not animate and that nature is subsequent to chance, for, in his view, the spontaneous initiates the motion, and only then are the various natural processes brought to pass. As for the Forms, for which our Epicurean criticizes Plato, Aristotle, who everywhere assails them and brings up against them every sort of objection in his treatises on ethics and on natural philosophy and in his exoteric dialogues, was held by some to be more contentious than philosophical in his attitude to this doctrine, aiming to undermine Plato's philosophy; so far was he from being a follower of him. How frivolous a man can be not to know of these men's views, then to father on them views they did not hold, and in the conviction that he is

[28] Colotes' works *Against Plato's Lysis* and *Against Plato's Euthydemus* have been preserved, partly and severely damaged, in two Herculaneum papyri, *PHerc.* 208 and *PHerc.* 1032 respectively. The papyri have been edited by Crönert (1906: 162–70). Colotes is also attested to have criticized Plato's myth of Er in *Republic* 10 (Proclus, *In Remp.* 2. 109. 11–12, 111. 6–17, 113. 9–10, 116. 19–20, 121. 19–122. 1; Macrobius, *In somn. Scip.* 1. 2. 3), possibly in a work named Περὶ τῶν παρὰ Πλάτωνι μυθικῶς πεπλασμένων or Πρὸς τοὺς Πλάτωνος μύθους, as Crönert (1906: 12) has argued. On Colotes and his work see Crönert (1906: esp. 11–16); Westman (1955: 26–40); A. Martini, 'Sulle opere polemiche di Colote', *Cr. Erc.* 6 (1976), 61–7.

exposing others to give proof of his own ignorance and recklessness when he asserts that men who differ from Plato agree with him and that men who attack him are his followers. (*Adv. Col.* 1114F–1115C; tr. B. Einarson- Ph. De Lacy modified)

The context into which the passage is integrated is the following.[29] It is part of Plutarch's criticism of Colotes' attack on the metaphysics of Parmenides and Plato, who distinguish between intelligible and sensible reality, that is, a realm of being and a realm of becoming, respectively (1113E–1114E). More precisely, it forms the initial part of Plutarch's attempt to disarm Colotes' attack on Plato's philosophy, starting with Colotes' criticism of Plato's theory of Forms by which Plato, as Plutarch argues, elaborates on the Parmenidean distinction between sensible and intelligible (1114F).

Plutarch contends that Colotes criticized Plato's identification of real beings with Forms apparently arguing that, by reserving 'being' only for the Forms (1115C–D), Plato had disputed the reality of sensible things. Such a view, Colotes claimed, makes this world unreal and normal life impossible (1116E), presumably because in this case we are living in a dream without being able to know anything and make decisions in everyday life.[30] In his defence of Plato, Plutarch argues that Plato hardly ever denied the existence of sensible entities, but rather denied that they qualify strictly speaking as beings (1115E–F). Plutarch appears to criticize Colotes for confusing the existential use of 'is' with the ontological one; in the first use, 'existing' is opposite to 'non-existing', while in the latter 'being' is contrasted with 'becoming' (1115D).

Plutarch considers the latter to be a basic philosophical distinction with which Colotes should have been familiar (1116B–D). In his view, for something to qualify as 'being', it must be stable and unchanging (1115E, 1116B). Material entities, Plutarch argues, do exist for Plato, that is, they have a degree of reality but do not qualify as 'being', because, given the nature of matter, they are subject to alteration and corruption (1115E–F). Plutarch claims that according to Plato it is the Form of a material entity that is on the full sense 'being', because it is this that is always identical and stable (*καθ' αὑτὸ καὶ ταὐτόν*; 1115E) and has never come to be (ibid.). Since material entities change, they do not hold firmly on to their Forms (1115E); as a result, they only resemble

[29] For a commentary on this passage see Düring (1957: 323–5).

[30] Westman (1955: 67–9) must be right to point out that Plutarch's reply at 1116E should reflect Colotes' initial criticism. Cf. the title of Colotes' work in n. 28.

their Forms in the way that Plato's image resembles Plato (1115F), and are as ontologically inferior as is a copy to its model. In this sense material entities are other than 'being' (ἕτερον; 1115Dfin, 1115Ffin). Yet this does not mean, Plutarch argues, that their existence is disputed, just as the existence of the copy is hardly disputed (1115F, 1116A–B). Plutarch's argument makes clear that he refers both to transcendent and to immanent Forms, as he distinguishes between Form and the Form in matter, and describes their relation as that between model and copy.

Now, as I said above, Colotes' argument against Plato's Forms involved the claim that Aristotle together with the Academics and other Peripatetics espoused these doctrines (τούτοις τοῖς δόγμασι ἐπηκολουθηκέναι; 1115Ainit.). This is a claim that Plutarch also wants to refute. As will be seen, Plutarch admits that Aristotle accepted immanent Forms, but to claim that he accepted Plato's Forms without any qualification, as Colotes did, in his own view plainly manifests ignorance and confusion. Aristotle, he argues, is the clearest example of someone who objected to Plato's transcendent Forms (πᾶσαν ἀπορίαν ἐπάγων; 1115Bfin) and contradicted Plato (ἀντιλέγων; 1115Cfin). Aristotle, Plutarch argues, rejected the transcendent Forms in works like the *De anima* and the *De caelo*, but also everywhere in his writings (πανταχοῦ κινῶν Ἀριστοτέλης), in his esoteric works, such as his ethical treatises and the works on natural philosophy, and also in his exoteric works, the dialogues, for instance.

Plutarch's testimony is a valuable piece of evidence which shows that in no part of his work did Aristotle adopt Plato's transcendent Forms, but raised various objections against such a theory (1115B). The fact that Plutarch, who was familiar with writings of Aristotle lost today, does not know of any early (exoteric) writing in which Aristotle appealed to transcendent Forms, strengthens the argument against Jaeger's view that Aristotle in his early works espoused such a view.[31]

Plutarch seems to distinguish two ways in which Aristotle rejected transcendent Forms, an implicit and an explicit one. That is, he distinguishes between instances in which Aristotle discusses philosophical issues without making any reference to transcendent Forms, when

[31] Jaeger (1948: 35–6, 126) argued that Plutarch's passage is similar with a passage from Proclus' work Ἐπίσκεψις τῶν πρὸς τὸν Πλάτωνος Τίμαιον ὑπ' Ἀριστοτέλους εἰρημένων (apud Philoponum *De aet. mundi* 31. 17–32. 8) and both derive from the same source and are founded on Aristotle's dialogue *On Philosophy*, where Aristotle criticizes Plato (fr. 10 Ross); cf. Westman (1955: 280–1). But Plutarch refers to 'dialogues' in plural, and nothing suggests that he had only this dialogue in mind.

such reference in Plutarch's view is mandatory, and instances in which Aristotle openly criticizes the existence of such Forms. As regards the latter, Plutarch must refer to some well-known passages in which Aristotle argues against the existence of transcendent Forms, such as in the *Nicomachean Ethics* 1. 6 (1096^a11–1097^a14), or in the *Metaphysics* 1. 9, 13. 1–9. However, in the *De caelo* and the *De anima*, both of which Plutarch mentions, Aristotle does not even discuss the transcendent Forms. Plutarch, I suggest, must refer to the fact that in these works Aristotle examines matters such as the world's coming into being without referring to the Forms, and thus he departs from Plato's thinking. In the next section I will try to show in what sense exactly, according to Plutarch, Aristotle departs from Plato's doctrine in these works. Here I want to draw attention to the fact that Plutarch emphasizes that Aristotle's difference from Plato in the *De anima* and the *De caelo* is more extensive. In them, he argues, Aristotle not only rejects the Forms, but also opposes Plato's views regarding as fundamental issues as coming into being, motion, the soul, the intellect, and the universe in the same way that other Peripatetics did (*Adv. Col.* 1115A–B).[32]

It is important to notice that Plutarch links together Aristotle's rejection of the transcendent Forms in the *De caelo* and the *De anima* with his departure from some other Platonic doctrines. This link becomes manifest already from the structure of Plutarch's argument. He starts out by claiming that Aristotle and the early Peripatetics rejected Plato's transcendent Forms, yet goes on to argue that they also contradicted Plato on questions of natural philosophy. Here Plutarch implies that Aristotle's rejection of the Forms in the *De caelo* and *De anima* is crucial to his difference of opinion from Plato in these areas, as is the case with other Peripatetics like Strato and Dicaearchus, and seems to believe that it was the rejection of the Forms that resulted in this difference. Plutarch's language clearly suggests that the difference is so considerable that it constitutes a strong opposition to Plato.[33]

Yet, however strong Plutarch's claims about Aristotle's opposition to Plato's philosophy are, they should not be seen as expressing hostility to Aristotle's philosophy or outright rejection of it as a whole. First, in this context Plutarch does not consider how Aristotle's philosophy compares in general with that of Plato's, but rather addresses a specific claim of

[32] Plutarch concludes that Aristotle and other Peripatetics both depart from Plato (*διαφερόμενοι*) *and* contradict (*ἀντιλέγοντες*) Plato (*Adv. Col.* 1115cfin).

[33] Notice the terms *ὑπεναντιούμενοι, μαχόμενοι τῷ Πλάτωνι*; *Adv. Col.* 1115A–B.

Colotes.[34] Secondly, Plutarch has a polemical purpose, to demonstrate Colotes' ignorance and thus invalidate his criticism against Plato. Plutarch shows Colotes' ignorance about the 'ancients', whom he professed to have studied (1107D, 1108D), also about the views of Democritus and Protagoras (ibid. 1109A) and Xenocrates. Regarding the last, Colotes was mistaken to think that also he had been committed to Plato's theory of Forms. However, Plutarch highlights the cases of Aristotle and the Peripatetics because these most clearly demonstrate Colotes' ignorance, since in their case Colotes takes contradictory positions to be identical (1115C). Such evidence serves Plutarch's polemical purposes best; his reader is prepared to admit that Colotes' criticism of Plato's philosophy, in this regard at least, is based on confusion and ignorance.

What also speaks against the view that Plutarch is hostile to Aristotle is the important fact that already within the present context Plutarch distinguishes Aristotle from the other Peripatetics, whom he collectively had presented as strongly opposing Plato. Talking about Strato's attitude to Plato's doctrine, Plutarch argues that Strato adopted views contrary to those of Plato about motion, the nature of soul, the intellect, generation, and the constitution of the universe. Plutarch's claim about Strato's views on the soul and the intellect is supported by independent evidence, while his claim that Strato disputed that the universe is animate (*Timaeus* 30b7–8) and that he denied the teleological view of the world which Aristotle adopted from Plato is less certain.[35] The crucial matter for us is that, according to Plutarch, Strato came to contradict Plato extensively because he departed from Aristotle's own doctrines.[36] Plutarch's implication apparently is that Aristotle is closer to Plato in many of the issues in which Strato and later Peripatetics diverge strongly from Plato.

[34] Plutarch differs considerably from Numenius and Atticus who regard Aristotle's departure from Plato's doctrine of Forms as a sign of his general departure from Plato's philosophy. Numenius' criticism of Cephisodorus who, like Colotes, ascribed the transcendent Forms to Aristotle too, suggests that for Numenius Aristotle's rejection of the Forms testifies to his contradiction of Plato's philosophy (fr. 26. 105–17 Des Places). Atticus explicitly argues this (frs. 2, 9 Des Places). See Chs. 3 and 4, pp. 137–44, 161–71.

[35] See frs. 32–4W; cf. Capelle (1931: 291, 299–310) and F. Wehrli, *Straton von Lampsakos*, Basel/Stuttart 1969, 54. On Strato's views on the soul see below.

[36] *καὶ μὴν τῶν ἄλλων Περιπατητικῶν ὁ κορυφαιότατος Στράτων οὔτε Ἀριστοτέλει κατὰ πολλὰ συμφέρεται καὶ Πλάτωνι τας ἐναντίας ἔσχηκε δόξας περὶ κινήσεως, περὶ νοῦ καὶ περὶ ψυχῆς καὶ περὶ γενέσεως, τελευτῶν τε τὸν κόσμον αὐτὸν οὐ ζῷον εἶναί φησι, τὸ δὲ κατὰ φύσιν ἕπεσθαι τῷ κατὰ τύχην ἀρχὴν γὰρ ἐνδιδόναι τὸ αὐτόματον εἶτα οὕτως περαίνεσθαι τῶν φυσικῶν παθῶν ἕκαστον.* *Adv. Col.* 1115B.

A further detail in the text also suggests that Plutarch draws a line between Aristotle's attitude to Plato and the other Peripatetics who strongly opposed Plato. Plutarch voices an apparently widespread claim according to which Aristotle showed a contentious spirit in his criticism of Plato's Forms, aiming to undermine Plato's philosophy as a whole (1115cinit.). This is exactly the claim Atticus later makes.[37] Plutarch shows reluctance to accept it.[38] He implies that acquaintance with Aristotle's work may suggest this view, rather than the one that Colotes takes, but he himself does not endorse it. This is of some further significance if we bear in mind that accusations of contentiousness were often raised against Academic sceptics, and that Plutarch, like Cicero, was concerned to refute them.[39]

The upshot of all this is that even in such a polemical context Plutarch tries to be fair to Aristotle. He does find some of Aristotle's doctrines at odds with those he considers Plato's, but he refrains from accusing Aristotle of hostility to Plato. Plutarch rather implies that Aristotle agreed with Plato on several issues to which later Peripatetics would object, especially as regards natural philosophy and psychology.

Before we discuss how Plutarch generally rates Aristotle's views on these subjects, it is important to notice that in the present context he appears to suggest that also in metaphysics Aristotle was aligned to some degree with Plato. Plutarch argues that Plato's distinction between the 'participant' and what it 'participates in' (cf. *Phaedo* 102b–103c), that is, between Form and the Form in matter, amounts to the distinction between genus and species, or to the distinction between common and individuating characteristics which, he argues, 'later philosophers' make. The first distinction must refer to Aristotle,[40] and the latter to the

[37] Frs. 6. 72, 7. 37, 9 Des Places; see Ch. 4, pp. 159–61. Cf. Proclus in Philoponus, *De aet. mundi* 32. 6–7.

[38] *φιλονεικότερον ἐνίοις ἔδοξεν ἢ φιλοσοφώτερον ἔχειν τῷ δόγματι τούτῳ, ὡς προθέμενος τὴν Πλάτωνος ὑπερείπειν φιλοσοφίαν·* (ibid. 1115Cinit.). *ὑπερείπειν* is a rare word (meaning 'undermine', 'subvert'; LSJ, s.v.) and Reiske's emendation instead of *ὑπεριδεῖν* of the MSS ('despise', 'disdain', 'overlook'; LSJ, s.v.), which ascribes to Aristotle a contentious spirit. The textual difficulty is not crucial for my argument here, because Plutarch refrains from endorsing this view.

[39] Arcesilaus, for instance, is defended from contentiousness (*Acad.* 1. 44, 2. 76); cf. Plutarch, *Cic.* 4. 3. For further references to Plutarch, see Opsomer (1999: 187). Numenius accuses Arcesilaus and Zeno of contentiousness (frs. 25. 11, 63, 133, 27. 57 Des Places).

[40] Westman (1955: 302) does not notice any reference to Aristotle here, while De Lacy in his review of Westman in *AJP* 77 (1956), 436, detects (wrongly in my view) an implied criticism of Aristotle here.

Stoics. Plutarch's terminology suggests that he refers to Aristotle's doctrine of substance, as presented in the *Categories* (2^a11–12), where Aristotle distinguishes between primary and secondary substances, that is, between individuals and species or genus. Yet Plutarch must allude also to Aristotle's doctrine of immanent Forms, which he considers to be the essences of things.[41] And in a different context, he refers to Aristotle's view that the intellect is the place of Forms.[42] It is still controversial whether the Aristotelian essential Form is universal or particular,[43] yet Plutarch apparently believed that it is universal and held that Plato and Aristotle agree in considering the Form to be the essence of a thing and 'being' (*ousia*) strictly speaking.[44]

Nevertheless, Plutarch argues, neither Aristotle nor the Stoics went 'higher', that is, to the transcendent Forms, because, he argues, they became involved with logical matters.[45] Plutarch's implication is that Aristotle, like the Stoics, lost sight of the metaphysical questions and the proper way to address them, that is, by making reference to the Forms. The language Plutarch uses suggests that for him the Forms constitute the higher causes; so by rejecting them, Aristotle's causal explanations are philosophically inadequate. For Plutarch, this is not a small shortcoming for a philosopher. As he argues in *De primo frigido*, the natural philosopher (φυσικός) differs from the practitioner, for example, a doctor, in that the former should be concerned with discovering the ultimate causes.[46] Apparently for Plutarch the natural philosopher is essentially a metaphysician, who not only seeks the ultimate causes but also accepts that these are, Plato's transcendent Forms. It is not surprising, then, that in the passage of *De primo frigido* cited above Plutarch does not mention Aristotle next to Plato as an example of a natural

41 See esp. *Met.* 1029b12–1032a11, 1032b15–1033a23.

42 *De Iside* 374E–F; (Aristotle, *De anima* 429^a27–8). Cf. *De Iside* 370A. See s. 4 below.

43 See C. Witt, *Substance and Essence in Aristotle* (Cornell, 1989), ch. 5, with reference to further bibliography.

44 The view that Aristotle followed Plato in espousing the immanent Forms was widely maintained at the time. Seneca presents Platonic and Aristotelian causes as unified, acknowledging the transcendent Forms as specifically Platonic (*Ep.* 65. 4–14). I discuss this passage in Ch. 7 (5. 2). On Plutarch's view on the Forms see Jones (1916: 101–5) and below, s. 4.

45 ἀνωτέρω δὲ οὐ προῆλθον [sc. Aristotle and the Stoics], εἰς λογικωτέρας ἀπορίας ἐμπεσόντες (*Adv. Col.* 1115E). Cf. Aristotle *Met.* 1078^b31–79a1 uses similar language to state that the Platonists moved there (ἐκεῖ προῆλθον), i.e. to the Forms, when searching for the causes of the sensibles.

46 τὰ πρῶτα καὶ ἀνωτάτω (*De primo frigido* 948B–C); cf. Alcinous, *Didasc.* 189. 15–16, *Atticus* fr. 9. 31–3 Des Places.

philosopher, although he does refer to Aristotle in the same context as the philosopher who corrected Anaximander's theories.[47] It emerges that Plutarch considers Aristotle's philosophy metaphysically wanting, a view which will be argued at length later by Atticus and Plotinus. Yet unlike them Plutarch is only mildly critical of Aristotle.

On the basis of the passage in *Adversus Colotem* we can conclude that: (*a*) Plutarch is aware that in natural philosophy and metaphysics Aristotle contradicted several of Plato's views. (*b*) He also is aware that Aristotle rejected Plato's transcendent Forms altogether, yet he considers Aristotle as being partly aligned with Plato's metaphysics to the extent that Aristotle espoused immanent Forms. (*c*) Unlike other Platonists who thought of Aristotle's opposition to Plato's Forms as an indication of a contentious spirit, Plutarch does not endorse such a view. (*d*) Plutarch maintains that Aristotle followed some of Plato's doctrines in psychology and natural philosophy, which later Peripatetics opposed. And finally, (*e*) the above passage shows that Plutarch would be the last to concede to Aristotle's views. When he espouses such a view, he does so because he considers it to be Plato's. This will be confirmed in the sections below, especially in section 5 on ethics.

4. NATURAL PHILOSOPHY, PSYCHOLOGY, AND EPISTEMOLOGY

As has been seen, Plutarch suggests in the *Adversus Colotem* that in the *De caelo* and the *De anima* Aristotle not only objects to Plato's transcendent Forms but that his objection goes along with an opposition to other Platonic doctrines. In this section I will try to show in which sense Plutarch considers Aristotle as rejecting the Forms in these particular works, and how according to Plutarch this position of Aristotle is linked with his departure from other Platonic tenets.

As far as the *De caelo* is concerned, Plutarch must refer to the fact that in it Aristotle discusses the constitution of the universe without making any reference to the Forms. To understand this we have to look briefly at

[47] *De primo frig.* 948A. At least since Posidonius there had been some discussion on how the philosopher differs from a scientist in the method of explanation. See Geminus apud Simplicium, *In Phys.* 291. 21–292. 31 (Posidonius fr. 18 E–K); cf. Plutarch, *De facie* 921D–E. See also Ch. 4, pp. 175–7.

Plutarch's interpretation of the role the Forms play in the *Timaeus*, a subject to which he dedicated entire treatises (lost today).[48]

Plutarch construes the cosmogony of the *Timaeus* in a literal way.[49] He argues that the world had been created at a certain point in time from a pre-existing, uncreated, material substratum, which the demiurge formed and fitted together.[50] The main reason why Plutarch takes this view is because he thinks that he can thus explain how the soul in Plato is said to be uncreated (*Phaedrus* 245c–e) and also created (*Timaeus* 34b–35a), a topic he discusses extensively in his *De animae procreatione in Timaeo* (cf. 1013A). Plutarch does this in the following way. In his view, before the world came into being, there was disordered matter (cf. *Timaeus* 30a, 48a–d, 52e–53b; *Politicus* 273b), which was governed by a world-soul, the evil world-soul of the *Laws* 10 (896d–e, 898c). To put order into matter, the demiurge first creates a benevolent world-soul by making the evil one partake in intelligence and reason.[51] Once the world-soul becomes rational, the demiurge initiates the ordering process of matter until the world comes eventually into being (*Plat. Q.* 1003A–B).

The crucial point for us in this process is that according to Plutarch (who follows the *Timaeus*) something comes into being as a result of the contact between matter and the intelligible realm.[52] The kind of contact between the two in the *Timaeus* is complex, if not obscure. Plutarch maintains that the world comes into being through 'the impression of the intelligible entities onto matter' (*De an. procr.* 1024C), as seals are impressed on material objects (*De Iside* 373A; *De Pyth. orac.* 404C; cf. *Timaeus* 52d–53c).[53]

[48] Cf. *Ποῦ εἰσιν αἱ ἰδέαι* (Where are the Forms; Lamprias no. 67); *Πῶς ἡ ὕλη τῶν ἰδεῶν μετείληφεν; ὅτι τὰ πρῶτα σώματα ποιεῖ* (How matter participates in the Forms; that it constitutes the primary bodies; Lamprias no. 68).

[49] Plutarch wrote a lost essay *Περὶ τοῦ γεγονέναι κατὰ Πλάτωνα τὸν κόσμον* (On the creation of the world according to Plato; no. 66 Lamprias). See Dillon (1977: 204–8); Baltes (1976: 38–45).

[50] *Plat. Q.* 1001B–C; *De an. procr.* 1013C–1014C; cf. *Timaeus* 30a, 52d–53b.

[51] Plutarch outlines his interpretation in the *De animae procreatione in Timaeo*, esp. 1013E–1014E; cf. also 1023D–1024A, *Plat. Q.* 1001B–C, 1003A. See Jones (1916: 78–100); Deuse (1983: 13–72); and Schoppe (1994: 88–109).

[52] See *De def. orac.* 435F–436A; *Quaest. Conv.* 720C; *Plat. Q.* 1001B; *De an. procr.* 1022E–1024B, *De Iside* 374D and the comments of Deuse (1983: 27–33).

[53] *γένεσιν δὲ τοῦ κόσμου μήπω γεγονότος οὐδεμίαν ἄλλην ἢ τὴν ἐν μεταβολαῖς καὶ κινήσεσιν οὐσίαν, τοῦ τυποῦντος καὶ τοῦ τυπουμένου μεταξὺ τεταγμένην, διαδιδοῦσαν ἐντεῦθεν τὰς ἐκεῖθεν εἰκόνας.* (*De an. procr.* 1024C). It is the precosmic soul which is placed between the Forms and the matter on which they are imposed, and the one which mediates and transmits the Forms from the intelligible to the sensible realm. See Baltes (2001: 263–4).

But where are the transcendent Forms before they inform the matter? Plutarch wrote an entire treatise on this question, lost today.[54] The rest of the evidence about him seems to articulate a clear answer: the Forms are in the soul of the demiurge. This is first suggested by the testimony of Syrianus according to which Plutarch, together with Atticus, believed that the Forms exist eternally in the divine soul.[55] In the myth of *De Iside* now, Osiris sows in matter, that is Isis, the *logoi* of himself (372E–F).[56] Given that Osiris is an intellect with soul, identified with God or with the Form of Good (372E–373B, 374F, 382C), it is reasonable to assume that the *logoi*, that is the Forms, exist in his soul. Now the Forms, Plutarch argues, are transmitted to the sensible realm and inform the matter through the mediation of the irrational pre-cosmic soul which receives the Forms (*De an. procr.* 1024C) and thus is partly itself transformed into an intelligent and benevolent soul (ibid. 1024A, C). The pre-cosmic soul transmits only images (εἰκόνας) of the transcendent Forms to the sensible world (ibid. 1024C), and as a result the entire sensible world is a copy of the intelligible realm of the Forms, which is the sense that a sealed object relates to the seal (ibid).

There seem to be two ways in which the world is modelled on the transcendent Forms, which appear to correspond to two stages in creation. First, the participation of matter in the Forms results in the formation of primary bodies or elements (*De an. proc.* 1025A–B; *Plat. Q.* 1001D–E) like water and fire (cf. *Timaeus* 53b).[57] Secondly, individual material entities come into being by being modelled on a Form (*De Iside* 372E–F, 373E–F).

The myth of Osiris and Isis seeks to explain this process of the participation of matter in the Forms, but several questions do remain.

[54] *Ποῦ εἰσιν αἱ ἰδέαι* (no. 67 Lamprias).

[55] τοὺς καθόλου λόγους τοὺς ἐν οὐσίᾳ τῇ ψυχικῇ διαιωνίως ὑπάρχοντας ἡγοῦνται [sc. Plutarch, Atticus, Democritus the Platonist] εἶναι τὰς ἰδέας. (Syrianus, *In Met.* 105. 36–8). Dörrie (1976: 220 n. 9) and Dillon (1977: 256) have claimed that in this passage reference is made to the world-soul; Baltes (1983: 48–9; 2000: 267–9) has argued, convincingly in my view, that the reference is to the soul of the demiurge. Dillon (1977: 201) has adduced as evidence that, in Plutarch's view, God comprises the Forms also, *De Sera* 550D. But the passage does not say this. It rather is concerned with virtue, and this is why it refers to *Theaetetus* 176a–b. God is said to be the model of the world in the sense that it is goodness in which the world participates. See also below, s. 5, pp. 122–3.

[56] Cf. *Quaest. conv.* 719A. See the discussion in Schoppe (1994: 139–81).

[57] Plutarch must have examined this process in his lost essay *Πῶς ἡ ὕλη τῶν ἰδεῶν μετείληφεν; ὅτι τὰ πρῶτα σώματα ποιεῖ* (Lamprias no. 68). See the reconstruction of it by Schoppe (1994: 217–23).

For instance, Plutarch seems to believe that each of the sensible entities participate in more than one Forms (cf. *Plat. Q.* 1001E), but nowhere does he explain how. Yet however this is, it is clear that in Plutarch's view the sensible world as a whole is brought about by God who imposes the transcendent Forms existing in him in matter through the mediation of the cosmic soul. In this sense the world is a copy of the intelligible paradigm of the *Timaeus* (cf. *Tim.* 29b, 30c–31b, 39e).

Aristotle's account in the *De caelo* appears to be seriously divergent from this picture, since the world for Aristotle does not come into being, and the transcendent Forms do not play any role in explaining how the world exists. But if this is so, presumably Plutarch disagreed with Aristotle also on the sense in which God is the principle of the world. This is because for Platonists since Xenocrates (cf. fr. 15 Heinze) the divine craftsman brings the world about having a model in mind, or in the case of Plutarch, having the *logoi*/Forms in soul. This model is the object of his thinking, and according to *Republic* 10 this is how any craftsman creates (cf. *Gorgias* 503e). All this, of course, is part of the bigger question of how the intelligible realm relates to the sensible one. For Plutarch, the fact that Aristotle accepted only immanent Forms presumably indicates Aristotle's insufficient appreciation of the way in which the two realms are related. It is in this sense, I think, that Plutarch perceives the *De caelo* as exemplifying Aristotle's rejection of Plato's Forms when he refers to it in the *Adversus Colotem*. If my reconstruction is correct, however, Plutarch's disagreement with Aristotle was more extensive than the one he states in the *Adversus Colotem*.

There are some further reasons to believe this. Plutarch was certainly aware of Aristotle's explicit criticism of Plato's description of the world's coming into being from an initial disorder.[58] And one can surmise that he devoted so much energy in explicating the *Timaeus* because he wanted to address Aristotle's objections. However, there is no evidence that Plutarch ever criticized Aristotle in this capacity. This is a feature of Plutarch's attitude towards Aristotle that we will encounter again. Plutarch appears to have regarded Aristotle as having departed from Plato's views on two other issues related to the constitution of the world, the aether and the issue of the divine providence, but he does not criticize Aristotle explicitly on them either.

[58] *De caelo* $280^{a}28$–32, $283^{a}4$–$284^{a}2$, $300^{b}16$–19. Cf. *De philosophia*, frs. 18, 19a–c Ross. I briefly discussed Aristotle's interpretation of Plato's cosmogony in the Introduction, s. 3, pp. 29–31.

In some parts of his work Plutarch comes to discuss the aether, because there was a question among Platonists as to whether the aether, of which Plato speaks in several parts of his work, is identical with that described by Aristotle in *De caelo*.[59] We can understand better the emergence of such a question if we bear in mind that already the early Academics postulated such an element, and in doing so they meant to remain true to Plato.[60] Besides, later sources often credited Plato with five elements.[61] Aristotle, however, differed from all Platonists in that he suggested that such an element must be distinct from the four standard ones, imperishable, and responsible for the eternal existence and the circular movement of the planets (*De caelo* 1. 2–3, 268b11–270b31). The Platonic passages on the other hand present the aether as being simply a mixture of air and fire. However, some Platonists apparently identified Aristotle's aether with the corresponding element of Plato already since Xenocrates (fr. 53 Heinze). Plutarch gives voice to such views, especially in his *De E apud Delphos*, where he presents speakers who consider Aristotle's view about the existence of aether as harmonious with Plato's conception of the aether.[62] These characters credit Aristotle with five elements, though clearly Aristotle never considered the aether as a substance which stands on the same footing as the other four, let alone ranks it fifth.[63] And they take these five elements to be hinted at in *Timaeus* 53c–57c and to correspond to the five solids discussed there and also to the five *megista genê* of the *Sophist* (256c–d).

Plutarch, however, appears to have had his reservations considering this view, without ever becoming overtly critical. In the *De E*

[59] Cf. *Timaeus* 58d1–2; *Phaedo* 109b9, 111b2; *Cratylus* 408d8; and also [Plato], *Epinomis* 984b–e where the aether is considered the second most important element after fire, and that from which the soul fashions animate creatures. It is generally assumed that the author of *Epinomis* is Philipp of Opus; see Dillon (2003: 179, 193).

[60] Speusippus appears to have accepted the aether as an originally Pythagorean doctrine espoused also by Plato (cf. fr. 4 Lang; 28. 1–13 Tarán). Apparently he assumed that the five solids of *Timaeus* 53c–57c correspond to five elements. Xenocrates also postulated a fifth element (fr. 53 Heinze). See Dillon (2003: 60–1, 128). The aether is ascribed to Pythagoras and the Pythagoreans in several sources: e.g. ps-Plutarch 2. 6. 2, Stobaeus 1. 186. 16–22 (*DG* pp. 333–4), 1. 476. 17–22 (*DG* p. 397); Philolaus fr. 12D–K; Timaeus Locrus 98a–99d (pp. 216–17 Thesleff). See Moraux (1963: 1176–93, 1226–31).

[61] e.g. Alcinous, *Didasc.* 171. 17 who accepts the aether as an element, although he does not mention it when he refers to the elements involved in the cosmogony (168. 11–13). Cf. Aetius 2. 6. 5; (*DG* p. 334).

[62] *De E* 389F–390C; cf. *De def. orac.* 422F–423A, 428C–430B.

[63] Aristotle standardly speaks of τὸ πρῶτον σῶμα (*De caelo* 270^{b}21). See Moraux (1963: 1196–1211).

Eustrophos' view is corrected (390C–D), and in the *De facie* it is disputed that the theory of a fifth element applies to the moon (928E–929A).[64] We do not know why Plutarch was sceptical about this doctrine. Presumably in his view Aristotle's doctrine does not solve any problem.[65] This is probably because for Plutarch the eternal nature and circular movement of the planets, allegedly guaranteed by the aether, are explained sufficiently in terms of the orderly arrangement of the universe by the demiurge. Yet the fact that Plutarch wrote a long treatise on the subject suggests that, like Antiochus, he found this a complex matter that cannot be exhausted in a mere approval or disapproval, but one that requires extensive discussion.[66] Plutarch states, though, that Aristotle followed Plato and Xenocrates in believing that everything in the sublunary realm consists of four elementary components.[67] This again shows that Plutarch tends to highlight Aristotle's agreement with Plato's doctrines rather than his departure from them.

There is another, more serious, issue to which Plutarch probably refers when he argues that Aristotle contradicted Plato on questions of natural philosophy in works like the *De caelo*. This concerns the limited degree of divine providence that Aristotle's God exercises. Plutarch maintains the existence of strong divine providence. This belief is part of his conviction that there is a tight relation between the intelligible and the sensible realm in the following sense. In his view, the world of becoming is closely linked with aspects of the creator's substance; God imparts intellect to the world-soul out of his own substance,[68] so the world-soul, which initiates the world's coming into being, is a fragment of God. It is in this sense that Plutarch understands the statement in *Timaeus* 28c2 that the demiurge is not only a ποιητής, but also a πατήρ,

[64] See Moraux (1963: 1238) and Donini (1988*b*); on the fifth element see also Ch. 7 s. 5. 4, pp. 285–7.

[65] *μυρίων οὐσῶν ἀποριῶν* (*De facie* 928F). Already the Peripatetic Xenarchus (1st c. BC) had raised several problems regarding Aristotle's aether in his work on the fifth element; see Moraux (1963: 1237; 1973: 198–206).

[66] *Περὶ τῆς πέμπτης οὐσίας*; in five books, Lamprias no. 44. On Antiochus see Ch. 1, p. 60, n. 48.

[67] See *Adv. Col.* 1111D–E; cf. *De primo frig.* 947E.

[68] *ἡ δὲ ψυχὴ νοῦ μετασχοῦσα καὶ λογισμοῦ καὶ ἁρμονίας, οὐκ ἔργον ἐστι τοῦ θεοῦ μόνον, ἀλλὰ καὶ μέρος, οὐδ' ὑπ' αὐτοῦ, ἀλλὰ καὶ ἀπ' αὐτοῦ καὶ ἐξ αὐτοῦ γέγονεν* (the soul, however, when it has partaken of intelligence and reason and harmony, is not merely a work but also a part of God, and has not been created by him but from him and out of his own substance *Plat. Q.* 2. 2, 1001C, Cherniss tr. modified); cf. *De an. procr.* 1023D. On the world-soul in Plutarch see Baltes (2000) and also below pp. 110, 114–15.

the father of the world (*De def. or.* 425F).[69] Since the world came into being through the interference of the creator's being, in a sense God is always present in it and responsible for the basic qualities of the world, order, intelligibility and goodness (*Plat. Q.* 1001 A–B; *Gorgias* 503e–504a; *Timaeus* 28a–b). And since the creator relates to the world as the father to his children, God cares for the world as much as fathers care for their children. Being inspired by *Laws* 10 where the world-soul takes an active interest in human affairs,[70] Plutarch regards God as being constantly involved with the world, exercising providence over everything in it.[71] That is, all changes are supervised by God, and, most importantly, God's will prevents the world's destruction. Aristotle's God, on the other hand, provides only for the essential in the world, that is, orderliness, and is not concerned with individuals or details, in the same way that the general provides for the army by maintaining its order, but not for every soldier in the army individually (*Met.* 1075ᵃ13–18). Plutarch appears to be critical of the limited extent of providence exercised by Aristotle's God in the following passage.

> [Lamprias speaks:] The real Zeus has a fair and fitting variety of spectacles in numerous worlds, not viewing the infinite void outside *nor concentrating his mind upon himself and nothing else, as some have imagined*, but surveying from above the many works of gods and men and the movements and courses of the stars in their cycles. In fact, the Deity is not averse to changes, but has a very great role therein, to judge, if need be, by the alternations and cycles in the heavens among the bodies that are visible there. Infinity is altogether senseless and unreasoning and does not pertain to God, but brings into the discussion the concepts of chance and accident. But the oversight and providence in a limited group and number of worlds ... seems to me to contain nothing involving less dignity or greater labour. (*De def. orac.* 426D–E; tr. F. Babitt modified)

The passage is part of Plutarch's discussion as to whether there exists one or many worlds (*De def. or.*, chs. 22–37), an issue set out in *Timaeus* 55c–d. Plutarch reviews the various possibilities and examines their plausibility.[72] One such possibility was Aristotle's view that there exists

[69] Porphyry understands God as father of the universe in a different sense. See Ch. 7, s. 5. 3. 3, pp. 279–83.

[70] Cf. *Laws* 10, 899d–900b, 903b–904b; Gods are said to be attentive to details, *Laws* 10, 900c8–10, 901c–d, 902a–e. See Solmsen (1942: 149–60).

[71] Cf. *De Iside* 382B–C; *De def. orac.* 435E–437C. See Babut (1969*a*: 310–17, 474–82); Kenney (1991: 44–51).

[72] There is a mix of singular and plural of the term κόσμος in the text which can be confusing. Editors change the MSS reading κόσμον in some instances (424Ffin, 426Cfin), for Reiske's κόσμων.

only one world (*De caelo* 276^{a}18–279^{a}18), a view that finds favour also in the *Timaeus* (31b). The Epicureans instead argued for the existence of many worlds.[73] The Epicureans may well be Plutarch's target in this passage, but it may extend also to Aristotle. This is because, parallel to the discussion about the number of worlds, the issue of the divine providence is discussed and it is suggested that God can govern even many worlds (*De def. or.* 425F–426A). Another indication suggesting that the passage is critical of Aristotle's God is the reference to a God engaged solely in thinking, which fits well with the God of *Metaphysics* 12. In fact, Plutarch may be concerned more with Aristotle than with the Epicureans here because he already dealt with both Epicurean and Stoic theology in the previous two chapters of the treatise (chs. 28–9). If Plutarch is in fact addressing Aristotle's view through Lamprias' voice, it is noticeable that he does not name Aristotle.

I would suggest that Plutarch's criticism of Aristotle is rather constructive. Plutarch seems to point out a mistake in Aristotle, his separation of God from the realm of change, thus postulating a God who is engaged solely in eternal thinking.[74] One possible way in which such a position can arise is if one takes the view that any contact of God with the realm of change would affect the divine status, something that is not proper to God. Such a view can lead to the denial of an all-pervasive divine providence, as is the case with Aristotle. Yet such a view may well be formed on the basis of a particular understanding of Plato's God, such that God is not in any kind of contact with the sensible realm.

We know that the way in which God relates to the world of becoming was controversial among Plutarch's contemporary Platonists, who interpreted Plato differently in this area. Some thought it not worthy of God to be concerned with material beings and postulated God's greatest possible distance from them. Notably Moderatus and Numenius understood God's transcendence in such a way that they raised God above the level of the demiurge. In Numenius, at least, the highest God exercises providence only through a second and a third God (see Ch. 3, s. 3). Plutarch on the other hand takes the view that God himself regulates the world while remaining outside it, in which case God's contact with the

73 See Epicurus, *Ep. Hdt.* 45. 73–4; Cicero, *De nat. deor.* 1. 53 [13A, C H Long and Sedley].

74 *Met.* 1074^{b}21–35. If Plutarch refers to Aristotle's God here, as I think he does, he fails to appreciate the role of the heavenly bodies which are part of Aristotle's notion of the divine and in a sense the efficient causes of all sublunary movement, as they mediate between the unmoved mover and the sublunary world.

world of change neither diminishes God's dignity nor compromises God's transcendence, as Aristotle may have thought.[75] The important thing for us is that Plutarch may have regarded Aristotle's view as representing a tendency within the Platonic school of thought on a vexed question which at his time still divided Platonists.

This is supported by the fact that elsewhere Plutarch appears to believe that Aristotle's conception of God, and even his limited extent of divine providence, captures much of the essence of Plato's doctrine, according to which God is indestructible, blessed, and benign. This must be appreciated against Plutarch's criticism of the relevant doctrines of Epicureans and Stoics.[76] Against the Stoic view that providence is immanent in Nature in particular, Plutarch argues that nature has been arranged in a certain way, and it is in this arrangement that the essence of divine providence lies (*De facie* 927c–d). If nature is self-arranged, Plutarch argues, God is useless, in the same sense that a tactician is useless if each soldier knows his position (ibid. 927b). This simile clearly is an allusion to Aristotle's analogy of God with the general providing for the army (*Met.* 1075^{a}13–18). The simile as well as Plutarch's other examples in the same context confirm that it is basically the providential arrangement of things which accounts for the nature of things and their function.

Plutarch's approval of Aristotle's conception of God and nature goes further than that. As we have seen, Plutarch considers Aristotle to be following Plato on the teleological explanation of the universe, which Strato later abandoned (*Adv. Col.* 1115b). This is confirmed by two pieces of evidence. First, Plutarch appears to endorse Aristotle's view that God is the object of universal striving (*Met.* 1072^{a}25–34).[77] This is

[75] Plutarch maintained that God's transcendence is not affected by the exercise of providence, since this happens through demons (*De Is.* 378A; cf. *De Stoic. rep.* 1052a). On Plutarch's demonology see Jones (1916: 24–40) and Dillon (1977: 216–25). Celsus appears to espouse Plutarch's position; see Frede (1994: 5208–10). A similar view is expressed by the Peripatetic author of *De mundo*. It is an open question to me whether Plutarch was familiar with this work, and whether he took it as reflecting Aristotle's views.

[76] See *De Stoic. rep.* 1051c–1052c. Antipater's citation from his *On Gods* in ibid. 1051d–f appears to capture what Plutarch regards as the essence of Plato's doctrine, which the Epicureans and Chrysippus contradicted.

[77] Plutarch's view that God is the object of universal love is to be inferred from *De Iside* 372a–e and from the following passage of *De facie* which is part of the eschatologial myth about the moon. *ἀποκρίνεται* [sc. the moon] *δ᾽ ἔρωτι τῆς περὶ τὸν ἥλιον εἰκόνος, δι᾽ ἧς ἐπιλάμπει τὸ ἐφετὸν καὶ καλὸν καὶ θεῖον καὶ μακάριον οὗ πᾶσα φύσις, ἄλλη δ᾽ ἄλλως, ὀρέγεται.* (It [sc. the moon] is separated by love for the image in the sun through which shines forth manifest the desirable and fair and divine and blessed towards which all nature in one way or another yearns; *De facie* 944e; Cherniss tr. modified). Cf. *Rep.* 507d–509d and Arist. *Physics* 192^{a}16–19.

an idea that Plotinus would also find appealing.[78] Second, Plutarch himself explains natural events in teleological terms (*De facie* 928C), and in this way he aims to do justice to Plato's account.

In conclusion, Plutarch appears to maintain a strong mutual relationship between God and the world, according to which not only does God care for the universe, as father does for son, but also the universe in turn strives for God.[79] Plutarch discerns this relationship in Aristotle, though not to the extent he finds it in Plato. But the above evidence suggests that in his view Aristotle preserves much of what Plutarch considered to be the substance of Plato's doctrine, that is, that God arranges the world providentially and is its final cause.

Compared with this, Plutarch's criticism of the Epicurean and the Stoic positions on the divine providence is a clear contrast. The common element in both philosophical systems, according to Plutarch, is that their misguided views on divine providence result from fundamentally mistaken theologies which, though different, equally contradict not only previous philosophy but also what Plutarch regards as universal theological conceptions.[80] In his view, the Epicurean denial of divine providence arises from their atheism,[81] while the Stoic view on providence rests on a materialist conception of God and their assumption of a universally pre-determined fate, since both Epicureans and Stoics are fundamentally mistaken about God's nature.[82] For this reason, Plutarch often criticizes the two schools jointly, although his criticism for each differs.[83]

Let me now turn to Plutarch's conception of Aristotle's psychology. In his *Adversus Colotem* he argued that Aristotle's rejection of the transcendent Forms becomes evident also in the *De anima*. The sense in which this is so is far from clear. One possible way in which Plutarch connected the transcendent Forms with the soul can be inferred from the testimony of Syrianus (*In Met.* 105. 36–8), according to which Plutarch and Atticus believed that the Forms exist eternally in the soul.[84] As we have seen, though, this testimony most probably concerns

[78] See Ch. 6, p. 237.

[79] Cf. *Gorgias* 507e–508a.

[80] *De Iside* 369A–B, *Adv. Col.* 1108C, 1123A, 1124E.

[81] See *Non posse suav. vivi* 1100E–1101C, 1103A–E, *Adv. Col.* 1123A, 1124E, *De def. or.* 420B.

[82] See *De def. or.* 425E–F; *De Pyth. or.* 402E (contrast *De def. or.* 434B–C: Aristotle's philosophy does not undermine divination). Plutarch criticizes Stoic theology extensively; on this see Babut (1969*a*: 453–65).

[83] See *De comm. not.*1075E–1076A, *De Stoic. rep.* 1051A–1052B.

[84] For interpretation of this passage see above n. 55.

the soul of the divine creator. Plutarch, like Atticus, maintained that an intellect cannot exist without soul[85] and that should be the case also with the divine intellect, as is specified in the *Phaedrus* 246d. I have mentioned above that the transcendent Forms are transmitted from the divine soul to the pre-cosmic one and through this to the sensible realm (*De an. procr.* 1024C). It is this latter soul to which Plutarch refers when he says that there are two constituent parts of the universe, soul and body (*Plat. Q.* 1001B). This evidence suggests that according to Plutarch the Forms cannot exist independently from a soul, whether it be the divine or the pre-cosmic soul.

As far as I know, we do not have any evidence about the relationship of Forms to human soul in Plutarch. Yet it would be reasonable to suppose that in his view human souls would also host the Forms, by which they would be able to achieve elementary cognition, that is, to perceive objects as such. We have found a similar view in Antiochus. He held that for one to perceive objects, one would need to be acquainted with the Forms of those objects in advance. Such a view is built on the Platonic suggestion in the *Meno* that we had been acquainted with Forms prior to birth.[86] Aristotle's doctrine of the soul as the *entelecheia* of the body is at odds with this Platonist theory of how the soul cognizes. In fact, he explicitly criticizes this theory.[87] According to Aristotle, the soul does not pre-exist the living body in any sense, as it cannot possibly exist separately from the body, which means that the soul is not acquainted with the Forms prior to birth, as the Platonists believed.

If this comes close to the sense in which Plutarch regarded Aristotle as rejecting the transcendent Forms in the *De anima*, one would expect that Plutarch also objected to Aristotle's conception of the soul. This expectation is strengthened by his claim in the *Adversus Colotem*, according to which in the *De anima* Aristotle contradicts Plato on several fundamental issues (1115A–B). The reference to the materialist theories on the soul of Dicaearchus and Strato, made in the same context,[88] suggests that Aristotle's doctrine of the soul may also be hinted at here.

[85] *Plat. Q.* 1002F–1003A; *De Iside* 377E; Plutarch relies on Plato's *Sophist* 248d–249a; *Philebus* 30c; *Timaeus* 30b, 46d–e; see also below. Atticus shares the same view, but he draws different conclusions regarding Aristotle's doctrine of the soul; see Ch. 4, pp. 172–4.

[86] On the soul's cognition according to Plutarch see Opsomer (1999: 193–212).

[87] *Pr. an.* 67^{a}22–7; *Post. an.* 71^{a}29–^{b}8; *On memory* 451^{a}18–^{b}11. See further on this in Ch. 7, s. 6. 3, pp. 301–3.

[88] See Dicaearch frs. 11–12W; Strato frs. 119–20, 122–7W. Cf. Capelle (1931: 303–8) and Gottschalk (1971).

However, nowhere in his extant work does Plutarch criticize Aristotle's doctrine. In the only occasion that it is explicitly mentioned, Plutarch is not critical. Discussing how Plato's view that the souls were sowed in earth and moon and all the remaining instruments of time (*Timaeus* 42d4–5) must be understood, Plutarch interprets instruments as meaning 'not the stars, but the bodies of living beings in the sense that Aristotle defined the soul as actuality of body, that is, natural, instrumental, and potentially living' (*Plat. Q.* 1006D; cf. *De anima* 412^{a}19–22). According to this interpretation, the souls would be disseminated in the appropriate instrumental bodies. Plutarch eventually rejects this possibility, but he does not criticize Aristotle's view.

Why did Plutarch refrain from criticizing Aristotle's position? The reason, I suggest, is that Plutarch understood Aristotle to be close to Plato in position. From *Platonic Questions* 1006D it becomes clear that Plutarch understood Aristotle's phrase *σῶμα ὀργανικόν* as 'a body which serves as an instrument' to the soul.[89] This interpretation of Aristotle's phrase is different from the modern one, according to which *σῶμα ὀργανικόν* is understood as 'a body equipped with organs',[90] which cannot exist separately from the soul. Apparently Plutarch held that according to Aristotle the soul can exist separately from the body, and when in body, the soul uses it as an instrument. Plutarch may have been able to trace such a view in early Aristotelian works like the *Eudemus*, where the soul is said to exist also independent of the body (frs. 3, 4, 8 Ross).

Indeed, Plutarch offers a lengthy quotation from this treatise in his *Consolatio ad Apollonium* 115B–E (fr. 6 Ross).[91] In this Silenus reveals to King Midas that it is best for people not to be born, or, if they must suffer this fate, to die as soon as possible after birth. Plutarch concludes: 'It is evident, therefore, that he made this declaration with conviction that the existence after death is better than life' (tr. F. Babbitt). Such evidence suggests that Plutarch considered Aristotle to hold that the soul is separable from the body, but in order to see, to hear, or to touch, it needs a certain body as an instrument. This means that Plutarch interpreted Aristotle's position in the *De anima* in the light of his statements in the *Eudemus*, where the soul is defined as form *simpliciter* which can be independent from the body (fr. 8 Ross).

[89] See Bos (1999), who also refers to a similar understanding of Aristotle's formulation by Diogenes Laertius 5. 33 and in Hippolytus, *Elenchur* 7. 24. 1–2.

[90] See for instance Hicks (1907: 51, 313), Ross (1961: 211–12).

[91] There is some doubt about the authenticity of this treatise. See K. Ziegler, 'Plutarchos von Chaironeia', in *RE* XXI (1951), 794–801.

This is amplified by further evidence. In a fragment from his work *On the Soul* (fr. 178 Sandbach), Plutarch describes the condition of the soul when one is awake as follows: the soul is extended to fit the body and dispersed through the organs of the sense. As has been noted, this is very close to the imagery used by Aristotle in a fragment of his *Protrepticus* (10b Ross).[92] In this passage Aristotle seems to be inspired by Plato's *Phaedo* 82d–e, where the soul is presented in similar terms. It is noticeable that Plutarch prefers to describe the soul not as 'glued to the organs' (*προσκεκολλημένην*), as is argued by both Plato (*Phaedo* 82d) and Aristotle (*Protrepticus* fr. 10b Ross), but as being 'dispersed through them' (*διατετάσθαι*), as only Aristotle argues. This evidence again shows that Plutarch took Aristotle to maintain that the soul is strongly linked to the body but remains separable from it.

In the same fragment (fr. 178) Plutarch also argues that the soul acquires knowledge when one is sleeping or even dead because it is not hampered by the connection with the body, and as we have seen he uses Aristotle's description of the soul in the *Protrepticus*. This seems to suggest that Plutarch took Aristotle as agreeing with Plato also in that the soul becomes acquainted with the Forms, as Plato had argued and some fragments of Aristotle's early works appear to testify (Themistius, *In de an.* 106. 29–107. 5; *Eudemus* fr. 1 Ross).

If this is so, then Plutarch's criticism in the *Adversus Colotem* of Aristotle's rejection of the transcendent Forms in the *De anima* would seem odd. How are we to explain it? One possibility is that Plutarch accuses Aristotle of taking in the *De anima* a less Platonic position than in his earlier works. Yet we have reasons to believe that Plutarch did not consider Aristotle's later position on the soul substantially different from his earlier one.

This is suggested by the fact that elsewhere Plutarch approves of Aristotelian views outlined in the *De anima*, or is inspired by them. First, Plutarch appears to consider Aristotle's doctrine that the soul has faculties (*dynameis*; cf. *De anima* 414^{a}29–34) as expressing Plato's position about the way in which the soul relates to the body and how it operates in the living body. This is to be inferred from the fact that

[92] Cf. Plutarch, *On the Soul* fr. 178 (p. 320 Sandbach): *χωρίζεται γὰρ ἐν τῷ καθεύδειν ἀνατρέχουσα καὶ συλλεγομένη πρὸς ἑαυτὴν ἐκ τοῦ διατετάσθαι πρὸς τὸ σῶμα καὶ διεσπάρθαι ταῖς αἰσθήσεσι.* Compare Aristotle *Proterpticus* fr. 10b Ross (the soul is compared with the prisoners tied to corpses by the Etruscan pirates) *οὕτως ἔοικεν ἡ ψυχὴ διατετάσθαι καὶ προσκεκολλῆσθαι πᾶσι τοῖς αἰσθητικοῖς τοῦ σώματος μέλεσιν.* See Santaniello (1999: 636–7).

Plutarch conflates parts of the soul with faculties when he talks of the spirited and appetitive parts alongside the vegetative and the perceptive.

Plutarch does this in several parts of his work.[93] He thought, like Plotinus and Porphyry would do later, that the soul develops faculties such as the perceptive, the nutritive, or the vegetative, when associating with the body so that it can carry out the living functions.[94] Presumably Plutarch maintained that the soul's use of the body mentioned above is through faculties. This does not mean that Plutarch borrows an Aristotelian doctrine; rather, he considers it Platonic, since already Plato used to talk in terms of faculties.[95] It is crucial to remember that while Plutarch agrees with Aristotle on the unity of soul and body, yet he holds against Aristotle's theory of the soul in the *De anima* the separability of the soul. There is also another fact which shows Plutarch's adherence to Plato. Plutarch does seem to think that it is better to speak of the soul in terms of faculties but he does not consider the acceptance of faculties as justifying Aristotle's criticism of the partition of the soul.[96] At one point he argues that the irrational aspect of the soul is not a part, as one would infer from Plato, but a faculty (Tyrwitt's frs. pp. 60–71 Sandbach). Apparently Plutarch finds Aristotle to be in accord with Plato's doctrine despite Aristotle's criticism of it. This feature is characteristic of Platonists who consider Aristotle as being part of the Platonic tradition. We will find it in Taurus (Ch. 4, pp. 179–85) and, especially, in Porphyry.

Further, Plutarch appears to have perceived Aristotle as staying close to Plato not only in the way in which the soul relates to the body but more generally on human constitution, and especially on the more elevated part of it, the intellect. In Plutarch's view, humans are composed of body, soul, and intellect, and, although both soul and intellect

[93] *De virt. mor.* 442B–C; *De def. orac.* 429E–F; *De E* 390F; *Plat. Q.* 1007E–1009B; see also H. Cherniss (ed.), *Plutarch Moralia*, 13.1, 20 (Cambridge Mass., 1976; Loeb). Cf. Ch. 4, p. 188.

[94] As Plutarch argues, these faculties sprout from the soul's association from the body *De virt. mor.* 442B, 450E, 451A. This view was taken up later by Plotinus, Longinus, and Porphyry (see Ch. 6, s. 2, p. 228, Ch. 7, s. 6. 3, pp. 300–2). See Baltes (2000: 258) and below. Later Platonists, like Numenius and esp. Atticus, do not consider this irrational soul as essential part of the soul. See Ch. 4, pp. 171–3.

[95] See Introduction n. 69.

[96] There is a question as to whom Aristotle criticizes for dividing the soul into parts in *De anima* (e.g. 432a23–b8, 433b1–6). Hicks (1907: 551) and Ross (1961: 316) maintain that he criticizes Plato, while Vander Waerdt (1987: 641–3) argues that he targets the anonymous Academics referred to in *Topics* 126^a6–14. See also Ch. 7, s. 6. 3.

are immortal, he regarded the intellect as superior to soul.[97] He thought that both the cosmic and the human soul originally are non-rational but eventually partake in intellect,[98] and this is characteristic of their affinity with the divine demiurge and their essential characteristic.[99] Plutarch appears to have considered Aristotle to be following Plato on the role and status of the intellect. Two pieces of evidence suggest that Plutarch construed Aristotle as considering the intellect to be not bodily located, immortal, the distinctive characteristic of humans, and man's link with the divine.[100] The first is that Plutarch explicitly approves of Aristotle's view that the intellect is the place of Forms.[101] Secondly, Plutarch ascribes to Plato a doctrine very similar to that, namely the view that the objects of intellection are the Forms (*Plat. Q.* 1001E). This suggests that he may well have regarded Aristotle as expressing Plato's own doctrine in passages where Aristotle describes the intellect as the place of Forms, or as being the Form of Forms (*De anima* 429^{a}27–8, 432^{a}2).

For Plutarch, the fact that Aristotle acknowledges the role of Forms in the intellect's cognition must have been an important point of his accord with Plato's relevant doctrine for two reasons. First, Plutarch must have considered Aristotle's idea about the way in which the intellect cognizes to be indicative not only of the similar way in which both Plato and Aristotle thought of the intellect's cognition, but also of their common belief in its immaterial nature. Secondly, Plutarch maintains that for Plato the cognition achieved by the intellect is particularly important and, at any rate, superior to the cognition performed by the soul. Intellectual perception includes thinking but also some kind of sense perception such as vision, while the soul's perception concerns some 'lower' kinds of sense perception such as touch.

On the basis of such evidence one can conclude that Plutarch probably believed that Aristotle comes close to Plato's position about the cognition of the soul through his doctrine of the intellect, since Aristotle allegedly attributes to the intellect what Plato credits also to the soul. And this may be the reason why he, as I suggested, did not consider

[97] Cf. *De facie* 943A, 944F–945A; *De genio Socr.* 491B. The relation between intellect and soul in Plutarch is complex. The entire myth in *De facie* means to illustrate his view of human nature. The body is supplied by the earth, the soul by the moon, and the intellect by the sun. See Deuse (1983: 45–7) and Opsomer (1999: 198–9).

[98] *De facie* 945A; *Plat. Q.* 2. 1001C, 4. 1003A; *De an. procr.* 1014D–E.

[99] *De an. procr.* 1026D; *De virt. mor.* 442A, 450E.

[100] See *De anima* 3. 5, *NE* 1096^{a}24–5, 1177^{b}26–1178^{a}8; *Protrepticus*, fr. 6 Ross; cf. *Plat. Q.* 1002A; *Adv. Col.* 1119A–B.

[101] *De Iside* 374E; cf. *De anima* 429^{a}27–8.

Aristotle's psychology of the *De anima* to be substantially different from his earlier doctrine and from that of Plato.

However, Plutarch may have had one difficulty with Aristotle's position on the intellect, especially as far as the divine intellect is concerned. The difficulty may arise from the fact that Plutarch, being inspired by the *Philebus* (30c9–10), the *Sophist* (248d–249a), and the *Timaeus* (46d–e), maintained that the intellect, to the extent that it implies life, must go along with the principle of life, namely the soul (*Plat. Q.* 1002F–1003A).[102] Thus he argued, as has been seen, that even the divine intellect is ensouled (*De Iside* 377E). This is an aspect that does not occur in Aristotle's theory about the divine intellect. Given that Plutarch interprets Plato in such a way, he is likely to have regarded Aristotle's view on the divine intellect as preserving only part of Plato's doctrine. A similar view can be found in Atticus.[103] Yet again, unlike him, Plutarch does not criticize Aristotle.

To sum up: in this section we have seen in what sense Plutarch may have considered Aristotle as rejecting Plato's transcendent Forms in the *De caelo* and the *De anima*, and how he linked this with Aristotle's departures from other Platonic doctrines on natural philosophy and psychology. It has emerged that Plutarch criticizes Aristotle's differences from Plato mildly and often not explicitly, and sometimes not at all, while he is prompt in highlighting the points which Aristotle shares with Plato, often treats Aristotle as preserving part of Plato's doctrine, drawing on Aristotle's work without acknowledging. These are salient features of Plutarch's attitude to Aristotle; they suggest that Plutarch considers Aristotle part of the Platonist tradition.

5. ETHICS

It is especially in ethics that Plutarch makes clear that he considers Aristotle part of the Platonist tradition. He highlights Aristotle's adherence to Plato's views on moral psychology and ethics in the *De virtute morali*. As his *Adversus Colotem*, this work also has a polemical aim, namely to refute Stoic ethics, which Plutarch, like Antiochus, regarded as diverging from Plato's ethics both in terminology and in substance.

[102] We find the same view in Alcinous, *Didasc.* 170. 3–4 and more strongly in Atticus fr. 7 Des Places.

[103] See Ch 4, p. 170.

To do this, he first sets out to draw a sharp line between Plato's ethics and Stoic ethics. Plutarch feels entitled to use Aristotle's work in his argument because he maintains that Aristotle preserves Plato's ethical doctrine. That is, Plutarch, like Antiochus, regards Aristotle as representing Plato's doctrine concerning the highest good, the nature of the human soul, and the nature of virtue. Let us see what this doctrine is for Plutarch and how in his view it differs from the Stoic one.

For Plutarch the crucial difference between the Platonic–Aristotelian stand on moral virtue and the Stoic one lies in their different conceptions of the soul.[104] The Stoics rejected the model of a soul consisting of a rational and an irrational element or part, which is found in *Republic* 4 and later dialogues, arguing that the soul is reason only. For the Stoics, emotions (*pathê*) are impulses to which the reasoning mind assents, and thus are essentially beliefs (*De virt. mor* 447A). And since for them emotions are excessive impulses, the reason's assent to them amounts to reason being directed in the wrong way.[105] The Stoics, then, believe that *pathê* are faulty rational judgements, and since virtue presupposes valid reasoning, it amounts to resisting and eliminating them (*apatheia*; 443c10).

Plutarch sets out to show that emotions are essential for attaining virtue, a view which, as he claims, both Plato and Aristotle maintained. His main thesis is that virtue is a state in which emotion is present as matter and reason as form (*De virt. mor.* 440D). In this sense, he argues, virtue amounts to the formation of emotion by reason, so that emotion is channelled in the right direction (443C, 444B–C, 451C), while vice arises from a mismatch between emotion and reason (443D). Plutarch is concerned to defend the model of partite soul which comprises an irrational element, the source of emotions, but first he explains how Aristotle's doctrine compares with Plato's in this respect. Let us examine this first. I quote the relevant passage.

> Aristotle largely[106] made use of these principles [i.e. the tripartite soul] as it becomes plain from his writings. But later he assigned the spirited part to the appetitive, on the grounds that anger is a sort of appetite and desire to cause pain in requital. Yet until the end he continued to treat the passionate and irrational part as distinct from the rational, not because this part is wholly

[104] *De virt. morali* 441C–E; cf. *De an. procr.* 1026C–D.

[105] Cf. DL 7. 110 (*SVF* iii. 412). One sense in which this is so is that emotions make people disobedient to reason (Galen, *PHP* 4. 6. 27; Stob. 2. 88. 8–9); see Sorabji (2000: 56–65), on the difference between Zeno and Chrysippus on this issue.

[106] Following the majority of MSS, I read ἐπὶ πλέον (instead of ἐπὶ πλεῖστον).

irrational, as is the perceptive part of the soul, or the nutritive and vegetative part (for these parts are completely non-submissive and deaf to reason and, so to speak, mere off-shoots of our flesh and wholly attached to body); though the passionate part is lacking in reason and does not participate in reason at all, yet otherwise is by nature fitted to heed the rational and intelligent part, to turn towards it, to yield to it, to conform itself to it, if it is not completely corrupted by foolish pleasure and a loose mode of life. (*De virt. mor.* 442B–C; tr. W. Helmbold modified)

The passage has been taken to suggest that Plutarch describes Aristotle's philosophical development from a Platonic phase, in which he adopted Plato's tripartite soul, to his mature, less Platonic views on the nature of the soul.[107] I will argue that this is not what Plutarch maintains.

Plutarch indeed distinguishes two phases in Aristotle's moral psychology in the passage in question. In the first phase, Aristotle largely (*ἐπὶ πλέον*) maintained Plato's view according to which the soul is tripartite, consisting of a rational, a spirited, and an appetitive part, while later in his career (*ὕστερον δέ*) he conflated the spirited with the appetitive part on the grounds that spirit is a kind of irrational desire; anger, for instance, essentially is a desire for requital (*De virt. mor.* 442B; cf. *De anima* 403^{a}24–31). However, Plutarch argues, Aristotle still upheld Plato's bipartition of the soul in a rational and an irrational part,[108] and still adhered to Plato's tenet that the irrational part is distinct from the rational, not in the sense that it is entirely insensitive to reason (*οὐ παντελῶς ἄλογον*) but that it does not guide its desires rationally and needs to be informed by reason.

Nothing in this passage, or in a later passage where again Plutarch says that at a later stage Aristotle abandoned some of his early views on moral psychology (*De virt. mor.* 448A), suggests that in Plutarch's opinion Aristotle actually changed his basic position in moral psychology. Even less does the quoted passage suggest that Aristotle's philosophy developed in general from a Platonist phase to a less Platonist philosophical profile, in the sense in which Jaeger argued. We have seen that such a development is ruled out also in the passage where Plutarch criticizes Colotes concerning the Forms (s. 3). In the present passage Plutarch's point is that Aristotle subscribed to Plato's position on moral psychology throughout his career, no matter whether he talked in terms of a bipartite or a tripartite soul, since, as Plutarch observes, Plato also

107 Düring (1957: 354–5) and Verbeke (1960: 238–40); cf. Jaeger (1948: 36).

108 See Babut (1969*b*: 140–1).

talked in both ways. Plato, he argues, distinguished a rational and an irrational part of the soul, and sometimes distinguished also two parts within the irrational part, the appetitive and the spirited (ibid. 442A). Indeed, in the *Republic*, for instance, the tripartition clearly is the extension of a basic bipartition (e.g. *Rep*. 439d–e), while in later dialogues Plato speaks more in terms of a bipartite soul.[109] Similarly Aristotle talks of a tripartite soul in some of his early writings (e.g. *Topics* 133^{a}30–2), while later, in the *Nicomachean Ethics*, for instance, he favours the model of the bipartite soul, but he already had done this in some of his early writings like the *Protrepticus* (fr. 6 Ross). Plutarch says precisely this, namely that Aristotle in his early career was largely in favour of the tripartite soul, and that later he, like Plato, favoured the model of the bipartite soul. His point is that Aristotle followed Plato's principles (*archai*) in moral psychology throughout his career.[110]

Once Plutarch has established the common ground between Plato and Aristotle, he relies heavily on Aristotle for presenting Plato's doctrine. He defines moral virtue as the state of absolute excellence (*akrotês*; *De virt. mor*. 444D; cf. *NE* 1107^{a}6–8) in which emotions are balanced by reason. In this sense, he argues, following Aristotle's definition, moral virtue is a mean state (*mesotês*; 443D–E, 444D–445B, 451F; *NE* 1106^{b}5–1107^{a}8).[111] Plutarch stresses, against the Stoics, that the absolute excellence of virtue is not at odds with its status as a mean, that not every virtue is a mean but moral virtue is, because one should be able to choose the right emotion among the large spectrum of emotions possible. Courage, for instance, is the virtue by which the person, though fearful, subordinates fear for a more elevated goal, such as fighting for one's country. Without some amount of fear, however, there can be no courage in the first place (451E–452A). For Plutarch this is a doctrine that Aristotle

109 Cf. *Timaeus* 41c–d, 69c–e; *Politicus* 309c; *Laws* 653b–c, 904b–c. Doxographers and Platonists of the imperial times often interchange tripartition and bipartition; cf. Alcinous, *Didasc*. 156. 35–7, 176. 6–177. 15, Apuleius, *De Platone* 1. 207–9. See Vander Waerdt (1985*b*); Dillon (1993: 149)

110 Actually, in this context Plutarch fends off Aristotle's differences from what he understands as Plato's doctrine, for instance, that Aristotle opposes the doctrine of the two cosmic souls (*De caelo* 284^{a}27–35), which, in Plutarch's view, corresponds to Plato's bipartition of the human soul (441F). Cf. *De an. procr*. 1026C; cf. ibid. 1014B–C. On this Plutarchean view see Opsomer (1994).

111 Cf. *Plat. Q*. 1009A–B; *Tranq. an*. 474C; *De sera* 551C. In *De superst*. 171F Plutarch defines piety as a mean between atheism and superstition. A similar view about virtue is taken by Alcinous, *Didasc*. 149. 4–5, 184. 14–20; Apuleius, *De Platone* 2. 227–8; and Taurus (in Gellius *NA*. 1. 26, fr. 16 Gioè with his comments (2002: 323–8) cf. Dillon (1993: 183–9).

shares with Plato.[112] Plutarch talks similarly also in a fragment from his work *On Anger*; he argues that Platonists and Peripatetics are right to hold that anger does not have to be eliminated, but that it can become an ally (*symmachos*) to bravery in the war if moderated.[113]

For Plutarch the upshot of such considerations is that emotions are crucial in achieving virtue, provided that practical reason rules them (*De virt. mor.* 444B–C). In his view the really virtuous man is the one who has the right emotion as a motivational force, as Plato and Aristotle maintained. This view makes a difference regarding ethical education, because, since virtue is a habit (*hexis*; 443D), one has to be trained in it.[114] On this aspect Plutarch finds Aristotle in agreement with the early Academics (*De comm. not.* 1069A). Yet further, to Plutarch's mind such considerations about virtue also confirm the existence of two opposing elements in our soul, a rational and an irrational one, a fact which, as he claims, the Stoics ignore. And as a result, he argues, they are not able to explain incontinence (*De virt. mor.* 445B–F).

Plutarch's arguments regarding Aristotle's agreement with Plato and the failure of Stoic ethics are questionable. To start with the latter, Plutarch is guilty of circular reasoning in his argument that virtue is a mean and that the soul consists of two parts. As regards Plutarch's argument against the Stoics concerning incontinence, Dillon has shown the grounds on which it is unsatisfactory.[115] So is Plutarch's suggestion that the Stoics essentially follow Plato and Aristotle in accepting emotions which they simply relabel *eupatheiai*, arguing that these are in accordance with reason (*De virt. mor.* 449B).[116] Plutarch

112 Cf. Plutarch, *De an. procr.* 1025D; *Cleom.* 9. 4. See Becchi (2004: 28–31).

113 *On anger* fr. 148 Sandbach. My interpretation is contingent on accepting Sandbach's reading <*κατορθοῦσι δὲ μάλιστα*> *οἱ παραδεξάμενοι τὸν θυμὸν ὡς σύμμαχον ἀρετῆς ἀπολαύοντες ὅσον αὐτοῦ χρήσιμόν ἐστιν ἔν τε πολέμῳ* ... For alternative readings and interpretations of the text see Becchi (2004: 34–40). Cf. *Republic* 440a–c.

114 *De coh. ira* 461c. Dillon (1977: 195) has argued that, unlike Aristotle who defines virtue as *hexis* (*NE* 1106^{b}36), Plutarch defines it as *kinēsis* or *dynamis* (*De virt. mor.* 444F5), a view that Aristotle rejects (*NE* 1105^{b}19–1106^{a}13). It seems to me that Plutarch does not define virtue as *dynamis* only, but in some senses as *dynamis*, that is, when virtue comes about, and in others as *hexis*, when one is accustomed to exercising virtue.

115 See Dillon (1983). Plutarch overlooks the Stoic argument that, no matter what impulse is present, it is always the mind that decides. For the Stoics, too, incontinence is possible, when the mind assents to an impulse. Plutarch overlooks this argument because in his view a false judgement is not what we mean by incontinence. And in this at least, I think, he may well be right.

116 On the role of Stoic *eupatheiai* and the Stoic moral ideal see Frede (1986); Striker (1991: 62–7); Annas (1993: 60–6); Sorabji (2000: 47–51, 207–8).

implies that either (*a*) *eupatheiai* are moderate *pathê*, which is the Platonic–Peripatetic position, in which case the Stoics contradict themselves, given that *pathê* according to them are excessive, or (*b*) *eupatheiai* are not *pathê* at all, in which case the Stoics are lying. Plutarch does not do justice to the fact that for the Stoics not all emotions are excessive but only those which ordinary people have (with the exception of *lypê*), and that only these are to be eradicated because only they affect rational decisions. The Stoic wise man can have emotions which are in accordance with reason, and thus are beneficial to him (*eupatheiai*). It is not then the case, as Plutarch argues, that the Stoic wise man is not moved by anything, a pilot in a ship where no winds strike (*De virt. mor.* 452B). If this is so, Plutarch is mistaken to claim that the Stoic *apatheia* is incompatible with moral virtue and hardly a moral ideal.

Of even less value is Plutarch's argument that Aristotle shares the same psychological model as Plato, by which he aims to justify his reliance on Aristotle as a source of Plato's doctrine. Because instead of explaining why Plutarch believes that Aristotle follows Plato's ethical doctrine, it rather is part of this belief. Plutarch simply assumes Aristotle's accord with Plato in this regard, because he has a certain fixed idea regarding what Plato's doctrine on virtue was, but he does not seek to argue for this point. Plutarch apparently believes that Plato's doctrine is outlined in places like *Republic* 4 and later dialogues, where it is suggested that moral virtue arises from the agreement between emotion and reason.[117] We know, though, that other Platonists argued that Plato had espoused the doctrine of *apatheia*,[118] which the Stoics developed, and that this can be discerned in several parts of Plato including the *Republic*. Plutarch may have justified the rejection of such a view referring to passages like *Philebus* 21d–e, where Socrates argues that if a life of thinking and knowledge is devoid of all affection it can hardly be considered as complete and happy (*Tranq. an.* 468D). Or, he could refer to passages like *Republic* 619a5–b1, or *Politicus* 284d–285a, where virtue is regarded as the correct measure. But whatever the rationale behind his view that for Plato moral virtue consists in the harmony between reason and emotion, it is because Plutarch finds this view articulated in Aristotle's ethics that he considers Aristotle to be a source

[117] Cf. *Republic* 430a–432a, 442c–d; *Laws* 653b–c.

[118] Cf. Anon., *In NE* 127. 3–8; Clement, *Strom.* 4. 23. 147. 1; Atticus, I will argue, appears to espouse exactly this view (frs. 2, 7 Des Places; see Ch. 4, s. 3); see Lilla (1971: 103–17).

of Plato's ethical doctrine. And he could probably justify his reliance on Aristotle by tracing back to Plato's dialogues the view that moral virtue is a mean between extreme emotions.[119]

Even then, however, Plutarch would have justified neither his understanding of Plato's ethical position nor his belief that Aristotle preserves it. It is because Plutarch takes Aristotle as representative Plato's doctrine, though, that he integrates into the Aristotelian doctrine Platonic ideas like the localization of the parts of the soul in bodily parts (*De virt. mor.* 450F) or the image of the charioteer (445B–C; *Phaedrus* 253c–d). To be explained similarly is his adoption of Aristotle's distinction between theoretical wisdom (*sophia*) and practical one (*phronêsis*; 443F–444A; cf. *NE* 1141^{a}5–8), a distinction that Plato does not make; for Plato *phronêsis* covers the whole span of rational activity including both theoretical and practical wisdom—the wise man is also *phronimos*.[120] Plutarch also endorses Aristotle's view that the temperate man (ἐγκρατής) is less virtuous than the *phronimos* who does the good without wavering (445C–D; *NE* 1151^{b}23–1152^{a}3), on the grounds that the harmony between action and feeling makes the latter state preferable to temperance or self-control. This may not be a view that is stated explicitly by Plato, but it is entailed by the doctrine of the unity of virtues, which we do find in Plato (e.g. in the *Protagoras*).

Such adjustments show neither unfamiliarity with Aristotle, as has sometimes been argued,[121] nor an effort to blend Platonic and Aristotelian elements. Rather, they show that Plutarch takes Aristotle to be recasting originally Platonic views and treats them as such. Scholars miss the point when they argue that Plutarch borrows from Aristotle in order to carry out his anti-Stoic polemic.[122] Even more untenable is the view of some scholars that Plutarch draws on Aristotle, though he is conscious of Aristotle's divergence from Plato in ethics, and speaks of his extra-Peripatetic or functional Aristotelianism.[123] To be sure, in order to argue against the Stoics, Plutarch needs to specify Plato's doctrine, and as has been seen he does this relying on Aristotle's testimony, but as the

[119] Cf. *Republic* 431c, 619a–b; *Philebus* 64d–e; *Laws* 728e, 792c–d. See Babut (1969*b*: 74–6).

[120] See *Philebus* 21a14–d10; *Phaedo* 79d7; cf. Alcinous, *Didasc.* 153. 7.

[121] For instance by Donini (1974: 71–80).

[122] Thus Becchi (1975); Babut (1996: 19–23); Donini (1999: 10, 16–19).

[123] Thus Dörrie (1971), who argues that Plutarch distances himself from Platonism when he espouses Aristotle's view: similarly, Becchi (1981) and Etheridge, as the title of his Ph.D. thesis shows (n. 26).

passage in the *Adversus Colotem* has shown, Plutarch would be the last to abandon Plato for Aristotle. Some other passages also show that Plutarch dismisses Aristotle's views when they contribute nothing to Platonist philosophy.[124] Similarly mistaken is the view that Plutarch considers Aristotle's position as being compatible with that of Plato.[125] As I have shown above with respect to Plutarch's argument in the *De virtute morali*, Plutarch rather believes that this *is* Plato's view.

The belief that Plutarch is a Platonist who tries to do justice to Plato's work as he understands it is confirmed by two further facts. The first is Plutarch's argument about human nature and good life. Plutarch takes a view remarkably similar to that of Antiochus in this regard, arguing that nature makes us be attracted (*οἰκειοῦσα*; *De comm. not.* 1060E) to some things for which it is natural to strive, which are divided into those of the soul, such as reason and virtue, and those of the body, such as health and beauty. Plutarch follows Antiochus in believing that one's final end is life in conformity with nature. Yet given his conception of nature Plutarch argues that such a life does not consist only in the attainment of virtue, but also in the satisfaction of other primary demands of nature which may involve the body. Like Antiochus, Plutarch maintains that this doctrine was upheld by Aristotle, Xenocrates, and Polemo (*De comm. not.* 1069E–F).[126] It is their understanding of human nature that shapes Plutarch's ethical doctrine, and it is against this understanding that he criticizes the Epicurean ideal of a life of pleasure[127] and the Stoic doctrine that there are no goods other than reason.[128] The fact that Plutarch takes the common doctrine of Aristotle, Xenocrates, and Polemo as a measure for judging the Epicureans and especially the Stoics suggests that he considers them to be expressing Plato's doctrine rather than their own, and this is why he relies on their collective authority.

The second piece of evidence to show that Plutarch seeks to do justice to Plato's philosophy and uses Aristotle only for such purposes is the fact that he does not dismiss those Platonic passages in which a life of

124 Aristotle is pronounced wrong about time (*Plat. Q.* 1007A) or about the movement of the planets (*De facie* 939A—with Cherniss's note, *Plutarch Moralia*, 12.1, p. 68).

125 As Babut (1996: 23) argues; cf. Donini (1974: 80–1).

126 On the value of this passage see Dillon (2003: 139–40, 161–2).

127 *Non posse suav.* 1091A–D (with reference to *Republic* 584b–586d), 1096C–E, *De comm. not.* 1060B–E.

128 *De comm. not.* 1060A–1062E; *De Stoic. rep.* 1038C–E, 1042A–E.

apatheia is suggested. He rather associates such life with the divine state.[129] Plutarch argues that the virtue of the purely rational mind which is uncontaminated by *pathē* does not come into being by observing the mean (*De virt. mor.* 444C–D). Being inspired by the *Phaedo* (64a–67e, 82c–83b) and the *Theaetetus* (176a–b), Plutarch defined man's end as assimilation to God (*De sera* 550D–E) and marks this end as blissful life (*μακάριον*).[130] This ideal is not distinct from that of a good life based on virtuous action, but rather the result of a consistently virtuous life. Apparently Plutarch, like Porphyry and later Platonists, maintained the existence of different levels of ethical life, and *apatheia* corresponds to the more exalted level, which involves a life contemplation devoted to the theoretical understanding of reality. Indeed, Plutarch seems to presuppose a distinction of kinds of virtues when speaking in terms of civic virtues (*politikas aretas*); he refers to them, arguing they are obtained by the subordination of emotions to reason (Tyrwitt frs. p. 68 Sandbach), as Plotinus will do later.

However, even as regards the more exalted level of virtue, Plutarch considers Aristotle to be following Plato. As he argues, for both Plato and Aristotle contemplation (*τὸ ἐποπτικόν*) is so crucial to philosophy that it constitutes philosophy's end (*De Is.* 382D–E).[131] Plutarch probably refers to Aristotle's remarks in *NE* 10 (e.g. 1178^{a}5–8), but also elsewhere to the effect that contemplation represents man's best life, as it does justice to man's distinctive element, the intellect.[132]

6. LOGIC

There is another piece of evidence to suggest that Plutarch follows Aristotle only when he considers his doctrines as being essentially Platonic. Plutarch seems to have been quite interested in Aristotle's

129 *De virt. mor.* 444D; *De def. or.* 470E; cf. *Timaeus* 90b–c. Scholars (e.g. Spanneut 1994: 4705–8) often argue that Plutarch wavers between these two views; but, as I argue, there is no real conflict between them. See Babut (1969*a*: 321–8) and Lilla (1971: 106–17).

130 *De def. or.* 470E; *De facie* 944E; *De genio* 593D.

131 The term *ἐποπτικόν* is Platonic (*Symp.* 210a1) with connotations of mystical religiosity. Aristotle never uses it. Cf. Plutarch, *Vita Alex.* 7, where he argues that Aristotle taught Alexander *διδασκαλίας ἐποπτικάς*.

132 Ross prints the passage as a fragment of *Eudemus* (fr. 10), but *Eudemus* may not be the only source of this, if at all. Cf. *Protrepticus*, frs. 6, 13–15 Ross. See Verbeke (1960: 241–2).

logic, as the writing of a treatise on the *Categories* suggests (*Διάλεξις περὶ τῶν δέκα κατηγοριῶν*; Lamprias no. 192). However, as with the *Topics*, he believed that the work was heavily indebted to Plato and thus in a sense Platonic. In the following passage Plutarch argues that Plato is the source of the categories.

whenever the soul touches anything that has being (*οὐσία*), either dispersed or indivisible, the soul is moved throughout herself and states that with which the object is identical, that which it is different from, in what relation (*πρός*), where (*ὅπῃ*) and how (*ὅπως*) it happens to be (*εἶναι*) or has an attribute (*πάσχειν*) in relation to each of the things that come to be. As in these words he [sc. Plato] simultaneously is also giving an outline (*ὑπογραφὴν*) of the ten categories, in the remarks that follow he clarifies the case still further (*De animae procr.* 1023E)

The Platonic passage referred to is *Timaeus* 37b1–c3, which is where the soul is discussed. According to this passage, the soul has the ability to distinguish the identity of any entity, perishable or eternal. Plutarch takes the opportunity to note in passing that in this passage Plato operates with what Aristotle later presented as his theory of categories. Plutarch probably found outlined in it the categories of substance (*οὐσία*), quality (*ὅπως*), relation (*πρὸς*), place (*ὅπῃ*), and being acted upon (*πάσχειν*).[133] This, of course, does not mean that Plutarch found traces of the categories solely in the *Timaeus*. He may have discerned traces of Aristotle's doctrine in several parts of Plato's work, as Alcinous does,[134] and perhaps he found traces of different aspects of Aristotle's doctrine, such as different categories, in various Platonic passages. By crediting Aristotle's theory of categories to Plato, Plutarch justifies his making use of it.[135] However, Plutarch would not have credited Plato with Aristotle's theory in the first place unless he found it philosophically attractive. It is beyond my present scope to speculate about this, but at least it should be noted that Plutarch disagrees with Eudorus' negative

133 *πάσχειν* here is used as in *Parmenides* 139e7, in the sense of 'to have a certain attribute'. On the passage of the *Timaeus* see Taylor (1928: 177).

134 Alcinous finds Aristotle's categories outlined in the *Parmenides* (*Didasc.* 159. 43–4, with Dillon 1993: 84–5), while the Anonymus in *Theaetetum* traces them in the *Theaetetus* (58. 35–48). Presumably Plutarch maintained that Aristotle had been inspired in this respect also by the *Sophist* (*Adv. Col.* 1115D–E). The term *ὑπογραφή* is used in the sense 'outline' later by Porphyry (*In Cat.* 60. 15–17, 72. 35, 73. 3, 111. 28–9).

135 Plutarch makes use of the distinction between 'being in a subject' and 'being said of a subject' (*Adv. Col.* 1120B); *Cat.* $1^a20–^b9$.

evaluation of the *Categories* and presumably with other contemporary Platonists.

Plutarch's remark is not very illuminating about his perception of Aristotle's logic. In an attempt to reconstruct Plutarch's rationale, I suggest that he may have been inspired by two main motives. First, his suggestion may be that in many respects Aristotle's philosophy essentially is Plato's philosophy, but one is in a position to realize this only if one knows about the origins of the former. Secondly, Plutarch's idea seems to be that, given the origins of Aristotle's philosophy, Aristotle through his interpretations of Plato's work often reveals the richness of Plato's texts. That is, given Aristotle's ability and familiarity with Plato's teaching, he was in a position to notice elements in Plato's dialogues, especially the late ones, which other contemporary readers of Plato did not capture and which Aristotle subsequently developed. If this is so, then one important benefit that the study of Aristotle's work was thought to offer to the Platonist is the appreciation of valuable elements of Plato's thought which Aristotle first noticed.

7. CONCLUSIONS

In conclusion, it turns out that Plutarch held that Aristotle often preserves Plato's doctrine in a more systematic form on a number of crucial issues in ethics, psychology, metaphysics, and epistemology. He considers Aristotle's ethics, for instance, to be a systematic account of Plato's relevant doctrine. A different kind of systematization is provided by the case of Aristotle's categories; this theory may be a new construction, but, in Plutarch's view, it is a development of originally Platonic elements. To the extent that Plutarch regards Aristotle as a source of Plato's doctrine, he feels free to draw on Aristotle's work. It is thus mistaken to hold that he used simply Aristotle as an ally in his polemic, compromising his Platonism.[136] Exactly because Plutarch is committed to Plato's philosophy, he shows great awareness of Aristotle's divergences from Plato's doctrines, and does not hesitate to criticize him. The fact, however, that Plutarch rarely criticizes Aristotle and that when he does so his criticism is implicit and when explicit it is mild and constructive

[136] Donini (1988b: 131); Babut (1996: 25).

suggests that he considers Aristotle to be part of the Platonist tradition, however divergent from Plato's doctrine.

Plutarch probably found it difficult to judge the issue of how Aristotle's philosophy compares with Plato's in its entirety, and appears to have thought that one could do justice to such a complex issue only by discussing different aspects of it separately. This attitude is characteristic of his more sophisticated position about the way Aristotle's philosophy compares with Plato's than the one that Antiochus maintained. This, along with the fact that Plutarch has a much wider appreciation of Platonic philosophy suggests that it is he, rather than Antiochus, who set the agenda for the subsequent discussion on Aristotle's philosophy.

3

Numenius

1. NUMENIUS' PYTHAGOREANISM AND HIS THESIS ON ARISTOTLE'S PHILOSOPHY

Numenius takes a position on Aristotle's philosophy which contrasts strongly with Plutarch's more balanced attitude towards it, and in doing so he may even be reacting to Plutarch specifically. Working about thirty years after Plutarch's death (AD 120), Numenius claims that Aristotle's philosophy must be separated altogether from Plato's doctrine and set aside (fr. 24. 67–70).[1] Numenius makes this claim in his treatise *Περὶ τῆς τῶν Ἀκαδημαϊκῶν πρὸς Πλάτωνα διαστάσεως* (*On the Dissension of the Academics from Plato*; frs. 24–8 Des Places) where he sets out to castigate what he considers the gravest departure from Plato's philosophy, namely Academic scepticism.

Numenius makes clear from the very start of his treatise that his project will be to separate Plato's philosophy from the philosophies of both Aristotle and Zeno the Stoic.[2] While this statement of intention indicates just how important this point was to him, nowhere in the preserved fragments does Numenius argue specifically about Aristotle's philosophy nor does he refer to any such argument. His only apparent reason for separating Aristotle's philosophy from Plato's is that Plato, unlike Aristotle, was a Pythagorean, a remark which suggests that Numenius is continuing Eudorus' argument on Aristotle. In the only

[1] I use the edn. of É. Des Places, *Numenius Fragments* (Paris, 1973). The literature on Numenius is rich. Most important are Beutler (1940); Dodds (1960); Waszink (1965); Merlan (1967: 96–118); Baltes (1975); Dillon (1977: 361–77); Deuse (1983: 61–80); and esp. Frede (1987*c*). The existing evidence does not allow Numenius' date to be determined more precisely; cf. Frede (1987*c*: 1038–9).

[2] *καὶ ὥσπερ ἐξ ἀρχῆς προὐθέμεθα χωρίζειν αὐτὸν* [sc. Plato] *Ἀριστοτέλους καὶ Ζήνωνος, οὕτω καὶ νῦν τῆς Ἀκαδημίας, ἐὰν ὁ θεὸς ἀντιλάβηται, χωρίζοντες ἐάσομεν αὐτὸν ἐφ' ἑαυτοῦ νῦν εἶναι Πυθαγόρειον·* (and as from the very start we intended to separate Plato from Aristotle and Zeno, now we separate him also from the Academy, if God helps us along, and having separated him from all of them, we will leave him as he really is, namely a Pythagorean); fr. 24. 67–70 Des Places.

other reference to Aristotle's philosophy in his preserved fragments, Numenius mentions the rejection of the transcendent Forms as the characteristic mark of Aristotle's departure from Plato (fr. 25. 105–17) and implies that anyone who regards Aristotle as a Platonist is deeply ignorant. But, as will be seen, this passage is a passing remark rather than part of, or a hint at, a fuller treatment. And one cannot immediately see how such a remark alone justifies the conclusion that Aristotle's philosophy is incompatible with Plato's. As shown in the previous chapter, Plutarch makes a very similar remark in the *Adversus Colotem* but still values Aristotle's philosophy highly.

One may be tempted to think that, since Numenius' thought is preserved only in fragments, we may be missing fuller discussions of Aristotle's philosophy that could have been contained somewhere in his body of works, perhaps already in the treatise *On the dissension of the Academics from Plato*. Yet it is quite improbable that this work contained such evidence. The preserved fragments clearly show that in this treatise Numenius sets out to criticize and parody any deviations from Plato's philosophy and that of Academic scepticism most especially. However, his general practice is not to justify why this, that, or the other interpretation of Plato constitutes a deviation. At best he gives hints, but nowhere does he supply arguments. The lack of such arguments against the sceptics, Numenius' main target, makes it quite improbable that he had made any concerning Aristotle either. As for the rest of his works, nothing in the existing evidence suggests that Numenius was seriously concerned with arguing against Aristotle's philosophy and against its use by Platonists. The fact that neither Eusebius, who had much respect for the work of Numenius and who appeared to know it well, nor any other apologist seeking evidence for the contradictions of Greek philosophers refers to anti-Aristotelian arguments drawn by Numenius, makes it unlikely that he presented any.[3] Furthermore, the existing evidence suggests that Numenius was more concerned with criticizing doctrines of the Academics (frs. 24, 28) and the Stoics (frs. 3, 4b, 24. 37–47, 52. 2–3) rather than those of the Aristotelians. This may suggest either that Numenius was not particularly hostile to Aristotle's philosophy, or that he was rather indifferent to it. But the fact that Numenius altogether rejects Aristotle's philosophy in his *On the dissension of the Academics from Plato*

[3] Eusebius follows his teacher Origen in his esteem of Numenius. His knowledge of Numenius' work becomes clear in several passages of the *Preparatio Evangelica*, (e.g. 9. 8. 10). It is difficult to believe that Eusebius would have left his anti-Aristotelian section devoid of Numenius' anti-Aristotelian arguments if there were any.

suggests that the latter is more likely. Apparently, for Numenius, Aristotle's divergence from Plato's philosophy was so considerable that it rendered Aristotle's philosophy devoid of any value.

Numenius' remark that Plato is a Pythagorean, however, does help us to understand how he considers Aristotle's philosophy as being incompatible with that of Plato. Given the state of our evidence, this remark is quite important as it reveals much about Numenius' philosophical predisposition. Understanding this is quite essential for any reconstruction of the grounds on which Numenius rejects Aristotle's philosophy.

Numenius was a Pythagorean, that is, he accepted Pythagoras as the ultimate philosophical authority whose doctrine is true in the sense that it was derivative of an ultimate, universally true account and probably a divinely inspired one at that.[4] A crucial aspect of Numenius' philosophical position is his view on the history of philosophy. Along with Eudorus and Moderatus, Numenius shares the view that all true philosophy originated with Pythagoras and was largely represented by Plato's philosophy—this explains why some ancient sources describe Numenius as a Pythagorean[5] and others as a Platonist.[6] According to Numenius, Plato appropriated Pythagoras' doctrine and communicated it widely through his own work (fr. 24. 56–62). Numenius appears to suggest that Plato came in contact with Pythagorean philosophy both directly and also indirectly through Socrates. As one of Socrates' pupils, Plato realized that Socrates was communicating Pythagorean doctrines (fr. 24. 47–59), most especially the doctrine of the three Gods (*Epist.* 2. 312e), which, as will be seen, Numenius considers to be a particularly crucial Pythagorean doctrine. But Plato was able to realize this, Numenius argues, because he already had become familiar with Pythagorean philosophy (πυθαγορίσας; fr. 24. 57). Numenius does not say how Plato had accessed this philosophy, but probably alludes to Plato's contacts with Pythagorean communities in his travels to southern Italy and Sicily, which are attested in the Platonic letters,[7] and also in Greece with Pythagoreans like Philolaus.[8]

[4] Cf. frs. 1a–1b Des Places and below.

[5] πυθαγορικός Eusebius *PE* 9. 7. 1 (fr. 1a), Nemesius, *De nat. hom.* 70. 1–2 (fr. 4b. 3), πυθαγόρειος, Origen, *C. Celsum* 1. 15, 4. 51, 5. 38 (frs. 1b–c, 53); cf. Chalcidius, *In Tim.* 297. 7–8; Waszink (fr. 52. 2).

[6] Cf. *V. Plot.* 14. 1–12; Iamblichus, *De anima* ap. Stob. 1. 374. 21 (fr. 43. 1 Des Places); Proclus, *In Remp.* 2. 96. 11.

[7] Cf. esp. [Plato] *Epist.* 7. 338c, 339b.

[8] Philolaus (*c.* 470–390) visited Thebes probably with some other Pythagorean followers. Cebes and Simmias are often seen as his followers, because they are said to be his associates in the *Phaedo* 61d–e. Yet this is not certain. On Philolaus see Burkert (1962).

Three points about this account need to be highlighted here. First, for Numenius the only substantial component in Plato's philosophy is Pythagorean doctrine, since even Socrates, who was often taken to have contributed the aporetic spirit in Plato's thought, in Numenius' view was a Pythagorean. Second, for Numenius Plato's Pythagoreanism was not a matter of interpretation of Platonic doctrines but rather a historical fact. Third, for Numenius the adoption of Pythagorean doctrine automatically endows Plato with philosophical authority, while at the same time specifying the limits of his authority. Since for Numenius the credit for the value of Plato's philosophy ultimately goes back to Pythagoras, Plato is less of an authority than Pythagoras (frs. 7. 5–7, 24. 16–22). Two further points confirm this. First, Numenius' idea probably was that Pythagoras had direct access to ancient universal wisdom, which he raised to objective philosophical truth.[9] Given that for Numenius secure knowledge (*epistême*) is a divine gift (fr. 14. 6–19),[10] Pythagoras' access to it indicates his privileged status as an intellectual. Secondly, Numenius maintains that Plato, even in his limited achievement of transmitting Pythagorean doctrines, was not faultless. Numenius criticizes him for being insufficiently clear and, as a result, also partly responsible for the departure of later Academics from his doctrine (fr. 24. 60–6).

The latter criticism apparently holds Plato responsible for concealing that he was a mere member and interpreter of the Pythagorean school, rather than an initiator of his own school of thought, as traditionally had been believed. The result of Plato's attitude, Numenius argues, was that the most essential aspect of Plato's philosophical outlook, his Pythagoreanism, had invariably been appreciated insufficiently by the Academics, and such an ignorance had caused sedition and secession from Plato's philosophy to varying degrees. Already the early Academics betrayed Plato's Pythagorean doctrines,[11] as they were carried away by confusion and ambition (fr. 24. 5–14), and this is even more the case with later Platonists like Antiochus who adopted doctrines alien to

[9] Cf. frs. 1a, 1b Des Places with the comments of Waszink (1965: 45–8) and Frede (1987*c*: 1047–8). The existence of such an account was maintained, among others, notably by Celsus (Origen, *C. Celsum* 1. 14, 3. 16), but he probably argued that Plato had direct access to it; see Frede (1994: 5192–9).

[10] See O' Meara (1989: 13) on this.

[11] Numenius argues that the early Academics 'did not abide by the first succession'. This succession clearly cannot be that of Speusippus or Xenocrates, despite the fact that both of them could be regarded as strongly Pythagoreanizing, so it must be Plato's. This seems to suggest that Numenius considered Plato as Pythagoras' successor.

Plato's thought (fr. 28. 14–16), which, as has been seen, included Stoic and Aristotelian ones. Yet, as I already have said, for Numenius the most serious of all departures from Plato's thought is the sceptical interpretation of Plato. Already the formulation of the title of his treatise shows this; the sceptic Academics did not simply move away from Plato but *against* Plato. This is suggested by the construction of the term διάστασις with πρός (διάστασις πρὸς Πλάτωνα) which comes close to the sense of revolt (στάσις).[12] Accordingly Numenius argues that the Academic sceptics launched a new philosophy.[13]

Numenius' concern with the sceptical interpretation of Plato's philosophy was strong first of all because this conception of Plato was particularly at odds with his own understanding of Plato as essentially Pythagorean, and secondly because it was upheld by several earlier Platonists or younger contemporaries of his, such as Plutarch, the *Anonymus in Theaetetum*,[14] and Favorinus.[15] Numenius' remark that Socrates propounded Pythagorean doctrines primarily targets their position that Plato's most essential aspect is the aporetic one, which Plato allegedly inherited from Socrates. Numenius may also have targeted Plutarch's view that the dialectical methodology of arguing on either side of a topic was an important element in Plato which Aristotle also shared (see pp. 86–7). Numenius may have wanted to discredit also certain historical claims such as Aristotle's depiction of Platonic philosophy as being a combination of Socratic and Pythagorean elements.[16] For Numenius both elements contributed equally to the formation of Plato's Pythagorean doctrine.

[12] See LSJ, s.v. sense 3; cf. Aristotle, *Politics* 1296ᵃ7–8, 1300ᵇ37; Eusebius, *PE* 1. 7. 16, 5. 4. 10, 15. 62. 16. The same term occurs in the title of Porphyry's treatise Περὶ διαστάσεως Πλάτωνος καὶ Ἀριστοτέλους (Elias, *In Isag.* 39. 7–8) but there the term is used in a more neutral sense, as I argue in Ch. 7, s. 2. Numenius' ideal is the Epicurean school which is 'without revolts' (ἀστασιαστοτάτῃ; fr. 24. 34). We know, however, that the Epicureans also disagreed with each other. See Philodemus, Πρὸς τοὺς[. . .], *P. Herc.* 1005, cols. IV, VI, XV Angeli.

[13] Cf. *kainotomia*; fr. 24. 31 Des Places.

[14] The date of the *Anon. in Theaetetum* is controversial. Brittain (2001: 249–54) has argued for a dating c.AD 100 against the earlier dating of Sedley and Bastianini (1995: 251–6: end of 1st c. BC). One important piece of evidence for the dating of Anonymus seems to me to be his concern with the unity of the Academy. Another is his concern with the Hellenistic debates. I am thus inclined to agree with an earlier dating.

[15] Favorinus' works include *Pyrrhonian modes* (where he presents the similarities between Academic and Pyrrhonian sceptics), *On Academic disposition*, *On Cataleptic impression*, *On Plato*. They are edited by A. Barigazzi, *Favorino di Arelate Opere* (Florence, 1966).

[16] See Aristotle, *Met.* 1029ᵃ31–2, 987ᵃ29–988ᵃ17, 989ᵃ28–991ᵇ4; cf. Antiochus' position that Plato appended Pythagorean doctrine to his Socratic system (*De fin.* 5. 87).

Although this doctrine is presented as being central to Plato's intellectual identity and crucial for the correct appreciation of his thought, we lack any coherent account of it in Numenius, which would allow us to measure any departures from it. And so we are left to wonder in what sense any philosophical outlook, especially that of Aristotle, could be incompatible with the Pythagorean doctrine as understood by Numenius.

2. IS PYTHAGOREANISM INCOMPATIBLE WITH ARISTOTLE'S PHILOSOPHY?

The question of the incompatibility between Pythagoreanism and Aristotelianism becomes more complicated by the fact that Pythagoras left no writings[17] and thus a certain fluidity of interpretation prevailed. Pythagorean philosophers differed considerably in their views and, as a result, took different or even contradictory attitudes to Aristotle's philosophy. This variation is due to one particular factor, namely that Pythagoreans were eager to appropriate doctrines of later philosophers, accusing the latter of having stolen them from Pythagoras. This was explicitly argued by Moderatus (Porphyry, *V. Pyth.* 53), who apparently sought to systematize Pythagorean doctrines in a comprehensive account.[18]

Pythagoreans drew their doctrines from two main kinds of sources which account for their doctrinal variation: the first, quite standard, source was Plato's work, on which Pythagoreans used to depend heavily; the second was other authors including the early Academics, Aristotle, and the Stoics.

The strong dependence of the Pythagoreans on Plato is to be explained by the fact that beliefs such as the immortality of the soul,[19]

[17] This was disputed by Pythagoreans (cf. DL 8. 6–7, 9), who created forgeries which they ascribed to Pythagoras. On this pseudo-Pythagorean literature see below.

[18] I refer to Moderatus' *Πυθαγορικαὶ σχολαί*. According to Stephanus Byzantius (s.v. Gadeira), it comprised five books, while according to Porphyry (*V. Pyth.* 48) it comprised ten or eleven (the MSS vary). The main sources of Moderatus' views are Porphyry, *V. Pyth.* 48–53 and Simplicius, *In Phys.* 230. 34–231. 12. On Moderatus see Dodds (1928: 53–4); Dillon (1977: 344–51); and Tarrant (1993: 165–73).

[19] Already in the 4th c. BC the belief in the transmigration of the soul is parodied by comedy writers as distinctly Pythagorean. Cf. also DL 8. 14; Porphyry, *V. Pyth.* 19. On the question Plato's debt to Pythagoreanism see Burkert (1962: 74–85). Doxography often presents Pythagoras and Plato in accord; cf. Aetius 1. 23. 1 (*DG*, p. 318), 4. 4. 1 (*DG*, p. 389), 1. 7. 2 (*DG*, p. 307), 4. 7. 5 (*DG*, p. 393), 4. 9. 10 (*DG* p. 397), 5. 20. 4 (*DG*, p. 432). See Burkert (1962: 51–2).

or the creation of the world by God,[20] which Plato propounds, were connected in some form with Pythagoreanism. The Pythagoreans perceived such doctrines not only as evidence of Plato's doctrinal similarity to Pythagoras,[21] but chiefly as evidence that Plato was recasting Pythagorean doctrines.[22] This belief becomes manifest in the fact that they forged works where Plato's views figure as originally Pythagorean, as is the case with the work of Timaeus Locrus.[23] Yet Pythagorean Platonists disagreed with each other as much as non-Pythagorean ones as to which are Plato's doctrines and how they should be construed. To mention one important difference, some Pythagoreans are monists, that is, they accept God as the only principle from which everything else including matter arises.[24] Numenius, though, like Plutarch, who had much sympathy with Pythagoreanism, is a dualist, postulating two distinct principles, God, who is pure form, and matter, which is independent in origin and co-eternal with God.[25] This doctrinal variation clearly resulted from different interpretations, primarily of the *Timaeus*. Related to this variation was their disagreement as to whether God is an intellect, as the *Timaeus* suggests, or above intellect and substance, as *Republic* 509b appears to indicate.[26]

Now some Pythagoreans, for one reason or another, found attractive certain doctrines of Aristotle and other thinkers whom they also came to

[20] Cf. Aetius 2. 1. 1 (*DG*, p. 327). DL 8. 48. See Burkert (1962: 68–9).

[21] This was widely acknowledged. Aristotle reports about Plato's debt to Pythagorean lore in *Met.* 1, 13, 14) and often treats Pythagorean and Academic views jointly; Speusippus and Xenocrates wrote treatises on Pythagorean doctrines (Iamblichus [?], *Theol. Arithm.* p. 82. 10–5 De Falco; fr. 4 Lang; 28 Tarán; DL 4. 13). For the Pythagoreanism in Plato's Academy see Burkert (1962: 46–73).

[22] Pythagorean Platonists assumed, for instance, that Timaeus, the speaker in Plato's dialogue, was Pythagorean, since he is said to be of south Italian origin (*Timaeus* 20a), so they regarded the doctrines of Plato's *Timaeus* as Pythagorean. They probably held that Plato copied the *Timaeus* from Philolaus' book (DL 8. 85); Timon of Phlius parodied Plato for this (in Aulus Gellius, *NA* 3. 17. 4).

[23] Proclus (*In Tim.* 1. 7. 17–8. 29) and probably also Iamblichus (fr. 74 Dillon) argued that the *Timaeus* was inspired by the work of Timaeus Locrus; see O'Meara (1989: 99, 179–81) and Dillon (1973: 363–4).

[24] Such as the Pythagoreans referred to by Alexander Polyhistor (DL 8. 25), by Sextus (*Adv. Math.* 10. 261–2), by Nicomachus of Gerasa (Iamblichus [?] *Theol. Arithm.* pp. 3. 1–5. 5 De Falco; apud Photium, *Bibl.* cod. 187, 143a24), by Eudorus (Simplicius, *In Phys.* 181. 7–30; frs. 3–5 Mazzarelli), and by Moderatus (ibid. 231. 6–24).

[25] This must be also Celsus' view. See Frede (1994: 5205); cf. Dillon (1977: 342–8). On this doctrinal variation among Pythagoreans see Rist (1965: 333–8) and Frede (1987*c*: 1054–5).

[26] Cf. ps-Brotinus in Syrianus, *In Met.* 166. 5–6, 183. 1–3 and the Pythagoreans referred to by Iamblichus *Theol. Arithm.* 3. 21–3 De Falco, and Origen, *C. Celsum* 7. 38; see Whittaker (1969: 97, 104).

regard as beneficiaries of Pythagorean wisdom, and thus felt entitled to draw from them. Such an attitude increased their doctrinal variation further. To begin with two well-known cases, Eudorus found Pythagorean doctrines preserved in Aristotle's doxographic accounts and in Stoicism,[27] while Moderatus argued that, like Plato, Aristotle, Aristoxenus, and Xenocrates stole their best doctrines from Pythagoras (Porphyry, *V. Pyth.* 53). Moderatus may have meant that all these philosophers appropriated their doctrines directly from Pythagorean sources, but he may also have wanted to suggest that Plato had initiated a tradition of appropriating doctrines from Pythagoras, which he then passed on to his students. This seems to be the view of the Platonist author of the pseudo-Plutarchean *De musica* (second century AD?) who depicts Aristotle as recasting the Pythagorean doctrine of cosmic harmony as presented in Plato.[28] Various other sources which assume the accord of Plato and Aristotle with Pythagoras take a similar position. Already Posidonius had argued that Plato and Aristotle share Pythagoras' view on the nature of soul against Chrysippus' one,[29] Plotinus claims that 'the ancients', that is, Plato and Aristotle, inherited Pythagorean doctrines, especially metaphysical ones (*Enn.* 5. 1. 9. 28–9), while similar views are common in doxography.[30]

Yet no matter how precisely the relationship between Platonic and Aristotelian philosophy was viewed by Pythagoreans, the crucial point for us is that they often claimed to have found Pythagorean doctrines in Aristotle and appropriated them, following practices similar to the ones I outlined for Plato. Indeed, several Pythagorean treatises accommodate Aristotle's doctrines in ontology, cosmology, physics, or ethics and present them as Pythagorean, as is the case with many Platonic doctrines.[31]

[27] See Ch. 1, pp. 82–3.

[28] *De musica* 1139B–1140B = Aristotle, *De Philosophia* fr. 25 Ross.

[29] In Galen, *PHP* 4. 7. 39 (test. 95 E–K).

[30] See Aetius 1. 11. 12 (*DG* p. 310): Aristotle is presented as being in accord with Pythagoras on the first causes being incorporeal. Aetius 5. 4. 2 (*DG*, p. 417): Pythagoras, Plato, and Aristotle agree on the force of seed being incorporeal. ps-Plutarch 4. 20. 1 (*DG*, p. 409): the three are in accord on the nature of sound. Clement, *Strom.* 5. 13. 88.1–2 records their accord on the intellect and on matter (ibid. 5–6). Photius, *Bibl.* cod. 249, 438b14–19 presents Plato and Aristotle as successors of Pythagoras (ninth and tenth, respectively).

[31] Cf. e.g. ps-Archytas, *De principiis* 19. 5–20. 17 Thesleff, where we find Aristotle's doctrine of matter and form, Ocellus, *De univ. nat.* 123. 3–138. 12 Thesleff, where Aristotle's cosmological doctrines are used. The evidence suggesting the dependence of Pythagorean treatises on Aristotle, his ontology and physics most especially, can be multiplied. The best available survey on the ps-Pythagorean literature is that of Moraux (1984: 605–83). On their ontology and physics in particular see Moraux (1984: 633–41).

As regards ethics in particular, a number of Pythagorean works adopt Aristotle's doctrines of *eudaimonia*, the nature of virtue and how this is achieved, in a way reminiscent of Antiochus and Plutarch.[32] Further, as was the case with Plato's *Timaeus*, Aristotle's *Categories* were claimed as originally Pythagorean in the forgery of pseudo-Archytas (first–second century AD).[33] It is quite remarkable that the Pythagorean author of this work takes the same interpretation as Eudorus, namely that the categories do not apply to the intelligible world but only to the sensible one,[34] and yet, unlike Eudorus, he finds Aristotle's doctrine of the categories valuable enough to maintain its Pythagorean origin.

The above evidence shows (*a*) that Pythagoreans neither subscribed to a fixed set of philosophical doctrines, (*b*) nor did they have a unified attitude toward Aristotle, and (*c*) that their attitude toward Aristotle depended on their interpretation of Plato's doctrines.

However, after Eudorus there emerges a stream of Pythagorean Platonists who appear to share a distinct doctrinal orientation to which also Numenius adheres.[35] They are primarily concerned with the structure of reality, especially the first principles, and agree in distinguishing a first principle, the One of Plato's *Parmenides* above the pair of limit and unlimited of the *Philebus*. Being inspired mainly by

[32] Ps.-Archytas and Euryphamus, for instance, argue that human soul has a rational and an irrational part and, given that man's nature is soul and body, good life must include goods other than virtue (ps-Archytas, *De vir. bon.* 11. 3–21; Euryphamus *De vit.* 86. 21–31, 87. 6–9 Thesleff). They come to distinguish between good life (εὐδαιμονία) and good luck (εὐτυχία); the latter depends on the possession of external goods which some of them consider, like Antiochus, complementary to good life (ps-Archytas, *De vir. bon.* 9. 26–10. 20; Euryphamus, *De vit.* 87. 6–19 Thesleff). Further, several define virtue as the mean between two excesses (ps-Archytas, *De vir. bon* 12. 7–10; Metopus, *De virt.* 119. 27–120. 24; Theages, *De virt.* 191. 25–192. 4 Thesleff), presumably because they saw Aristotle's theory as a corollary of the Pythagorean conception of the soul as harmony (*Phaedo* 85e–86c) and even criticize the Stoic doctrine of *apatheia* (ps-Archytas, *De educ.* 41. 9–18 Thesleff). The proximity to the thought of Antiochus and Plutarch suggests a likely date for these treatises the 1st c. AD. See Moraux (1984: 643–66) and Centrone (1990: 21–44) for a detailed discussion.

[33] On ps-Archytas' treatise *On the Categories* see Szlezák (1972: 17–19); Moraux (1984: 608–22). The date of the work is debated. Szlezák (1972: 14–17) sets it in the 1st c. BC, while Moraux (1984: 608, 614) finds a dating in the first two centuries AD more plausible. Hippolytus, *Elenchus* 6. 24. 2, 8. 14. 9, Iamblichus (in Simplicius, *In Cat.* 2. 9–25) and others (see Szlezák 1972: testimonia) also present the categories as Pythagorean. See Mueller (1994: 148); O'Meara (1989: 68–9, 180); Mansfeld (1992: 50–1, 57–77). Ps-Archytas also claims that Aristotle's *De interpretatione* relies on a Pythagorean original (31. 10–14 Thesleff).

[34] Ps-Archytas 22. 31–23. 41, 30. 17–31. 5 Thesleff. On this interpretation see Kotzia (1992: 241–4).

[35] Eudorus in Simplicius, *In Phys.* 181. 7–30; frs. 3–5 Mazzarelli.

the *Timaeus*, the *Sophist* and the *Republic*, Moderatus and Numenius share a belief in a hierarchy of intelligible hypostases, considered divine, which account for the structure of the sensible and intelligible world. This hierarchy appears to comprise three hypostases. The first one is an intellect which is identified with the Form of the Good in *Republic* 6 (508e), something that implies its absolute goodness, and placed above the demiurgic intellect of the *Timaeus*. This demiurgic intellect is the second hypostasis, and it either comprises the Forms (Numenius), or is identical with them (Moderatus).[36] The third hypostasis can correspond either to the world-soul, as is the case in Moderatus, or can be identified with a third intellect, as is the case in Numenius, but in either case it is concerned with the maintenance of the world.[37]

We have good reasons to believe that, when Numenius refers to Plato's Pythagoreanism to account for the separation of Aristotle's philosophy from that of Plato, he is primarily referring to this doctrine of the three intelligible hypostases. First, he focuses on this doctrine in a way that suggests that he considers it to be the backbone of Plato's philosophy and its primary debt to Pythagorean wisdom. For instance, he refers constantly to Plato's texts (frs. 7, 17, 20, 22) in order to demonstrate that this doctrine is plainly present in Plato and he emphasizes its importance (e.g. fr. 17). Second, Numenius' sole example of a Pythagorean doctrine with which Plato became acquainted is that of the three Gods (fr. 24. 51–2). Its importance is highlighted by the fact that according to Numenius this doctrine was a principal one also for Socrates from whom Plato took it over (fr. 24. 57–9). Third, later philosophers appear to assume that Pythagoreanism essentially consists in this very doctrine. Longinus refers to this very doctrine when he argues that Plotinus explained 'Pythagorean and Platonic principles' better than Numenius had (*V. Plot.* 20. 71–6) and surely it was precisely this doctrine for which Plotinus was accused of plagiarizing Numenius (ibid. 17. 1–6, 21. 1–6). Now we have to see how Aristotle was perceived as opposing this metaphysical doctrine which Numenius finds so essential in Plato's thought.

3. METAPHYSICS

Most of what follows is work of reconstruction and as such remains, at best, only probable. Let us start however with the little firm evidence we

36 In Porphyry apud Simplicium, *In Phys.* 230. 34–231. 5

37 For the origins of this interpretation see Dodds (1928) and Whittaker (1987: 94–104).

have. As I said in the beginning of the chapter, Aristotle's rejection of the transcendent Forms is the only point which Numenius mentions to explain Aristotle's alleged estrangement from Plato. This testimony shows that Numenius' objections to Aristotle's philosophy to some extent at least concern metaphysics. Let us look at this more closely.

In the surviving testimony, Numenius refers to a certain Cephisodorus, a student in Isocrates' school. Seeing his teacher being criticized by Aristotle, Cephisodorus set out to attack Aristotle.[38] However, Numenius argues, Cephisodorus was familiar only with Plato's philosophy and remained ignorant of Aristotle's doctrines; yet he assumed that Aristotle, as a student of Plato, necessarily adhered to views such as the theory of Forms. Cephisodorus thus criticized Aristotle by attacking Plato's theory of Forms, Numenius claims. I quote the passage in question.

Zeno was conducting his fight [against Arcesilaus] with solemnity and gravity, but not better than Cephisodorus, the orator. Cephisodorus realized that his teacher, Isocrates, had been attacked by Aristotle, but he neither had any knowledge of, nor direct familiarity with, Aristotle's views. Yet since he realized that Plato's doctrines were respected and believed that Aristotle followed Plato in philosophy, he tried to attack Aristotle but was in fact criticizing Plato. He started his accusations with the Forms and finished with matters he did not understand, believing that they concern what he thought they did. However, in this way Cephisodorus argued not against the person he wanted to attack [sc. Aristotle], but against the one he did not wish to take on [sc. Plato]. (Numenius fr. 25. 105–17 Des Places).

Numenius argues that Cephisodorus did not intend to criticize Plato's philosophy, but eventually did so, because in his view Plato's doctrines were espoused by Aristotle too (*κατὰ Πλάτωνα τὸν 'Αριστοτέλην φιλοσοφεῖν*). We do not really know what Cephisodorus' argument actually was, and we should be cautious in drawing inferences from Numenius on this subject. Presumably Cephisodorus was motivated in his attack by two considerations: first, he considered Aristotle as upholding Plato's doctrine of Forms; second, he considered his own criticism of this doctrine as an effective polemical means against Aristotle, because this doctrine was well known among his contemporaries. However Cephisodorus arrived at his claim about Aristotle, the point which

[38] Cephisodorus wrote a work of four books against Aristotle *c.* 360. This contained also personal invectives. The *testimonia* are collected by Düring (1957: 379–80; cf. ibid. 389–90). Aristocles partly refutes his attacks on Aristotle (in Eusebius *PE* 15. 2. 7; fr. 2. 40–3 Heiland, 12. 7 Chiesara). Cf. Dionysius Halicarnaseus, *Ad Pomp. Gem.* 1. 16–17.

Numenius underscores is that it indicates how little understanding he had of Aristotle's work (ἀμαθὴς καὶ ἄπειρος).

Cephisodorus appears to match the case of Colotes whom Plutarch criticizes; both were ignorant enough to assume that Aristotle had followed Plato's doctrine of transcendent Forms. Their difference lies in the fact that Cephisodorus wanted to attack Aristotle, whereas Colotes had sought to criticize Plato. But as with the testimony of Colotes, the one about Cephisodorus should not be taken as suggesting that Aristotle in his early works was defending Plato's theory of Forms, as Jaeger thought.[39] If indeed Cephisodorus did launch such a criticism, his assumption that Aristotle had espoused Plato's view of the Forms could be sufficiently accounted for by the fact that Aristotle was an Academic. And especially considering the period in which he was writing, Cephisodorus was entirely justified in making this claim.

Numenius suggests that Cephisodorus also criticized other doctrines of Plato which he again assumed that Aristotle shared, and was so confused that he attacked doctrines which were not about what he thought he was attacking (τὰ νομιζόμενα ἀμφ᾽ αὐτῶν ᾗ λέγεται ὑπονοῶν). As a result, Cephisodorus made criticisms which did not apply to Plato, since they concerned doctrines which, in Numenius' view, Plato had never maintained. The text is quite unclear as to what exactly Numenius means here, but it seems that there are two possible ways in which Cephisodorus was confused: either he ascribed to Aristotle Platonic doctrines, or he criticized Aristotle for original Aristotelian doctrines, which he took to be Plato's views also, on the assumption that Aristotle in general tends to follow Plato.

The parallel with Zeno, with whom Numenius compares Cephisodorus (fr. 25. 105–19), makes the latter option more likely. Zeno, Numenius argues, made the mistake of thinking that Arcesilaus followed Plato's views, and in order to attack Arcesilaus' scepticism, he turned to criticizing Plato (fr. 25. 120–8, 140–8). In this case Numenius puts the blame partly on Arcesilaus, who had projected his scepticism back to Plato. The important point for us is that Numenius understood both Cephisodorus and Zeno as having championed views foreign to Plato, mistakenly assuming them to have been originally Platonic and criticizing them in this capacity. And they also erred, Numenius claims,

[39] Jaeger (1948: 37) argued that Cephisodorus' view resulted from his familiarity only with Aristotle's dialogues. Ross, *Arist. Fragm. Sel.* p. 5, prints the passage as a testimony of Aristotle's dialogues. But there is nothing to suggest that this is the case. On the contrary, Cephisodorus is criticized here for his *general* ignorance of Aristotle's philosophy.

in regarding as Platonists people who departed from Plato's doctrines in one way or another, such as Aristotle and Arcesilaus.

There are some further conclusions to be drawn from the passage cited above regarding Numenius' understanding of Aristotle. One conclusion is that according to Numenius any reliance on Aristotle for understanding Plato is as mistaken an approach as relying on the Academic sceptics, or on the Stoics for that matter. This is so, because, in Numenius' view, neither do Aristotle's doctrines reflect Plato's own nor does Aristotle report correctly on Plato's philosophy. Presumably the message Numenius seeks to impart is that one should try to understand Plato's philosophy only through Plato's texts, and he aspires to set the example by citing Plato frequently in his own writings.[40] A further conclusion is that Numenius considers ontology in general, and the doctrine of transcendent Forms most especially, to be important enough to take their rejection not only as evidence of Aristotle's disagreement with Plato on ontology but as evidence of Aristotle's distance from Plato's philosophy as a whole.[41] In order to understand how this can be so, we first have to briefly review Numenius' ontological views.

To begin with, Numenius, like Plutarch, maintains that only immaterial, intelligible entities qualify as being, because only these remain stable (frs. 4a7, 6. 15, 7. 2), while nothing material qualifies as such because it is subject to change (fr. 3. 8–12). Also like Plutarch, Numenius assumes the existence of uncreated matter (fr. 52. 7, 58–60), which is co-eternal with God (fr. 52. 13) and which, as it is by nature in a fluid condition (frs. 4a6–7, 11.16), *a fortiori* hardly qualifies as being (fr. 3. 10–12). Numenius considers disorder and division as the essential characteristics of matter, and accordingly he terms it *dyas* (frs. 11. 15, 52. 6; cf. *Parm.* 149d2). For Numenius order is characteristic of goodness; since matter lacks order, he considers it evil, and to the extent that this disorder goes against the orderly nature of the world, matter is regarded as the source of all evil (fr. 52. 37–9),[42] and is said to be animated by an evil world-soul (fr. 52. 64–5), as is suggested

[40] Cf. frs. 1a4, 6. 13, 7. 7–12, 8. 8, 14. 19, 17. 2, 19. 12, 20. Atticus will follow Numenius' practice.

[41] Similarly with Stoic philosophy, Numenius focuses his criticism on Stoic first principles, which he regarded as opposite to Platonic ones (fr. 52), and on Stoic ontology (frs. 3, 4b).

[42] Numenius' views on matter are discussed in detail by Frede (1987*c*: 1051–3); cf. Waszink (1965: 67–71) and Baltes (1975: 255–7).

in *Laws* 10.[43] In Numenius' view, order is inherent in intelligible entities; hence only these can account for unity, coherence, and order in material entities, that is, for their existence. He argues that bodies, for example, exist as such due to the coherence and unity bestowed by a soul (fr. 4b. 1–14), a view inspired by Plato's *Laws* 10 (see below, p. 144).

Similarly for the world there must be an immaterial principle to account for its order, its unity, and coherence, wherein eventually the goodness of the world lies (*kosmos*). Since this principle accounts for the relative goodness of the world, some Platonists took the step of identifying it with the Form of the Good of *Republic* 6 (508e). Platonists also traditionally maintained that the world came into being through the imposition of Forms on matter by the demiurge of the *Timaeus* (30a), leading some Platonists to identify the demiurge with the Form of the Good.

Numenius resisted this tactic. He held that goodness varies in degree depending on simplicity and unity, and these qualities become stronger the greater the distance from matter, the source of disorder. Numenius denied that the principle which primarily accounts for the unity and the goodness of the world is the demiurge of the *Timaeus*, for two basic reasons. First, because contact with matter inevitably divides and taints, and this would be inappropriate for the divine principle which accounts for all that exists. And second, because while an intellect such as the creator's must think of the Forms, such thinking brings about multiplicity, thus violating the principle of absolute simplicity which accounts for the unity and order of the world. In his view, it is such an ultimately simple principle which must be the principle of good.

Thus Numenius postulated an intellect, which is above the demiurgic intellect (frs. 16, 17, 19–21) and does not do anything, but is inert (ἀργόν; fr. 12. 13; cf. fr. 15. 2) and utterly simple (fr. 11. 11–14). This is the first God (fr. 11. 11–12) or first intellect (fr. 20. 12) which qualifies as the being itself (αὐτοόν; fr. 17. 4), the source of being (fr. 16. 1–2, 9–10), and goodness itself (αὐτοάγαθον; frs. 16. 9–10, 14, 20. 12), and is identical with the Form of the Good (fr. 20. 4–5, 11–12).[44] But as an intellect, the first God is bound to think, so one wonders how he could remain simple. The question is sharpened in view of Proclus' report that

[43] Waszink (1965: 68–9) perceptively remarks that Numenius, unlike Plutarch, does not distinguish clearly between evil world-soul and matter, but rather seems to conflate the two, probably because for him a soul cannot be really evil; cf. fr. 52. 65–7 Des Places.

[44] On Numenius' theology see Baltes (1975: 257–68); Frede (1987*c*: 1054–70); Kenney (1991: 59–74).

Numenius' first God is identical with the intelligible living substance (ζῷον) of the *Timaeus* 39e7–9 which contains all Forms (*In Tim.* 3. 103. 28–9; fr. 22. 1), which means that Numenius maintained that the Being of *Timaeus* 52d amounts to God plus the Forms.[45] On the other hand this first intellect eventually appears to account for the creation of all beings (fr. 16. 1–2, 9–10), so the other question is how this is to be understood, especially since this intellect is supposed to remain inert.

The two questions are closely connected. Although the status of the evidence does not permit certainty and much remains controversial, an answer based on the testimonies and fragments of Numenius' doctrine can be outlined as follows. Numenius maintains that, since demiurgic activity is not proper to the first intellect, the highest God, this God brings about a second one (fr. 21. 7) and uses this second, demiurgic intellect as an instrument by which the first God thinks (fr. 22. 1–2). There is a question concerning the sense of this 'use', but it cannot be addressed here.[46] For the present purpose it is important to note two things; first that it is the second intellect that thinks of the Forms and sets out to impose them on matter (fr. 18), thus being the demiurge of all generated entities (δημιουργὸς τῆς γενέσεως; fr. 16. 4–5), and second, that in Numenius' view the Forms are in some sense also comprised by the first intellect, in the following two senses.

First, as it is the Form of the Good which governs over all intelligible entities (fr. 20. 4–5, 11–12), all other Forms participate in this very Form (frs. 16. 2–5, 46b–c).[47] Second, the first intellect is said to be thinking of the Forms through using the second one. Since the first intellect in some sense comprises the Forms, this is considered to be the demiurge of all substance (ὁ τῆς οὐσίας δημιουργός; fr. 16. 9). Yet it is the second God, the one who actually thinks the Forms, who creates and who governs over both intelligible and sensible entities (fr. 15. 5). The highest God, though ultimately responsible for the creation, does not actually create, nor does he actually think but only in a very qualified sense: being the Form of the Good and an intellect, his being and object

[45] For the identification of the first God with the living substance see Frede (1987*c*: 1062); cf. Baltes (1996: 80–1). Holzhausen (1992: 253) appears to question it.

[46] The evidence of Proclus *In Tim.* 3. 103. 28–32 (fr. 22 Des Places) is controversial. See Baltes (1975: 266); Frede (1987*c*: 1070). Holzhausen (1992: 250–5) disputes the evidence of Proclus, arguing that it cannot be possible for the first God to be in need of the second one.

[47] Numenius maintained that intelligible entities can participate into other such entities (frs. 46b–c). His view was followed later by Amelius, Iamblichus, Syrianus, and, more systematically, by Proclus; for a brief discussion see Dillon (1973: 348–9).

of thought are identical. For these reasons the highest God remains utterly simple and hence also pure goodness, while the second God is good only to the extent that it participates in the first God (frs. 16. 8–10, 19. 8–13, 20. 7–12).[48]

Exactly because this second, demiurgic intellect turns to matter to create, he inevitably suffers the consequences of such contact, that is, division (fr. 11. 11–16). Thus he splits into two, becoming both the proper demiurgic intellect which continues contemplating the Forms and another intellect which deals with the sensible world, imposing the Forms on matter and eventually bringing the world about (frs. 11. 14–20, 16. 10–12, 21. 4–5). The demiurgic intellect then creates through a third God, a third intellect (frs. 21. 4–7, 22. 3–4), who is thinking discursively (διανοούμενον; fr. 22. 4), that is, he is planning and desiring (fr. 18. 13). This intellect is also active in maintaining the world (frs. 12. 14–19, 18, 52. 91–8), an activity which Platonists such as Plutarch and, later, Plotinus ascribed to the world-soul. Numenius thus appears to have postulated a hierarchy of divine intellects, in which the first one is the source of everything and goodness itself, as, in his view, is the Form of Good in the *Republic*, while the second is identical with the demiurge of the *Timaeus*.

On this basis we can now try to reconstruct some of Numenius' possible objections to Aristotle's ontology and theology. First, Numenius must have considered Aristotle's God to be insufficiently transcendent. As we know, Aristotle's God is an intellect which accounts for the constitution of the world as the general accounts for the order in the army (*Met.* 1074^{b}13–17). Some Aristotelian passages actually appear to suggest that God is in some contact with the world.[49] But according to Numenius it is inappropriate to make God directly involved in the world's coming into being, because this would undermine God's utter simplicity and goodness. As has been seen, in his view there must be a second God who accounts for the world's coming into being (frs. 12. 1–9, 15), and to this God pertains the desire to bring the world about and maintain it. This desiring aspect is granted to the divine intellect by Plato, Aristotle, and Numenius (frs. 11. 20, 18. 13), yet the latter maintains that desire implies some kind of division and pertains to matter (fr. 11. 14–20), causing in his view the split of the demiurgic

[48] As Edwards (1991*b*: 163) points out, there are two kinds of participations involved here, the first God imparts goodness to the second God and also beauty to the world (Numenius fr. 16. 15–17).

[49] *De caelo* 1. 9, esp. 278^{b}12–15, 279^{a}28–30; cf. ibid. 286^{a}8–12, 292^{a}20–8.

intellect into two. This happens when the demiurgic intellect starts to plan what it originally contemplated (fr. 11. 16–20); the third intellect apparently carries on with the planning and the execution of the plan and the second one with the contemplation (frs. 12. 19–22, 16. 10–12). The crucial point for us is that Numenius considers Plato's highest God, as he understood it, to be distanced from the qualities of a creative intellect. In this view the providential aspect and the intellectual contemplation of Aristotle's God constitute characteristics inappropriate for the highest God. Numenius anticipates Plotinus in this. We know though that Plotinus relied much on Aristotle's theory of intellect for formulating his own (see Ch. 6, p. 237), and this may be true also about Numenius' conception of the second God.[50]

The second and most crucial matter regarding which Aristotle must have appeared to be mistaken to Numenius is that, by denying the existence of the transcendent Forms, he had failed to appreciate the very nature of the highest God, which Numenius identifies with the Form of the Good. As is known, Aristotle explicitly rejects the existence of such a thing as a Form of the Good, arguing that nothing accounts for goodness universally, but such a quality depends on the thing to which it applies.[51] For instance, the good for the world is its order, while for man qua man the good is virtue. Aristotle's rejection becomes particularly significant in Numenius' eyes because for him this is the most sublime entity of the intelligible realm on which all reality causally depends. This means that Aristotle's conception of the structure of reality is fundamentally different from what Numenius takes to be Plato's.

Numenius may well have maintained that Aristotle's denial of the transcendent Forms had some further serious consequences. Aristotle must have appeared to him to hold a fundamentally different view from Plato in the *Timaeus* as to how the world came into being and is constituted, and also as regards divine providence. Regarding the latter, we have some further evidence. Numenius, being inspired by *Politicus* 272d–e, argues that the second God exercises providence over the world by using the Forms as instruments (ταῖς ἰδέαις οἰακίζων; fr. 18. 10; cf. fr. 12. 19). The language which Numenius uses here, which is essentially Plato's language, makes his actual view obscure, but clearly the Forms again play an essential role, this time in the maintenance of the universe.

50 Kalligas (2004*a*: 48) argued that Numenius used Aristotle in order to formulate his own tripartite division of divinity, but I find this rather farfetched. At any rate, the available evidence does not allow secure conclusions on this.

51 *Met.* 1031^{b}4–14; *NE* 1096^{a}19–29; *EE* 1217^{b}23–5; *Topics* 107^{a}3–17; *Cat.* 14^{a}23–5.

If I am right so far, Numenius might have considered Aristotle's ontology as involving two kinds of errors: first Aristotle postulates a God imperfectly transcendent and good and also insufficiently provident, and second he is misguided about the way the universe and everything in it has come into being and has seen maintained.

There is a crucial aspect in Numenius' metaphysics which explains why he should have taken Aristotle's denial of the transcendent Forms to amount to such a strong divergence from Plato's ontology. Numenius does not seem to have assigned any important role to immanent Forms. For him these do not account for the unity and the essence of a material entity. This role rather is ascribed to the soul, which is the agent of coherence and formation (fr. 4b. 5–9). In his view, the soul permeates the whole body (διήκουσα δι' ὅλου τοῦ σώματος; fr. 4b27) and gives unity and coherence to it in a fashion similar to the manner in which the world-soul or the demiurgic intellect gives unity to the world. Numenius is inspired by *Laws* 10 where the soul is presented as being the principle of material entities (892a–c) and the cause of all things (896d–e).[52] This text must have inspired to the Stoics the idea that Nature gives unity and coherence to the world, as *pneuma* does this to particular entities.[53] The crucial point for us here is that Numenius, unlike the Stoics, assumes that the unifying principle should be transcendent, and only the latter are truly immaterial substances (fr. 4b11–13). Numenius appears to believe that only transcendent entities can sufficiently account for a sensible being, and also that only they have essences or natures, not sensible beings. Such a conception of the Forms explains why Numenius is unlikely to have thought of Aristotle's doctrine of immanent Forms as evidence for his proximity to Platonic ontology, as Antiochus and Plutarch did. Plotinus, as will be seen, follows Numenius' ontological view and his argument against Aristotle's conception of substance may be largely inspired by Numenius.[54] For both Numenius and Plotinus, Aristotle's rejection of transcendent Forms basically amounts to rejecting Plato's entire intelligible realm. This view is definitely crucial for the formation of their conviction that Aristotle's philosophy is strongly at odds with that of Plato.

[52] Cf. *Laws* 899b; Numenius' position will be adopted by Atticus (fr. 8 Des Places) but will be rejected by Plotinus; see Ch. 4, p. 164, Ch. 6, pp. 236–7.

[53] Cf. *SVF* ii. 439, 441, 444, 1029. Noticeably Alexander, *De mixtione* 223. 25–36 (*SVF* ii. 441) equates the Stoic *pneuma* with Aristotle's essences; see Long and Sedley (1987: i. 282–3).

[54] See Ch. 6, ss. 2 and 4.

4. PSYCHOLOGY

Numenius' understanding Plato's doctrine of the nature of the soul is quite distinct from that of other Platonists of the time and, in my view, partly responsible for the development of his belief that Plato's philosophy must be sharply separated from that of Aristotle.[55] According to Numenius the soul which enlivens the human body is a transcendent entity of a particular kind, namely an intellect (*nous*). In his view this soul which accounts for man's essence (reason) must be sharply distinguished from other souls. Numenius actually distinguishes between two kinds of souls, the rational one of grown-up humans and the irrational one of children and animals.[56]

This is reported by several ancient sources. One of them is Porphyry who distinguishes between those Platonists who divided the soul into two or three parts, and Numenius who speaks of two souls.[57] Porphyry seems to classify both doctrines as interpretations of Plato's theory of the partite soul and rejects them invariably for reasons I will examine later.[58] Numenius' view, however, was not inspired by Plato's passages on the division of the soul such as *Republic* 4, but by the section of *Timaeus* on the creation of the human soul (35b–37c), which suggests that the soul's constitution is like that of the creator God (36d–e). Numenius is actually attested to have

[55] For Numenius' psychology I am largely indebted to Frede's exposition (1987*c*: 1070–4).

[56] Philoponus, *In de anima* 9. 35–8 (fr. 47) argues that Numenius distinguished also a soul for the plants (φυτικήν; fr. 47. 3), but we cannot judge the truth of this. If Numenius distinguished only two souls, then this may correspond to the distinction between two world-souls, the good, or rational, and the evil, or irrational, which, as the individual ones, neither coexist as two aspects of the same soul nor does the rational stem from the irrational. See fr. 52. 64–75 and Macrobius, *In somnium Scipionis* 1. 12. 5–7. Numenius' understanding of the world-soul is discussed by Deuse (1983: 68–73, 79–80); cf. Baltes (1975: 247–54).

[57] Ἄλλοι δέ, ὧν καὶ Νουμήνιος, οὐ τρία μέρη ψυχῆς μιᾶς ἢ δύο γε, τὸ λογικὸν καὶ τὸ ἄλογον, ἀλλὰ δύο ψυχὰς ἔχειν ἡμᾶς οἴονται, ὥσπερ καὶ ἄλλα, τὴν μὲν λογικὴν τὴν δὲ ἄλογον. (Others like Numenius maintained not that there are three or two parts of the soul, the rational and the irrational one, but that we have two souls, as is the case with other aspects, the rational and the irrational one; Porphyry *On the faculties of the soul* in Stob. 1. 350. 25–351. 4; fr. 44). Des Places (fr. 44) accepts Wachsmuth's conjecture and reads ὥσπερ καὶ ἄλλα, meaning 'other elements we have in two' (i.e. eyes, ears; similarly Dillon (1973: 376), while Smith (fr. 253) prefers the reading ὥσπερ καὶ ἄλλοι (which is what Zambon 2002: 216 also assumes). Yet ἄλλοι does not make sense here; rather, it blurs the distinction which Porphyry makes. For a discussion of the passage see Zambon (2002: 216–21).

[58] I examine Porphyry's view in detail in Ch. 7 (s. 6. 3).

argued that the soul does not differ from that of Gods (fr. 41. 15–16). Numenius' belief in the inherent rationality of the soul is confirmed by Porphyry's statement that Numenius talked in terms of an 'assenting faculty' (συγκαταθετικὴν δύναμιν; fr. 45. 1), that is a faculty which monitors all conscious action. The term συγκαταθετικὸς is Stoic and suggests that Numenius was inspired to some extent by the Stoic theory of soul,[59] but we must remember that this can also be found in Plato, and it reflects the Socratic conception of the soul, which the Stoics inherited.[60]

Numenius' view of the human soul becomes clearer in the testimonies of Iamblichus and Macrobius. The former argues that Numenius did not see the two souls as being linked but rather as being opposed to each other.[61] Iamblichus draws a line between the view of Numenius and that of Plutarch and Atticus who, however much they may distinguish the rational from the irrational part, still see them as bound together, and he seems to suggest that Numenius considered both immortal. Iamblichus adds that Numenius spoke of elements attached to the soul (ἔξωθεν προσφυόμεναι; fr. 43. 8),[62] a point elucidated in Macrobius' text (*In somnium Scipionis* 1. 12).

Macrobius describes the descent of the soul from the sky to the earth, from its disembodied state to its bodily entrance, a story basically inspired by the *Republic* (614b–618e) and the *Timaeus* (42a–e).[63] In the descent through the planetary spheres, the soul acquires several capacities necessary for its function in a body (*In somn. Scip.* 1. 12. 13–14).[64] It first acquires the capacity of theoretical thinking (*logistikon*) in the sphere of Saturn, then, in Jupiter's sphere, practical thinking (*praktikon*), spirit (*thymos*) in Mars, in Sun the ability to perceive (*aisthêtikon*) and imagine (*phantastikon*), in Venus the appetite (*epithymêtikon*), in Mercury the linguistic ability (*hermêneutikon*), and finally

[59] See LSJ s.v. *syngatathe-sis, -tikos*; cf. *SVF* i. 39, ii. 40, Aetius 4. 21. 1–4 (*SVF* ii. 836). See Long and Sedley (1987: i. 315–321, ii. 238).

[60] Celsus apparently shared the same view (Origen, *C. Celsum* 8. 49).

[61] Iamblichus, *De anima* apud Stobaeum 1. 374. 21–375. 1 (fr. 43 Des Places).

[62] Cf. *Timaeus* 42c6; *Phaedo* 82d; see Waszink (1965: 41).

[63] The descent of the soul through the planets was maintained also by Plutarch, *De facie* and Celsus (in Origen, *C. Celsum* 6. 21). See Frede (1994: 5211).

[64] It is controversial as to how much of Macrobius' text reflects Numenius' views. E. Leemans, *Studie over Wijsgeer Numenius van Apamea* (Brussells, 1937), test. 47 and Dodds (1960: 8) believe that the whole chapter (1. 12) goes back to Numenius, because it forms a continuous exposition and because the doctrines attested are characteristic of Numenius, while Des Places in his edn. follows Beutler (1940: 676) and prints only the section 1. 12. 1–4. It makes good sense to me that at least the part 1. 12. 5–7 also reflects Numenius' view on the descent of the soul, as Ley (1972) and Deuse (1983: 72–3) have suggested. The question is discussed extensively by Elferink (1968: 3–7) and Ley (1972) with contradicting conclusions.

in the moon the vegetative functions (*phytikon*). The fact that all these abilities, which include rational and irrational ones, are acquired suggests that they are incidental to the soul and that none of them determines its nature. In fact, they are said to be a burden on the soul (frs. 43. 7–9, 48), acquired only so that the soul can operate within the body. The soul, however, remains one and unchanging (fr. 42), an intellect whose essential function is intuitive thinking.[65]

This is a significantly different position from the one we find in Plutarch and may have entailed a different evaluation of Aristotle's view on the soul. For Numenius the soul primarily is that by which man thinks, not that by which man is alive, as it is for Aristotle but also for Plutarch. Apparently Numenius maintained that a thinking entity by definition is alive, and its kind of life should not be described in terms simply of living but in terms of thought, a view inspired by Plato (e.g. *Sophist* 248d–249a) that Atticus also takes (see Ch. 4, pp. 171–4).

Against this view, Aristotle's psychological doctrine appears to be mistaken in the following sense. For Numenius the fact that Aristotle defined the soul as the form of the living body suggests that Aristotle identified the soul with what Numenius calls 'elements attached to it'. According to Numenius, Aristotle's crucial mistake is that he did not consider the soul in its essence, that is, the intellect. That Aristotle in the *De anima* does consider the intellect to be only a faculty of the soul and not its essence, as Numenius holds, appears to confirm this. What is more, for Numenius such a position creates further problems, because if the intellect is just another faculty, there is nothing to account for the unity of the soul. This is a problem for somebody like Numenius who thinks that the unity of something must be accounted for by a transcendent entity.

It must be for such reasons that Numenius should not have considered Aristotle's doctrine in *NE* 10, which was highly valued by Plutarch, as being close in spirit to that of Plato. Numenius would not side with Plutarch also because he had reasons to disapprove of Aristotle's view of man's nature, according to which there is also an irrational part of the soul from which non-rational desires stem. As has been seen, for Numenius the soul is essentially reason and has only rational desires.

[65] There is a question as to what happens to the non-rational soul. Numenius accepts the idea expressed in *Republic* 10 and elsewhere (e.g. *Phaedrus* 248c–249d; *Laws* 904d–e, 906b) that the non-rational soul will have more lives after death (frs. 48–9) in which it will be rewarded or punished depending on its earthly life. Porphyry will follow Numenius on this. See Ch. 7, pp. 269, 292.

Atticus seems to follow Numenius against Aristotle in this respect and I defer further discussion for the next chapter.

Finally, I would like to add that such a position on the soul presumably entailed also an ethical doctrine according to which man, as an essentially rational being, achieves his end by living a life of intellectual contemplation, like God does and strives to become like God (*Theaet.* 176a–b). This is probable in view of three facts. The first is that Numenius identifies the first God with the Form of the Good, which suggests that he considers moral goodness as the only actual good and thus sufficient for happiness, a position that also Atticus advocates. The second is that, according to Numenius, man's soul does not differ from that of God in essence (frs. 31. 25–6, 41. 15–16). The third is that Plotinus, who also identifies man's true self with intellect,[66] takes the view that man's final end amounts to life of intellectual contemplation[67] and, as will be seen in Chapter 6, he criticizes Aristotle's doctrine of *eudaimonia*. If Numenius took a similar position, as may well be the case, he may have targeted views expressed in the Pythagorean ethical writings such as those attributed to Archytas, Euryphamus, or Metopus, which are largely inspired by Aristotle's ethics in that they claim Aristotle to have preserved Pythagorean ethical doctrines.

5. CONCLUSION

To conclude, let me emphasize what I said in the beginning of the chapter, namely that we actually know next to nothing about Numenius' attitude to Aristotle, not even if he had one. I have argued that Numenius does not show hostility to Aristotle, and does not even display much concern for his thought. The existing evidence, though, shows that Numenius did voice a warning to Platonists to the effect that Aristotle's philosophy is substantially different from that of Plato, and that any concession to his views on the assumption that he preserves Plato's doctrines can cause sedition and secession from Plato's actual philosophical spirit.

Since Numenius does not specify on what grounds Aristotle's philosophy is to be rejected, I tried to indicate several points on which Numenius might have disagreed with Aristotle. I argued that according

[66] Cf. Plato, *Republic* 589a. Plotinus argues that 'the perfect life, the true, real life is found in the intelligible nature' (*Enn.* 1. 4. 3. 33–5). See Ch. 6, s. 3, pp. 229–33.

[67] See *Enn.* 1. 4. 4–14, 1. 4. 16. 11–15, and Ch. 6, s. 3.

to Numenius' interpretation of Plato's ontology, which he considers to be essentially Pythagorean, there is a hierarchy of intelligible hypostases, in which the first God is the Form of the Good and the source of all substance. Given such a view, for Numenius the rejection of the transcendent Forms on the part of Aristotle would indicate that the latter is fundamentally mistaken both about the structure of reality as a whole and about the nature of God more especially. In this sense Aristotle appears to contradict Plato's metaphysics, which Numenius considered to be the most important part of Platonic philosophy. I also argued that Numenius might have considered Aristotle's views on psychology substantially different from what he took to be Plato's. This is because for Numenius the soul is essentially a transcendent, rational entity, which accounts for man's rational nature, while all living functions are simply attached to it, whereas for Aristotle the soul is an immanent entity which accounts for the functions of the living body. Finally, Numenius' view according to which the human soul is essentially an intellect may have entailed a position denying the relevance of Aristotle's external goods for achieving good life and would rather postulate as man's end a life of sole virtue and intellectual contemplation which is the ideal envisaged in Plato's *Phaedo* (64b–65d; 82c–83b) and *Theaetetus* (176a–b).

With his critical stance against Aristotle, Numenius appears to harden the line that Eudorus had initiated on the part of the Pythagoreans. He may have addressed Pythagoreans, such as the authors of several treatises influenced by Aristotelian doctrines, and also Platonists, such as Plutarch or even Antiochus, who had favoured Aristotle's views and sometimes relied on his work in order to reconstruct Plato. Several of Numenius' views will have a strong impact on later Platonists and will play a role in the subsequent discussion of Aristotle's philosophy. I have already referred to Plotinus' debt to Numenius' doctrine of the Forms and to Atticus' debt to Numenius' psychology. Besides, the view that Aristotle's God is not as sufficiently transcendent as Plato's is, championed by Numenius, will be adopted by later Platonists and Plotinus in particular. The same view may have played a role in the formation of the critical attitude of Christian Platonists like Origen and Eusebius toward Aristotle's philosophy, as they were inclined to identify Numenius' first God with the Christian God-Father.[68] Aristotle's theology would then appear as being at odds with both the Platonic and Christian conception of God.

[68] Edwards (1991*a*) has established some tentative connections between the Platonism of Justin Martyr and Numenius. If this is so, the appreciation of Numenius' thought, especially of his theology, was even stronger and more lasting among Christian Platonists than has been previously thought.

4

Atticus

1. ATTICUS' CRITICAL TREATISE

Atticus takes the same position as Numenius in maintaining that Aristotle's philosophy is in fundamental conflict with that of Plato and that the two are to be kept separate. Yet unlike Numenius, and indeed any of the ancient Platonists we know of, Atticus argues for his view extensively and in a strong polemical manner.[1] His basic claim is that Aristotle opposes Plato on all crucial philosophical issues, rejecting Plato's most important doctrines such as the immortality of the soul and the theory of Forms, and for this reason, he contends, Aristotle's work cannot possibly assist anyone (least of all Platonists) in understanding Plato's philosophy.

Atticus seems to be making also the stronger claim that no part of Aristotle's work, such as in logic or in natural philosophy, has philosophical value and that philosophers cannot possibly benefit from it in any way since it is either largely mistaken, as is the case with logic, or of purely scientific interest, as is the case with natural philosophy. There is no need to resort to Aristotle in the first place, Atticus contends, because Plato had already addressed all areas of philosophy sufficiently.

[1] We know almost nothing about Atticus himself. According to Eusebius' *Chronicle* his *floruit* was c. AD 176–80. This may be taken as an indication that Atticus occupied the chair of Platonic philosophy created by Marcus Aurelius in 176 (cf. Dillon 1977: 248), but no evidence confirms it. It has also been remarked that the name 'Atticus' may suggest 'an Athenian origin or a long period of residence in Athens' (Glucker 1978: 143–5) or an insistence on the Greekness of Plato's philosophy against those Pythagoreans like Numenius who argued for the derivation of Plato's philosophy from Pythagoras (Kalligas 2004*a*). References to Atticus' fragments are to the (unsatisfactory) edn. of É. Des Places, *Atticus Fragments* (Paris, 1977). As Baltes (1983) has shown, Des Places has left out several passages which should be connected with Atticus. On Atticus and his philosophy see Dillon (1977: 247–58); Moraux (1984: 564–82); Moreschini (1987), and especially Baltes (1983); on his interpretation of the *Timaeus* see Baltes (1976: 45–63) and on his psychology Deuse (1983: 51–61).

Atticus makes these claims in the excerpts which Eusebius preserves in the eleventh (fr.1 Des Places) and the fifteenth (frs. 2–9) book of his *Praeparatio Evangelica*.[2] We have good reasons to believe that Eusebius' excerpts, which are all we have from Atticus himself, come from the same treatise. Such reasons are the coherence of the existing fragments, the unity of their theme, and the consisting tenor of the discourse: with the exception of the first fragment, all the remaining ones strongly criticize Aristotle's philosophy in the same terms and style, and Eusebius quotes them all as evidence that Aristotle's philosophy is substantially different from Plato's and from Hebrew philosophy, which Plato, in his view, had anticipated (*PE* 15. 4–9, 12–13). The first fragment instead is fairly constructive, as it stresses Plato's exceptional role in the growth of philosophy. Yet it is closely connected with the rest, since it sets out the plan of the treatise, which is to show that Plato covered sufficiently well all areas of philosophy, that is, physics, ethics, and logic.

Eusebius introduces the first of the excerpts from Atticus with the following words:

> *Θήσω δὲ τὰ ἀρέσκοντα Πλάτωνι ἀπὸ τῶν τὰ αὐτοῦ πρεσβευόντων, ὧν Ἀττικὸς, διαφανὴς ἀνὴρ τῶν Πλατωνικῶν φιλοσόφων ὧδέ πῃ τὰ δοκοῦντα τῷ ἀνδρὶ διέξεισιν ἐν οἷς ἵσταται πρὸς τοὺς διὰ τῶν Ἀριστοτέλους τὰ Πλάτωνος ὑπισχνουμένους.* (*PE* 11. 1. 2)
>
> I will present the doctrines of Plato relying on his followers, one of whom is Atticus. He is an eminent Platonist who outlined Plato's doctrines in his work against those who promise to expound Plato's doctrines relying on Aristotle's writings.

Scholars have often taken the phrase *πρὸς τοὺς διὰ τῶν' Ἀριστοτέλους τὰ Πλάτωνος ὑπισχνουμένους* as the title of Atticus' treatise,[3] but most probably this is not so. Eusebius is usually very precise in his references; he gives the titles of the works he uses, specifying also the target of the work and the book from which he quotes.[4] The fact that the phrase in

[2] On the structure of Atticus' treatise and the order of the fragments see Mras (1936: 186–7); Des Places (1977: 8–9).

[3] See Mras (1936: 187–8); Des Places (1977: 8, 38); Baltes (1976: 50; 1983: 38); Moraux (1984: 564 n. 3); Gottschalk (1987: 1149).

[4] See how Eusebius introduces titles in the case of Numenius: ... *ἀπὸ τοῦ πρώτου Περὶ τἀγαθοῦ τάδε παραθήσομαι* (*PE* 9. 7. 1), ... *ἐν τῷ Περὶ τῶν Πλάτωνι ἀπορρήτων* (*PE* 13. 4. 4; cf. 14. 4). When he quotes from Plotinus, for instance, Eusebius specifies both the title of the work and its target: *Πλωτίνου, ἐκ τοῦ Περὶ ἀθανασίας ψυχῆς δευτέρου, πρὸς Ἀριστοτέλην ἐντελέχειαν τὴν ψυχὴν εἶναι φήσαντα* (*PE* 15. 10). (From Plotinus' second treatise on the immortality of the soul against Aristotle who maintained that the soul is the actuality of the body (= *Enn.* 4. 7)).

question does not present all these features suggests that it most probably is Eusebius' report of what Atticus' treatise was about, rather than its actual title, and represents his own understanding of its content and aim.

The question to ask now is what Eusebius' description suggests about the content of Atticus' treatise. There is also a question as to whether this description is correct, which can be addressed after we examine Atticus' argument as it can be reconstructed through his fragments. So let me start with the first one.

According to Eusebius, Atticus wrote his work to take a position (*ἵσταται*; cf. LSJ, s.v. sense B.2) against (*πρός*) certain people (*τοὺς ὑπισχνουμένους*). The verb *ὑπισχνοῦμαι* can mean 'promise' or 'profess' (LSJ, s.v.). It is used once more in the preserved fragments (fr. 2. 3–5) with the former meaning,[5] and is also used somewhat ironically in Plato for what the sophists 'professed' to do.[6] Crucial for understanding what the people addressed are criticized for are the phrases *τὰ Πλάτωνος*, *τὰ Ἀριστοτέλους*, which occur often in the preserved fragments, but which are quite ambiguous, as they can mean either 'the doctrines of Plato/ Aristotle' or the 'writings of Plato/Aristotle'. On closer inspection, Atticus appears to use the phrase *τὰ Πλάτωνος* in the former sense, while in the only instance that he uses the phrase *τὰ Ἀριστοτέλους*, he appears to use it rather in the latter.[7]

It seems that Atticus wants to preserve the ambiguity of these phrases, so that he can cover all various ways of using Aristotle as a guide to Plato, which had been widespread at his time. His fragments show that he addresses philosophers who used to treat Aristotle as a kind of back up for what they considered as Plato's doctrine or for understanding better a Platonic doctrine.[8] They could do this either by relying on

[5] *Τῆς γὰρ συμπάσης φιλοσοφίας κοινῇ γνώμῃ τῶν φιλοσοφησάντων τὴν ἀνθρωπίνην εὐδαιμονίαν ὑπισχνουμένης* ... (philosophers share the view that philosophy as a whole promises happiness to humans); fr. 2. 3–5 Des Places.

[6] *Prot.* 319a4; *Meno* 90d2, 91b3, 94c2–3; *Theaet.* 178e8; *Soph.* 232d2.

[7] The phrase *τὰ Πλάτωνος* occurs in frs. 5. 36, 38, 7. 9, 9. 29, *τὰ Ἀριστοτέλους* occurs in fr. 4. 49.

[8] e.g. *τίνα τρόπον* ... *ἄλλους* ... *ἐπιρρώσει ποτέ* [sc. on moral virtue] (fr. 2. 109–11); *ποθ' ἡμᾶς δι' αὐτῶν* [sc. Aristotle's divisions] *προσάξεις τῷ Πλάτωνι* (fr. 2. 125); *ἢ πῶς ἂν ἐφ' ἃ βούλεται Πλάτων παρακαλέσαι καὶ πιστώσαιτο τὰ εἰρημένα* (fr. 3. 30–1); *τίς ἡμῖν τῶν Περιπατητικῶν ταῦτα βεβαιοῖ* (on the world being imperishable; fr. 4. 42); *πόθεν ἐκ τῶν Ἀριστοτέλους λάβωμεν βοήθειαν* (fr. 4. 49); *τοσοῦτον ἀποδεῖ διὰ τούτων* [sc. through Aristotle's doctrines] *βοηθεῖν* (fr. 4. 57–8); *εἰς τὴν ἀπόδειξιν τοῦ τέσσαρας εἶναι τὰς πρώτας τῶν σωμάτων φύσεις* ... *οὐκ ἂν συντελοῖ τι ὁ Περιπατητικός*, (fr. 5. 15–18); *τὰ Πλάτωνος βεβαιούμενος*; (on the four elements; fr. 5. 36). *Τίς οὖν ἡ βοήθεια τῷ τὴν ψυχὴν ἀθάνατον εἶναι θέλοντι παρὰ τοῦ τὴν ψυχὴν ἀποκτιννύντος; τὶς δ' ἡ διδασκαλία τοῦ τρόπου τῆς κινήσεως, καθ' ὃν αὐτοκίνητον αὐτήν φαμεν* (fr. 7. 67–71).

Aristotle's reports about Plato in order to identify the latter's doctrines, or by considering Aristotle's own doctrines as being essentially Platonic. At any rate, Atticus addresses philosophers who were promising to teach Plato's doctrines to their students (and they actually did this) by relying, in one way or another, on Aristotle. Indeed, the fragments contain indications that those addressed philosophers were active in teaching philosophy.[9] The present tense of the verb ὑπισχνοῦμαι suggests that these philosophers were Atticus' contemporaries, or that they were practising such an approach to Plato's philosophy quite regularly, or both.

One question that naturally arises is who the criticized philosophers are. Are they Platonists, Peripatetics, or both? Scholars have been divided between those who have argued that these philosophers are Platonists and those who maintain that Atticus targeted mainly Peripatetics.[10] Eusebius' description suggests that the philosophers addressed shared two basic assumptions, that Platonic and Aristotelian philosophies are doctrinal systems, a feature which Atticus stresses,[11] and that they are at least partly in accord so that one can rely on Aristotle for accessing some of Plato's tenets. As has been seen so far, both Platonists and Peripatetics shared such assumptions, and I will argue below that we have reasons to think that Atticus criticized both. Yet Atticus must have meant primarily to criticize Platonists because only they would promise to teach Plato. As the cases of Antiochus and Plutarch have shown, Platonists used the works of Aristotle systematically in teaching and interpreting Plato, while for Peripatetics, like Aristocles, for instance, the teaching of Plato was rather incidental. Yet Atticus appears to be addressing a Peripatetic philosopher.

2. ATTICUS' ADVERSARY

In the first of his critical fragments (fr. 2), Atticus argues that from all those who contradict Plato, 'the Peripatetic' does it most strongly

[9] Cf. διδάσκειν (fr. 2. 7, 83), διδάσκαλοι (fr. 4. 112), διδασκαλία (fr. 7. 69–70).

[10] In favour of the view that Atticus addresses Platonists are Praechter (1922: 115); Merlan (1934: 264; 1967: 73), Donini (1974: 49–50), Des Places (1977: 5–9); Moraux (1984: 564 n. 3). The view that Atticus addresses mainly Peripatetics is maintained mainly by Dillon (1977: 248–9) and Baltes (1983: 38 n. 2).

[11] Cf. the occurences of the words δόγμα (frs. 2. 83, 113, 149, 4. 9, 60, 7. 10, 12, 25), δόξα (fr. 3. 99), δίδαγμα (fr. 2. 138), δοκεῖν (frs. 3. 99, 4. 17, 5. 37, 7. 35).

(fr. 2. 6–9),[12] and later on, in a direct address, he asks: 'tell us, Peripatetic (*ὦ Περιπατητικέ*) how can you teach these doctrines [sc. Plato's ethical doctrines], how can you guide to them the friends of Plato (*φιλοπλάτωνας*)' (fr. 2. 50–2).[13] The Peripatetic addressed is sometimes taken to be Aristotle,[14] but the following considerations suggest that this is quite unlikely.

First, quite generally Aristotle is hardly ever referred to as 'the Peripatetic'; this term is always used to refer to a follower of Aristotle's philosophy.[15] Secondly, Atticus addresses this Peripatetic in the second person throughout fragment two (fr. 2. 50–63, 96–9, 122–45), which must come from the first part of his treatise, arguing that his teaching of Aristotelian doctrines, such as the division of goods (fr. 2. 122–8, 132–4), the distinction between final and instrumental ends (fr. 2. 130–2), and the categories (fr. 2. 136–8), does not help the least in understanding Plato's ethical doctrine (*γνώμη*). It becomes fairly clear that Atticus addresses a follower of Aristotle, rather than Aristotle himself, when he distinguishes between the anonymous Peripatetic and the heads (*ἡγεμόνες*) of his school (fr. 2. 57–63).[16] Here Atticus must refer to Aristotle, whose ethical treatises he mentions in this connection (fr. 2. 63–5), but presumably also to Theophrastus. Later on in his treatise, Atticus refers again to the anonymous Peripatetic in order to argue that his teaching of the doctrine of aether, which Aristotle had maintained (fr. 5. 9–13), is useless for the Platonists (fr. 5. 15–18; cf. fr. 4. 42).

[12] *τοσοῦτον ἀποδέων ἐν τούτοις τοῦ διδάσκειν τι τῶν Πλάτωνος Περιπατητικὸς ὀφθήσεται ὥστε, πλειόνων ὄντων οἳ διαφέρονται Πλάτωνι, μάλιστ' ἐναντιούμενος αὐτὸς φανεῖται* (the Peripatetic will appear in the following to be so far from teaching any of the Platonic doctrines, that from all those who differ from Plato he contradicts him most strongly; Atticus fr. 2. 6–9 Des Places).

[13] *φράσον ἡμῖν, ὦ Περιπατητικέ, πῶς ἐκδιδάξεις ταῦτα; πῶς ὁδηγήσεις ἐπ' αὐτὰ τοὺς φιλοπλάτωνας*; (Atticus fr. 2. 50–2 Des Places).

[14] Moraux (1984: 562), for instance, who considers Atticus' fr. 2. 50–2 to be parallel to Nicostratos' address of Aristotle in the second person (apud Simplicium, *In Cat.* 368. 12–26).

[15] This is the result of a TLG search. See e.g. Plutarch, *Cat. Min.* 67. 3 and Strabo 14. 2. 19 who by 'Peripatetic' refer to a specific Peripatetic other than Aristotle (sc. Demetrius of Phaleron mentioned in *Cat. Min.* 65. 6, Aristo of Ceos in Strabo 14. 2. 19). Cf. Alexander, *In de sensu* 101. 15–23 on which see below.

[16] *Τὶς οὖν ἡ παρὰ σοῦ πρὸς ταῦτα τοῖς νέοις βοήθεια; καὶ πόθεν τίς ὁ τῆς ἀρετῆς συναγωνιστὴς λόγος; ἐκ ποίων γραμμάτων Ἀριστοτέλους; τίνος ἀπ' αὐτοῦ; . . . ἀλλὰ γὰρ οὔτ' ἔχεις εἰπεῖν οὔτ' ἂν ἐπιτρέψαι σοι τῶν ἡγεμόνων τῆς αἱρέσεως οὐδείς*. (How can you help the young understand these doctrines? And what would be the reasoning in favour of virtue? In what Aristotelian writings or of his successors? But you have nothing to say, neither would any of the heads of your school allow you; Atticus fr. 2. 57–63 Des Places).

If it is not Aristotle, as the above evidence shows, who can this Peripatetic be? Scholars have been divided on this. Mras suggested Alexander of Aphrodisias,[17] while Dillon rejected this on chronological grounds and suggested instead Aristocles of Messene.[18] The first thing to note is that each of the suggestions relies on a different assumption about what promising Plato's doctrines through those of Aristotle involves. Dillon assumes that this involves the belief that Plato's philosophy is in essential accord with that of Aristotle and presupposes a strong approval of Plato, which is attested for Aristocles,[19] while Mras assumes that such a move would involve only a limited approval of Plato's philosophy, such as that shown by Alexander. Alexander, as is known, does not hesitate to observe that Aristotle diverged from Plato's doctrines, and some times argues that Aristotle surpassed them so much that these are of mere historical interest.[20] However, he often outlines Plato's doctrines in his Aristotelian commentaries, especially in the one on *Metaphysics*, prompted by Aristotle's own references.[21] Particularly noteworthy are Alexander's quotations of Aristotle's reports from early works like the *On the Good* (frs. 2, 4, 5 Ross) and *On the Forms* (frs. 3, 4, 5 Ross) concerning Plato's views on the first principles and on the Forms.[22]

As I said above, Atticus does not exclude such a use of Aristotle. Quite the opposite. We must also bear in mind that Alexander contends that Aristotle's accounts of Plato's views are more objective than those of Platonists, which Alexander sometimes strongly disputes, as is the case with Taurus' interpretation of the *Timaeus*.[23] However, Alexander is unlikely to be Atticus' adversary, not so much on chronological grounds,[24] but rather because his profile is quite at odds with that

[17] See Mras (1936: 187). [18] Dillon (1977: 250).

[19] See Introduction, pp. 37–41.

[20] See for instance his argument on how obsolete is Plato's method of division compared with Aristotle's syllogism; Alexander *In An. Pr.* 333. 10–334. 14; cf. *In Top.* 540. 17–541. 6.

[21] Cf. *In de sensu* 11. 7–9, 33. 1–6 (both passages quote from the *Timaeus*); *In Soph. El.* 4. 6–7.

[22] For a discussion of the nature of Alexander's report of Aristotle's *Περὶ ἰδεῶν* see G. Fine, *On Ideas* (Oxford, 1993), 30–6, who also edits and translates Alexander's text.

[23] See Philoponus, *De aet. mundi* 212. 16–216. 23; Simplicius, *In de caelo* 297. 1–298. 20. On Alexander's criticism of Taurus' interpretation see Baltes (1976: 71–6) and Sharples (1987: 1178–9); cf. Dillon (1989: 59).

[24] Nothing precludes Alexander from being active in the last two decades of the 2nd c., when Atticus could still be writing. The only secure evidence for the dating of Alexander is the dedication of his *De fato* to the emperors Severus and Caracalla (i.e. 198–208). But we do not know at what age Alexander wrote this.

which Atticus seems to be addressing. As has long been suggested, in some parts of his work Alexander appears to be responding to Atticus' criticisms.[25] Quite conspicuously, he criticizes 'those who promise Plato's doctrines' (τοὺς τὰ Πλάτωνος ὑπισχνουμένους; *Quaest. et Solut.* 1. 2. 21) for claiming that Aristotle lacks a doctrine of divine providence, and sets out to explain what this is. Alexander appears to be responding to Atticus also when he speaks with a sneer of 'the friends of Plato' (φιλοπλάτωνας; *In Top.* 530. 12), whom Atticus quite notably mentions (fr. 2. 51). Alexander seems to allude to Atticus also on another occasion. Addressing fellow Peripatetics he comes to discuss doctrines which may appear strange to the layman, such as that of aether, arguing that Aristotle presents arguments for it (*In de sensu* 101. 11–102. 2). If someone, Alexander argues, addresses you saying 'Dear Peripatetic (ὦ Περιπατητικέ), Aristotle guides you to a strange doctrine by claiming that heavens consists of a fifth element, tell him that this appears strange because most people are prejudiced in favor of a different doctrine' (ibid. 101. 23–102. 2). Quite remarkably, Atticus uses the same form of address (fr. 2. 50). Another relevant piece of evidence is a fragment in which Alexander refutes a Stoic, who claims that Aristotle strongly opposed Plato's doctrines. Alexander argues that Aristotle, unlike the Stoics, agrees with Plato that God and the soul are incorporeal, yet Alexander does not deny the doctrinal difference between Aristotle and Plato, claiming rather that there is much more disagreement between the Stoics and Plato.[26] Such evidence suggests that Alexander was concerned to defend Peripatetic doctrines, and in doing that he was critical of Platonists, while Atticus addresses a Peripatetic who sees little difference between Platonic and Aristotelian philosophy and aims to teach Plato to 'the friends of Plato' (φιλοπλάτωνας).

Aristocles seems to be a more likely candidate, because he was such a friend of Plato and often portrayed Platonic and Aristotelian doctrines as being unified. The fact that Atticus highlights the difference between Platonic and Aristotelian philosophy from the standpoint of ethics

[25] His account on divine providence (*Quaestio* 2. 21) and his criticism of the incorruptibility of the world of the *Timaeus* (*Quaestio* 1. 19) were probably prompted by Atticus (frs. 3, 4 Des Places). See Merlan (1969: 90); Sharples (1987: 1212, 1216). Donini (1974: 49–50) has suggested that Alexander's views on the intellect were also prompted by Atticus' objections (fr. 7. 72–87).

[26] ὅτι δὲ πλείων ἢ κατὰ ταῦτα [sc. on God and soul] διαφωνία τοῖς ἀπὸ Στοᾶς ἢ Ἀριστοτέλει πρὸς Πλάτωνα, παντί που γνῶναι ῥάδιον (that the difference between the Stoics and Plato is greater on these matters [sc. on God and soul] than that between Aristotle and Plato is easy for almost everyone to know; Alexander fr. 2, Vitelli 1902: 93).

(cf. fr. 2. 27–8) also speaks for Aristocles as his target, because, as has been seen,[27] he was particularly concerned with ethics and maintained the accord of Platonic and Aristotelian ethical doctrines. Further, Aristocles presents Plato's philosophy (fr. 1 Heiland/Chiesara) in terms similar to those of Atticus (fr. 1), as was noticed by Eusebius who cites the one after the other.[28]

All that this evidence shows, however, is that Atticus addressed a Peripatetic close to Aristocles' philosophical profile, not him specifically. Atticus is actually likely to have deliberately refrained from specifying his adversary. Instead, he could have addressed an effigy representing the rival school.[29] In such a way Atticus would be criticizing a wide variety of positions. This is likely because, as I argued above, Atticus' criticisms are formulated so that they could apply to various philosophers who made different uses of Aristotle's work. In the name of a Peripatetic adversary Atticus could criticize different Peripatetics and Platonists who relied on Aristotle for understanding Plato's doctrines, either through Aristotle's references to them, or on the assumption that Aristotle recasts them in his own work in a more systematic way. Atticus also criticizes the use of Aristotle for those philosophical areas which Plato supposedly had not studied systematically, such as logic and natural philosophy. Yet he is much more concerned with the former than with the latter way of using Aristotle and in the extant fragments he argues primarily against this. To this argument I now pass.

3. ATTICUS' ARGUMENT AGAINST USING ARISTOTLE'S PHILOSOPHY AS A GUIDE TO THAT OF PLATO

Atticus repeatedly emphasizes that Aristotle is of no 'help' or 'use' in guiding one through Plato's philosophy, either as a source of Plato's views outside the dialogues or as an interpreter of Plato's tenets.[30]

[27] See above pp. 37–41.

[28] Eusebius cites Atticus (fr. 1 Des Places) in *PE* 11. 1. 2–2. 5 and Aristocles (fr. 1 Heiland/Chiesara) in *PE* 11. 2. 6–3. 9. On Aristocles' view on Plato see Introduction, s. 5, pp. 37–41. On Atticus' fr. 1 see below, s. 5, pp. 174–5.

[29] This has been suggested Kalligas (2004*a*: 50).

[30] Cf. e.g. *πόθεν ἐκ τῶν Ἀριστοτέλους λάβωμεν βοήθειαν* (fr. 4. 49); *τοσοῦτον ἀποδεῖ διὰ τούτων* [sc. through Aristotle's doctrines] *βοηθεῖν* (fr. 4. 57–8); *ὥστ' οὐδαμῇ χρήσιμος πρὸς τὰ τοῦ Πλάτωνος* (fr. 5. 37–8).

Atticus presents two basic reasons against using Aristotle as a guide to Plato's doctrines. The first is that there is no need to resort to Aristotle in the first place, since Plato specified his views (ἕκαστα ἠκρίβωσε; fr. 1. 35) in his dialogues. Atticus indeed appears to believe that Plato had made his views sufficiently clear in his work. This is suggested by the fact that he, like Numenius, specifies Plato's view on an issue by simply referring to, or citing from, a Platonic dialogue, without giving any other justification.[31] Atticus actually speaks as if it would be sufficient to contrast Aristotle's views with those of Plato so that any misinterpretations arising under the influence of Aristotle's doctrines are ruled out—in this way Atticus means to defend Plato's original views.

However, what Atticus takes to be Plato's view involves his personal interpretation for which he does not argue. One may think that this is a special feature of his polemical treatise, since Atticus himself admits that he is not concerned to show how Aristotle's doctrines are mistaken (fr. 2. 17–22), but rather to prove the extent of their difference from those of Plato. Yet it turns out that this feature characterized Atticus' approach more generally. Later generations of Platonists regarded him as being shortsighted as to what Plato's doctrines are, criticizing him for being focused on certain parts of Plato's work only,[32] and speaking of his attachment to the letter of Plato's texts.[33] This attitude partly accounts also for Atticus' superficial treatment of Aristotle's doctrines. In the case of Aristotle, however, there is another reason for this treatment, namely Atticus' conviction that Aristotle contradicted Plato systematically and in a spirit of opposition. This is what I take to be Atticus' second reason against using Aristotle as a guide to Plato, and the one which underlies his whole polemic against Aristotle.

A close look at his fragments shows that, according to Atticus, Aristotle's contradictions to Plato's doctrines are systematic in two senses. First, Aristotle did not simply happen to contradict Plato's philosophical doctrines but rather purposefully did so.[34] Second, Aristotle did not contradict Plato's doctrines in isolation, but rather built an entire doctrinal system opposite to that of Plato.

[31] Cf. frs. 3. 17–23, 3. 19–22, 4. 19–23, 4. 26–9, 4. 93, 7. 17–19, Des Places.

[32] Philoponus, *De aet. mundi* 606. 16–22; fr. 39 Des Places.

[33] Cf. Proclus, *In Timaeum* 3. 247. 12–15; fr. 14, ibid. 1. 381. 26–382. 12; fr. 23, Philoponus, *De aet. mundi* 6. 211. 1–18 and 13. 519. 22–5; frs. 38a–b, and Proclus, *In Tim.* 1. 284. 14.

[34] See frs. 5. 9–15, 54–5, 6. 45–8, 7. 31–4, 9. 14–16 Des Places.

Let me start from the latter, which I take it to be more significant. We first have to bear in mind that Atticus maintained that Plato's philosophy is a system in which all parts are connected as the parts of a living organism, which means that all doctrines are interdependent, so one cannot reject a doctrine without thus affecting the whole system.[35] Aristotle's contradiction of this or that Platonic doctrine could still be in a sense accidental, namely in the sense that Aristotle somehow misunderstood a Platonic view and his criticism or his diverged view arose from such a mistake, a point which Taurus and Porphyry, as we will see, sometimes make. Atticus strongly denies this, claiming that Aristotle's opposition to Platonic doctrines lies at a deeper level. If Aristotle contradicts Plato here and there, this is because he created a rival philosophical system from which such contradictions result. Atticus appears to believe that such a system arises from a conception of the world and the human nature different from that of Plato, and that it is this difference that the particular doctrinal differences manifest.[36]

Even stronger is Atticus' claim that Aristotle intended to construct a philosophical system independent from that of Plato, not only because of his different philosophical conception of the world, but also because of so base a motivation as Aristotle's contentious spirit (*φιλονικῶν ἐφιλονίκησε*; frs. 5. 15–30, 6. 72–3, 7. 37–9) and eristic nature (frs. 6. 83–4, 7. 87–9).[37] In support of his conclusions Atticus adduces the fact that Aristotle was the first to oppose Plato's philosophy, and that for some of his doctrines only Aristotle has done so (frs. 5. 18, 5. 29–30, 7.

[35] *ὅτι μὲν Πλάτων πρῶτος καὶ μάλιστα συναγείρας εἰς ἓν πάντα τὰ τῆς φιλοσοφίας μέρη τέως ἐσκεδασμένα καὶ διερριμμένα ὥσπερ τὰ τοῦ Πενθέως μέλη, καθάπερ εἶπέ τις, σῶμά τι καὶ ζῷον ὁλόκληρον ἀπέφηνε τὴν φιλοσοφίαν, δῆλα παντὶ λεγόμενα* (that Plato first and foremost brought together into one all parts of philosophy previously scattered and thrown away like Pentheus' limbs, as someone has said, and declared philosophy to be a certain body and a complete animal being, is obvious to everyone; Atticus fr. 1. 19–23). A very similar picture is given by Apuleius, *De Platone* 1. 187. Later on Atticus will claim that Plato's doctrines actually depend on one, that on the immortality of the soul (fr. 7. 25–8; text cited in n. 47 below); cf. fr. 9. 31–3, 49–50 on Plato's Forms.

[36] See below in this section and s. 4.

[37] Atticus presents Aristotle as being driven to taking positions only because these were opposite to those of Plato, as the following passages show: *ὁ δ' ἀντιτίθησι πανταχόθεν καταβάλλειν δεῖν ἡγούμενου τἀκείνου* (the other [sc. Aristotle] opposes himself in all possible ways believing that he has to refuse his views [sc. Plato's]; fr. 6. 83–4); *καὶ τὴν μὲν ψυχὴν τοῦ σώματος οὐκ ἀξίωσεν ἐκβαίνειν, ὅτι Πλάτωνι τοῦτ' ἤρεσε, τὸν δὲ νοῦν ἀπορρήγνυσθαι τῆς ψυχῆς ἠνάγκασεν, ὅτι ἀδύνατον ἔγνω Πλάτων τὸ τοιοῦτον* (and he [sc. Aristotle] maintained that the soul does not depart from the body, because this was Plato's doctrine [*Phaedo* 77d], but he postulated the separation of the intellect from the soul because Plato believed that this is impossible; fr. 7. 87–9).

28–31). Atticus indeed goes as far as to argue that Aristotle would have opposed even more Platonic doctrines, such as the circular motion of the universe, had he been able to (fr. 6. 45–8).

Quite crucial for presuming Aristotelian hostility to Plato was Atticus' assumption that Plato's philosophy represents the objective philosophical truth (fr. 1. 32–7). Only if this assumption is granted, can one's systematic opposition to Plato's philosophy then mean either incompetence, or else contentiousness and hostility to the truth. Whichever may be the case, the implication is that such views are not worth serious discussion. Atticus actually claims that hostility rather than incompetence was involved in the case of Aristotle. The reason is that this would probably appeal more to Platonists who tended to consider Aristotle's work as a source of Plato's doctrines despite his frequent criticism of them. Atticus' message is that Aristotle, hostile as he is to Plato, should be altogether distrusted.[38]

Atticus' conception of Aristotle's philosophy as being hostile to that of Plato entails a superficial treatment of Aristotle's views. Atticus offers a polemical response to Aristotle, which he presumably considered justified. Indeed, Atticus' work is full of the devices of polemic, such as rhetorical questions (e.g. frs. 2. 50–2, 57–8, 132, 4. 42, 7. 31), irony (e.g. fr. 5. 9–15), overstatements (e.g. frs. 7. 37–9, 9. 5–7), and also some distortion of the truth. A case of such distortion is Atticus' criticism of Aristotle's doctrine of divine providence. Atticus maintains that, in Aristotle's system, human affairs are not ruled by divine reason, but by a 'certain nature' (fr. 3. 81–5), and appears to suggest that Aristotle denies divine providence in the same strong way that Epicurus does, ruling out the existence of Gods altogether. Indeed, he argues that Aristotle was basically as atheist as Epicurus (fr. 3. 52–102). But even Eusebius, who cites Atticus with approval, admits that Aristotle's God exercises some providence, though one limited to the superlunary realm (*PE* 15. 5. 1), and refrains from saying that Aristotle is an atheist.[39]

Atticus' strong claim about Aristotle's position on divine providence is integrated with his argument that Aristotle's divergences from Plato

[38] I note, though, that Atticus also accuses Aristotle of incompetence (fr. 5. 54–61), but it is the criticism of Aristotle's hostility that looms large.

[39] Origen, *C. Celsum* 1. 21. 9–11, 2. 13. 25–8 also compares Epicurus with Aristotle on this but admits that Aristotle is less radical, as he denies only that God is provident of individuals (ibid. 3. 75. 22–4). Another case of distortion of the truth is Atticus' presentation of Aristotle's view of the soul, as he claims that Aristotle denied the existence of the soul, thus contradicting Plato more than any other (fr. 7. 28–34). On this see below pp. 166–7, 171–4.

are not to be seen in isolation, but as part of an extensive opposition between the two doctrinal systems, as extensive as that between Platonic and Epicurean philosophy. More specifically, Atticus' claim about Aristotle's view on divine providence is part of his argument about Aristotle's departure from Plato's ethics, and I will demostrate how presently. This turns out to be an important argument in his work, and perhaps his main thrust against Aristotle. Two pieces of evidence suggest this: first Atticus' polemic most probably opens up with his argument concerning ethics (fr. 2). This is probable in view of the fact that it is in this that we find several rhetorical devices and also a straightforward appeal to the anonymous Peripatetic, features which we would expect at the beginning of a polemical treatise. Secondly, Atticus' only reference to Aristotelian works is to his ethical ones, and this is remarkably informed, as he mentions all of them (fr. 2. 63–5). This indeed is the earliest mention of all of them ascribed to Aristotle, and the first occurrence of the titles *Nicomachean Ethics*, *Eudemean Ethics*, and *Magna Moralia*.[40]

Atticus' fragments offer some further clues regarding his strong concern for ethics. As with Hellenistic philosophers and Antiochus, Atticus assumes that the purpose of philosophy is to lead us to a good life. Such an assumption is suggested by the fact that, like Antiochus, he argues that different conceptions of man's final end result in entirely different philosophical systems.[41] If Aristotle's ethical position can be proved to be substantially different from that of Plato, then, in Atticus' view, the opposition between the philosophy of Aristotle and that of Plato would be established. It is such a rationale which accounts for Atticus' strong concern with ethics in his polemical treatise.

Atticus' argument for why Aristotle's ethics are of no use for the followers of Plato does not so much consist in stressing the difference between Aristotle's position and what he takes to be Plato's doctrine, as in showing what this difference actually involves. Atticus' central claim is that according to Plato virtue is the sole intrinsic good and thus

[40] See Dirlmeier (1958: 102–3); Gauthier and Jolif (1970: 84); and Moraux (1984: 565 n. 7). Before Atticus it is Cicero, *De fin.* 5. 12, or Piso, representing Antiochus, who refer to the *Nicomachean Ethics*, but not by its title and even express some doubt if this is to be attributed to Aristotle or to Nicomachus. This doubt is rather dispelled in what follows, since Piso speaks of Aristotle's ethical views.

[41] ἀνάγκη κατὰ τὴν διαφορὰν τοῦ τέλους καὶ τὴν ἐπὶ τοῦτ' ἄγουσαν φιλοσοφίαν διάφορον εἶναι (according to the difference in the final end the philosophy that leads to it also necessarily differs; Atticus fr. 2. 27–8 Des Places).

sufficient for achieving a good life,[42] a doctrine which, he argues, Aristotle abandoned for the view that the attainment of good life requires that virtue be supplemented by other goods such as health and beauty (fr. 2. 12–17, 74–7). As a result, Atticus argues, Aristotle's conception of good life (*eudaimonia*) is substantially different from that of Plato, and this he emphasizes throughout fragment two. What seems to be a scandal for Atticus is that the good life according to Aristotle is to some degree dependent on fortune and not entirely up to us (fr. 2. 97–108). He actually refers with contempt to Aristotle's example in the *Nicomachean Ethics* (1101^{a}6–8) according to which one cannot be blissful if one has fallen to Priamic misfortunes (fr. 2. 85–7). Here Atticus blurs the distinction between good and blissful life that Aristotle makes in this passage and equates the two.[43]

Nowhere does Atticus explain why virtue is sufficient for good life or why the latter must be up to us. Yet several passages suggest that, according to Atticus, Plato's ethics result from a metaphysical position which Aristotle rejected. Atticus appears to have had a particular conception of how Plato understood the goodness of life (*eudaimonia*). In his view, for one to reach *eudaimonia* it is necessary to participate in the Form of the Good (fr. 9. 20–4). If we want to make sense of this view, we should also take into account Atticus' later claim that man becomes *eudaimōn* through knowledge (fr. 9. 50–3), where clearly knowledge of the Forms is meant. This claim shows that according to Atticus virtue or goodness can be grasped rationally, and presumably this can be achieved if one has some knowledge of the good in order to recognize the circumstantial good, that is, the virtue a situation may require. It remains obscure how in Atticus' view one can achieve this knowledge of the good, given that the Form of the Good, according to *Republic* 509b, lies outside the realm of being. Yet, however this is, it becomes fairly clear that, according to Atticus the Form of the Good represents an objective standard of goodness really existent.

If we now recall that Atticus identified God with the Form of the Good of *Republic* 6 and the demiurge of the *Timaeus*,[44] we understand

[42] See fr. 2. 68–72 Des Places. Cf. e.g. *Gorgias* 507c, *Republic* 387d–e.

[43] *εὐδαιμονία, φησίν,* [sc. Aristotle] *ἐπὶ τροχὸν οὐκ ἀναβαίνει οὐδ' ὁ ταῖς πριαμικαῖς τύχαις συνεχόμενος δύναιτ' ἂν εὐδαίμων καὶ μακάριος εἶναι;* (good life, he says, does not mount on the wheel of fortune, neither can he who falls on priamic misfortunes be happy and blissful; Atticus fr. 2. 85–7). Cf. Plotinus' similar objection in *Enn.* 1. 4. 5. 5–9. See Ch. 6, s. 3.

[44] Porphyry in Proclus, *In Timaeum* 1. 305. 6–16 (fr. 12); cf. ibid. 1. 359. 22–7, 1. 393. 31–394. 12 (fr. 28), 1. 431. 19–20 (fr. 34. 4–5). On this doctrine of Atticus see below s. 4, pp. 169–70.

that for him this standard also has a divine status; it is the cause of all that exists, the cause of the goodness of the world, which God is concerned to maintain and promote. If this is so, we understand that the reason why Atticus was so much concerned to maximize Aristotle's difference from Plato on divine providence is because this doctrine bears significantly on ethics. Atticus argues that the upshot of Aristotle's view of the divine providence is that man is encouraged to give in to his desires and even to regard pleasure as a good, as Epicurus does (fr. 3. 43–8; fr. 3. 57–71). This is Atticus' rhetoric at work again, but his criticism of the Aristotelian conception of divine providence results from the assumption that Plato takes a view about providence similar to that of the Stoics (cf. fr. 8. 17–20 and *SVF* ii. 1029). And like the Stoics, Atticus believes that different conceptions of divine providence entail different conceptions of good life.

Now Atticus' claim that the knowledge of the Form of the Good leads us to good life suggests two things. First, it suggests some strong connection between virtue or goodness and the Form of the Good, such that virtue is derived from, or is determined by the latter, and secondly it suggests that man's goodness amounts to a link with the divine. To begin with the connection between virtue and the Form of the Good, in this view, specific virtues such as justice and honesty are part of virtue or goodness, such that one cannot really be virtuous or good unless one possesses all virtues. Atticus apparently upheld the mutual implication of virtues, which is defended by Socrates in the *Protagoras* (e.g. 349 b–d) and rests on the assumption that virtue is knowledge.[45] We thus gain some more insight as to what Atticus' claim that only virtue is intrinsically good means: in metaphysical terms it means that virtue is ontologically dependent on the Form of the Good, which entails that virtue qualifies as good strictly speaking, and in epistemological terms it means that virtue is grasped through knowledge of the Good.

From this standpoint Aristotle's rejection of the Forms and the Form of the Good most especially, means that Aristotle dismissed Plato's metaphysical and epistemological foundations of his ethics. This practically means for Atticus: (*a*) that since Aristotle does not know what the principle of good is, he is not in position to realize what good is, and this is why he does not realize that virtue is good in a sense that no other advantage is, and thus is sufficient for happiness; (*b*) that if we accept Aristotle's rejection of the Form of the Good, then virtue can neither be

[45] This view is also upheld by Plotinus. See Ch. 6, s. 3, pp. 229–33.

defined nor attained, and thus good life or happiness is impossible. Atticus' claim that Aristotle's rejection of the Forms leaves Plato's philosophy bare (fr. 9. 31–3) must mean that in Aristotle's view one cannot possibly realize what a good life consists in, let alone live it.

Let me return to Atticus' argument. As I mentioned above, his view that the Form of the Good leads us to good life also suggests that the attainment of good life requires man's link with the divine, and this belief, I have argued, is partly responsible for Atticus' critical evaluation of Aristotle. Yet there is more in this belief of Atticus. We have reasons to assume that for Atticus the highest good is assimilation to God, which must amount to both a virtuous life and also a life of intellectual contemplation. Although no explicit statement to such an effect survives on his part, this can be inferred first from Atticus' identification of God with the Form of the Good and his argument to the effect that *eudaimonia* requires knowledge of the Good, and secondly from his claim that Plato's aim was to attract the souls towards the divine, that is, he explains, towards the virtue and the good (fr. 2. 46–9).[46] Crucial in this regard is Atticus' interpretation of Plato's doctrine of the immortality of the soul. Atticus appears to have considered the human soul as being tightly connected with the world-soul which exercises providence over the world. Being inspired by *Laws* 10, he appears to suggest that human souls are fragments of or derivatives from the world-soul (frs. 7. 17–19, 8, 11), which confirms that Atticus reckoned the human soul to constitute man's link with the divine (cf. fr. 28. 10). This belief accounts for the importance he assigns to the doctrine of the immortality of the soul, which becomes clear when he argues that all other Platonic doctrines depend on this very doctrine, and whoever denies it overturns the entire philosophy of Plato (fr. 7. 10–15, 25–8),[47] that is basically his ethics, as in this context Atticus makes clear that Plato's ethics is based on this very doctrine.[48]

[46] Cf. *Republic* 533d.

[47] *Πάντων τῶν Πλάτωνος δογμάτων ἀτεχνῶς ἐξηρτημένων καὶ ἐκκρεμαμένων τῆς κατὰ τὴν ψυχὴν θειότητός τε καὶ ἀθανασίας, ὁ μὴ συγχωρῶν τοῦτο τὴν πᾶσαν ἀνατρέπει φιλοσοφίαν Πλάτωνος* (Since all Plato's doctrines depend on and follow from the doctrine of the divinity and immortality of the soul, the one who does not admit that overthrows Plato's entire philosophy; Atticus fr. 7. 25–8 Des Places).

[48] *σχεδὸν γὰρ τὸ συνέχον τὴν πᾶσαν τἀνδρὸς τοῦτ' ἔστιν* [sc. the immortality of the soul]. *Ἥ τε γὰρ τῶν ἠθικῶν δογμάτων ὑπόθεσις ἐπηκολούθησε τῇ τῆς ψυχῆς ἀθανασίᾳ, τὸ μέγα καὶ λαμπρὸν καὶ νεανικὸν τῆς ἀρετῆς διὰ τὸ τῆς ψυχῆς θεῖον σῶσαι δυνηθείσης* (for this is almost what holds together Plato's entire doctrine. The ethical doctrines followed the immortality of the soul, as the former could save the great, splendid, and youthful character of virtue due to the divine character of the soul; Atticus fr. 7. 10–15 Des Places).

Atticus does not explain his claim, but the ethical significance of the doctrine of the nature of the human soul must be along the following lines. First, man, by being virtuous, supports divine providence, as this contributes to the maintenance of the goodness of the world, a view very similar to the Stoic position. Second, Atticus holds that the soul, immortal as it is, is subject to rewards and penalties in afterlife, and this, which is the work of divine providence, in his view, is a strong motivation for man to become virtuous (fr. 3. 25–38). Third, man has to do justice to his divine nature and accordingly live a life of virtue and intellectual contemplation. That Atticus considered this as an ideal is supported by the fact that in his view the soul is reason (fr. 7. 60–3).[49] Accordingly Atticus must have maintained that virtue lies in the extirpation of all emotions (*apatheia*),[50] being inspired by the Socratic ethical ideal, which also inspired the Stoics in constructing their ethics, but also by Plato's mature dialogues like the *Phaedo* (64a–67e, 82c–83b).

From Atticus' point of view, then, Aristotle's rejection of the immortality of the soul is perceived as depriving the soul of its divine character and also as undermining any motivation for virtue (fr. 3. 33–8). Besides, Aristotle's doctrine amounts to denying the possibility of knowledge to the soul, that is knowledge of the Forms, since for Plato knowledge is partly recollection, which presupposes the soul's immortality (fr. 7. 19–25). For Atticus, Aristotle's doctrine of the soul matches the one of divine providence in that both presuppose the separation between the divine and the human realm and both undermine man's assimilation with the divine (fr. 3. 38–62), which for Atticus is also impaired by Aristotle's rejection of the Forms.

Atticus' placement of the ethical doctrines of Plato and Aristotle in the framework of metaphysics, instead of attempting to show which Plato's ethical doctrine is and how it compares with that of Aristotle, is dictated by his belief that only with such a perspective does their degree of difference become manifest. His argument would target Platonists like Plutarch and Taurus, or even Antiochus, depending on how far back he looks. There were also Pythagorean authors of ethical treatises

[49] Atticus identifies the soul with its deliberating part: *ὅταν γάρ ἴδωμεν τὸ σῶμα καὶ τὰς τούτου δυνάμεις καὶ ἐνθυμηθῶμεν δὲ τὰς τοιαύτας ἐνεργείας ὡς οὐ σώματος, δίδομεν εἶναί τι ἐν ἡμῖν ἕτερον τὸ βουλευόμενον, τοῦτο δ' εἶναι τὴν ψυχήν* (when we consider the body and its faculties and we think that such activities cannot come from the body, we admit that there is another element in us, the deliberating, and this is the soul; fr. 7. 60–3 Des Places).

[50] For the connection between *apatheia* and assimilation to God see Lilla (1971: 109–17).

who drew on both Platonic and Aristotelian ethics, with whom presumably already Numenius took issue, and Peripatetics, like Aristocles, Aspasius, and Adrastus, who held that in ethics Aristotle follows Plato.

Actually Atticus addresses a counterargument characteristic of some of these philosophers. He argues against the belief that Aristotle comes close to Plato by considering virtue as the most essential aspect of a good life (fr. 2. 77–82). This in his view does not diminish in the least the disparity between the two philosophers in ethics, because, as he argues, good life then becomes a matter of fortune (fr. 2. 87–108). Atticus cannot accept this argument because, as I have shown, he has a strong conception of goodness and divine providence.

It is characteristic of Atticus' polemical stance that, once he rejects Aristotle's conception of good life, he tries to demolish Aristotle's ethics altogether. He thus challenges the value of Aristotle's distinctions like that between dispositions and habits, or his divisions of goods into absolute and relative or into those of the soul, of the body, and the external ones, arguing that these hardly advance our understanding of Plato's ethical doctrines (fr. 2. 132–8). We know that these distinctions held some attraction to philosophers at the time. Division in general was used widely for definition,[51] and Diogenes Laertius' presentation of the so-called *divisiones Aristoteleae* as part of Plato's doctrine shows that some Platonists regarded Aristotle's divisions as expressing the spirit of Plato's divisions in the *Sophist* or the *Politicus* (DL 3. 80–109).

Atticus' argumentation contains some further hints to widespread views at his time that he probably meant to target. The stance of the Peripatetic author of the *De mundo*, for instance, who argued that Aristotle's God, though transcendent, exercises providence through a mediating power derived from him, is likely to be addressed (fr. 8. 21–5). Atticus holds that this divine power pertains to the world-soul which Aristotle rejects (fr. 8. 25–9). Relying on *Laws* 10 like Numenius, he argues that this soul permeates everything and accounts for the unity and the coherence of the world (fr. 8. 17–20). Atticus also criticizes those who maintained that Aristotle's doctrine of the immortal intellect is analogous to Plato's belief in the immortality of the soul, thus suggesting Aristotle's proximity to Plato (fr. 7. 72–5). This is a view we detected in Plutarch but we also find in Clement (*Strom.* 5. 13. 88. 1–2) and

[51] Alcinous *Didasc.* 157. 4–10; Clement *Strom.* 8. 17. 4–5; Galen, *PHP* 9. 5. 11–17; Seneca, *Epist.* 58. 8–16 are evidence of the wide use of division for definitions at the time; cf. Sextus *PH* 2. 211–13; ps-Galen, *Phil. Hist.* 14. See Mansfeld (1992: 78–92); Dillon (1993: 74).

Origen (*C. Celsum* 3. 80. 15–17),[52] who probably echo Platonist sources, and as will be seen is maintained later by Porphyry.

Atticus has a special argument for why this view is not compatible with that of Plato, which rests on his assumptions about what Plato's relevant doctrine is, that I will present below.[53] He addresses Platonists who might be tempted by Aristotle's apparent Platonism, arguing that loyalty to Plato crucially involves defending the doctrine of the immortality of the soul (fr. 7. 8–11, 55–7). To stress his point, Atticus goes as far as to suggest that Aristotle denied the existence of the soul (fr. 7. 37–9), a doctrine which, in his view, inspired Dicaearchus to eliminate the soul altogether from his ontology (fr. 7. 51–3).[54] For Atticus, apparently rejecting the view that the soul is a separable substance and thus immortal, as Aristotle did, amounts to denying the existence of the soul, and at any rate is a shameful doctrine because it denies man's resemblance of the divine (cf. fr. 7bis). Further, Atticus argues that Aristotle's doctrine of the intellect is least satisfactory as such and quite obscure, as it does not make clear where the intellect comes from and where it returns after man's death (fr. 7. 75–81).

Atticus' conviction that the immortality of the soul is an essential Platonic doctrine which was contradicted by Aristotle was quite widespread at the time. The example of Justin Martyr is worth mentioning in this regard. After he was convinced by his interlocutor that Plato's view on the immortality of the soul rested on mistaken argumentation, Justin left Platonism for the Christian faith (*Dialogue with Trypho* 4–5; cf. *Apologia* 2. 12–13). It is noticeable that his interlocutor argued against Plato's doctrine using recognizably Peripatetic arguments.[55]

Atticus also addresses Platonists who took seriously Aristotle's objections against Plato's cosmogony in the *Timaeus* and maintained that also according to Plato the world is uncreated (fr. 4. 14–35, 57–64).[56] This is a different case from the ones I have presented so far, since the

[52] Cf. Theodoretus, *Cur. aff gr.* 5. 28.

[53] See below, s. 4, pp. 171–4. For a commentary on Atticus fr. 7 Des Places see Dörrie-Baltes (2002), Baustein 152. 1, 173–7.

[54] This is suggested also by Simplicius, *In Cat.* 216. 12–13; fr. 8gW. On this see Gottschalk (1971: 184–5).

[55] Grant (1956: 247–8) points out similarities between the arguments used in this text and arguments used against the immortality of the soul maintained by Strato and other Peripatetics. On Justin's Platonism see Andersen (1952/3). Hippolytus, *Elenchus* 1. 20 (*DG*, p. 570) also argues that the only Platonic doctrine which Aristotle clearly opposes is that concerning the immortality of the soul.

[56] Cf. Proclus, *In Tim.* 1. 286. 18–20. Baltes (1983: 46) argued that here Proclus draws from Atticus. Des Places has left this out from his collection of fragments.

Platonists in question defended Plato against Aristotle's objections. But it is a relevant one because, as Atticus argues, they accepted Aristotle's belief that the world has to be uncreated, if it is to be everlasting, and came up with various interpretations of Plato's text in order to show Aristotle's objections are not valid (fr. 4. 57–64). Against them Atticus argues that Plato's text is hardly ambiguous in this regard, as it indicates that the creator's will is sufficient to account for the eternity of the world, and this in his view makes good sense, since God is powerful enough to prevent the corruption of the world and maintain it for ever (fr. 4. 35–95; cf. *Timaeus* 41a–b). Atticus considered Aristotle's objections as being part of his systematic opposition to Plato (and thus devoid of any philosophical value) and he regarded those Platonists who were seriously concerned with them as not being convinced of such an opposition.

4. METAPHYSICS AND PSYCHOLOGY

We have seen so far how Atticus argues that Aristotle contradicted Plato's philosophy systematically, and I have referred to particular doctrines on the basis of which Atticus illustrates this. Now I would like to show some of the fundamental assumptions that Atticus makes concerning Plato's metaphysics and psychology, which suggested to him that Aristotle had opposed Plato's philosophy systematically.

One important set of such assumptions concerns Plato's principles and especially the transcendent Forms. Atticus has a particular conception of Plato's intelligible realm which basically results from a literal interpretation of the *Timaeus*. On the basis of such an interpretation, Atticus, like other contemporary Platonists, distinguished three principles, God, matter, and Forms, all of which originally subsist (cf. e.g. *Timaeus* 28a–c, 30a, 39e, 52d).[57] Now, there is a set of questions regarding the specific character of these principles, how they operate, and how they relate to each other. Atticus follows the *Timaeus* in thinking that matter subsists only prior to creation while God and the Forms subsist also after it. Unlike matter, then, God and the Forms are eternal, intelligible beings which serve in maintaining the world.

[57] See frs. 23, 26 Des Places. Porphyry criticized Atticus on this. See Proclus, *In Tim.* 1. 305. 6–16, 391. 4–12 (fr. 26 Des Places), 431. 20–23. Cf. Deuse (1981: 238–45). I discuss Porphyry's views in Ch. 7 (s. 5. 3. 3).

Following the *Timaeus*, Atticus held that God uses the Forms as models (*paradeigmata*; fr. 9. 41) for the creation of all sensible entities (frs. 13, 28. 5–7). This happens when God imposes the Forms on pre-existing disordered matter (frs. 4. 19–23, 23, 26; cf. *Timaeus* 29a–30a, 50c–53c).[58] As a result, the nature of each entity is determined in accordance with its corresponding Form which remains unchanged, and this is why for Atticus the Forms are the principal and primary beings (fr. 9. 14–16, 32–4, 42–3).

Atticus' position as to how the Forms relate to God plays an important role in his evaluation of Aristotle's metaphysics. Let us first see what this position is. The existing evidence gives us a rather confusing picture. Porphyry tells us that according to Atticus the Forms subsist by themselves lying outside the divine intellect (Proclus, *In Tim.* 393. 31–394. 8; fr. 28).[59] Yet Atticus himself implies that the demiurgic intellect thinks of the Forms in order to create (fr. 9. 35–42). We also know from Porphyry that Atticus identified God, the demiurge of the *Timaeus*, with the Form of the Good (fr. 12). Finally, Syrianus tells us that according to Atticus and Plutarch the Forms subsist in the soul (*In Met.* 105. 36–8; fr. 40).[60]

How are we to reconcile these testimonies? To answer this, we first have to take into account that Atticus presumably distinguished between the divine intellect and the divine soul, as Plutarch had done. This is suggested by the fact that Atticus talked in terms of divine soul θεία ψυχή (fr. 35. 3)[61] and also by his claim that the divine intellect has a living power (δύναμις ἔμψυχος; fr. 8. 18). It is this divine soul which created the world and also the human soul from a rational and an irrational part (frs. 11, 35) and which maintains it and governs everything in it (fr. 8. 3–9). Atticus' distinction between a divine intellect and a divine soul does not seem to have been as sharp as that of Numenius and other Platonists who postulated distinct divine hypostases of intellect and soul.

[58] τὰ τοῦ θεοῦ νοήματα πρεσβύτερα τῶν πραγμάτων (God's thoughts pre-exist things fr. 9. 40). Atticus construed *Timaeus* 28a6–7 in a way that he postulated that God looks always at the Forms. See Baltes (1983: 39).

[59] αἱ ἰδέαι κεχωρισμέναι τοῦ νοῦ καθ' αὑτὰς ὑφεστήκασιν (the Forms subsist by themselves separated from the intellect; fr. 28. 2–3). The question whether the Forms exist independently was discussed in Plotinus' seminar (*V. Plot.* 20. 90–104). Plotinus for the most part maintained that the Forms exist in the demiurgic intellect, thus disagreeing with Longinus (Syrianus, *In Met.* 105. 25–6; Proclus, *In Tim.* 1. 322. 24–5). See Armstrong (1960: 394–7) and Dillon (1973: 317–18).

[60] On the testimony of Syrianus see Ch. 2, p. 102 n. 55, pp. 109–10.

[61] Cf. *Phaedrus* 246d, *Timaeus* 30b. See Baltes (1983: 49–51); Deuse (1983: 52–3).

Rather, as will be seen presently, he argued for the ontological proximity of soul and intellect, yet his motivation presumably was similar to theirs—that is, the wish to maintain the simplicity of the demiurgic intellect. Presumably Atticus did this by placing the Forms outside the divine intellect but in the divine soul; thus the Forms are not external to God but remain subordinated to him.[62]

If this is so, then Atticus may have identified only the divine intellect with the Form of the Good, but not the divine soul, because only the former is simple, while the latter, as it thinks of the Forms, is characterized by multiplicity. Atticus' divine intellect, then, corresponds to Numenius' first God, which is utterly simple, while the divine soul is like Numenius' second God. Atticus' divine intellect uses the Forms in order to create, presumably in a similar way that in Numenius the first God uses the second one, that is, as an instrument, while the existence of the Forms in the soul of the demiurge after the creation presumably serves the maintenance of the world, a function which in Numenius is carried out by his third God. Given his position on how God relates to the Forms, Atticus holds that it is God rather than the Forms that accounts for everything that exists (fr. 3. 16–18), hence God is the primary cause (frs. 9. 35–9, 13), and the Forms only secondary causes (παραίτια; fr. 9. 43).[63]

Such a position may have motivated Atticus to resist the view that Aristotle's God resembles Plato's in that it is an intellect where the Forms exist, a view upheld by Platonists like Ammonius Saccas and Alcinous (see next chapter, s. 5). For Atticus Aristotle's God is quite unlike Plato's in three important respects: (*a*) Plato's God is not only an intellect, as Aristotle's is, but rather an intellect with a soul; (*b*) Plato's God is identical with the Form of the Good, which Aristotle rejects, and this amounts to rejecting God's nature; (*c*) there is nothing to suggest that Aristotle's God thinks of the Forms; rather, Aristotle's rejection of Plato's transcendent Forms shows the opposite. In Atticus' view, then, all this means a major gap in metaphysics between Plato and Aristotle, because the latter appears to reject Plato's intelligible realm.

Yet this needs to be qualified. Atticus does not claim that Aristotle denies the existence of intelligible entities, but rather argues that he has a

[62] Atticus' position is succinctly presented by Dillon (1977: 254–5); Kenney (1991: 85–7); and Dörrie and Baltes (1998), Baustein 125 (fr. 9), 128. 2 (fr. 28), 217–26, 269–70.

[63] The term παραίτιον was used by the Stoics in connection with their doctrine of human responsibility and divine fate; see Plutarch, *De Stoic. rep.* 1041D2–4, 1049E1–4, 1050B6 (Chrysippus; *SVF* iii. 289, ii. 1125).

very mistaken picture about them and their order (fr. 9. 4–16). Atticus was certainly aware that Aristotle accepted a divine intellect which was pure actuality (fr. 7. 72–81), and he does refer to Aristotle's acceptance of immanent Forms (fr. 9. 7–15). However, Atticus, unlike Plutarch, does not consider this as evidence of Aristotle's proximity to Plato's doctrine.[64] This is because Atticus has a special understanding of immanent Forms. He considers them to constitute *dynameis* of the transcendent Forms.[65] In his view, immanent Forms are dependent on the transcendent ones in the sense that the former are not only modelled on the latter, as Plutarch argued; rather, Atticus believed that the transcendent Forms operate through the immanent Forms, so the latter *are* essentially the former. This view of the Forms recurs later in Plotinus who postulates a similar relationship between the hypostasis soul and individual souls. This view would be adopted also by Porphyry.[66] They argue that individual souls are *dynameis* of the hypostasis Soul, so the Soul *is* the individual souls in some strong sense.

The crucial thing for us is that to Atticus, given his view on immanent Forms, Aristotle appears to accept only derivative intelligible entities which are manifestations of the original and primary ones, and hence to maintain a considerably different conception of the intelligible realm. Since for Atticus this is the realm of real beings, he perceives Aristotle as having a very different view about the structure of reality. And this, in his view, has further consequences, such that Aristotle's causal explanations are different from Plato's and that Aristotle takes a considerably different position in ethics from that of Plato, as he does not appreciate the role of the Form of the Good.

Atticus' views on psychology are an integral part of his metaphysical view of the world and tightly connected with the above. Like Plutarch,

[64] Atticus' views about the Forms would be strongly at odds also with the position of Alexander of Aphrodisias on the matter. For Alexander the Forms are intelligible entities embodied in matter but actualized only through the activity of an intellect; the only immaterial, unchanging Form, is the divine intellect. See Alexander, *De anima* 87. 24–88. 16, 90. 2–11 and the comments of Donini (1974: 26–34) and Sharples (1987: 1199–1202).

[65] οὐ γὰρ δυνάμενος ἐννοῆσαι διότι τὰ μεγάλα καὶ θεῖα καὶ περιττὰ τῶν πραγμάτων παραπλησίου τινὸς δυνάμεως εἰς ἐπίγνωσιν δεῖται . . . ἀπέγνω τινὰς εἶναι ἰδίας φύσεις, οἵας Πλάτων ἔγνω . . . (Not being able [sc. Aristotle] to fathom that what is great, divine, and extraordinary, requires a similar power in order to become known . . . he denied the existence of particular natures which Plato recognized; fr. 9. 7–15.) Plotinus often takes the same view about the immanent Forms (cf. *Enn.* 3. 6. 17. 19–21, 5. 8. 2. 21–3).

[66] See below, Ch. 6, s. 2, pp. 218–29 and Ch. 7, s. 6. 2, pp. 267–98.

Atticus maintains that human soul comprises two parts, a rational and an irrational one, the latter of which results from the association of the soul with the body (frs. 10, 35). Yet, unlike Plutarch, Atticus believes that the entire soul essentially is rational (ὅλη ψυχή; fr. 11. 2; cf. fr. 36. 3). Apparently Atticus relies on the *Republic* where Socrates, talking of the conversion of the soul after being released from the cave, speaks of 'the whole soul' (ὅλη ψυχή; *Rep.* 518c8). As becomes clear in this context, Socrates speaks of the soul as the subject of cognition, and 'the whole soul' is the soul with all its cognitive powers, the rational soul. Atticus considers only this soul to be immortal (fr. 15), while the irrational part is not a soul strictly speaking but what he calls 'irrational life' (ἄλογος ζωή; fr. 15. 2).[67] Such a view clearly contrasts that of Plutarch who argued that the irrational part is a faculty of the soul (Tyrwitt's frs. pp. 60–71 Sandbach). It is, however, very close to Numenius' position that the human soul is a transcendent entity, an intellect, which is immortal, because it is not bodily dependent, while all other capacities of the soul are later attached to the soul. It may well be the case that Atticus was influenced by Numenius in forming his conception of the soul.

However this may be, though, the crucial point is that Atticus probably perceived Aristotle's view of the soul as the actuality of the living body to be mistaken on grounds similar to those I averred for Numenius; that is, he may have considered Aristotle as confusing what the soul essentially is with what is accidental in an ensouled body, that is, its living functions.[68] For Atticus the result of this confusion is that Aristotle regards the soul as being inseparable from the living body, as life is, which in his view is a 'shameful' doctrine (fr. 7bis), for reasons I have argued above.[69]

There is a further assumption which underlies Atticus' conception of the soul. Like Plutarch and Numenius, Atticus maintains that a rational principle, an intellect, somehow involves a soul, and hence life, because thinking presupposes life, so it requires a soul which is the principle of

[67] See Ch. 3, s. 4. Baltes (1983: 53–5) has perceptively suggested that ἄλογος ψυχή (fr. 11. 4–5) refers to the irrational world-soul, while ἄλογος ζωή refers to the irrational bodily bound human soul, as the contrast in fr. 15. 1–2 suggests. Cf. Iamblichus, *De anima* (ap. Stob. 1. 384. 19–28, 1. 375. 17).

[68] Aristotle defines the soul as a principle of life (ζωή); *De anima* 412^{a}13–22.

[69] See p. 167. This passage (*PE* 15. 11) is authored by Atticus and not Porphyry, as I argue in Ch. 7 s. 6. 2, pp. 297–8.

life (fr. 7. 82–7).[70] Yet this Platonist view about the connection between intellect and soul allows for variations.[71] Atticus seems to believe that the intellect cannot exist without a soul, because it is essentially associated with the soul, and in this sense the intellect is inseparable or even indistinguishable from the soul. And he actually argues that this is Plato's doctrine (fr. 7. 82–3). It is conspicuous that in our limited evidence Atticus always talks in terms of the soul, not of the intellect; the term *nous* occurs only in association with Aristotle's concept of intellect (fr. 7. 72–89) and once in a report by Proclus (*In Tim.* 3. 234. 9–18; fr. 15 Des Places), who compares the views of Alcinous and Atticus and may not be very precise.[72]

Atticus speaks always in terms of the soul because, unlike Plutarch who considered thinking as a distinctive activity performed specifically by the intellect, he does not distinguish thinking from other rational functions such as desiring and remembering. For him, even rational desires, like the desire to read literature or to go to the theatre, are like thinking. This is suggested by the fact that Atticus puts together as functions of the rational soul deliberation, thinking, memory, and reasoning (fr. 7. 42–5, cf. ibid. 58–60). Besides he, like Plutarch, apparently maintained that the soul contains the general *logoi* by means of which the soul is able to recollect, learn, and recognize things (fr. 7. 19–25). This seems to suggest that for him thinking is an activity like remembering or recognizing. One reason for this may be that thinking involves such functions or is a combination of them. But whatever his reasoning was, Atticus did not find it necessary to distinguish sharply between a separate faculty for thinking, that is intellect, and a rational soul, which accounts for the other rational psychological functions, as Plutarch did or even Numenius, but rather maintained that the rational soul involves the intellect. It is on the basis of such a view, I believe, that Atticus considers Aristotle's distinction between the intellect and the soul as being indicative of his difference from Plato's relevant doctrine (fr. 7. 82–90). If this is so, it turns out that Atticus found Aristotle's view of the intellect mistaken in the following two regards: first, because Aristotle distinguishes between the intellect and

[70] They rely for this view on *Timaeus* 30b, 46d–e; *Philebus* 30c; *Sophist* 248d–249a.

[71] We have to allow for variations not only in how one understands this, but also in how strongly one espouses this view. Noticeably Alcinous says that 'perhaps *nous* cannot exist without a soul' (*Didasc.* 170. 3–4). This may well stem from his concern to see Aristotle close to Plato's views. See Loenen (1956: 318).

[72] Cf. *In Tim.* 1. 381. 26–382. 12 (fr. 23 Des Places), where Proclus talks about Plutarch and Atticus together.

the soul, and second, because he distinguishes between thinking and other rational activities.

It must be on the basis of the above view about the nature of the soul as primarily rational that Atticus came to assume that God too, like all living entities, has a soul which does the thinking, that is, thinks the Forms in order to create. We can now understand better Atticus' theology and his reasons for his critical evaluation of Aristotle's God, and also why Plutarch, who had a view of the soul similar to that of Atticus, was eventually much more sympathetic to Aristotle's theology.

5. ATTICUS AGAINST USING ARISTOTLE'S PHILOSOPHY AS A SUPPLEMENT TO PLATO'S: NATURAL PHILOSOPHY AND LOGIC

As I mentioned earlier, Atticus appears to reject a more general way of exploring Aristotle's work, namely using it for aspects of philosophy which Plato allegedly had not studied, such as specific aspects of natural philosophy and especially logic. Peripatetics, like Alexander, argued that in those areas Aristotle had surpassed Plato's philosophy (see above, p. 155), and this to some extent was conceded by Platonists, like Plutarch, who as has been seen did make use of Aristotle's relevant works, sometimes justifying their practice by arguing that in them Aristotle develops doctrines prefigured in Plato (Ch. 3, ss. 2, 6). Atticus now claims that Aristotle's work in these areas has no value and maintains that it is unnecessary to resort to it. Let us see how he justifies this claim.

In the fragment which appears to be part of his prologue (fr. 1), Atticus argues that Plato appropriately brought together all parts of philosophy which had been scattered or treated in isolation, developed certain parts himself, such as ethics, and bound them all in such a way that philosophy was revealed in its entirety and organic unity (*ὁλόκληρος*; fr. 1. 19–23, 34). Atticus emphasizes that Plato brought philosophy to completion and perfection (*ἐντελὴς φιλοσοφία*; fr. 1. 8), as if it were a process of divine revelation (fr. 1. 34–5);[73] the effect of this

[73] *Τούτοις* [sc. the Presocratics] *δ' ἐπιγενόμενος Πλάτων, ἀνὴρ ἐκ φύσεως ἀρτιτελὴς καὶ πολὺ διενεγκών, οἷα καταπεμπτος ὡς ἀληθῶς ἐκ θεῶν, ἵν' ὁλόκληρος ὀφθῇ ἡ δι' αὐτοῦ φιλοσοφία.* (After them [sc. the Presocratics] came Plato, a man perfected by nature and much superior to them, really sent down by Gods so that he reveals philosophy in its entirety; Atticus fr. 1. 32–5 Des Places). On Atticus fr. 1 see Dörrie-Baltes (1994), Baustein 100, 379–85.

was that Plato did not leave anything of philosophical significance unspecified or unexamined (fr. 1. 35–7). Rather, Atticus maintains, Plato had covered, all branches of philosophy, physics, ethics, and logic, hence Platonists have Plato's doctrines to guide them in all these areas.[74]

As regards the study of nature, an area to which Aristotle, as is known, paid special attention, Atticus appears to suggest that there is no need to resort to Aristotle, not only because Plato covered it well enough, but also for two other reasons. The first is that Aristotle did not have a correct view about nature. Atticus tells us what his view on nature is: nature is identical with the world-soul (fr. 8. 1–11). Like Numenius, Atticus is inspired by *Laws* 10 where the soul is considered as the principle of all material entities (892a–c).

Atticus' second reason for rejecting Aristotle's philosophy of nature is that Aristotle's approach is not properly philosophical. Atticus has a certain understanding of what qualifies as a philosophical approach, according to which an inquiry qualifies if it is part of a comprehensive investigation of reality. For Atticus the Presocratics, for instance, were not philosophers strictly speaking, because, unlike Plato, they had not developed philosophy into a system (fr. 1. 24–32). Atticus' view that an approach to an issue qualifies as philosophical only when it is part of a systematic investigation into reality indicates that for him an account is properly philosophical only if it has a metaphysical dimension. And as in the case of Plutarch, with Atticus, too, such a metaphysical aspect involves reference to ultimate realities or causes. Indeed, he defines natural philosophy as 'aiming at the knowledge of the divine reality and the first causes' (fr. 1. 14–17). In Atticus' view, Aristotle's inquiries fall short of qualifying as philosophical, because he offers a low-level explanation of how nature works, relying on the testimony of sense (*αἴσθησις*) rather than on reason (fr. 6. 34–44; cf. fr. 7. 45–57). Aristotle, he argues, is good only at making observations about nature, on animals, plants, or stars, and hence qualifies as an 'explorer' or 'secretary of nature'[75] rather than a philosopher. For this reason, Atticus

[74] *'Επεὶ τοίνυν πάντων ἔφαμεν μετεῖναι τῷ Πλατωνικῷ καὶ φυσιολογοῦντι καὶ περὶ ἠθῶν λέγοντι καὶ διαλεγομένῳ, φέρε καθ' ἕκαστον ἐπισκεψώμεθα.* (Because we claim that the Platonist has share in all parts of philosophy, namely in natural philosophy, ethics, and dialectic, let us examine each of them; Atticus fr. 1. 37–40). The same division of philosophy is attributed to Plato in Alcinous *Didisc.* 153. 25–154. 9; cf. Cicero *Acad.* 1. 19.

[75] *τῆς φύσεως εὑρετής*; fr. 3. 82; *ὁ τῆςφύσεως . . . γραμματεύς*; fr. 7. 46–7 Des Places.

contends that Aristotle's views on nature should not be considered as proper philosophical doctrines,[76] and that only Plato qualifies as natural philosopher (*φυσιολογών*) strictly speaking,[77] because he alone had a sufficiently philosophical approach, as only he realized the ultimate causes of reality (fr. 9. 31–3, 40–5).

Atticus identifies the ultimate causes of reality with the transcendent Forms, and in his view, there is a strong sense in which one can neither understand the nature of a thing, nor have knowledge of anything, unless one understands the 'principal and primordial natures' of the Forms (fr. 9. 25–33). We have seen how, in his view, this is so as regards ethics, but he also applies it to natural philosophy (frs. 1. 14–17, 9. 25–33). Atticus does not explain how this is the case, but as I have said in the previous section, for Atticus the nature of everything that exists is determined by the corresponding Form which remains unchanging. What I want to stress here is that the reason why Atticus claims that Aristotle's views on nature do not count as philosophical doctrines is because he has certain expectations about the terms in which philosophical explanation is to be given, that is, in terms of the Forms, which he understands as being primarily transcendent. For Atticus the fact that Aristotle argues against the existence of such Forms, acknowledging only immanent ones, is evidence of his failure to go beyond the realm of observable entities. It is not the case then that Aristotle's work generally, and his philosophy of nature in particular, lacks a metaphysical dimension because of its exclusive focus on observation, but rather because it does not provide metaphysical explanations of a special kind, namely those given in terms of transcendent Forms, which Atticus favours.

If Aristotle's writings on nature fall outside the scope of philosophy, as Atticus claims, the implication is that philosophers do not need to use them, unless they have specific scientific interests. One may indeed want

[76] *μὴ συνιδὼν* [sc. Aristotle] *δ' ὅτι οὐ νομοθετεῖν δεῖ φυσιολογοῦντα, τὰ δὲ τῆς φύσεως ἐξιστορεῖν*. (failing to understand that the natural scientist should not issue laws but rather inquire into nature; fr. 5. 13–15). The verb *νομοθετεῖν* here has to be understood in the sense 'present doctrines'. As I argued in the Introduction p. 13, in late antiquity the philosopher was paralleled with the legislator (cf. DL 3. 51 and Des Places's n. 3 in his edn. of Atticus p. 56). Clement also contrasts Aristotle, the student of nature (*ὁ φυσικός*), with Plato, the 'philosopher' (*Stromata* 6. 16. 101. 4).

[77] The term never occurs in Plato. Aristotle uses it to refer to the inadequate investigation of natural causes by the Presocratics and Plato (*Met.* $988^{b}26$–8, *De anima* $406^{b}26$, $426^{a}20$; *NE* $1157^{a}7$). It seems that Atticus uses the term with a different sense when he applies it to Platonists (fr. 1. 38), and by implication to Plato, and with a more base one when he applies it to Aristotle (fr. 5. 14).

to pursue such interests and thus use Aristotle, but Atticus seems to think that such study would be of little value.[78] Atticus' criticism of Aristotle's natural philosophy seems to reflect a general rise of interest in science in the second century, which Aristotle's scientific works to some extent would satisfy. This interest was strong both among philosophers but also outside philosophical circles. Galen and Ptolemy, for instance, to mention two prominent cases, studied Aristotle's scientific works quite closely.[79] And as we saw in Chapter 2, Plutarch already had a first-hand knowledge of Aristotle's science and made frequent use of the relevant treatises.

Atticus' criticism of Aristotle's logic must have been prompted by an equally wide interest in it.[80] We learn that Atticus was critical of specific doctrines in the *Categories*, such as the one on homonymy (frs. 41–42b). The composition of any form of commentary on the *Categories* by such a hostile critic as Atticus is quite improbable, especially since his interest in the treatise appears to have been very limited.[81] The sole view of his which is reported by Porphyry (*In Cat.* 66. 34–67. 2; fr. 42b) and, probably through him, Simplicius (*In Cat.* 32. 19–21; fr. 42a), is that homonyms, that is, things which have a name in common but differ in definition (*Cat.* 1^{a}1–3), result from only one way, which is analogy, arguing that metaphor too is a kind of analogy. Porphyry and Simplicius agree that Atticus confuses metaphor and analogy.

More specifically, metaphor occurs if the same term designates different things when there are distinct words for each of them (the 'feet' of a mountain instead of its slopes), while homonymy occurs if there is only one term which designates one thing strictly speaking (foot) and another through an analogy ('foot' of a table; Porphyry, *In Cat.* 67.

[78] Atticus would call studies which Plato did not cultivate 'useless' (ἄχρηστον; fr. 1. 37). Proclus, *In Tim.* 1. 7. 6–13 maintains a similar view.

[79] For Galen's use of Aristotle see Moraux (1984: 687–808, esp. 729–35); Galen counted Aristotle among the 'ancients' together with Plato and Hippocrates (*De nat. fac.* 2. 116. 7–117. 10 Kühn).

[80] The rising interest in Aristotle's logic is reflected in Galen who wrote commentaries on several of Aristotle's logical works (see Appendix II), but also in the parody of a Peripatetic's knowledge of the categories in Lucian's *Demonax* 56.

[81] Des Places (1977: 81, 90) suggested that Atticus wrote a commentary; cf. M. Baltes, 'Attikos', *Der Neue Pauly*, (Stuttgart, 1997), 246. Praechter (1922: 131) argued that Atticus, following Nicostratus, wrote a critical monograph of the *Categories*. The evidence about Atticus' attitude to Aristotle makes both suggestions improbable. As I argue in Ch. 7, s. 9, pp. 324–6 a commentary presupposes approval of the main doctrine of the text and appreciation of its philosophical value.

15–31). Apparently Atticus argued that these two modes of speaking are essentially the same. We do not know more about his view in question, but, to judge from the scant attention it received by later commentators, it was probably of little significance. Atticus may also have argued that Aristotle's categories do not apply to the noetic world, but only to the sensible one.[82] Although the details again escape us, his overall aim apparently was to diminish the importance of the theory of categories, which had such a strong impact on contemporary philosophers including Platonists, as one can infer from his remark that the *Categories* are pedantic and do not advance in the least our understanding of Plato's philosophy.[83]

Atticus' remarks on the *Categories* and on a wide range of Aristotelian doctrines suggest that he had quite some familiarity with Aristotle's work. Scholars tend to deny this, arguing that doxography would be sufficient for Atticus' treatment of Aristotelian philosophy.[84] Yet the fact that Atticus treats Aristotle's philosophy in a superficial way for polemical purposes, and, as I argued, often misrepresents it, does not mean that he necessarily had a second-hand knowledge of Aristotle's work. As I have mentioned, he is the first to give a full reference to the three Aristotelian treatises on ethics (fr. 2. 63–5). Of course, this reference alone does not mean that Atticus had studied them closely.[85] But the reference serves a purpose; Atticus wants to present himself as being well-versed in Aristotle's work and more specifically his ethics, which he discusses at some length. His reference to Aristotle's example in *NE* 1101ª6–8 to the effect that one fallen in severe misfortunes cannot be blissful (fr. 2. 85–7) also suggests some direct knowledge of Aristotle's ethical works, and the same is suggested by his reference to Aristotle's view that it is not the soul but the man that moves, learns, or thinks (fr. 7. 45–51; cf. *De anima* 408ª34–ᵇ18).[86] We should also remember that Atticus addresses philosophers well acquainted with Aristotle's work. So if he wanted his

[82] Simplicius places Atticus next to Nicostratus (*In Cat.* 105. 36–8; fr. 41 Des Places), which may suggest that Atticus elaborated on Nicostratus' criticism rather than came up with one of his own.

[83] κἂν τὰς δέκα δὲ κατηγορίας παρὰ σοῦ μάθῃ τις δεκαχῇ διανέμειν τἀγαθόν, τί ταῦτα πρὸς τὴν Πλάτωνος γνώμην τὰ διδάγματα; (and even if one learns the ten categories from you in order to distinguish ten kinds of good, how this doctrine would help to understand Plato's view? Atticus fr. 2. 136–8 Des Places).

[84] e.g. Moraux (1984: 566–9, 580).

[85] Dirlmeier (1958: 103) and Moraux (1984: 566–8) have shown that Atticus most likely draws from Arius Didumus in his account on the division of goods (ap. Stob. 2. 134. 20–137. 12).

[86] Atticus not only renders Aristotle's thought well, but he does so in Aristotelian terms. As Moraux (1984: 577) notes: 'Damit gibt Atticus eine Lehre aus *De anima* ziemlich getreu wieder'. (Herewith Atticus renders a doctrine of Aristotle's *De anima* quite accurately.)

criticism to be credible, he must have had at least some direct knowledge of Aristotle.

6. TWO POSSIBLE PLATONIST TARGETS OF ATTICUS' CRITICISMS: TAURUS AND SEVERUS

So far it has emerged that Atticus criticizes both Platonists and Peripatetics who used Aristotle for accessing Plato's thought, and this evidence shows that Eusebius' description of Atticus' work is fitting. Atticus' targets in the Platonist camp must have included Platonists who ascribed to Plato Aristotle's doctrines, as did the Platonist author of the *De fato* attributed to Plutarch, who presented Aristotle's view on chance as Platonic (572A–B; *Physics* 197^{a}5–6) and who apparently also held that Aristotle's doctrine of divine providence is similar to Plato's,[87] or Apuleius who also credits Plato with Aristotelian doctrines.[88] Quite intriguing are the cases of two Platonists who lived around Atticus' time, and whose philosophical profiles fit with those of the Platonists addressed in his treatise.

The first of these Platonists is Taurus, who must have been a generation older than Atticus.[89] Like other Platonists of his age (e.g. Apuleius), Taurus employed Aristotle's works in his teaching of science and perhaps also of rhetoric in his school (Gellius, *NA* 19. 4–6, 20. 4). Taurus is attested to have regarded some of Aristotle's explanations as insufficient (*NA* 19. 6. 2–3), but, unlike Atticus, who rejects Aristotle's causal explanations altogether, he still found Aristotle's work of some

87 See *De fato* 572A–574A and Moraux (1984: 495–505).

88 Apuleius mixes Aristotelian with Platonic definitions of justice (*De Platone* 2. 229; *NE* 1130^{a}9–10) and ascribes to Plato Aristotle's theory of mixed constitution (*De Platone* 2. 260–1; *Politics* 1265b33–1266a30).

89 See Praechter (1934: 58); Dillon (1977: 248; 1988*a*); According to the testimony of Hieronymus (T2 Gioè; cf. Suda s.v. Taurus; T3 Gioè), Taurus' *floruit* must be *c.* AD 145. On Taurus see Praechter (1934); Dörrie (1973: 310–23) (pages in Dörrie 1976); Dillon (1977: 237–47); Lakmann (1995); and now Gioe (2002: 223–376). Dillon (1988*a*: 197) conjectures that Atticus' emphasis on Greek identity ('we Greeks'; fr. 4. 18) may have been meant to sound like a sneer at Taurus who came from Beirut and his Greek may not have been good enough. This is possible, especially if Atticus' name suggests correct use of Greek. Kalligas (2004*a*: 53) has argued that Atticus' emphasis on the Greek identity may be a reaction to Numenius and other Neopythagoreans who were insisting that Plato had followed alien wisdom. But Pythagoras was considered to be Greek, and Numenius' point was that his philosophy was in accord with, rather than drawn from other ancient wisdom. Yet Atticus may well have targeted Neopythagoreans who made use of Aristotle.

value, as also Plutarch had. Further, Taurus follows Antiochus and Plutarch in strongly criticizing the Stoic doctrine of *apatheia*, arguing that lack of emotions not only cannot be an ethical ideal but rather is a sign of insensibility (*analgêsia*; *NA* 1. 26. 10–11, 12. 5. 10).[90] Like them, Taurus maintains that for Plato moral virtue consists in the mean of an emotion (*NA* 1. 26, 12. 5. 5–10). His argument (*NA* 12. 5. 7–9) shows so much similarity with that of Antiochus (*De fin.* 5. 24–40) and of Plutarch (*De comm. not.* 1060C–E, 1069E–F.), that, despite the lack of firm evidence, we can reasonably infer that like them he considered Aristotle rather than the Stoics to be expressing Plato's view on moral psychology, on what virtue consists in, and on what good life amounts to.[91] And this is precisely what Atticus means to argue against.

One other issue on which Taurus appears to be in conflict with Atticus and quite inspired by Aristotle is his interpretation of Plato's cosmogony in the *Timaeus*. Taurus argues against the literal interpretation of cosmogony according to which this was an event which had taken place in the past. Like the early Academics, Taurus argues that Plato implies that the world is uncreated (ἀγενές),[92] that is, not generated, although it is said to be 'created' (*Timaeus* 27c5). He perhaps went so far as to alter the text to that effect.[93] In his view, Plato talked of the world as 'created' because he wanted to affirm that the world is governed by divine providence and for the sake of clarity, since most people understand causality in temporal terms, that is, the cause as being prior in time to its effect (Philoponus, *De aet. mundi* 187. 4–15). But according to Taurus this does mean that the creation has to be understood as temporal. 'Temporal' (κατὰ χρόνον, χρόνῳ) can mean: (*a*) taking place in time (weak sense), or (*b*) taking place in time and have some duration (strong sense). The weak sense covers cases when something comes about in time all at once, while the strong one refers to cases where this happens as the result of a process. According to the *Timaeus* (e.g. 37e3–4, 38b6, 38c2–6), time comes into being together

[90] Cf. Plutarch, *De virtute morali* 452D.

[91] On Taurus' ethics see Gioè (2002: 323–48). He presumably criticized the Stoic ontology in his Περὶ σωμάτων καὶ ἀσωμάτων (*Suda* s.v. Taurus), like Porphyry in *Sententia* 42. See Ch. 7, s. 8, pp. 308–10.

[92] Philoponus *De aet. mundi* 187. 12, 188. 23–4.

[93] *De aet. mundi* 186. 20–3. According to Philoponus, Taurus read εἰ γέγονεν εἰ καὶ ἀγενές ἐστιν (Philoponus and Burnet in OCT read ἢ καὶ ἀγενές ἐστιν); cf. Dillon (1989: 57–9); Baltes (1976: 113–14), though, argues that Taurus simply understood ἢ καὶ in a concessive sense. This is more plausible in view of what Philoponus says in *De aet. mundi* 191. 22–6.

with the world, so, it is implied, the world came about outside time. To resolve this Atticus, who held that the world came into being as a result of a process, postulated pre-cosmic time, apparently because he found it strange to have a process, which by definition involves time, taking place outside time.[94] In either of the above senses, though, 'temporal' basically means 'having a beginning'. This is the construal on which Aristotle founded his objections and which Taurus among others reject,[95] although nothing remains of Taurus' criticism of Aristotle.

To avoid the difficulties into which one may run through the literal interpretation of Plato's text, Taurus argues that nothing in Plato's text necessitates such a construal and that there is room for several interpretations which must be outlined and judged. In this Taurus was inspired by Aristotle's remark (*De caelo* 280^{b}1–6) that the term γενητὸς is a word with many senses (πολλαχῶς λεγόμενον) which Taurus tried to identify. As a verbal adjective in -τος it can take at most three senses, an actual sense and two potential ones, an active and a passive.[96] γενητός, though, can take one actual and only one potential sense. Yet these senses can be multiplied as a result of philosophical interpretations. Taurus listed the possible senses leaving the temporal one aside as improbable.[97] Let us look at his list.[98]

1. Something is said to be 'created' (γενητός) which in fact is not created (= generated). Rather, it belongs to the same genus as things created—for example, we describe something as 'visible', although it has not been seen, nor is now being seen, nor will ever be seen, like a body at the centre of earth (Philoponus, *De aet. mundi* 146. 8–13). A note is needed here before we go further. As Philoponus realized (ibid. 149. 27–150. 22), Taurus confuses two different uses of the adjective, the potential and the actual one, each of which supports

[94] In Proclus, *In Tim.* 1. 277. 3–7; fr. 19 Des Places. This view was encouraged by several temporal terms found in the dialogue (e.g. *Timaeus* 28b6–7, 39e3–5). Probably Plutarch did not postulate pre-cosmic time (*Plat. Q.* 1007c); thus Baltes (1976: 44); Sorabji (1983: 270) argues that he did.

[95] Cf. Alcinous, *Didasc.* 169. 32–5. Notably Alcinous avoids the term δημιουργεῖν in his theological chapters and uses κοσμεῖν to preclude any inferences of actual creation; see Loenen (1956: 303).

[96] This is the case with some middle verbs. For instance, μεμπτός(<μέμφεσθαι) can mean someone who is blamed, who can blame, or who can be blamed.

[97] Philoponus, *De aet. mundi* 145. 1–8.

[98] *De aet. mundi* 146. 2–147. 25; the section is translated and discussed by Dillon (1977: 242–4). For a detailed analysis, see Baltes (1976: 106–20), and Gioè (2002: 346–55).

different interpretations. Only what is actually created belongs to the genus of created entities, whereas what is potentially created does not. The analogy with 'visible' does not work, because something potentially visible does belong to the genus of visible entities.[99]

2. Something is called 'created' which in thought (ἐπινοίᾳ) is composite, even if it has not in fact been combined—for example, the middle note in music is a combination of the higher and the lower one, but not the result of an actual combination of these two. In the world there is a kind of combination which we can analyse only in theory into a primary substratum and something else, such as Forms, for example, by abstracting various qualities from the substratum (*De aet. mundi* 146. 14–20).
3. The world can also be 'created' as being always in becoming (*gignesthai*)—as Proteus is always in the process of changing shapes. In the case of the world, the earth and everything up to the moon is continuously changing forms, while the bodies above the moon change only their relative positions, as the dancer does (ibid. 146. 20–147. 5).
4. The world can also be said to be 'created' because its existence is dependent on an external source, i.e. God, who brought it into order—even if the world is eternal, just as the moon's light is created, as it comes from the sun, but always has come from the sun and since there never was a time when it first came to have light (ibid. 147. 5–9).

The actual and potential sense of γενητός are represented by senses 1 and 2 (if we set aside Taurus' confusion about sense 1), while the other two senses in the list result from a particular philosophical understanding of γίγνεσθαι. Sense 3 rests on the distinction between 'being' (εἶναι) and 'becoming' (γίγνεσθαι), highlighting the ontological difference between an immaterial substance which never changes and a material one which does. Sense 4 results from a certain construal of 'coming into being' according to which an entity does so if its being is accounted for by a certain principle external to it, for example, the world-soul is eternal (*Phaedrus* 245c–e), but also 'created' (*Timaeus* 34b–35a), that is, dependent on God.

[99] See Praechter (1934: 63–4) on this.

Taurus apparently preferred the third and fourth senses, which he considered to be complementary.[100] In his view, the world has an *ἀρχή* (*Timaeus* 28b6–7) only in the sense of principle or cause, and this is the demiurge. Regarding his preference for the third sense, Taurus referred to the *Timaeus* (28b8) where it is argued that the world 'has a body'; if the world is of corporeal nature, it is a composite, and as such it is always in the process of becoming (*gignesthai*), which means that it belongs to the realm of becoming.[101] The upshot of this is that according to Taurus it is not only God's will which prevents the world from perishing but also its nature. Yet Taurus' conception of God's nature is heavily influenced by the Aristotelian view that God essentially is pure actuality—all that God can do is being done (*Met.* 1071^{b}12–22). This is explicitly denied by Atticus who holds that God's will alone determines the nature of things and suffices for the preservation of the world.[102]

Quite noticeably, the senses of 'coming into being' which Taurus considered probable are in accordance with Aristotle's understanding of coming into being and perhaps influenced by his accounts in the *De caelo* or in the *De generatione*; they also are compatible with the claim that the universe is eternal. This seems to suggest that for Taurus there is no actual conflict between the Platonic and the Aristotelian position on the world's coming into being. In fact, Taurus defended Aristotle quite explicitly. He argued that Aristotle had rested his literal interpretation of cosmogony, on the basis of which he had then raised objections to Plato, on the work of the Pythagorean Timaeus Locrus rather than on the

100 *De aet. mundi* 147. 15–25. Similar is Alcinous' view in *Didasc.* 169. 32–5.

101 *De aet. mundi* 147. 21–4; cf. *Timaeus* 28a–29a. See Baltes (1976: 110–12).

102 Notice the very similar language of Taurus in Philoponus, *De aet. mundi* 189. 6–9 and Atticus fr. 4. 59–64, which strongly suggests in my view that Atticus probably targeted Taurus: ... *καθὸ μὲν οὖν γενητὸν αὐτόν* [sc. the world] *ὑποτίθεται, ἄφθαρτος ἔσται διὰ τὸν θεόν, καθὸ δὲ ἀγένητον οἶδεν, ἄφθαρτος ἔσται διὰ τὴν αὐτοῦ φύσιν, ὡς καὶ τἆλλα πάντα ἀγένητα ἄφθαρτα ἐστιν* (as far as he assumes the world to be created, this is imperishable due to God, but as far as he pronounces it uncreated, it is imperishable because of his own nature, as all other uncreated entities are imperishable; Taurus ap. Philoponum, *De aet. mundi*: 189. 6–9). *ὥστ᾽ ἤδη τινὰς καὶ τῶν περὶ Πλάτωνος ἐσπουδακότων φοβήσας οἷς εἶπεν* [sc. Aristotle] *ἀπέστησεν τοῦ δόγματος, οὐ δυνηθέντας συνιδεῖν ὅτι κατὰ μὲν τὴν αὐτῶν φύσιν τῶν πραγμάτων ἦν, ἄνευ θεοῦ βουλήσεως καὶ δυνάμεως, ἐπινοῆσαι οὔτε το γενόμενον ἄφθαρτον οὔτε τὸ μὴ φθαρησόμενον γενητόν* (he [sc. Aristotle] already intimidated some of Plato's disciples with his statements and made them shift from their doctrine, as they were not able to understand that it is impossible to conceive what is created imperishable or what is imperishable and yet created according to the nature of things without the divine will and power; Atticus fr. 4. 59–64 Des Places). See the comments of Gioè (2002: 360–1) about Taurus' interpretation as opposed to that of Atticus.

Timaeus (Philoponus, *De aet. mundi* 145. 15–20).[103] Apparently Taurus found it difficult to believe that Aristotle, given his sensitivity to the ambiguity of the term γενητός, had not examined the possibility that Plato may have meant it in a non-literal sense. Taurus' suggestion shows that he did not regard Aristotle as actually disagreeing with Plato on this issue, despite his objections in the *De caelo*, but rather as misunderstanding Plato. Presumably it was for this that he refrained from criticizing Aristotle's interpretation of the cosmogony of *Timaeus*.

We know though that Taurus did maintain that Aristotle had departed from Plato's doctrine in some issues, and outlined such doctrinal differences in a special treatise.[104] I have mentioned that he criticized Aristotle for not giving philosophically satisfying explanations. We also know that he found Aristotle's doctrine of aether at odds with what he took to be Plato's view (*De aet. mundi* 520. 13–521. 4). Further, his claim that Plato had talked of a created world because he had wished to affirm the strong role of providence in it (ibid. 187. 4–15) may contain a critical overtone concerning Aristotle's limited divine providence. Yet no explicit criticism by Taurus survives on the matter. Even if Taurus did criticize Aristotle, most probably he did not regard such differences as part of a systematic opposition to Plato on the part of Aristotle, as Atticus did.[105] This is suggested by the fact that Taurus did not hesitate to use Aristotle's work in general and in interpreting Plato in particular, and that he attributed Aristotle's criticism of the *Timaeus* to misunderstanding rather than doctrinal discord. The avoidance of criticizing Aristotle is a feature that we encountered in Antiochus and Plutarch, which suggests that Aristotle is considered as being part of Plato's school of thought. This is exactly the position Atticus rejects, denying the value of Aristotle's work as a whole and arguing against any use of Aristotle as a source of help for identifying or construing Plato's doctrines.

Atticus' argument against those who, under Aristotle's influence, claim that the world is actually 'uncreated' may have targeted also the

[103] Taurus argues that Theophrastus realized that perhaps Plato had chosen to speak of a cosmogony only for the sake of clarity and instruction (*De aet. mundi* 145. 20–4), but, he continues, eventually Theophrastus, like Aristotle, maintained that this is not the case (ibid. 188. 9–18).

[104] *Περὶ τῆς τῶν δογμάτων διαφορᾶς Πλάτωνος καὶ Ἀριστοτέλους* (*Suda*, s.v. Taurus).

[105] Praechter (1934: 61–5) is wrong to infer that Taurus was as critical as Atticus of Aristotle.

little known Platonist Severus, who must have been roughly Atticus' contemporary.[106] Severus' construal of the cosmogony in the *Timaeus* was also shaped by his consideration of Aristotle's objections against it. Like Plutarch and Atticus and indeed most Platonists, Severus gave credit to Plato's affirmation in the *Timaeus* that the world by its nature is subject to corruption but God's will holds it eternally together (Proclus, *In Tim.* 3. 211. 25–212. 11), but unlike them, Severus upheld that no cosmogony had actually taken place. Like Taurus, he argued that the 'created' character of the world has to be understood in the sense that as a sensible entity the world belongs to the realm of becoming and thus changes, for instance, it moves. If one looks at specific periods of time the world is moving, and in this sense is γενητός, but in the long term, he argues, the world remains eternally the same due to God's will (Proclus, *In Tim.* 1. 289. 6–13).[107]

As Proclus reports, Severus found inspiration for this interpretation in the central myth of the *Politicus* (270b–274e), according to which the universe sometimes evolves in its present direction and sometimes in the opposite one, as God, 'the captain of the universe' (272e3) sometimes guides it and sometimes lets it go. Thus Severus tried to show that there is a way in which the world in some sense is perishable and in some other eternal, which means that the 'created' character of the world does not necessarily amount to its being perishable. The implication of such a position seems to be that Aristotle's objections, though not philosophically empty,[108] do not actually apply to Plato. This in turn suggests that Severus' interpretation of the *Timaeus* may have been informed by Aristotle's criticisms, which, as I said, Atticus altogether rejected as philosophically worthless. Severus is likely to be Atticus' target if we consider that Atticus probably discarded the relevance of the *Politicus* to the understanding of the 'created' character of the world; he was criticized for focusing on the *Timaeus* and not paying any attention to

[106] Severus' chronology is uncertain, but all indications suggest that he lived in the 2nd half of the 2nd c. On Severus see Praechter (1923); Dillon (1977: 262–4); Lilla (1992: 68–71); and now Gioè (2002: 379–433) who offers a collection of his fragments with commentary.

[107] On the interpretation of this passage see Dörrie-Baltes (1998: Baustein 137. 9, 419–21). On Severus' interpretation of the *Timaeus* see also Baltes (1976: 102–5) and Gioè (2002: 406–12).

[108] Nevertheless contemporary Peripatetics argue against Severus' view (Proclus, *In Tim.* 3. 212. 10–11). Simplicius' criticism of Alexander gives us a picture of the overall argument (*In Phys.* 1122. 6–25).

the *Politicus* regarding the world's coming into being.[109] It may be in defence of this view that he stated that 'Plato maintained the creation of the world neither by using enigmas, nor for the sake of clarity' (fr. 4. 23–4).

Some other instances show that Severus took Aristotle's work into serious account in his study of Plato, which is what Atticus criticizes. A passage preserved by Proclus (*In Tim.* 1. 227. 13–17) suggests that Severus was familiar with Aristotle's *Categories* and used them in his interpretation of Plato's *Timaeus*. More specifically, Severus, commenting on the sentence of *Timaeus* 27d6–7 which he considered to be affirmative, put being and becoming under the same genus. The existing evidence does not allow certainty about the view that Severus held, or how he judged Aristotle's doctrine of the *Categories*.[110] Nevertheless his use of it in his interpretation of Plato is exactly what Atticus criticizes as being futile (fr. 2. 136–8).

Another instance is also telling of Severus' use of Aristotle in his study of Plato. Severus held a particular ontological view according to which there is a sequence of interconnected levels from the level of being, that is, of intelligible entities, to the level of becoming, that is, of sensible ones, with the mathematical units as the binding links. As a crucial link between the two realms Severus regarded the world-soul. Since according to the *Timaeus* (35a) the world-soul is created by a combination of divisible and indivisible substance, Platonists maintained that it is either a mathematical or a geometrical magnitude (cf. *Timaeus* 36b–d).[111] Severus, we know, took the latter view, perhaps because he believed

[109] *Οὐκ ἔδει τοὺς περὶ Ἀττικὸν εἰς τὰ ἐν Τιμαίῳ μόνα βλέπειν τὸν ἀπόντα ποτὲ παρόντα ποιοῦντα οὗ ἀπῆν, ἀλλὰ καὶ εἰς τὰ ἐν Πολιτικῷ τὸν παρόντα ποτὲ ἀπόντα ποιοῦντα ἐκείνου ᾧ παρῆν* (Atticus should not have considered only the *Timaeus* [53b] where God is absent one time and then present where he was absent before, but also consider the *Politicus* [273d–e] where God is present one time and then absent where he was present; Philoponus, *De aet. mundi* 606. 16–20; fr. 39 Des Places). Philoponus' point is that Atticus' argument shows not only that the world came into being but also that it will perish.

[110] Praechter (1923: 2007–8 and Dillon (1977: 262) have argued that Severus was a critic of the *Categories*. Gioè (1993: 50–3; 2002: 402–6) rightly distinguishes between Severus' possible critical attitude of the *Categories* and the anti-Aristotelianism of critics such as Nicostratus. See also Dörrie and Baltes (1996: Baustein 104. 8, 288–9).

[111] The issue was discussed already by Speusippus and Xenocrates but also the Pythagoreans; see Plutarch, *De an. procr.* 1012B–F, Numenius ap. Proclum, *In Tim.* 2. 153. 21–5 (fr. 39 Des Places), Aetius 4. 2. 3 (*DG* p. 386). See Jones (1916: 72–5); Cherniss (1945: 44–6); Elferink (1968: 9, 20); Dillon (1973: 330–1). Plutarch (*De an. proc.* 1013C–D) criticizes those Platonists for confusing the discourse about the substance of the soul with that about how the soul came into being (i.e. according to number, proposition, harmony).

that thus it becomes clear that the world-soul mediates between the intelligible and the sensible realm.[112] The crucial point for us is that, as Syrianus reports (*In Met.* 84. 23–7), Severus, like some others, formed his view on the role of the mathematical entities in Plato by relying on the authority of Aristotle.

Most probably Severus relied on the *De anima* 407^{a}2–19 where Aristotle discusses Plato's views in the *Timaeus* about the composition of the soul and criticized Plato for presenting the soul as being a spatial magnitude (μέγεθος) which is continuous and has parts. In this passage Aristotle also criticizes Plato for his conception of the cosmic soul on the grounds that such a description does not explain how the soul thinks, and suggests that Plato would have faired better had he described the soul as an intellect. For Severus, this passage presumably served as a source of help for understanding the complex section of Plato's *Timaeus* on the world-soul and especially for understanding what the world-soul is like, namely a geometrical magnitude. Those who argued that according to Plato the soul is a mathematical magnitude could rely instead on *De anima* 404^{b}16–30, where the powers of the soul are assimilated to numbers; understanding (*nous*) is identified with the number one, knowledge with two, opinion with three, perception with four. Aristotle prefaces this report of Plato's position with the remark that 'in similar manner the matter was also explained in "on philosophy" ' (ἐν τοῖς περὶ φιλοσοφίας; ibid. 404^{b}19). Critics since antiquity have wondered whether Aristotle here refers to his own work *On Philosophy* or to lectures of Plato on philosophy.[113] Several Platonists took the latter to be the case.[114] Yet, however one takes this reference, Aristotle clearly professes to present Plato's views. We do not know why Severus preferred to rely on this particular Aristotelian comment on the *Timaeus* and how, if at all, he justified his view about what the world-soul is like. But for us the important thing is that he most probably did rely on Aristotle, and in doing so Severus was following a widespread tendency.

112 In Proclus, *In Tim.* 2. 152. 24–32, 153. 15–25; cf. Iamblichus, *De anima* in Stob. 1. 363. 26–364. 5. On these passages see the commentary by Gioè (2002: 412–19).

113 See Ross (1951: 209–10; 1961: 177–9); Cherniss (1944: 14–15; 1945: 565–80). Iamblichus (*De anima* in Stob. 1. 364. 12–18) and Hicks (1907: 15, 222) take it to be a reference to Plato's lectures; Themistius, *In de an.* 11. 18, Philoponus, *In de an.* 75. 34–6 (cf. Simplicius, *In de an.* 28. 6–8), and Cherniss to Aristotle's treatise.

114 Already Crantor probably relied on this passage (Plutarch, *De an. procr.* 1012F–1013A.) and later Iamblichus (*De anima* in Stob. 1. 364. 12–18); see Praechter (1923: 2009); Dillon (1973: 330).

Severus appears to have found also Aristotle's work in psychology useful for interpreting Plato's relevant doctrine. In the only fragment from his treatise *On the soul*, which Eusebius preserves (*PE* 13. 17. 1–7), he argues against the view that human soul consists of a mixture of an unaffected or immortal part and a part subject to affection, that is, mortal, which accounts for the affections of the living body.[115] If the soul is composite, Severus argues, it would be subject to dissolution and thus mortal, like all composites, especially those which consist of contraries, as the soul is supposed to (ibid. 13. 17. 1–3). He then suggests that Plato's division of soul into parts, as appears in the *Timaeus*, for instance, was a concession to a popular view (ibid. 13. 17. 5–6). Being inspired by the *Phaedo* (80a–b), Severus rather maintains that the soul is simple and incorporeal and as such not subject to affections; however, though simple (*PE* 13.17. 4), the soul in his view is a cluster of faculties (δυνάμεις) which enable us to perform a variety of activities (ibid. 13. 17. 6). He thus rejects both the dualist and the materialist view of the soul, but unfortunately his argument does not survive.

Severus appears to have been inspired by Aristotle's *De anima*, which speaks about the soul in terms of faculties. He probably considered this doctrine as reflecting Plato's position on the soul, as several of his contemporaries did.[116] As in the case with the interpretation of the *Timaeus*, Severus may have been motivated to take such a position by Aristotle's criticisms of Plato's partition of the soul in *De anima* $432^a23–^b8$, $433^b1–6$. He tried first to save Plato by arguing that his actual doctrine is preserved in the *Phaedo*, where the soul is presented as simple and unaffected (79b), and secondly to make Plato's doctrine philosophically more credible.[117] If we now compare Severus with Atticus, we must recall that the latter criticized specifically views on the soul which had been inspired by Aristotle (fr. 7), while he himself took a strongly dualist position on the matter (frs. 10, 11, 15).

[115] Severus' views on the soul are discussed by Merlan (1960: 19–24); Deuse (1983: 104–8); and Gioè (2002: 425–33).

[116] See e.g. *De anima* 413^b25, $414^a29–34$ $416^a19–20$, $433^a31–^b3$. Aristotle's conception of the soul as a unity with multiple faculties was considered Platonic by Plutarch (see Ch. 2, pp. 112–13) and Porphyry (*On the faculties of the soul* in Stob. 1. 350. 8–354. 18; fr. 253 Smith—see Ch. 7, s. 6.3, pp. 298–301). It was found attractive by Tertullian (*De anima* 14. 3, p. 18 Waszink); Galen (*Meth. Med.* 10. 635. 6–10 Kühn); the Platonist Democritus (in Iamblichus, *De anima* in Stob. 1. 370. 1–2); Longinus (in Porphyry, *On the faculties of the soul* in Stob. 1. 351. 14–19; fr. 253. 37–42 Smith).

[117] Severus appears to think of the soul in terms of faculties also in a fragment preserved by Proclus, *In Tim.* 1. 255. 3–9.

On the whole Severus, like Taurus, did not hesitate to rely on Aristotle's work when he thought either that Aristotle preserves Plato's doctrine, even amidst criticism, or maintains it. This is particularly remarkable in view of the fact that for the most part Severus appears to have disagreed with Aristotle. Even if Severus was not one of Atticus' targets, as I think he was, we get an idea about the kind of Platonists that Atticus must have addressed.

7. CONCLUSIONS

To conclude: Atticus writes with the aim of castigating the widespread use of Aristotle's work by Platonists and Peripatetics, who tended to use Aristotle as a guide to Plato's philosophy on the assumption that Aristotle preserves Plato's doctrines and/or often also follows them. Atticus argues that Aristotle opposed Plato's philosophy systematically and no doctrine of his can be of help for understanding Plato, or for doing philosophy in general. He holds such a view because, like Numenius, he construes Plato's philosophy as a system based on the metaphysics of the transcendent Forms which determine all entities including ethical values, and considers immanent Forms derivative from them. Also crucial for the evaluation of Aristotle's doctrine is his tendency to rely on Stoicism for the reconstruction of Plato's doctrines, as is the case with his view on the divine providence or with his view that the soul is essentially rational and yet a separable substance (against the Stoics). For Atticus, Aristotle's difference on the Forms, the providence, and the nature of the soul entails a substantially different position in ethics. Since for Atticus ethics is the purpose of all philosophy, Aristotle's divergence from Plato in this is taken as indicative of the fundamental conflict between Aristotle and Plato. This in turn suggests to Atticus that Aristotle's position deserves polemic rather that philosophical refutation, and this is precisely what Atticus offers in his treatise. His abundance of rhetoric and polemical devices such as the instances in which he shows prejudice against Aristotle establish the polemical character of his work. As we have seen, he maintains that Aristotle denied the existence of a soul, that he was an atheist, and that he ruled out divine providence.

Contemporary Peripatetics, such as the Anonymous in *NE* (127. 3–8, 248. 15–29; fr. 43 Des Places) and especially Alexander reacted to Atticus (see above p. 156). His works were studied in Plotinus' seminar

(*V. Plot.* 14. 12), but Platonists like Porphyry and Proclus were often critical of his views and exegetical methods.[118] A critical evaluation of Atticus was probably first launched by Ammonius Saccas, to whom I now turn.

[118] Porphyry argued against Atticus' interpretation of the *Timaeus*, but also against his view concerning the relation between God and the Forms. See Baltes (1976: 44–5); Deuse (1983: 51).

5

Ammonius Saccas

1. INTRODUCTION

Ammonius Saccas (*fl.* early third century), Plotinus' acclaimed teacher, is a notoriously shadowy figure and given the state of the relevant evidence he is bound to remain so.[1] One of the few things we know about him is that he held the view that the philosophy of Aristotle is in agreement with that of Plato on most essential philosophical issues. We are also told that this view distinguished him from all his contemporaries and that it was transmitted to his students, Plotinus, Longinus, the pagan Origen, and perhaps also his Christian namesake, being the characteristic of his school of thought.[2] All this suggests that this view was one of Ammonius' central doctrines. Yet the value of the evidence for this view has been questioned in various ways. Since my discussion of Ammonius largely relies on this evidence, I will start out by arguing that it deserves to be taken seriously.

2. THE EVIDENCE ABOUT AMMONIUS' THESIS

The evidence that Ammonius held such a view comes from the *Bibliotheca* of Patriarch Photius (ninth century AD), who reports on the

1 Ammonius was active at least until Plotinus left his seminar at 242/3. The bibliography on Ammonius is rich, but it must be used with caution because it contains too much speculation; see mainly Dörrie (1955) = (1976*b*: 324–60); Theiler (1966*a*); Schwyzer (1983); Baltes (1985); and Schroeder (1987).

2 It has been seriously disputed that the Christian Origen was a disciple of Ammonius Saccas. Edwards (1993), taking over from Dörrie (1955), argues that he was rather the pupil of the Peripatetic Ammonius (*V. Plot.* 20. 49). It is possible that Origen was tutored by a different Ammonius but unlikely that this was the Peripatetic one, given Origen's Platonism and his contempt for Aristotle's philosophy. For an argument in favour of one Ammonius teacher of both Origens see Schroeder (1987: 502–9). Yet, nothing in my argument depends on this issue. For the rest of Ammonius' students, we have the testimony of *V. Plot.* 3. 24–30 and 20. 36–8 (for Longinus); see Kalligas (1991: 96–9, 158–60) and Fowden (1977: 365 n. 26).

treatise *On Providence* by the Platonist Hierocles (written *c.*412).[3] Photius' report appears in two distinct accounts, codex 214 and codex 251. At the end of his first account (cod. 214), Photius quotes the table of contents of Hierocles' book. According to this table, in his sixth book Hierocles elaborates on what appears to be Ammonius' conviction, which Hierocles himself espouses, namely that there is a fundamental agreement between the philosophy of Plato and that of Aristotle, while in the seventh and final book Hierocles discusses the continuation of Ammonius' intellectual tradition by his students and later eminent Platonists (cod. 214, 173a18–40). Photius' report of Hierocles' table of contents turns out to be largely a verbatim excerpt from Hierocles' work, and as such it is of particular value.[4] It runs as follows:

> In the sixth book Hierocles takes up all philosophers after Plato until Ammonius of Alexandria, whose most illustrious disciples are Plotinus and Origen, and considers Aristotle to be the most important among them. He takes as being in accord (*ὁμοδοξία*) with Plato's judgement all philosophers after Plato and up to those just mentioned who made a name for their wisdom. Yet he considers to be unworthy and harmful those who tried to break the accord between Plato and Aristotle. Although they acknowledged Plato as their teacher, they considerably corrupted (*νοθεῦσαι*) Plato's works, and the same happened with the writings of Aristotle at the hand of those who claimed to belong to his own school. And they contrived all this with no other purpose, but in order to make the Stagirite be in conflict with the son of Aristo. The seventh book examines a new subject; it focuses on the school of the above mentioned Ammonius. Plotinus, Origen, Porphyry and Iamblichus and their successors, who, as he [i.e. Hierocles] says, are of the same divine lineage, and up to Plutarch of Athens, whom he acknowledges as his teacher and to whom he ascribes similar doctrines, all are in harmony with Plato's purified philosophy. (*Bibl.* cod. 214, 173a18–40) [testimony I]

Unfortunately Photius does not excerpt anything from books 6 and 7 of Hierocles' work, where Ammonius' position regarding the relationship between Platonic and Aristotelian philosophies was outlined. Yet in his report in codex 251 Photius preserves a fragment of Hierocles which appears to summarize Ammonius' position and contains several

[3] There has been a significant growth in the literature on Hierocles, as scholars have taken interest in Hierocles' non-Plotinian Platonism. See the old important studies by Elter (1910) and Praechter (1913), and more recently Kobusch (1976); I. Hadot (1978); O'Meara (1989: 109–18); Aujoulat (1986); Schibli (2002). On the scope and content of Hierocles' *On Providence* see Schibli (2002: 21–31).

[4] This has been argued by Elter (1910); Schwyzer (1983: 40) summarizes well Elter's argument.

significant points about how according to Ammonius the philosophy of Aristotle compares with that of Plato. I quote the relevant passage.

Many of the disciples of Plato and Aristotle employed their zeal and study to show their teachers to be in conflict with each other (συγκρούειν ἀλλήλους) in their fundamental doctrines, and went so far in their quarrel and daring as to corrupt (νοθεῦσαι) the writings of their teachers in order to show them to be contradicting (μαχομένους) each other even more. This passion was constantly present in philosophical schools until Ammonius of Alexandria, the one taught by God (τοῦ θεοδιδάκτου). He was the first who had a godly zeal for the truth in philosophy and despised the views of the majority, which were a disgrace to philosophy. He apprehended well the views of each of the two philosophers and brought them under one and the same *nous* and transmitted philosophy without conflicts (ἀστασίαστον) to all of his disciples, and especially to the best of those acquainted with him, Plotinus, Origen, and their successors. (*Bibl.* cod. 251, 461a24–39) [testimony II]

The two testimonies quoted above complement each other as far as Ammonius' position is concerned, but testimony II also indicates that Ammonius' thesis differed from that of Hierocles. For according to testimony I, Hierocles argued that not only Aristotle but also all renowned philosophers up to Plotinus had been in accord with Plato, while testimony II suggests that Ammonius upheld only the accord between Platonic and Aristotelian philosophy.[5] The third testimony on Ammonius confirms that this was his claim.

Regarding those who set these men [i.e. Plato and Aristotle] in discord, he [i.e. Hierocles] argues that they were most mistaken about the intention of the men and departed from the truth, some of them deliberately, being themselves victims of contentiousness and mindlessness, others because they were slaves to prejudice and ignorance. And he claims that all those formed a long chorus, until the moment that Ammonius' wisdom shone, whom Hierocles honours by calling taught by God (θεοδίδακτον). For Ammonius purified the doctrines of these ancient men and dispensed with the superfluous claims sprouting from both sides. He thus declared that the thought of Plato is in accord with that of Aristotle (σύμφωνον ... τὴν γνώμην ἀποφῆναι) as regards the essential and most necessary doctrines. (*Bibl.* cod. 214, 171b38–172a8) [testimony III]

As we can see, there is a striking similarity between testimony III and testimony II. This is due to the fact that both are drawn from the same part

[5] Presumably Hierocles included the Stoics in those who are in accord with Plato, as he defended as Plato's ethical doctrines the views that the Stoics had advocated; see Praechter (1913: 1483–5). He also maintained the accord between Platonic and Pythagorean philosophy; see O'Meara (1989: 115–18).

of Hierocles' work, namely the introduction (προθεωρία), where the author outlined the basic ideas that he sought to expound in his work and also announced its plan. However, as Elter (1910) has established, the two testimonies differ in their nature: testimony III is a report of Photius based on Hierocles' introduction, while testimony II is a fragment excerpted from Hierocles' introduction.

To sum up Photius' evidence as far as Ammonius is concerned: codex 251 preserves an excerpt from Hierocles' introduction (461a24–39; testimony II), while codex 214 contains Photius' report on it (171b38–172a8; testimony III), as well as an excerpt from Hierocles' work containing his table of contents (173a18–40; testimony I).[6]

Now there are several indications suggesting the reliability of this evidence. The fact that all of Photius' testimonies about Ammonius agree so much with each other and complement one other so well is one reason for considering Photius' preservation of Hierocles' report on Ammonius to be reliable. Besides, Photius himself approved of Ammonius' thesis on the accord between Platonic and Aristotelian philosophies,[7] and may have taken special care to preserve a view similar to the one he himself upheld. Indeed, this factor may account for Photius' special selection of Hierocles' quotations. It may also partially account for the fact that Photius, relying only on Hierocles' introduction, was keen to project Hierocles' view, as is presented in books 6 and 7 (test. III), onto Hierocles' entire work when outlining his central argument. Against the evidence of the table of contents, Photius claims that Hierocles' entire treatise was about reconciling the philosophy of Plato with that of Aristotle,[8] and he did not hesitate to insert the name of Aristotle next to that of Plato on a couple of occasions (172a12–14, 172b7–8), though by that stage Hierocles had not yet talked about Aristotle. Although Photius is somewhat misleading regarding the scope of Hierocles' work, this does not diminish the value of his testimony on

[6] See Elter (1910: 190–3). Photius here exhibits some of his characteristic features as a source of information for the books he read. See T. Hägg, *Photios als Vermittler antiker Literatur* (Uppsala, 1975), 196–204.

[7] See Elter (1910: 198). Photius follows Porphyry in the interpretation of the *Categories* and perhaps took a view similar to Arethas' who maintained the accord between the philosophies of Plato and Aristotle; see M. Share, *Arethas of Caesarea's Scholia on Porphyry's Isagogê and Aristotle's Categories* (Athens, 1994), 94. 10, 96. 29, 203. 21–2. Essential research on this subject is still to be done.

[8] Photius, *Bibl.* cod. 214, 171b33–8. Then follows testimony III. See Elter (1910: 198–9) on how Photius may have been carried away in describing Hierocles' work in such a way.

Ammonius but in a way enhances it, because it turns out that he paid special attention to Ammonius' thesis. Thus there is no reason either to discredit Photius' testimony or to doubt its reliability. Quite the contrary. Yet it may be the case that Hierocles' report on Ammonius, on which Photius draws, is unreliable.

This, I think, is unlikely, first because Hierocles did not have any reasons to make up the information he presents about Ammonius, and secondly because his report is limited to generalities, which suggests that it communicates what was common knowledge about Ammonius. Hierocles does not seem to know anything about Ammonius other than his most salient features, that is, his drive for the philosophical truth and his claim that the philosophies of Plato and Aristotle are in accord. The latter in particular is a feature in which Hierocles himself was much interested, since he saw in Ammonius the initiator of the tradition to which he himself aspired to belong. Apparently, though, Hierocles did not preserve any of Ammonius' arguments as to which views Plato and Aristotle share, presumably because he did not know them, which is quite natural since Ammonius most probably had not written anything (*V. Plot.* 20. 17–47). There is still a question as to how Hierocles knew anything at all about Ammonius. Any answer on this is destined to remain speculative.[9] But our ignorance about this does not necessarily affect the value of Hierocles' account; rather, I think, it deserves our credit because it is modest and focused on features in which Ammonius had a special interest and may have become well known by Hierocles' time.

[9] Beutler (1953: 282–3) and Dörrie (1955: 343–7) have argued that Hierocles drew on Porphyry and did not know of Ammonius. Their theory was taken up by I. Hadot (1978: 75–6); Schwyzer (1983: 45); Schroeder (1987: 511–12); O' Meara (1989: 113); Schibli (2002: 28–9). Langerbeck (1957) on the other hand has argued that Hierocles relied primarily on Origen's writings; cf. Dodds (1960: 28). Langerbeck's view is unlikely because for the generalities that Hierocles knows, he did not have to rely on the writings of an immediate pupil of Ammonius. I find more likely the view that Porphyry was a source of Hierocles' report, despite the fact that Hierocles himself distanced himself from the Platonism of Plotinus and his circle. This does not diminish, though, the value of Hierocles' report, as has often been thought. It rather adds to its credibility, because Porphyry himself was very scholarly, very much interested in Plotinus' intellectual roots, and especially concerned with the topic of how Aristotle's philosophy compares with that of Plato. Finally, to dismiss Hierocles' report on the grounds that it is trivial, as Schroeder (1987: 511), for instance, has done, arguing that the accord of Plato and Aristotle 'was a common theme in Middle Platonism' which does not tell us much about Ammonius, misses the point; as this book hopefully shows, this topic was quite controversial, and especially so in Ammonius' time.

3. AMMONIUS' PLATONISM AND THE TARGETS OF HIS CRITICISM

I now turn to examine the evidence presented above and to make some sense of it. My aim is to give some historical and philosophical content to Ammonius' claim that the Platonic and Aristotelian philosophies are in fundamental accord. The first question I would like to address is in what sense Ammonius' claim was such a central characteristic of his philosophical profile (*Bibl.* cod. 214, 172a3–4) that it was crucial both in his search for the truth in philosophy (cod. 251, 461a33) and in the restoration of Platonic philosophy (cod. 214, 172a2–8, cod. 251, 461a24–39).

Let me start from the fact that all our testimonies draw a clear contrast between Ammonius on the one hand and those Platonists and Peripatetics on the other, presumably both predecessors and contemporaries of his, who argued that there was a conflict between the philosophies of Plato and Aristotle and falsified either of them. Unlike them, Ammonius is said to have restored both philosophies (test. III), or only the one of Plato (test. I), or philosophy in general (test. II). Such a discrepancy leaves us wondering what Ammonius' position precisely was but also what was the historical context in which he took it. There are three prominent questions here: (*a*) what was the mistake of those Platonists and Peripatetics; (*b*) who are these philosophers; and (*c*) how did Ammonius differ from them?

As regards the first question, Hierocles reports that several Platonists and Peripatetics up to Ammonius' time had presented Plato and Aristotle as being in conflict as a result of some form of prejudice which became manifest as a partiality (cod. 214, 171b38–172a2). Hierocles divides them into two groups of culprits: (i) those who were motivated by a quarrelsome spirit (*ἔριδι*) and lack of sense (*ἀπόνοια*), and (ii) those who were blinded by prejudice (*προλήψει*) and ignorance (*ἀμαθίᾳ*). The formulations in our testimonies suggest some determination and obstinacy on the part of the philosophers involved and indicate a distortion of the truth.[10] Their attitude, we are told, amounted to departing from the doctrine of Plato and Aristotle rather than defending it.

[10] Notable are the terms used for expressing the setting of Plato and Aristotle in conflict: *ἔστησαν* (*Bibl.* cod. 214, 171b39), *ἐπεχείρησαν . . . μεμηχανῆσθαι* (cod. 214, 173a26–31), *σπουδὴν καὶ μελέτην εἰσενηνοχότες* (cod. 251, 461a25–7).

Here we need to remember that philosophers at the time, especially Platonists, used to assume that the doctrines of their school authority amounted to the truth in philosophy, at least as regards the fundamental issues, and they criticized all divergences from such doctrines for falling short of, or contradicting the truth. As a result, for philosophers of the time the defence of their school authority involved the criticism of other philosophical authorities. Philosophers came to regard this criticism as indication of loyalty to their school authority. This ideology motivates the polemics of Plutarch and Taurus against the Stoics and the Epicureans, of Numenius and Atticus against Aristotle and the Stoics, and also that of Alexander of Aphrodisias who criticizes Platonists and Stoics alike. Yet as has been seen, all of the above make strong assumptions about the doctrines they consider as Platonic or Aristotelian, which for the most part they do not justify sufficiently, if at all.

Numenius and especially Atticus are two prominent examples of this attitude. Indeed their profiles match well those criticized by Ammonius.[11] Both Numenius and Atticus considered Aristotle's philosophy as being strongly at odds with that of Plato, and their defence of the latter involved the rejection of the former. Further, both Numenius and Atticus made unjustified claims about which Plato's doctrines are and they required other Platonists to be loyal to them, arguing that it is these doctrines which amount to true philosophy.[12] Numenius assumed that true philosophy meant Pythagoreanism, and his judgement about which doctrines are alien to Plato's philosophy rests on the further assumption that the latter is essentially Pythagorean. His understanding of Plato's metaphysics and psychology resulted from an interpretation of the dialogues which, though philosophically interesting, is by no means compelling. Atticus' interpretations of Plato on the other hand were even less justified and even in antiquity were criticized for their perceived partiality. And as we have seen in the previous chapter, it was such interpretations that sustained Atticus' criticism of Aristotle. This becomes manifest in his misrepresentation of Aristotle' ethics as being similar to that of Epicurus (fr. 3. 49–71), or in his criticism of Aristotle

[11] The linguistic hints I point out in the following should only be taken as indicative of the spirit which Ammonius opposes, because, even if Photius faithfully conveys Hierocles' spirit and language (at least in the excerpts *Bibl.* cod. 214, 173a5–40, cod. 251, 461a24–39), this is at best Hierocles' own language.

[12] Both Numenius (fr. 24. 16–18) and Ammonius (in *Bibl.* cod. 214, 173a22–6) were concerned with ὁμοδοξία and with putting an end to philosophical quarrels (ἀστασίαστον; Numenius fr. 24. 34–5, Ammonius in *Bibl.* cod. 251, 461a34–8). Some similarities between the two have been noticed by O'Meara (1989: 113).

for being contentious and hostile to Plato (frs. 5. 15–30, 6. 45–8) and also audacious (τολμᾶν; frs. 2. 71, 7. 42, 9. 16). Such evidence testifies to Atticus' spirit of quarrelsomeness,[13] which is exactly the spirit that Ammonius criticizes for motivating those who tried to show Plato and Aristotle in discord.[14] It seems reasonable to conclude then that Numenius and especially Atticus probably were two of Ammonius' targets.

According to Hierocles' account, there were also Peripatetics who exhibited such an attitude, and as I have suggested above, Alexander's profile fits that of the philosophers criticized. As has been seen in Chapter 4 (s. 2), he was eager to advocate Aristotle's philosophy against any critics including Platonists, and this often caused him to emphasize the differences between Platonic and Aristotelian philosophy and also to criticize Plato. Sometimes he actually showed an eristic spirit against contemporary Platonists.[15] Yet Ammonius may have also known other Peripatetics in Alexandria who took an attitude similar to that of Alexander, for instance, some of his disciples.

According to our testimonies, some of those prejudiced philosophers reportedly went as far as to corrupt or to falsify (νοθεῦσαι; 173a27, 461a28) their own master's writings. By means of such 'corruptions', we are told, Platonists and Peripatetics aimed to show loyalty to their school authorities. This is because in such a way they managed to enhance the conflict between Plato and Aristotle, which they assumed in the first place.[16] And since they also assumed that their school authorities represented the entire philosophical truth, any conflict with it amounted to divergence from the truth, which was a demolishing criticism of the doctrines of the rival philosophical school.

Such a description fits the altering of the text of Platonic dialogues, especially the *Timaeus*, which several Platonists attempted in order to support their personal interpretation of the cosmogony described in the dialogue.[17] In particular, it applies to manipulations of the text by

13 Photius' word for the setting of Plato and Aristotle in conflict ἔστησαν is the onethat Eusebius uses when introducing Atticus quotations: Πρὸς ὃν [sc. Aristotle] ὅπως ἔστησαν διεψευσμένην αὐτοῦ τὴν ὑπόληψιν ἀπελέγχοντες οἱ Πλάτωνος γνώριμοι (*PE* 15. 3. 1).

14 Cf. φιλονεικία καὶ τόλμη (*Bibl.* cod. 251, 461a27–8); ἔριδι (cod. 214, 171b41).

15 See Ch. 4, p.156; cf. Introduction p. 43.

16 *Bibl.* cod. 251, 461a29–30; cf. cod. 214, 173a25–7. One reason why philosophical books were corrupted was δι' εὔνοιαν τῶν μαθητῶν (Olympiodorus, *Proleg.* 13. 7–8), that is, the aim was to attract more students. νοθεύειν appears to be a *terminus technicus* for both corrupted and spurious texts. See DL 2. 124, 3. 62; Olympiodorus *Proleg.* 13. 36–14. 4; Philoponus, *In Cat.* 7. 16–26.

17 See Dillon (1989: 56–72).

Platonists who supported the literal interpretation of the cosmogony, an interpretation on which Aristotle founded his objections, who apparently wanted to make the conflict between Plato and Aristotle as strong as possible.[18] It may also apply to instances like Eudorus' alteration of Aristotle's text in order to credit Plato with Pythagorean metaphysical monism (Alexander, *In Met.* 58. 31–59. 8; fr. 2 Mazzarelli). In both types of cases the falsifications were partly inspired by the wish to distance Plato's doctrine as strongly as possible from that of Aristotle. But given such a motivation, this practice involved sacrificing the philosophical truth.

The preceding considerations show that philosophers like Numenius, Atticus, Alexander, or Eudorus could be considered with some reason as sacrificing the impartial philosophical inquiry to school polemic in one direction or the other, and thus as distorting the doctrines of Plato, Aristotle, or both. This seems to be the mistake that Ammonius criticizes. He castigates the tendency of those philosophers to do polemics rather than philosophy. According to Ammonius this tendency led philosophers to attack the doctrines of the authority of the rival school without actually examining their sense and value as well as misrepresent the doctrines of their own master, and hence to do harm to philosophy as a whole. We still have to see how Ammonius differed from such philosophers. But we now can understand, at least to some extent, why Ammonius' commitment to the truth in philosophy was connected with the discussion of the issue of how Plato's philosophy compares with that of Aristotle and with his project to restore Platonist philosophy in its actual, pure form.

4. AMMONIUS' THESIS AND HIS SPECIAL CHARACTERISTICS AS A PHILOSOPHER

Ammonius differed from the above group of philosophers both as regards the practice of philosophy as a whole and as regards the sense of commitment to the philosophy of Plato. We are told that, unlike his

[18] I primarily refer to alterations like that of forms of γίγνομαι to forms of γεννάω (e.g. γενητός to γεννητός) throughout the dialogue. Yet similar alterations, especially of *Timaeus* 27c5, were also introduced by partisans of the non-literal interpretation of the cosmogony. See the *apparatus criticus* of Burnet's OCT *ad loc* and Dillon (1989: 57–60); see also Introduction pp. 29–31, Ch. 4 pp. 180–6, and Ch. 7 s. 5. 2 for a discussion of the alternative interpretations.

contemporaries, who were strongly committed to a specific authority embodying philosophical truth, Ammonius was committed to the truth in philosophy, wherever this lay (cod. 251, 461a33–4). It is for this reason, we are told, that Ammonius came to study the philosophies of both Plato and Aristotle deeply enough as to understand them well (*εἶδε καλῶς τὰ ἑκατέρου*; 461a35). I take the phrase *τὰ ἑκατέρου* to refer to 'doctrines' rather than to 'writings', because it is only in this sense that it fits as the object of both *εἶδεν* and *συνήγαγεν* in the crucial phrase *συνήγαγεν εἰς ἕνα καὶ τὸν αὐτὸν νοῦν*. Construed in this manner, the phrase *εἶδε καλῶς τὰ ἑκατέρου* suggests a profound understanding of Platonic and Aristotelian doctrines. And one can surmise that Ammonius' own *dogmata* (*V. Plot.* 3. 27), whatever these were, may have resulted from such an understanding.

However, the will to reach this understanding is one thing, the ability to achieve it quite another. According to Hierocles, the crucial quality that accounted for Ammonius' unbiased interpretation of Plato, and for his conclusion that the philosophies of Plato and Aristotle are in essential agreement, was his ability to see beyond the letter to the philosophical sense underlying the philosophical texts of the ancient authorities.

This is epigrammatically conveyed in the phrase *εἶδε* [sc. Ammonius] *καλῶς τὰ ἑκατέρου* [sc. Plato's and Aristotle's doctrines] *καὶ συνήγαγεν εἰς ἕνα καὶ τὸν αὐτὸν νοῦν* (461a35–6). Though too short to provide us with the necessary information for understanding what Ammonius was precisely doing, this phrase clearly suggests two steps. Ammonius first made good sense of the doctrines of Plato and Aristotle through the study of their texts, and then, on the basis of such an understanding, he concluded that the *nous* behind their doctrines was the same.

The question now is what the *nous* is. It is fairly safe to say that *nous* is the opposite of *lexis*, the linguistic formulation, which can be misleading either because the author is not precise enough, or because his terminology is obscure. Ammonius may well have argued that the language of Plato or Aristotle had misguided several who had come to think that the stated views of the two philosophers were diverse or even contradictory. We are familiar with this type of argument. Antiochus used to argue that the Stoics dressed in new terminology essentially Platonic doctrines (*De fin.* 5. 22, 89), and that in epistemology in particular they developed Plato's views (*Acad.* 1. 35, 43). Ammonius may similarly have argued that Aristotle's philosophy is not essentially different from that of Plato, despite some Aristotelian novelties or discrepancies, including even Aristotle's criticisms of Plato. And he may have explained away such differences as only apparent, or unimportant, being convinced that the substance of their doctrines is similar.

Such a practice is likely to have been employed also by Ammonius given that this is attested for several of his disciples and contemporaries. Plotinus, for instance, is reported as being able to figure out the sense of a text by focusing on the underlying thought (*V. Plot.* 14. 16–17), and we are told that Plotinus in his philosophizing followed his teacher's approach, that is, Ammonius' (ibid. 14. 15–16).[19] Porphyry actually contrasts Plotinus' approach with that of Longinus. He tells us that Plotinus criticized Longinus' attention to the letter in his interpretation of the 'ancients' and considered him to be a philologist rather than a philosopher (ibid. 14. 19–20).[20] Plotinus' criticism may well be parallel to Ammonius' criticism of Platonists like Atticus who, as we have seen, was a typical example of such a literal interpretation.[21] The Christian Origen also stressed the distinction between the letter and the spirit of an author.[22] He generally objected to the practice of literal interpretations of a text, and was especially critical of Celsus' tendency to do so.[23] More specifically, Origen criticized Celsus for ascribing to Plato a certain doctrine simply by means of quoting Plato without any argument to such effect (e.g. *C. Celsum* 6. 9), a practice reminiscent of Numenius and especially of Atticus (see Ch. 4, s. 3).

Yet, however characteristic of Ammonius and his circle the emphasis on the underlying thought of a text was, it was not confined to them; rather, it was widely regarded as a crucial feature of the philosopher in

[19] Porphyry also tells us that Plotinus was able to realize the spirit of a complex thought and to summarize it with a few words (*V. Plot.* 14. 16–17). On this point see Baltes in *Gnomon*, 56 (1984), 207. For some discussion of the relevant passage of *V. Plot.* see Romano (1979: 68–9) and Kalligas (1990: 142–3).

[20] Cf. Proclus, *In Tim.* 1. 86. 19–25. Plotinus was not the only one who thought of Longinus like this. Longinus was widely known as ὁ κριτικός (Proclus *In Tim.* 1. 14. 7). A look at his few fragments confirms his focus on the letter of a text (Proclus, *In Tim.* 1. 59.10–19, 1. 94. 4–14); see Frede (1990: 85–7) and esp. Männlein-Robert (2001: 46–58, 77–86).

[21] See Atticus frs. 4, 19, 23, 38a–b Des Places.

[22] See Torjesen (1986: 138–47).

[23] Origen argues that Celsus' criticisms of the biblical style show someone who focuses at the level of *lexis*. He also remarks that this is a more general problem, because even Plato, whose style is more sublime, is largely construed by philologists too (*C. Celsum* 6. 2. 1–18). Celsus' attention to the *lexis* is criticized in several passages (e.g. ibid. 4. 38. 18–24, 6. 19). See also the next note.

late antiquity.[24] Everyone took himself to be focusing precisely on the thought behind a philosophical text, using the *lexis* only as an instrument for unveiling it. Hence this feature as such did not pertain only to Ammonius and cannot be credited exclusively to him. His alleged achievement then must be something else.

Hierocles seems to suggest that Ammonius' characteristic ability consisted in the discovery of an underlying doctrinal content in the texts of the ancient authorities rather than in his focused search for it. As I have said earlier, the object of the verbs εἶδεν/συνήγαγεν is the doctrines of Plato and Aristotle, so their *nous* must refer to a specific doctrine on a given issue. Ammonius' main achievement must have been precisely this.

To discover this doctrine, Ammonius had to set aside details or obscure points. Also, he must have been able to detect such a doctrine through its various versions. For example, he may have been able to specify Plato's view on the creation of the world through the accounts of the *Timaeus* and the *Politicus*, or to determine Plato's ethical doctrine despite the variety of suggestions made in his dialogues. Ammonius may have gone further. He presumably aimed to discover the sense that an author is getting at, given his general philosophical outlook and the language he uses. The term *nous* is indeed used in this sense in philosophical texts.[25] It has a meaning similar to that of γνώμη which occurs in the phrase σύμφωνον...Πλάτωνός τε καὶ Ἀριστοτέλους τὴν γνώμην ἀποφῆναι (cod. 214, 172a8–9).[26] In this use *nous* amounts not only to one's basic doctrine on a given matter but also to the intended one.

This receives some confirmation from Hierocles' report. Part of the error of Ammonius' predecessors was their misunderstanding of the intention of Plato and Aristotle (*Bibl.* cod. 214, 171b39–41). This is

[24] Seneca, for instance, *Epist.* 108. 23 laments that the study of philosophy has become the study of words (*Itaque quae philosophia fuit, facta philologia est*), which as he argues in *Epist.* 88. 42–3 does harm to the discovery of truth (*Audi quantum mali faciat nimia subtilitas et quam infesta veritati sit* (Let me tell you how much it harms exaggerated exactness and what an enemy it is of truth; tr. Gummere modified); and he shows how a philologist differs from a philosopher (*Epist.* 108. 30–7). Cf. Epictetus *Enchir.* 49, *Diss.* 3. 2. 12, and Justin, *Dialogue with Trypho* 3 (where the φιλόλογος is contrasted with the φιλόσοφος, who is the true lover of truth, φιλαλήθης).

[25] See LSJ s.v. *nous* sense III. For a similar use see Philoponus, *In de anima* 489. 11–12 καὶ ἔστιν ὁ νοῦς ὅλου τοῦ ῥητοῦ οὗτος, Origen, *C. Celsum* 2. 6. 9, Athanasius, *Contra Arianos* 1. 52.

[26] See LSJ, s.v. γνώμη. Numenius (fr. 24. 34) and Atticus (frs. 2. 138, 3. 90, 5. 36) also use γνώμη to refer to a philosopher's intended doctrine on an issue.

also supported from the practice of Ammonius' students. In attempting to specify Plato's doctrine on the status of the soul, Plotinus looks at the *βούλημα* of Plato (*Enn.* 4. 8. 28), and similarly does Longinus (Proclus, *In Tim.* 1. 83. 19–20). Origen also employs terms like *τὸ βούλημα* or *ὁ σκοπὸς* to describe his focus on the mind of an author[27] and criticizes readers like Celsus for having misread Plato's myth, thus failing to realize his intention (*τὸ βούλημα τοῦ Πλάτωνος*; *C. Celsum* 4. 39. 43–51).[28] This practice becomes widespread later with Porphyry and especially with Iamblichus (see e.g. Proclus *In Tim.* 1. 204. 76–9), but it may well have been characteristic already of Ammonius. However, this orientation clearly has its antecedents in Platonists like Plutarch, Numenius, and Atticus who were concerned to determine Plato's general philosophical position. What really seems to distinguish Ammonius is the method by which he achieved this.

A crucial step towards the recovery of the actual doctrines (*δόξας*) of Plato and Aristotle certainly was the rejection of false doctrines imposed on them by later interpreters (*Bibl.* cod. 214, 172a4–8, cod. 251, 461a34–6). These were unfounded claims (*λῆροι*), the result of short-sightedness and prejudice, and as such, shameful to philosophy (*Bibl.* cod. 251, 461a34–5).

Yet one account of the story (*Bibl.* cod. 214, 172a4–8) seems to suggest more than that.[29] It aims to justify why, according to Hierocles, Ammonius should be considered inspired by God and to show how he concluded the accord of Plato and Aristotle. This account appears to suggest two things: (i) that Ammonius purified (*διακαθάραντα*) the doctrines of the ancients, and (ii) that he dismissed (*ἀποσκευασάμενον*) the false doctrines forged by later interpreters which were projected back onto the 'ancients' as being their original doctrines.[30]

[27] For instance, in *C. Celsum* 2. 76. 47, 3. 53. 19.

[28] Celsus is also criticized for not realizing the intention (*βούλημα*) of the Bible (*C. Celsum* 4. 17. 10–12, 4. 44. 1–2); Torjesen (1986: 144–5 and n. 34).

[29] *Τοῦτον γὰρ τὰς τῶν παλαιῶν ἀνδρῶν διακαθάραντα δόξας, καὶ τοὺς ἑκατέρωθεν ἀναφυόμενους ἀποσκευασάμενον λήρους, σύμφωνον ἐν τοῖς ἐπικαίροις τε καὶ ἀναγκαιοτάτοις τῶν δογμάτων Πλάτωνός τε καὶ Ἀριστοτέλους τὴν γνώμην ἀποφῆναι.* (*Bibl.* cod. 214, 172a4–8). See the tr. of this passage on p. 193 (test. III).

[30] Iamblichus proceeds similarly. Before he determines a doctrine, he dispenses with faulty statements. *Ζητῶν δὲ τὰς νοερωτέρας περὶ τῆς ποιότητος αἰτίας ὁ Ἰάμβλιχος πρῶτον μὲν ἀποσκευάζεται τὰς μὴ καλῶς εἰρημένας, εἶθ' οὕτως τῷ Ἀριστοτέλει συμφιλοσοφῶν τὰς καθαρωτέρας ἐννοίας ἐκφαίνει περὶ αὐτάς.* (Inquiring about the most elevated causes regarding quality, Iamblichus first discards the mistaken ones and then, philosophizing in the spirit of Aristotle, he presents the clearest ideas about them; in Simpl. *In Cat.* 216. 6–8.)

Now the question is whether (i) and (ii) are the same. This depends on whether the *καὶ* is epexegetic or not. If it is not, then Ammonius made two steps in order to recover the actual doctrines of Plato and Aristotle.

Some reflection may help us to decide. Hierocles' evidence does not leave doubts that Ammonius cleansed the doctrines of Plato and Aristotle from the mistakes ascribed to them by later generations, but the question is whether this was sufficient for the discovery of their actual doctrines? This is unlikely in view of the fact that often another step was needed to restore the doctrines of the 'ancients'. We know that Platonists tried to identify Plato's tenets setting aside anything which could disguise or obscure them, such as Plato's myths, allegories, or enigmatic utterances.[31] Platonists often admit that Plato is obscure,[32] as do Platonist commentators about Aristotle, yet they maintain that in such a way Plato or Aristotle appeal only to higher, philosophically oriented minds.[33] This means that obscurity was not always considered a negative feature in late antiquity; it could have been due to the subject matter, or, when it was due to the author, it could serve an educational purpose.[34] But no matter how obscurity occurred, it was the duty of ancient interpreters to set it aside and make the master's views more intelligible, first because in such a way they educated their students and

[31] Plutarch admits that Plato had disguised his doctrine of the first principles (*De Is. et Os.* 370F) and had expressed himself with riddles (*De def. orac.* 420F). Similarly Plotinus says that sometimes Plato speaks with riddles (*ᾐνιγμένως Enn.* 4. 2. 22. 1, cf. 6. 2. 22.13), or with allegories and allusions (*Enn.* 1. 6. 8. 18–20, 3. 4. 5. 3–4). Porphyry wanted to articulate what Plato had intended to argue in his lecture *On the Good* and to show how it squares with the *Philebus* (Simpl. *In Phys.* 453. 25–8; fr. 174 Smith) and he also accepted that Aristotle had recast Plato's ideas written in mystical or symbolic form (*V. Pyth.* 41, see Introduction p. 26 n.77). The concern to clarify the obscurity of an ancient authority was characteristic of philosophical exegesis in late antiquity. Epictetus (*Enchiridion* 49) criticizes those who take pride in clarifying the doctrines of Chrysippus, arguing that 'if Chrysippus had not written obscurely, this man would have no reason to put on airs'.

[32] Apart from the references mentioned above, see also Plutarch fr. 186 Sandbach, Numenius (fr. 24. 60–66 Des Places) and Plotinus claim that Plato was obscure (*Enn.* 3. 6. 12. 1–11, 4. 4. 22. 10–13, 4. 8. 1. 23–8), but Numenius is the most critical of them.

[33] See Simplicius, *In Cat.* 3. 26, 6. 30–7. 22; Olympiodorus, *Proleg.* 11. 21–12. 17; Philoponus, *In Cat.* 6. 17–18; Elias, *In Cat.* 125. 16; David, *In Isag.* 106. 17. Such an attitude can be traced back to Philodemus *Πρὸς τοὺς*[...] (*PHerc.* 1005, col. XVI Angeli). See Erler (1991: 85–6) for a valuable discussion on this matter.

[34] See Cicero, *De fin.* 2. 15, who distinguishes between *rerum et verborum obscuritas* and also deliberate and accidental obscurity. Deliberate obscurity can be equivalent to philosophical profundity, but also to non-sense; this is how Varro means it referring to Stoic doctrines in *Acad.* 1. 7 and Atticus to Aristotle's doctrine of the intellect (fr. 7. 75–81 Des Places). See Erler (1991: 84, 87–8).

secondly because they also responded to critics who tended to argue that nothing important lies behind an obscure formulation.[35]

Sometimes, however, a more serious issue was involved. We know of Platonists and Peripatetics who rejected views that Plato and Aristotle themselves held, believing that not everything that Aristotle or Plato had maintained was correct. Xenarchus is a well-known example of a Peripatetic critic of Aristotle.[36] Surprising as it may seem, there were also Platonists who found mistakes in Plato. As we have seen (Ch. 3, ss.1, 2), Moderatus and Numenius held that there is nothing sacrosanct about Plato's writings, and Numenius in particular did not hesitate to criticize Plato.

There are several ways in which Platonic and Aristotelian views can be wrong, some of which have been suggested in earlier chapters. If one believes that Plato has doctrines, as Ammonius apparently did, the fact that Plato's main speakers commit themselves to different positions is a problem. One may think that some of them are more defensible than others, or that some of them represent Plato's mind better. One may think, for instance, as Antiochus clearly did, that Plato's early dialogues do not preserve Plato's actual views as well as later ones do. But one may also think that the way Plato (i.e. one of his protagonists) argues on a particular occasion is wrong, although his eventual conclusion is right.[37]

In view of such evidence, it is possible that Ammonius, apart from dismissing mistaken interpretations of Plato and Aristotle made by later interpreters, also set aside aspects of Platonic and Aristotelian philosophy that obscured what he regarded as their actual doctrines. And this may not only have involved the elucidation of Platonic and Aristotelian doctrines, but also the rejection of some of them which obscured what he considered to be the principal ones. This may be what was involved in Ammonius' alleged 'purification' of the doctrines of the 'ancients', which was characteristic of his critical attitude towards Aristotle but also Plato. If Numenius did this as a result of his allegiance to Pythagoras, Ammonius may have done it because of his commitment to the truth in philosophy.

35 Atticus criticized Aristotle for obscurity on his doctrine of the intellect (fr. 7. 78–81 Des places), but his point clearly is that no important doctrine lies behind this obscurity.

36 Xenarchus wrote an entire treatise against Aristotle's fifth element (*Πρὸς τὴν πέμπτην οὐσίαν*; fragments in Simplicius, *In de caelo*), in which he also criticized Aristotle's unmoved mover. Xenarchus' objections against Aristotle's arguments in *De caelo* 1. 2 and *Met.* 12 are discussed by Moraux (1973: 198–206).

37 One may agree with Plato's overall argument in the *Meno* about a priori knowledge, without endorsing his argument on recollection, for instance.

Now if this is so, Ammonius' commitment to Plato was different from that of most Platonists. Although he accepted Plato as a philosophical authority, for him Plato's *ipsissima verba* were not sacrosanct, as they were for neither Moderatus or Numenius. What was more important for him was independence of thinking and the search for the truth. It may have been Ammonius' weaker commitment to Plato's philosophy that entailed not only a certain detachment from interschool polemics but also an indifference regarding traditional school loyalty and a distance from contemporary philosophical schools.[38] It may be for his different sense of commitment that Ammonius is portrayed as an unconventional philosopher in our sources. Such a feature explains why he was rather isolated, as Porphyry reports (*V. Plot.* 3. 7–13). And it may also explain why Ammonius was regarded as inspired by God (*θεοδίδακτος*, *Bibl.* cod. 214, 172a4, cod. 251, 461a32).[39] It may then be Ammonius' weak commitment to Plato that primarily accounts for his attention to the philosophy of Aristotle.[40]

Another element suggesting Ammonius' impartiality is that he is not presented as trying to prove that Plato and Aristotle are in accord, as his contemporaries sought to prove the opposite thesis; rather, as both accounts of Hierocles suggest (*Bibl.* cod. 214, 172a7–9, cod. 251, 461a35–36), Ammonius realized that on certain crucial issues Plato and Aristotle share the same view,[41] which they present in

[38] Contrast this with Atticus' attachment to Plato's philosophy which led him to argue that this represents the whole truth in an almost religious sense (fr. 1. 32–7 Des Places), and this view in turn motivated his claim that Aristotle's philosophy is useless since it is opposite to that of Plato.

[39] W. Inge, *The Philosophy of Plotinus* (London, 1929), i. 115 n. 1 suggested that *θεοδίδακτος* amounts to *αὐτοδίδακτος* (I owe the reference to Dodds 1960: 30). Yet there are hardly any parallels for such usage. Besides, Ammonius' profile is different from that of people who are described as *αὐτοδίδακτοι* in philosophy (Dion. Halicarn. *Rom. Antiq.* 5. 12). *θεοδίδακτος* means 'inspired by God' (cf. 1 *Epistle to Thess.* 4. 9, Clement, *Strom* 4. 18. 166), which is also supported by the phrase *ἐνθουσιάσας πρὸς τὸ τῆς φιλοσοφίας ἀληθινόν* (being divinely inspired for the truth in philosophy; *Bibl.* cod. 251, 461a33), which means that Ammonius was committed to the truth in philosophy. See Schibli (2002: 30).

[40] Views like those of Dörrie (1955) or of Fowden (1977: 369–70) that Ammonius was a distinguished philosopher being a Pythagorean or a highly religious figure have no foundation in the existing evidence.

[41] Note the use of singular: *σύμφωνον . . . τὴν γνώμην ἀποφῆναι* (*Bibl.* cod. 214, 171a7–9), *συνήγαγεν εἰς ἕνα καὶ τὸν αὐτὸν νοῦν* (cod. 251, 461a36). He maintained the *ὁμοδοξία* of Plato and Aristotle (cod. 214, 173a25).

different ways.[42] And he was able to understand what this view was, that is, to make some philosophical sense of it (*γνώμη*, *νοῦς*), by going beyond what was explicit in the texts of Plato and Aristotle. Yet as Hierocles' report implies, this was only a small step besides the deep understanding of their philosophical doctrines, which was Ammonius' main achievement.

Ammonius' thesis does not suggest that he denied the existence of points of disagreement between Plato and Aristotle. Quite the contrary. He was interested, however, only in their views on the most crucial philosophical issues. According to Hierocles' account, he not only upheld the harmony of Plato and Aristotle on them (*Bibl.* cod. 214, 172a7–9), but also had views as to which doctrines are the crucial ones (*τὰ ἀναγκαιότατα τῶν δογμάτων*). This is hardly surprising. Already Antiochus and Atticus had similar views. Yet the evidence for such a belief in the case of Ammonius suggests that he not only opposed those who maintained the conflict between the Platonic and the Aristotelian philosophy on the most crucial issues (*Bibl.* cod. 251, 461a25), but he also argued that their agreement on them has some significance, namely that Aristotle follows in Plato's philosophical tradition. A similar thought underlies Origen's claim that 'the disagreement between philosophical schools is substantiated by reference to their differences on the most crucial issues'.[43] Once Ammonius reached such a conclusion about Aristotle, he then could study Aristotle's work systematically without compromising his Platonism.

42 Ammonius' approach differs considerably from that of Plutarch of Athens who used to read Plato into Aristotle. This is suggested by the following passage. *καὶ ὁ Πλούταρχος δὲ ἁμαρτάνει ἰδίαν ἁμαρτίαν διότι τὰ Πλάτωνος Ἀριστοτέλει προσάπτει. Πλάτων γάρ ἐστιν ὁ οἰόμενος τὸν τῶν παίδων νοῦν καθ' ἕξιν εἶναι καὶ λόγους ἔχειν τῶν πραγμάτων, οὐ μὴν Ἀριστοτέλης· ὁ δὲ Πλούταρχος καὶ αὐτὸν οἴεται τὸν Ἀριστοτέλην ταῦτα λέγειν. καὶ πῶς οὐ ψεύδεται, ὅπου γε Ἀριστοτέλης ἐλέγχει αὐτὸν* (Plutarch makes a specific mistake, as he attributes Plato's doctrines to Aristotle. For Plato, unlike Aristotle, maintained that the mind of children is shaped by habits and contains the Forms of things. Yet Plutarch maintains that also Aristotle says this. And does he not lie, since Aristotle's work proves him wrong; Philoponus, *In de anima* 519. 37–520. 5). See Taormina (1989: test. 35, 123–6). Hierocles seems to follow his teacher Plutarch rather than Ammonius (cf. the verbs *συνάγει*/*ἀνάπτει* in *Bibl.* cod. 214, 173a13–18).

43 *ἡ ἐν ταῖς αἱρέσεσι τῶν φιλοσοφούντων διαφωνία οὐ περὶ μικρῶν καὶ τῶν τυχόντων ἀλλὰ περὶ τῶν ἀναγκαιοτάτων* (*C. Celsum* 5. 61. 7–8). See also Ch. 7, p. 251.

5. METAPHYSICS THE QUESTION OF THE FIRST PRINCIPLE

Unfortunately, Hierocles (or Photius) does not tell us on which issues Ammonius argued that there is a fundamental agreement between the philosophies of Plato and of Aristotle, let alone which views, according to Ammonius, Plato and Aristotle share. Photius reports that Hierocles sought to show the accord between Plato and Aristotle 'not only in their accounts of providence but also in their theories about the heavens and the world' (*Bibl.* cod. 214, 171b35–8). We have seen, though, that Photius' report is misleading regarding the scope and goal of Hierocles' treatise as a whole (see p. 194). Hierocles in his sixth book may well have maintained the agreement of Plato and Aristotle on the issues which Photius lists but, as has been argued above (s. 2), his project in the sixth book was much more ambitious than that of Ammonius (173a18–19). We should therefore resist the temptation to attribute to Ammonius all the issues on which Hierocles sought to reconcile Plato and Aristotle, at least in the absence of further supporting evidence.

From the remaining information we have about Ammonius, it can be seen that one issue which was definitely of importance to him was the status of the first principle. Ammonius appears to be a monist in the sense that he accepted the existence of only one divine hypostasis. That is, he identified this hypostasis with the demiurge of the *Timaeus* and the Form of the Good in *Republic* 6 (508e),[44] maintaining that below the demiurge there are only demons, and below them souls (cf. *Bibl.* cod. 251, 461b12–17). Indirect though it may be, the evidence suggests that Ammonius held such a view. We know that his pupil, the pagan Origen, wrote a treatise with the title Ὅτι μόνος ποιητὴς ὁ βασιλεύς (*V. Plot.* 3. 32). The title indicates that only the highest God can be the creator of the universe, in other words, that there is only one divine being. The fact that in this publication and in his *On demons* (Περὶ τῶν δαιμόνων, *V. Plot.* 3. 31), Origen followed Erennius in violating the pact amongst Ammonius' students (i.e. themselves and Plotinus), not to disclose Ammonius' doctrines, suggests that in these works Origen upheld doctrines of Ammonius himself.[45] And as their titles suggest, these doctrines were

[44] On Ammonius' monism see Weber (1962: 74–96); Theiler (1965: 9–12); Baltes (1985).

[45] The fact that Longinus counts Origen among those who did not systematically write philosophical works suggests that Origen's two treatises were presumably regarded as popularizing Ammonius' doctrines (*V. Plot.* 20. 35–40).

nothing else but the two main aspects of Ammonius' monism, the belief in the existence of one divine hypostasis and the existence only of demons below this hypostasis. Longinus, who also was Ammonius' student, probably held the same view (Proclus, *In Tim.* 1. 322. 18–6), one which he presumably expounded in his work *On Principles* (*V. Plot.* 14. 18). This also is Hierocles' view on the matter, and one may think that this was a reason why he adhered to Ammonius' tradition.

If Ammonius was a monist, which seems quite likely, he may have taken issue with Platonists like Moderatus and Numenius, who postulated a God above being on the basis of *Republic* 508e, distinct from the demiurge of the *Timaeus*, or even with Platonists like Alcinous who talks of three entities, a God, an Intellect, and a Soul (*Didasc.*, 164. 7–36).[46] Hierocles may well reflect Ammonius when he criticizes Platonists for their misconception of the demiurge (*Bibl.* cod. 251, 460b23–5). Against them Ammonius may have argued that there was nothing higher than the demiurgic intellect to understand, and these Platonists were mistaken to think that this is an issue in which Aristotle differs from Plato. One reason for postulating only one God as the cause of the universe and of all beings is one's concern to claim that God is the sole cause of the universe and that God's goodness is directly imparted to the world. Yet the crucial question for us is how, if at all, this monistic view of Ammonius played a role in forming his thesis about the accord between the philosophies of Plato and Aristotle.

Ammonius may have found Aristotle's position in *Metaphysics* 12 very close to his own understanding of Plato's view on the first principle as presented in the *Republic* and the *Timaeus*. Aristotle appears to share with Plato (in the *Timaeus*) several concerns and assumptions regarding the highest principle. One such assumption is that the highest principle is the ultimate source of everything that exists and the source of intelligibility, which means that all other intelligent beings, like the stars and humans, derive their intelligence from this. After Parmenides, this principle was identified with a thinking intellect. For Aristotle, like Plato, this principle is an active intellect, which, being nothing but form, is an unchangeable (*Met.* $1074^{b}26$) immaterial entity (*Met.* $1074^{a}35$–6) whose being consists in thinking (a *nooun*) and is also an object of thought (a *noêton*; *Met.* $1072^{b}20$–1, $1074^{b}21$–35). Aristotle's

[46] It is tempting to consider Ammonius as reacting against Numenius on this issue. Dörrie (1976*b*: 394) argued that Origen's treatise on the first principles was a polemic against Numenius. But this is not necessary.

unmoved mover is like Plato's God in the *Timaeus* also in that it is sheer actuality, that on which 'heaven and nature depend' (*Met.* 1072^{b}7–14), an intellect which, being itself good, is responsible for the goodness and perfection of the universe (cf. *τελεώτατον*; Hierocles in *Bibl.* cod. 214, 172a28, cod. 251, 461b11). Since Ammonius was probably a monist, for him one crucial point of agreement between Plato and Aristotle may have been their acceptance of an intellect with such features as the first principle.

Some further common ground also appears possible if one takes this interpretative line. For Aristotle this intellect comprises the entire intelligible reality, since heavenly bodies may be eternal but still are sensible substances.[47] Now one may be tempted to think that Aristotle's God is like Plato's if one makes the following two assumptions: first, that Plato's God comprises the entire intelligible realm in that the Forms are thoughts of the divine mind (cf. *Timaeus* 30c–d, 39e); second, that Aristotle's God, being an intellect, also has thoughts which are immaterial, and these are the Forms (*Met.* 1074^{b}21–35). Such a step may be justified on the basis of Aristotle's approval of Plato's alleged view that the intellect is the place of Forms (*τόπος εἰδῶν*; *De anima* 429^{a}27–8) and Aristotle's own statement that the intellect is the Form of Forms (*εἶδος εἰδῶν*; ibid. 432^{a}2). If Ammonius made the above assumptions, then Aristotle's objections to transcendent Forms would have appeared relatively unimportant to him. He could actually justify this by arguing that Aristotle in his criticisms of the Forms had disregarded the demiurgic intellect of the *Timaeus* (cf. *Met.* 991^{a}20–3). Ammonius may have held then that (for both Plato and Aristotle) the divine intellect is identical with the realm of intelligibles.

This development, which paved the way for the doctrine that we find fully articulated in Plotinus,[48] is detectable already in Philo of Alexandria and in Alcinous.[49] The origins of such a view remains

[47] Cf. *Met.* 1073b1–8, 1074 a24–34; regarding the intellect see also *De anima* 431^{b}17–19.

[48] *Enn.* 3. 9, 5. 9. 3; Longinus did not share this view, but rather argued that the Forms exist outside the divine intellect (*V. Plot.* 18. 10–11, 20. 89–95); cf. Frede (1990: 87–90); Männlein-Robert (2001: 68–73, 537–40). Porphyry wrote a special treatise arguing against such a view. It may well be that the book of 'Refutation of Longinus on the Intelligence and the Intelligible' testified by Al–Nadim *Fihrist* i. 253 Flügel is the same as the work 'Against those who separate the Intelligibles from Intellect' (Op. 24 Smith).

[49] Philo, *De opif. mundi* 5. 20–2, Alcinous *Didasc.* 163. 14–34, 164. 29–31. See Armstrong (1960: 394–404); Dillon (1993: 94–5).

controversial.[50] Ammonius cannot be the author of such doctrine, but he may well be one of the first to see in this a point in which Plato and Aristotle agree. This is likely first because such a view shows interest in metaphysics and presupposes good knowledge of Platonic and Aristotelian metaphysics, that is, features attested for Ammonius, and secondly, because Plotinus and later Porphyry adopt this view, and by doing so they largely rely on Aristotelian theology.[51] As Armstrong has convincingly argued, Plotinus was stimulated to formulate his own doctrine by Alexander.[52] The latter identified the active intellect of *De anima* 3. 5 with Aristotle's God of *Met.* 12, and he suggested that the divine intellect is identical with its thoughts. Porphyry on the other hand explicitly maintains that this doctrine is characteristic of the agreement between Platonic and Aristotelian metaphysics (see Ch. 7, ss. 5. 2, 8). If Ammonius held such a view at all, then, and given that he accepted the existence of only one divine hypostasis, the divine intellect, he may have argued that Aristotle subscribes entirely to Plato's doctrine of the intelligible realm. And for a philosopher like Ammonius who was so much oriented towards metaphysics, this would clearly be a very important aspect of Aristotle's accord with Plato.

The above reconstruction is supported by the following considerations. Ammonius' position about the status of the first principle was thought to be closer to Aristotle already in antiquity. Proclus argued that the view of the pagan Origen on the first principle, which, as I have argued, reflects Ammonius' belief on the matter, was foreign to Plato's philosophy and yet full with Peripatetic doctrine.[53] Besides, if this were Ammonius' position, it would be strongly at odds with those of Numenius and Atticus, whom, as it has emerged so far, he would probably have targeted, and perhaps it was meant to be a response to them. Ammonius would reject both Numenius' view that the Forms are the

[50] Loenen (1957: 45–6) argued for Alcinous' originality. Armstrong (1960: 402–5) has expressed some doubts and Göransson (1995: esp. 128–36) has argued convincingly against it. See also Rich (1954: 126–9).

[51] It also occurs in the Christian Origen, e.g. in his *Comm. In Ioannem* 1. 24. 1–7. See Lilla (1990: 38–41).

[52] Alexander, *Mantissa* 108. 7–9, 16–19, 109. 23–110. 3, 112. 18–113. 2. See Armstrong (1960: 405–12).

[53] Proclus, *Plat. Theol.* 2. 4. 9–22, p. 31 Saffrey–Westerink (fr. 7 Weber). On this text see Aujoulat (1986: 55–61); Schibli (2002: 48–50). Schibli (2002: 51) disputes that Origen was following Ammonius on this matter, and argues that the latter maintained a transcendental One above the demiurgic intellect. But if this is so, it is difficult to see how Ammonius managed to reconcile Platonic and Aristotelian metaphysics, which he must have regarded as essential for their overall unanimity.

thoughts of a second God in a divine hierarchy and that of Atticus that the Forms exist not in the divine intellect but in the divine soul, arguing that both result from misconceptions of the demiurge and his role in the creation and maintenance of the world (*Bibl.* cod. 251, 460b23–5), which distort Plato's doctrine and guide them to reject Aristotle unnecessarily.

6. THE COSMOGONY OF THE *TIMAEUS* AND THE QUESTION OF THE NUMBER OF PRINCIPLES

Ammonius may have differed from Numenius and Atticus also regarding the role of the demiurge as principle in the cosmogony. Being a monist, he accepted only one principle, the divine intellect, from which everything else derives, including matter and Forms. Such a view would be part of a certain interpretation of the cosmogony of the *Timaeus*, aspects of which can be inferred with various degrees of probability. In view of what has been said so far about Ammonius' interpretative methods, we can be fairly sure that he opposed the literal interpretation of the *Timaeus*, championed by Platonists like Plutarch and Atticus, according to which the world was the result of a certain process which took place in the past. Rather, he must have sided with those Platonists (Alcinous, Apuleius, Celsus, Taurus) who maintained that the world is 'created' only in the sense that it has a cause outside itself, namely God.[54]

Hierocles outlines some of the difficulties one runs into if one accepts the literal interpretation of the *Timaeus* (*Bibl.* cod. 251, 460b26–461a23), difficulties which perhaps were mentioned by Ammonius himself.[55] The most serious of these is that, if God created the world at a certain point, this means that he changed his mind and, since the world is good, it also means that God had not always wanted to do the good, a suggestion which contradicts God's perfection and goodness. As was seen in the previous chapter (5.6), Platonists like Taurus and Severus argued that the world's 'created' character should be understood

[54] On this matter see Introduction pp. 29–31, Ch. 4, s. 6, and further Ch. 7, s. 5. 3.

[55] Some of these difficulties are outlined by Porphyry in his argument against the literal construal of the *Timaeus* (in Proclus, *In Tim.* 1. 394. 11–31). See Ch. 7, s. 5. 3, pp. 281–3. On Hierocles' conception of the demiurge and the creation see Schibli (2002: 58–72).

in a purely perfective sense without implications about the past. These Platonists had a conception of God's nature which is essentially Aristotelian in that it assumes that God is pure actuality. They understood God as a principle (*archê*; *Timaeus* 28b6–7) that brings about the world without any special activity, but merely by being what it is, a thinking intellect. In this sense God is the world's ultimate explanation. Hierocles appears to share a similar view when he argues that God's activity accounts for the existence of the world but that the world has been there all along (ἐξ ἀϊδίου ἐνεργοῦντα; *Bibl.* cod.251, 460b27, 461a13).

Ammonius is likely to have argued for the world being created in this sense, because he is likely to have shared the Aristotelian conception of God's nature. Some further details enhance this possibility. Hierocles addresses certain Platonists who believed that God can create only with the aid of uncreated matter, which means that they held matter also to be a principle. Against them Hierocles argues that God was the only principle of creation (*Bibl.* cod. 251, 460b25–9).[56] In his view, matter and Forms were provided by God, and in this sense God did not only set order on pre-existing matter, as some Platonists were suggesting, but also brought everything into being including matter (*Bibl.* cod. 251, 460b30–2; cf. *Timaeus* 28c). According to Hierocles, matter is not an entity, because it lacks unity, and so it cannot be uncreated and co-eternal with God (*Bibl.* cod. 251, 460b33–8), and he points to further difficulties arising from the assumption of uncreated matter (461a8–23). One such difficulty is that on such an assumption God's absolute perfection and self-sufficiency is undermined.

We do not know whether all this reflects Ammonius, but this is possible first because such a position would contradict the views of Numenius and Atticus, whom, as I have argued, Ammonius must have criticized;[57] secondly, Ammonius' metaphysical monism would be compatible with Hierocles' position about the role of the demiurge and also with the view that Longinus probably held, namely that God created the Forms and then (in a non temporal sense) the sensible substances (Proclus, *In Tim.* 1. 322. 24–6).[58] In such a case Ammonius would maintain Aristotle's adherence to what he took to be Plato's doctrine that God is the only principle which accounts for everything

[56] See Schibli (2002: 68–72).

[57] This has been suggested by I. Hadot (1978: 78–83).

[58] See Frede (1990: 92). The evidence about Longinus' views on the creation of the world has been collected and discussed by Männlein-Robert (2001: 76–7, 447–8, 600–3).

coming into being (*Bibl.* cod. 214, 172a26) and always has been so, as there has never been a time that the world was not there.

If this is so, then Ammonius may have considered Aristotle to be following Plato not only about God but also regarding his role as cause of the world, intelligible and sensible alike. This suggests as a possibility that, for Ammonius, Plato and Aristotle further agreed as to how the two realms relate to each other. And one may be tempted to think that Hierocles' claim that these realms are joined appropriately in harmonious relationship (*συντεταγμένη δημιουργία*; *Bibl.* cod. 214, 172a27, cod. 251, 461b10–11), such that there is in fact one world in two versions, may reflect Ammonius' position.[59] In view of what has been said so far, it is possible that Ammonius held that this is a doctrine that Plato and Aristotle had shared.

7. CONCLUSIONS

I have argued that Ammonius was an independent thinker who, though a Platonist, had a weaker commitment to Plato than most of his contemporary Platonists and hence was uninterested in interschool polemics. His concern rather was to search for the truth in philosophy, which led him to study the works of both Plato and Aristotle and appreciate them according to their merits. Focusing on the underlying thought behind the texts, Ammonius left aside doctrines forged by later philosophers, points of detail, and also certain flaws of the philosophers themselves, and reached an understanding of Platonic and Aristotelian philosophy as a whole, concluding that their basic doctrines are essentially the same. We do not know which these doctrines were, but I have proposed that one such doctrine was that Plato and Aristotle maintain that there is only one God, that is, an intellect which accounts for both

[59] *κόσμον...διπλοῦν ἅμα καὶ ἕνα* (*Bibl.* cod. 251, 461b11–12). One would be tempted to see here an analogy with the union of soul and body. Nemesius, *De nat. hom.* 69. 11–70. 5, 129. 8–132. 2 attributes certain views on this question to Ammonius, which are very similar to those of Plotinus (see next chapter, s. 2). Ammonius is credited with the doctrine that the soul unites the body but, being an intelligible entity, remains distinct from it and is not affected by the body. It has been argued that these views are actually Porphyry's. See von Arnim (1887: 276–85); Dörrie (1959: 276–85); Dodds (1960: 25); Schwyzer (1983: 45–65); Schroeder (1987: 512–17); Edwards (1993: 177). It is true that Porphyry holds similar views, but the possibility remains that he appropriated Ammonius' views, which he presumably knew through the work of Ammonius' students, Longinus, Plotinus, or Amelius, as Igal (1979: 332) has argued.

the intelligible and the sensible reality, and this principle summarizes the entire intelligible realm, on the assumption that the transcendent Forms constitute the divine thoughts. I have also argued that Ammonius is likely to have considered the two philosophers in accord also on how God accounts for the existence of the world and how the intelligible and the sensible realm relate to each other. An agreement on such issues would have suggested to him that Aristotle was attached to the essence of Plato's philosophy, which for him consisted in metaphysics.

Ammonius' thesis may have triggered some discussion. We hear that his contemporary Platonist Eubulus wrote a work entitled *On Aristotle's objections to Plato's Republic* (*V. Plot.* 20. 42–3), but we do not know anything about it.[60] Plotinus, however, disagreed with the unqualified acceptance of Ammonius' thesis and, as we will see in the next chapter, he often criticizes Aristotle for departing from Plato's doctrines. Yet the fact that he did pay considerable attention to Aristotle and his Peripatetic commentators may well attest to Ammonius' impact on him.

[60] On Eubulus and his treatise see Kalligas (1991: 145), and Männlein-Robert (2001: 290–1).

6

Plotinus

1. INTRODUCTION

In his biography of Plotinus, Porphyry tells us that 'Plotinus' works are shot through with Stoic and Peripatetic doctrines in a hidden form' (*V. Plot.* 14. 4–7).[1] Indeed, a casual look at the *apparatus fontium* of the Henry-Schwyzer editions of Plotinus suffices to convince us of the truth of this statement.[2] This evidence, however, should not be taken as implying Plotinus' agreement with either Aristotelian or Stoic views. As we know, he criticizes both Aristotle and in particular the Stoics throughout his works. This critical attitude does not amount to rejection either. On the contrary, Plotinus seems to have considered a philosophical view critically when he found it to be of merit. This is suggested by the following.

First, it is quite indicative that Plotinus hardly ever argues against the Epicureans (as Plutarch had done), the Pyrrhonian or the Academic sceptics (as Numenius had done). One may argue that Epicureanism or scepticism were no longer perceived as a threat to Platonism by Plotinus' time. This can also be said, however, of Aristotelianism or Stoicism; we do not know of any significant Peripatetic philosopher after Alexander of Aphrodisias, let alone of any Stoic. Secondly and most importantly, Plotinus himself offers some evidence suggesting that the doctrines of Aristotle and the Stoics are important enough to merit critical discussion. In his treatise 'On time and eternity' (*Enn.* 3. 7), Plotinus turns to consider the Aristotelian and Stoic conceptions of time in detail but dismisses the relevant Epicurean doctrine, arguing at the end of his critical section that he is not doing history but rather seeks out the truth

[1] *ἐμμέμικται δ' ἐν τοῖς συγγράμασι καὶ τὰ Στωικὰ λανθάνοντα δόγματα καὶ τὰ Περιπατητικά· καταπεπύκνωται δὲ καὶ ἡ "Μετὰ τὰ φυσικὰ" τοῦ 'Αριστοτέλους πραγματεία.* (*V. Plot.* 14. 4–7).

[2] I use the edition minor of P. Henry and H.-R. Schwyzer, *Plotini Opera*, i–iii (Oxford, 1964–82: OCT). The bibliography on Plotinus is rich. A valuable introduction is that of O'Meara (1993). See also Armstrong (1940), (1960).

of the matter (3. 7. 10. 9–17),[3] and for this reason he takes into account only views of some value (τὰ μάλιστα ἀξίως λόγου; 3. 7. 7. 15–16). While Plotinus eventually disagrees with both Aristotle and the Stoics, his theory of time draws especially on the Aristotelian account (see s. 5).

This attitude differs considerably from that of Numenius and Atticus, and also, as far as we know, from that of Ammonius Saccas, and it is much more complex than theirs.[4] Plotinus' critique of Aristotle's doctrines can take many forms, ranging from strong criticism in some places to modified acceptance in others. It seems then that Porphyry's statement about the shaping effect of Aristotle's philosophy on Plotinus, general as it is, indicates a far more complicated situation than is sometimes thought. To shed some light on it we first need to address the question of why Plotinus is preoccupied with Peripatetic and Stoic philosophies more than with any others.

One reason why Plotinus does this is because he often considers them as a means for explicating Plato's doctrines. Like Antiochus and Plutarch, Plotinus also appears to believe that Aristotle and the Stoics drew much from Plato but failed to acknowledge their debt. This is suggested by the fact that Plotinus sometimes treats Aristotelian and Stoic views as possible reconstructions or interpretations of Plato's doctrines, which could have been adopted by a Platonist. This, as will be seen, is the case with Aristotle's view of how the soul operates in the body and his conception of the intellect. Yet sometimes Plotinus, in rushing to Plato's defence, launches an attack on Aristotelian or Stoic tenets exactly because he considers them as being at odds with what he takes to be Plato's doctrine. This tactic pervades several Plotinian treatises, such as his 'On the immortality of the soul' (*Enn.* 4. 7). As we will see in the following section, in this work Plotinus tries to elucidate Plato's doctrine on the soul partially by criticizing Stoic and Aristotelian views.

[3] Ἀλλ' ἐπειδὴ οὐ τί μὴ ἔστι ζητοῦμεν ἀλλὰ τί ἐστιν, εἴρηταί τε πολλὰ πολλοῖς τοῖς πρὸ ἡμῶν καθ' ἑκάστην θέσιν, ἃ εἴ τις διεξίοι, ἱστορίαν μᾶλλον ἂν ποιοῖτο, ὅσον τε ἐξ ἐπιδρομῆς εἴρηταί τι περὶ αὐτῶν ... εἴη ἀνακόλουθον εἰπεῖν, τί ποτε δεῖ νομίζειν τὸν χρόνον εἶναι (But since we are not trying to find what time is not but what it is, and since a great deal has been said by a great many of our predecessors on every theory of its nature, and if one went through it and all one would be making a historical rather than a philosophical inquiry ... it would be in order to say what one ought to think time is; *Enn.* 3. 7. 10. 9–17; tr. Armstrong).

[4] I disagree with Praecther (1922: 137) who sees Plotinus as simply continuing the line of Nicostratus and Atticus. The following account will hopefully show that this is far from being the case.

At no point in his career, however, did Plotinus examine systematically Aristotelian or Stoic philosophy in the same way that he did Gnosticism, for example. He never set out to write a treatise such as the ones that Taurus, Atticus, or Porphyry wrote on the question of how to compare the Platonic and the Aristotelian philosophies. Nor did he offer even a general judgement of either, as Plutarch did in his *Adversus Colotem* on Aristotle's philosophy addressing Colotes' unhistorical claims. So if we are interested in Plotinus' overall verdict on Aristotelian or Stoic philosophy, we have to reconstruct it on the basis of his dispersed criticisms, judgements, uses of, or allusions to them.

A series of specialized studies have equipped us better for this task, and indeed they have given some content to Porphyry's statement about Plotinus' debt to Aristotle and the Stoics.[5] Yet, while Plotinus' attitude to the Stoic philosophy has been studied in some detail by Andreas Graeser,[6] no attempt has been made so far to outline an answer to the question of how Plotinus saw the relationship between Platonic and Aristotelian philosophies. One reason for this is that Plotinus absorbed so much from Aristotle and in so many different ways that the question about his stance to Aristotle's philosophy inevitably becomes very complex. My aim here is not to address this question in its full complexity. I will look instead exclusively at the instances in which Plotinus compares, in one way or another, Peripatetic and Platonic views and I will try to sketch a preliminary answer to the above question. My treatment will avoid several complicated questions concerning Plotinus' attitude to Aristotle, and I will refer the reader to more specialized studies when available.

2. PSYCHOLOGY

In his inquiry on the subject of the soul Plotinus paid considerable attention to the relevant views of Aristotle. This has to do with two basic facts. The first is that while Plato's dialogues suggest that the soul is an immaterial, transcendent, and thus immortal entity, which uses the

[5] I refer especially to the studies of Blumenthal (1972); Szlezák (1979); Emilsson (1988); Corrigan (1996); Chiaradonna (2002). For a review of recent studies on Plotinus' critique of Aristotle see Chiaradonna (1998*b*).

[6] Graeser (1972).

body,[7] they do not offer much illumination as to how this happens or how the soul enters the body in the first place. In his own study of the soul, Plotinus sought to shed light on what Plato had intended but not stated explicitly, and also sought to elaborate on it.[8] The second fact is that Plotinus, as a philosopher, was very much interested in determining the ontological status of the soul because he perceived this issue as a crucial one for his metaphysics.

The reasons for Plotinus' interest in the ontological status of the soul are quite complex. One principal reason was his belief, found already in Plato (*Phaedo, Phaedrus, Timaeus*), that the soul bridges the intelligible and the sensible realms, since the soul is an intelligible entity, yet often connected with material ones. In this conception the role of the soul becomes crucial for discussing the metaphysical question of how the intelligible world relates to the sensible one. This was an important question for all Platonists but Plotinus was especially engaged with it, as he was concerned to work out Plato's ontology in a systematic way. As has been noticed, Plotinus seems to have approached the relationship between intelligible and material reality in terms of the soul–body relationship.[9] That is, he seems to have deemed the soul–body relationship crucial for understanding how the intelligible realm relates to the material one. One further reason for Plotinus' concern with the ontological status of the soul was his interest in ethics. We have encountered this already in Platonists like Atticus—and it is easily explicable. Already for Plato the question of what the human soul is and how it relates to the intelligible realm was crucial for determining how man should live his life and how he should achieve happiness.

Plotinus' first step towards specifying Plato's doctrine on the soul was to disprove theories, such as the Stoic and the Aristotelian ones, which he considered considerably divergent from it. In one of his earliest treatises (*Enn.* 4. 7. 8⁵ [2]) Plotinus provides a detailed criticism of Aristotle's conception of the soul as the *entelecheia* of the living body.[10] Plotinus is more concerned with the Stoics than with Aristotle, because he finds the Stoic doctrine that the soul is corporeal more mistaken than that of Aristotle, that is, more at odds with and more distortive of Plato's

[7] τῷ σώματι προσχρῆται; *Phaedo* 79c3; cf. *Phaedrus* 246b–c.

[8] See esp. *Enn.* 1. 1. 2–3, 4. 3. 22, 6. 7. 4.

[9] O'Meara (1993: 13).

[10] Plotinus repeats this criticism in *Enn.* 4. 2. [4] 1. 3–7, where he apparently refers to 4. 7. 8⁵.

own belief.[11] From the Platonist point of view, Aristotle fared better because he at least did not deny the immaterial status of the soul. Yet Aristotle did deny the soul's independent existence and transcendence, and Plotinus, like Atticus earlier, accuses him precisely of this.

Plotinus presents the following objections to the Aristotelian doctrine.[12] First, if the soul is the form of the living body, as Aristotle argues in the *De anima*, then cutting a piece from the body would amount to cutting a corresponding part of the soul, which for Plotinus is absurd. As he argues elsewhere, when a body is cut and the living being feels pain, this is precisely because the soul itself has not been cut, as it is not in the body (*Enn.* 4. 4. 19. 19–29). Secondly, Plotinus argues that on Aristotle's conception of the soul we cannot explain the soul's departure (*anachorêsis*) when we fall asleep. Plotinus seems to be saying that, when we fall asleep, the living body is not actual in the same sense as when we are awake since the soul departs from it, a point already made by Plutarch (fr. 178 Sandbach). This, in his view, shows that the soul is not the actuality of the living body, as Aristotle maintained in the *De anima* but separable from it. Finally, Plotinus argues, Aristotle's view that the soul is the actuality of the body may seem justified if we consider functions which involve both soul and body, such as movement and perception, but is hardly justified if we consider mental events such as reason's opposition to desire and especially thinking, because in his view these activities involve only the soul. For Plotinus the evidence of such activities where the soul operates independently of the body, or even against the body, shows that the soul is not the actuality of the living body but rather subsists independently from it. It is this defect, Plotinus argues, that Aristotle tried to cover by postulating an intellect which subsists, being a transcendent entity that exists separately from the body (*Enn.* 4. 7. 8^5. 15–18).

Plotinus' objections to Aristotle's doctrine of the soul seem to me to be either wrong or else to rest on several strong assumptions. Wrong is Plotinus' objection that on Aristotle's doctrine cutting a piece from the body also amounts to cutting part of the soul. For first, in the view of Aristotle (and also of Plato) the immanent Form is an immaterial entity which is not to be identified with the shape of an individual thing, but rather is what makes the thing to be what it is, in the case of the living body to be alive. If this is so, cutting a piece from the body hardly

[11] See Graeser (1972: 25–6).

[12] For a short discussion of Plotinus' argument see O'Meara (1993: 15–19).

amounts to cutting part of the Form, because this as such is indivisible. It may be the case that by cutting one piece of the living body, the body subsequently dies because the form of being alive is seriously impaired, but this obviously would not happen with any piece.[13] As regards Plotinus' objection regarding sleep, he seems to ignore Aristotle's distinction between first and second actuality, which corresponds to the distinction between possession and exercise of knowledge. As is well known, in Aristotle's view the soul is the actuality of the body in the first sense, and in this sense a sleeping man still is alive (*De anima* 412^{a}21–6).

Let me now pass to the assumptions that Plotinus makes regarding the soul, which are crucial for appreciating Plotinus' criticism of Aristotle's doctrine. Plotinus assumes: (*a*) that something cannot be a substance unless it is a transcendent entity; (*b*) that the soul is such an entity and as such is ontologically prior to the body; (*c*) that the soul is not a mere principle of animation of the body but rather a special kind of such principle, namely a rational one, capable of reasoning and thinking; (*d*) that thinking is an activity which does not involve the body.[14]

Now, while the soul's transcendence was upheld by all known Platonists, the assumption that the soul is essentially rational was specifically made by Numenius and Atticus. As has been seen in previous chapters, the point of such a view is that the human soul is unlike other souls in that it accounts for man's rational character, and it was thought that being alive is implied in rationality, as the case of the divine intellect shows.

It is this particular assumption which stirs Plotinus' criticism of Aristotle's doctrine of the soul. Plotinus' claim that the soul departs when we fall asleep results from the belief that the soul is mainly reason, and this is why he stresses so much the role of reason and thinking in his discussion of Aristotle's doctrine. Actually Plotinus takes the rational status of the soul as proof of its transcendent status. His claim that the evidence of thinking proves Aristotle's conception of the soul to be

13 Blumenthal (1972: 345) advanced another objection. He argued that if a piece of the living body is cut, the soul would not be able to do the things that require the missing part; for instance, he argued, the actuality of a man without an arm would not be the same as that of a man with both arms, but still this is a living man. This is a bad objection, because even a man with one arm can do all the things required for a genuinely human life.

14 The first two assumptions are supported by the evidence of dialogues like the *Phaedo* (77b–78d, 99d–100a) and the *Timaeus* (37c–d, 38b), and while the third and fourth on passages like *Sophist* 249a; *Timaeus* 41c, 69c; *Philebus* 30c.

wrong shows that Plotinus takes for granted that thinking is an activity not only independent from the body but also characteristic of a transcendent entity which is essentially rational; as a consequence, if the soul is such an entity, then it exists independent from the body. That Plotinus takes the rational status of the soul as evidence for its transcendence becomes evident on several other occasions, most famously when he maintains that a part of ours remains in the intelligible realm even when we go about our daily business (*Enn.* 4. 8. 8. 1–3).

However, much as Plotinus criticizes Aristotle's conception of the soul as being the form of the living body, in some places of his work he appears to be more amenable to such a view. In one of his last works (*Enn.* 1. 1 [53]), for instance, Plotinus examines various solutions to the question of how the soul relates to the body and comes to consider Aristotle's suggestion that the soul is the Form of the living body (*Enn.* 1. 1. 4. 18). But then the question is how the soul, being a separable Form, relates to the body.

To answer this we must note first that Plotinus concedes that the soul is the Form of the living body in the same way that a piece of iron is an axe in virtue of the Form of the axe (*Enn.* 1. 1. 4. 18–25), which is Aristotle's example in the *De anima* (412^b10–17). As an axe is such in virtue of its Form which enables it to cut, without which it is not an axe any more, similarly the living body is living in virtue of the soul, without which it is not a living body any more.[15] For Plotinus this means that the body is a certain kind of body (*toionde soma*), namely living, as Aristotle himself

15 *᾿Αλλ᾽ ὡς εἶδος ἐν ὕλῃ ἔσται* [sc. the soul] *ἐν τῷ σώματι; πρῶτον μὲν ὡς χωριστὸν εἶδος ἔσται, εἴπερ οὐσία, καὶ μᾶλλον ἂν εἴη κατὰ τὸ χρώμενον. εἰ δὲ ὡς τῷ πελέκει τὸ σχῆμα τὸ ἐπὶ τῷ σιδήρῳ, καὶ τὸ συναμφότερον ὁ πέλεκυς ποιήσει ἃ ποιήσει ὁ σίδηρος ὁ οὕτως ἐσχηματισμένος, κατὰ τὸ σχῆμα μέντοι, μᾶλλον ἂν τῷ σώματι διδοῖμεν ὅσα κοινὰ πάθη, τῷ μέντοι τοιούτῳ, τῷ φυσικῷ, ὀργανικῷ, δυνάμει ζωὴν ἔχοντι· καὶ γὰρ ἄτοπόν φησι* [sc. Aristotle] *τὴν ψυχὴν ὑφαίνειν λέγειν, ὥστε καὶ ἐπιθυμεῖν καὶ λυπεῖσθαι ἀλλὰ τὸ ζῷον μᾶλλον.* (Will it then be in the body like form in matter? First of all, it will be like a separable form, assuming it to be a substantial reality, and so will correspond still more exactly to the conception of it as a 'user'. But if we assume it to be like the shape of an axe imposed on the iron (in this case it is the compound of matter and form, the axe, which performs its functions, that is to say the iron shaped in this particular way, though it is in virtue of the shape that it does so) we shall attribute all the common affections rather to the body, but to a body 'of a specific kind', 'formed by nature', 'adapted to the use of the soul', 'having life potentially'. Aristotle says that it is absurd 'to talk about the soul weaving', and it follows that it is also absurd to talk about it desiring or grieving; we should attribute these affections rather to the living being; *Enn.* 1. 1. 4. 18–25; tr. Armstrong); cf. Aristotle, *De anima* 408^b12–13, 412^a19–^{b}17. See the comments of Kalligas (1994: 154–5, 167–9).

argued,[16] rather than a mixture of soul and body (1. 1. 4. 1–3). Plotinus makes this clearer in *Ennead* 4. 4 [28]. 18–21, where he argues that there is no body as such but rather a certain kind of body (*toionde soma*), which is informed by the soul in the same way that the heated air is informed by the heat (4. 4. 18. 1–9).

How shall we explain this evidence? Clearly a developmental hypothesis would not do, since Plotinus appears to be indebted to Aristotle's doctrine already in a treatise from his middle period, that is *Ennead* 4. 4 [28].[17] Is he then only speaking of the soul in Aristotelian terms while in fact diverging from Aristotle's doctrine?

To decide this, we first need to remember that Plotinus' assumptions about what the soul essentially is leave unanswered the question of how the soul relates to the body and how it operates in it. Plotinus was much interested in this, as was his student, Porphyry, who for three successive days asked Plotinus how the soul is present in the body (*V. Plot.* 13. 10–11), because, as I have already said, they were not satisfied with Plato's treatment of this issue,[18] and also because this issue was crucial for addressing the question of how intelligible entities relate to material ones. Besides, it bears on philosophical questions concerning human perception, memory, and imagination. Philosophy and science since Aristotle had been much preoccupied with such questions. As a result, the philosophical discussion had been modernized, while science had made some important discoveries, such as Herophilus' discovery of the nervous system.[19] There was a need then to interpret and also to revise Plato's position in this light.

Aristotle was a good candidate for accomplishing such a revision, because he gives a systematic account of the relationship between soul and body, while maintaining the immaterial status of the soul. Already Plutarch and Severus, as we have seen, had paved the way. The fact that Platonists rejected Aristotle's doctrine of what the soul essentially is did not prevent them from taking seriously into account Aristotle's theory

[16] ἀναγκαῖον ἄρα τὴν ψυχὴν οὐσίαν εἶναι ὡς εἶδος σώματος φυσικοῦ δυνάμει ζωὴν ἔχοντος. ἡ δ' οὐσία ἐντελέχεια. τοιούτου ἄρα σώματος ἐντελέχεια. (*De anima* 412^{a}19–22).

[17] Yet as Igal (1979: 316–27) has discerned, there is some development in Plotinus' doctrine, which he started to expound in *Enn.* 6. 4 [22]. See below.

[18] See *Enn.* 4. 4. 22. 10–13. The separability of the soul from body is maintained in *Phaedo* 64c–65d, 80b–81e, *Phaedrus* 246a–249d, but more crucial for the relation between soul and body are *Timaeus* 41d–46c and also *Laws* 895c–899a; on the influence of the *Laws* on Plotinus see O'Meara (1985: 249–51). Cf. also *Epinomis* 981a.

[19] See Igal (1979: 334–5) on how Plotinus is aware of this development. Cf. *Enn.* 4. 3. 23. 9–27.

on how the soul relates to body. This does not mean that Plotinus accepted Aristotle's doctrine as such. Rather, by placing it in a Platonist framework he adapts it to his own metaphysical assumptions. Let us see how.

If we work with Plotinus' terms about the soul, the question as to how the soul relates to the body becomes a metaphysical question of a particular kind, namely how a transcendent entity can somehow become immanent. For both Platonists and Peripatetics in late antiquity a fairly common way to address such a problem was to postulate a mediating *hypostasis* derived from the transcendent one. Such a way was inspired by Plato himself, who in the *Timaeus* 35a defined the world-soul as an entity mediating between the indivisible soul and the souls of particular individuals. To give some examples, Atticus seems to think that the immanent Forms are mere powers (*dynameis*) derived from the transcendent ones (fr. 9. 7–15 Des Places), while the Peripatetic author of the *De mundo* argued that Aristotle's transcendent God of *Metaphysics* 12 is also immanent in the world through a mediating *dynamis* (397^{b}23–30, 398^{b}20–2). Similarly mediating between the transcendent God and the world is the world-soul in Moderatus or the second God in Numenius' theology. Now in Numenius and especially in Plotinus this becomes a more complex idea, as they postulate a hierarchy of *hypostases*, each of which produces the lower by means of an outgoing power, and through this procession everything in the intelligible world comes about: the One produces the Intellect (cf. *Enn.* 5. 4. 2. 23–6), the latter the Soul (cf. 5. 1. 6. 46–7), while the Soul in turn gives rise to the individual souls including the world-soul.

If we concentrate on the soul, Plotinus maintains that this, being an immaterial, transcendent entity, is not present in the body it enlivens except in a very qualified sense.[20] The soul, he argues, does not fully descend into the body which it enlivens, but rather enlivens the body through an outgoing power, a *dynamis*. Plotinus describes the power by means of which the soul enlivens the body in many different ways, as an image, a reflection, a beam of light, a shadow, or a trace of the soul.[21]

[20] Plotinus denies that the soul *is* in the body (*Enn.* 4. 3. 22. 8–10)

[21] *Εἴδωλον Enn.* 4. 3. 10. 38–40, 4. 5. 7. 61, 6. 4. 16. 40–6, *ἴνδαλμα* 2. 1. 5. 7, 4. 4. 19. 4–5, 6. 2. 22. 32–7, *οἷον φῶς*, *ἔλλαμψις* 1. 1. 7. 4, 4. 4. 22. 7, 6. 4. 15. 10–18, 6. 7. 7. 9–17; cf. 1. 1. 10. 10–11, *σκιά* 4. 4. 18. 7, 3. 2. 15. 48–9, *ἴχνος* 6. 4. 15. 15, 4. 4. 18. 30, 20. 15–16, 28. 8–9, 11, 16, 19–21, 52–3, 56, etc. Schwyzer (1974: 243–4) draws attention to the fact that Plotinus does not speak explicitly in terms of *dynamis*, but rather describes the soul in terms of a power descending of its own will (*ῥοπῇ αὐτεξουσίῳ*; *Enn.* 4. 8. 5. 26). Plotinus' views on how the soul relates to the body are discussed by Blumenthal (1971: esp. 15–18); Igal (1979); and O'Meara (1985).

The soul, he argues, informs the body so that it becomes living in the same way that the heat of the fire makes something hot, or the light of the sun illuminates the air in the sky.[22] The heat of a substance like water or the daylight are side effects of the fire and the sun respectively, qualities derivative from the essential ones of the heat of the fire and the light of the sun. The fire or the sun are active in a primary way which is essential to them, that is, in producing heat or light, and in a secondary or derivative one, that is, in having the water heated or the earth illuminated. In a similar sense, the soul has an inner, essential activity, in being alive, and a secondary one, in producing life in the form of the embodied soul in a living body, and this happens effortlessly, without the soul's substance being diminished.

The imagery Plotinus uses is indicative of his conception of the ontological relation between the transcendent and the embodied soul. It suggests that the latter is inextricably bound to the former, in fact, it is substantially identical with it,[23] and that only the transcendent soul (the Soul) is a *hypostasis*, that is, it subsists of itself, while the embodied soul is an entity derivative of the transcendent one.[24] More precisely, the imagery suggests that the embodied soul relates to the transcendent one as immanent Forms relate to transcendent ones. The imagery also is meant to show that the transcendent soul neither is present as such in the living body, nor is diminished by being divided in individual bodies, a point which Plotinus makes in several parts of his work.[25] The crucial gain so far is that the soul can be embodied without compromising its transcendence.

The second important gain is that the embodied soul retains the characteristics of the transcendent soul as an animating power. More importantly, the embodied soul gives the body a unity such that each part of the living being contributes to the well-being of the whole.[26] Further, the embodied soul endows the body with powers (*dynameis*)

[22] *Enn.* 1. 1. 7. 1–6, 4. 3. 10. 31–3, 22. 1–7, 4. 4. 14. 1–9, 18. 4–6, 29. 1–17. Nemesius attributes the analogy of the relation between light and illuminated air to that between soul and body to Ammonius Saccas (*De nat. hom.* 133. 5–134. 9), but it is controversial whether it goes back to him or to Porphyry (Porphyry fr. 261. 1–25 Smith; on this see Ch. 5, n. 59). For the origins of the light analogy see Kalligas (1994: 173). Plotinus often uses the analogy of the heat of fire and the heated object for showing the difference between hypostasis and its power; cf. *Enn.* 5. 4. 2. 30–3.

[23] *Enn.* 4. 9. 1–3, 4. 9. 5. 1–2.

[24] Cf. *Enn.* 4. 4. 22. 28–31.

[25] See *Enn.* 4. 2. 1. 65–76.

[26] See Kalligas (2000: 34–5) on how the features of the transcendent soul are transmitted to the embodied one.

which allow it to sustain itself, to operate, to perceive, and to reproduce (*Enn.* 4. 3. 23. 3–22).

This is a recognizable Aristotelian position which Platonists like Plutarch and Severus espoused because they considered it Platonic. Plotinus follows this tradition but he goes further in his reliance on Aristotle with regard to how the embodied soul relates to body. Plotinus turns out to accept two crucial Aristotelian premises. First, the human body is not an object that becomes alive but rather is a certain kind of body (*toionde soma*), that is a natural body equipped with organs which exists in a certain form, that is, as living.[27] Secondly, this form is accounted for by the soul,[28] as is the soul that shapes and informs the body so that it becomes living.[29]

Plotinus appears to distinguish two stages in this process. First the body is shaped and moulded by the world-soul so that it becomes a suitable organic body, and then the individual soul enlivens it.[30] Thus the body acquires a life of its own (*Enn.* 4. 4. 29. 14–15), which is an image of the life of soul (4. 3. 10. 38–40). As I have mentioned above, Plotinus presents the body as being informed by the soul so that it becomes living in the way the light informs the air (1. 1. 7. 1–6, 4. 3. 22. 1–7, 4. 4. 14. 1–6, 18. 4–6) or the heat of the fire informs the heated water (4. 4. 14. 6–9, 29. 1–17). Now such analogies suggest not only that the embodied soul relates to the transcendent one in the way immanent Forms relate to transcendent ones, but also that the embodied soul relates to the body in the way that the immanent Form of an entity relates to that entity. Against this one can bring as evidence Plotinus' claim that the soul does not relate to the body as immanent Form to matter, but that it imposes Form on matter, being different from that Form (4. 3. 20. 36–9). Yet in this passage, I think, Plotinus talks about the transcendent soul, which is separable even while being present in the body (1. 1. 10. 7–11). Plotinus

[27] The body is said to be suitable (ἐπιτήδειον) for accommodating the soul (*Enn.* 4. 3. 23. 3).

[28] Cf. *Enn.* 4. 7. 2 (there can be no body without some formative principle), and 6. 4. 15. 9–18.

[29] *ἔστι γὰρ ἡ φύσις πρὸ τοῦ τοιόνδε σῶμα γενέσθαι, αὕτη γὰρ ποιεῖ τὸ τοιόνδε πλάττουσα καὶ μορφοῦσα* (for nature exists before the qualified body has come into being, since it itself makes the qualified body, shaping it and forming it; [Armstrong's tr.]). *Enn.* 4. 4. 20. 23–5). Plotinus clarifies that what we call nature is the soul 'which gives the trace of soul to the body' (*Enn.* 4. 4. 20. 15–16). Cf. 2. 5. 3. 13–17.

[30] See *Enn.* 4. 3. 17. 1–3, 6. 4. 15. 8–29. See Igal (1979: 328). Plotinus maintains that matter itself cannot form any body, let alone a living one without an intellect and a soul to give shape to matter, and not even matter would exist (*Enn.* 4. 7. 3. 14–35). Plotinus is obviously inspired by the *Timaeus* here.

makes clear that he considers the living being (τὸ ζῷον) to be a complex entity (τὸ συναμφότερον or τὸ σύνθετον) consisting in Form and matter.[31] That is, the embodied soul accounts for the living body in the same way that the Form of a book, for instance, accounts for the being of a book qua book.

There is a difficulty, though, with the analogy of the heat and the heated water or the one of the light and the air. The heat is the Form of the heated water, and as such is inseparable from it qua heated water, but the heat accounts only for a quality of the water, that is, its being hot, not for the water itself, the substance. In the case of the book, though, the Form of the book accounts for the being of the book.

Plotinus' analogies are revealing of the way in which he thought of the immanent Forms. As I explain below (s. 4), Plotinus assumed that the immanent Form is not a substance but only an image (εἴδωλον) of the real substance which must be transcendent, and in the case of sensible entities, more especially, it is the *logos* or the intelligible Form (*Enn.* 6. 3. 15. 26–39). In the case of the soul, it is the transcendent soul which is substance, while the embodied one is a power derived from the former, and as such a mere image or a shadow of the soul, as the sensible substance is the shadow of the intelligible one (6. 3. 8. 30–7). However, this does not mean that the embodied soul is a mere quality, as the above analogies appear to suggest. Plotinus argues expressly against such an idea (6. 4. 1. 17–29; cf. 4. 2. 1). The reason why such an idea is rejected is that the transcendent soul remains one and the same even when it is divided in individual souls (4. 2. 1, 6. 1. 1).[32]

The upshot of all this is that Plotinus did conceive of the relation between the embodied soul and the living body in terms of the relation between immanent Form and matter, that is, as Aristotle had thought of them, yet his metaphysics of this relation differs much from that of Aristotle. For Aristotle the immanent Form, which corresponds to the embodied soul, is a substance, that which makes something what it is, whereas for Plotinus it is the transcendent soul which is substance, while individual, embodied souls are substances derivative from it, in the same sense that sensible substances are such because they are accounted for by intelligible ones (see more below, s. 5). It is because Plotinus believes

[31] *Enn.* 1. 1. 7. 1–2, 1. 1. 11. 1–3, 4. 3. 26. 1, 6. 8. 2. 13. The term συναμφότερον is inspired by Plato's *Alcibiades* 130a9. Plotinus and later Porphyry use it to denote the composite of matter and Form (e.g. *Enn.* 2. 5. 13, 6. 7. 4. 19, *Sent.* 21, p. 13. 5 Lamberz); see Schwyzer (1974: 232) and below p. 249.

[32] I am grateful to Professor Emilsson for drawing my attention to these passages.

that immanent Forms are qualities that he rejects Aristotle's doctrine of the soul as being the Form of the living body. If the soul is like a quality, similar to colour or shape, Plotinus argues, there would be many subjects of sense perception, but obviously this is not so, so the soul is not a quality and thus Aristotle, according to Plotinus, is wrong.[33]

Plotinus appears to be adopting Aristotle's doctrine while at the same time rewriting its metaphysics; he adapts Aristotle's hylomorphism to fit his dualism, while Aristotle was a monist. Such an interpretation comes in clear contrast with that of Alexander, which Plotinus presumably had in mind when criticizing Aristotle.[34] With this strategy Plotinus manages to preserve both the transcendence of the soul and a high degree of unity of the soul–body compound, and thus, in his view at least to disarm Peripatetics who argued only for the latter.

Plotinus appears to make use of Aristotle also on other issues regarding the soul. For instance, he draws on several Aristotelian views concerning specific ways in which the soul operates within the body. Plotinus maintains that the soul operates in the body by means of faculties, as Aristotle does in the *De anima*, a view already adopted by Plutarch and Severus, but unlike the latter he also accepts the division of the soul into rational and irrational parts (*Enn.* 4. 4. 28. 62–76; cf. *De anima* 432^{a}22–b8). Plotinus is particularly indebted to Aristotle in his account of sense perception, which he considers a common function of soul and body (4. 3. 26. 1–9).[35] He takes over Aristotle's distinction between sense perception and thinking, arguing that the former requires material, bodily organs in order to capture material entities, while thinking does not.[36] As regards sense perception, Plotinus argues that the soul represents the craftsman and the body the tool (4. 3. 26. 4–5). For Plotinus the bodily organs are the recipients of the sensibles. That is, they receive the sense impression (*typôsis*) on the body and transmit it to the soul (4. 3. 26. 6–8). As a result, a kind of affection (*homopatheia*) between the soul and the sense-objects is established.[37]

What kind of affection is this? Plotinus argues that the soul does not receive impressions of external objects, so when he uses the word *typos* he does not refer to impressions in a literal sense, like those of seals for

[33] *Enn.* 4. 2. 2. 4–10. I am indebted here to Emilsson (2005).

[34] See Alexander, *De anima* 14. 24–15. 5. I am indebted to Riccardo Chiaradonna who drew my attention to this passage.

[35] See Emilsson (1988: 67–70).

[36] *Enn.* 4. 3. 23. 3–7, 34–5, 4. 4. 23. 1–6, 4. 5. 1. 6–13.

[37] *Enn.* 4. 5. 1. 6–13. For a discussion of this passage see Kalligas (2004*b*: 69–70).

instance.[38] Plotinus follows Aristotle in arguing that the way in which the sense organ receives the sensible is by receiving its Form.[39] This means that for Plotinus all perceptions of the soul are determined by the world of the intelligible Forms.

Interestingly, such a view leads Plotinus to disagree with Aristotle's conviction that when we remember, a kind of impression (*typos*) of the sensation (*aisthêma*) occurs in the soul.[40] Aristotle proposed this as a solution to the question of how we remember an absent thing, that is, how an affection is present while the object absent. Plotinus construes Aristotle's reply literally and argues against the idea that the soul can have impressions in this sense.[41] Indeed, his short treatise *On perception and memory* (*Enn.* 4. 6 [41]) targets specifically Aristotle's *On memory* $450^{a}27–450^{b}1$.

From the above considerations some conclusions emerge. Plotinus maintains that Aristotle's doctrine of the soul as the actuality of the living body contradicts that of Plato, and thus he criticizes the former. Yet Plotinus finds Aristotle's doctrine of the soul compatible with the Platonic metaphysics of the soul when limited to the way the embodied soul relates to the body and how it operates within it. In this matter Plotinus does not hesitate to draw on Aristotle for reconstructing Plato's relevant doctrine, but in doing so he strips Aristotle's doctrine of the soul from his metaphysical underpinnings.

3. ETHICS

Plotinus' belief that the soul is essentially rational shapes his ethical views and determines his stance towards Aristotle's ethics.[42] To put it briefly, Plotinus is critical outright of Aristotle's position in ethics, as

[38] *Enn.* 3. 6. 1. 1–11, 19–20, 37–9, 4. 3. 26. 26–33. See Emilsson (1988: 78–82). Porphyry, however, defines perception precisely as impressions of the seals *In Ptol. Harm.* 14. 14–18. See Ch. 7, s. 6. 3, pp. 301–3.

[39] *Enn.* 4. 4. 23. 20–1, Aristotle, *De anima* $424^{a}17–21$; see also Emilsson (1988: 71–2).

[40] *ἔτι τῶν αἰσθήσεων τυπώσεων οὐκ οὐσῶν, πῶς οἷόν τε τὰς μνήμας κατοχὰς τῶν οὐκ ἐντεθέντων οὐδὲ τὴν ἀρχὴν εἶναι;* (when sense perceptions are not impressions, how could memories be retentions of imprints which were never made [in the soul] at all? Armstrong's tr.; *Enn.* 4. 6. 3. 55–7).

[41] See Emilsson (1988: 76–8).

[42] On Plotinus' ethics see Dillon (1983: 92–105; 1996: 315–35); Smith (1999: 227–36).

outlined in the first books of the *Nicomachean Ethics*. He argues that Plato's conception of happiness or good life (*eudaimonia*) has nothing to do with the state which Aristotle described, according to which happiness consists in a life of virtue but also the enjoyment of other goods, such as health, beauty, having children and friends. In *Ennead* 1. 4, one of Plotinus' late treatises (no. 46), Plotinus makes a sharp distinction between *euzôia*, which in his view is the state that Aristotle describes, and *eudaimonia*, which, he argues, is the state of real happiness.[43] Plotinus maintains that *eudaimonia* is a state not subject to improvement (*Enn.* 1. 4. 3. 30–1, 1. 4. 4. 30–1). Living longer, he argues, does not increase happiness, which should not be counted by time but by eternity (1. 5. 7, 22–4); nor do bodily or external advantages increase happiness. For these, Plotinus argues, have nothing to do with our true self, the intellect, but are simply necessary for everyday life;[44] since Aristotle failed to realize this, he failed in his aim to outline how one can live a good life.

To understand Plotinus' criticism we must first make sense of his conception of virtue. This in turn is rooted in his understanding of human nature. Plotinus distinguishes between the inner man, whom he identifies with the human intellect, and the outer man, who consists of all other living functions (*Enn.* 1. 1. 10. 5–15).[45] Relying on *Phaedo* 115c–d. and *Alcibiades* 1. 130a–c, Plotinus argues that man's self is his rationality, that is, the transcendent, intellective soul (*Enn.* 4. 4. 18. 10–12)[46] which the demiurge of *Timaeus* (34c–37c) created as rational, immortal, and divine, destined to think and contemplate.[47] The soul, Plotinus argues, stays always in contact with the transcendent realm (*Enn.* 4. 8. 8), having its eye continuously fixed upon true Being, even if we are not aware of

[43] *Enn.* 1. 4. 14, 1–7, 1. 4. 16. 11–15.

[44] *Enn.* 1. 4. 4. 22–9, 1. 4. 5, 1. 4. 15.

[45] This distinction constitutes an attempt to reconcile passages of Plato which suggest that man is essentially an intellect (e.g. *Sophist* 248d-e–249a) with those which assume that man is more complex (*Philebus* 21d–e).

[46] *ἡ δὲ ψυχὴ ἡ τοιαύτη ἡ ἐγγενομένη τῇ τοιαύτῃ ὕλῃ, ἅτε οὖσα τοῦτο, οἷον οὕτω διακειμένη καὶ ἄνευ τοῦ σώματος, ἄνθρωπος, ἐν σώματι δὲ μορφώσασα κατ' αὐτὴν καὶ ἄλλο εἴδωλον ἀνθρώπου ὅσον ἐδέχετο τὸ σῶμα ποιήσασα, ὥσπερ καὶ τούτου αὖ ποιήσει ὁ ζωγράφος ἔτι ἐλάττω ἄνθρωπόν τινα* (And the soul of this kind which enters into matter of this kind, just because this is what it is, being in a way disposed like this even without the body, is man; it makes shapes in body according to itself, and makes another image of man as far as body allows, just as the painter in his turn makes yet another image of this, a kind of still lesser man; *Enn.* 6. 7. 5. 11–17; tr. Armstrong).

[47] Cf. Plato, *Rep.* 589a. For Plotinus 'the perfect life, the true, real life is found in the intelligible nature' (*Enn.* 1. 4. 3. 33–5; cf. 1. 2. 7. 6–13).

that, trying to conform to this reality and thus achieve happiness (*Enn.* 1. 4. 10. 10–24). The body on the other hand is not an essential part of human nature but simply attached to man (*prosērtēmenon*; 1. 4. 4. 27; cf. 1. 1. 12. 18–20, *Timaeus* 42c–d) or used by man (*Enn.* 6. 7. 5. 24–5), a position reminiscent of that of Numenius (cf. fr. 43 Des Places). As a result, Plotinus identifies virtue with thinking and he believes that man becomes happy only if he does justice to his rational nature, and this would essentially involve thinking.

There are, however, different levels of knowledge and thinking, already distinguished in Plato's work. Plotinus considers different levels of thinking to correspond to different levels of virtue. As he values philosophical understanding higher than practical knowledge, he also values theoretical virtues more than political or practical ones (*Enn.* 1. 2. 1. 22–3). Within each of the two levels Plotinus distinguishes further grades of virtue. At the level of political virtue he distinguishes between the practical (1. 2. 1. 17–21) and the cathartic virtue (1. 2. 3. 15–19), that is, the stage in which the soul is purified from bodily concerns and thus attains more virtue, because, as is suggested in the *Phaedo* (66b–d, 69b–e), the body prevents the soul from seeing reality.[48] At the theoretical level of virtue Plotinus distinguishes between intellectual contemplation (*theōria*, 1. 2. 6. 12–27) and intellection (*noēsis*; 1. 2. 7. 3–6).[49]

At this point one can object that also for Aristotle intellectual contemplation is an activity essential to a good life, and as has been seen, both Antiochus and Plutarch appreciated this Aristotelian doctrine. What is more, this Aristotelian view rests on the belief, found in several passages of the *Nicomachean Ethics*, especially in *NE* 10, that man's real self consists in reason. The question that arises is why Plotinus does not acknowledge this aspect of Aristotle's ethics. One could further argue that also in Aristotle's ethics one can detect different levels of virtue, corresponding to different levels of good life, and one can claim that also for Aristotle good life can increase, if one, for instance, not only is virtuous but also dedicates oneself to philosophical contemplation.[50] This actually seems to be Porphyry's view, as I will argue in the next chapter (pp. 303–8), while the issue remains controversial in modern scholarship.[51]

[48] See *Enn.* 3. 6. 5. 13–20 where Plotinus explains from what the soul is to be purified.

[49] On the hierarchy of virtues see Sorabji (2000: 205–10).

[50] This is argued by Heinaman (2002: 137–41).

[51] See e.g. Heinaman (2002).

Plotinus does not address such a question. One reason for this may be his belief that Aristotle's accounts of happiness in *Nicomachean Ethics* 1 and 10 are contradictory, and on these grounds Aristotle's ethics is a failure. This would not be an entirely unfair criticism. Also in modern times it is often argued that Aristotle's accounts of *eudaimonia* in *NE* assume different conceptions of virtue which are difficult to reconcile. Plotinus may have regarded the two Aristotelian accounts as contradictory because on Aristotle's conception of happiness in *NE* 10 virtue is not subject to improvement, while in the one assumed in *NE* 1–9 this is less clear. For Plotinus this may be due to the fact that the two Aristotelian accounts rest on considerably disparate conceptions of human nature. We know that Plotinus rejected the Aristotelian definition of man as a rational animal, because 'animal' means 'a compound of body and soul' (*Enn.* 6. 7. 4. 10–18),[52] while for him this compound corresponds only to the outer man, the lower human part, which he identified with the embodied soul. Presumably, from Plotinus' point of view, Aristotle seems to retain Plato's doctrine in *NE* 10, but denies it in the rest of the *NE*. Aristotle then appears to Plotinus as the Stoics appear to Plutarch, as self-refuting Platonists. From this point of view, Aristotle's ethics is useless for a Platonist.

Plotinus' conception of virtue does not involve correlative degrees of virtue and happiness or good life. Rather, such a life is obtained only at the ultimate level of virtue because only at this level can one grasp the truth and thus realize one's real self. For Plotinus this amounts to ascending to the level of intellect and becoming like God (*Enn.* 1. 2. 6. 3–7, 3. 4. 2. 13–15), which implies a life of freedom, virtue, and intellectual contemplation, as suggested in *Republic* 10, the *Phaedo* (64b–65d, 82c–83b) or the *Theaetetus* (176a–b). All other kinds of life are simply likenesses (*indalmata*) of the perfect life (*Enn.* 1. 4. 3. 33–40). This suggests that according to Plotinus lower virtues are preparatory for developing the higher ones but not sufficient for happiness. This is why Plotinus was little concerned with the nature of practical virtue and how to achieve it.[53]

This does not mean that he was disinterested in practical virtue, however. His personal example shows that for him commitment to the intellectual level does not mean indifference to the ethics of everyday

[52] This has been pointed out by Emilsson (1988: 26).

[53] Cf. *V. Plot.* 9. 12–22, 11. 12–15. On Plotinus' view of practical virtue see Smith (1999).

life. Quite the contrary. Plotinus rather believes that the ultimate virtue implies also the lower ones, because the life of the intellect, when achieved, informs our entire life. He seems to hold that a philosopher does not need to think especially about his duty when he sees an elder lady trying to cross the road; his intellectual concern with virtue would make it natural, almost instinctive for him to help. Plotinus argues that philosophical reflection (*theōria*) leads to such action, while such action does not lead to philosophical reflection (*Enn.* 3. 8. 6. 1–6). Like the Stoic sage, the Plotinian wise person knows what virtue is and is able to identify the good in all circumstances. But in the case of Plotinus the wise man is always guided by *theōria* in his actions and it is precisely this which lends value to them (3. 8. 4. 31–40). But this *theōria* does not only involve knowledge of the good but rather living at the level of the intellect, aspiring to become assimilated to the divine which is identified with the Form of the Good of the *Republic* (*Enn.* 1. 7. 1. 14–22). It seems then that Plotinus' conception of *theōria* rests on metaphysical postulates which Plotinus did not find in Aristotle.

This is reminiscent of Atticus, who, as has been seen, was inspired by the view of virtue being sufficient for a good life, which is found in Platonic dialogues and was taken over by the Stoics. Like them, Plotinus holds that knowledge transforms man so completely that one's virtuous disposition enables one to possess all virtues.[54] In such a way one's actions are at an altogether different level from that of the ordinary person. Plotinus turns out to agree with Atticus (and presumably also with Numenius) about Plato's ethical doctrine and his criticism of Aristotle's doctrine is launched from a similar point of view. His only difference from them is that he strives to integrate and systematize all elements found in Plato, so that Plato's doctrine emerges coherent and complete. But this makes Plotinus' rejection of Aristotle's ethics even more striking because it suggests that there is almost nothing in it to help understand Plato. And this is because Plotinus believes, following earlier Platonist critics, that Aristotle's ethics underlies metaphysical doctrines considerably different from those they attributed to Plato.

[54] Plotinus maintains that virtues imply one another: *'Αντακολουθοῦσι . . . ἀλλήλαις αἱ ἀρεταὶ ἐν ψυχῇ* (*Enn.* 1. 2. 7. 1–2). We find this view also in Atticus (see Ch. 4, s. 3, p. 163); Arius Didymus in Stob. 2. 142. 6–14; Alcinous, *Didasc.* 183. 3. See Lilla (1971: 82–3).

4. METAPHYSICS

Plotinus' most important and detailed criticism of Aristotelian philosophy concerns its metaphysics, more precisely Aristotle's doctrine of the *Categories*.[55] Plotinus discusses Aristotle's theory in his *Enneads* 6. 1–3, but does not criticize Aristotle in all of them. His criticism is mainly contained in the first twenty-four sections of *Ennead* 6. 1.

Like earlier Platonist critics such as Lucius and Nicostratus, Plotinus considers Aristotle's *Categories* to be an ontological work in which Aristotle addresses the question 'how many and what kinds of beings there are'. Plotinus reviews Aristotle's theory in order to show its weaknesses. His main objection is that in the *Categories* Aristotle does not take into account what is being *par excellence*, the intelligible entities.[56] This is a serious defect if Aristotle is outlining a general ontology, as Plotinus believes. Plotinus considers the possible answers as to why the intelligible entities are not mentioned in the *Categories*. One possible answer would be that Aristotle's ten *genera* of being apply to both sensible and intelligible entities. Yet for Plotinus this is impossible, given their ontological disparity (*Enn*. 6. 1. 1. 15–30).[57] As Pierre Hadot has argued, Plotinus's objection is that the term substance (*ousia*) cannot be used synonymously both for the intelligible substances, those which are only Form, and also those which consist in both Form and matter, such as the sensible ones, but only homonymously.[58] Since Plotinus considers Aristotle to be mistaken in this, he regards Aristotle's doctrine of substance as fundamentally mistaken (*Enn*. 6. 1. 2. 8–18, 6. 1. 3. 21–3).

Plotinus' objection underlies the belief that a real genus cannot include items which are prior and posterior to each other, as intelligibles and sensibles are. As has been argued, this is an idea that Plotinus takes

[55] Plotinus' criticism of Aristotle's *Categories* has engendered some controversy lately. See mainly Lloyd (1955: 68–72); Henry (1973); Strange (1987: 965–74); Chiaradonna (1996: 55–76); De Haas (2001); and Chiaradonna (2002: 8–54). I disagree with De Haas's argument that Plotinus and Porphyry take very similar positions. I hope that this will be convincingly shown in this and the next chapter (esp. s. 8). The thrust of Plotinus' criticism goes back to Nicostratus; see Praechter (1922: 115–22, 131–3).

[56] οὐ πάντα ἄρα τὰ ὄντα διαιρεῖσθαι ἐβουλήθησαν, ἀλλὰ τὰ μάλιστα ὄντα παραλελοίπασι (so they did not want to classify all beings, but left out those which are most authentically beings; Armstrong's tr.; *Enn*. 6. 1. 1. 27–30).

[57] On this criticism of Plotinus see Strange (1987: 965–70).

[58] Hadot (1990: 126).

over from Aristotle himself.[59] Scholars have shown how Aristotle and Plotinus understand this view. Plotinus, unlike Aristotle, understands natural priority not only as ontological dependence, but also as causal priority.[60] The important point, though, is that Plotinus does not accuse Aristotle of inconsistency, nor does he even consider this as a possibility; rather, he takes it for granted that Aristotle's categories do not apply to the intelligible realm and he maintains that Aristotle left out intelligible entities. Given the impossibility of having one genus spanning both the intelligible and the sensible realm, Plotinus argues, we have to devise another series of categories applicable only to the intelligible realm (*Enn.* 6. 1. 12. 51–3, 6. 3. 1. 3–6, 19–21). The most important item in this series would be the category of being. This is one of the five *megista gênê* of the *Sophist* (254b–255d), which for Plotinus are the categories of the intelligible world, as for several other Platonists before him (cf. Plutarch, *De an. proc.* 1013D). In his view, the category of being would replace Aristotle's conception of substance. But if this is so, then Aristotle's theory of the categories turns out to be inadequate also as regards the sensible realm.

It is not immediately clear why this is so. Nor is it clear why Plotinus did not consider the possibility that Aristotle simply had omitted intelligible substances because, for instance, he wanted to concentrate only on the sensible ones.

The reason must be the following. In Plotinus' view, one cannot possibly account for the sensible beings without reference to the intelligible ones. This must be the view which guides Plotinus' entire polemics.[61] Plotinus argues that Aristotle does not actually talk at all about substance in his *Categories*; what he rather talks about, Plotinus argues, is peculiar properties of substances (*Enn.* 6. 1. 3. 19–22).[62] Plotinus finds Aristotle's view of substance untenable exactly because he regards Aristotle's conception of immanent Form as mistaken. For Plotinus, Aristotle is right to hold that the Form is substance and also

[59] Lloyd (1990: 76–85), Strange (1987: 966–8).

[60] Strange (1987: 967).

[61] See Chiaradonna (2002: 117–46) for a detailed analysis.

[62] *ἀλλὰ ταῦτα μὲν* [sc. the immanent Forms] *ἴδια ἄν τις λέγοι πρὸς τὰ ἄλλα καὶ διὰ τοῦτο εἰς ἓν οὕτω συνάγοι καὶ οὐσίας λέγοι, ἓν δέ τι γένος οὐκ ἂν λέγοι, οὐδὲ δηλοῖ πω τὴν ἔννοιαν τῆς οὐσίας καὶ τὴν φύσιν.* (But one might say that these are peculiar properties of substances as compared with other things, and for this reason one might collect them into one and call them substances, but one would not be speaking of one genus nor would one yet be making clear the concept and nature of substance; *Enn.* 6. 1. 3. 19–22; tr. Armstrong).

to hold that this is what accounts for the existence of all sensible entities, but is wrong to maintain that it is the immanent Form that amounts to substance. In his view Aristotle's sensible substance is a mere conglomeration of matter and qualities (*Enn.* 6. 3. 8. 19–23) and Aristotle's immanent Form is one such quality or the sum of such qualities (6. 3. 15. 24–9), not substance, as Alexander had argued. Plotinus seems to admit that such a quality or sum of qualities partly accounts for the existence of a sensible entity. But he argues that this is only an image (εἴδωλον) of the real substance, which is the *logos* or the intelligible Form, the one that sufficiently accounts for a sensible being (6. 3. 15. 26–39). For Plotinus as substances qualify only the transcendent Forms and other transcendent entities, all of which eventually are accounted for by the presence of the One. This is because Plotinus believes that sensible entities do not have natures or essences and that only transcendent entities have, since the former change while the latter do not. That is, in his view a sensible entity becomes F but never truly is F.

This conviction was shared by Numenius and Atticus and can be traced back to Plato. It explains why for them the sensible or physical world cannot be adequately explained except with reference to the intelligible world. For Plotinus in particular, the cause of everything is the One.[63]

This feature of Plotinus' philosophy is crucial if we want to understand his attitude to Aristotle's categories in *Enn.* 6. 3. There Plotinus is much less polemical towards Aristotle, but this does not mean that he accepts Aristotle's categories as valid for the sensible realm. If Plotinus eventually integrates Aristotle's categories and his notion of substance, in particular, in *Enn.* 6. 3, he does so while placing them in a Platonist ontological framework, which redresses the insufficiencies of Aristotle's theory. And this framework would justify his use of Aristotle's distinctions between 'in a subject' and 'said of a subject', that is, between property and substance (*Enn.* 4. 5. 6. 11–13; *Cat.* 1^{a}20–5). This should not obscure the fact that Plotinus finds Aristotle's doctrine essentially flawed for the reasons I have explained above. As with psychology, Plotinus eventually integrates Aristotle's views of sensible reality in his own conceptual framework, but the entire metaphysics behind Aristotle's doctrine of the *Categories* is seriously altered.

Given Plotinus' conception of the One as the ultimate cause of everything, he overtly rejects Aristotle's doctrine according to which

[63] See Wagner (1996: 136) and esp. Chiaradonna (2002: 249–71).

the first entity by nature on which all else depends is an intellect, the unmoved mover. Plotinus maintains that this is an untenable doctrine because the intellect already implies multiplicity in two senses: first, there is the multiplicity of objects of thought, and, secondly, there is also a duality of thinking and object of thought. On these grounds the intellect is composite, and as such it cannot be first by nature. Plotinus' objection rests on the assumption found already in Alcinous, that the demiurgic intellect, the creator of the *Timaeus*, who may be compared with Aristotle's God, thinks of the Forms. Plotinus posits instead the One as superior, prior to the Intellect, and argues that it is on it that everything else depends. The One is beyond being, as the Form of the Good is in Plato (*Rep.* 509b), while the Intellect is not.

Yet Plotinus' conception of the Intellect is much influenced by the Aristotelian account of the divine intellect in *Metaphysics* 12, as has been shown in detail by Thomas Szlezák.[64] Plotinus, Szlezák argues, follows Aristotle (*Metaphysics* 12. 9) in presenting the Intellect both as an *hypostasis* in which subject and object of thinking are identical (*Enn.* 5. 3. 5), and also as a self-thinking *nous*. Furthermore, Plotinus is guided by *Metaphysics* 12. 7 in his argument about the goodness of the Intellect (*Enn.* 6. 6. 7. 19–22). He follows Aristotle in presenting the Intellect as the object of universal striving and love (6. 7. 20. 20–4). Already Plutarch had implied this (see Ch. 2, p. 108), but Plotinus explores the matter further, because he is more interested in describing in detail the intelligible realm.

One instance is quite indicative of Plotinus' respect for Aristotle's *Metaphysics*. He argues that the Intellect is not desired qua Intellect but qua good, but the definition of the good which he cites in this context turns out to be Aristotle's.[65] This is a feature which we have encountered in Platonists like Plutarch or Alcinous who believed that sometimes Aristotle recasts Platonic doctrines or interprets Plato correctly. Apparently Plotinus thought similarly in this case and this is why he endorsed Aristotle's conception of the divine intellect. Such a treatment of Aristotle is striking in three other instances where Plotinus refers with approval to Aristotle by a mere φησὶν or φασίν, the kind of reference usually reserved for Plato. We have already encountered one when discussing Plotinus' doctrine of the soul (see above, n. 15). The two other instances

[64] Szlezák (1979: 126–32). I refer the reader to Szlezák's work for an extensive discussion of the matter.

[65] *Enn.* 6. 7. 19. 9–10; cf. *NE* 1098^{a}16–17.

are the following: *Enn.* 2. 1. 6. 25 (referring to *De gen. et corr.* 335^{a}1–2 on the composition of the earth), *Enn.* 4. 4. 15. 19–20 (referring to *Phys.* 221^{a}8–9 on place and time).[66]

5. PHYSICS

Plotinus' disagreement with Aristotle's metaphysics becomes evident again in his criticism of various aspects of Aristotle's physics, such as the Aristotelian doctrine of time and change. Plotinus accuses Aristotle of simply describing the physical world instead of explaining it. This is a criticism Plutarch had already implied and Atticus had made forcefully; Plotinus' conception of causal explanation has similarities with theirs. According to this, the physical world can be explained adequately only by reference to the intelligible world, and in particular to the One.

This can be seen first in Plotinus' criticism of Aristotle's theory of time. Plotinus argues that Aristotle, among others, does not explain but merely describes the real nature of time. Plotinus relies on Aristotle's report of the various views of philosophers about time (*Physics* 218^{a}30–^{b}20), which he summarizes as follows: time is said to be either 'the so-called movement, or what is moved, or something which pertains to movement' (*Enn.* 3. 7. 7. 18–19). Plotinus rejects all this for the view stated in *Timaeus* 37d–38b that time is the 'image of the eternity', and comes to argue against Aristotle's position that time is the number of movement.[67] Plotinus finds several flaws in Aristotle's argument, which were already noticed by Peripatetics themselves.[68] First, he argues, if we adopt Aristotle's definition of time as number of the movement, we cannot measure irregular movement; for this reason, Aristotle's term 'measure' (*metron*) of movement is preferable (*Enn.* 3. 7. 9. 2–15: *Phys.* 221^{a}1). But if time is a measure of different types of movement, like a number which can apply to horses and oxen, or of different types of things, like liquids and solids, then what is the difference between time and numbers (3. 7. 9. 15–17)? Further, Plotinus accuses Aristotle of not specifying what time is as such, the measured distance or the measure by means of which we calculate (3. 7. 9. 17–31). His point is that Aristotle

[66] Plotinus' citation of Aristotle in *Enn.* 2. 1. 6. 25 has been identified by Dufour (2002).

[67] *Physics* 219^{b}1–2; cf. *De caelo* 275^{a}14–15; *Enn.* 3. 7. 9. 1–2.

[68] e.g. Eudemus frs. 82b, 86 Wehrli. See Chiaradonna (2003: 229–33).

tells us what kind of thing time measures but not what kind of thing time is. This is Plotinus' most crucial argument against Aristotle.

As Plotinus argues, time is not essentially the measure of movement but only accidentally (*Enn.* 3. 7. 12. 41–3). Movement, he argues, does not bring time about (3. 7. 12. 49–52), nor does time need movement in order to exist, but rather movement makes time manifest (ibid.), since it takes place in time (3. 7. 8. 56–8). For Plotinus time essentially is the activity of the soul. It is not easy to understand what he means by this and it is beyond the scope of this study to explain it in detail, but a brief explanation might be the following.

Plotinus' view about time has to do with the fact that for him the sensible world is accounted for, and maintained by the Soul, one of the three intelligible hypostases. For Plotinus it is the Soul that sets everything in motion;[69] the motion that takes place in the sensible world is an imitation of that of the Soul. Such a view is clearly inspired by the *Phaedrus* (245c–d) and the *Timaeus* (36b–c) where the soul is presented as being self-moved. It is the movement of the Soul, Plotinus argues, which generates time (3. 7. 13. 45–7). But why does the Soul generate time? Plotinus' answer is that this is because the Soul was unable to contemplate the totality of intelligibles all at once but only gradually (3. 7. 11).

Yet although Aristotle is found culpable of considering time only in relation to sensible movement, Plotinus refrains from castigating him. In a remarkable passage near the end of his treatise Plotinus argues that Aristotle is obscure in his written work but he may have been clearer to his audience (*Enn.* 3. 7. 13. 13–18). This is quite striking because Plotinus takes a view about Aristotle's explanation of the physical world similar to that of Atticus, and yet his tone is considerably more lenient than that of Atticus. Besides, as already referred to, Plotinus does not hesitate to refer to Aristotle's views on time and place with approval (*Enn.* 4. 4. 15. 19–20; *Phys.* 221^{a}8–9).

Plotinus' criticism of Aristotle's doctrine of change rests on the same basic idea that Aristotle does not offer sufficient explanations. Plotinus finds the Aristotelian distinction between *kinêsis* and *energeia* questionable.[70] As is known, for Aristotle *energeiai*, such as life, pleasure, sight do not become complete at a given time, but are in fact always so (*Met.* 1048^{a}25–^{b}35; *NE* 1174^{a}14–^{b}10). Anytime something is seen, for

[69] *Enn.* 3. 7. 13. 34–5, 3. 6. 4. 38–43.

[70] Plotinus' criticism of Aristotle's doctrine of change is discussed in detail by Chiaradonna (2002: 147–225). I refer the reader to Chiaradonna's analysis.

instance, it also has been seen completely. *Kinêseis* on the contrary, involves a process, a transition from one point to another, for instance from being white to being some other colour, or being at my house to being in the library. Before reaching one of these end-points the motion, according to Aristotle, is incomplete. Accordingly he considers *kinêsis* as an incomplete *energeia* (*Physics* 201^b31–2). Plotinus rejects the idea that motion itself is an incomplete *energeia* and argues that something's being in motion is completely actual or real at any time it moves. What remains incomplete is not the walking, for instance, but the walking of a certain distance, for example, up to the library (*Enn.* 6. 1. 16. 10–17). On the other hand, Plotinus argues, both the *kinêsis* and the *energeia* of sensible objects are in time, but both can take place outside time (6. 1. 16. 23–31). Plotinus implies that Aristotle's distinction between *kinêsis* and *energeia* makes little sense because both take place in time. He seems to believe that *kinêsis* merely is an extended *energeia* (6. 1. 16), and that there is a contradiction inherent in Aristotle's view that an *energeia* does not take time but is in time.

As has been noted,[71] Plotinus is wrong in this. There is no contradiction in Aristotle's doctrine. Yet for Plotinus *kinêsis* is one of the *megista gênê* of the *Sophist* (254d) which are constitutive of the intelligible world, so the distinction in his view must be made in ontological terms (*Enn.* 6. 2. 8. 25–49). Once again it turns out that Plotinus' criticism of Aristotle is based on strong metaphysical assumptions. The interesting point here is that Plotinus is intrigued by Aristotle's distinction; he seems to find some value in it and this is why he wants to modify it, so that it could be integrated into Platonist metaphysics, which he does in *Enn.* 6. 3. 22.[72]

One other question in which Plotinus considers Aristotle's positions quite carefully is that of matter, as has been shown in detail by Kevin Corrigan.[73] Plotinus believes that matter is privation, non-being, and evil, as Numenius did, but he argues that the Peripatetic notions of ultimate matter have to be interpreted similarly (*Enn.* 2. 4, 2. 5). This brings him to believe that Plato's conception of matter, especially his notion of the receptacle, and Aristotle's relevant doctrine are compatible, a view already taken by Plutarch (*De def. orac.* 414F). Plotinus appears to

[71] Chiaradonna (2002: 164–5). See also Wagner (1996: 139–42).

[72] Plotinus' strategy in *Enn.* 6. 3. 22 is expounded in detail by Chiaradonna (2002: 195–221).

[73] I am indebted to Corrigan's analysis (1996: esp. 108–16), to which I refer the reader for an interesting and detailed account.

endorse some important Aristotelian principles. He accepts that matter is potentially everything but he specifies that potentiality is always potentiality of something, which is to be explained by reference to the eventual actual state of the subject (*Enn.* 2. 5. 1–2). It is intelligible entities, *logoi* or Forms, which account for the actuality of a subject. This is a doctrine which will play a crucial role in the shaping of Porphyry's interpretation of the cosmogony of the *Timaeus* (see Ch. 7, s. 5. 2).

Plotinus himself shows little interest in the debate about the cosmogony of the *Timaeus*, although he clearly sides with the non-literal interpretation of it.[74] Unlike Atticus, Plotinus finds the view that the world is eternal thanks to God's will hardly satisfactory. He rather argues that such a view does not solve the problem because we still have to explain why some parts of the universe are eternal and some others not (*Enn.* 2. 1. 1. 33–40). In this context Plotinus does not hesitate to accept Aristotle's doctrine of the eternity of the world, though he rejects that this could be due to an incorruptible element such as the Aristotelian aether (2. 1. 2. 12–16; cf. 2. 1. 8. 15–16, 2. 5. 3. 18–19).

7. CONCLUSION

The above outline is hardly sufficient for appreciating Plotinus' attitude to Aristotle in full, but some conclusions seem to emerge. First, Plotinus knew Aristotle's work very well and took it seriously into account in all main areas of philosophy. Second, Plotinus' attitude to Aristotle's doctrines is complex and differs from case to case. Third, in general Plotinus is cautious in accepting Aristotelian views and when he does so he subjects them to critical judgement. This cautiousness results from his belief that Aristotle's metaphysics is considerably different from that of Plato and results in serious problems and inconsistencies, which Plotinus sets out to show, often targeting Alexander's interpretation of Aristotle. Yet, fourth, despite this, Plotinus does not show hostility to Aristotle; quite the opposite, he sometimes rather refrains from criticizing him, as is the case in *Enn.* 3. 7. 13.

I have noted several different uses of Aristotle by Plotinus, which I list below.

[74] Cf. *Enn.* 2. 1. 1, 2. 9. 6–7, 3. 7. 6. 50–4, 4. 3. 9. 12–19. See Baltes (1976: 18–25, 123–36); Chiaradonna (2003: 243); and esp. Kalligas (1997: 281–7).

(*a*) Plotinus finds Aristotle's views of philosophical value but not quite right (as far as the metaphysics is concerned), that is, not expressing exactly Plato's doctrine, and so he adapts their metaphysics to fit the Platonist framework (e.g. Aristotle's view on time, on motion and *energeia*, on matter).

(*b*) He finds Aristotle's views to be of interest but strongly at odds with Plato's doctrine (again, as far as the metaphysics is concerned) and refers to them in order to specify and defend the latter (e.g. Aristotle's doctrine of the soul, of happiness, of substance as outlined in the *Categories*).

(*c*) He finds Aristotle's work useful for reconstructing Plato's doctrine (e.g. Aristotle's views on how the soul operates in the body, on perception, on the Intellect), but he modifies considerably the metaphysics of the Aristotelian doctrines.

(*d*) He simply takes Aristotle's view to express that of Plato (e.g. Aristotle's definition of the good in *Enn.* 6. 7. 19, 9–10).

In Porphyry use (*b*) turns out to be noticeably absent. This is what I turn to argue next.

7
Porphyry

1. INTRODUCTION

Porphyry was much more involved in the study of Aristotle's work than any other Platonist before him had been, including Ammonius and Plotinus.[1] He not only drew much from Aristotle, but was engaged in a systematic evaluation and study of Aristotle's philosophy. At least four commentaries on Aristotelian works are credited to him with certainty, two commentaries on the *Categories* and a commentary on the *De Interpretatione* and the *Physics*. He also produced an introduction to the *Categories* (the *Isagogê*), he wrote on Aristotle's ethics, on the *Sophistici Elenchi*, on the *Prior Analytics*, and on *Metaphysics* 12, but from the existing evidence it is unclear what the form of these writings was. Finally, Porphyry is attested to have written two works on how Aristotle's philosophy compares with that of Plato, that is *Περὶ τοῦ μίαν εἶναι τὴν Πλάτωνος καὶ Ἀριστοτέλους αἵρεσιν ζ* (*Suda*, s.v. Porphyry; henceforth *ΠΠΑ*), and *Περὶ διαστάσεως Πλάτωνος καὶ Ἀριστοτέλους* (Elias, *In Porphyrii Isag*. 39. 7–8; henceforth *ΠΔΠΑ*).

Had these works survived, Porphyry's attitude to Aristotle's philosophy would be clear, but on the basis of the existing evidence there is an uncertainty and even confusion among scholars as to what precisely was Porphyry's attitude. Let me start with the uncertainty aspect.

Andrew Smith, an expert on Porphyry, has argued that 'Porphyry's stance is not easy to determine' and that it 'is not entirely clear'.[2] On some issues, Smith says, Porphyry approved of Aristotle's views, while he was critical of Aristotle on several others. Smith's claim that Porphyry was critical of some Aristotelian doctrines rests on the following three pieces of evidence: (*a*) a fragment from Porphyry's treatise against

[1] Porphyry was a student of Longinus (*c.* 210–72) in Athens, where he stayed until his thirtieth year, and later of Plotinus (*c.* 204–70) with whom he spent five years (263–8). On his career see Bidez (1913); Beutler (1953: 275–8); Smith (1987: 719–22).

[2] Smith (1987: 754–5; 1992: 183).

Boethus which is critical of Aristotle's view of the soul as the *entelecheia* of the body (in Eusebius *PE* 15. 11. 4; 249F);[3] (*b*) the title of a work attacking Aristotle's same doctrine;[4] (*c*) the title *Περὶ διαστάσεως Πλάτωνος καὶ Ἀριστοτέλους* which he takes to suggest a Porphyrian argument for the discord between Aristotelian and Platonic philosophy.

Smith is one of the very few to have given some attention to the matter. Most scholars have proven content with vague formulations about Porphyry's attitude to Aristotle's philosophy without examining the evidence.[5] Smith apparently believes that Porphyry maintained the compatibility of Aristotle's *Categories* with Plato's ontology, since he interpreted this work as dealing with logic, but in metaphysics, in ontology, and psychology in particular, he considered Aristotle to have departed from Plato's doctrine and thus criticized Aristotle's positions. This is a view some other scholars seem to share.[6] A close look at the evidence, though, will show that this view rests on very weak grounds. Regarding the first piece of evidence which allegedly suggests Porphyry's critical stance toward Aristotle, I will argue that the author is not Porphyry but Atticus (see pp. 296–8). As for the polemical title of a work criticizing Aristotle's psychological doctrine, it resulted from an inference by a misguided reader of Eusebius (see p. 298). Finally, the title of Porphyry's treatise *ΠΠΑ*, I will argue, is not evidence of a Porphyrian argument for the disagreement between Platonic and Aristotelian philosophy and hence of a critical attitude toward Aristotle (s. 2). If I am right, then no Porphyrian criticism of Aristotle survives.

This is hardly accidental. Rather, it is due to the fact that, as I will show in this chapter, Porphyry maintained the accord between Aristotelian and Platonic philosophy in all crucial philosophical questions, such as those in physics, psychology, ethics, and especially in metaphysics. I say 'especially in metaphysics', because, as it will emerge, the agreement between Aristotle and Plato, which Porphyry maintained in physics or in psychology, appears to rest on what he takes to be their common ontological position. This may sound surprising, given that Porphyry essentially adopted Plotinus' interpretation of Plato's

[3] I use the edn. of A. Smith, *Porphyrius Fragmenta* (Stuttgart, 1993). I indicate fragments in this edn. in the way that Smith does: e.g. 249F = fr. 249 Smith, 2T= testimony 2 Smith.

[4] *Πρὸς Ἀριστοτέλην περὶ τοῦ εἶναι τὴν ψυχὴν ἐντελέχειαν*; in *Suda*, s.v. Porphyry.

[5] e.g. Beutler (1953: 285); Romano (1979: 136–7); Ebbesen (1990*a*: 145); Sorabji (1990: 2, 17).

[6] See, for instance, Dörrie (1959: 9–11, 73); Theiler (1965: 112); Lloyd (1967: 275–6, 281).

philosophy, but a careful examination of the existing evidence will show, I hope, how this is the case. Several scholars have already headed in this direction, arguing that Porphyry approves, at least partly, of Aristotle's ontology[7] and of some related aspects of his metaphysics.[8] The examination of a neglected passage from Porphyry's commentary on Ptolemy's *Harmonics* will shed some further light on how Porphyry tried to square the views of Plato with those of Aristotle. I will start out, though, by examining the evidence concerning Porphyry's two works on how Aristotle's philosophy compares with that of Plato, as there is some confusion in scholarship about them.

2. PORPHYRY'S TWO TREATISES ON HOW ARISTOTLE'S PHILOSOPHY COMPARES WITH PLATO'S

In his edition of Porphyry's fragments, Smith casts doubt on the status of the two Porphyrian works (*ΠΠΑ*, *ΠΔΠΑ*) by printing a question mark next to their titles.[9] Smith issues such a warning for works of dubious existence, such as Porphyry's commentary on Aristotle's *Metaphysics* (op. 8 Smith). Yet it is not immediately clear what reasons cause his suspicion in the case of the *ΠΠΑ* and the *ΠΔΠΑ*. In his apparatus Smith treats the two treatises as one, and refers us to Augustine, *Contra Academicos* 3. 19. 42 and Hierocles in Photius' *Bibliotheca* cod. 214, 173a18–32, 171b33–172ᵃ8, to justify this. The claim made in these passages is that Plato's philosophy is in accord with that of Aristotle. By referring to them, Smith implies that these passages reflect Porphyry's position on the question of how the two philosophies compare. Smith's suggestion apparently is that perhaps Porphyry wrote just one work in which he argued that Aristotle's philosophy is in accord with Plato's, and this work must be the *ΠΠΑ* because its title fits with Porphyry's assumed position; he thus basically doubts the existence of the *ΠΔΠΑ*, and the question mark next to the titles indicates the editor's puzzlement about the existence of two titles for the same work. But how credible is this suggestion and how much can be justified by the passages invoked?

At the root of Smith's suggestion lies the belief that the titles of the two treatises represent contradictory attitudes towards Aristotle's

7 Chiaradonna (1998*a*); De Libera (1999: 9).

8 Hadot (1990).

9 Opera 29, 30; 238T, 239T Smith.

philosophy, and this would not be likely to be shared by the same author. Such a belief rests on the conviction that in treatises bearing titles like the ones ascribed to Porphyry the author argues for the thesis embodied in the title.[10] Such reasoning dictates that in the *ΠΠΑ* Porphyry argued for the agreement of Plato's doctrines with those of Aristotle, whereas in the *ΠΔΠΑ* he maintained the opposite position. Given Porphyry's Platonism, then, in the *ΠΠΑ* Porphyry allegedly approved of Aristotle's philosophy, whereas in the *ΠΔΠΑ* he was critical of it. Since these two positions are incompatible, however, Porphyry is unlikely to have held both, and as a solution Smith suggests that Porphyry wrote only the *ΠΠΑ*. Elsewhere, though, Smith admits that for Porphyry to take both approaches towards Aristotle would be 'intriguing but not impossible'.[11]

A number of assumptions are involved here. One is that titles formulated like the ones ascribed to Porphyry suggest that the author espouses the thesis embodied in the title. This is clearly unfounded. In the case of Plotinus' *Περὶ τῆς ἐκ τοῦ βίου εὐλόγου ἐξαγωγῆς* (*Enn.* 1. 9), for instance, the author argues against the thesis embodied in the title. Even if we assume, however, that the two Porphyrian titles embody positions espoused by the author, one first has to show what these positions precisely are, before one can claim that they are incompatible. Now it is quite unlikely that Porphyry's position is captured in any of the passages to which Smith refers. The first passage probably reflects Antiochus' view, which Augustine knew through Cicero's *Academica*. While in the second one, Hierocles, as we have seen in Chapter 5, reports on the views of Ammonius Saccas. We do not know whether Hierocles was influenced by Porphyry; no evidence suggests that he knew Porphyry's works, and he does not seem to have had access to works of Plotinus and his students either.[12] But even if Hierocles relies on Porphyry, he draws on Porphyry's reporting Ammonius' position, not his own, unless we assume a further confusion here.

But even if all these passages reflect Porphyry's position in the *ΠΠΑ*, how do they tell us anything about the *ΠΔΠΑ*? Smith's suggestion that the two titles stand for one work, the *ΠΠΑ*, rests on the further assumption that Porphyry was committed to one rather than to the

[10] Smith (1987: 754; 1992: 186).

[11] Smith (1992: 186).

[12] For Hierocles' dependence on Porphyry argue Dörrie (1955: 343–7) and I. Hadot (1978: 75–6), (cf. Ch. 5, p. 195 n. 9, p. 214 n. 59). Theiler (1966*b*: 166) connects the passages of Augustine and Hierocles with the *ΠΠΑ* and also claims that Porphyry draws on Ammonius, but he does not give any argument for either.

other thesis. This assumption was first made by Busse,[13] who claimed that both titles refer to the same work, the *ΠΠΑ*. Busse's sole reason is that the 'Neoplatonic' tendency to 'harmonize' Plato and Aristotle goes back to Porphyry, so, he implies, a Porphyrian work arguing for their discord is incompatible with this and thus immediately suspect. Yet Busse does not wonder how the occurrence of the *ΠΔΠΑ* should be explained in Elias (*In Isag.* 39. 7–8), given that Elias, as Busse himself admits, favours the thesis of the fundamental accord between Plato and Aristotle, and in this he follows Porphyry. Is Elias unreliable here? Did he have in mind Porphyry's *ΠΠΑ* instead? But how could such confusion possibly arise, given that the titles of the two works are so different?

Busse treated the whole issue in a footnote, but his explanation gained wide scholarly approval. Immisch,[14] Praechter,[15] and Beutler[16] subscribed to his hypothesis without adding any further argument. Obviously the evidence concerning the attested Porphyrian treatises has been viewed in the light of Porphyry's assumed attitude to Aristotle's philosophy. Even Smith, who, as has been seen, remains sceptical as to what Porphyry's stance to Aristotle's philosophy was, and others who share his scepticism still consider Busse's view seriously.[17] Yet, as I will argue in the following, there is neither compelling evidence suggesting that the two works argued for incompatible positions nor any other reason to discredit the testimonies suggesting the existence of two separate Porphyrian works. There is rather much which shows that they are authentic and complementary.

To begin with, the existing evidence suggests that the two treatises were quite different in scope. The *ΠΠΑ* must have been a scholarly work, the *ΠΔΠΑ* an introductory one. One feature speaking in favour of such a difference is their indicated length. The *Suda* indicates that the *ΠΠΑ* comprised seven books. For the *ΠΔΠΑ*, on the other hand, Elias does not give any figure, but this lack of figure often suggests that the work in question comprises only one book.[18] The different length and scope of the two works is supported by some strong evidence.

13 Busse (1893: 268 n.1).

14 Immisch (1906: 3–4).

15 F. Ueberweg and K. Praechter, *Grundriss der Geschichte der Philosophie* (Berlin, 1920¹¹), 636.

16 Beutler (1953: 285). Wallis (1972: 24) gives Elias as the reference for the treatise attested in the *Suda*! Lloyd (1967: 275, 284) is similarly confused.

17 Theiler (1965: 112); Romano (1979: 143–4); Sorabji (1990: 2). Bidez (1913: 68*), however, treats the two treatises as distinct. Ebbesen (1990*a*: 145) also maintains their difference in scope.

18 This is the case with Porphyry's *Isagogê* mentioned in the *Suda* (s.v. Porphyry) as *Περὶ γένους καὶ εἴδους καὶ διαφορᾶς καὶ ἰδίου καὶ συμβεβηκότος*.

The introductory nature of the *ΠΔΠΑ* is suggested by the fact that it was addressed to Chrysaorius,[19] who was a beginner in philosophy and often asked for Porphyry's help.[20] Porphyry wrote some other introductory treatises of only one book for him, like the *Isagogê*, the short commentary on the *Categories*, and the work *On what is up to us*.[21] As Porphyry himself reveals, in these works he tried to write as simply as possible, tailoring the argument to the level of his addressee. In the *Isagogê*, for instance, he admits a limited scope, which leads him to leave aside problems of metaphysics (*Isag.*1. 8–16), and in his short commentary on the *Categories* he does the same.[22] His lost commentary on the same work addressed to Gedaleius, on the other hand, was more sophisticated and much longer (seven books). Simplicius, who knew both well, says that in the short commentary 'Porphyry aimed to expound only the mere concepts discussed by Aristotle' (*In Cat.* 1. 10–13), while in the long one he 'took pains to provide a full-scale interpretation of the work and to give solutions to all problems in seven books' (ibid. 2. 6–7). The similarities of the *ΠΔΠΑ* with the *Isagogê* are emphasized by Elias, who draws attention to common features, such as their introductory nature and their address to Chrysaorius, in order to assure us with this evidence of the authenticity of the *Isagogê* (*In Isag.* 39. 4–8). The testimony of Elias does not only show the introductory nature of the *ΠΔΠΑ*, but leaves little doubt about its authenticity either, as he chooses to mention this particular work among others (*καὶ ἄλλαι* [sc. *πραγματεῖαι*]) addressed to Chrysaorius. A work of disputed authenticity would hardly do for his argument.

To pass to the testimony of the *Suda* which preserves for us a catalogue of Porphyry's works including the *ΠΠΑ*, it is difficult, if not impossible, to speak in general about the reliability of the lists of works provided by this tenth-century compilation, as it varies considerably

[19] Chrysaorius was probably a Roman aristocrat, a descendant of the family of Symmachi (cf. Elias, *In Isag.* 39. 8–11, 93. 17–19; David, *In Isag.* 93. 13–14, 107. 26–7). See Bidez (1913: 58–60); R. Goulet (ed.), *Dictionnaire des Philosophes Antiques* (Paris, 1994), ii. 323–4.

[20] Ammonius, *In Isag.* 22. 12–22 (28T Smith); Elias, *In Isag.* 39. 8–19 (29T).

[21] *Περὶ τοῦ ἐφ' ἡμῖν* (268F–271F Smith). We do not know how long this treatise was, but it may also have comprised only one book, given its elementary character.

[22] Porphyry says that he avoids speaking about a 'deep' issue such as the difference between universals and accidents because it is 'beyond the level of comprehension of a beginner' (*In Cat.* 75. 24–6). Probably there were also some differences in the philosophical perspective between his two commentaries in *Cat.* See below s. 8, pp. 312–18.

from one case to another.[23] The *Suda*'s list of Porphyry's works, as in the case of most other such lists in the *Suda*, is selective,[24] containing twenty-three items; ten of them are confirmed by other sources, twelve are mentioned only by the *Suda*,[25] among them the *ΠΠΑ*, and one is spurious.[26] Important evidence for the reliability of the list is the figures provided about the length of Porphyry's works; to the extent of our knowledge, these figures are confirmed from external evidence.[27] So there is not much reason to doubt the length of the *ΠΠΑ*, or its existence (which has never been seriously disputed).

The different scopes of the two Porphyrian works in question are suggested also by the titles themselves. The *ΠΠΑ* appears to address a more general topic, while the *ΠΔΠΑ* a very specific one. Let us see which these are. The word *αἵρεσις*, which occurs in the *ΠΠΑ*, in the case of philosophy denotes a philosophical school,[28] but not a school in its institutional sense; rather, it indicates a philosophical system or persuasion. Our sources do distinguish between a philosophical school in the institutional sense (*σχολή*, *διατριβή*) and a *hairesis*,[29] and often a line is drawn between being a member of a philosophical institution and adhering to a *hairesis*. Antiochus and Numenius, for instance, argued,

[23] An instance of misinformation occurs in the entry 'Plotinus', where we read that Plotinus wrote other works apart from the *Enneads*. See Henry (1937: 154–62). There are also some signs of interpolations, as the duplication of the list of works for Syrianus and Proclus suggests. See Praechter (1926: 261–2).

[24] The *Suda* mentions about one third of the known Porphyrian works (72 titles; 11 survive extant) from three categories of his writings, philosophical, rhetorical, grammatical, leaving out the exegetical works.

[25] In the first category I include the title by which the *Suda* knows the *Isagogê* (see n. 18 above). I accept the identification of the work *Φιλολόγου ἱστορίας ε´* with the treatise *Φιλόλογος ἀκρόασις* (cf. Smith 1992: 185; Beutler 1953: 288), and I number it under the first class of works.

[26] This is *Πρὸς' Αριστοτέλην < περὶ > τοῦ εἶναι τὴν ψυχὴν ἐντελέχειαν*. See my argument below, s. 6. 2, pp. 296–8.

[27] This is the case with the following: *Φιλόσοφος ἱστορία δ´*, *Περὶ τοῦ γνῶθι σαυτόν δ´*, *Περὶ ἀποχῆς ἐμψύχων δ´*; from *Κατὰ τῶν Χριστιανῶν ιε´* we have fragments from books 3 and 14 (frs. 39 and 9 Harnack), but the evidence about this work remains controversial. We also have fragments from the first four books of *Σύμμικτα ζητήματα ζ*, the first book of *Περὶ ψυχῆς πρὸς Βόηθον ε´* (*PE* 11. 27. 20; 242F), the first book of *Φιλόλογος ἀκρόασις ε´* (*PE* 10. 3; 408F), and the second book of *Περὶ ὕλης στ´* (Simplicius, *In Phys.* 230. 34–231. 24; 236F).

[28] The term literally means 'choice' (LSJ, s.v.). On its use in philosophy and medicine see the detailed discussion in Glucker (1978: 166–92) and also von Staden (1982).

[29] e.g. *Index Acad.* cols. XVIII–XIX Dorandi where Speusippus and Polemo are said to lead their own *haireseis*, while Arcesilaus is said not to have introduced one but to have preferred to criticize the *haireseis* of the others; cf. Dion. Halicarn. *Ad Amm.* 7. See Glucker (1978: 160–6).

each one in his own way, that the sceptic Academics, though officially members of Plato's Academy, had deserted the Platonic *hairesis*,[30] that is, dogmatic Platonism. Porphyry's use of the term *hairesis* suggests then that his work was not about the Academic and Peripatetic schools as institutions, as sometimes has been argued.[31]

Nevertheless in order to specify the subject that Porphyry addresses in his *ΠΠΑ*, we have to look at the term *hairesis* in more detail, since it admits of different scopes within its non-institutional sense. It may denote a philosophical system or school of thought (broad scope), but also a certain persuasion within the same school of thought (narrow scope).[32] The latter is the case with different Platonists who are divided into various *haireseis* with reference to a particular issue (Stob. 1. 378. 1–6); we also hear of Platonists leading their own *haireseis* (*Index Acad.* col. XVIII–XIX Dorandi) and of Chrysippus' *hairesis* within the Stoic school, from which Posidonius allegedly departed. Divisions into *haireseis* in this sense amount to differences in opinions within a school of thought, but whether these differences should be regarded as deviations from an alleged orthodoxy depends on the importance of the issue in question.[33] In the broad sense, now, the term *hairesis* denotes a philosophical persuasion, or a school of thought, which may cut across philosophical schools. The term is used thus by Galen, who argues that Hippocrates and Plato belong to the same *hairesis*.[34] But Hippocrates and Plato can be considered as belonging to the same *hairesis* only if somebody takes their accord on a certain issue as so crucial as to outweigh other differences. For Galen this was their conception of the human soul. Galen sets out to show that in this respect also Posidonius belongs to the same *hairesis* with Plato and Aristotle despite their difference in ethics (*PHP* 5. 7. 10–11). The same broad use of *hairesis* underlies Antiochus' claim regarding the agreement between Plato and Aristotle, which is argued from the standpoint of ethics and epistemology and, in his view, as has

30 There were also people who led their own institutions but denied that they had established a new *hairesis* (e.g. Cleitomachus).

31 Romano (1985: 26–7); Sorabji (1990: 2); Smith (1992: 186). In fact, the distinction between *haireseis* was one of the standard topics discussed by Platonist commentators in their introductions to their Aristotelian commentaries. See Praechter (1916: 42) and more extensively Plezia (1949).

32 Glucker (1978) does not make this distinction, although his collected evidence clearly suggests it.

33 The *hairesis* of the Stoic Aristo was regarded as a deviation from Stoicism (Galen, *PHP* 7. 1. 9–15), while that of Chrysippus obviously was not.

34 Cf. *PHP* 5. 6. 42–4.

been seen in Chapter 1, is such that it outweighs other differences. In the *ΠΠΑ* Porphyry must employ *hairesis* in the broad sense of 'school of thought', so the question he examines is whether Plato and Aristotle belong to the same school of thought, despite the fact that they led their own schools.

The question about what belonging to the same school of thought amounts to is a difficult one. Most philosophical (and medical) *haireseis* lacked a normative self-definition, and the criterion for distinguishing them varies.[35] However, as I have already stated, adherence to fundamental doctrines was crucial. Galen talks about the core (*στοιχείωσις*) of a *hairesis* (*PHP* 9. 6, p. 586. 33 De Lacy), Atticus about Plato's cardinal doctrines (frs. 4, 7, 9 Des Places), while Ammonius (in Photius, *Bibl.* cod. 214, 172a7) and Origen (*C. Celsum* 5. 61. 7–10) talk about the most necessary doctrines (*τὰ ἀναγκαιότατα*) which determine one's membership in a *hairesis*. In Porphyry's time the doctrines associated with metaphysics were crucial in such a discussion. This does not mean that the *ΠΠΑ* dealt only with them, as Bidez and Smith appear to suggest.[36] Ethical doctrines, for instance, also were regarded as being crucial, and Porphyry in particular showed strong interest in them (see s. 7). At any rate, if the question regarding the adherence to the same school of thought was about such crucial doctrines, then Porphyry's discussion was about a *special* type of doctrinal agreement. It is quite different, for instance, from the comprehensive agreement indicated by the term *συμφωνία*, which was often used to describe the agreement between Platonic and the Pythagorean philosophy, or between Plato and other ancient sources such as Homer.[37] Porphyry in particular must have been sensitive to various forms of agreement ranging from the one between Plato and Pythagoras, which, as will be seen, he accepted (cf. *V. Plot.* 21. 5–7), to the limited unanimity between members of Plotinus' school (cf. ibid. 17. 4–7, 42) and of Platonists more generally, who often disagreed with each other on many issues. His phrasing of the title of the *ΠΠΑ* indicates an inquiry into the modest question of whether Aristotle agrees with Plato on those crucial issues which in his view

[35] The prologue of Diogenes Laertius (1. 13–21) reflects the different ways in which one could divide *haireseis*.

[36] Bidez (1913: 68*) and Smith in his edn. p. 258 classify it under Porphyry's metaphysical works.

[37] Cf. Syrianus' work *Συμφωνίαν 'Ορφέως, Πυθαγόρου καὶ Πλάτωνος περὶ τὰ λόγια, ί* (*Suda*, s.v. Syrianus); see O'Meara (1992: 123). Cf. also Hierocles in Photius, *Bibl.* cod. 214, 173a13–15.

determine a school of thought.[38] Commitment to such a thesis could clearly allow for considerable diversity among the two philosophers.

Diversity among philosophers could be indicated in many ways in Greek, depending on its importance and its extent. Most relevant are the terms *διαφωνία*, *διαφορά*, and *διάστασις*, which is the term Porphyry uses in the *ΠΔΠΑ*.[39] From the term alone, it is unclear which kind of doctrinal differences Porphyry discussed, since the term sometimes is used to indicate strong differences which occur between members of different philosophical schools, but also differences which, however important, are allowed within the same school.[40] Nothing necessitates that Porphyry used the term to indicate strong differences, as Smith and others suppose, and two considerations suggest that he may well have used it for a disagreement that can take place within the same school of thought. First, *διάστασις* was sometimes used to indicate differences between Platonists themselves.[41] Amelius, for instance, uses this term when he admits his doctrinal divergence from his teacher Plotinus (*διάστασις ἀπὸ τῶν τοῦ καθηγεμόνος ἡμῶν δογμάτων*; *V. Plot.* 17. 42).[42] But clearly Amelius still considered himself a loyal student of Plotinus and a committed Platonist. Secondly, *διάστασις* can be constructed in various ways, which give different meaning (e.g. *περί*, *πρός*,

[38] Porphyry's title is often translated as 'On the Unity of Doctrine in Plato and Aristotle' (Shiel 1990: 370) or 'On the school of Plato and Aristotle being one' (Sorabji 1990: 2); cf. Romano (1985: 31). Walzer (1965*a*: 285) suggests that 'Porphyry set out to demonstrate the ultimate identity of Plato's and Aristotle's philosophies'. As I argue above, the title does not support any of these interpretations.

[39] The term *διαφωνία* often indicates a disagreement as extensive as the accord suggested by the term *συμφωνία*, and was widely used by Christians like Eusebius and Theodoretus who set out to argue that the ancient philosophy cannot have claims to be true since ancient philosophers strongly disagree with each other (*PE* 1. 8. 14, 14. 1. 1, 14. 2. 7, *Cur. Aff. Graec.* 4. 31; cf. Origen, *C. Celsum* 5. 61. 7–10). This is an argument which the Christians borrowed from ancient sceptics. Simplicius uses the same term when he denies that the conflicts between Plato and Aristotle are substantial (*In De Caelo* 640. 27–8; cf. *In Cat.* 7. 23–32). Cf. Philoponus, *De aet. mundi* 31. 8, 32. 8–9.

[40] The term is used to indicate strong disagreement generally, e.g. Eusebius *PE* 14. 2, or on a particular question, e.g. on God, *PE* 14. 16. 11, on the criterion, Sextus, *Adv. Math.* 7. 46. 3, 8. 2. 5, 8. 177. 8 sometimes interchangeably with *διαφωνία*, ibid. 8. 11. 1.

[41] Platonists are said to differ (*διαστασιάζουσιν*) in psychology (Iamblichus, *De anima* in Stob. 1. 374. 21–5).

[42] Amelius wrote on the doctrinal differences between Numenius and Plotinus (*Περὶ τῆς κατὰ τὰ δόγματα τοῦ Πλωτίνου πρὸς τὸν Νουμήνιον διαφορᾶς*; *V. Plot.* 17. 5). Platonists speak of their differences (*διαφορὰ τῶν Πλατωνικῶν δογμάτων*, David, *In Isag.* 115. 4–5), but differences suggested by the term *διαφορὰ* can be accepted within the same school (cf. Posidonius' difference from Chrysippus; Galen, *PHP* 5. 2. 8–10). Taurus may have discussed such differences in his work *Περὶ τῆς τῶν δογμάτων διαφορᾶς Πλάτωνος καὶ Ἀριστοτέλους* (*Suda*, s.v. Taurus).

εἰς, ἀπό, ἐν) or with bare genitive(s), like in Porphyry's title. In construction with πρὸς (and εἰς) and accusative διάστασις suggests a strong opposition, as in Numenius' title *Περὶ τῆς τῶν Ἀκαδημαικῶν πρὸς Πλάτωνα διαστάσεως*, coming close to the sense of rebellion (στάσις), of which Numenius accuses the Academics.[43] This idea of opposition between Aristotle and Plato is absent from Porphyry's title; his construction of διάστασις with two genitives is the most neutral one available, indicating a discussion of doctrinal differences between Plato and Aristotle, real or alleged.

Even if Porphyry accepted that such differences exist, this does not necessarily entail a hostile attitude to Aristotle, as these differences could be only minor and even if important they could well be differences which occur among adherents of the same school of thought, as was the case with the difference between Amelius and Plotinus. Yet whichever these differences are, the *ΠΔΠΑ* was a treatise focused specifically on them. Clearly, though, the evidence we have about Porphyry shows that such differences do not exhaust the relation between Platonic and Aristotelian philosophies, as he believed that there are also points of agreement between the two. Presumably then the treatment of the relation in the two philosophies in their entirety was reserved for the *ΠΠΑ*, which was the longer and more scholarly of the two treatises.

In conclusion, the evidence of the titles has shown that, the *ΠΠΑ* discussed the larger question of 'whether Plato and Aristotle belong to the same school of thought', while the *ΠΔΠΑ* was a brief work focused only 'on what Plato and Aristotle differ', tailored to the needs of a beginner like Chrysaorius. This treatment of the same subject both in a brief and in a fuller way was not unusual for Porphyry.[44]

The question now is what position Porphyry took in each of these works. This is not clear from the titles. There are four possibilities: (*a*) Porphyry espoused the view that Plato and Aristotle belong to the same school of thought, and also maintained that they differ in some respects, (*b*) he espoused the former but opposed the latter view, (*c*) he opposed the former and espoused the latter; (*d*) or he denied both. Since within a *hairesis* there was room for doctrinal diversity and differences were tolerated, option (*a*) is a possibility and, as I have argued above, nothing

[43] Cf. Aristotle, *Politics* 1296ᵃ7–8, 1300ᵇ37; *PE* 1. 7. 16, 5. 4. 10, 15. 62. 16; Numenius frs. 23. 6, 24. 34, 63 Des Places.

[44] This was the case with the two commentaries on the *Categories*, for instance, or with his works *Περὶ ἀρχῶν β´* and *Περὶ ὕλης ς´* (opera 26, 28 Smith).

in the titles or generally rules it out. Quite the contrary: the above discussion has shown that this option is probable.

Some external evidence also suggests that option (*a*) is actually quite probable. In his commentary on the *De Interpretatione* Boethius presents his ambitious plan in philosophy, which he never fulfilled.[45] This plan comprised the translation of the entire work of Plato and Aristotle and Porphyry's *Isagogê*, the writing of commentaries on the basic texts, and, among other studies, the composition of a treatise demonstrating the accord between Platonic and Aristotelian philosophy. He describes the latter as follows:

> his peractis non equidem contempserim Aristotelis Platonisque sententias in unam quodammodo revocare concordiam non ut plerique dissentire in omnibus sed in plerisque et his in philosophia maximis consentire demonstrem. (*In De Interpretatione* 2. 79. 16–19 Meiser).

> after I finish with all this, I would very much like to draw attention to the accord which somehow exists between the doctrines of Plato and those of Aristotle, and thus to demonstrate not that they disagree in everything, as many think, but rather that they agree in most issues and indeed the philosophically most important ones.

We know that Boethius draws heavily on Porphyry whenever there was a work of his available on a subject Boethius was treating, and in his commentary on Aristotle's *On interpretation* most especially.[46] If he ever were to write the work announced above, he may well have intended to rely on Porphyry, and Porphyry's most relevant work was his *ΠΠΑ*. Boethius' testimony quoted above may recast a Porphyrian statement, or, more probably, it may reflect Porphyry's general view on the matter. We notice that Boethius wanted to show that Plato and Aristotle do not agree on everything but do agree on the most crucial philosophical issues. Although this is still a very general idea within which many positions are possible, it lends some support to the view I have suggested above that Porphyry may have argued that the two philosophers agree on fundamental issues and yet differ in some regards. One important question to ask while reviewing the evidence in the following sections is to what kind of differences Porphyry referred. For the moment, though,

[45] It is unclear whether Boethius even intended to fulfil this plan. See Kappelmacher (1928: 216–25); Shiel (1990: 370); Ebbesen (1990*b*: 374–5).

[46] Boethius' debt to Porphyry is well discussed by Ebbesen (1990*b*). Boethius draws systematically on Porphyry's commentary on the *De interpretatione*, and this is something he admits, as he mentions Porphyry very often in his work (see Boethius, *In de Int.* 2. 7. 5–9, 2. 11. 7–11 75T–76T).

we can be content with the provisional answer that these can be such that they would not undermine the essential agreement between Plato and Aristotle. So the two works of Porphyry on the relation between the Platonic and the Aristotelian philosophy may well have presented complementary positions. This is still to be proved.

Unfortunately no trace of these Porphyrian works has survived in the Greco-Roman tradition. In the search for remains attention has been drawn to the Arabic tradition in which the accord between Plato and Aristotle is often maintained. Al-Fârâbi (ninth–tenth century) wrote a treatise on this with the title *Treatise on the Harmony between the views of the two sages, the divine Plato and Aristotle*;[47] Al-Kindî (ninth century) makes remarks in some of his works to the effect that Plato and Aristotle are in agreement, and Al-Amirî (tenth century), a pupil of Al-Kindî, sometimes in his works places Platonic with Aristotelian passages next to each other in order to show that they are in agreement. Walzer has argued that these sources rely on Porphyry's *ΠΠΑ* both in terms of content and presentation of the material.[48] He has claimed that the Arabic treatises are modelled on Porphyry's work, which was full of quotations from Plato and Aristotle, but, unlike the Arabic ones, Porphyry framed the quotations by the argument he aimed to illustrate and sustain.

Walzer's thesis is not convincing. Let us review the evidence first. It is true that the Arabs appear to have possessed some of Porphyry's works in translation,[49] and authors like Al-Fârâbi and Al-Amirî do refer to Porphyry and deal with some of the questions with which he was concerned. In his introduction to the treatise mentioned above Al-Fârâbi states that he will show how Plato and Aristotle agree on the creation and the eternity of the world, the existence of God, the survival of the soul and its reward or punishment after death, in which it was claimed that they had disagreed.[50] His discussion extends further to

[47] Al-Fârâbi argues this also in other writings like *The Philosophy of Plato and Aristotle*; see Mahdi (1969: 5). I am indebted to Dr Fritz Zimmermann for expert advice on this section.

[48] Walzer (1965*a*: 284–96; 1965*b*). He seems to follow Busse in assuming that Porphyry wrote only the *ΠΠΑ*.

[49] According to the Fihrist of Al-Nadim, apart from the *Isagogê*, there were available translations of the *Epistle to Anebo*, the *History of Philosophy*, the commentary on the *Categories* and the *Physics*, and treatises lost today like the one *Against those who distinguish the intelligible from the intellect*. See B. Dodge (ed.), *The Fihrist of Al-Nadim* (New York and London), ii. 598–9, 603, 606, 610 (3aT–3hT Smith).

[50] See Mallet (1989: 57–8).

logic, metaphysics, and psychology. Although he refers explicitly to Porphyry only once concerning a remark of his on Aristotle's ethics,[51] Al-Fârâbi focuses on areas in which, as will be seen, Porphyry maintained Aristotle's agreement with Plato; so his use of Porphyry is possible. Also intriguing is the view of Al-Kindi that there is no real difference between the position of Plato and that of Aristotle on the soul.[52] As for the work of Al-Amirî, Walzer admits that, despite its reference to Porphyry, it probably echoes rather than relies on him.[53] This is because it includes quotations from Plato and Aristotle without comments or arguments, because it deals with Platonic or Aristotelian passages in an uncoordinated manner, while often its quotations from Porphyry's reports on Aristotle are not coupled with any references to Plato. Besides, Al-Amirî's work deals only with ethical and political philosophy, leaving aside areas such as psychology or ontology, which must have been central to Porphyry for determining membership in the same school of thought; and even in ethics, as Walzer admits, the relation between Plato and Aristotle is rarely discussed.

Nothing in this evidence, though, proves that the Arabs drew directly on Porphyry, let alone from the *ΠΠΑ*, and nothing in it is distinctly Porphyrian. Quite the contrary is the case. The attested views were widespread among Platonists after Porphyry. As is known, Porphyry's views gained wide approval among later generations of Platonists, and they often drew from his work without acknowledgement. The Arabs may well have acquired a general knowledge of Porphyry's views and interpretative methods on the topic of the accord between Plato and Aristotle from such intermediary sources. Indeed, Al-Fârâbi refers specifically to a treatise by Ammonius Hermeiou, which argues for the accord of Plato and Aristotle on God, and scholars have noticed some similarity between the views of Al-Fârâbi and those of Ammonius on this issue.[54] So Walzer's suggestion remains speculative. Yet Walzer is

[51] See Mallet 78. Smith omits this testimony. The Arabs must be responsible for some adjustments; e.g. when Al-Fârâbi claims that the two philosophers agree in religion, it is probably meant that they agree on God, the first principle.

[52] See Walzer (1965*a*: 289–90). Also Al-Fârâbi maintains the accord of Plato and Aristotle on the soul and appeals to the beginning of *Post. an.* (71^{a}1–17), seeking to show that Aristotle shares Plato's theory of recollection. See Mallet (1989: 80–3).

[53] Walzer (1965*a*: 290–4).

[54] See Mallet (1989: 86). Sorabji (1990: 182–3, and more fully in 1988: 273–81) argues that Ammonius' view on God surivives in Al-Fârâbi. Also Philoponus' works were available in Arabic (Sorabji 1988: 259–60). We also find a reference to Themistius and Ammonius on logic (p. 69 Mallet).

close to the truth when he claims that Porphyry's method in the *ΠΠΑ* was to compare Platonic and Aristotelian texts and argue on this basis that the two philosophers agree in substance. A neglected piece of evidence comes as confirmation of his hypothesis.

3. A PORPHYRIAN ARGUMENT FOR THE AGREEMENT BETWEEN PLATO AND ARISTOTLE (PORPHYRY, *IN PTOLEMAEI HARMONICA*, PP. 45. 21–49. 4 DÜRING)

The evidence comes from Porphyry's *Commentary on the Harmonics of Ptolemy*, which is an interesting work in many regards.[55] It is most famous as an important source of fragments of earlier Greek musical theorists (e.g. Aristoxenus), but it has never been examined on its own terms. However, it contains much of philosophical interest, such as sections on physics, epistemology, and also metaphysics.[56] Porphyry's interest in Ptolemy's work on music was dictated by a deep metaphysical interest which music aroused in most Platonists of late antiquity, especially Platonists of Pythagorean inclination. For them music exemplified the numerical basis of reality and suggested the existence of balanced proportions in the world. In their view, the study of music confirms that everything is set up according to a rational ordering cause and that nature in all its aspects is the work of a divine mind (pp. 12. 18–20, 24. 22–8 Düring).

Porphyry seems to be interested in certain issues raised by Ptolemy rather than in the entire work. This is why his commentary is very unevenly written.[57] A central issue that occupies Porphyry's work is the perception of sound. The main question concerns the role that reason (*λόγος*) and sense (*αἴσθησις*) play in how sound is perceived. There had been a discussion on their relative role among the two most important schools of musical theorists in antiquity, the Pythagoreans and the

55 I use the edn. of I. Düring, *Porphyrios Kommentar zur Harmonielehre des Ptolemaios* (Göteborg, 1932). The work as it is preserved today extends only up to Ptolemy's book 2, ch. 7, but it is unclear whether Porphyry left it unfinished or had intended to write only that far.

56 See Gersh (1992: 141–55). Gersh does not refer to the section I discuss in the following.

57 Half of the commentary, as we have it, is devoted on the first four chapters of Ptolemy's first book.

Aristoxenians. Porphyry follows Ptolemy in maintaining that neither the senses nor reason alone are sufficient to make judgements about sounds, but that the senses must be informed by reason (ibid., p. 16. 15–21).[58] This, he argues, also is the view of the 'ancients' (*οἱ παλαιοί*), that is, Plato and Aristotle.[59]

Porphyry's commentary is particularly important for the present study because it contains evidence for his approval of the agreement of Plato and Aristotle in areas such as ontology and epistemology (see s. 8), and also because it contains an explicit attempt to show their accord, which has so far passed unnoticed. Porphyry argues that the two philosophers are unanimous on how pitch comes about, despite their apparent disagreement. This suggests that Porphyry in general may have admitted the existence of differences between the two philosophers and have still held that these differences do not undermine their essential agreement. Since this is the only surviving occasion on which Porphyry specifically tries to show how Aristotle's view is in accord with that of Plato, we should examine the relevant section quite closely.

Porphyry devotes one third of his commentary (*In Ptol. Harm.* 29. 27–78. 2 Düring) to the third chapter of Ptolemy's work which deals with the physics of sound and more specifically with how high and low pitch are produced. The question is part of the bigger issue of how qualities in general are produced. It is argued that qualities can be produced either by qualities or by quantities (ibid. 44. 11–16, 45. 13–14). The quantity of matter (i.e. in a chord), for instance, can account for qualities like thickness, thinness, diffuseness, or density, and certain combinations of these qualities in turn can account for qualities of sound (44. 19–45. 13). So differences between sounds can be either qualitative or quantitative, and the question is that of how differences in pitch can be classified. Ptolemy follows the Pythagoreans in explaining high and low pitch ultimately in terms of quantity (37. 6–8). The force with which an instrument is blown, for instance, would result in a difference in pitch. Even more important is the speed of the air's motion (29. 27–33).[60] For the Pythagoreans and Ptolemy, high and low pitch result from a rapid and slow motion respectively (ibid.). Porphyry argues that Ptolemy is indebted to the view of Plato and

[58] On Ptolemy's position on the role of reason and the senses in the perception of sound see Barker (2000: 14–32). I am grateful to Professor Barker for valuable advice in this section.

[59] *In Ptol. Harm.* 11. 4–19, 14. 1–16. 21, 17. 13–31; see s. 8, pp. 310–12.

[60] Ptolemy's views on pitch are presented with clarity by Barker (2000: 33–53).

Aristotle on the matter (38. 5–7) and repeats this also later on (49. 5–8). At some point (45. 17–20), though, he contends that Ptolemy's view is different from that of the 'ancients', that is of Plato and Aristotle, and moves on to establish what their view is.

Porphyry argues that for the 'ancients' the swiftness of the sound's movement does not cause high pitch, but is identical with it. This, he claims, is the view of Plato and Aristotle (*ἥ τε Πλάτωνος καὶ Ἀριστοτέλους δόξα*; 45. 30; cf. 45. 27). But Porphyry's text confuses us, because two distinct views are presented as *the view* of the 'ancients'. The first is that speed is the cause of high and low pitch (45. 23–5),[61] which turns out to be Aristotle's view that also Ptolemy follows. The second is that high and low pitch are essentially rapid and slow movements respectively (45. 27–30), which is Plato's view and the one that Porphyry seeks to establish.[62] The first view regards high and low pitch as basically qualities, while the second understands them to be quantities or, at least, qualities resulting from quantities, since rapid and slow movements with which they are identical are also quantities.[63] So what is presented as one view clearly amounts to two distinct views, of Plato and of Aristotle respectively. Instead of acknowledging their difference, Porphyry says that their one view needs to be clarified (45. 30–46. 2) and goes on to quote the relevant passages from Plato and Aristotle (*Timaeus* 67a–c; *De anima* 420ᵃ26–ᵇ4).

Later on, however, Porphyry states that Aristotle not only holds a different view, but also that he meant to oppose that of Plato (*ἀντιλέγων τῷ Πλάτωνί φησιν*; *In Ptol. Harm.* 48. 12)—although Aristotle does not say

[61] *Ταύτῃ τῇ αἰτίᾳ καὶ οἱ παλαιοὶ ἐχρῶντο, ἐφ' ἣν μεταβέβηκε* [sc. Ptolemy] *παρεὶς τὴν προτέραν. τὴν γὰρ ταχύτητα αἰτίαν τῆς ὀξύτητος ἀπεδίδοσαν καὶ τὴν βραδύτητα τῆς βαρύτητος* (This was the cause also according to the 'ancients' which Ptolemy endorsed, abandoning the one he had believed earlier. For they considered high speed the cause of high pitch and slow speed the cause of low pitch; *In Ptol. Harm.* 45. 17–24). This is Aristotle's view.

[62] *καὶ εἴπερ ἐν ποσῷ ἡ ταχύτης καὶ ἡ βραδύτης, αἴτιον μὲν τὸ ποσὸν ὀξύτητος καὶ βαρύτητος δοίη ἄν τις. οὐ μὴν πάντως ἐκ τούτου συνάγεται τὸ εἶναι τοῦ ποσοῦ τὴν ὀξύτητα καὶ τὴν βαρύτητα, εἰ μέντοι ὡς οἴεται Ἀριστοτέλης καὶ ὁ Πλάτων οὐκ αἴτιον τὸ ταχὺ ἐτίθετο τοῦ ὀξέος, ἀλλ' αὐτὸ τὸ ὀξὺ ταχὺ καὶ αὐτὸ τὸ βαρὺ βραδύ* (and since high and low speed are quantities, one would consider quantity as the cause of high and low pitch. But it does not follow from this that high and low pitch are quantities, unless one considers, like Aristotle and Plato, not the high speed as the cause of high pitch but that high pitch itself is fast and low pitch slow; *In Ptol. Harm.* 45. 24–8). This is Plato's view.

[63] Cf. *οὐ μὴν πάντως ἐκ τούτου συνάγεται τὸ εἶναι τοῦ ποσοῦ τὴν ὀξύτητα καὶ τὴν βαρύτητα* and *εἴη ἂν τοῦ ποσοῦ τὸ ὀξὺ καὶ βαρύ, εἴπερ ποσὰ τὸ ταχὺ καὶ τὸ βραδύ.* ('it does not follow from this that high and low pitch are quantities' and 'high and low pitch would be quantities if high and low speed are quantities;' *In Ptol. Harm.* 45. 25–6, 28–9).

anything like this. This time the difference between Plato and Aristotle is not only admitted but highlighted. Only now do we start to realize that the two positions are being compared, and this comparison is being carried out in order to show that they are fundamentally in agreement. By then Porphyry has quoted the relevant Platonic and Aristotelian passages which he has also paraphrased and explained, aiming to make their *one* view clearer. Until the point at which Porphyry admits their difference, we are not told that an argument to this effect has been going on. In fact, we are led to believe that there was hardly any need for such an argument, since Plato and Aristotle hold the same view. Does Porphyry eventually justify his claim that the two views are one? Let us first look at the passages from Plato and Aristotle which Porphyry quotes.

The third part of perception within us which we have to describe in our survey is that of hearing, and the causes whereby its affections are produced. In general, then, let us lay it down that sound (φωνή) is a stroke (πληγή) transmitted through the ears by the action of the air upon the brain and the blood reaching to the soul. And that motion caused thereby, which begins in the head and ends about the seat of the liver, is 'hearing'; and that every rapid motion amounts to a sharp sound, and every slower motion amounts to a deeper sound, and that uniform motion to an even and smooth sound and the opposite kind of motion to a harsh sound. And that large motion amounts to a loud sound, and motion of the opposite kind to a soft sound. The subject of concords of sounds must be treated in a later part of our exposition. (*Timaeus* 67a–c; tr. R. G. Bury modified) [quoted *In Ptol. Harm.* 46. 5–13]

Porphyry paraphrases this, arguing that for Plato (*Timaeus* 64b–c, 67a–b) sound is the result of a stroke (πληγή) which strikes us by the action of the air on the brain through the ears (*In Ptol. Harm.* 46. 14–15). According to this description, hearing (ἀκοή) involves an external motion, the sound's transmission through the air, as well as an internal motion, the one from the ears to the brain (ibid. 47. 2–5).[64] The air then is the efficient cause of sound, and therefore the qualities of sounds (like sharp and deep, smooth and harsh, loud and soft) are to be explained in terms of the characteristic motion of the air. Porphyry is right to argue that for Plato slow and rapid motion are not an causes of low and high pitch respectively, but rather amount to low and high pitch, and in this sense high and low pitch are essentially quantities (47. 5–12). This is maintained in the passage quoted above and becomes clearer in *Timaeus* 80a, where we read that rapid and slow sounds appear

[64] Taylor (1928: 477, 576) argues that both motions play a role in hearing.

as high and low pitch respectively.[65] Plato's view is probably to be understood in a sense similar to our modern view that a certain sound amounts to a certain wavelength. In the same way that a certain wavelength is (it does not cause) a sound in a scientific description, similarly for Plato a rapid movement of air struck in a certain way is a sharp sound.

After Porphyry's paraphrase of Plato's text comes a quotation from Aristotle.

The differences between things that sound are revealed in the actual sound (ψόφος); for just as colours are not seen without light, so sharp and flat in pitch are not perceived without sound. These are so spoken of by transference from tangible objects; for that which is sharp moves the sense to a great extent in little time, while that which is flat moves it little in much time. Not that the sharp is quick and the flat slow, but the movement in the one case is such because of speed, in the other because of slowness. There seems to be an analogy with the sharp and blunt in the case of touch. For the sharp, as it were, stabs, while the blunt, as it were, thrusts, because the one produces motion in a short time, the other in a long, so that the one is incidentally quick, the other slow. (*De anima* 420^{a}26–^{b}4; tr. D. W. Hamlyn) [quoted *In Ptol. Harm.* 47. 15–23]

Porphyry paraphrases also this passage, admitting that Aristotle's view is contrary to that of Plato (*In Ptol. Harm.* 48. 12). For Aristotle, he says, rapid and slow motion are causes of high and low pitch respectively, but are not identical with them (ibid. 48. 10–17). Porphyry again is close to the truth. For Aristotle the differences between sounds are to be explained in terms of their effect on our senses (ἐν τῷ κατ' ἐνεργείαν ψόφῳ; *De anima* 419^{b}9). The analogy of the sharp and blunt objects illustrates that the difference in sensation is due to the speed with which these objects move, given their nature; the sharp object moves the sense much in little time, while the blunt one moves it little in much time. The speed of motion, though, clearly does not account for their being blunt or sharp. Similarly with high and low pitch; speed plays a causal role in the resulting sensation, as our senses are affected rapidly or slowly. This, of course, does not mean that high pitch amounts to the air's rapid speed. It is open to discussion how important for Aristotle the causal role of speed exactly is. Aristotle, unlike Plato, believes that the air is only the medium of sound, not its efficient cause (*De anima*

[65] καὶ ὅσοι φθόγγοι ταχεῖς τε καὶ βραδεῖς ὀξεῖς τε καὶ βαρεῖς φαίνονται (*Timaeus* 80a3–4). Cf. Plutarch, *Plat. Q.* 1006A–B, Alcinous, *Didasc.* 174. 4–6. Doxographers have these Platonic passages in mind; see ps. Plutarch 4. 16. 4; Stobaeus 1. 53. 1 (*DG* 406); ps. Plutarch 4. 17. 19 (*DG* 407–8).

419^b19–25, 420^a3–5). For him sounds are incorporeal *energeiai*, forms which do not really move but travel through the air, in the same sense that a man travels in the train remaining seated.[66] If this is so, it is tempting to think that speed is a property of sound which plays a relatively small causal role in the perception of sound.[67] The crucial point for my purposes, however, is that Aristotle rejects Plato's view that high and low pitch amount to rapid and slow motions, respectively, for the view that rapid and slow motion are causes of high and low pitch.

Porphyry admits Aristotle's departure from Plato's view. So, one wonders, how the two views can be identical, as Porphyry appears to consider them? I translate part of Porphyry's relevant argument.

The sharp sound is analogous to a sharp object, and the low sound to a blunt object. The sharp object moves our sense much in a short time; similarly the sharp sound penetrates our sense of hearing much because of the speed of the stroke. The blunt object moves our sense little in much time, because it pushes rather than cuts; similarly the deep sound penetrates our hearing little because of the slow movement of the sound's impact. In the case of tangible objects, the sharp is fast and the blunt is slow, while with sounds rapidity is the cause of sharp sounds and slowness the cause of deep ones. It makes a difference whether you account for the occurrence in terms of causes or things affecting, or in terms of things caused or affected (*διαφέρει δ' ἢ περὶ τὸ αἴτιον καὶ τὸ ποιοῦν ἡγεῖσθαι τὸ συμβαῖνον ἢ περὶ τὸ αἰτιατὸν καὶ τὸ πάσχον*). Aristotle explains the event in terms of its cause, and for this reason in the sounds the rapidity of the stroke of the air, which is the cause of sound, produces sharpness according to him. As for the tangible objects, sharpness, for instance of the iron, which is the cause, brings about the rapidity, similarly in the case of deepness and of bluntness the corresponding is the case. Yet Plato talks in terms of the thing caused, 'for when the sound is rapid, it becomes sharp, when it is slow, it becomes deep'. But if, according to Plato, something is affected as the cause acts on it and vice versa, then whatever occurs in the affected thing pre-exists effectively in the cause. Thus on this issue the two philosophers would eventually agree. (*In Ptol. Harm.* 48. 17–49. 4)

Porphyry not only rules out that the two views are in conflict, but argues that they are rather complementary, and that the two philosophers differ

[66] On this point see Burnyeat (1995: 429–30).

[67] This is also how Philoponus, *In de anima* 373. 14–374. 35, and Simplicius, *In de anima* 147. 1–148. 8 and esp. 148. 22–3 understand the passage. A stronger causal role is assumed by Themistius, *In de anima* 66. 9–14. Simplicius, *In de anima* 147. 7–10 maintains that Aristotle addresses Plato, which suggests that he probably knows Porphyry's section that I refer to. Cf. Psellus, *Opusc.* 13, p. 55. 10–28 O'Meara; see also Hicks (1907: 384).

only in perspective. His claim that Plato talks in terms of the thing caused (*περὶ τὸ αἰτιατόν*) and Aristotle in terms of the cause of the event (*περὶ τὸ αἴτιον*) must mean that Plato looks at how sharp and deep sounds strike us, and argues that the rapid ones are sharp and the slow ones are low (*τὸ ταχὺ ὀξύ*; *In Ptol. Harm.* 47. 9–10; cf. *Timaeus* 67b6), while Aristotle looks at how sharp and low sounds are sensed, and argues that sharp sounds are rapid and low ones are slow (*τὸ ὀξὺ ταχύ*; *In Ptol. Harm.* 48. 24; cf. *De anima* 420^{b}2–4). This, Porphyry argues, is suggested by Aristotle's analogy with the tangible objects which, by being sharp or blunt, either stab or thrust (*In Ptol. Harm.* 48. 27–32).

Porphyry's argument is far from being clear. He seems to suggest that Plato and Aristotle adopt these different perspectives because they in general take different approaches towards the effect of sound. One is from the point of view of the sound, another from the point of view of how our senses are affected by it. Porphyry's suggestion apparently is that Plato explains how the sound (sharp or deep) strikes (rapidly or slowly), while Aristotle examines how our senses are affected by it (sharply or deeply). The obscurity of the argument is partly due to the ambiguity of the term *πληγή*,[68] which can be used in at least four senses: (*a*) the blow of something against something else, which results in sound (active sense 1; *De anima* 419^{b}9–11); (*b*) the air being struck (passive sense; *In Ptol. Harm.* 46. 20–1); (*c*) the sound's striking our senses (active sense 2; *Timaeus* 67b3, *De anima* 419^{b}17), and (*d*) the effect of the sound upon our senses (resultative sense). Porphyry distinguishes between the latter two senses with reference to Plato's text, arguing that Plato takes the word in the active sense 2, that is, how the sound strikes (*In Ptol. Harm.* 46. 22–3; cf. 53. 8–11), which includes the sound's movement outside and inside the human body. Porphyry seems to imply that Aristotle uses the term *πληγὴ* in the resultative sense, that is, he investigates how the sound strikes our senses. According to Porphyry, then, Plato is more concerned with kinds of sound produced and their perception, while Aristotle examines the cause of the kinds of sounds we sense. This is why, Porphyry argues, Plato explains rapid

[68] *τῆς πληγῆς διχῶς λεγομένης κατά τε τὸ πλήττειν, ὅ ἐστιν ἐνεργεῖν εἰς ἄλλο … κατά τε τὸ πλήττεσθαι, ὅ ἐστι πάσχειν ὑπ' ἄλλου … ὅτι πλήσσει ἡμῶν τὴν αἴσθησιν ὁ ἀὴρ πληγεὶς καὶ αὐτὸς πρότερον καὶ διαφέρων τὴν πληγὴν εἰς ἡμᾶς* (blow is used in two senses, in that of striking, that is, acting on something else, … and in that of being struck, that is, being acted upon by something else … because the air strikes our senses, having been struck itself before and transmitting the strike to us; *In Ptol. Harm.* 46. 16–18, 29–30). In other passages Porphyry confers the two senses; ibid. 38. 23–39. 9, 53. 4–11.

movement by reference to sound's sharpness, while Aristotle explains the sound's sharpness by reference to rapid movement.

Porphyry maintains that if this difference in perspective is set aside, Aristotle turns out to agree with Plato. And he tries to explain away Aristotle's difference from Plato by means of a certain interpretation of the analogy with tangible objects, arguing that for Aristotle too the sharp is rapid and the blunt is slow (*In Ptol. Harm.* 48. 17–25). But when Aristotle says that the sharp is rapid, he does not mean that sharpness is the same as or that it amounts to rapidity, but rather that rapidity is a property of the sharp object, which plays a causal role in the way it affects us. Aristotle, as we have seen, strongly denies that rapid motion is identical with high pitch (*De anima* 420^{a}31–2). The thrust of Porphyry's argument seems to be confined to the hypothesis that Plato would accept Aristotle's causal thesis according to which high pitch affects us in the way it does because of rapidity—not only that it amounts to a rapid motion (*In Ptol. Harm.* 49. 2–4).[69] It is on this basis that the two philosophers would be in agreement.

This suggestion, though, is baseless and also contradicts Porphyry's earlier claim that Plato denies the causal relation between speed and pitch (ibid. 47. 10–11). What is worse, Porphyry is inconsistent about what the 'agreed' thesis is. The initial agreement (45. 27–30) was in terms of the identity thesis, that is, that high pitch amounts to rapid motion, and against the causal one, while at the end of the section Porphyry claims that Plato would agree with Aristotle's causal thesis (49. 2–3). So now Ptolemy appears to be in agreement with the 'ancients' (49. 5–8), while earlier on (45. 17–18) Porphyry considered his view as conflicting with that of the 'ancients'. Porphyry is inconsistent as to what the agreed thesis of the 'ancients' on pitch is throughout this section and indeed throughout his entire commentary.[70] On the whole Porphyry

[69] *εἰ δὲ κατὰ τὸν Πλάτωνα ὡς ποιεῖ τὸ ποιοῦν, οὕτω πάσχει τὸ πάσχον καὶ ἔμπαλιν, εἴη ἂν τὰ περὶ τὸ αἰτιατὸν συμβαίνοντα προϋπάρχοντα ποιητικῶς ἐν τῷ αἰτίῳ* (*In Ptol. Harm.* 49. 2–4). Porphyry's formulation is cryptic. See my tr. above p. 262.

[70] *καλῶς καὶ τοῦ Ἀριστοτέλους αἰτίας μὲν ὀξύτητος καὶ βαρύτητος τὰ τάχη καὶ τὰς βραδύτητας παραδεξαμένου, μηκέτι δὲ προσεμένου τὸ ταχύτητα εἶναι ἢ ταχεῖαν γε τὴν ὀξεῖαν φωνὴν ἢ βραδεῖαν τὴν βαρεῖαν* (Aristotle has done well to accept high and low speed as the causes of high and low pitch respectively, yet he did not concede that high pitch amounts to high speed or to being fast and low pitch to slow speed or to being slow; *In Ptol. Harm.* 58. 13–16). This contradicts Plato's view as presented in ibid. 47. 8–11; *σαφῶς οὖν ὁ Πλάτων ... τὴν ταχεῖαν φωνὴν τίθεται ὀξεῖαν, καὶ τὴν βαρεῖαν βραδεῖαν. ἀλλ' οὐ τὴν ταχύτητα αἰτίαν γίνεσθαι τῆς ὀξύτητος ἢ τὴν βραδύτητα τῆς βαρύτητος* (clearly Plato declared the fast sound to be sharp and the slow to be low, and not that high speed is the cause of high pitch and slow speed the cause of low pitch).

appears to insinuate rather than to prove the agreement between Plato and Aristotle on that matter, and their difference is hardly resolved. Yet Porphyry considers his conclusion established. He goes on to conclude that the agreement extends from Pythagoras to Plato, to Aristotle and Ptolemy (*In Ptol. Harm.* 49. 5–8), and he appears to refer to his conclusion also elsewhere (Simplicius, *In Cat.* 213. 20–2; 70F. 17–20).

The whole section is instructive in many regards. First, it emerges that Porphyry does not miss an opportunity to show how Plato and Aristotle are in accord, though the context hardly invites such an argument. The formulation of his conclusion shows that he was strongly concerned with demonstrating the unanimity of Plato and Aristotle (καὶ ταύτῃ ὁμόφωνοι εἶεν ἂν ἀλλήλοις οἱ φιλόσοφοι). Second, it turns out that, in Porphyry's view, Aristotle's objections to Plato (ἀντιλογίαι; *In Ptol. Harm.* 48. 12) do not always amount to disagreement (διαφωνία, ἀντίθεσις); sometimes the relevant arguments of Plato and Aristotle rather suggest, in his view, that there exists an essential agreement, which may be obscured by some difference in perspective. In the present case, the discord is reduced to a difference in explanatory direction; although, Porphyry suggests, Aristotle thought he was contradicting Plato's view, in fact he essentially agrees with it. This is presumably why Porphyry does not acknowledge their difference from the start.

The above instance shows that in his *ΠΔΠΑ* Porphyry may well have dealt with differences which do not undermine the essential accord of the two philosophers, such as misguided objections to Plato on Aristotle's part. Hence he could have espoused both positions embodied in the titles of *ΠΔΠΑ* and *ΠΠΑ* without contradicting himself. In the light of the above evidence, it becomes most probable that Porphyry's two works on the relation between Platonic and Aristotelian philosophies presented complementary positions.

The section is also instructive regarding Porphyry's method of reconciling Plato's views with those of Aristotle's. It involved the integration of long quotations from Plato and Aristotle, followed by paraphrase and explanation of each passage and then a concluding argument asserting the compatibility of the two philosophers. Occasionally Simplicius follows the same strategy when he tries to show that the disagreement between Plato and Aristotle is only apparent.[71] Quite generally,

[71] e.g. *In de caelo* 454. 23–456. 5; cf. ibid. 87. 3–28.

Porphyry often gives quotations to illustrate a point,[72] and throughout his commentary on Ptolemy's *Harmonics* quotations abound. Quotations from Plato (especially the *Timaeus*) and musical theorists, Aristoxenians and especially Pythagoreans, predominate. Yet we also find quotations from Aristotle (the *Categories*, the *De Anima*, the *De audiendis*), from Theophrastus (pp. 61–5), and Adrastus' commentary on the *Timaeus* (pp. 7, 96).

It seems that the method of quotation–paraphrasis–argument was used by Porphyry especially in exegetical projects with two opposite sides, such as between Aristoxenians and Pythagoreans, or between Plato and Aristotle, and it may well have been employed in his works on the relation between the philosophies of the latter. However, as his commentary on the *Harmonics* clearly shows, quotation and paraphrasis are framed by the argument and constitute part of it.[73] So the present section lends some support to Walzer's hypothesis about Porphyry's use of quotations, but also suggests that the Arabic sources are rather unlikely to have drawn on Porphyry directly, since they do not present any argument along with the quotations from Greek philosophers. It is possible, of course, that they simply were not interested in the arguments.

4. FURTHER EVIDENCE ON PORPHYRY'S WAYS OF SHOWING PLATO AND ARISTOTLE IN ACCORD

A passage from the Byzantine philosopher Michael Psellus (eleventh century), who had a good knowledge of Porphyry's work, corroborates the belief that one of Porphyry's strategies for showing Plato and Aristotle to be in accord was to reduce their differences to differences of explanatory direction.[74] I quote:

[72] In *V. Plot.* Porphyry quotes long passages from Longinus (chs. 17, 19, 20) and the entire oracle about Plotinus' soul (ch. 22). Several quotations are found in the *De abstinentia* and his early *De philosophia ex oraculis haurienda*. On Porphyry's tendency to quote from his sources see Smith (1987: 743, 748–9).

[73] Porphyry's method reminds us of Origen's in his *Stromateis* where Christian views were compared with those of pagan philosophers (Plato, Aristotle, Numenius), and also of Eusebius' method in the *PE.*

[74] Smith leaves out the above passage from his edn. Psellus' good knowledge of Porphyry's work becomes clear from his frequent references to it; e.g. op. 8, pp. 29. 55–30. 2 Duffy, op. 46, pp. 166. 12–167. 8 Duffy, op. 48, p. 174. 67–76 Duffy, op. 16, pp. 76–82 O'Meara, *De omnifaria doctrina*, ed. L. G. Westerink (Nijmegen, 1948), chs. 60, 64–6, 87, 115.

Ὁ θεῖος οὗτος πατὴρ πάσαις ταῖς Ἀριστοτελικαῖς καὶ Πλατωνικαῖς πραγματείαις ὡμιληκώς, νῦν μὲν οὕτως, νῦν δὲ ἄλλως περὶ τῶν αὐτῶν διατάττεται· ἐπειδὴ γὰρ ἐκεῖνοι νῦν μὲν τὸ αἴτιον λόγον φασὶ τοῦ αἰτιατοῦ, νῦν δὲ τὸ αἰτιατὸν τοῦ αἰτίου, πρὸς ὃ βούλεται καὶ καταλλήλως ἔχει τῷ λόγῳ τὸ νόημα, ταῖς ἐκείνων ἀποχρῆται φιλοσοφίας. (*Theol. Opusc.* 97, p. 379. 25–9 Gautier)

This divine father [sc. Porphyry] has become acquainted with all Aristotelian and Platonic treatises, and approaches the same subjects one time this way, the other time in a different way. For since they [sc. Plato and Aristotle] sometimes explain the thing caused in terms of the cause, and some other times the cause in terms of the things caused, depending on what Porphyry wants to show and what fits to the argument, he makes use of their philosophy accordingly.

Psellus maintains that quite generally Platonic and Aristotelian explanatory accounts may present matters either in terms of the cause or in terms of the effect, and that Porphyry took advantage of this ambiguity in order to justify his own exegetical variation. Psellus approves of Porphyry's approach and he seems to imply that this was a standard Porphyrian approach towards Platonic and Aristotelian works by means of which Porphyry claimed to be doing justice to the multiple perspectives involved in them. One thing which emerges from both this passage and the section from the commentary on the *Harmonics* is that Porphyry' exegesis of Plato involved discussion of the relevant views of Aristotle. This was presumably motivated from his belief that Aristotle largely followed Plato, in which case Aristotle's views were useful for understanding Plato. But, as has been seen, Porphyry's exegetical strategies do justice neither to Plato nor to Aristotle; rather, he falls into contradictions, his argument is obscure and convoluted, and tends to explain away differences rather than prove the essential accord of Plato and Aristotle.[75]

Sometimes Porphyry does not give any argument as to why 'the ancients' (*οἱ παλαιοί, οἱ ἀρχαῖοι*), that is, Plato and Aristotle are in accord, but simply states it. Such statements may rest on an argument made at some other part of his work. For instance, Porphyry states the accord of the 'ancients' on sound in his long commentary on *Categories* (Simplicius, *In Cat.* 213. 20–2; 70F. 17–20), but his argument is preserved, as has been seen, in his commentary on Ptolemy's *Harmonics*. In the same work we find sections discussing epistemological or

[75] Elsewhere Psellus refers to a similar argument by means of which the differences between Plato and Aristotle are explained away, but Porphyry is not explicitly mentioned (*Philosophica Minora*, op. 13, p. 71. 13–16 O'Meara).

metaphysical questions, yet some of these conclusions are stated in the *Sententiae* where no argument is given.[76]

One instance in which Porphyry assumes the agreement of the 'ancients' without argument occurs in *De Abstinentia* 3. Porphyry endorses Plato's idea of the transmigration of human souls into animal bodies,[77] and moves on from this to argue for the rationality of animals. He claims that animals share both linguistic discourse (*logos prophorikos*) and discursive thinking (*logos endiathetos*; *De abst.* 3. 2. 1), arguing that animals understand each other, some of them also imitate human language (ibid. 3. 3. 4, 3. 4. 4, 3. 4. 7, 3. 5. 2), while also having the ability to learn and to remember, all of which suggest that they think rationally (3. 10. 3). Porphyry holds that his views are supported by the authority of the 'ancients', namely Aristotle, Plato, Empedocles, Pythagoras, and Democritus (3. 6. 7), among whom Aristotle is presented as prominent, probably because of his research into animals (3. 6. 5).

However, Aristotle denies reason to animals, and in this he largely follows Plato. Both Plato and Aristotle share a strong notion of rationality, according to which reason (*logos, logistikon, nous*) is capable of finding out the true or right thing by means of reasoning, and take this rationality to be the special characteristic of humans.[78] In their view, animals only partake of *phronêsis* or *synesis*, which is a form of cognition in virtue of which they are able to learn and do certain things, and thus cope with the problems of their lives.[79] But to Plato and Aristotle this does not suggest a share in reason, as it does to Porphyry, and both sharply distinguish animal *phronêsis* from human reason and the activities of thinking and understanding.[80] Aristotle in particular clearly

[76] *In Ptol. Harm.* 11. 1–15. 27, 17. 13–31, 18. 1–23; cf. also *Sent.* 42, p. 53. 7 Lamberz. See below s. 8.

[77] Cf. *Phaedo* 81b–82b; *Rep.* 620a–d; *Timaeus* 42b–d, 91d–92c.

[78] Cf. *De anima* 429^a23–5; esp. *NE* 1097^b32–1098a15. However, the concept of reason developed from Plato to Aristotle is still debated. See Sorabji (1996) for a recent discussion.

[79] Cf. Plato, *Rep.* 375e–376a–c; *Theaetetus* 186b–d; *Politicus* 263d; Aristotle, *De anima* 427^b7; *Met.* 980^a27–$^b28$; *Hist. Anim.* 608^a17; *De Part. Anim.* 660^a35–$^b2$. I owe some of the references to Sorabji (1993), but I disagree with his view that Plato wavers on his denial of reason to animals. As I argue, the acceptance of transmigration of the soul does not suggest that animals have reason, as he believes, but rather the opposite. This is how Plotinus understands the transmigration of the soul (*Enn.* 3. 4. 2. 19–30, 3. 4. 6. 10–30).

[80] *Symp.* 207a–c; *Rep.* 441a–b; *De anima* 404^b1–6, 427^b6–10. To animals the cause of movement can never be *nous*, but either desire (*orexis*) or *phantasia* (*De anima* 433^a10–27).

denies language in animals,[81] and Porphyry is misleading when he implies the opposite.

How, then, did Porphyry come to assume that Plato and Aristotle attribute reason to animals? As far as Plato is concerned, Porphyry reached such a conclusion simply because in various places in his work Plato talks about the transmigration of souls (*Phaedo* 81b–82b, 107c–d; *Rep.* 620a–d; *Timaeus* 42c, 91d–92c). Porphyry interprets these passages as implying the rationality of animals.[82] But this interpretation does not do justice to what seems to be Plato's position, because for Plato the souls of animals are punished souls, confined in animal bodies and unable to exercise their rational faculty, since the mind has escaped. This is actually the point of their punishment. In this sense animal souls are essentially irrational.

Porphyry is convinced of Aristotle's agreement with the view he attributes to Plato because, according to Porphyry, Aristotle considers reason to be not man's special difference from other animals but only a gradated distinction, in the same sense that Gods differ from men only in the degree of their reason (*De abst.* 3. 7. 1–2; cf. ibid. 3. 8. 6–7, 3. 9. 1). Aristotle, however, explicitly rejects such a view. In the only passage in which he speaks about gradated difference between man and animal, he refers to temperament and makes clear that regarding intellectual ability the difference is substantial (*Hist. Anim.* $588^a18–^b4$). If this is so, then, Aristotle follows Plato against Porphyry's claim that animals possess reason.[83]

This instance seems to be of further interest. What Porphyry tries to do here is not only to assimilate Aristotle's position to that of Plato, but also to bring Plato and Aristotle into line with Pythagoreanism. He

[81] Aristotle distinguishes between voice (φωνή), which animals have (*De anima* 420^b32), and language (διάλεκτος), which is characteristic of man only, although some animals have voice which is language-like (ὥσπερ διάλεκτον; *Hist. Anim.* 536^a21, $^b11–12$). Later the Stoics will develop Aristotle's distinction. They will distinguish between pronounced speech (προφορικὸς λόγος), which animals may have, and internalized speech, or reasoning (ἐνδιάθετος λόγος), which only men have. (Sextus, *Adv. Math.* 8. 275; *SVF* ii. 135, 223). Cf. Philodemus, *On Poems I*, fr. 26, cols. i–ii Sbordone (=cols. 114–15 Janko). See further Sorabji (1996: 323–5).

[82] On Porphyry's acceptance of the transmigration of souls see Augustine, *Civ. Dei* 10. 30. 1–2 (300F). Porphyry follows Plotinus on this (see n. 79) but he goes beyond Plotinus' interpretation. See also the comments of Deuse (1983: 129–67) and Smith (1987: 725–7). See also below p. 292.

[83] Porphyry may be the author of a passage often attributed to Aristotle's *Protrepticus* (Iamblichus, *Protr.* 36. 7–13 Pistelli), which talks in terms of gradated difference between man and animal, ascribing to the latter 'shadows of reason' (λόγου . . . αἰθύγματα); cf. *In Ptol. Harm.* 16. 17. See Jaeger (1948: 62).

makes the same claim in the section from his commentary on *Harmonics*, arguing that Ptolemy follows Pythagoras and also Plato and Aristotle (49. 5–8). Porphyry may have taken a similar position in his *History of Philosophy*, in which he outlined the evolution of philosophy, starting with Pythagoras and stopping apparently with Plato.[84] Porphyry stopped with Plato probably because in his view philosophy reached its perfection with him. This, however, should not necessarily mean that he excluded Aristotle from his account altogether. Porphyry may have discussed Aristotle's philosophy briefly in the section on Plato, suggesting that Aristotle largely follows Plato and belongs to his school of thought. This may well be the reason why Aristotle does not get separate treatment in Porphyry's history.

So far it has emerged that Porphyry was seriously engaged with how Aristotle's views compare with those of Plato, and had developed special ways to deal with the question. Now, taking a more microscopic approach, I turn to examine Porphyry's views on how Aristotle's doctrines in physics, psychology, ethics, and metaphysics/logic compare with those of Plato.

5. PHYSICS

5.1. Introduction

Porphyry wrote a commentary on Aristotle's *Physics*,[85] being the first Platonist to pay such close attention to the treatise. Yet he does not seem to have commented on the entire work as we have it. The last extracts preserved by Simplicius, our sole witness for this commentary, come from a summary of the fifth book (*In Phys.* 802. 8; 159F. 2), with which the commentary apparently stopped (ibid. 918. 11–15; 162T). The question, of course, is why. Simplicius' report gives us an insight, which strengthens us in the belief that Porphyry's detailed commentary stopped with book 4. Porphyry, Simplicius says, divided Aristotle's

[84] The work comprised four books (Eunapius, *Vit. Soph.* 2. 14–18; 198T). The first book, apart from Pythagoras, also treated the seven sages and Homer (201T–203T); book 2 dealt possibly with the Presocratics (208F), book 3 with Socrates (210F–218F), book 4 with Plato (219F–223F).

[85] See Moraux (1985: 225–39). The fragments have been collected by Romano (1985), with Italian translation appended, and by Smith (1993: 118F–162F). Two fragments from Porphyry's commentary are not included in Smith's edn. i.e. Simplicius, *In Phys.* 336. 28–9 and *In Phys.* 378. 17–21.

Physics into two parts, the 'physics' (φυσικά), comprising books 1–4, and 'on movement' (περὶ κινήσεως), covering books 5–8, thus resisting the tendency to reckon books 1–5 as the φυσικὰ and books 6–8 as the περὶ κινήσεως (*In Phys.* 802. 7–13; 159F).[86] This means that Porphyry considered his commentary on the 'Physics' complete at the end of the fourth book, and this is why he stopped with this.[87]

It turns out that Porphyry concentrated on the part which is more loaded with metaphysics. Presumably this was exactly what attracted his interest in the work in the first place.[88] In the sole fragment from the preface to his commentary (Simplicius, *In Phys.* 9. 10–27; 119F), he argues that the search for principles in nature is not the concern of the naturalists (οἱ φυσικοί), but of the metaphysician (ὁ ἀναβεβηκώς; ibid. 9. 10–13; 119F. 1–3). Porphyry's statement stops here, but Simplicius' explanation that follows helps to understand its sense. To begin with, the term φυσικὸς is ambiguous; it can mean, generally, the one who inquires into the nature of things (e.g. a scientist, like a doctor), or the natural philosopher (cf. LSJ, s.v.). Porphyry must use it in the former sense, because Simplicius in his comment makes a contrast between the scientist, such as a doctor or a mathematician, who has a specialized knowledge, and someone with a higher, philosophical knowledge (ὁ ἀναβεβηκώς; cf. *In Phys.* 15. 34).[89] Scientists, Simplicius argues, refer to certain principles in order to explain why something is so, but they take for granted these principles and neither inquire into them nor into the force (*dynamis*) each of them has. That is, they do not seek to determine the role of each principle and its relative importance. The principles of the human body, for instance, is not the concern of the doctor, but of the *physiologos*, the natural philosopher, while the principles of nature is

[86] This division is adopted also by Simplicius, *In de caelo* 226. 19, Philoponus, *In Phys.* 2. 16, Olympiodorus *In Meteor.* 7. 13; see also Smith's *apparatus fontium* at 159F. This division goes back to Andronicus and perhaps can be traced further back to Theophrastus, as Simplicius, who approves of it, suggests (*In Phys.* 923. 7–16; cf. 802. 7–13). See D. Ross, *Aristotle's Physics* (Oxford, 1936), 1–2 and Moraux (1984: 314).

[87] This is supported by the testimony of Al-Nadim in *Fihrist* (118T); see also Romano (1985: 53–6).

[88] The first five books of the *Physics* were often mentioned with the title Περὶ ἀρχῶν, e.g. Adrastus apud Simplicium, *In Phys.* 4. 11–12; cf. Ross's *apparatus criticus* concerning the title of *Physics* in the OCT.

[89] Already Plutarch in *De primo frigido* 948B–C makes a similar distinction between the φυσικός, who seeks the ultimate causes, and the practitioner, such as a doctor. Note though that in Plutarch the φυσικός is the natural philosopher. Plutarch describes the ultimate causes as ἀνωτέρω (*Adv. Col.* 1115E), τὰ πρῶτα καὶ ἀνωτάτω (*De primo frigido* 948B–C); cf. Atticus frs. 5. 13–15, 9. 31–3, 42–5 Des Places; Alcinous, *Didasc.* 189. 15–16. See below pp. 275–7 on how Porphyry differs from them.

the business of the metaphysician, the 'first philosopher', and such explanations are given in terms of form and matter.

Simplicius then suggests that the *Physics* is not a treatise on 'first philosophy', an inquiry into the being as such (*Met.*1026^{a}30), as it does not examine each principle separately (119F. 16–22); in this sense Aristotle's treatise is not metaphysical. But Porphyry presented as the metaphysician's aim the identification of the principles of nature, not the examination of the role of each principle. This is confirmed by Simplicius who argues that in this work Aristotle is doing metaphysics only in the sense that he outlines the principles from which any inquiry into natural matters should start, leaving the investigation of each principle *per se* for his *Metaphysics* (119F. 19–22), and he cites Aristotle stating this (*Physics* 192^{a}34–5) in support of his opinion. It is this narrow sense of metaphysics which attracts Porphyry's interest in the *Physics*. His suggestion seems to be that this work, though not properly metaphysical, may be valuable for the metaphysician. Let us see how this can be so.

5. 2. Porphyry on Platonic and Aristotelian Causes

Porphyry comments on the first lines of the *Physics* (184^{a}10–16), in which Aristotle argues that one cannot reach systematic knowledge of a thing, unless one first grasps its primary causes (αἰτίαι), its principles (ἀρχαί), and its elements (στοιχεῖα). Similarly, Aristotle argues, in the case of nature, one needs first to specify its principles. Porphyry sets out to explain the various ways in which Aristotle understands principles (Simplicius, *In Phys.* 10. 25–11. 17; 120F). One way to understand principles is in the sense of 'origin'. The principles of a house or of a ship are, in this sense, the founding stones and the keel respectively. A more sophisticated way in which Aristotle understands principles is in terms of the nature or the art which, depending on the case, accounts for the coming into being of natural entities and artifacts, the purpose for which a thing comes about, the matter it consists of, and also its Form. These four principles account in different ways for the being of a thing.

Porphyry focuses on the latter way of understanding principles and relates Aristotle's doctrine to what he takes to be the corresponding doctrine of Plato, although nothing in the text invites such a comparison. He argues that Aristotle differed from Plato in two respects. First, Aristotle considered only the Form which is immanent in a thing (τὸ ἐν τῇ ὕλῃ εἶδος), while Plato had also postulated the separable Form (χωριστὸν εἶδος). This latter, Porphyry argues, constitutes a distinct principle, that he calls paradigmatic (παραδειγματικὴ ἀρχή), which Plato first had established.[90] Porphyry's formulation here suggests that for him the transcendent Form is the model (*paradeigma*) upon which a material entity was based, in the same way that the idea of the bed is the model for a carpenter who sets out to create a bed—I will take this up below. The second aspect in which Aristotle differs from Plato, according to Porphyry, is that Plato also understands as principle the instrument by means of which something comes about. In Porphyry's view, then, Plato's set of principles is richer than Aristotle's by two.[91] Interestingly, though, no conflict between Plato and Aristotle is implied. Quite the opposite is the case. Porphyry suggests that Plato amended, as it were, Aristotle's version of principles by adding two more (προσείγαγε). This means that Aristotle adopted an incomplete set of Plato's principles. The upshot is that the doctrine outlined in Aristotle's text must be credited entirely to Plato, but also that the two versions are compatible and complementary.[92]

The above piece of evidence is striking in many regards. To begin with, it is quite remarkable that Porphyry departs from Plotinus' view about Aristotle's doctrine of substance and the Aristotelian conception of immanent Form. First, Porphyry differs from Plotinus in maintaining that Aristotle did not reject Plato's transcendent Forms, but rather omitted them. Secondly, Porphyry does not follow Plotinus in criticizing the Aristotelian immanent Form for being a mere quality which does not account for the being of a thing.

Porphyry's account is puzzling. We would be surprised if a modern commentator presented things the way Porphyry did. This is first because we do not believe that Plato had a system of five causes, as Porphyry suggests, and also believe that Aristotle reacted against Plato's

[90] ἀλλ' ὁ μὲν Ἀριστοτέλης τὸ ἐν τῇ ὕλῃ μόνον θεασάμενος εἶδος τοῦτο ἔλεγεν ἀρχήν, ὁ δὲ Πλάτων πρὸς τούτῳ καὶ τὸ χωριστὸν ἐννοήσας εἶδος τὴν παραδειγματικὴν ἀρχὴν προσείγαγε. (Simplicius, *In Phys.* 10. 32–5; Porphyry 120F. 11–15 Smith). The text continues in the next footnote. On the term *paradeigma* see below, pp. 275–6.

[91] τετραχῶς οὖν ἡ ἀρχὴ κατὰ τὸν Ἀριστοτέλην . . . κατὰ δὲ Πλάτωνα καὶ τὸ πρὸς ὅ, ὡς τὸ παράδειγμα καὶ τὸ δι' οὗ ὡς τὸ ὀργανικόν (Simplicius, *In Phys.* 10. 35–11. 2; 120F. 15–19).

[92] Later Platonists, probably drawing from Porphyry or an intermediary source, attribute to Plato six causes, three main ones (final, paradigmatic, efficient) and three auxiliary ones (*synaitia*: organic, formal, material); cf. Philoponus, *De aet. mundi* 159. 5–14, Simpl. *In Phys.* 316. 22–6, Olymp. *In Phaed.* 207. 28–208. 14.

ontology and modified it considerably. That is, we take it that Aristotle criticized Plato's suggestion that there can be Forms existing separately from particulars. Aristotle's work offers plenty of solid evidence for this,[93] including his specific criticism of the view that the world has come about when matter was informed by transcendent patterns or models (*paradeigmata*; *Met.* 991^{a}20–3). One wonders, then, why and on what grounds Porphyry fends off Aristotle's rejection of Plato's transcendent Forms and presents their sets of principles as being compatible. To give an answer to this, we must briefly look at the background to his view, which is based on antecedent Platonist positions.

One such position can be detected behind the practice of conflating Platonic with Aristotelian causes, which are presented by means of prepositions (ἐξ, διά, ὑπό, etc.);[94] the four Aristotelian causes are assumed to be common to Plato and Aristotle, while that of the paradigmatic Forms is presented as specifically Platonic. A clear case of such a conflation is found in Seneca (*Epist.* 65. 4–14), who presents the causal theory of the Platonic–Aristotelian tradition, as he says, in order to criticize it from the Stoic point of view.[95] For Stoics like Seneca, the Platonic–Aristotelian notion of cause is intrinsically wrong, because a cause, strictly speaking, must be active, that is, must do something to something else;[96] a necessary condition for something (like matter, for instance) does not qualify as a cause in this sense.[97] In Seneca's view, the Platonic–Aristotelian 'swarm of causes' (*turba causarum*) are too many to count as sufficient causes and too few to count as accessory ones, since they do not comprise all necessary conditions for something to come about (*Epist.* 65. 11–14). The crucial point for us is that Seneca was familiar with a tradition, possibly a Platonist one, of unifying Platonic and Aristotelian causes into one scheme, acknowledging only the paradigmatic Forms as specifically Platonic. Apparently Seneca and his source consider Aristotle's immanent Forms to be originally Platonic,

[93] For Aristotle's objections against Plato's separate Forms see *Met.* 990^{b}8–992^{a}10, 1078^{b}12–34, and esp. *Met.* 7 (e.g. 1031^{a}28–1031^{b}11). See Fine (1986) on the metaphysics involved behind Aristotle's objections.

[94] On this way to formulate metaphysical relations see Theiler (1964: 19–30); cf. Dörrie, 'Präpositionen und Metaphysik', in 1976: 125–36 and Dillon (1993: 62) with further references.

[95] *Epist.* 65. 7–8. Cf. ibid. 58. 18–21; Philo, *Cherubim* 125; Alcinous, *Didasc.* 163. 40–2. For a commentary on Seneca's passage see Frede (1987*d*: 133–5).

[96] *Stoicis placet unam causam esse, id, quod facit.* (Seneca, *Epist.* 65. 4). Thus for the Stoics three of the Platonic/Aristotelian causes amount to one in the Stoic system, namely *logos* (*ratio scilicet faciens, id est deus*; Seneca, *Epist.* 65. 12).

[97] See Frede (1987*d*) on the Stoic conception of cause.

and given the evidence of the *Phaedo* (100d4–8, 105b–c), the *Republic* (472d5), or the *Parmenides* (131b1), they are certainly justified in doing so. Apart from Seneca, this also is what Plutarch and Alcinous maintain.[98] The same view underlies Porphyry's comment on the beginning of the *Physics*. Like his predecessors he was justified in considering Aristotle's immanent Form as being originally Platonic.

Another relevant position is found in Platonist accounts on three principles, matter, God, and the Forms,[99] and concerns an understanding of the Forms which we also find in Porphyry, namely as paradigms. As I have already said, the term 'paradigm' refers both to transcendent and to immanent Forms. Plato uses the term *paradeigma* sometimes in the former sense (*Rep.* 592b2, *Tim.* 48e5) and at other times in the latter one (*Rep.* 472d5, 561d6).[100] Yet, more importantly, the term indicates a particular understanding of the relation between the two kinds of Forms. We know that several Platonists used the term to indicate that the Form of x is both the model for x, which is separate from x, that is transcendent, and the actual Form of x, which is immanent.[101] For them this is one and the same Form which exists in two different ways, as transcendent and as immanent, that is, as model and copy, in a sense analogous to the existence of the engraved form of a seal and the form imprinted on what is sealed. Indeed, Porphyry uses precisely this analogy to describe their relation.[102] For these Platonists there are not two causes, but only one that exists in two versions.

This Platonist understanding of Forms, however, may lead one to criticize Aristotle's rejection of transcendent Forms in the way that Plutarch does in his *Adversus Colotem* (1115B–C). There Aristotle is criticized for mistakenly thinking that he could isolate the immanent aspect of Plato's Forms and adhere to this only. Aristotle is criticized for this because a Platonist would run into difficulties regarding the interpretation of the cosmogony in the *Timaeus*. For, in order to bring the

[98] Cf. *Adv. Col.* 1115D–E; see Ch. 2, pp. 98–9 for discussion. Cf. τὰ μὲν πρῶτα [sc. νοητά] ὑπάρχει, ὡς αἱ ἰδέαι, τὰ δὲ δεύτερα ὡς τὰ εἴδη τὰ ἐπὶ τῇ ὕλει. (Alcinous, *Didasc.* 155. 39–40); *Etiam hunc si aliam desideras distinctionem, idos in opere est, idea extra opus nec tantum extra opus est, sed ante opus.* (Seneca, *Epist.* 58. 21); cf. Porphyry's formulation in Simplicius, *In Phys.* 10. 32–5.

[99] Taurus apud Philoponum *De aet. mundi* 147. 19–20; Alcinous, *Didasc.* 163.11–14; Apuleius, *De Platone* 1. 190; cf. Dillon (1993: 93–4).

[100] In the former sense the term occurs also in *Timaeus* 29b4, 31a4. Aristotle uses the term in connection with the Forms in *Met.* 991a21–31, 1013a27. For a discussion of the different interpretations of the term see Cherniss (1944: 257 n. 66).

[101] Cf. Plutarch, *De an. procr.* 1024C; *Plat. Q.* 1001E; Alcinous, *Didasc.* 163. 21–4.

[102] Porphyry, *In Ptol. Harm.* 14. 17–21.

world about, the divine craftsman to some extent operates as any other craftsman, namely in so far as he is a thinking intellect (cf. Xenocrates fr. 15 Heinze). Like the craftsman of *Republic* 10 who creates a bed having a certain model in mind, the divine one must bring the world into being in an analogous way, that is, by imitating a model which is the object of his thinking.[103] The relation between the object of the creator's thinking and the divine intellect itself was, as we know, debated among Platonists,[104] but for us the important thing is that Platonists considered themselves to be justified in setting aside Aristotle's objections to transcendent Forms on the grounds that these are indispensable to creation, and in criticizing his rejection of them. This is apparently what Xenocrates first did (fr. 30 Heinze).[105]

The strong connection between transcendent and immanent Forms which some Platonists since Xenocrates assumed is understood in an even stronger way by those who use the term 'paradigmatic' for the Forms. This is a term Plato never uses, but already Xenocrates does.[106] They maintain that there has never been the one kind of Form without the other. It is noteworthy that those who use this term for the Forms, namely Xenocrates (fr. 30 Heinze), Alcinous (*Didasc.* 163. 21–4), and Porphyry, believe that the world has always existed and that the cosmogony of the *Timaeus* was a fiction. The term 'paradigmatic' was presumably coined in order to emphasize that God has always used the transcendent Forms to create, since these Forms are thoughts of the divine intellect on which immanent Forms have always been modelled. For these Platonists, the former have never existed without the latter, since the world has always existed. Hence Platonists like Alcinous, but also Taurus (in *De aet. mundi* 147. 19–20) and Apuleius (*De Plat.* 1. 192–3) contradicted Platonists like Atticus, who argued that the Forms served as paradigms at some particular point (e.g. frs. 9. 41, 38a–b Des Places), although they had always existed in the divine mind (frs. 9. 40, 40).

[103] The assumption of an analogy between the human and the divine mind as one which played a crucial role in the formation of this view has been discussed by Rich (1954: 127–33) and Dillon (1993: 93–5).

[104] The Platonist views on this issue depended much on the interpretation of the *Timaeus*; see Baltes (1996: 82) and also Rich (1954). Cf. Ch. 4, pp. 168–71, Ch. 5, pp. 208–10.

[105] See Cherniss (1945: 257); Dillon (2003: 118–21). The way of understanding Plato's Forms was debated in the Academy. See Cherniss (1945: 33–48) for a discussion of the different views in circulation.

[106] He speaks of *paradeigmatikê archê* (ap. Proclum *In Parm.* 136 Cousin; fr. 30 Heinze); see Dillon (1993: 96–8; 2003: 119–20).

Such a Platonist interpretation may well have been formed in response to Aristotle's objections.

As I have argued in Chapter 5, some of the representatives of the above understanding of Forms may have believed that Aristotle, despite his objections, also had accepted transcendent Forms, since his God is also an intellect whose activity is thinking (*Met.* 12. 7). Porphyry, I submit, takes exactly this view. He maintains that Aristotle accepted transcendent Forms as thoughts of the divine intellect, and that these are related to the immanent ones as he believed they are in Plato. It is because Porphyry takes such a view that he does not criticize Aristotle for rejecting the transcendent Forms, as Plutarch did. The evidence for this Porphyrian belief is twofold; first, his interpretation of the world's coming into being in the *Timaeus*, which shows that Porphyry considers the Platonic and the Aristotelian schemes of principles to be essentially the same; secondly, some Porphyrian comments to the effect that Plato and Aristotle agree in ontology.[107] Let us look first at Porphyry's interpretation of the *Timaeus* in some detail.

5. 3. Porphyry on the 'Created' Character of the Platonic Cosmos and on Aristotle's Interpretation of the Cosmogony in the *Timaeus*

Porphyry wrote a large-scale commentary on the *Timaeus* in which he presented his views regarding how the cosmogony described in the dialogue should be interpreted and also how one has to look at Aristotle's criticisms of it.[108] As we have seen so far, Platonists were divided between those who took the cosmogony in the *Timaeus* literally, arguing that the world is the result of a certain cosmogonical process, and those who argued that no such process was involved and considered the cosmogony described as being fictional.[109] Partisans of the first, literal construal, like Atticus, criticized Aristotle for contradicting Plato, while the followers of the second, non-literal one accepted Aristotle's argument as valid but maintained that it does not apply in the case of Plato, because for Plato the world was never actually created but has always

107 See s. 8 below.

108 Proclus and Philoponus made extensive use of Porphyry's commentary. The fragments are collected by A. R. Sodano, *Porphyrius In Platonis Timaeum commentariorum fragmenta* (Naples, 1964).

109 The first party was represented by Plutarch (Ch. 2, pp. 101–3) and Atticus (Ch. 4, pp. 168–70), the latter by Taurus, Severus (Ch. 4, pp.179–86), Alcinous (*Didasc.* 169. 32–5).

existed, and that the world has an origin (*archē*) only in the sense that God is the principle accounting for its existence. As has been seen in Chapter 5, the partisans of the non-literal construal held that the literal one gives rise to enormous interpretative difficulties. One such difficulty was the question Aristotle had asked which is why the world did not come about earlier. Another was the question why God postponed doing the good by setting order in chaos and thus bringing the world about. As has been seen in Chapter 4 (s. 6), Taurus argued that the literal interpretation is not compelled by Plato's text, and in the search for the best possible non-literal construal he listed all possible senses that the verbal adjective γενητός can admit. Taurus suggested that the world is corporeal, and as such a composite, and thus always in the process of becoming (*gignesthai*), which means that it belongs to the realm of becoming.[110] As I noted in Chapter 4 (s. 6), such a sense of 'created' is in accordance with Aristotle's understanding of coming into being.

Porphyry seems to have found Taurus' work on the interpretation of the *Timaeus* useful and he takes it up.[111] He agrees with Taurus that one first has to map out the various possibilities before one commits oneself to an interpretation, since, he argues, Plato talks only about the extremes, the eternal being and the created, leaving out what is being and also in some sense created (Proclus, *In Tim.* 1. 257. 2–8; fr. XXXI Sodano).[112] Unlike Taurus, though, Porphyry understands *Timaeus* 27c5 and 28b6–8 as being entirely open to interpretation. In this spirit, he adds three more senses to Taurus' list, including temporal ones (Philoponus, *De aet. mundi* 148. 7–149. 16).[113] In his view, the interpretative task for a Platonist consists in finding the sense of 'created' which fits Plato's overall account of how the world comes about and Plato's metaphysics in general (*De aet. mundi* 154. 6–19, 172. 15–20).

Porphyry subscribes to Taurus' view that according to the account in the *Timaeus* the world is 'created' in the sense that God is the origin and cause of the world's existence.[114] The problem which Taurus did not seriously consider, though, is that matter and Forms also account for the world's existence in some sense, as they are necessary for the world's

110 In Philoponus, *De aet. mundi* 147. 21–4; cf. *Timaeus* 28a–29a. See Baltes (1976: 110–12).

111 See Baltes (1976: 136–63) and Verryken (1988).

112 Cf. *Rep.* 477a, 478e1–2; *Phaedo* 78c6–8, 79a9–10.

113 Porphyry includes examples of temporal creation in both the strong and the weak sense, i.e. with and without process; an example of the latter is lightning (*De aet. mundi* 149. 2–3; fr. XXXVI Sodano).

114 Proclus, *In Tim.* 1. 277. 10–16; cf. *De aet. mundi* 172. 5–20 (172F Smith).

coming into being. The question then is what is the difference between the contribution of matter and Form on the one hand and that of the divine creator on the other in the constitution of the world, and how this translates into the physics of the cosmogony.

Porphyry appears to assume that there must be one ultimate cause which comprises or accounts for all others, and in this sense is sufficient (αὐτάρκης; Proclus *In Tim.* 1. 457. 11; fr. LVI Sodano). In the case of the world, only God, in Porphyry's view, is a principle strictly speaking (κυρίως; *De aet. mundi* 172. 14–15), which means that God is the main cause of the world's existence.[115] This is because only God can account for the most basic quality of the world, that is order and goodness, since only God, by being goodness, can bring about something good such as the world.[116]

Now, God being the main cause in this context seems to suggest three things:

(*a*) that God does something rather than merely contributes to something's coming about, i.e. he is an efficient cause,[117]
(*b*) that God accounts for matter and Forms too,[118] and

[115] *De aet. mundi* 172. 4–5; Proclus, *In Tim.* 1. 366. 15–27; fr. XLVI Sodano, and next footnote. Porphyry must have discussed the question of the different ways one can talk about principles in his work Περὶ ἀρχῶν, which must have covered the same area as the work of the Christian Origen with the same title. The pagan Origen also wrote a work with such a title (*V. Plot.* 14. 18) but nothing survives.

[116] ἀλλ' εἰ αὕτη κυριωτάτη κόσμου ἀρχὴ καὶ οὕτως ἤρξατο γίνεσθαι ὡς οὐκ ἐκ ταυτομάτου οὐδὲ αὐτοτελὴς ἑαυτῷ ἀλλ' ἀπὸ θεοῦ παρελθὼν καὶ ἀπὸ τῆς οὐσίας γενόμενος, οὐσία δὲ θεοῦ ἡ ἀγαθότης, θεὸς αὐτοῦ κυρίως εἴη ἀρχή (but if this is the main principle of the world and it started coming into being neither at random nor of itself but rather by God and by being, and given that God's essence is goodness, then it is God mainly its principle; Porphyry in Philoponus, *De aet. mundi* 172. 11–15).

[117] δηλοῖ γὰρ ὡς ὃν τρόπον τὸ αἴτιον κυρίως καὶ διαφέροντι τρόπῳ τὸ ποιοῦν ἐστιν, οὕτως καὶ ἡ ἀρχή, ἡ δὲ ὕλη οὐκ ἀρχή. διο καὶ τοῖς περὶ Πλάτωνα ἐλέγετο μία, ὅτι ἡ ἀρχή (and it is clear that as the cause is mainly and distinctly the efficient one, similarly the principle, while matter is not a principle. This is why Plato declared that there is only one which is the principle; Simplicius, *In Phys.* 248. 15–18; 146F. 29–32). Cf. τὸ αἴτιον τοῦ εἶναι ὅπερ λέγεταί ἐστιν τὸ αἴτιον τοῦ ἐντελεχείᾳ εἶναι καὶ μὴ μόνον δυνάμει (the cause of being is the cause of what is in actuality and not only potentially; Porphyry in Simplicius, *In Phys.* 277. 29–30; 148aF. 6–8).

[118] τὴν ἀνωτάτω ἀρχὴν οὐ ταύτῃ μόνον χαρακτηρίζειν δεῖ τῷ μὴ ἔχειν ἄλλην ἀρχὴν . . . ἀλλὰ τῷ πάντα ἐξ αὐτῆς. εἰ δὲ τοῦτο, οὐκ ἂν εἶεν ἀρχαὶ πλείους μιᾶς. ἔσται γὰρ οὕτως οὐ πάντων αἴτιος ὁ θεός, ἀλλὰ τινῶν. εἰ δὲ καὶ τῆς ὕλης ἄρχοι, μία ἡ ἀρχὴ καὶ οὐ πολλαί (the characteristic feature of the highest principle must be not only its independence from any other principle . . . but also that everything comes into being by it. If this is the case, then there cannot be more than one principle. For then God will be the cause of some things and not of everything. But if he also governs matter, then the principle is one and not many; Porphyry in Proclus, *In Tim.* 1. 392. 17–25).

(*c*) that God is the world's final cause.[119]

As regards the last aspect, Plato's explanation of the world's coming into being is analogous with the role of God as a final cause in Aristotle's explanation of the world. This aspect was upheld already by Plutarch (*De facie* 944E) and Plotinus (*Enn.* 6. 7. 20. 20–4). More crucial is the sense in which, in Porphyry's view, God accounts for matter and Forms, because this specifies the sense in which God is an efficient cause of the world.

Porphyry argues that God, being an intellect, has in himself the demiurgic *logoi*, that is, the Forms of everything (Cyril, *Contra Iulianum* 1. 32d, 552B1–2; 223F. 4–5), as is the case with seed or semen, which contain everything needed for the constitution of the complete plant or animal. These seminal *logoi* exist in God's mind as his thoughts and, as Porphyry stresses criticizing Atticus, do not exist separately from God (Proclus, *In Tim.* 1. 392. 2–4). Given that God is an immaterial entity, these divine demiurgic *logoi*, unlike the *logoi* contained in the seed, are also entirely immaterial. God, Porphyry argues, hardly needs even a negligible amount of matter in order to bring the world about (ibid. 1. 396. 5–26); rather, God does this without pre-existing matter (ἀύλως; ibid. 1. 396. 6, 23), by merely thinking, that is, by unfolding his thoughts, the Forms.[120] These are instantiated in matter, which also comes into being to the extent that is needed (ibid. 1. 440. 1–16). In such a way the entire multiplicity of sensible substances comes into being.[121] In this sense everything comes about by God alone (πάντα ἐξ αὐτῆς [sc. τῆς ἀρχῆς]; ibid. 1. 392.22), including matter.

This is to be understood properly. For Porphyry no timely process is needed for the world's creation. Rather, the world, he argues, comes about all at once (ἀθρόως; Proclus, *In Tim.* 1. 395. 21), that is, matter and its order come into being together (ὁμοῦ τῇ τάξει συνυφεστός [sc. matter];

[119] ἡ μὲν γὰρ ἀρχὴ φησὶν ὁ Πορφύριος ἐπινοεῖται καθὸ προηγεῖται, τὸ δὲ αἴτιον καθὸ ποιεῖ τι καὶ ἀποτελεῖ τὸ μεθ' ἑαυτό, ὄντος καὶ τοῦ αἰτίου δυνάμει ἀρχικοῦ καὶ τῆς ἀρχῆς δυνάμει τελικῆς (Porphyry argues that the principle is thought of in terms of being prior, while the cause in terms of acting and producing what comes after it, as the cause is potentially initial and the principle potentially final; Porphryry in Simplicius, *In Phys.* 11. 6–8; 120F. 20–5). Cf. also n. 128.

[120] I translate as 'unfolding' the term προϊοῦσαν (in Proclus, *In Tim.* 1. 439. 32). Cf. *De cultu simuclacrorum* apud Eusebium *PE* 3. 9. 3; 354F. 43–51: Ζεῦς δὲ καθὸ νοῦς, ἀφ' οὗ προφέρει πάντα καὶ δημιουργεῖ τοῖς νοήμασιν . . . ὅτι νοῦς ἦν καθ' ὃν ἐδημιούργει καὶ λόγοις σπερματικοῖς ἀπετέλει τὰ πάντα (Zeus to the extent that he is intellect from which everything comes and creates through the thoughts . . . because it was an intellect through which he created and brought everything into being by means of seminal *logoi*). For the Plotinian origins of this see *Enn.* 3. 2. 2. 15–48.

[121] In Proclus, *In Tim.* 1. 396. 21–6, 1. 439. 40–440. 3.

ibid. 1. 395. 9–10). Nor did God have to engage in a special act of creation at a particular point in time. For Porphyry, God's mere being is sufficient for the world to come about, since God is an intellect and as such his being amounts to thinking, which involves thinking of the Forms of all entities.[122] This means that the world's creation is not something that happened at some point; rather, God has always been involved in the act of creating, since God's thinking alone entails the world's creation.[123] In this sense God is not only the 'creator' of the world, but also its father (*Timaeus* 28c3; cf. Alcinous, *Didasc.* 164. 40–2), because like a real father he provides both matter and Form for the world to come into being (ibid. 1. 300. 1–6; fr. XL), and this is in the nature of God to do (*σύμφυτον*; ibid. 1. 393. 11).

According to this interpretation, which is largely Plotinus' own,[124] there was neither a point that the world did not exist nor were there distinct phases in the world's coming into being.[125] Porphyry seems to think that there are two sets of reasons against such a literal construal which Plutarch and Atticus took (Philoponus *De aet. mundi* 200. 4–23; fr. XXXIV Sodano), and in favour of the one outlined above.

The first set of reasons has to do with the nature of God, and is close in spirit to Aristotle's arguments in *De philosophia* (frs. 16, 18–19c

[122] *αὐτῷ τῷ εἶναι τὸν θεῖον νοῦν ἐπιμελούμενον . . . τῷ παρεῖναι μόνον ἐνεργῆσαν, . . . τί θαυμαστὸν τὸν δημιουργὸν αὐτῷ τῷ νοεῖν τὸ πᾶν ὑπόστασιν παρέχεσθαι τῷ αἰσθητῷ, ἀύλως μὲν παράγοντα τὸ ἔνυλον* (the divine intellect takes care by its mere existence . . . it acts by being only present . . . what is the wonder if the creator brings everything into being in the sensible realm through thinking alone, hence bringing about the enmattered immaterially; Proclus, *In Tim.* 1. 395. 11–13, 28, 1. 396. 5–7). Sorabji (1983: 290–4, 313–14) shows how Porphyry's view is taken over by Gregory of Nyssa and finds its way to Berkeley. Cf. Deuse (1981: 239–51), and below, nn. 146, 198.

[123] *ὁ δημιουργὸς αἰωνίως ποιεῖ καὶ ὁ κόσμος ἀίδιός ἐστι* (the creator creates eternally and the world is 'everlasting'; Proclus, *In Tim.* 1. 366. 22–3); *ἀεὶ τὰ εἴδη προιόντα φησὶν εἰς πλῆθος ὑποφέρεσθαι καὶ διαίρεσιν καὶ χωρεῖν εἰς ὄγκον καὶ μερισμόν παντοῖον* (he says that the Forms flowing eternally give rise to multiplicity and division and are hosted into every kind of size and partition; ibid. 1. 439. 31–3). The divine intellect and the world exist *ἀχρόνως* (Cyril, *Contra Iulianum* 1. 32d, 552c6; 223F. 18; cf. Proclus, *In Tim.* 1. 395. 18).

[124] See *Enn.* 2. 9. 1. 3, 3. 2. 2, 5. 9. 9; cf. Baltes (1976: 123–36).

[125] This interpretation presupposes a certain view about how eternal entities can have a cause, a problem which was puzzling also for Plotinus. Porphyry follows Plotinus in admitting causal relations between eternal entities. See Strange (1987: 967–8). Strange refers to Augustine, *City of God* 10. 31, where he mentions a Platonist who clarified the notion of causal relations between eternal entities with the following example: if a foot had been implanted in sand from eternity, one would say that the foot is the cause of the footprint, although it was not temporally prior to it. Strange argues that the Platonist may well be Porphyry. I am inclined to agree with him.

Ross). It would be absurd to believe, Porphyry argues, that God brought the world about at a certain point, because, given that the world is good, either God had not been willing to do the good, or was incapable of setting matter in order at an earlier point. But neither of these alternatives is tenable, so the ordered world has always been there (Proclus, *In Tim.* 1. 394. 12–25). It makes much better sense to assume that the world's creation amounts to God's thinking, Porphyry argues, because this is in accordance with God's nature; and as this is not something that happened at some time but has always been the case, it follows that the world has always existed. Plato, Porphyry argues, distinguishes phases in the creation of the world, that is, the creation of elementary bodies from matter, and from these bodies the creation of the world (*Timaeus* 69b–c), in order to teach us with clarity the difference between the two, not because he actually maintains a process of creation (*De aet. mundi* 164. 20–165. 16; 547. 5–25). Similarly the pre-existing disorder, on which Aristotle based his objections, aims to teach us the distinction between what has been subject to order (*genesis*) and what has been ordered (*taxis*), while in reality, Porphyry argues, there has never been such a disorder (Proclus, *In Tim.* 1. 394. 25–395. 30).

The second set of reasons against the existence of actual stages in Plato's cosmogony concern the way in which Forms relate to matter. Porphyry argues that the priority of matter to its being formed is a purely conceptual one, as is the case with Aristotle's accounts of what comes into being.[126] This is particularly the case with living bodies. A human body is not an object that becomes living, but rather life is its form without which it has never existed. Similarly with the world, there has never been a *substratum* which at some point becomes the world's body. Rather, the world has a body suitable (ἐπιτήδειον) for the form it has (*kosmos*), in the same sense that man has a body suitable for being alive.[127] According to Porphyry, this is how the corporeal nature of the world is to be understood.

[126] ἡ γὰρ ὕλη ἀειδὴς καὶ ἄμορφος κατ' αὐτὸν Πλάτωνα καὶ μόγις νόθῳ λογισμῷ λαμβανομένῃ (matter is without form and shape according to Plato and conceivable just by a false thought; *De aet. mundi* 547. 6–7; ibid. 165. 11–16). See *Sent.* 20, p. 10. 12–11. 2 Lamberz: Τῆς ὕλης τὰ ἴδια κατὰ τοὺς ἀρχαίους τάδε· ἀσώματος ... ἀνείδεος, ἄλογος, ἄπειρος (the properties of matter are the following according to the ancients: incorporeal ... uninformed, irrational, unlimited). Cf. Porphyry, *In Ptol. Harm.* 16. 23–4.

[127] See Proclus, *In Tim.* 1. 394. 15–25, 395. 13–24. Porphyry does not make exactly the above claim, but he talks in similar terms in *Ad Gaurum* about the relation between the soul and the body (e.g. ἐπιτηδείου τοῦ σώματος; 49. 9) and Philoponus who, as we will see (s. 6. 2 p. 296), draws on Porphyry's views on the soul does the same (e.g. ἐπιτηδειότης τῆς ὕλης; *In de an.* 14. 5–15. 8).

Such an argument already suggests that, according to Porphyry, Plato had meant the creation of the world in the way Aristotle did, that is, as a composition of matter and Form which never underwent a process of actual combination (Philoponus *De aet. mundi* 149. 18–20, 153. 17–155. 4). Philoponus confirms that the sense of 'created' which Porphyry approved most (*μάλιστα συγκατατίθεται*; ibid. 154. 3–5) is the Aristotelian sense of hylomorphic composition. And Proclus reports that Porphyry explicitly acknowledged that the most charitable interpretation of Plato's sense of creation is the Aristotelian one.[128] This sense of 'created' corresponds to the second sense in Taurus' list, but is not quite the same. It rather is the Aristotelian sense of hylomorphic composition which Porphyry distinguishes from other senses of composition, such as the one according to which something is a composite but its parts can exist separately (e.g. a syllable or a triangle; ibid. 148. 9–15).[129] Unlike composites of that kind, in hylomorphic ones, Porphyry argues, the elements of the composite, matter and Form, do not subsist by themselves but only in thought (*ἐπινοίᾳ*; ibid. 153. 17). So they neither exist separately, nor does a composition actually take place—and this is important because all actual composites eventually perish (*Sent.* 14).

If the world is created in this sense, then, not only do Aristotle's objections fail to apply, but he turns out to be quite in accord with Plato. It further emerges that not only do Plato and Aristotle accept the same set of principles, as Porphyry argues in his commentary on the *Physics*, but they also provide similar causal explanations. In the case of the world, both explain its constitution in terms of a formal, a material, a final, an efficient cause. What is more, in Porphyry's view, both consider the efficient cause as the main principle.

As has been seen, though, Porphyry understands the divine intellect as an efficient cause in that it accounts for matter and Forms; the latter, in particular, are thoughts of the divine intellect. This is a view which Porphyry inherited from Plotinus, one based on a particular interpretation of the *Timaeus* according to which God is identical with the real

128 *ἀλλ' ὡς αὐτὸς* [sc. Aristotle] *τὸ ἀνείδεον ὁρᾷ πρὸ τῶν εἰδῶν, εἰ καὶ μηδέποτε ἔστιν ἐκείνων χωρίς, οὕτω το εἰδοπεποιημένον μέν, ἔτι δὲ ἀδιάρθρωτον εἴληπται πρὸ τῆς τάξεως ἦν, ἀλλ' ὁμοῦ τῇ τάξει συνυφεστός* (but Plato conceives the uninformed as Aristotle does, as that which is before the occurrence of the Forms, even if it never exists without the Forms, so similarly what is informed is thought of as being unstructured before the imposition of order, but it comes about together with order); Proclus, *In Tim.* 1. 395. 6–10.

129 On these distinctions see Verrycken (1988: 286–9).

being, the Forms.[130] The fact that this interpretation of Plato's cosmogony is meant to be acceptable by Aristotle's criteria (ὥς αὐτός [sc. Aristotle]; Proclus, *In Tim.* 1. 395. 6) suggests that Porphyry considered Aristotle's God to be an efficient cause in the sense in which Plato's is, and hence to also accept transcendent Forms as thoughts of the divine intellect. If this is so, then, according to Porphyry, the two philosophers share the same principles and agree not only on how the world comes about but quite generally on how everything comes into being.

One can start to suspect that Porphyry's commentaries on the *Physics* and on the *Timaeus* are closely connected. Indeed, Simplicius who reports on the former, suggests that Porphyry related his comments on Aristotle's text to the *Sophist* and the *Timaeus* (*In Phys.* 134. 14–18, 135. 1–14, 136. 33–137. 7; 134F Smith). Besides, in Porphyry's commentary on the *Physics* we find views about Forms and matter similar to those advanced in his commentary on the *Timaeus* (148a–bF, 151F, 152F Smith). Such evidence suggests that Porphyry regarded the *Physics* as a work not only compatible with the *Timaeus*, but also useful for its interpretation and, more generally, valuable for anyone who wants to understand physics and how it relates to metaphysics. This is why he commented on it in the detail that he appears to have done.

Porphyry, then, differs much from earlier generations of Platonists, who either deny that Aristotle's work has a metaphysical aspect,[131] or suggest that this is limited.[132] He also differs from Plotinus who used to consider Aristotle as contradicting the doctrines of the *Timaeus*. Later Platonists, like Simplicius, must be inspired by Porphyry in prioritizing the study of *Physics* and *De caelo* to that of *Timaeus*.[133] They adopt Porphyry's interpretation of the *Timaeus*, and this involves the belief that for both Plato and Aristotle there is only one main principle, God, which is the efficient and final cause of the universe, while matter and Forms are merely auxiliary principles.[134]

[130] See Simplicius, *In Phys.* 230. 34–231. 24 (236F); Porphyry, *Sent.* 43, 44; cf. Plotinus, *Enn.* 5. 5. 1–2, 5. 9. Plotinus was inspired by Numenius' second God who comprises the Forms.

[131] Atticus e.g. frs. 5. 13–15, 9. 31–3, 40–5 Des Places.

[132] Plutarch, *De primo frig.* 948B–C; *Adv. Col.* 1115D–E; cf. Taurus apud Gellium *NA* 19. 6. 2–3. See Ch. 2, pp. 99–100, Ch. 4, pp. 179–80.

[133] See I. Hadot (1987*b*: 276–85).

[134] Simplicius, *In Phys.* 11. 29–32, 179. 13–14, 21–2, 1154. 3–1169. 9, 1360. 24–32; cf. Philoponus, *In Gen. et. Corr.* 136. 33–137. 3.

5. 4. Porphyry on the Fifth Element

The existence of an element other than the four standard ones which Aristotle had suggested (*De caelo* 1. 2–3, 268b41–270b31) was connected with the issue of the constitution and the eternity of the world. As I argued in Chapter 2 (s. 4, pp. 104–5), there had been some controversy among Platonists as to whether Aristotle's aether is identical with, or different from Plato's aether (*Timaeus* 58d1–2; *Phaedo* 109b9, 111b2), which is a mixture of air and fire. As has been seen, a wide range of Platonist views were in circulation. Antiochus and Plutarch appear to have found the whole issue difficult to judge; especially the latter was quite sceptical about the Platonic credentials of such a doctrine. Given his polemical agenda, Atticus was more outspoken, arguing that this was not Plato's view and criticized Aristotle for departing from it (fr. 5. 9–15 Des Places). Taurus also rejected the aether as a Platonic doctrine but he seems to have altogether refrained from criticizing Aristotle in this matter.[135] Plotinus also rejected the aether (*Enn.* 2. 1. 2), though he did not offer detailed criticisms or arguments. Porphyry is like Taurus in this regard; he appears to believe that this doctrine is not Platonic but most probably he did not criticize Aristotle.

Commenting on *Timaeus* 31b4–32c3, Porphyry argued that, according to Plato, the world is constituted of only four elements for reasons pertaining to the world's nature (Philoponus, *De aet. mundi* 521. 25–522. 4). The body of the world, he argues, contains fire and earth, but in order to be properly bonded by geometrical proportion it needed two further terms, water and air (ibid. 522. 7–9). Any further element would destroy the proportion which is essential for the stability of the world's body, as it is for any body, if it is to be a living one.[136] Anything else that exists, Porphyry argues, is only one of various combinations (συνδέσματα; ibid. 522. 15) of the four elements, and he concludes that those who maintain the existence of a fifth element as a constituent of the planets follow their own doctrine (ἴδιον δόγμα), not Plato's (*De aet. mundi* 522. 2–9). Among the authors of this doctrine Porphyry mentions Aristotle and also Archytas, who, he infers (ὥστε), departed from Plato's view (ibid. 522. 20–2).

[135] Philoponus *De aet. mundi* 520. 23–521. 4. Philoponus states that Taurus criticized Theophrastus for maintaining the fifth element, and goes on to mention that Theophrastus is an Aristotelian, so that Taurus' objection applies to Aristotle. But this suggests that Taurus probably did not criticize Aristotle. cf. Dillon (1977: 244–5).

[136] Cyril, *C. Iul.* 1. 48, 573 AB (460F. 1–4).

Noticeably no criticism follows Porphyry's claim. Given that the late Philoponus was a fierce critic of the Aristotelian aether,[137] he was more likely to include such criticisms, if there had been any. But, as his report suggests, Porphyry in his own work was concerned with explaining Plato's view.[138] This is strengthened by the fact that Porphyry discusses a doctrine ascribed not only to Aristotle but also to Archytas. Porphyry's favourable attitude towards Pythagoreanism makes it quite improbable that he criticized one of their doctrines. Presumably Porphyry, like Plutarch, held that this Peripatetic doctrine creates problems rather than solves any as regards the world's constitution, but he did not find it pertinent to offer any criticisms.[139]

It is notable that Porphyry's account of world's constitution is very similar to those of Pythagorean texts, such as those of Timaeus Locrus and Ocellus, which, however, do accept such an imperishable element.[140] Both these texts admittedly show Aristotelian influence; their authors apparently upheld Aristotle's dependence on Pythagorean wisdom in his cosmology and regarding the fifth element in particular. And one way in which they could explain Aristotle's dependence on Pythagorean doctrines was to assume his reliance on the *Timaeus*, a dialogue which they considered to be largely Pythagorean in its content. In this view, then, Aristotle's introduction of aether resulted from a construal of Plato's dialogue. As a result, these Pythagoreans upheld the existence of the aether because they approved of Aristotle's construal of Plato's text. But, as has been seen, Porphyry believes that Plato and Aristotle shared a view which explains the eternity of the world sufficiently without making any reference to an indestructible element.[141] So for Porphyry the introduction of aether by Aristotle and also by Archytas rests on a

[137] By 'late' I refer to Philoponus' career after 529; before that date he used to approve of Aristotle's aether (e.g. *In Gen. et. Corr.* 135. 1–2). See Moraux (1963: 1243–4); Verrycken (1990); and more fully C. Wildberg, *John Philoponus' Criticism of Aristotle's Theory of Aether* (Berlin and New York, 1988).

[138] Porphyry's formulations suggest the same; *κατὰ τὸ ἑπόμενον δόγμα τῷ Πλάτωνι* (*De aet. mundi* 522. 3), *κατὰ Πλάτωνα* (ibid. 522. 7); cf. ibid. 522. 13, 18.

[139] An indication for a contradiction may be preserved in Simplicius, *In Phys.* 264. 27–32 (147F). Porphyry must have known the work of Xenarchus who had raised such difficulties about Aristotle's doctrine.

[140] *δεσμῷ κρατίστῳ συνεδήσατο* (Timaeus Locrus 99a5; 217. 5–6 Thesleff) *τὸ μὲν οὖν πῦρ καὶ ἡ γῆ ἄκρα, τὸ δὲ ὕδωρ καὶ ὁ ἀὴρ μεσότητες* (Ocellus 28; 131. 30–132. 3 Thesleff). For other references to Pythagoreans who accepted the fifth element see Ch. 2, s. 4, p. 104 n. 60.

[141] Origen *C. Celsum* 4. 60. 8–13 must echo a widespread view when he says that this element was invented to account for the world's eternity.

mistake, most probably a mistaken interpretation of Plato, especially of the *Timaeus*, according to which in this dialogue Plato suggests the existence of a fifth element.[142] But for Porphyry these are the kinds of mistake which may occur within the same school of thought. The further conclusion that can be made from the above is that Porphyry distances himself from Plotinus' practice of explaining or defending Plato's alleged doctrine by criticizing Aristotle; this is conspicuous in cases like the above in which there is ground for criticizing Aristotle but Porphyry refrains from doing so.

6. PSYCHOLOGY

6. 1. Introduction

As I mentioned in the beginning of the chapter, it is in psychology that scholars have found Porphyry to maintain a critical attitude towards Aristotle. However, I will argue that in fact Porphyry rather approves of Aristotle's psychological views and considers them to be close to those of Plato. The argument that follows is detailed and complex partly because Porphyry's position needs to be reconstructed from the relevant evidence, which is fragmentary and not as straightforward as is the case with Plotinus. But the undertaking is worthwhile, because, given the importance that psychology has for Platonists of this age, an agreement between Plato and Aristotle in this regard would be crucial for deciding whether the two philosophers belong to the same school of thought.

6. 2. Porphyry on the soul being the *entelecheia* of the body

Porphyry inherited Plotinus' strong interest in questions regarding the soul and much of his philosophy deals with them. On the questions of how the soul relates to the body and how it operates within it, Porphyry takes as starting point Plotinus' relevant views.[143] As has been seen (Ch. 6, s. 2), in one of his last works (*Enn.* 1. 1 [53]), Plotinus considers the

142 Iamblichus accepts the aether as Platonic, since it is indisputably in Plato (Simplicius, *In de an.* 49. 31–4, *In Phys.* 1165. 19–39), and Simplicius does the same arguing that it is composed of the purest parts of the four elements, which presumably suggests that in his view aether is not an element (*In de caelo* 12. 28–30 and *passim*). See Moraux (1963: 1240–5); Sorabji (1988: 117–19); Hoffmann (1987).

143 Porphyry's views on the soul are discussed by Dörrie (1966b); Smith (1974); and Deuse (1983: 129–230). His works are listed by Smith (1974: 151); Beutler (1953: 289–90) discusses their status.

possibility that the soul is the form of the living body (1. 1. 4. 18–25), and speaks of the powers (δυνάμεις) of the soul by means of which it operates in the body (e.g. *Enn.* 4. 3. 23). I have argued that the soul to which Plotinus refers is the embodied one, which is a power (*dynamis*) derivative from the transcendent one. Porphyry shares Plotinus' belief that the embodied soul is a power derivative from the transcendent one (the Soul),[144] a reflection or shadow of the Soul,[145] by means of which the latter enlivens the human body without descending itself to the body.[146]

Porphyry makes the distinction between transcendent and embodied soul sharper than Plotinus. One way he does this is by distinguishing between Soul in itself (καθ' ἑαυτήν) and soul in relationship (κατὰ σχέσιν), that is, in relationship with the body.[147] Porphyry inherits from Plotinus the view that, like the embodied soul, the body does not subsist by itself. He realizes that, like the material substratum of the world, the 'world's body', the human body is not an object which becomes alive, but rather exists in a certain form, namely as living, and this is accounted for by the soul (cf. *On the faculties of the soul* 259F. 67–74). The lifeless body is either an abstraction or, in the case of the dead one, only homonymously a body.[148] The body, Porphyry argues, cannot be affected unless it is a living one, while the soul, being immaterial, cannot be affected either. So one has to speak in terms of the compound, the living body,[149] because it is this that is subject to affections.[150]

[144] *Enn.* 4. 3. 10. 38–40, 4. 8. 8. 2–3, 5. 1. 10. 13–18, 6. 2. 22. 30–3, Porphyry, *Sent.* 4, 11, 28.

[145] Plotinus characterizes the embodied soul as εἴδωλον, ἴνδαλμα ψυχῆς or σκιὰ ψυχῆς; see Ch. 6, s. 2, p. 224 n. 21 for references. Porphyry maintains that the mode in which anything exists in body is εἰδωλικῶς (*Sent.* 10. 3). See also next note.

[146] τὰ καθ' αὑτὰ ἀσώματα ὑποστάσει μὲν καὶ οὐσίᾳ οὐ πάρεστιν οὐδὲ συγκίρναται τοῖς σώμασι, τῇ δὲ ἐκ τῆς ῥοπῆς ὑποστάσει τινὸς δυνάμεως μεταδίδωσι προσεχοῦς τοῖς σώμασιν. ἡ γὰρ ῥοπὴ δευτέραν τινὰ δύναμιν ὑπέστησε προσεχῆ τοῖς σώμασιν. (The real incorporeals are not present with their hypostasis or their being, neither do they mix with bodies. Rather, through their hypostasis which is radiating they transmit a certain power attaching to the bodies. For this radiation brings into being a second power attaching to the bodies; *Sent.* 4; cf. *Sent.* 30). As Smith (1974: 7) notes, the passage implies also a first *dynamis* which corresponds to the activity of the transcendent Soul.

[147] *On the faculties of the soul* 253F. 114–15, 261F. 56–60; cf. *Sententia* 3.

[148] *Sent.* 12, *On the faculties of the soul* 248F. 5–6; cf. *De anima* 412^{b}21.

[149] Like Plotinus, Porphyry uses the term συναμφότερον for the living being (*Sent.* 21, p. 12. 10 Lamberz) but also the term σύνθετον (*Sent.* 21, p. 13. 8 Lamberz). For the former see Ch. 6, p. 227. The latter is inspired by Plato's *Phaedo* 78c1 but also Aristotle, *Met.* 1023^{b}2, 1043^{a}30, 1051^{b}27. Both terms are used to denote the composite of matter and Form (e.g. *Enn.* 6. 7. 4. 19, *Sent.* 21, p. 13. 5 Lamberz); see Schwyzer (1974: 232).

[150] ὥστε οὔτε ἡ ὕλη πάσχει ἄποιος γὰρ καθ' ἑαυτήν οὔτε τὰ ἐπ' αὐτῆς εἴδη εἰσιόντα καὶ ἐξιόντα, ἀλλὰ τὸ πάθος περὶ τὸ συναμφότερον. (so neither is matter affected, since it is without qualities, nor the forms which enter and leave matter, but only the compound can be affected; *Sent.* 21, p. 12. 8–11 Lamberz).

To find out what kind of compound this is and how the soul exists in it, we need to examine how the soul actualizes the body being a *dynamis* of the transcendent soul. Since the Soul for the Platonists has essentially the capacity to enliven a body, the fact that the embodied soul is a derivative power of the Soul entails that its capacity to enliven must be a derivative one. This was Plotinus' view to which Porphyry subscribes, and he illustrates the relation between transcendent and embodied soul and between soul and body with similar analogies. The Soul, Porphyry argues, is like the fire or the sun and its *dynamis*, the embodied soul, like the heated water or the daylight. As the heat of the water or the daylight are side effects of the fire and the sun respectively, produced effortlessly by them without being diminished, similarly the Soul produces the embodied soul without being diminished.[151] And as the heat of the heated water is the form of the water, similarly, Porphyry argues, the embodied soul is the form of the living body, that is its life, and inseparable from it as form is from matter (*Sent.* 21, p. 13. 4–8 Lamberz).[152]

For Porphyry, then, the soul relates to the living body as immanent Forms relate to matter in sensible entities, and as immanent Forms derive from the transcendent ones, similarly the souls are derivative of the transcendent soul. The life of the soul and the body which the soul enlivens is derivative from that of the Soul, which explains why Porphyry does not distinguish between the life of the soul from that of the living body, while he does distinguish between the life of the transcendent soul and the embodied one (*Sent.* 12).

So far Porphyry follows Plotinus closely. But there is one crucial point in which Porphyry differs from Plotinus, and leads him first to be more committed than Plotinus to Aristotle's view that the soul is the actuality of the body (*De anima* 412^{a}19–22), and as a consequence to refrain from criticizing Aristotle for rejecting the immortality of the soul.

This point has to do with Porphyry's conception of the ontological status of the embodied soul. This becomes manifest through Porphyry's

[151] Porphyry, *Symm. Zet.* in Nemesius, *De nat. hom.* 133. 5–137. 4 (261F), *Against Boethus* in Eusebius, *PE* 15. 11. 2–3 (248F). Gottschalk (1986: 250–1) and Sodano (1993: 150–1) wrongly maintain that these analogies are part of the theory Porphyry argues against. As I argue below, Porphyry accepts a limited application of these analogies (248F. 12–15), that is, regarding only the embodied soul. Plotinus uses the same analogy concerning the *nous* (*Enn.* 4. 3. 22. 1–7, 5. 4. 2. 30–3; cf. 1. 2. 1. 31–5). Porphyry uses these analogies for immanent Forms in *In Cat.* 95. 23–9, 106. 31–3, 132. 8–11. See below pp. 292–6.

[152] Note also that αἱ φύσεις καὶ αἱ δυνάμεις correspond (like the soul) to the immanent Forms in *Sent.* 42, p. 53. 6–9 Lamberz; see Smith (1974: 14–15).

analogy with the musician (*Sent.* 18). As harmony, Porphyry argues, exists separately from the chords, but also is inseparable from the musician, being his form (ἐναρμόνιον; *Sent.* 18, p. 9. 8 Lamberz), similarly the soul exists separately from the living body, namely in the transcendent soul, but as the form of the living body (that is, ἔμψυχον) is inseparable from it.[153] And as the harmony makes the musician an actual or accomplished one, because he has the harmony in himself, even when he is not manifesting it, so the soul makes the body an actual, complete, body, and in this sense the soul is the *entelecheia* of the living body, and the two are distinct only in thought.[154] If this is so, Porphyry subscribes to Aristotle's view that the soul is *entelecheia* in the sense which corresponds to the possession of knowledge, not its exercise; for as the musician, in Porphyry's analogy, is such even when asleep or drunk, so the body is living even when asleep or otherwise unconscious (*De anima* 412^{a}22–8).[155]

The purpose of this analogy partly is to show that only the embodied soul, not the transcendent one, is the completion (*entelecheia*) of the body. But there is more in this. While the harmony of the musician and the embodied soul are immanent Forms derived from transcendent entities, the separate harmony and the transcendent soul respectively, yet the embodied soul is the essence of the living being, as the harmony is the essence of a musician. This is a difference from Plotinus who considered the embodied soul to be a substance only because it is derivative from a substance *par excellence* (a hypostasis), namely the transcendent soul, and he criticized Aristotle's conception of the soul as the essence of the living body. Porphyry's position has ontological underpinnings in his distinction between accidental and essential qualities (e.g. the heat of the heated water as opposed to that of the fire)—I will discuss this in section 8. Here it suffices to say that for Porphyry the embodied soul is an essential quality, the essence of the living body, and on this he regards Aristotle as being in agreement with Plato.

[153] The analogy of the soul as harmony, an originally Pythagorean view, is used differently by Aristotle who criticizes it (*De anima* 408^{a}4–28), and Plotinus 4. 7. 8[4]. Porphyry is closer to *Enn.* 3. 6. 4. 41–52.

[154] *Μεριστὸν οὖν τὸ ζῷον εἰς τὴν ἐπίνοιαν αὐτοῦ καὶ τοῦ σώματος παραλαμβανομένου* (the animal is divisible only in thought also when it receives the body; Porphyry, *On the faculties of the soul*, in Stob. 1. 354. 7–8; 253F. 110–11).

[155] We must note that Porphyry argues that the soul is like the harmony of the musician, not that it is the harmony of the bodily materials, a view Aristotle argues against on the grounds that the soul causes movement while a harmony cannot (*De anima* 407^{b}34–408^{a}1).

To arrive at this, we have to look first at Porphyry's argument in his treatise against the Peripatetic Boethus.[156] In this Porphyry distinguishes the transcendent soul from the form of the living body, the embodied soul, which he terms *ἐμψυχία*.[157] The term, which is of Hellenistic origin, indicates the character of being alive,[158] which means that the *ἐμψυχία* involves soul and body in such a way that the one cannot be separated from the other. This is striking if we consider that Porphyry's aim in this treatise is to defend the immortality of the soul. Porphyry sets out to show this in a manner reminiscent of Plotinus' argument in *Enn.* 4. 7, being guided by the third argument of Plato's *Phaedo* (77d–84b). More precisely, he relies on the concepts in question (*τὰ τῶν ἐννοιῶν*) and the evidence of the soul's activities (*τὰ τῆς ἱστορίας*; *Against Boethus* 246F. 2–3). Artistic or scientific activities of the soul (*ἐνέργειαι*; ibid. 242F. 31, 244F. 17), or movements (*κινήσεις, ῥοπαί*; 243F. 9, 247F. 10) like willing, desiring rational desires, thinking (247F) suggest, Porphyry argues, a remarkable similarity of man to the divine.[159] This similarity, he contends, manifests that man's substance, that is the soul, is very much like (*ὁμοιότατον*; 244F. 1) the divine one.[160] The implication is that, like the divine soul, man's soul also is immortal.[161]

156 Most scholars maintain that this is the Peripatetic Boethus; e.g. Beutler (1953: 289); Gottschalk (1986: 255–7); Sodano (1993: 137–8. Only Moraux (1973: 172–6) argues that this is the Stoic Boethus, and that there are no indications suggesting the Peripatetic one as Porphyry's adversary. But already the fact that Eusebius cites from this work in the anti-Aristotelian section clearly suggests the opposite. As I argue, only against the Peripatetic Boethus does Porphyry's argument make sense.

157 Porphyry in Eusebius' *Preparatio Evangelica* 15. 11. 3; 248F. 12 Smith.

158 It was used by Epicurus in Sextus, *Adv. Dogm.* 1. 267; *PH* 2. 25; Zeno in Sextus, *Adv. Math.* 9. 104; Chrysippus, *On nature* in Plutarch, *De stoic. rep.* 1053B. We also find it in Theon of Smyrna 187. 13–26, 188. 3–7 Hiller. In coining the term Porphyry was probably inspired from Plotinus' formulations that the body is in soul (*τὸ σῶμα ἐν τῇ ψυχῇ*; *Enn.* 4. 3. 22. 9). He uses the term often in *Ad Gaurum* (17. 5, 7, 45. 19, 56. 24, 57. 20, 59. 23, 25). Later Platonists borrow the term from Porphyry. See below, n. 178.

159 Cf. Porphyry's expressions *ἐμφερές τῷ θεῷ* (similar to God; 244F. 16); *πρὸς τὸν θεὸν ὁμοιότης* (the similarity to God; 243F. 16); *ἀποδεικνὺς τὸν θεῖον καὶ θεῷ παρισωμένον ἐν αὐτῷ νοῦν* (demonstrating the divine and equal to the divine intellect; 245F. 15–16).

160 *ὥσπερ γὰρ τὰ ταῖς ἐνεργείαις τῷ θεῷ ἀνόμοια εὐθὺς καὶ τῇ συστάσει τῆς οὐσίας ἐξῄλακτο, οὕτως ἀκόλουθον εἶναι τὰ τῶν αὐτῶν πως ἐνεργειῶν μέτοχα φθάνειν τὴν ὁμοιότητα τῆς οὐσίας κεκτημένα. διὰ γὰρ τὴν ποιὰν οὐσίαν ποιὰς εἶναι καὶ τὰς ἐνεργείας, ὡς ἂν ἀπ' αὐτῆς ῥέουσας καὶ αὐτῆς οὔσας βλαστήματα* (For as those entities which are different from God in terms of their activities differ also in their being, it follows that also those which somehow participate in the same activities are similar in their being. For the activities are of such a kind because of their kind of being, as they flow from it or spout from it; Porphyry, *On the faculties of the soul* 242F. 31–7).

161 Porphyry, *On the faculties of the soul* 244F. 14–20, 245F. 1–5, 15–16.

Porphyry's argument suggests that the soul to which he refers is the transcendent one, the intellective soul, whose immortality Plotinus defended with similar arguments. As in Plotinus and earlier in Numenius (Ch. 3, s. 4), in Porphyry too this soul is essentially an intellect (*nous*; *Against Boethus* 243F. 13, 245F. 16). Throughout the few existing fragments of his work against Boethus, Porphyry maintains that the intellect is the most essential element to human nature, which makes us similar to God.[162] This becomes plain when he contrasts the basic living functions with the intellectual abilities which distinguish man from other animals (245F). Apparently Porphyry, like Plotinus, takes Plato's arguments in the *Phaedo* as concerning the immortality of the intellect, while he may also rely on *Republic* 10 (611b–e) and on *Timaeus* 41c6–7, where the affinity (*συγγενής*) of man's soul to God is stated.[163]

One reason why Porphyry takes this view is because, like Numenius and Plotinus, he believes that the intellect, unlike the other aspects of the soul, operates independently of any bodily organ, and this shows its independence from the living compound.[164] Another reason is the belief Porphyry shares with Plotinus that true happiness amounts to becoming like God, which is suggested in the *Phaedo* (64b–65d, 82c–83b) and the *Theaetetus* (176a–b), and this ethical ideal cannot be attained unless the intellect is immortal. Like Plotinus, then, Porphyry holds that the intellect is our self, the aspect of the soul which never really descends but rather has the ability to ascend to the Intellect, that is, to separate itself from body and contemplate.[165] For Platonists since Plutarch who were inclined to believe that it is mainly the intellect which is immortal, there had been a question as to whether the irrational soul survives.[166] Like Numenius, Porphyry holds that it does survive in some form,[167] but it is the immortality of the intellect which matters to him, and in his view to Plato too, because this is the soul strictly speaking. Porphyry takes this view about human immortality also in his work *On knowing yourself* where he argues that man's

[162] Cf. 242F. 3–8, 23–35, 244F, 245F with *Phaedo* 80a2–b5, 81a4–10, 84a7–b2.

[163] See Introduction p. 10, n. 27.

[164] Porphyry *On the faculties of the soul* in Stobaeus 1. 49. 24; 251F. 9–18.

[165] See *Enn.* 1. 1. 3. 21–5, 4. 8, 4. 8. 8. On this see Smith (1974: 20–39) and my section on Ethics below pp. 303–8.

[166] Atticus, for instance, maintained that it does not (Proclus, *In Tim.* 3. 234. 9–18; fr. 15 Des Places).

[167] Stobaeus 1. 384. 19–28 (453F); cf. Numenius fr. 46a Des Places. For a discussion of the issue see Smith (1974: 56–68).

essence is the intellect and knowing ourselves amounts to knowing the intellect or the (intellective) soul, which is immortal.[168]

Porphyry, then, defends in his work against Boethus the immortality of the intellect or the intellective soul. I say 'he defends' because he takes this to be the position of the *Phaedo* which Boethus criticized. Boethus apparently followed up Strato's objection to the argument for the soul's immortality in the *Phaedo* which shows that the soul cannot admit death, nor that it survives it. The Peripatetic objection is that the soul does not die, but this does not necessarily mean that it is immortal.[169]

In Porphyry's terms, these Peripatetics made the mistake of confusing the soul strictly speaking, which is an intellective, transcendent entity, with the *empsychia*, the form of being alive. Throughout his treatise *Against Boethus* Porphyry tries to show that ψυχή, the intellective soul, is not an immanent Form or an essential quality, as the ἐμψυχία, on his own admission, is (248F), because the intellect, unlike the other living functions of the living body, is not dependent on the body.[170] This means that for Porphyry, while the *empsychia* is the *entelecheia* of the body, as is suggested from the analogy of the musician, the intellective soul is not. Porphyry's point is that Boethus failed to make precisely this distinction, and this failure guided his objection to Plato's argument for the immortality of the soul in the *Phaedo*. Boethus apparently took a materialist view of the soul, from which he did not exclude the intellect, maintaining that this is merely a quality of the living body and explicable in physical terms (*Against Boethus* 248F). Boethus' view was typical of the Peripatetics of his age. It represents a Peripatetic tradition which goes back to Dicaearchus and Aristoxenus to become consolidated with Strato, and which was continued by Alexander of Aphrodisias.[171] It is because the Peripatetics fail to understand the distinction between the

[168] τὸ μὲν οὖν γιγνώσκειν ἑαυτὸν τὴν ἀναφορὰν ἔοικεν ἔχειν ἐπὶ τὸ γιγνώσκειν δεῖν τὴν ψυχὴν καὶ τὸν νοῦν, ὡς ἐν τούτῳ ἡμῶν οὐσιωμένων (*On knowing yourself*, in Stobaeus 3. 582. 13–16; 275F. 22–4); cf. *De abstinentia* 1. 29. 4, 1. 30. 6–7.

[169] See Strato fr. 123 W (= Olympiodorus, *In Phaed.* p. 183 Norvin). Cf. Gottschalk (1987: 1118–19).

[170] οὐδὲ ἡ τοῦ σώματος ἐμψυχία, ἥτις ἔοικε τῇ βαρύτητι καὶ τῇ περὶ σῶμα ποιότητι, ἡ ψυχὴ ἡ ἐν σώματι καταταχθεῖσα, δι' ἣν καὶ πνοῆς τινος ζωτικῆς μετέσχε τὸ σῶμα. (The being-alive of the animal body, which is like the weight or the other qualities connected with body, is not the soul which descended into the body, through which the body partakes of life (vital breath)); Porphyry, *On the faculties of the soul* in Eusebius, *PE* 15. 11. 3; 248F. 12–15. The only scholar I know of who construed Porphyry's point correctly is Igal (1979: 346). See also above n. 151.

[171] B. Sharples offers a good overview of this tradition in his paper 'Peripatetics on Soul and Intellect', which he kindly allowed me to read before its publication.

soul as the form of the living being and the soul as a transcendent entity, Porphyry argues, that they cannot understand that the soul in the latter sense, the soul strictly speaking, is immortal, while the *empsychia* is not, at least not in the same sense.

A crucial piece of evidence from Simplicius' (?) commentary on Aristotle's *De anima* not only confirms this, but also shows that Porphyry perceived the view that the intellective soul is immortal as being not only Plato's doctrine but also Aristotle's,[172] which means that for him Plato and Aristotle would agree against Boethus. I quote the passage.

καλῶς γὰρ καὶ τὸ ἀίδιον προστέθεικεν [sc. Aristotle] *ὡς ὁ Πλάτων τὸ ἀνώλεθρον ἐν τῷ Φαίδωνι, ἵνα μὴ ὡς ὁ Βόηθος οἰηθῶμεν τὴν ψυχὴν ὥσπερ τὴν ἐμψυχίαν ἀθάνατον μὲν εἶναι ὡς αὐτὴν μὴ ὑπομένουσαν τὸν θάνατον ἐπιόντα, ἐξισταμένην δὲ ἐπιόντος ἐκείνου τῷ ζῶντι ἀπόλλυσθαι.* ([Simplicius], *In de anima* 247. 23–6)

[Aristotle] has done well to add the term 'everlasting', as Plato added the term 'imperishable' in the *Phaedo*, so that we should not, like Boethus, think that the soul is immortal in the same sense that the *empsychia* is, that is in the sense that it does not suffer death when this comes, but withdraws when [death] comes upon the living being, and thus perishes.

The passage belongs to a context in which the author, Simplicius or Priscian,[173] argues that Aristotle agrees with Plato on the immortality of the intellect.[174] Boethus is contrasted with this view, as he argued that the soul is immortal only in the sense that it is not affected by death, since it departs from the living being by the time death occurs. Boethus is criticized for his view because it suggests that the soul is mortal, while, it is argued, only the *empsychia* is mortal, not the soul, that is, the intellect. There are several strong indications that the passage reflects Porphyry's argument against Boethus. First is the reference to Plato's view in the *Phaedo* about the immortality of the soul; second, the term *ἐμψυχίαν* which is characteristically Porphyrian; and third the reference to Boethus' belief in the soul's mortality. If this is so, the passage confirms

172 Cf. *De anima* 429^{b}4–5, 429^{b}30–1, 430^{a}22–5, *NE* 1178^{a}22.

173 Steel (1978) has ascribed this work to Priscian; see his introduction. See also Blumenthal (2000: 1–7).

174 *Ἐπιστῆσαι ἄξιον τῷ παντὶ λόγῳ,* < *ᾧ* > *θαρρῶν τὸν οὐσιώδη λόγον τῆς ψυχῆς νοῦν ἀθάνατον καὶ ἀίδιον ἀποφαίνεται* [sc. Aristotle], *ἵνα καὶ ταύτῃ τὴν πρὸς Πλάτωνα συμφωνίαν θαυμάσωμεν* (It is noteworthy that Aristotle by all means is bold enough to pronounce the essential form of soul to be an immortal and everlasting intellect, so that we marvel at his agreement with Plato also in this regard; [Simplicius], *In de an.* 246. 16–23; cf. 247. 13–15).

that in his *Against Boethus* Porphyry defended the immortality of the intellect, arguing that Boethus opposes a doctrine which Aristotle shares with Plato (cf. ἀΐδιον; *De anima* 413^b27, 430^a23). Apparently Porphyry goes on the assumption that Aristotle's active intellect of *De anima* 3. 5 refers either to the human intellect alone, or both to human and divine intellect.

Modern commentators are justified in considering this passage as a fragment from Porphyry's work against Boethus, but they are mistaken in thinking that in it Porphyry criticizes Aristotle for his theory of *entelecheia* to which Boethus adheres.[175] Porphyry rather criticizes a particular understanding of this theory according to which the intellect is inseparable from the living body as it is part of the *empsychia*. For Porphyry, Aristotle's view of the soul as the *entelecheia* of the living body is compatible with the doctrine of the immortality of the intellect, which he may have discerned also in Aristotle's remark about the sailor in the ship (*De anima* 413^a8–9), as it will to later Platonists.

The question now is how Porphyry can follow Plotinus and also maintain that Aristotle agrees with Plato on the immortality of the soul. The answer seems to me to be the following. While Plotinus believed that Aristotle's active intellect is the divine one, Porphyry assumed that it is also the human. It seems to me that their different conceptions of Aristotle's intellect result from a further difference. Unlike Plotinus who distinguished between the transcendent, intellective soul (the hypostasis) and the version of it present in man, Porphyry considers the soul to be one in the transcendent and the immanent realm in a stronger sense than Plotinus assumed. As Porphyry argues in *Sententia* 5, the intellect does not become partite, while the soul does. This, I take it, means that the soul divides itself in individual *empsychiae*, while the soul as intellect does not. That Porphyry considers the intellective soul to be one in the transcendent and the immanent realm is confirmed by the analogy with the musician discussed above, in which the harmony is both a separate one and derivative as the immanent Form of the musician.

Porphyry's view that Aristotle's active intellect is immortal and applies to the human one is shaped also by his belief that there is little difference between the hypostasis of Intellect and that of the Soul. Porphyry was

[175] e.g. Gottschalk (1986: 250–4); Sodano (1993: 156–8); Moraux (1973: 173) argues that the phrase ὥσπερ τὴν ἐμψυχίαν is obscure and suggests the reading ὡς μερικὴν ἐμψυχίαν. But clearly there is hardly any need for such an alteration.

known in antiquity for his view that the Soul essentially is Intellect,[176] a mere function of the former.[177] Such a view may have suggested to him that Aristotle's disregard of the transcendent soul is of little importance, since he accepted the immortality of the intellect. Porphyry may have also argued that Aristotle's *De anima*, given its topic, limited itself to the realm of *empsychia*, and his few remarks about the intellect aim to solely clarify his general position.

There is a piece of evidence, however, which is quite at odds with the view I have ascribed to Porphyry. In a passage from his *Against Boethus* Porphyry appears to criticize Aristotle using strong language, characterizing his doctrine of the soul as 'shameful' (αἰσχρός, αἰσχύνης γέμων; Eusebius, *PE* 15. 11. 4; 249F). This passage cannot be Porphyrian for many reasons. First, nowhere else does Porphyry use such language about Aristotle's doctrines. Second, the fragment is entirely different both in tone and in content from the rest of the preserved fragments of his *Against Boethus*; it criticizes Aristotle concerning the soul, while Porphyry criticizes Boethus concerning the intellect. Third, the reference to the *Laws* in this suggests an altogether different direction from that of Porphyry's argument which, as has been said, is based on the *Phaedo*.

There are also external indications which speak against the Porphyrian authorship of this fragment. To begin with, an Arabic fragment, which may well belong to Porphyry's work *Againt Boethus* (436F), distinguishes between functions of the soul which perish, including Aristotle's passive intellect, and intelligence which does not. Further, later Platonists like Philoponus, who generally draw on Porphyry, use the term *empsychia* in an argument to the effect that Aristotle follows Plato on the soul, on the grounds that Aristotle allegedly upheld the immortality of the intellect as Plato had done.[178] Further, in one

[176] Iamblichus, *De anima* in Stob. 1. 365. 7–21 (441F). Iamblichus disagreed on this and sharply distinguished Soul and Intellect. On the sense and significance of the Porphyrian view see Dörrie (1959: 195–7; 1966: 170–9); Lloyd (1967: 287–9); Hadot (1968: 338–9); Steel (1978: 23–32); Deuse (1983: 208–10).

[177] See *Sent.* 16, pp. 7. 5–8. 3 Lamberz: εἰς δὲ ἑαυτὴν εἰσδῦσα [sc. ἡ ψυχή] πρὸς τὸν νοῦν ἐν ταῖς νοήσεσι γίνεται (as the soul goes back to herself towards the Intellect she enters the realm of thoughts). Cf. *Enn.* 1. 1. 8. 1–3, Nemesius, *De nat. hom.* 135. 7–9. See Deuse (1983: 175–7).

[178] Philoponus, *In de anima* 10. 7–11. 31, 12. 10–11, 524. 6–11, 572. 3–12. Also Olympiodorus distinguishes between the *empsychia* which perishes, i.e. the compound of soul and body that corresponds to form and matter, and the soul (*In Phaedonem* 62. 2–4, 80. 16–21 Norvin). Simplicius, *In Phys.* 421. 24–422. 8, 638. 1–3 and David, *In Isag.* 183. 27–184. 3 distinguish between separable and inseparable motion, as Porphyry implies in *PE* 11. 28. 6–10; 243F Smith. As regards Philoponus, I am indebted to U. Lang, who kindly gave me access to his doctoral thesis.

instance Porphyry refers explicitly to Aristotle when characterizing the soul as the *entelecheia* of the body. Rather than criticize the idea, Porphyry approves of the ontology underlying it.[179]

What is more, Porphyry's position as outlined above is corroborated by his epistemological and ethical views, which I will discuss below, and also by the following evidence. Addressing the question at what stage the soul develops the *nous* (*Ad Gaurum* 50. 12–15), that is, the understanding pertaining to intellect, he argues that Aristotle bears witness to Plato's belief (*Timaeus* 41c) that the *nous* grows at a later stage in life and in some people not at all.[180] In the same context (*Ad Gaurum* 50. 23–6), Porphyry argues that Plato and Aristotle agree on the divine origin of *nous*, referring to the descent of the souls in *Phaedrus* 246c, 248c and to Aristotle's θύραθεν νοῦς (*De gen. anim.* 736^{b}28), and this, he argues, shows the soul's ability to acquire knowledge of God. This is part of the Platonic theory which Porphyry expounds in *Ad Gaurum*, according to which the embryo is ensouled from outside while it lives as a plant in the mother's uterus.

If Porphyry maintained the unanimity of Plato and Aristotle on the soul, who, then, is the author of this fragment in which Aristotle is criticized? It fits perfectly with the language and the argument of Atticus, from whom Eusebius quotes also in the adjacent sections (*PE* 15. 12, 13; Atticus frs. 8–9 Des Places). As has been seen in Chapter 4, it is Atticus who uses such a strong language against Aristotle, is inspired by the *Laws*, attacks Aristotle's doctrine of the soul and assimilates it to that of Dicaearchus (fr. 7. 34–52)—which is quite the opposite from what Porphyry does. Indeed, the reference to the 'others' (249F. 2) must be to other Peripatetics.

It is not clear whether Eusebius is simply mistaken in attributing to Porphyry a fragment of Atticus, or he is deliberately misleading.[181] The following considerations speak for the latter option. To begin with, Eusebius' excerpts leave out the view for which Porphyry argued in his *Against Boethus*; it is quite conspicuous that the quoted passage from

[179] Porphyry, *In Cat.* 56. 19–24; cf. *In Ptol. Harm.* 47. 32–48. 2.

[180] ἀλλὰ ... καὶ τὸν Πλάτωνα τοῦ λόγου ἐπαγόμενος μάρτυρα καὶ σὺν τούτῳ γε Ἀριστοτέλην, ὡς ὀψὲ νοῦς ἀνθρώποις παραγίνεται καὶ οὐδὲ πᾶσιν οὕτως, σπάνιος δὲ ὅτῳ ἐπιτηδεία ψυχὴ πρὸς νοῦ γίνεται συνουσίαν (But he brings Plato and also Aristotle as witness to the argument that the intellect grows at a later stage in life and in some people not at all, and only rarely does one have a soul suitable for the accommodation of the intellect; *Ad Gaurum* 50. 12–15).

[181] Mras in his edn. of the *PE* ii, p. 374 and (1936: 184) attributes the fragment to Porphyry; Moraux (1973: 173–4); Gottschalk (1986: 245); Smith (1993: 267); Sodano (1993: 155, 174) followed him, relying on Eusebius' ascription. Merlan (1967: 73) first raised doubts and attributed it to Atticus; Des Places (1977: 65–6) attributes the fragment

[Simplicius]' commentary where the agreement between Plato and Aristotle on the immortality of the soul is stated, is the only one drawn from Porphyry's work which does not come from Eusebius.[182] Further, the citation from Porphyry's work in the context of the refutation of Aristotle's doctrine of the soul,[183] with a heading which suggests that Porphyry follows Plotinus,[184] is highly deceiving. Porphyry's position is assimilated to that of Atticus and Plotinus, when in fact it is the opposite. Finally, in the section adjacent to the allegedly Porphyrian passage (249F) Eusebius quotes from Atticus, but he does not give any reference to Atticus whatsoever, and the heading misleadingly suggests that Atticus has the same target as Porphyry, that is Aristotle.[185] Given Eusebius' presentation of the material, it is no surprise that a misguided reader came to think that Porphyry's fragments from his *Against Boethus* quoted in this connection (*PE* 15. 10, 11, 15; 247F–250F) derive from a treatise against Aristotle's theory of the soul being the *entelecheia* of the body (*Πρὸς Ἀριστοτέλην περὶ τοῦ εἶναι τὴν ψυχὴν ἐντελέχειαν*; *Suda*, s.v. Porphyry), that is, from a treatise entitled in the way Eusebius subtitles Plotinus' quotation from *Enn.* 4. 8.[186]

6. 3. The Activity of the Embodied Soul

Porphyry's approval of Aristotle's view of how the soul is associated with the body and how it accounts for the functions of a living body becomes

to Atticus (fr. 7 bis) with reservations; cf. his edn. of the *Praeparatio*, *Eusebe La Préparation Evangélique, livres XIV–XV* (Paris, 1987), 299 n. 5.

[182] There is also an Arabic fragment which may derive from this Porphyrian work (436F).

[183] That is, after Atticus, *PE* 15. 9 (fr. 7 Des Places) and Plotinus, *Enn.* 4. 7. 8[5]; *PE* 15. 10.

[184] Eusebius' heading is *Πορφυρίου περὶ τοῦ αὐτοῦ*, which refers us to his heading on Plotinus *Περὶ ἀθανασίας τῆς ψυχῆς πρὸς Ἀριστοτέλην ἐντελέχειαν τὴν ψυχὴν εἶναι φήσαντα* (*PE* 15. 10). The first heading can only mean that Porphyry deals with the immortality of the soul, but the context suggests to the reader that he has the same target as Plotinus. Manuscript Ib adds *ἀπὸ τὸ πρὸς Βόηθον περὶ ψυχῆς*. This may be either an inference of the scribe on the basis of the content of Porphyry's fragments or part of Eusebius' original title, but the latter is less likely given the evidence presented above.

[185] Eusebius' heading runs as follows *Πρὸς τὸν αὐτὸν* [i.e. Aristotle] *διενεχθέντα τῷ Πλάτωνι καὶ ἐν τῷ περὶ τῆς καθόλου ψυχῆς* (i.e. 'On Aristotle opposing Plato on the universal soul')—MS Ib adds *ἀπὸ τῶν αὐτῶν* (i.e. from Porphyry's work!).

[186] Henry (1937: 154–62), Schwyzer (1951: 582–3), and Beutler (1953: 289) have argued that the title of this work most likely was a mistake made by someone who checked through Eusebius' list of contents. Smith (1992) disputes that Eusebius was always the source of the *Suda* and accepts the work as genuine (240T). But the point here is primarily philosophical not palaeographical. Porphyry could not have written such a work, while such a mistake could be made very easily, given Eusebius' presentation of the matter.

manifest in his work *On the faculties of the soul.*[187] In this Porphyry argues that, since soul and body relate to each other as form and matter, every single part of the living body partakes of the soul, which means that the soul is everywhere in the living body but not located anywhere in it;[188] rather, the soul informs the body so that it becomes living, and in this sense the body is assimilated to the soul. This is what Porphyry means when he argues that the presence of the soul in the living body is assimilating (ἐξομοιωτική; *Sent.* 35, p. 40. 10 Lamperz).

The question now is how the soul, as the essence of the living body, accounts for activities as diverse as motion, perception, memory, and thinking, all of which are part of the living form (*On the faculties of the soul* 253F. 102–4). Porphyry admits that there had been controversy on this issue among philosophers in general and among Platonists in particular (ibid. 251F). The tripartition of the soul which several Platonists espoused was, in his view, misguided, resulting from a literal interpretation of the statement in *Timaeus* 35a that the soul is both indivisible and divisible. Such a view entails the existence of many agents in the soul, and this would mean, for instance, many subjects of sense perception (ibid. 253F. 33–7). Actually the very aim of the partition is to postulate different sources of motivation (in *Rep.* 4, for instance). But the problem is how the same agent is able to do many different things. Besides, partition applies to quantities, and for this reason cannot possibly apply to the soul (253F. 62–76).

Already Plotinus rejected the view that the soul is partite, arguing that the soul's local existence does not imply division into spatially distinct parts.[189] Porphyry, while in agreement with Plotinus, also brings Aristotle into the discussion. He argues that the doctrine of the partition of the soul was upheld by both Plato and Aristotle but it meant to explain human motivation and not how the soul accounts for the various living functions (*On the faculties of the soul* 253F. 11–15). Porphyry appears to make a stronger distinction than Plotinus between the concerns of moral psychology and those of theoretical one,[190] but the crucial thing is that unlike Plotinus he endorses Aristotle's criticism of the partition of the soul in *De anima* 432^{a}23–^{b}8, 433^{b}1–6 (253F. 29–33). Porphyry recasts

187 Fragments are preserved by Stobaeus (1. 49. 24–26, 3. 25. 1); I refer to fragments in Smith's numeration.

188 *Sent.* 31, p. 21. 14–15L, 31, p. 22. 10L; *Symm. Zet.* 261F. Cf. *Enn.* 4. 3. 20, 6. 4. 4. 27–34.

189 *Enn.* 4. 2. 1. 69–77, 4. 1. 14–22. On this see Emilsson (2005).

190 Cf. Plotinus e.g. *Enn.* 1. 2. 1. 16–20; see Blumenthal (1971: 21–38).

Aristotle's argument, arguing that the three parts do not exhaust the range of the soul's abilities, as they leave out aspects such as the perceptive, the vegetative, and the intellective (253F. 15–18; cf. *De anima* 432^{a}23–432^{b}8, 433^{b}1–6). Following Aristotle's criticism of those who distinguish an irrational and a rational part of the soul, he criticizes Numenius who distinguished two souls (253F. 18–21).

Porphyry endorses Aristotle's criticism either because he considered it as not being levelled against Plato,[191] or because he took it to rest on a mistaken interpretation of Plato's doctrine of the soul. Porphyry's argument suggests that the latter is more likely. Let us look at this more closely.

Porphyry maintains that the best explanation of how the soul acts in the body is that the soul has powers or faculties, *δυνάμεις* (*On the faculties of the soul* 253F. 29–31). This doctrine, which Aristotle had outlined in the *De anima*, was upheld already by Plutarch, Severus, the Platonist author of Tyrwitt's fragments, and Plotinus.[192] Porphyry's difference from them is that he ascribes this doctrine explicitly to Aristotle, probably on the assumption that Aristotle represents Plato's thought on the matter.[193] The other interesting feature is that Porphyry does not refer to Plotinus in this connection, but rather to Longinus who argued that, since the soul is the soul of a body, it is characteristic of it to have parts, while the soul as such (*καθ' ἑαυτήν*), i.e. the transcendent one, has only faculties (253F. 37–42; cf. *Enn.* 4. 7. 14. 6–12). Longinus, Porphyry reports, did not argue for the existence of parts of the soul in a quantitative but in a qualitative sense, that is the sense in which, for instance, philosophy has parts (253F. 88–94).

Porphyry agrees with this view, which he interprets in a certain way. He argues that the *dynameis* are not located in parts but rather their

[191] It is controversial whether the criticism is directed against Plato or against Academics. Hicks (1907: 551) and Ross (1961: 316) maintain that it applies to Plato, while Vander Waerdt (1987) argues that Aristotle's criticism is directed against the anonymous Academics referred to in *Topics* 126^{a}6–14.

[192] Plutarch, *De virt. mor.* 442B–C, Tyrwitt's fragment pp. 60–71 Sandbach; (see Ch. 2, pp. 112–13); Severus in Eusebius, *PE* 13. 17. 6 (see Ch. 4, p. 188); Plotinus, *Enn.* 4. 3. 23. 3–22.

[193] *Ῥητέον δὲ ὡς δύναμις μέρους διήνεγκεν, ὅτι τὸ μὲν μέρος ἐκβέβηκε κατὰ γένος τὸν χαρακτῆρα τοῦ ἄλλου μέρους, αἱ δὲ δυνάμεις περὶ τὸ αὐτὸ στρέφονται γένος. διὸ τὰ μὲν μέρη παρῃτεῖτο Ἀριστοτέλης ἐπὶ τῆς ψυχῆς, τὰς δὲ δυνάμεις οὐκέτι* (We must say that a faculty is different from a part because a part differs in genus from the character of another part, while faculties are of the same genus. This is why Aristotle abandoned the parts with regard to the soul but not the faculties; Porphyry *On the faculties of the soul* 253F. 29–33). Plato does speak of *dynameis* of the soul (see Introduction p. 23 n. 69).

activities (*energeiai*) take place in different bodily parts.[194] His idea is that the soul gives life by imparting different *energeiai* to different bodily parts in the same way that the pulse is imparted to the body.[195] This view comes very close to Aristotle's understanding of the way in which the soul operates in the body.[196] Porphyry takes such a view because he considers the *dynameis* of the soul part of the form of the living body. A *dynamis*, he argues, is merely the disposition (*hexis*) of the construction of the living body, which allows it to operate in a certain way.[197]

From this Porphyry infers two things. The first is that the *dynameis* manifest the unity and structure of the organism (*On the faculties of the soul* 253F. 68–71). That is, while life activities take place in parts (253F. 105–11), the soul as well as the living being have no parts—but only in thought (ἐπινοίᾳ; 253F. 110; cf. *De anima* 432ᵃ26–432ᵇ7). The second inference that Porphyry draws is that the soul does not have to engage in special activities in order to produce different *energeiai*; rather, these come about by its mere presence,[198] in the same sense in which the hypostasis-Soul does not do anything in order to produce an individual soul. The form of life imposed on the body accounts for life activities in it in the same way that the form of the car accounts for motion and acceleration without the form of the car actually doing anything.

Porphyry appears to have investigated the role of specific faculties in works now lost.[199] In a fragment from his treatise *On the faculties*

194 *On the faculties of the soul* 253F. 82–7, 105–20; cf. *Enn.* 4. 3. 23. Longinus' interpretation is discussed by Männlein-Robert (2001: 620–3).

195 Porphyry's term is ἔνδοσις (253F. 112); it occurs in *De mundo* 398b27 and, with reference to pulse, in Synesius, *Aeg.* 1. 98B. See also Porphyry's reference to pulse in Proclus, *In Tim.* 1. 393. 2–8, cited in n. 198.

196 *De anima* 412ᵃ12, 417ᵃ13–18, 425ᵇ26, 426ᵃ4–5.

197 δύναμις δὲ τῆς κατασκευῆς ἕξις ἀφ ἧς ἐνεργεῖν δύναται, καθ' ὃ κατασκεύασται ἕκαστον (Porphyry, *On the faculties of the soul* 253. 60–62F).

198 ὅτι αἱ ἀληθεῖς δυνάμεις αὐτῷ τῷ εἶναι ἐνεργοῦσι, καὶ ἡ αὐξητικὴ δύναμις καὶ ἡ θρεπτικὴ αὐτῷ τῷ εἶναι τρέφει τὸ σῶμα καὶ αὔξει. οὕτω δὴ οὖν καὶ ἡ ψυχὴ ψυχοῖ καὶ ζωοποιεῖ καὶ κινεῖ τὸ ὄργανον ἑαυτῆς. οὐ γὰρ προελομένων ἡμῶν αἰσθάνεται ἢ σφύζει τὸ σῶμα, ἀλλ' ἡ παρουσία τῆς ψυχῆς ἀποτελεῖ τὰς ἐνεργείας ταύτας (true faculties act by merely existing, so the faculties of growth and nourishment feed the body by being present in it. Similarly the soul ensouls and enlivens and moves its instrument. For the body perceives and pulses without our consent, but the presence of the soul accomplishes these activities; Porphyry in Proclus, *In Tim.* 1. 393. 2–8).

199 I refer to *Περὶ αἰσθήσεως* (Nemesius, *De nat. hom.* 182. 3; 264F.1) and *Περὶ ὕπνου καὶ ἐγρηγόρσεως* (Al Nadim, *Fihrist*; 265T), but their authenticity is doubtful.

of the soul he discusses memory (Stob. 3. 25. 1; 255F). We have seen that Plotinus rejected the Aristotelian account according to which memory is generated by a kind of impression occurring in the soul.[200] Porphyry, however, describes memory in Aristotelian terms, arguing that memory is 'the having of an image (*phantasia*) regarded as a copy of that of which it is an image' (Sorabji's translation).[201] According to this Aristotelian view accepted by Porphyry, memory is a *hexis* in two senses: (*a*) as the soul's having of an image, and (*b*) as a certain state of the soul.[202] From this Porphyry infers that memory involves both soul and body (*συναναφορά*); this is what he assumes for all faculties of the soul, and the case of memory demonstrates it best. The picture Porphyry gives about memory is in accordance with that outlined in a fragment from his work *On Styx* (in Stob. 1. 427. 13–18; 378F. 10–15), where he makes reference to *Philebus* 34a–b. This suggests that Porphyry probably regarded Aristotle as following Plato's image theory according to which memory involves seeing internal pictures.[203]

Porphyry's belief in Aristotle's reliance on Plato in this regard is suggested by another remark of his. He mentions that Aristotle distinguished memory from recollection on the grounds that the later is deliberate[204] and also structured, a form of inquiry (*ζήτησις*; *On memory* 453ᵃ6–14), pertaining to man only (255F. 15–23). This is famously maintained in *Meno* 81c5–d5 and *Phaedo* 73a–74d. Aristotle certainly draws on Plato's heritage in this regard,[205] so Porphyry would be justified in considering this as an instance of Aristotle's acceptance of Plato's doctrine.

One can object, however, that, while Aristotle is indebted to the *Meno* and the *Phaedo* for the view that learning involves association of ideas, he criticized the belief that learning is recollection in the sense of relearning, arguing that it is instead learning for the first time through the recovery of previous knowledge. That is, knowledge of universals

200 See Ch. 6, s. 2, pp. 228–9.

201 Porphyry, *On the faculties of the soul* in Stobaeus 3. 606. 1–3; 255F. 5–8, making reference to Aristotle's *On memory* 451ᵃ14–17.

202 I am indebted to Sorabji's analysis in his (1972: 87).

203 *Phaedo* 73d; *Philebus* 38e–39d; *Timaeus* 26d; see Sorabji (1972: 4–5).

204 *ἐξ αὐτοῦ κινηθῆναι* (*On memory* 452ᵃ11); cf. *Meno* 85b9–c1.

205 *τὸ γὰρ ζητεῖν ἄρα καὶ τὸ μανθάνειν ἀνάμνησις ὅλον ἐστιν* (*Meno* 81d4–5). Porphyry seems to conflate the Platonic and Aristotelian accounts on memory also *In Ptol. Harm.* 13. 27–14. 1.

guides us towards knowledge of particulars through the process of induction.[206] What did Porphyry think about this? Unfortunately we do not know, but once again Porphyry may have refrained from castigating Aristotle for his objections to Plato.[207]

The above discussion has shown that probably for Porphyry Aristotle's criticism of Plato's partition of the soul rested on a mistake. This seems to be the view of Platonists like Plutarch, Severus, Longinus, and Plotinus. Porphyry follows them in believing that Plato had thought that the soul operates in the body as Aristotle theorized, that is, through faculties. And perhaps he also believes that in this case Aristotle is closer to Plato than he admits.

7. ETHICS

Porphyry's emphasis on ethics, which he seems to have considered the end of philosophy, was well known.[208] This means that his view on the relationship between Platonic and Aristotelian ethics would be quite crucial for forming his general position about how the two philosophies compare. We have seen that Plotinus was critical of Aristotle's ethics, arguing that the final end according to Plato was *eudaimonia*, while Aristotle maintained merely *euzôia*. Porphyry, however, takes a much more positive view of Aristotle's ethics, while agreeing on the whole with Plotinus' understanding of Plato's ethics. Let us see how he does this.

As has been seen, Porphyry follows Plotinus in distinguishing between the transcendent, intellective soul and the embodied one (the *empsychia* in Porphyry's terms). On the basis of this distinction Porphyry distinguishes, like Plotinus, between the inner man, the intellect, which he considers to be man's true self, and the outer man, the man of all other living functions.[209] Porphyry sides with Plotinus also in believing

[206] *Pr. an.* 67^{a}22–7; *Post. an.* 71^{a}29–^{b}8; cf. *On memory* 451^{a}18–^{b}11. See also Sorabji (1972: 37–9).

[207] This is the line of Philoponus, *In an. post.* 7–18 where he passes the issue over in silence, while *In an. pr.* 464. 25–465. 2 he notices Aristotle's difference from Plato but he explains it away, arguing that induction does not preclude recollection, as Aristotle implies, but rather the latter makes part of the former.

[208] See Smith (1974: chs. 4–5); Sorabji (2000: 205–10, 284–7). Proclus, *In Tim.* 1. 19. 24–5 reports that even Porphyry's exegesis of the *Timaeus* was guided by ethical concerns; cf. also Praechter (1922: 187–90).

[209] Porphyry, *On what is up to us*, in Stobaeus 3. 581. 17–18 (275F); cf. *Enn.* 1. 1. 10. 5–6.

that virtue identifies with thinking and that different levels of virtue amount to different levels of thinking. In ascending order these are the political/moral and the theoretical/cathartic virtues. Porphyry eventually distinguishes four levels: the political, cathartic, theoretical, and paradigmatic (*Sent.* 32).[210]

Porphyry, however, differs from Plotinus in two important respects. The first is that Porphyry does not consider Aristotle's ethical ideal to be a failure, as Plotinus did, but rather appears to think that Aristotle's doctrine that virtue consists in the mean between extreme emotions expresses Plato's view in practical ethics. We have some solid evidence for that. In *Sententia* 32 Porphyry argues that at the level of civic life virtue amounts to *metriopatheia* (p. 23. 4–6 Lamberz), while in his work *On what is up to us*, he urges Chrysaorius to have his emotions guided by reason so that he avoids excesses but seeks the mean (διώκειν τὸ μέσον; in Stobaeus 2. 168. 10–11; 271F. 1–2). In this passage Porphyry tries to explain to Chrysaorius Plato's ethical doctrine (271F. 20, 38–40). Apparently Porphyry, like Plutarch before him, traced Aristotle's doctrine back to Platonic passages like *Republic* 619a5–b1 or *Politicus* 284d–285a. Yet surely also Plotinus knew these passages. The question then is why Porphyry took a line different from that of his teacher.

Scholars have noted that Plotinus never uses the term *mêtriopatheia*,[211] yet Porphyry's difference from Plotinus is not terminological but substantial. This is confirmed by the fact that Porphyry considers Aristotle to be expressing Plato's view in moral psychology (*On the faculties of the soul*, in Stobaeus 1. 350. 19–22; 253F. 11–15), as Plutarch did (*De virt. mor.* 442B–C). Porphyry placed the emphasis slightly differently from Plutarch, arguing that Aristotle follows Plato in moral psychology because he subscribes to Plato's view about virtue: it is because Aristotle understands virtue as being produced in the way Plato does that he considers the soul partite—not the other way round. From this one can plausibly infer that Porphyry, like several earlier Platonists, considers Aristotle's view that virtue lies in the mean between two extreme emotions as being Plato's own doctrine regarding civic virtue.[212]

The above evidence suggests that Porphyry differs from Plotinus in one crucial respect. Unlike Plotinus who maintained that happiness is

[210] Schwyzer (1974: 225–7) notes the differences between Plotinus and Porphyry in this regard.

[211] As Schwyzer (1974: 225) has noted, although Plotinus comes close to the concept in *Enn.* 4. 4. 34. 1–7.

[212] *Sent.* 32, p. 23. 8–12 Lamberz; cf. *Republic* 434c8–9, 443b1–5, 619a.

obtained only at the ultimate level of virtue, Porphyry appears to think that all levels of virtue not only have their realm of application but also amount to different degrees of happiness. This rests on the assumption that happiness is subject to degrees, which Porphyry clearly made, as his phrase 'perfect happiness' shows.[213] This may betray a different way of reconciling the various views about happiness which exist in Plato's dialogues from that of Plotinus.

Porphyry's difference from Plotinus has the following important consequence. Aristotle's diverse views about happiness in *Nicomachean Ethics* 1 and 10 could now be perceived as complementary because they could be considered as referring to different degrees of happiness, in the same sense that Plato's ethical doctrines in the *Republic* 4 and the *Phaedo* (64b–65d, 81c–83b) or the *Theaetetus* (176a–b) allegedly are. This is what Porphyry seems to assume, thus differing from Plotinus who apparently considered Aristotle's ethics a failure.[214] Porphyry's formulations suggest that he finds Plato's alleged view that the intellect is man's essential element and that the perfect *eudaimonia* consists in intellectual contemplation, stated in Aristotle.[215] On the substance of this Porphyry follows Plotinus closely, arguing that intellectual contemplation involves the knowledge of our real self (*On knowing yourself* 274F–275F), which presupposes the soul's release from the bodily desires (*Sent.* 8, 9, *Ad. Marc.* 34). And like Plotinus, he considers this to be the state in which man attains similarity to God[216] and to amount to the salvation of the soul (*Ad. Marc.* 8, 24).[217] But Porphyry seems to have

[213] *τελεία εὐδαιμονία*; Porphyry, *On what is up to us* 274F. 34.

[214] *Sent.* 32, p. 28. 6–29. 7 Lamberz; 274F. 23–34; *De Abst.* 1. 29. 4. Cf. *Enn.* 6. 7. 35. 4–6, 6. 9. 3. 22–5.

[215] *τὸ γὰρ οἰκεῖον ἑκάστῳ τῇ φύσει κράτιστον καὶ ἥδιστόν ἐστιν ἑκάστῳ· καὶ τῷ ἀνθρώπῳ δὴ ὁ κατὰ τὸν νοῦν βίος, εἴπερ τοῦτο μάλιστα ἄνθρωπος. οὗτος ἄρα καὶ εὐδαιμονέστατος.* (what is dear to the nature of some being, this is best and most pleasant for each being, and in the case of man, the life of the intellect, since this is what man principally is. So this life is also the best one; *NE* 1178^{a}5–8); cf. *NE* 1098^{b}24^{a}5, 1103^{a}5, 1139^{b}17, 1177^{a}24–33, 1179^{a}30–2. Cf. Porphyry in Stobaeus 3. 21. 27; 274F. 30–4: *ἡ γὰρ τεῦξις τῆς ὄντως οὔσης οὐσίας ἡμῶν καὶ ἡ ταύτης ἀληθὴς γνῶσις σοφίας ἦν τεῦξις . . . διὰ σοφίας δὲ ἡ τῆς τελείας εὐδαιμονίας γίγνεται κτῆσις* (for the attainment of our real being and the true knowledge of it amounts to achieving wisdom.. for the perfect happiness can be reached only through wisdom). Cf. 275F. 22–4; *Sent.* 40.

[216] Porphyry, *On knowing yourself*, in Stobaeus 3. 21. 27; 274. 18–28; *Ad Marcellam* 16, 24; cf. 245F. 15–16.

[217] Yet this deification is not an otherworldly matter, at least not entirely so, as largely is the case in Christianity, but rather a prospect attainable during earthly life; cf. *De abst.* 2. 46, 4. 20. 11–16. *Ad Marc.* 32–3.

found this ideal not only in the *Phaedo* (64c–67b) and the *Theaetetus* (176a–b), but also in *Nicomachean Ethics* 10 (e.g. 1177^b28–34).[218]

This is corroborated by some Porphyrian comments on the *Nicomachean Ethics* which survive in the medieval Arabic tradition and are ascribed to a commentary of his on the *NE*. It is doubtful, however, that Porphyry wrote such a commentary.[219] When Arab writers say that they quote Porphyry interpreting Aristotle (165F(ii), 166F), this does not necessarily mean that they draw on a Porphyrian commentary. This rather is our inference. One possibility is that Porphyry commented on passages from the *NE* in some of his works on different subject matter. Yet, although we cannot determine the source of these fragments, there is no reason to doubt their Porphyrian authorship. The Arabs knew Aristotle's *Nicomachean Ethics* and, being concerned with understanding it, kept an eye open for erudite comments such as Porphyry's.[220] These occur in Al-Amirî's anthology and Miskawaih's *The Refinement of Character*.[221] It is not always clear, though, how much in these works comes from Porphyry; here we have to confine ourselves to those instances where he is explicitly cited. No testimony compares Aristotelian and Platonic views, but some seem to assume that the two philosophers share common ground in ethics.

In one of those fragments, Porphyry argues that the person who is entitled to leadership is the one who has control over himself and his

[218] Cf. *Rep.* 500c–d, 613a–b; *Timaeus* 90b–c; *EE* 1249^b16–23.

[219] Such a commentary is attested by Al-Nadim *Fihrist*, ed. Flügel, 1. 251 (3eT). Yet Al-Nadim, the blind bookseller in Baghdad, is not always accurate. Also a bibliographer like him would have been tempted to infer the existence of a Porphyrian commentary from comments of Porphyrian authorship. None of the Arabic authors which preserve Porphyry's comments suggest that these come from a commentary; they may well have come from doxographic material. This is how their knowledge of Platonic quotations, for instance, is to be explained. Walzer (1965*a*: 282; 1965*b*); F. Peters, *Aristoteles Arabus* (Leiden, 1968), 52–3; Smith (1993: 161) maintain the existence of such a commentary.

[220] Plenty of evidence suggests that Aristotle's *Nicomachean Ethics* were translated into Arabic and were available in the book market. See J. Arberry, 'The *Nicomachean Ethics* in Arabic', *Bulletin of the School of Oriental and African Studies*, 17 (1955), 1–9, D. M. Dunlop, 'The *Nicomachean Ethics* in Arabic Books', *Oriens*, 15 (1962), 18–34. Al-Farabi in his *Treatise on the Harmony between the views of the two sages, the divine Plato and Aristotle* refers to Porphyry's interpretation of the *NE* (Mallet 1989: 78). See Gauthier-Jolif (1970: 107–11). I acknowledge Dr F. Zimmermann's assistance in this section.

[221] Tr. C. Zurayk, *The Refinement of Character: A translation from the Arabic of Miskawayh Tahdhib al-Akhlaq* (Beirut, 1968). Walzer, 'Some Aspects of Miskawaih's Tahdhib Al-Akhlaq', in *Greek into Arabic* (Oxford, 1962), 220–35 and (1965*a*: 294–6) argues that chs. 3–5 largely reflect Porphyry's views. Walzer may overstate his case here, but it seems that much more than the fragment that Smith prints (166F) in his edn. must go back to Porphyry (e.g. the section on the division of goods pp. 70–2 Zurayk).

house, and then parallels him with the craftsman who reaches perfection in his art (165F(iv)). Porphyry refers to the ability to dominate over one's emotions by means of reason, which should characterize everyone who lives in a community (*Sent.* 32, p. 23. 4–8 Lamberz) and especially the politician. It is not clear which part of Aristotle's ethics Porphyry is referring to here. He may allude to the view found in Plato and Aristotle that only those who are able to rule themselves can rule.[222] Although Aristotle does not endorse Plato's political views as presented in the *Republic*, for instance, he does hold that political competence is the same *hexis* as prudence (*phronesis*) but applies to deliberating and acting in public affairs rather than in private matters (*NE* 1141^b23–1142^a11, *EE* 1218^b13–14). According to Aristotle, a wise man, like Pericles, can recognize the good not only for himself but for the others too (*NE* 1140^b6–11).

Aristotle's account of happiness as an intellectual activity is alluded to in a passage where Porphyry comments on the notion of happiness, which I quote below:

> Porphyry said: Happiness is the perfection of man's form. Man's perfection—as a man—lies in his voluntary actions. [On the other hand] man's perfection—as a divine being and intellect—lies in contemplation. Related to its object, each of these two kinds of perfection is perfect [in itself], but if they were compared to each other, the human perfection would be found deficient.[223]

Porphyry appears to speak of two kinds of human perfection, that of voluntary actions and the perfection of contemplation, each of which is honourable, but the latter, we are told, is more sublime. The passage suggests that Porphyry found in Aristotle both levels of good life which he distinguishes in Plato, and that he also considers Aristotle to value intellectual contemplation as the most complete form of a good life, alluding clearly to *NE* 10 (esp. 1177^b30–1178^b22).

This is supported by another piece of evidence. This is an otherwise unknown Aristotelian text, probably a pseudo-Aristotelian one, on the degrees of virtue, which is cited by Miskawaih, and its source may well be Porphyry. According to this text, man's virtue culminates when all his

222 Cf. *Republic* 435b–444a; *NE* 1140^b6–11, 1177^b12–16, 1180^a10–1181^b1.

223 I follow the translation of A. A. Ghorab, 'The Greek Commentators on Aristotle quoted in AL-Amiri's 'AS-SA 'ADA WA'L-AS 'AD', in *Islamic Philosophy and the Classical Tradition* (Oxford, 1972), 77–88, esp. 79. Smith (165F(i)) left out an important part of the passage.

actions become divine.[224] Porphyry is presented as reporting Aristotle's views. I quote:

> When all man's actions become divine, all of them originate in his essence and his true being, namely his divine intellect, which is true being... This condition is the ultimate degree of the virtues. In it man adopts the actions of the First Principle, the Creator of the Universe... His 'being itself' is identical with divine activity itself... This is the aim of philosophy and supreme bliss... Then he is filled with divine gnosis and divine longing, and acquires through what is established in his soul, that is, his being which is identical with the intellect, certainty of the divine matters. [tr. Rosenthal]

Although the evidence is not conclusive, it strongly suggests that Porphyry perceived Aristotle as following Plato in what constitutes virtuous life and in holding that the highest degree of happiness is the activity of the contemplating intellect. In this he differed significantly from Plotinus. Yet this may well be part of a more considerable difference between Plotinus and Porphyry as regards Aristotle's doctrine of the active intellect; as has been seen in the previous section, Porphyry maintains that Aristotle subscribes to Plato's doctrine of the immortality of the intellect. Given that for Porphyry this ethical ideal constitutes the main aim of philosophy,[225] this was an important point of agreement between Aristotle and Plato. As in physics and psychology, so in ethics Porphyry stresses Aristotle's similarities with Plato, passing his differences over in silence. This strengthens the view that Porphyry's argument about the accord between Platonic and Aristotelian philosophies focused on what was considered essential.

8. METAPHYSICS/LOGIC

Porphyry's treatment of physics, cosmology and psychology has shown that he considered Platonic and Aristotelian ontology to be not only

[224] pp. 77–81 Zurayk included in F. Rosenthal, *The Classical Heritage in Islam* (Berkeley, Calif., 1975), 97–103. S. Pines, 'Un texte inconnu d'Aristote en version arabe', in *Archives d'histoire doctrinale et litteraire du Moyen Âge*, 31 (1956), 5–43, and Walzer, 'Aristutalis', *Encyclopedie de l'Islam*, i. 653b, attribute the text to the *Protrepticus*, while P. Moraux, *Le Dialogue 'Sur la Justice'* (Louvain, 1957), p. xii and Gauthier-Jolif (1970: 110 n. 83) maintain that it is pseudo-Aristotelian.

[225] In Stobaeus 3. 580. 17–581. 10; 274F. 13–30; *Ad Marcellam* 31.

compatible but largely in agreement.[226] In this section I will discuss some further evidence which confirms this claim. I will then recapitulate my findings, in order to ascertain Porphyry's understanding of Aristotle's metaphysics as precisely as possible.

In *Sententia* 42 Porphyry distinguishes between two kinds of 'incorporeals' (ἀσώματα), proper and catachrestic ones. The former, Porphyry argues, are those which are not bodily but which exist in relation to bodies (πρὸς τὰ σώματα ὑφίσταται). Such incorporeals do not subsist by themselves but exist only in a thing, such as immanent Forms, natures, powers (*dynameis*), time, and place, and can be abstracted from bodies only in thought (*Sent.* 42, p. 53. 8 Lamperz).[227] Incorporeals of the latter kind, such as the intellect and its thought (νοερὸς λόγος; cf. *Sent.* 19),[228] subsist by themselves separately from bodies.[229] Porphyry makes, or implies, the same distinction elsewhere.[230] In the context of *Sententia* 42, however, he is targeting the Stoics who accepted incorporeals only of the first kind.[231] Quite noticeably, Porphyry carries out his criticism by contrasting the Stoic view with that of 'the ancients'.

226 Like many scholars, I remain sceptical about the Porphyrian authorship of the Anonymous Turin Commentary on the *Parmenides*, claimed for Porphyry by P. Hadot (1968), and I do not take it into account in the present discussion. Some strong doubts have been raised by Smith (1987: 740–1), who does not include the relevant fragments in his edn., and Edwards (1990). Dillon (1992: 357 n. 6) follows Hadot in maintaining its Porphyrian authorship. The most recent discussion of the question by G. Bechtle, *The Anonymous Commentary on Plato's* Parmenides (Berne, 1999), 77–8 leaves it open whether it is pre- or post-Plotinian. See the review of the *status quaestionis* by Zambon (2002: 35–41).

227 Ἀσώματα τὰ μὲν κατὰ στέρησιν σώματος λέγεται καὶ ἐπινοεῖται κυρίως, ὡς ἡ ὕλη κατὰ τοὺς ἀρχαίους καὶ τὸ εἶδος τὸ ἐπὶ τῆς ὕλης, ὅταν ἐπινοῆται ἀποληφθέν ἀπὸ τῆς ὕλης, καὶ αἱ φύσεις καὶ αἱ δυνάμεις· οὕτως δὲ καὶ ὁ τόπος καὶ ὁ χρόνος καὶ τὰ πέρατα. τὰ γὰρ τοιαῦτα πάντα κατὰ στέρησιν σώματος λέγεται. ἤδη δὲ ἦν ἄλλα καταχρηστικῶς λεγόμενα ἀσώματα, οὐ κατὰ στέρησιν σώματος, κατὰ δὲ < τὸ > ὅλως μὴ πεφυκέναι γεννᾶν σῶμα (Incorporeals are called and thought of those private of bodies. According to the ancients such are matter and enmattered Form when conceived abstracted from matter, and also natures, faculties, as well as place, time and limits. All such things are called incorporeals in virtue of being private of body. There are also other incorporeals in a similar catachrestic sense, not in virtue of being private of bodies but in virtue of not being able to generate a body; *Sent.* 42, p. 53. 6–13 Lamberz).

228 On *Sententiae* 19 and 42 see Dörrie (1959: 183–7), Schwyzer (1974: 229–30), De Libera (1999: 11–15).

229 Porphyry's distinction seems to correspond to his distinction between χωρίζεσθαι and χωρίς εἶναι. The former holds true of a substance, the latter largely of accidents. The fragrance may be separate from bodies, but cannot exist separately from a body (*In Cat.* 79. 23–34). On this see Ellis (1990: 290–3).

230 *Sent.* 5, 19; *In Ptol. Harm.* 14. 17–21, 17. 13–17.

231 The Stoics accepted as incorporeals void, *lecton*, time and place; Sextus, *Adv. Math.* 10. 218 (*SVF* ii. 331).

Porphyry implies that 'the ancients' not only accept incorporeals of the first kind (e.g. matter and immanent Form); they also accept incorporeals of the second kind (i.e. proper intelligible substances). As has been seen so far, for Porphyry the 'ancients' include Plato and Aristotle. Porphyry repeats here his claim that Plato and Aristotle consider matter and immanent Form to be causes, which he argues in his commentary on the *Physics* (120F Smith). But here he also goes further. He not only suggests that Plato and Aristotle accepted proper intelligible substances, he also specifies these as the intellect and its thoughts, not the transcendent Forms. This evidence confirms my claim (in s. 5. 3, pp. 283–4) that Porphyry upheld Aristotle's adherence to Plato's principles, which include the transcendent Forms as thoughts of the divine mind.

This conclusion is confirmed by two other pieces of evidence. First, in a passage of his commentary on the *Categories*, Porphyry counts among intelligible substances the intellect and its thought, while he expresses some scepticism over the existence of transcendent Forms (*In Cat.* 91. 14–17).[232] Secondly, and more importantly, in a passage from his commentary on Ptolemy's *Harmonics*, Porphyry provides some discussion of the various kinds of intelligibles including the ones just mentioned, and specifies that only incorporeals in the catachrestic sense count as proper intelligible substances.

Λέγεται τοίνυν νοητὸν ἰδίως, ὃ κατ᾽ αὐτὴν τὴν οὐσίαν διενήνοχε τῶν αἰσθητῶν, ὡς ἐστι μόνα τὰ ἀσώματα νοητὰ καὶ καθάπαξ ὅσα μὴ σώματα. ἐλέγετο γοῦν ὁ περὶ τῶν τοιούτων παρὰ τοῖς ἀρχαίοις λόγος περὶ τῶν νοητῶν. λέγεται ἑτέρως νοητόν, ἐφ᾽ ὃ δύναται ἐπίστασις γενέσθαι νοῦ καὶ ἀντίληψις. Οὕτω δὲ καὶ τὸ αἰσθητὸν ἔσται νοητὸν καὶ ἅπαν γε . . . κατὰ δὲ τὸ δεύτερον σημαινόμενον καὶ τὰ κατὰ τοὺς φθόγγους αἰσθητά ἐστι νοητά, ὅτι δύναται καὶ περὶ τούτων ὁ λόγος ἐπιστῆσαι, ὃν κοινότερον οἱ παλαιοὶ καὶ νοῦν προσηγόρευον. (*In Ptol. Harm.* 17. 13–17, 27–9).

What is called intelligible strictly speaking is that which differs in substance from sensibles, and thus only the incorporeals and at any rate non bodies. Such kinds of entities were defined as intelligibles by the ancients. Alternatively

[232] Reply: *Λέγω ὅτι αἰτιῶνται* [Praechter; *αἰτιῶμαι* mss] *αὐτόν, ὅτι κυριώτατα κατὰ αὐτὸν καὶ μάλιστα καὶ πρώτως λεγομένων πρώτων οὐσιῶν τῶν νοητῶν οἷον τοῦ νοητοῦ θεοῦ καὶ τοῦ νοῦ καί, εἴπερ εἰσὶν ἰδέαι, καὶ τῶν ἰδεῶν, παριστὰς ταύτας πρώτας οὐσίας ἔφη τὰς ἐν τοῖς αἰσθητοῖς ἀτόμους* (I reply that some object that on his own [i.e. Aristotle's] showing it is the intelligibles that are said most strictly and above all and primarily to be substances in the primary sense, i.e. the intelligible god and intellect and the Forms, if there are Forms, but he ignores these, and claims that the individuals in sensibles are primary substances; *In Cat.* 91. 14–17, Strange's tr. slightly modified). On this passage see also Chiaradonna (1996: 89–90)).

something is called intelligible which can be known and understood by the intellect. In this sense every sensible entity is also an intelligible one... According to the second definition intelligibles are also the properties of meaningful sounds, because they can also be known by reason, which is what the ancients used to term intellect.

In the section from which the text quoted is taken, Porphyry attempts to distinguish between the various kinds of intelligibles, which include those mentioned in *Sententia* 42. One such kind includes entities essentially different from sensibles, for example, the *nous* or the *noeros logos*. Another kind are those which can be grasped by the intellect. Among these are meaningful sounds (*φθόγγοι*), that is, sayings whose meaning can be apprehended by reason, which is what the 'ancients' called 'intellect' in a wider sense, argues Porphyry. The basic underlying distinction here seems to be between the intellect itself and its contents, which include thoughts, perceptions, and understanding of linguistic terms. Porphyry appears to be implying here that the intelligibles can either be substances such as intellects and souls, or else exist in substances, as do thoughts within the intellect. These two categories correspond to the two classes of incorporeals mentioned above, namely catachrestic and proper ones. Porphyry again implies that the 'ancients' agree in accepting both kinds of intelligibles.

That Porphyry believed this is further supported by his conviction that the complementary ontological views of Plato and Aristotle lead to their agreement in epistemology. This is repeatedly emphasized in Porphyry's commentary on the *Harmonics*, in which he argues that their agreement involves accepting the relative importance of both sense and reason. That is, Porphyry suggests that Plato and Aristotle agree in maintaining that accurate perceptual knowledge is possible when sense is informed by reason.[233] And in Porphyry's view, both Plato and Aristotle believe that we, as humans, grasp the essential Forms through the intellect, and thus come to know the things around us. The connection between the epistemological position of the 'ancients' and the ontological one is that, as Porphyry argues, both Plato and

[233] *Κριτήρια οὐ μόνον τῶν περὶ τοὺς ψόφους διαφορῶν καὶ τῆς τούτων ἁρμονίας αἴσθησιν καὶ λόγον οἱ παλαιοὶ ἐτίθεντο, ἀλλὰ καὶ πάντων ὁμοίως τῶν αἰσθητῶν. τὰ μὲν γὰρ λόγῳ κρινόμενα μὴ πάντα αἰσθήσει κρίνεσθαι, τὰ δ' αἰσθήσει πάντως καὶ λόγῳ* (The ancients set sensation and reason as rules not only concerning the differences between sounds and their harmony, but similarly about all sensibles. For not everything that is judged by reason can be judged by sensation, while those judged by sensation can be judged by reason); *In Ptol. Harm.* 11. 4–7. Cf. ibid. 14. 1–28, 16. 15–21.

Aristotle consider primarily the Forms to be *ousiai*.[234] This is quite at odds with Plotinus' view regarding Aristotle's conception of substance, but it does square with Porphyry's belief that proper intelligible substances are the intellect and its thoughts, since he identities the latter with the Forms (cf. pp. 283–4). This is further illustrated in Porphyry's comments on Aristotle's *Categories*, where the agreement between Platonic and Aristotelian ontology is strongly defended.

Porphyry wrote two commentaries on this work; a short one for Chrysaorius, and a more comprehensive one in seven books, surviving only in some fragments of Simplicius.[235] As for modern commentators on the *Categories*, for Porphyry determining the subject matter or purpose of Aristotle's treatise is absolutely crucial, especially because the long exegetical tradition engendered by the work had been marked by controversy and disagreement on this. Quite crucial in this regard is the meaning of the term *κατηγορία*. By Porphyry's time, three different interpretations had emerged regarding the meaning of the term, and, accordingly, the purpose of the treatise in general. In the first interpretation the term refers to words; in the second, to meanings of words or concepts; and in the third, to things, that is, to beings. The latter interpretation is the one which Plotinus assumed in his criticism of Aristotle's work (*Enn.* 6. 1–3).

As we saw in Chapter 6, Plotinus considered the *Categories* to be a work on ontology, that divided all beings into a number of classes or kinds. For Plotinus, Aristotle's account is seriously incomplete, because it leaves out intelligible beings, which he considers to represent actual beings. In Plotinus' view, the term 'substance' strictly speaking applies only to intelligible beings like intellect and soul, and only homonymously to sensible ones.

Porphyry, though, argues that Aristotle's work is not in fact about ontology and does not aim to classify beings. He claims that titles like *Περὶ τῶν γενῶν τοῦ ὄντος* or *Περὶ τῶν δέκα γενῶν* result from a serious misunderstanding of the subject matter of the *Categories* (*In*

[234] *τοῦ γὰρ εἴδους ἡ αἴσθησις καθ' ὃ ἔνυλον . . . ὁ δὲ λόγος χωρίζων αὐτὸ ἀπὸ τῆς ὕλης. ἔνθεν καὶ δοκεῖ τισιν τὸν μὲν τῆς οὐσίας εἶναι κριτικόν — οὐσίας γὰρ τὰ εἴδη καὶ οἱ παλαιοὶ ὑπελάμβανον* (sense is of the Form of something which is material . . . reason instead separates Form from matter, and this is why it is considered to be the faculty apprehending substance—for the ancients regarded the Forms as substances); *In Ptol. Harm.* 11. 13, 31–3.

[235] 45T–74F Smith. Porphyry's preserved commentary breaks off at Ch. 9, which he probably considered to be the end of Aristotle's genuine work. See Frede (1987*a*: 13–17).

Cat. 56. 18–57. 15).[236] In Porphyry's view, Aristotle's treatise examines rather how words relate to the things they signify.[237] The aim of the work, Porphyry argues, is suggested by the term *κατηγορία* which, in his view, indicates a 'significant expression applied to things'; 'whenever a simple significant expression is employed and said of what it signifies, this is called a predicate' (*κατηγορία*; *In Cat.* 56. 8–9, Strange tr.).[238] Porphyry justifies his view by referring to Aristotle's claim according to which what is said without any combination (*κατὰ μηδεμίαν συμπλοκήν*; *Cat.* 1^{b}25–7) signifies (*σημαίνει*) an entity which falls under one of the ten categories, namely substance, quantity, quality, etc. He also refers to the passage in which Aristotle argues that only the combination of the categories can lead to affirmation, while each category separately is not affirmed (*ἐν οὐδεμίᾳ καταφάσει λέγεται*; *Cat.* 2^{a}4–7; cf. *In Cat.* 87. 31–5). The verb 'signify' (*σημαίνει*) and the reference to affirmation, Porphyry argues, shows that Aristotle is dealing with words, because only words can signify and only the combination of significant words produces affirmation. He thus concludes that the categories concern significant words, not classes of beings (*In Cat.* 57. 6–12).

In order to specify the subject matter of the treatise more precisely, Porphyry finds it crucial to determine the kind of words with which Aristotle is concerned. Porphyry distinguishes between words of first and second imposition. In the first class belong those words which signify things in the world, like 'stone', 'tree', 'animal' (the thing, i.e. what is an animal), while words of the second class signify words, like 'noun', 'verb', 'animal' (the word, e.g. ' "animal" in this context is ambiguous').[239] The two classes correspond to two uses of language, object-language and meta-language. The words of first imposition are the most basic ones, because they signify things. These are, as Porphyry

[236] The various titles with which the *Categories* were known in antiquity corresponded to different interpretations of Aristotle's work. Apart from the above mentioned, other titles included *Πρὸ τῶν τόπων*, *Πρὸ τῶν τοπικῶν* which Porphyry equally rejects. See Frede (1987*b*: 17–21). For Porphyry's criticism on his predecessors, including Plotinus, see Kotzia (1992: 31–7).

[237] On Porphyry's interpretation of the categories see mainly Strange (1987: 957–63); Hadot (1990: Lloyd (1990: 36–70); Ebbesen (1990*a*); Kotzia (1992: 21–50); Chiaradonna (1998*a*); De Libera (1999).

[238] *ὥστε πᾶσα ἁπλῆ λέξις σημαντικὴ ὅταν κατὰ τοῦ σημαινομένου πράγματος ἀγορευθῇ τε καὶ λεχθῇ, λέγεται κατηγορία* (*In Cat.* 56. 8–9).

[239] *In Cat.* 57. 32–58. 4. As examples of words of the second imposition Porphyry adduces only 'noun' and 'verb', but Dexippus, who draws on Porphyry, adds more (*In Cat.* 15. 5–16. 13). See Ebbesen (1990*a*: 161).

puts it, like messengers which announce things (*In Cat.* 58. 23–5). Apart from these two classes of words, there are also others such as articles or prepositions. These are needed for constructing full sentences and for expressing complex meanings, but they do not belong to any of the categories because they are not significant but merely connectives.[240]

According to Porphyry the subject matter of the *Categories* precisely concerns significant words of first imposition, words to the extent (*καθό*) that they signify things in the world.[241] Porphyry does not hesitate to acknowledge that this view was upheld by Peripatetic commentators, such as Boethus, Alexander's teacher Herminus, and Alexander himself (*In Cat.* 59. 17–33).[242]

What, then, are the ten categories, according to Porphyry? They are ten classes of words into which all significant words of first imposition are divided (*In Cat.* 58. 3–15, 71. 22–6), or ten kinds of predication (ibid. 58. 29–31). The ten classes of words signify substance (e.g. man), quality (e.g. white), quantity (e.g. three), relation (e.g. father), place (e.g. in the Lyceum), time (e.g. last year), doing (e.g. hit), being affected (e.g. being hit), having (e.g. wearing shoes), position (e.g. sitting; ibid. 87. 24–7).

Porphyry goes on to argue that these classes of words are divided into two groups, namely substance and accident, into which all other categories apart from substance fall (*In Cat.* 95. 13–16). The difference between the two groups is illustrated in the difference between saying 'Socrates is a man' and 'Socrates is white'. White exists only as property of a subject, that is, it requires a substratum in order to be realized, and this is why all accidents are *in* a subject (*Cat.* 1^a20–1) and cannot exist separately from it (*In Cat.* 78. 13–21, 79. 19–27). In the sentence

[240] *In Cat.* 57. 3–8, Simplicius, *In Cat.* 10. 20–11. 22 (46F). Cf. Dexippus, *In Cat.* 32. 30–33. 7

[241] *ἔστι τοίνυν ἡ πρόθεσις τοῦ βιβλίου περὶ τῆς πρώτης θέσεως τῶν λέξεων τῆς παραστατικῆς τῶν πραγμάτων· ἔστιν γὰρ περὶ φωνῶν σημαντικῶν ἁπλῶν, καθὸ σημαντικαί εἰσι τῶν πραγμάτων, οὐ μὴν τῶν κατὰ ἀριθμὸν ἀλλήλων διαφερόντων ἀλλὰ τῶν κατὰ γένος* (The subject of this book is the primary imposition of expressions, which is used for communicating about things. For it concerns simple significant words insofar as they signify things –not however as they differ from one to another in number, but as differing in genus; *In Cat.* 58. 5–8; Strange's tr.) Cf. Simplicius, *In Cat.* 10. 20–11. 22 (46F). The words of the second imposition are discussed in the *De interpretatione* (*In Cat.* 58. 32–3) on which Porphyry also commented. His views are preserved by Boethius and Ammonius (75T–110T). See Kotzia (1992: 26–9).

[242] This was also the view of an editor of Aristotle's corpus, presumably Andronicus, who made the *Categories* the first of Aristotle's logical works. See Moraux (1973: 99–101).

'Socrates is a man' on the other hand, 'man' signifies the essence of Socrates, which can be said of Socrates as such (*Cat.* 1ª20). Accordingly, there are two kinds of predication, accidental and essential.[243] As regards the latter, in the sentence 'Socrates is a man', Socrates is a particular substance, while 'man' is a universal predicated of it, which tells us what Socrates essentially is, i.e. a man. As is known, Aristotle distinguishes in the *Categories* between particular substances, which he considers to be primary, such as Socrates, and universal ones, which he considers to be secondary, that is, a genus or a species, such as animal or man (*Cat.* 2ª11–16). And he argues that particular substances are substances most of all (μάλιστα οὐσίαι; *Cat.* 2ᵇ17), because they exist separately and are prior in nature (ibid. 2ᵇ12–20, 14ᵇ11–13), while universal substances, such as genus, or species, like animal or man, exist only to the extent that individual men or animals exist, and in this sense are posterior in nature (ibid. 2ᵇ6).

Now this, at least *prima facie*, should be a problem for the Platonist who assumes the ontological priority of the transcendent Forms and the ontological dependence of particular substances on them. And it surely was a problem for generations of Platonists in late antiquity. Eudorus, Lucius, Nicostratus, and Plotinus had thought that with this view Aristotle denies the priority of the intelligible substances over the sensible ones. In Chapter 6 we have seen how Plotinus argued this out.

Porphyry, however, takes a different view, one based on his conviction that the subject matter of Aristotle's treatise is about significant words. He distinguishes between the term 'animal' which is predicated of someone in the phrase 'Socrates is an animal', and 'animal' not being predicated of anything.[244] 'Animal' in its first use, as a predicate, signifies the essence of the thing it is predicated of; it tells us that Socrates essentially is an animal. In ontological terms, the predicate 'animal' amounts to the immanent Form of Socrates which, as Porphyry argued in his commentary on Ptolemy's *Harmonics* (11. 31–3), for Plato as well as Aristotle amounted to the essence of a thing. This Form is not

243 In the *Isagogê* (3. 5–20) Porphyry distinguishes three kinds of predications, essential (ἐν τῷ τί ἐστι), qualitative (ἐν τῷ ποῖόν τί ἐστι), and dispositional (πῶς ἔχον). On this distinction see De Libera (1999: 22–6) and esp. Barnes (2003), 84–92.

244 In his major commentary on the *Categories* Porphyry speaks in terms κατατεταγμένος (= allocated) and ἀκατάτακτος (= unallocated; apud Simplicium, *In Cat.* 53. 4–9; 56F, 79. 25–30; 59F). 'Allocated' is the predicate as predicated of a subject (e.g. Socrates is an animal), while 'unallocated' is the predicate (e.g. animal) not being predicated of anything, the unqualified term. On this distinction see Ebbesen (1990*a*: 147), 157–9); Lloyd (1990: 65–6); and Chiaradonna (1998: 591–5).

separable from a particular substance but, as Porphyry argues, it can only be mentally abstracted (*In Cat.* 91. 2–7; *In Ptol. Harm.* 14. 1–14). As regards the other use of 'animal', the one outside predication, this can amount either to the concept 'animal', which we use when we think of an animal, or to the transcendent Form, which, in Platonist terms, accounts for the existence of all animals.

Porphyry appears then to distinguish between (*a*) animality, the transcendent Form which accounts for the very being of the class of animals, (*b*) 'animal' as a universal concept, an abstraction, which we apply to all animals by subtracting their *differentiae*, and (*c*) a specific man being an animal (the immanent Form, or essence).[245] These in some sense represent three kinds of universals, but in fact only (*b*) is a genuine universal, because, according to Aristotle at least, a universal essentially is something which is predicated of many things (*De Int.* 17^{a}39–40); (*c*) rather is the immanent Form which differs in different species, while (*a*), the transcendent Form, is the common cause for the existence of all animals, rather than a universal. In Porphyry's view Aristotle is not at all concerned with the latter in the *Categories* (or with any other intelligible beings), precisely because his subject matter is limited to words used in predication, that is (*c*). And according to Porphyry no inference can be drawn about Aristotle's ontology from the fact that he does not refer to transcendent Forms in his *Categories* (*In Cat.* 91. 14–27); given its subject matter this is a justifiable omission.

A Platonist can still raise the question of why Aristotle comes to consider as primary substances the particular ones, when traditionally according to Platonists universal substances are prior to particulars. A Platonist could also object that the immanent Forms, which are the essence of a thing and which correspond to the genus or species, are also ontologically prior to individual substances. One can further object in this connection that if Socrates is eliminated, man is not eliminated, whereas if man is eliminated, every particular man is also eliminated, which shows that the universal is prior to the particular substance (*In Cat.* 90. 12–26).

[245] Elias, *In Isag.* 48. 15–49. 23 formulates the above distinction in the following terms: (*a*) *χωριστά τὰ πρὸ τῶν πολλῶν*, (*b*) *ἐν τοῖς αἰσθητοῖς τὰ ἐν τοῖς πολλοῖς*, (*c*) *περὶ ταῦτα ὑφεστῶτα τὰ ἐπὶ τοῖς πολλοῖς*. Cf. Ammonius, *In Isag.* 41. 10–42, 68. 25–69; Simplicius, *In Cat.* 69. 19–71. 2, 82. 35–83. 20. See also Porphyry, *In Cat.* 124. 6–13, where he distinguishes between the white colour (the abstraction) and the particular white thing. On Porphyry's distinction of three kinds of universal see Lloyd (1990: 67–8) and De Libera (1999: 18–21).

Porphyry's answer is that by 'particular substance' Aristotle does not refer to a particular substance, for instance, a single man, but rather refers to the whole class of men on the basis of which we form the concept of man (*In Cat.* 90. 29–91. 2; cf. 80. 24–5). It is this class of substances that is prior to universal substance, not the particular one. As Porphyry argues, we cannot conceive of a universal predicate, e.g. 'man', as existing apart from its class-extension, the class of men (*In Cat.* 90. 29–91. 7). What is more, Aristotle, prioritizes particular substances in the *Categories* because he deals with significant words. Originally, Porphyry suggests, words were invented to signify particular substances which we encounter first in nature; hence words primarily (πρώτως) signify individuals (ibid. 91. 5–12, 19–27). With respect to significant words then, Porphyry argues, primary substances are individuals, while intelligible substances are primary with respect to nature (ibid. 91. 23–5).[246] This is why, Porphyry contends, given the subject matter of the *Categories*, Aristotle does not prioritize intelligible substances.

Porphyry thus shows that the criticisms of previous Platonists against Aristotle for not prioritizing intelligible substances fail to apply.[247] Further, he appears to believe that Aristotle was right to hold that universals (e.g. 'man') are posterior to particulars. In his commentary on Ptolemy's *Harmonics* (p. 14. 1–4 Düring) Porphyry argues that universals exist only as concepts, that is, as mental abstractions of the immanent Forms, which we form from the perception of particulars. It is from the perception of particulars that we come to conceive of universals, and if particulars are eliminated, universals will not exist either (*In Cat.* 91. 2–7; cf. *Cat.* 2^a37–8). But these universals are not to be confused with the kind of universals that are the Platonic Forms. These, as I have said above, are in Porphyry's view not at all at issue in the *Categories*.

From the above outline of Porphyry's argument it emerges that, despite his claims about the limited scope of the *Categories* to significant expressions, he seems to have accepted that the treatise has some ontological implications. This is already implied in Porphyry's

246 Cf. Dexippus, *In Cat.* 51. 14–15; Simplicius, *In Cat.* 104. 21–2, both of whom, as Lloyd (1990: 66) has suggested, must echo Porphyry. Porphyry's position is well outlined by Strange (1987: 362–3). Cf. Chiaradonna (1996: 86–9). Porphyry appears to apply here Aristotle's distinction between what is prior in nature and what is prior in relation to us (*Post. an.* 71^b33–5).

247 Porphyry replies to critics such as Lucius and Nicostratus (apud Simplicium, *In Cat.* 73. 15–28), and Plotinus (*Enn.* 6. 1. 1. 15–30). On Porphyry's interpretation of Aristotle's views on intelligible substances see also below.

statement that Aristotle's treatise is not about classes of beings but about the correspondence between them and predications (*In Cat.* 59. 31–3). Porphyry avoided discussion of the ontological implications in the preserved short commentary, as he wanted to clarify Aristotle's basic claims to a beginner in philosophy like Chrysaorius. He probably discussed these implications and the possible objections to them in his long commentary on the *Categories*.[248] In this Porphyry possibly discussed also the role of concepts in some detail, which, as has been seen, he considered to be universals strictly speaking. In particular, he may have examined how we use a concept in order to classify a specific substance, as when we use 'animal' to predicate it of an individual. And he may have tried to reconcile the Platonic priority of universals with the Aristotelian view of the priority of individual substances, arguing that words signify in virtue of, or with reference to concepts.[249]

But even if Porphyry discussed all this, it does not change the fact that he perceived Aristotle's work as one which outlines an elementary philosophical theory that forms the beginning of Aristotle's logic and is a prerequisite for understanding the latter.[250] Nor does it change the fact that, as the above analysis has shown, the ontological implications of the work do not contradict Plato's ontology but rather are compatible with it. Porphyry perceived the *Categories* as an important work for students of philosophy, on the grounds that it presents a philosophical theory about language, and apparently, in his view, anyone who studies philosophy must know how language works, if he is to make any progress in philosophy.

The above examination of Porphyry's interpretation of the *Categories* has shown that his defence involved the defence of its ontological implications which he found to be compatible with Plato's ontology, a view which, as has been seen, he also maintains in *Sententia* 42 and in

[248] Cf. Simplicius *In Cat.* 21. 2–21 (50F), 29. 24–30. 15 (51F), 30. 16–31. 21 (52F). See Ebbesen (1990*a*: 146–62); Kotzia (1992: 44–50). In this work Porphyry dealt in detail with previous criticisms of the *Categories*. Dexippus, who sets out to respond to Plotinus' objections (*In Cat.* 5. 2–3), clearly draws from it.

[249] Thus Ebbesen (1990*a*: 143–62). Cf. Simplicius, *In Cat.* 13. 11–18 (48F).

[250] *στοιχειωδέστατον γὰρ τοῦτο καὶ εἰσαγωγικὸν εἰς πάντα τὰ μέρη τῆς φιλοσοφίας τὸ βιβλίον* (This work is a most elementary one, and serves as an introduction to all parts of philosophy); *In Cat.* 56. 28–9. *Ὅτι πρὸς εἰσαγωγικοὺς ἔγραψε τὴν τῶν Κατηγοριῶν στοιχείωσιν, πρὸς δὲ τοὺς ἤδη τελείους < τὰ > Μετὰ τὰ Φυσικά* (Because he wrote the *Categories* as an elementary work for beginning students, while the *Metaphysics* was written for advanced students; *In Cat.* 134. 8–9; Strange's tr.). Cf. *Isag.* 1. 10–16.

his commentary on the *Harmonics*. Let me now summarize Porphyry's view about the relation between Platonic and Aristotelian metaphysics.

As has been seen in section 5.2, in his commentary on Aristotle's *Physics* (120F Smith) Porphyry advanced the view that Plato and Aristotle share a scheme of four causes, the material, the formal, the efficient, and the final one, but Plato additionally assumes the so-called paradigmatic cause, the transcendent Forms, and the organic or instrumental one, that is the instrument by means of which something comes about. Porphyry apparently did not criticize Aristotle for rejecting the transcendent Forms. I have argued that this is because he found them implied in Aristotle as thoughts of the divine Intellect, which is how in his view they also exist in Plato. We have seen that there are four pieces of evidence which suggest this: in *Sententia* 42 and in the passage from his commentary on the *Harmonics* I discussed above, Porphyry implies that the 'ancients' agree in accepting proper intelligible substances, such as the intellect and its thoughts, and that the intellect comprises all intelligibles; in his short commentary on the *Categories* (91. 14–17) Porphyry appears to count as intelligible substances the intellect and its thought, and expresses scepticism about the existence of separate transcendent Forms; finally, Porphyry in his interpretation of the world's coming into being (outlined in his commentary on the *Timaeus*) appears to assume that Plato and Aristotle are unanimous in believing that the Forms are thoughts of the divine Intellect (see section 5. 3).

It turns out that Porphyry considered Plato and Aristotle to agree that the world, like any other material substance, is a composite of matter and Form, but no composition actually took place. In his view, both matter and Form are mere mental abstractions, so the world's body, like the human one, is not an object that becomes alive; rather, it exists in a particular form. Hence any inference about a primordial disorder is misguided. The world, Porphyry argues, has always existed, and is causally dependent on God in the same sense for both Plato and Aristotle. God, as an intellect who does not actually engage in any activity other than thinking, has in him the *logoi* of all kinds of beings, and thinking that it is good for everything to come into being, he has brought about the world's entities by unfolding his thoughts in matter. Given that God has always been good and engaged in thinking, at no moment did creation take place; rather, the world has always existed, being dependent on God, who is its cause. In Porphyry's view, this shows not only that Aristotle's objections to Plato about the cosmogony in *Timaeus* were misplaced, but also that Plato understood the world's coming into being in the same way that Aristotle did (see s. 5. 3, pp. 283–4). Porphyry's interpretation clearly suggests, I think, that he assumed Aristotle's acceptance of transcendent Forms as thoughts (*logoi*) in God's mind, on the grounds that Aristotle's God is an intellect, whose being is identical with thinking and also pure actuality.

Now, the world's coming into being included the coming into being of the Soul and the individual souls. Since for Porphyry the world, both intelligible and sensible, has always existed, all individual souls have always existed in some form.[251] As has been seen, Porphyry maintains that the individual souls are powers (*dynameis*) derivative from the transcendent soul, which means that they have always existed in the latter (cf. *Sent.* 37, pp. 44. 16–45. 1 Lamberz). This is analogous to the world's coming into being through the flow of *logoi* from God's mind. In both cases a lower *hypostasis* emanates from the higher one without the latter actually doing anything. As regards the individual soul, Porphyry follows Numenius and Plotinus in identifying this with intellect. The evidence from his treatise *Against Boethus* suggests that Porphyry regarded Aristotle as following Plato in maintaining the immortality of the soul in that Aristotle had propounded the immortality of the intellect, which for Porphyry is essentially the soul. This suggestion underlies the belief that Aristotle refers to individual intellect in *De anima* 3. 5, a view that Alexander rejected. As for the rest of the soul, the so-called *empsychia*, Porphyry approved of Aristotle's view that it is the *entelecheia* of the living body, and as such it cannot subsist by itself. Further, following a long tradition of Platonists, Porphyry agreed with Aristotle that the soul operates within the body through faculties.

Clearly, though, Aristotle denies the existence of the transcendent soul, and there is no evidence to show what Porphyry's position was on this. As I have suggested, we have reasons to believe that he considered Aristotle's divine intellect to correspond to the transcendent soul. This is a possibility because, as far as we know, Porphyry did not consider the divine intellect to be a *hypostasis* clearly distinct from the Soul, but he often designated it 'hypercosmic soul' (Prolcus, *In Tim.* 1. 306. 31–307. 14). Presumably for him Aristotle's active intellect is the principle

[251] One of the arguments against the immortality of the soul advanced by the interlocutor of Justin Martyr is that the soul cannot possibly be immortal, since it is part of the world which had a beginning, which means that the souls also had a beginning (*Dialogue with Trypho* 5). But for Porphyry, as for many other Platonists, the world did not have a beginning, and thus souls have also always existed.

accounting for all individual intellects; and as we have seen, for Porphyry individual souls are essentially intellects.

As I have argued in section 6.2, Porphyry believed that the relationship between transcendent and embodied soul is analogous to that between transcendent and immanent Forms; as the transcendent Forms account for the immanent ones, so the transcendent Soul accounts for the individual souls. Besides, Porphyry defends the ontological implications of Aristotle's *Categories*, arguing that Aristotle's immanent Forms are *ousiai*, as they are also in Plato, not qualities or properties, as Plotinus had argued. This seems to be a crucial divergence from Plotinus, which shapes Porphyry's view about the relation between Platonic and Aristotelian ontology. This point has not been fully appreciated. Porphyry deviates from Plotinus' view that only the transcendent *hypostases* are *ousiai*, while the entities derivative from them are not. Nor does he hold that the former simply give rise to the latter; rather, he holds that the former exist also in the immanent entities, that is, the same entity exists in both realms in different ways, as the shape of a seal exists in the seal and on what is sealed. Individual souls and immanent Forms are versions of the Soul and the transcendent Forms respectively, and in this sense are *ousiai*. They may be derivative *ousiai*, or essential qualities (οὐσιώδεις ποιότητες), but not simply qualities, as Plotinus had argued. This makes a considerable difference in one's perception of Aristotle's ontology, because one can claim that Aristotle's candidate for *ousia*, the immanent Forms, is correct. But this rests on the assumption which we have detected in Porphyry that Aristotle's Forms are a version of a transcendent entity, the *logoi* in the divine mind, in which case they are like Plato's Forms.

If I am right about this, then Porphyry possibly maintained that Aristotle, like Plotinus, retains a hierarchy of substances. This is quite likely given that such a classification of substances is found in Dexippus' commentary on the *Categories* (41. 7–18) which draws heavily on Porphyry.[252] When discussing Plotinus' objection to the *Categories* that substance does not signify the same thing in the case of the intelligible and sensible beings (ibid. 40. 12–13), Dexippus' answer is twofold: first, that Aristotle's treatise deals with significant words, which is Porphyry's answer; secondly, that Aristotle, like Plotinus, subsumes

[252] Dillon (1990: 75) has discussed the passage in a learned note, arguing that Dexippus relies on Iamblichus here. But this does not exclude Porphyry's influence, since Iamblichus drew much on Porphyry.

the multiplicity of substances under Substance, which is the God of *Metaphysics* 12 (*Cat.* 40. 13–42. 12). That is, Dexippus and his source relate Aristotle's division in unmoved substance, sensible corruptible substance, and sensible eternal one (*Met.* $1069^a30–^b2$, $1071^b3–6$) to Plotinus' division between intelligible, physical, and sensible, and show them to be in accord. If Porphyry is Dexippus' source, as Pierre Hadot has argued,[253] then Porphyry appears to believe that Aristotle assumes a hierarchy of substances similar to that of Plotinus, at the top of which lies the One. In this view Aristotle resembles Plotinus in founding being in general, including sensible substances, on intelligible beings.

This idea finds some support in the fact that Philoponus and Olympiodorus draw attention to Aristotle's remark at *Met.* 12, 1076^a4 arguing that the aim of Aristotelian philosophy is to establish that there is only one principle.[254] And they make clear that this is not the sole principle that explains the world's coming into being, but the only principle in a more specific theological sense. Such a remark may well reflect Porphyry's idea about Aristotle's philosophy, especially if he did not distinguish sharply between the One and the Intellect, as is sometimes reported.[255]

There are surely many points in need of clarification in such a picture. Yet if this reconstruction is right, Porphyry would find Aristotle subscribing to Plato's metaphysics almost completely. I say 'almost' because we do not need to assume that Porphyry was blind to all Aristotelian discrepancies from Plato, but that he did consider Aristotle as agreeing essentially with Plato despite such discrepancies.

9. CONCLUDING REMARKS

The examination of the evidence has shown, I hope, that nowhere does Porphryry criticize Aristotle, but that he considers him to have agreed with Plato in all crucial philosophical issues in physics, psychology, ethics, and metaphysics. As has been seen, however, Porphyry did not

253 Hadot (1990).

254 Cf. Philoponus, *In Cat.* 5. 34–6. 2; Olympiodorus, *Proleg.* 9. 14–30; Elias, *In Cat.* 119. 30–120. 12.

255 See *Sent.* 43; *Hist. Philos.* in Cyril, *Contra Iul.* 1. 32cd (223F); Damascius, *In Princ.* 86. 8–15 Ruelle (367F). See Hadot (1965: 131–2, 146–7); Lloyd (1967: 287–93); Dillon (1992: 357–8) expresses his reservations that this was Porphyry's position, but he mostly relies on the Anonymous commentary on the *Parmenides* which is not certainly Porphyrian.

deny that Aristotle sometimes contradicted Plato. What he denied was that these contradictions undermine their essential accord. In Porphyry's view, most of Aristotle's disagreements with Plato can be reduced either to difference in perspective, or to Aristotle's misunderstandings of Plato, or to misunderstandings of Aristotle by later interpreters.

The latter applies to Aristotle's theory of categories. Porphyry argues against earlier Platonists, including Plotinus, that Aristotle in the *Categories* deals with logic, not with ontology, and this is why he does not discuss intelligible beings and does not prioritize universals of the kind that the transcendent Forms are. Further, Porphyry appears to maintain that sometimes Aristotle's opposition to Plato does not necessarily suggest that Aristotle actually departs from Plato's view. The evidence from Porphyry's commentary on Ptolemy's *Harmonics* has shown that Porphyry may consider both views to be right, reducing their difference to difference in perspective. In this way Porphyry attempts to square Plato's explanation of pitch with that of Aristotle in his commentary on Ptolemy's *Harmonics*.

Porphyry examines also the possibility that Aristotle misunderstood Plato but in fact agrees with him. This is according to Porphyry the case with the world's coming into being. For Porphyry, Aristotle's criticism of the world's coming into being in the *Timaeus* results from Aristotle's misunderstanding of Plato, while Plato had meant this in the same way as Aristotle did. Other cases of Aristotle's misunderstanding of Plato according to Porphyry possibly include Aristotle's criticism of the tripartition of the soul, of learning as recollection, and of the existence of Forms. I have argued that Porphyry's practice was anticipated by Taurus who seems to have distinguished between actual and alleged doctrinal conflict due to Aristotle's misinterpretation of Plato.[256]

Finally, there are instances in which Porphyry seems to have disagreed with Aristotle and considered him wrong. This is clearly the case with Aristotle's theory of the aether. Even then, though, Porphyry does not seem to criticize Aristotle. Absolute certainty is impossible here, because we rely on reports from later sources, not on Porphyry's own testimony. But it is significant that we hear of no criticism, although Porphyry is cited by sources hostile to Aristotle like Philoponus. Presumably for Porphyry these instances were not important enough to undermine Aristotle's essential accord with Plato.

[256] In Philoponus, *De aet. mundi* 145. 15–147. 25. See pp. 180–4.

The evidence shows that Porphyry did not compromise his Platonism by adopting Aristotle's views. As a matter of fact, he did not distance himself substantially from Plotinus, either. Porphyry largely adopts Plotinus' interpretations of Plato in ontology, cosmology, psychology, and theology, but modifies them in some important respects which I have outlined in this chapter. Such differences play a crucial role in shaping Porphyry's belief in Aristotle's adherence to Plato's most important doctrines.

For Porphyry, the question was not simply whether Aristotle agrees with or contradicts Plato, since he thought that both are true to some extent. In his view one crucial question was how to use Aristotle with profit, given the wealth of Platonic material that he preserves and the extent in which he agrees with Plato, *malgré lui*. It was the view that Aristotle's work is valuable for Platonists which motivated Porphyry to undertake his bulky exegetical work on Aristotle. I shall argue that Porphyry was the first Platonist to write commentaries on Aristotle's works.[257] Platonists did write on Aristotle's works, mainly the *Categories*, before Porphyry, but nothing in the extant evidence suggests that they wrote commentaries as he did. This is because nobody had developed a view about Aristotle of the kind I have ascribed to Porphyry.

By 'commentary' here, I refer to the exegetical treatise which aims to expound the entire work of an ancient authority or, at least, a very substantial part thereof, proceeding line-by-line on the source text. Examples of such commentaries are those of Aristarchus on Homer, of Galen on Hippocratic works, of Alexander, Porphyry, or Simplicius on Plato or Aristotle. This is a specific kind of exegetical work among the many which can be indicated by the Greek term for commentary (ὑπόμνημα).[258] An author of *hypomnêma* is not necessarily one of a commentary in the sense specified above. Similarly the term ἐξηγητής attributed to early commentators of Aristotle's works,[259] or to any other commentators, does not necessarily suggest authorship of such commentaries. Indeed, there are many possibilities here, too. References to X's views on a question discussed by Plato or Aristotle should not imply

[257] Not just the first Neoplatonist one, as is commonly thought. This was argued already by Praechter (1922: 182) and is still maintained; see Sorabji (1990: 17); D'Ancona-Costa (2002: 213–15).

[258] Sense II. 5c in LSJ. Other possibilities include an exegetical monograph, like Plutarch's work *De animae procreatione in Timaeo* or a collection of notes. Originally the term *hymomnêma* means 'treatise' (see LSJ, s.v. sense II. 5). See Karamanolis (2004b: 92–3).

[259] e.g. Simplicius, *In Cat.* 159. 31–4.

more than a comment on it in passing.[260] Yet such views may well take the form of a monograph. Plutarch, for instance, qualifies as commentator (ἐξηγητής) of the *Timaeus* on the basis of his *De animae procreatione in Timaeo*.[261]

Now we have reasons to believe that no Platonist before Porphyry wrote commentaries in this sense.[262] One such reason has to do with the nature of the running commentary, which is analysable in two main features. The first is its didactic character. The commentary aims to elucidate to students an authoritative text. The commentator assumes the role of the teacher, and the commentary becomes his instrument for teaching.[263] The object of teaching is the main doctrine of the source text, which the commentator seeks to elucidate. This is why he regularly sets out to clarify the author's aim or subject matter (*skopos*). In order to do that, the commentator strives for the best possible interpretation of the author's argument. But, to pass to the second main feature of the commentary, this presupposes the commentator's commitment to the authority of the source text. It is actually this commitment that motivated the teaching of it with a commentary in the first place. The commentator meant not only to expound the source text, but also, and I would say primarily, to recommend it to the students as philosophically valuable.

If this is so, there is no point in writing a commentary on a text marred with faults. Who would want to teach a text considered useless? Figures like the Stoics Athenodorus and Cornutus, or the Platonists Eudorus, Lucius, Nicostratus, or Atticus cannot be authors of commentaries, because they strongly criticized Aristotle for serious mistakes in his central doctrine of the *Categories* but also in points of detail. While the author of a commentary typically took issue with alternative interpretations, which may diminish or destroy the value of the source text, these figures did quite the opposite; their aim was to demolish Aristotle's

260 See Blumenthal (1974).

261 Sedley (1997: 114 n. 11) seems to think that ἐξηγητής suggests an author of a commentary and considers Crantor as such. But the interpretation of Plato took many forms in antiquity and that of the commentary became popular only in late antiquity.

262 This is probably the case also with the Platonic dialogues; they commented on the part which interested them most, and perhaps Porphyry was the first to practise detailed exegesis of Plato's texts. See Dillon (1973: 54–7). Göransson (1995: 57–60) argues against this view.

263 Ancient philosophical commentaries contain plenty of evidence suggesting their connection with teaching; see e.g. Alexander, *In An. Pr.* 1. 8–9; Simplicius, *In Cat.* 3. 18–19. See further Plezia (1949: 9–30). On the didactic character of ancient commentaries see also Sluiter (1999: 187–200).

doctrine. Lucius and Nicostratus, we are told, used strong language in criticizing Aristotle's doctrine (Simplicius, *In Cat.* 1. 18–2. 1), while Atticus was outright polemical, arguing for the uselessness of the *Categories* and of Aristotle's philosophy as a whole.[264] Besides, these figures show a limited interest in, and knowledge of, the *Categories*. They repeat similar objections, such as that regarding Aristotle's doctrine of homonymy. This limited interest again suggests the polemical character of their enterprise.

If we now look at the existing evidence, nothing in it suggests any of these philosophers wrote a commentary, however short, on Aristotle's *Categories*. Quite the opposite is the case. As regards the Stoics critics of the *Categories* Athenodorus and Cornutus, we know with certainty that they wrote treatises.[265] As for the Platonists, although the evidence is inconclusive as regards the form in which they made their criticisms of Aristotle's *Categories*, Simplicius who reports on them distinguishes between the critical comments (ἀπορίαι) of Lucius and Nicostratus, Plotinus' discussion (ἐξέτασις) in *Enneads* 6. 1–3, and the commentaries of Porphyry and Iamblichus (ἐξήγησις ἐντελῆς; *In Cat.* 1. 18–2. 10). The rest of the evidence corroborates this picture. All we have from Eudorus' objections to the *Categories*, for instance, is eight short citations from Simplicius, but we do not hear of a title of a treatise.[266] Similar is the case with the evidence about the objections of Lucius and Nicostratus.[267]

As regards those Platonists before Porphyry who approved of Aristotle's doctrines, none of them is attested to have written commentaries. Plutarch wrote on the *Categories*, but we learn that this was a *dialexis*, a discourse, most probably a monograph (no. 92 in Lamprias's catalogue).

[264] Gioè (2002: 119–209) has collected, translated, and commented on the fragments of Lucius and Nicostratus. Despite what Des Places assumes, Atticus is a very unlikely candidate for a commentator in this sense (cf. frs. 41–42b = Simplicius, *In Cat.* 30. 16–17, 32. 19–21, Porphyry, *In Cat.* 66. 34–67. 2). See Gottschalk (1990: 79–80). I list the Platonist writings on Aristotle's works from the 1st c. BC to 3rd c. AD in Appendix II.

[265] Ἀθηνόδωρος . . . ὁ Στωικὸς βιβλία γράψας πρὸς τὰς Ἀριστοτέλους κατηγορίας, Κορνοῦτός τε ἐν ταῖς Ῥητορικαῖς τέχναις καὶ ἐν τῇ πρὸς Ἀθηνόδωρον ἀντιγραφῇ (Athenodorus . . . the Stoic wrote books against Aristotle's *Categories*, and also Cornutes in his *Rhetorical art* and in his reply to Athenodorus; Porphyry, *In Cat.* 86. 22–4; cf. Simplicius, *In Cat.* 62. 25–8). Cornutus apparently argued against Athenodorus' interpretation of Aristotle. See Moraux (1984: 587–601).

[266] Eudorus' fragments have been collected by Mazzarelli (1985). See my discussion in Ch. 1, pp. 82–4. Praechter (1922: 510–11) and Moraux (1973: 520) argue that Eudorus is unlikely to have written a commentary of any kind. See also Dillon (1977: 133–4) and Gioè (2002: 144, 152).

[267] See the collection of the evidence in Gioè (2002).

For Antiochus and Taurus there is no evidence that they ever wrote a commentary on any Aristotelian treatise. The only commentaries from non-Peripatetics until Porphyry are Galen's, but since they are lost we do not know how extended they were. And, at any rate, Galen is not a Platonist philosopher strictly speaking. Porphyry, then, most probably was the first Platonist to write full commentaries on Aristotle, and this is because he maintained that Aristotle's philosophy is compatible with and complementary to Plato's. It is because Porphyry took this view that he wrote commentaries on Aristotle in a systematic way.

There is something else which makes this hypothesis probable. One of Porphyry's innovative ideas was that Aristotle explored areas which Plato had not systematically investigated, most importantly, logic. As I have said, Porphyry first had to show that Aristotle does not really contradict Plato's ontology. Once this was granted, Porphyry's implication was that a Platonist can and actually should study Aristotle's work. This may not be Platonic philosophy strictly speaking, that is, an articulation of Plato's views, but it nevertheless is a philosophical theory worth studying on its own merits. One can say that it still is philosophy written in the spirit of Plato, or even inspired by Plato, but for Porphyry this philosophy is not Plato's. No matter how much Plato anticipated Aristotle' logic, one should recognize that Aristotle expounds a complex philosophical theory of his own, and this is what Porphyry urges his fellow Platonists to do. It is not accidental that in Porphyry there is almost no trace of the kind of argument favoured by earlier Platonists, that this or the other Aristotelian theory is foreshadowed in Plato.[268] This is, I think, because for Porphyry the issue rather was the correct appreciation of Aristotle's logic on its own terms, and this, in his view, was philosophically both demanding and beneficial. It is also this view, I think, which motivates Porphyry to write commentaries on Aristotle.

A broader understanding of philosophizing emerges. For Porphyry, to do philosophy did not solely amount to studying Plato but also to studying Aristotle, who now becomes an authority in some philosophical areas. His aim may still be the understanding of Plato's doctrine, while Aristotle's philosophy remains instrumental, as it had been for earlier generations of Platonists. But Porphyry legitimizes this by show-

[268] Zambon (2002: 321–3) argues for a similar position. Porphyry notices Plato's anticipation of Aristotle's definition of relation (*In Cat.* 111. 27–9), as Boethus had already done, but this concerns one small point, not Aristotle's general doctrine.

ing how important Aristotle's philosophy is, and by doing this, he does not see himself as being disloyal to Plato.

There is a question as to what the main source of Porphyry's inspiration in this direction was. Theiler argued that Porphyry was probably inspired by Ammonius Saccas.[269] This to some extent may be true. There are several similarities between the two. Like Ammonius, Porphyry maintains the accord between Plato and Aristotle primarily in metaphysics. They presumably shared the belief that the two ancients had maintained that the Forms are thoughts in the divine mind. As we have seen, Porphyry very probably took this view, and Ammonius is also likely to have espoused it. Besides, Porphyry appears to share Ammonius' characteristic focus on the main doctrine (*ἡ γνώμη*) or the purpose (*ὁ σκοπός, τὸ βούλημα*) of an ancient authority. We have seen that Porphyry dismissed some of Aristotle's objections to focus on his main philosophical point, and he also appears to have been seeking Plato's view behind the text.[270]

Undoubtedly, Porphyry was considerably indebted also to Plotinus in his study of Aristotle, as he was in his study of Plato. We have good reasons to believe that Plotinus discussed with his students Aristotle's works in his seminar and commented on them (*V. Plot.* 14). Presumably Porphyry considered himself as continuing on the same track when he set out to write commentaries on Aristotle's works. This for him was a rather small step ahead from Plotinus' practice, and it may well be the case that some of these commentaries were prepared for former disciples of Plotinus.[271] This speaks against a distinction between a Platonic and an Aristotelian period in Porphyry's scholarly life. His Aristotelian commentaries may come from his last period of life, in which he may also have written some of his Platonic commentaries.[272] If this is the case, his interpretations of Plato and Aristotle examined in this chapter represent his mature views.

Yet, while for Plato Porphyry could rely on a rich Platonist exegetical tradition, there was no such tradition among Platonists as far as Aristotle's work was concerned. Instead, Porphyry stood against a tradition

[269] Theiler (1965*b*). Zambon (2002) has examined in depth Porphyry's relation with earlier Platonists except for Ammonius Saccas.

[270] Cf. Ammonius in Hierocles in Photius *Bibl.* cod. 214, 172a8–9, (cf. Ch. 5, pp. 200–7); Porphyry in Stobaeus 2. 167. 19–20 (270F. 1–2), Stobaeus 2. 169. 21–22 (271F. 39). Porphyry appears to have applied this method also in his study of Homer; *De antro nymph.* p. 21. 31 Westerink *et al.*

[271] See Saffrey (1992: 42–3).

[272] On the dating of Porphyry's works see Zambon (2002: 31–4).

of Platonists from Eudorus to Atticus who were critical of Aristotle and disputed his Platonism. Porphyry's exegetical work on Aristotle manifests that he relied on the Peripatetic exegetical tradition from Andronicus to Alexander in his attempt to expound Aristotle's work to Platonists. In doing this, Porphyry followed his master Plotinus, who also had taken the Peripatetic commentators seriously into account. Yet Porphyry's point of view was different from that of Plotinus; while Plotinus had meant to defend Platonic philosophy by exposing the weaknesses of the Aristotelian one, Porphyry sought to show their essential agreement, despite Aristotle's occasional mistakes.

Porphyry's position on Aristotle's philosophy had an enormous impact on the later Platonist tradition, and contributed to the shaping of the new philosophical framework I described in the beginning of this book. This was acknowledged already in antiquity. Later Platonists regarded him as the authority on Aristotelian exegesis (e.g. Simpl. *In Cat.* 2. 5–6). Iamblichus (*c.* 242–325), Porphyry's younger contemporary and perhaps his student, also contributed considerably to the setting of this framework. We know that he considered the writings of both Plato and Aristotle to be full of Pythagorean philosophy.[273] It is difficult to compare Porphyry's contribution on the formation of the new framework with that of Iamblichus, and at any rate I am not in a position to do it. We know, though, that Iamblichus himself followed Porphyry. His commentary on the *Categories* was modelled on the one of Porphyry (Simpl. *In Cat.* 2. 9), and perhaps he was inspired by Porphyry in other works too. This is indicative of Porphyry's influence on his contemporaries.

From the next generation on, Platonists take up the views of Porphyry and Iamblichus as starting points and for the most part they dispense with the previous tradition. This is clearly the case already with Dexippus (fl. *c.*330), and becomes even clearer with Philoponus and Simplicius. It would require a separate study to show this in detail, but in this chapter I have often alluded to the fact that the views of Simplicius and the early Philoponus in physics, cosmology, and psychology correspond to those of Porphyry. Simplicius in particular relies on Porphryry most closely when claiming that Aristotle agrees with Plato, if one understands Platonic and Aristotelian views correctly (see Introduction p. 3 n. 7).

These Platonists who came to regard Aristotle as an authority next to Plato were no less Platonists for that, nor did they try to make a

273 See Larsen (1974: esp. 6–9, 20–5) and O'Meara (1989: 68–9, 96–105).

synthesis of the two. They rather studied Aristotle because they considered him instrumental to understanding Plato, either because Aristotle presents Plato's doctrines, or because he expounds philosophical theories compatible with those of Plato, which were valuable for the Platonists. This is manifested in the fact that Plato is named as the authority in metaphysics, and Aristotle in logic;[274] since for Platonists metaphysics is the summit of philosophy, Plato's authority in it amounts to his indisputable primacy.

It is this understanding of philosophizing which lies behind the formation of the Platonist syllabus I described in the beginning of this book. This remains the situation until the Renaissance. When Renaissance humanists revive ancient philosophy, especially Platonism, as happened in Renaissance Florence, they re-establish this very model. Few other shifts in the history of Western philosophy are of such significance as the one which we, quite rightly, attribute to Porphyry.

[274] Aristotle's primacy in logic becomes evident in statements like the following: *συλλογισμοῖς μέν καὶ ἄλλοι πρὸ τοῦ Ἀριστοτέλους ἐχρήσατο, ὥσπερ οὖν καὶ Πλάτων καὶ... ἄλλοι πλεῖστοι... οὐδεὶς μέντοι πρὸ τοῦ Ἀριστοτέλους παραδέδωκεν τὴν συλλογιστικὴν μέθοδον* (syllogisms were used by philosophers earlier than Aristotle, like Plato and... many others,... but no one before Aristotle did transmit the syllogistic method; Ammonius, *In An. Pr.* 7. 6–10). Platonists now turn out to agree with Peripatetics like Alexander who argued that Plato had used syllogisms but it was Aristotle who founded logic (Alexander, *In An. Pr.* 22. 7–9).

APPENDIX I

The Platonism of Aristotle and of the Early Peripatetics

In this section I have two aims. First, I will argue that Antiochus' belief that Aristotle and his school revered Plato's philosophy and were inspired by it has a historical foundation—although, as I stressed in Chapter 1, this in itself hardly justifies the use of Aristotle for the reconstruction of Plato's doctrines. Secondly, I will argue that some early Peripatetics had views on how the two philosophies compare.

As I said in the Introduction, Plato did not impose any interpretation of his work or any other kind of doctrinal unity on the basis of which Academic loyalty was judged.[1] We know that Academics often disagreed with views considered as Plato's. Most conspicuously, Speusippus, whom Plato appointed as his successor in the Academy, rejected the Forms in favour of mathematical entities.[2] Eudoxus on the other hand, who probably was appointed acting head of the Academy while Plato was in Sicily (367–365 BC; *Vita Marciana* 11), identified man's highest good with pleasure (*NE* 1172^{b}9–25; cf. 1101^{b}27–32), a view to which Plato objected (*NE* 1172^{b}28–31) most clearly in the *Philebus* (20e–22b, 60a–c).[3] Unlike Eudoxus, and perhaps opposing him, Speusippus distinguished sharply between pleasure and good,[4] while Aristotle specified his own position distancing himself equally from both Academics' views.[5]

Like other Academics, Aristotle was not expected to hold the same views as Plato. The fact that he developed positions different from, or even critical of, Plato's, did not make him less of a Platonist. On the contrary, Aristotle may well have seen himself as remaining faithful to Plato's spirit of philosophical inquiry, which arguably was the essential element of Academic membership. In fact, Aristotle is much nearer to Plato in spirit, and increasingly so as he progresses in his career, than the early Academics.[6] His decision to have his own circle of students may have been motivated by his different ideas about how Plato's

[1] The lack of doctrinal unity in the Academy has been emphasized by Cherniss (1945: 65–85).

[2] Cf. *Met.* 1069^{a}33–5, 1076^{a}19–22, 1083^{a}20–1.

[3] On Eudoxus (*c.* 395–342) and his relations with Plato and his Academy see F. Lasserre, *Die Fragmente des Eudoxos von Knidos* (Berlin, 1966), 137–47.

[4] See *NE* 1152^{b}8–10, 1153^{b}1–9; cf. *Philebus* 60a–c. See now Dillon (2003), 64–77.

[5] In *NE* 7, 10. Other issues on which Academics had diverse views include the theory of Forms and the nature of the human soul. See Cherniss (1945: 73–83) and Dillon (1977: 12–30).

[6] This has been argued convincingly by Owen (1986).

philosophy was to be continued. We know that Aristotle disagreed with the views of Speusippus and Xenocrates.[7] Perhaps he also disliked their efforts to systematize Plato's philosophy, which changed considerably the intellectual climate in the Academy. It is tempting to surmise that it was in reaction against this climate that Aristotle decided to have his own students[8] when he came back to Athens from Macedonia (in 335).[9]

Actually several Academics also had their own circles of students, notably Eudoxus (DL 8. 87, 89), Heraclides of Pontus, and Menedemus (*Index Acad.* col. VII Dorandi). Heraclides is a particularly interesting case in this regard. Initially a member of the Academy and admirer of Plato's works (DL 5. 86), Heraclides left the Academy when he was narrowly defeated by Xenocrates in the contest for the scholarchate (*c.* 339; *Index Acad.* col. VII Dorandi; fr. 9Wehrli). For some years he had his own pupils, but later joined Aristotle's circle.[10] Besides, Aristotle himself had had a circle of students already in Mieza in Macedonia (Plutarch, *Alexander* 7. 3–4) before he did the same in Athens. Two conclusions seem to emerge from this evidence. First, teaching a community of people, as Aristotle did, does not necessarily indicate a reaction to Plato; on the contrary it was a rather usual practice for eminent Academics. Second, Heraclides' attitude suggests that entering Aristotle's circle did not amount to distancing oneself from Plato's philosophical spirit, but rather to departing from the Academy of his successors. Other Peripatetics had a similar attitude. Theophrastus, for instance, also seems to have distinguished between Plato's work, which he appreciated (he wrote an epitome of the *Republic*; DL 5. 43), and that of the Academics, whom, like Aristotle, he criticized in works such as his *Πρὸς τοὺς ἐξ Ἀκαδημείας α´* (DL 5. 49).[11]

The only report which claims that Aristotle started his own school with the aim to oppose Plato comes from a man of manifestly aggressive temperament and as such quite unreliable. This is Aristotle's student Aristoxenus, who, as has been seen (Introd., s. 4, pp. 40–1), argued that Aristotle had founded the Lyceum while Plato was still alive in a spirit of spitefulness against him.[12] Being himself a

[7] Aristotle criticized Speusippus and Xenocrates in a special work (DL 5. 25). Cf. *Met.* 1028^{b}18–24, 1072^{b}30–4, 1083^{a}20–31, 1091^{a}31–^{b}1; *NE* 1153^{b}1–6, 1173^{a}5–13; *De anima* 404^{b}27–30, 409^{a}25–30; *De caelo* 279^{b}32–280^{a}5.

[8] Yet Aristotle did not found a school strictly speaking, since he was debarred by law from possessing property (no school is mentioned in his will; DL 5. 11–16). A school in this sense started life with Theophrastus, Aristotle's appointed successor (Gellius *NA* 13. 5), who bought property (DL 5. 39) in order to establish the Peripatetic school. See Brink (1940: 905); Lynch (1972: 95–105).

[9] At the time Xenocrates was head of the Academy (DL 5. 2). See Jaeger (1948: 311–16).

[10] Heraclides does not seem to have founded a school of his own. See Gottschalk (1980: 2–5).

[11] According to one tradition, Theophrastus also moved from Plato's school to Aristotle (DL 3. 46, 5. 36).

[12] Aristocles apud Eusebium *PE* 15. 2. 3 (Aristocles fr. 2. 20–6H; 2. 3 Ch) *Vita Marciana* 9, 25 (frs. 64–65bW).

Pythagorean,[13] Aristoxenus was generally hostile to Plato in favour of Pythagoras (frs. 61–68W).[14] He showed bitterness also against Socrates (frs. 51–60W) and even against Aristotle; he is attested to have insulted Aristotle's memory when he was not appointed head of the Lyceum (fr. 1W). Aristoxenus' claim about Aristotle's departure from Plato's school apparently was meant to suggest that Plato was not worthy of respect and to praise Aristotle for leaving his school. Given its polemical purpose, Aristoxenus' view lacks credibility and already in antiquity was distrusted; the historian Philochorus (*c.* 340–260) argued that it was a fabrication.[15]

Aristoxenus was an exception among early Peripatetics. They, following the example of Aristotle himself,[16] generally showed as great respect for Plato as the Academics and were inspired by Plato's philosophy as much as the Academics were. In this sense, early Peripatetics were as much Platonist as the Academics. And although some of them appear to be more attached to Plato's work, all of them show quite some interest in it.

To begin with, Peripatetics often write on Plato's works in the same way that Academics do. The *Republic* was particularly popular. Theophrastus, Clearchus, and Eudemus studied it,[17] as the Academics did (see e.g. *Suda*, s.v. Xenocrates). The same was the case with other works of Plato. Both Academics and Peripatetics show zeal in studying the *Timaeus*, which was particularly interesting for the latter, given their strong interest in natural philosophy. Aristotle was much concerned with it,[18] Clearchus addressed questions arising from it, which the Academic Crantor also discussed (Plutarch, *De an. procr.* 1022c–d; fr. 4W), and Eudemus also commented on the dialogue (ibid. 1015D; fr. 49W). Inspired by Plato's dialogues, early Academics and Peripatetics discuss the same philosophical issues. Pleasure was one such issue. We know of a series of writings on pleasure, by Speusippus (DL 4. 4), Xenocrates (DL 4. 12), Aristotle (DL 5. 24), Heraclides, (frs. 55–61W), Philip of Opus (*Suda*, s.v. *philosophos*), Theophrastus (DL 5. 44), and also Strato (DL 5. 52) and Chamaeleon (frs. 8–9W). Plato's dialogues on friendship (*Lysis*) and its special form, erotic love (*Phaedrus* and *Symposion*), also triggered much discussion among

13 Aristoxenus' work included a *Life of Pythagoras* (fr. 11W), *On the Pythagorean Life* (frs. 26–32W), *Pythagorean Decrees* (frs. 33–41W).

14 Aristoxenus accused Plato of plagiarizing Protagoras for his *Republic* and an early Pythagorean source for his *Timaeus* (Gellius, *NA* 3. 17. 4). His hostility is manifested in his report that Plato wished to burn all of Democritus' writings after he had plagiarized them (DL 9. 40; fr. 131W).

15 Cf. Jacoby *Fragm. Hist. Gr.* 328 F 223. Aristoxenus is also refuted by Diogenes Alic. *Ad Ammaeum* 7. 733; cf. Düring (1957: 256–9). Later sources which present Aristotle as being motivated by hostility to Plato (e.g. Origen, *C. Celsum* 2. 12; Aelian, *Var. Hist.* 4. 19; DL 5. 2) draw on Aristoxenus or intermediary sources.

16 Cf. *NE* 1096^{a}12–17 and his epigram to Plato (Ross, *Arist. Fragm. Sel.* p. 146).

17 DL 5. 43; Athenaeus 9. 393a; Clearchus fr. 3W. For Eudemus see below.

18 Bonitz's *Index Aristotelicus* lists more than forty references to the *Timaeus*; Cherniss (1945: 71–2) highlights the importance of this dialogue for Aristotle.

Academics and Peripatetics.[19] Other issues included the nature of the soul, justice, and the eternity of the world as described in the *Timaeus*. Clearly, there was hardly any unanimity on these matters, but it is wrong to believe that the disagreement was polarized between early Academics and Peripatetics as groups. Rather, different views were in circulation which were inspired by different Platonic dialogues and were competing with each other within and between both groups. The fact that so many writings were composed and several interpretations were in circulation shows that there was no authoritative line associated specifically with Plato.

Like Academics, early Peripatetics often expressed their approval of Plato's philosophy. Eudemus showed much appreciation of Plato's mathematics,[20] asserting Plato's superiority over his predecessors (Simpl. *In Phys*. 7. 10–11, fr. 31W; cf. frs. 35–7W). As Simplicius' excerpts show, Eudemus quite generally acknowledged Plato's pioneering work in philosophy, most especially in physics and metaphysics. Quite noticeably Eudemus employs Aristotelian terminology in his descriptions of Plato's teaching. He argues, for instance, that Plato was the first to distinguish the efficient, final, and paradigmatic cause (i.e. the Forms),[21] between potential and actual, and between accidental and essential (Simpl. *In Phys*. 242. 28–9; fr. 37bW). Such evidence suggests that Eudemus regarded these Aristotelian doctrines as an expansion and systematization of Plato's teaching. In view of Simplicius' stance towards Aristotle, we may want to be cautious about his testimony regarding Eudemus. Yet we also have the report of Proclus, who was rather critical of Peripatetics. Besides, views similar to those ascribed to Eudemus are attested also for other Peripatetics.

In Clearchus of Soloi we encounter not only appreciation and approval of Plato's work, but also admiration of Plato. He wrote a *Eulogy of Plato* (*Πλάτωνος ἐγκώμιον*; DL 3. 2; frs. 2a–bW), like Speusippus (DL 4. 5), but also like Aristotle (Ross, *Arist. Fragm. Sel.* p. 146, fr. 2). Like Eudemus, Clearchus also studied Plato's mathematics and wrote a work on the mathematics of the *Republic*.[22] His approval of Plato's philosophy becomes more manifest in his dialogue *On sleep* (frs. 5–10W), where, being inspired by the *Phaedo* and

[19] Works on friendship (*Περὶ φιλίας*) were written by Speusippus (DL 4. 4), Xenocrates (DL 4. 12), Theophrastus (DL 5. 45), Clearchus (frs. 17–18W), and Philip of Opus (*Suda* s.v. *philosophos*). Aristotle (DL 5. 22), Theophrastus (DL 5. 43), and Heraclides (frs. 64–66W) wrote an *Ἐρωτικός*, Clearchus wrote *Ἐρωτικά* (frs. 21–35W). Heraclides and Clearchus approved of Plato's treatment of the subject, while Dicaearchus was critical (*Tusc. Disp*. 4. 71–2; fr. 43W); see Wehrli (1961: 331–2).

[20] Proclus, *In prim. Eucl. Lib.* p. 64 Friedlein (fr. 133W). It is not certain that this report goes back to Eudemus; see F. Wehrli, *Eudemus von Rhodos* (Basel, 1966), 114–15.

[21] Simplicius, *In Phys*. 7. 10–17 (fr. 31W). Simplicius' presentation makes it unclear whether the whole of this report goes back to Eudemus. If it does, Eudemus would maintain an accord between Plato and Aristotle extending to theology.

[22] *Περὶ τῶν ἐν τῇ Πλάτωνος Πολιτείᾳ μαθηματικῶς εἰρημένων* (Athenaus 9. 393a; fr. 3W).

Republic 10, he argues that the soul is separable from the body, exists separately from it, and uses the body as a shelter.[23] Quite remarkably, the main speaker in this dialogue who maintains these views is Aristotle.[24] Clearchus tells us in this work the story of the resurrection of a man who was able to report what his soul saw after leaving the body.[25] Following Plato's myth of Er in *Republic* 10, Clearchus talks about the judgement of the souls, the punishment of the unjust, and the reward of the just souls (*Rep.* 614c–615c; cf. fr. 10W). Remarkably similar are Heraclides' views, who also maintained the immortality and transmigration of the soul (DL 8 .4; fr. 89W). In his work *Περὶ τῆς ἄπνου* (frs. 76–89W), Heraclides talks about a woman who had been dead for thirty days before Empedocles resurrected her.[26]

Clearchus, Heraclides, and Eudemus seem to have regarded Aristotle's philosophy as being largely in accord with, and as a development of, that of Plato. Nonetheless early Peripatetics were also critical of Platonic views. Dicaearchus, for instance, criticized Plato's dialogues in terms of style and content (frs. 42, 71W), and together with Aristoxenus argued against Plato's teaching that the soul is a separable entity. He maintained that the soul rather is a manifestation of the appropriate functioning of the bodily parts of an organism, and apparently defined the soul as a mixture of the four elements in the body (frs. 8–12W). Aristoxenus followed on, arguing that the soul is a special tuning of the body analogous to musical harmony.[27] But if we set Aristoxenus aside, who, as has been said, was biased against Plato, it is not necessary to detect a spirit of opposition behind other Peripatetic criticisms of Plato. In fact, the evidence speaks against such a view. Dicaearchus showed quite some interest in Plato's personality and work (frs. 40–1W, *Index Acad.* col. II–III Dorandi), which rules out any suspicion of hostility to Plato. Eudemus, too, criticized aspects of the *Timaeus* (fr. 49W), but, as has been seen, he also valued Plato's philosophy. One may argue that Academics never criticized Plato, and in this sense their loyalty to Plato was considerably different. This seems to be true. But the reason behind this may be that, unlike Academics, early Peripatetics, much as they respected Plato, did not bestow on his views in the dialogues an authoritative status, because for them Plato's philosophical spirit consisted primarily in a constant search for the truth. Dicaearchus may have explicitly argued this in his life of Plato.[28] So for the

[23] Proclus, *In Remp.* 2. 122. 22–8 (fr. 7. 1–6W).

[24] Ibid. 2. 122. 6–12.

[25] Ibid. 2. 113. 19–32 (fr. 8W).

[26] DL 8. 60 (fr. 77W). See Gottschalk (1980: 15–33, 98–100).

[27] Cf. frs. 120a–cW. For a discussion of their views on the soul, see Gottschalk (1971).

[28] Dicaearchus is likely to be the source on which Philodemus draws for the composition of his Plato's life, which includes the remark that Plato set problems to his students, especially mathematical ones (*Index Acad.* col. Y Dorandi). Thus Gaiser (1988: 152, 307–44). Dorandi (1991: 207–8) is less certain. If Dicaearchus is the source of the text, then his view on Plato was similar to that of Eudemus on Plato's contribution in mathematics (fr. 133W).

Peripatetics to criticize Plato did not make them less Platonists, just as their disagreements with Aristotle hardly made them less Aristotelians.

Later generations of Peripatetics distanced themselves from Plato's spirit. Strato not only rejected Plato's arguments for the soul's immortality in the *Phaedo*,[29] but also argued that the intellect is mortal and that thinking is as dependent on body as sensing is. This also is the case with later Peripatetics like Andronicus and Boethus (Galen, *Quod animi mores* 4. 782K), which is why Antiochus (*Acad.* 1. 33–4; *De fin.* 5. 12–14) and Plutarch (*Adv. Col.* 1115A–B) distinguish sharply between Aristotle and later Peripatetics. But as the above considerations have shown, Antiochus was not entirely unjustified in regarding Aristotle as a Platonist and the early Peripatos as a Platonist school.[30]

[29] In Olympiodorus, *In Phaed.* 221. 22–228. 12 (frs. 122–7W).

[30] Aristotle is mentioned together with Xenocrates and/or Speusippus also by Plutarch, *De comm. not.* 1069A; *Adv. Col.* 1111D; Boethius, *In de Int.* 24. 15–17; Apuleius, *Florida* 36 calls Theophrastus, Eudemus, and Lyco *Platonici minores.*

APPENDIX II

List of Works of Platonists on Aristotle's Philosophy

I append here a list of the works of Platonists up to the time of Porphyry dealing with Aristotle's philosophy. I divide them into three classes: (*a*) works on the relation between Platonic and Aristotelian philosophy, (*b*) critical works on Aristotle's philosophy, (*c*) exegetical ones. Now, given that often the work in question is lost (e.g. Plutarch's works listed), such a distinction appears to rest on shaky grounds. In the cases of Eudorus, Aristo, Nicostratus, Lucius, we do not even know the title of their works, and for this reason we cannot be certain about their nature. Sometimes even the assumption of the existence of an independent treatise is not entirely justified. Some Platonists may have included some comments on this or the other Aristotelian doctrine in one of their treatises with a Platonist subject matter. The objections to Aristotle's *Categories* by Eudorus and Lucius, for instance, may have been raised in such treatises. Or, to take a different example, we do not know in what form Porphyry made his remarks on Aristotle's ethics, if he did at all. But we do have a picture about the attitude of those Platonists to Aristotelian philosophy and, as I have argued in Ch. 7, s. 9, those who were hostile to Aristotle are very unlikely to have written any kind of exegetical work on an aspect of his philosophy or on an Aristotelian treatise.

The list does not include treatises in which Aristotle's philosophical doctrines do not form the main subject, though they were discussed at some length. Thus I exclude Plotinus' *Enneads* 6. 1–3 because the critical discussion of the Aristotelian as well as the Stoic categories there serves Plotinus' own exposition on the issue of the classes of being. From the first class of works, with the exception of Atticus' fragments, all works in the list are mere titles to us. From the second class, we have only fragments, while from the third one we possess Porphyry's short commentary on the *Categories* and fragments from some of his other exegetical works on Aristotle.

A. Works on the Relation Between Platonic and Aristotelian Philosophy

Atticus, <πρὸς τοὺς διὰ τῶν Ἀριστοτέλους τὰ Πλάτωνος ὑπισχνουμένους> (ap. Eusebium *PE* 11. 1, 15. 4–9, 11–13; frs. 1–9 Des Places).

Calvenus Taurus, *Περὶ τῆς τῶν δογμάτων διαφορᾶς Πλάτωνος καὶ Ἀριστοτέλους* (*Suda*, s.v. Taurus).

Eubulus, *Περὶ τοῦ Φιλήβου καὶ τοῦ Γοργίου καὶ τῶν 'Αριστοτέλει πρὸς τὴν Πλάτωνος Πολιτεία ἀντειρημένων* (*V. Plot.* 20. 42).

Porphyry, *Περὶ τοῦ μίαν εἶναι τὴν Πλάτωνος καὶ 'Αριστοτέλους αἵρεσιν ζ* (*Suda*, s.v. Porphyrius).

Porphyry, *Περὶ διαστάσεως Πλάτωνος καὶ Ἀριστοτέλους < πρὸς Χρυσαόριον >* (Elias, *In Porphyrii Isagogē* 39. 6–7 Busse).

B. Critical Works on Aristotle's Philosophy

Eudorus of Alexandria, on Aristotle's *Categories* (ap. Simplicium, *In Cat.* 159. 32–3, 174. 14–15, and *passim*; see Kalbfleisch's *Index Nominum*, s.v. Eudorus).

Lucius, on Aristotle's *Categories*, (ap. Simplicium, *In Cat.* 1. 19 and *passim*; see Kalbfleisch's *Index Nominum*, s.v. Lucius).

Nicostratus, on Aristotle's *Categories*, (ap. Simplicium, *In Cat.* 1. 20 and *passim*; see Kalbfleisch's *Index Nominum*, s.v. Nicostratus).

C. Exegetical Works on Aristotle's Philosophy

Aristo of Alexandria [*RE* 54], on Aristotle's *Categories* (ap. Simplicium *In Cat.* 159. 32–3, 188. 31–2, 202. 1–2; fragments in Mariotti 1966: 14–16).

Aristo of Alexandria, on Aristotle's *Prior Analytics* (ap. Apuleium *De interpretatione* 193. 16–20 Thomas; fragment in Mariotti 1966: 16–17).

Plutarch, *Περὶ τῆς πέμπτης οὐσίας βιβλία ε΄* (no. 44 in Lamprias catalogue).

Plutarch, *Τῶν Ἀριστοτέλους Τοπικῶν βιβλία η΄* (no. 56 in Lamprias catalogue).

Plutarch, *Διάλεξις περὶ τῶν δέκα Κατηγοριῶν* (no. 192 in Lamprias catalogue).

Porphyry, *Εἰς τὰς Ἀριστοτέλους Κατηγορίας κατὰ πεῦσιν καὶ ἀπόκρισιν*, ed. Busse, *CAG* iv 1.

Porphyry, *Εἰσαγωγή*, ed. Busse, *CAG* iv 1.

Porphyry, < *Εἰς τὰ Ἀριστοτέλους Κατηγορίας* > ἐν ἑπτὰ βιβλίοις (fragments in Smith, 45T–74F).

Porphyry, *In Aristotelis De interpretatione* (fragments in Smith 75T–110T).

Porphyry, *Introductio ad syllogismos categoricos* (i.e. on Aristotle's *Prior Analytics*, ap. Boethium, *De syllogismo categorico* 829D and *passim*; 111T–114T Smith).

Porphyry, *In Aristotelis Sophisticos elenchos* (ap. *Anonymum Aurelianensem II De Paralogismis*; 115F–117F Smith).

Porphyry, *In Aristotelis Physica* (ap. Simplicium, *In Phys.* 9. 10–27 and *passim*; 118T–162T Smith; also in Romano 1985).[1]

Porphyry, on Aristotle's *Metaphysics* 12 (ap. Simplicium, *In De caelo* 503. 22–34. 506. 8–16; 163F–164F Smith).

Porphyry, on Aristotle's ethics (frs. 165F–166F Smith).

[1] A later work in which Aristotle's views are discussed is Proclus' *Ἐπίσκεψις τῶν πρὸς τὸν Πλάτωνα Τίμαιον ὑπ' Ἀριστοτέλους ἀντειρημένων* (ap. Philoponum, *De aet. mundi* 31. 7).

Bibliography

A. Editions, Translations, and Collections of Fragments and Testimonies

ALBINUS

Isagoge in Platonem, ed. C. F. Hermann, *Platonis Dialogi* (Leipzig, 1892), vi. 147–51.

ALCINOUS

Didascalicos, Alcinoos, *Enseignement des doctrines de Platon*, ed. J. Whittaker, tr. P. Louis (Paris, 1990).

Alcinous, The Handbook of Platonism, tr. J. Dillon (Oxford, 1993).

ALEXANDER OF APHRODISIAS

In Aristotelis Metaphysica commentaria, ed. M. Hayduck (CAG i; Berlin, 1891).

In Aristotelis Topicorum libros octo commentaria, ed. M. Wallies (CAG ii/2; Berlin, 1883).

In librum De Sensu commentarium, ed. P. Wendland (CAG iii/1; Berlin, 1901).

De Anima liber cum Mantissa, ed. I. Bruns (CAG suppl. ii/1; Berlin, 1887).

Quaestiones, ed. I. Bruns (CAG Supplement ii/2; Berlin, 1892).

ANONYMUS, *IN THEAETETUM*

Commentarium in Platonis Theaetetum, ed. G. Bastianini and D. Sedley, in *Corpus dei papiri filosofici greci e latini*, iii. *Commentari* (Florence, 1995), 227–562.

ANONYMUS, *IN ETHICA NICOMACHEA*

In Ethica Nicomachea VII, ed. G. Heylbut (CAG xx; Berlin, 1892).

ANTIOCHUS OF ASCALON

Testimonies: *Der Akademiker Antiochos*, ed. G. Luck (Berne and Stuttgart, 1953), 73–94.

'Philon von Larissa und Antiochos von Askalon', ed. H. J. Mette, *Lustrum*, 28/9 (1986/7), 30–55.

ARISTO OF ALEXANDRIA

Testimonies: *Aristone d'Alessandria*, ed. I. Mariotti (Bologna, 1966).

ARISTOCLES

Aristoclis Messenii reliquiae, ed. H. Heiland (Geissen, 1925).
Aristocles of Messene: Testimonies and Fragments, ed. M. L. Chiesara (Oxford, 2001).

APULEIUS

De Platone et eius dogmate, Apulée, Opuscules philosophiques (Du Dieu de Socrate, Platon et sa doctrine, Du monde) et fragments, ed. J. Beaujeu (Paris, 1973).

ARISTOTLE

Aristotelis Ethica Nicomachea, ed. I. Bywater (OCT; Oxford, 1894).
Aristotelis Categoriae et Liber De Interpretatione, ed. L. Minio-Paluello (OCT; Oxford, 1949).
Aristotelis Physica, ed. W. D. Ross (OCT; Oxford, 1950).
Aristotelis Fragmenta Selecta, ed. W. D. Ross (OCT; Oxford, 1955).
Aristotle, Parva Naturalia, ed. W. D. Ross (Oxford, 1955).
Aristotelis De Anima, ed. W. D. Ross (OCT; Oxford, 1956).
Aristotelis Metaphysica, ed. W. Jaeger (OCT; Oxford, 1957).
Aristotelis Topica et Sophisti Elenchi, ed. W. D. Ross (OCT; Oxford, 1958).
Aristotelis Analytica Priora et Posteriora, ed. W. D. Ross, with L. Minio Paluello (OCT; Oxford, 1964).
Aristote Du Ciel, ed. P. Moraux (Paris, 1965).
Aristotelis Ethica Eudemia, ed. R. R. Walzer and J. M. Mingay (OCT; Oxford, 1991).

ASPASIUS

In Aristotelis Ethica Nicomachea, ed. G. Heylbut (CAG xix/1; Berlin, 1889).

ATTICUS

Atticus. Fragments, ed. É. Des Places (Paris, 1977).

AULUS GELLIUS

Noctes Atticae, Aulus Gellius. Attic Nights, ed. J. Rolfe, i–iii (Loeb; Cambridge, Mass., and London, 1927).

CICERO

De Re Publica—De Legibus, On Republic—On Laws, ed. C. W. Keyes (Loeb; Cambridge, Mass., and London, 1928).

Tusculanae Disputationes, Tusculan Disputations, ed. J. E. King (Loeb; Cambridge, Mass., and London, 1945^{2}).

Academica, Academics, ed. H. Rackham (Loeb; Cambridge, Mass., and London, 1956).

M. Tulli Ciceronis De Officiis, ed. M. Winterbottom (OCT; Oxford, 1995).

M. Tulli Ciceronis De Finibus Bonorum et Malorum, ed. L. Reynolds (OCT; Oxford, 1998).

De Finibus Bonorum et Malorum, ed. H. Rackham (Loeb; Cambridge Mass., and London 1931^{2}).

CLEMENT OF ALEXANDRIA

Clemens Alexandrinus Stromata, ed. O. Stählin (3rd edn. by L. Früchtel and U. Treu), i–ii (Berlin, 1960–85).

DAVID

In Porphyrii Isagogen, In Aristotelis Categorias, ed. A. Busse (CAG xviii/2; Berlin, 1904).

DEXIPPUS

In Aristotelis Categorias, ed. A. Busse (CAG iv/2; Berlin, 1888).

DIOGENES LAERTIUS

Vitae Philosophorum, Lives of Eminent Philosophers, ed. R. D. Hicks, i–ii, (Loeb; Cambridge, Mass., and London, 1925, repr. 1972).

DOXOGRAPHI GRAECI

Doxographi Graeci, ed. H. Diels (Berlin, 1879).

ELIAS

In Porphyrii Isagogen, In Aristotelis Categorias, ed. A. Busse (CAG xviii/1; Berlin, 1900).

EUDORUS

Fragments and Testimonies: 'Raccolta e interpretazione delle testimonianze e dei frammenti del medioplatonico Eudoro di Alessandria', ed. C. Mazzarelli, *Rivista di filologia neoscolastica*, 72 (1985), 197–209, 535–55.

EUSEBIUS

Praeparatio Evangelica, Eusebius Werke. Die Praeparatio Evangelica, ed. K. Mras, i–ii (Berlin, 1954–6; 2nd edn. by É. Des Places, 1982–3).

GALEN

Scripta Minora, ed. J. Marquardt, I. Müller, and G. Helmreich, i–iii (Leipzig, 1884–93).
De Placitis Hippocratis et Platonis, ed. P. de Lacy, i–iii (= Corpus Medicorum Graecorum 5/4/1/2; Berlin, 1978–84).

IAMBLICHUS

Iamblichus In Platonis Dialogos Commentariorum Fragmenta, ed. J. Dillon (Leiden, 1973).
Jamblique de Chalcis, exégète et philosophe, ii, *Testimonia et Fragmenta Exegetica*, ed. B. D. Larsen (Aarhus, 1972).

NEMESIUS

De Natura Hominis, ed. M. Morani (Lerpzig, 1987).

NUMENIUS

Fragments and testimonies: *Numénius. Fragments*, ed. É. Des Places (Paris, 1973).

OLYMPIODORUS

Prolegomena, In Aristotelis Categorias, ed. A. Busse (CAG xii/1; Berlin, 1902).
In Platonis Phaedonem Commentaria, ed. W. Norvin (Leipzig, 1913).

ORIGEN

Contra Celsum, Contre Celse, ed. M. Borret, i–iv (Paris, 1967–9).
De principiis, On First Principles, tr. G. W. Butterworth (London, 1936).

PERIPATETICS

F. Wehrli, *Die Schule des Aristoteles* (Basel/Stuttgart, 1944–59), i–x (2nd edn. 1969): i. *Dikaiarchos*; ii. *Aristoxenos*; iii. *Klearchos*; iv. *Demetrios von Phaleron*; v. *Straton von Lampsakos*; vi. *Herakleides Pontikos*; viii. *Eudemos von Rhodos*; ix. *Phainias von Eresos, Chamaileon, Praxiphanes*; x. *Hieronymos, Kritolaos, und seine Schüler.*

PHILODEMUS

Philodems Akademica, ed. K. Gaiser (Supplementum Platonicum, 1; Stuttgart and Ban Cannstatt, 1988)
Filodemo: Storia dei filosofi. Platone e l'Academia (PHerc. 1021 e 164*)*, ed. T. Dorandi (Naples, 1991).

PHILOPONUS

De Aeternitate Mundi contra Proclum, ed. H. Rabe (Leipzig, 1899).
In Aristotelis De anima, ed. M. Hayduck (CAG xv; Berlin, 1897).

PHOTIUS

Bibliotheca, *Photius.Bibliothèque*, ed. R. Henry, v. i–viii (Paris, 1959–77).

PLATO

Opera, tetralogiae I–II, ed. E. A. Duke, W. F. Hicken, W. S. M. Nicoll, D. B. Robinson, and J. C. G. Strachan, i (OCT; Oxford, 1995).
Opera, tetralogiae III–IX, ed. J. Burnet, ii–v (OCT; Oxford, 1905–15).

PLOTINUS

Opera, ed. P. Henry and H.-R. Schwyzer, i–iii (OCT; Oxford, 1964–82).
Plotinus, ed. A. H. Armstrong, i–vii. (Loeb; Cambridge, Mass., and London, 1966–88).

PLUTARCH

Moralia, ed. H. Cherniss and W. Helmbold, xii (Loeb; Cambridge, Mass., and London, 1957).
Moralia, ed. P. De Lacy and B. Einarson, vii (Loeb; Cambridge, Mass., and London, 1959).
Moralia, ed. B. Einarson and P. De Lacy, xiv (Loeb; Cambridge, Mass., and London, 1967).
Plutarque, De la vertu éthique, ed. D. Babut (Paris, 1969).
Moralia, ed. H. Cherniss, xiii/1 (Loeb; Cambridge, Mass., and London, 1976).
Moralia, ed. H. Cherniss, xiii/2 (Loeb; Cambridge, Mass., and London, 1976).
Fragmenta, ed. F. H. Sandbach (Loeb; Cambridge, Mass., and London).

POLEMO

Polemonis Academici Fragmenta, ed. M. Gigante (Naples, 1977).

PORPHYRY

Isagogē et in Aristotelis Categorias commentarium, ed. A. Busse (CAG iv/i; Berlin, 1887).
Porphyry The Phoenician, Isagogē, tr. E. Warren (Toronto, 1975).
Porphyry. On Aristotle's Categories, tr. S. Strange (London, 1992).
Die neuplatonische, fälschlich dem Galen zugeschriebene Schrift Πρὸς Γαῦρον περὶ τοῦ πῶς ἐμψυχοῦται τὰ ἔμβρυα, ed. K. Kalbfleisch (Anhang zu den Abhandl. d. König. Preuss. Akad. d. Wiss. zu Berlin vom Jahre 1895; Berlin, 1895).

Porphyrios, Kommentar zur Harmonielehre des Ptolemaios, ed. I. Düring (Göteborg, 1932).

Vita Plotini, in *Plotini Opera*, ed. P. Henry and H.-R. Schwyzer, i (OCT; Oxford, 1964). *Πορφυρίοῦ, Περὶ τοῦ Πλωτίνου Βίου*, ed. P. Kalligas (Athens, 1991).

Neoplatonic Saints. The Lives of Plotinus and Proclus by their Students, tr. M. Edwards (Liverpool, 2000).

In Platonis Timaeum commentariorum fragmenta, ed. A. R. Sodano (Naples, 1964).

Porphyry The Cave of the Nymphs in the Odyssey, collective work under the guidance of L. G. Westerink (New York, 1969).

Sententiae ad intelligibilia ducentes, ed. E. Lamberz (Leipzig, 1974).

Porphyre, De l'abstinence, ed. J. Bouffartique and M. Patillon, i. *Introduction. Livre I* (Paris, 1977); ii. *Livres II–III* (Paris, 1979); iii. *Livres IV* (Paris, 1995).

Porphyre Vie de Pythagore, Lettre à Marcella, ed. É. Des Places (Paris, 1982).

Porphyrius. Fragmenta, ed. A. Smith (Stuttgart, 1993).

POSIDONIUS

Posidonius. The Fragments, ed. L. Edelstein and I. Kidd, i–iii (Cambridge, 1972–88).

PROCLUS

In Platonis Rem Publicam Commentarii, ed. G. Kroll, i–ii (Leipzig, 1899–1901).

In Platonis Timaeum Commentarii, ed. E. Diehl, i–iii (Leipzig, 1903–6).

PSELLUS MICHAEL

Michael Psellus Theologica Opuscula, ed. P. Gautier (Leipzig, 1989).

Michael Psellus Philosophica Minora I, ed. J. M. Duffy and D. J. O'Meara (Leipzig, 1992).

Michael Psellus Philosophica Minora II, ed. D. J. O'Meara (Leipzig, 1989).

PSEUDO-ARCHYTAS

T. A. Szlezák (ed.), *Pseudo-Archytas über die Kategorien* (Peripatoi, 4; Berlin and New York, 1972).

PSEUDO-ARISTOTLE

De Mundo, On the world, ed. D. J. Furley (Loeb; Cambridge, Mass., and London, 1955).

Divisiones Aristoteleae, ed. H. Mutschmann (Leipzig, 1906).

PSEUDO-PLUTARCH

De Fato, [Plutarco] Il Fato, ed. E. Valgiglio (Naples, 1993).

PYTHAGOREAN TEXTS

H. Thesleff (ed.), *The Pythagorean Texts of the Hellenistic Period* (Abo, 1965).

B. Centrone (ed.), *Pseudopythagorica Ethica. I trattati morali di Archita, Metopo, Teage, Eurifano* (Naples, 1990).

SENECA

Seneca Ad Lucilium Epistulae Morales, ed. L. D. Reynolds, i–ii (OCT; Oxford, 1965).

Seneca Ad Lucilium Epistulae Morales, ed. R. G. Gummere, i–iii (Cambridge, Mass., and London, 1918–25).

SEXTUS EMPIRICUS

Pyrrhoneae Hypotyposes, Outlines of Pyrrhonism, ed. R. G. Bury, i (Loeb; Cambridge, Mass., and London, 1933).

Adversus Mathematicos, ed. R. G. Bury, ii–iv (Loeb; Cambridge, Mass., and London, 1935–49).

SIMPLICIUS

In Aristotelis De Caelo commentaria, ed. J. L. Heiberg (CAG vii. 1; Berlin, 1894).

In Aristotelis Categorias, ed. C. Kalbfleisch (CAG viii; Berlin, 1907).

In Aristotelis Physicorum libros quattor priores commentaria, ed. H. Diels (CAG ix; Berlin, 1882).

In Aristotelis Physicorum libros quattor posteriores commentaria, ed. H. Diels (CAG x; Berlin, 1895).

In Aristotelis De Anima commentaria, ed. M. Hayduck (CAG xi; Berlin, 1882).

SPEUSIPPUS

De Speusippi Academici Scriptis, ed. P. Lang (Bonn, 1911; repr. Darmstadt, 1965).

Speusippus of Athens, ed. L. Tarán (Philosophia Antiqua 39; Leiden, 1981).

SYRIANUS

In Aristotelis Metaphysica Commentaria, ed. W. Kroll (CAG vi; Berlin, 1902).

STOBAEUS

Ioannes Stobaeus Anthologium, ed. C. Wachsmuth and O. Hense, i–v (Berlin, 1884–1923; repr. 1974).

STOICS

Stoicorum Veterum Fragmenta, ed. J. von Arnim, i–iv (Leipzig, 1905–24): i. *Zeno et Zenonis discipuli*; ii. *Chrysippi Fragmenta Logica et Physica*; iii. *Chrysippi Fragmenta Moralia; Fragmenta Successorum Chrysippi*; iv. *Indices*.

TAURUS

Der Platoniker Tauros in der Darstellung des Aulus Gellius, ed. M.-L. Lakmann (Leiden, 1995).

THEODORETUS OF CYRRHUS

Graecarum Affectionum Curatio, Théodoret De Cyr, *Thérapeutique des Maladies Helléniques*, ed. P. Cavinet (Paris, 1958), i–ii.

VITA ARISTOTELIS MARCIANA

I. Düring (ed.), *Aristotle in the Ancient Biographical Tradition* (Göteborg, 1957), 96–106.

XENOCRATES

Xenokrates, Darstellung der Lehre und Sammlung der Fragmente, ed. R. Heinze (Leipzig, 1892; repr. Olms, Hildesheim, 1965).

B. Secondary Literature

Ackrill, J. (1963), *Aristotle Categories and the De Intepretatione* (Oxford).

Andersen, C. (1952/3), 'Justin und der Mittelplatonismus', *Zeitschrift für die neutestamentliche Wissenschaft*, 44: 157–95.

André, J.-M. (1987), 'Les Écoles philosophiques aux deux premiers siècles de l'Empire', in *ANRW* ii/36/1. 5–77.

Annas, J. (1988), 'The Heirs of Socrates', *Phronesis*, 33: 100–12.

—— (1990), 'The Hellenistic Version of Aristotle's Ethics', *Monist*, 73: 80–96.

—— (1992), 'Plato the Sceptic', in J. Klagge and N. Smith (eds.), *Methods of Interpreting Plato and his Dialogues* (*OSAP* suppl. vol.; Oxford), 43–72.

—— (1993), *The Morality of Happiness* (Oxford).

—— (1999), *Platonist Ethics Old and New* (New York).

Armstrong, A. H. (1940), *The Architecture of the Intelligible Universe in the Philosophy of Plotinus* (Cambridge).

—— (1960), 'The Background of the Doctrine "That the Intelligibles are not outside the Intellect" ', in *Les Sources de Plotin* (Entretiens Fondation Hardt, 5; Vandoeuvres and Geneva), 391–425.

—— (1970) (ed.), *The Cambridge History of Later Greek and Early Medieval Philosophy* (Cambridge).

—— (1991), 'Aristotle in Plotinus: The Continuity and Discontinuity of *psychê* and *nous*', (*OSAP* suppl. vol.; Oxford), 117–27.

Arnim, H. von (1887), 'Quelle zur Überlieferung über Ammonios Saccas', *Rh. Mus.* 42. 276–85.

—— (1921), 'Kleitomachos', *RE* xi/1. 656–9.

Aujoulat, N. (1986), *Le Néo-Platonisme Alexandrin; Hiérocles d'Alexandrie* (Leiden).

Babut, D. (1969*a*), *Plutarque et le Stoicisme* (Paris).

—— (1969*b*), *Plutarque, De la Vertu éthique* (Paris).

—— (1996), 'Plutarque, Aristote et l' Aristotélisme', in Luc Van der Stockt (ed.), *Plutarchea Lovaniensia: A Miscellany of Essays on Plutarch* (Leuven), 2–28.

Baltes, M. (1975), 'Numenios von Apamea und der platonische *Timaeus*', *Vigiliae Christianae*, 29: 241–70.

—— (1976), *Die Weltentstehung des platonischen Timaios nach den antiken Interpreten*, part 1 (Philosophia Antiqua, 21; Leiden).

—— (1983), 'Zur Philosophie des Platonikers Attikos', *Jahrbuch für die Antike und Christentum*, Ergänzungsband 10: 38–57.

—— (1985), 'Ammonios Saccas', in *Reallexicon für Antike und Christentum*, suppl. vol. iii. 323–332.

—— (1996), '*Γέγονεν* (Platon *Tim.* 28B7): Ist die Welt real entstanden oder nicht?', in K. Algra, P. van der Horst, and D. Runia (eds.), *Polyhistor: Studies in the History and Historiography of Ancient Philosophy presented to Jaap Mansfeld on his Sixtieth Birthday* (Leiden), 75–96.

—— (2000), 'La dottrina dell'anima in Plutarco', *Elenchos*, 21: 245–69.

Barker, A. (2000), *Scientific Method in Ptolemy's Harmonics* (Cambridge).

Barnes, J. (1989), 'Antiochus of Ascalon', in M. Griffin and J. Barnes (eds.), *Philosophia Togata*, i (Oxford), 51–96.

—— (1997), 'Roman Aristotle', in M. Griffin and J. Barnes (eds.), *Philosophia Togata*, ii. *Plato and Aristotle at Rome* (Oxford), 1–69.

—— (1999), 'Aspasius: An Introduction', in A. Alberti (ed.), *The Earliest Extant Commentary on Aristotle's Ethics* (Berlin and New York), 1–40.

—— (2003), *Porphyry: Introduction* (Oxford).

Becchi, F. (1975), 'Aristotelismo ed antistoicismo nel *De virtute morali* di Plutarco', *Prometheus*, 1: 160–80.

—— (1981),'Platonismo medio ed etica Plutarchea', *Prometheus*, 7/2: 125–45.

—— (1984), 'Sui presunti influssi Platonici e medioplatonici nel commento di Aspasio all'*Etica Nicomachea*', *Sileno*, 10: 63–81.

—— (1997), 'Plutarco e la dottrina dell' *'ΟΜΟΙΩΣΙΣ ΘΕΩΙ* tra Platonismo ed Aristotelismo', in I. Gallo (ed.), *Plutarco e la religione* (Naples), 321–36.

—— (2004), 'Plutarco e il Peripato: Tre esempi di filologia filosofica', *Prometheus*, 30: 26–42.

Beutler, R. (1940), 'Numenios', in *RE* suppl. vii. 664–78.

—— (1953), 'Porphyrios', in *RE* xxii/1. 275–313.

Bidez, J. (1913), *Vie de Porphyre, le philosophe néo-platonicien* (Ghent).

Blumenthal, H. J. (1971), *Plotinus' Psychology: His Doctrines of the Embodied Soul* (The Hague).

—— (1972), 'Plotinus' Psychology: Aristotle in the Service of Platonism', *International Philosophical Quarterly*, 12: 340–64.

—— (1974), 'Did Iamblichus Write a Commentary on the *De anima*?', *Hermes*, 102: 540–56.

—— (1986), 'Alexander of Aphrodisias in the Later Greek Commentaries on Aristotle's *De Anima*', in J. Wiesner (ed.), *Aristoteles' Werk und Wirkung* (Berlin), 90–106.

—— (1990), 'Themistius: The Last Peripatetic Commentator of Aristotle?', in R. Sorabji (ed.), *Aristotle Transformed* (London), 113–23.

—— (2000), '*Simplicius' On Aristotle on the Soul 3.1–5* (London).

Bos, A. P. (1999), 'Plutarch's Testimony to an Earlier explanation of Aristotle's definition of the soul', *Plutarco, Platon y Aristóteles: Actas del V Congresso Internacional de la IPS* (Madrid), 535–48.

Bostock, D. (1986), *Plato's Phaedo* (Oxford).

Bowersock, G. W. (1969), *Greek Sophists in the Roman Empire* (Oxford).

Boyancé, P. (1971), 'Ciceron et les parties de philosophic', *REL* 49: 127–54.

Brink, K. O. (1940), 'Peripatos', in *RE* suppl. vii. 899–949.

Brittain, C. (2001), *Philo of Larissa* (Oxford).

Burkert, W. (1962), *Weisheit und Wissenschaft: Studien zu Pythagoras, Philolaos und Platon* (Erlangen).

Burnyeat, M. (1970), 'Plato on the Grammar of Perceiving', *CQ* 26: 29–51.

—— (1995), 'How Much Happens When Aristotle Sees Red and Hears Middle C? Remarks on *De anima* 2. 7–8', in M. Nussbaum and A. O. Rorty (eds.), *Essays on Aristotle's De anima* (Oxford), 421–34.

Busse, A. (1893), 'Die neuplatonischen Lebensbeschreibungen des Aristoteles', *Hermes*, 28: 252–76.

Capelle, W. (1931), 'Straton der Physiker', in *RE* ii/7. 278–315.

Cardullo, L. (1986), 'Syrianus' Lost Commentaries on Aristotle', *Bulletin of the Institute of Classical Studies*, 33: 112–24.

Centrone, B. (1990), *Pseudopythagorica Ethica. I trattati morali di Archita, Metopo, Teage, Eurifano* (Naples).

Cherniss, H. (1944), *Aristotle's Criticism of Plato and the Academy* (Baltimore).

Cherniss, H. (1945), *The Riddle of the Early Academy* (Berkeley, Calif.).

Chiaradonna, R. (1996), 'L'interpretazione della sostanza in Porfirio', *Elenchos*, 17: 55–94.

—— (1998*a*), 'Essence et prédication chez Porphyre et Plotin', *Revue des sciences philosophiques et théologiques*, 82: 577–606.

—— (1998*b*), 'Plotino interprete di Aristotele. Alcuni studi recenti', *Rivista di filologia e istruzione classica*, 126: 479–503.

—— (2002), *Sostanza, movimento, analogia: Plotino critico di Aristotele* (Naples).

—— (2003), 'Il tempo misura del movimento? Plotino e Aristotele (*Enn.* III 7 [45])', in *Platone e la tradizione Platonica: Studi di filosofia antica, Acme*, 58: 221–50.

—— (ed.) (2005), *Plotino sull'anima* (Naples).

Chiesara, M. L. (2001), *Aristocles of Messene: Testimonies and Fragments* (Oxford).

Clarke, M. L. (1971), *Higher Education in the Ancient World* (London).

Cooper, J. (1985), 'Aristotle on the Goods of Fortune', *Philosophical Review*, 94: 173–96, cited from his *Reason and Emotion* (Princeton, 1999), 292–311.

Corrigan, K. (1996), *Plotinus' Theory of Matter-Evil and the Question of Substance: Plato, Aristotle, and Alexander of Aphrodisias* (Leuven).

Crönert, W. (1906), *Kolotes und Menedemos* (Studien zur Palaeographie un Papyruskunde 6: Leipzig).

D'Ancona-Costa, C. (2002), 'Commenting on Aristotle: from late Antiquity to the Arab Aristotelianism', in W. Geerlings and C. Schulze (eds.), *Der Kommentar in der Antike und Mittelalter* (Leiden), 201–51.

De Haas, F. (2001), 'Did Plotinus and Porphyry Disagree on Aristotle's *Categories*?', *Phronesis*, 46: 492–526.

De Ley, H. (1972), *Macrobius and Numenius* (Collection Latomus, 125; Brussels).

De Libera, A. (1999), 'Entre Aristote et Plotin: L'*Isagogê* de Porphyre et le problème des catégories', in C. Chiesa and L. Freuler (eds.), *Métaphysiques Médiévales: Études en l' honneur d' André de Muralt* (Neuchâtel), 7–27.

Decleva-Caizzi, F. (1992), 'Aenesidemus and the Academy', *CQ* 42: 176–89.

Deuse, W. (1981), 'Der Demiurg bei Porphyrios und Jamblich', in C. Zintzen (ed.), *Die Philosophie des Neuplatonismus* (Darmstadt), 238–78.

—— (1983), *Untersuchungen zur mittelplatonischen und neuplatonischen Seelenlehre* (Wiesbaden).

Dillon, J. (1973), *Iamblichi Chalcidensis in Platonis Dialogos Commentariorum Fragmenta* (Philosophia Antiqua, 23; Leiden).

—— (1977), *The Middle Platonists: A Study of Platonism 80 BC to 220 AD* (London, repr. 1996).

—— (1983), '*Metriopatheia* and *apatheia*: Some Reflections on a Controversy in Later Greek Ethics', in J. Anton and A. Preuss (eds.), *Essays in Ancient Greek Philosophy*, ii. 508–17.

—— (1986), 'Plutarch and Second Century Platonism', in A. H. Armstrong (ed.), *Classical Mediterranean Spirituality* (New York), 214–29.

—— (1988*a*), ' "Orthodoxy and "Eclecticism": Middle Platonists and Neo-Pythagoreans', in J. M. Dillon and A. A. Long (eds.), *The Question of Eclecticism* (Berkeley, Calif.), 103–25.

—— (1988*b*), 'Plutarch and Platonist Orthodoxy', *Illinois Classical Studies*, 13: 357–64.

—— (1989), 'Tampering with the *Timaeus*: Ideological Emendations in Plato, with Special Reference to the *Timaeus*', *AJPh* 110: 50–72.

—— (1990), *Dexippus On Aristotle* Categories (London).

—— (1992), 'Porphyry's Doctrine of the One', in *Σοφίης Μαιήτορες: 'Chercheurs de sagesse'. Hommage à Jean Pepin* (Paris), 356–66.

—— (1993), *Alcinous. The Handbook of Platonism* (Oxford).

—— (1996), 'An Ethic for the Late Antique Sage', in L. Gerson (ed.), *The Cambridge Companion to Plotinus* (Cambridge).

—— (2003), *The Heirs of Plato: A Study of the Old Academy (347–274 BC)* (Oxford).

Dirlmeier, F. (1958), *Aristoteles Magna Moralia* (Berlin).

Dodds, E. R. (1928), 'The *Parmenides* of Plato and the Origin of the Neoplatonic One', *CQ* 22: 129–42.

—— (1960), 'Numenius and Ammonius', in *Les Sources de Plotin* (Entretiens Hardt, 5; Vandoeuvres and Geneva), 3–61.

Donini, P. L. (1974), *Tre studi sull' aristotelismo nel II secolo d. C.* (Turin).

—— (1986*a*), 'Lo scetticismo accademico, Aristotele e l'unità della tradizione platonica secondo Plutarco', in G. Cambiano (ed.), *Storiografia e dossografia nella filosofia antica* (Turin), 203–26.

—— (1986*b*), 'Plutarco, Ammonio e l'Academia', in F. E. Brenk and I. Gallo (eds.), *Miscellanea Plutarchea* (Ferrara), 97–110.

—— (1988*a*), 'The History of the Concept of Eclecticism', in J. M. Dillon and A. A. Long (eds.), *The Question of Eclecticism* (Berkeley, Calif.), 5–33.

—— (1988*b*), 'Science and Metaphysics: Platonism, Aristotelianism, and Stoicism in Plutarch's *On the Face in the Moon*', in J. M. Dillon and A. A. Long (eds.), *The Question of Eclecticism* (Berkeley, Calif.), 126–44.

—— (1994), 'Testi e commenti, manuali e insequamento: la forma sistematica e i metodi della filosofia in età postellenistica', in *ANRW* ii/36/7. 5027–5100.

—— (1999), 'Platone e Aristotele nella tradizione pitagorica secondo Plutarco', in *Plutarco; Platon y Aristôteles: Actas del V Congresso Internacional de la IPS* (Madrid), 9–24.

Dorandi, T. (1986), 'Filodemo e la fine dell'Academia (*PHerc.* 1021 XXXIII–XXXVI)', *Cronache Ercolanesi*, 16: 113–18.

—— (1991), *Filodemo: Storia dei filosofi. Platone e l'Academia (PHerc. 1021 e 164)* (Naples).

Dörrie, H. (1955), 'Ammonius der Lehrer Plotins', *Hermes*, 83: 439–77.

Dörrie, H. (1959), *Porphyrios' Symmikta Zetemata* (Zetemata, 20; Munich).
—— (1966*a*), 'Die Schultradition im Platonismus und Porphyrios', in *Porphyre* (Entretiens Hardt, 12; Vandoeuvres and Geneva), 3–25.
—— (1966*b*), 'Die Lehre von der Seele', ibid. 165–87 (= *Platonica Minora*, 441–53).
—— (1971), 'Die Stellung Plutarchs im Platonismus seiner Zeit', in *Philomathes: Studies and Essays in the Humanities in Memory of Ph. Merlan* (The Hague), 36–56.
—— (1973), 'L. Kalbenos Tauros. Das Persönlichkeitsbild eines Philosophen um die Mitte des 2. Jahrh. n. Chr.', *Kairos*, 15: 24–35 (= *Platonica Minora*, 310–23).
—— (1976*a*), 'Der Platonismus in der Kultur- und Geistesgeschichte der frühen Kaiserzeit', in *Platonica Minora*, 166–210.
—— (1976*b*), *Platonica Minora* (Munich).
—— and M. Baltes (1993, 1996, 1996, 2002), *Der Platonismus in der Antike* (Stuttgart-Bad Cannstatt), vols. iii–vi.
Dufour, R. (2002), 'Une citation d'Aristote en "Enneade" II, 1, 6, 25', *REG* 115, 405–8.
Düring, I. (1957), *Aristotle in the Ancient Biographical Tradition* (Göteborg).
Ebbesen, S. (1990*a*), 'Porphyry's Legacy to Logic: A Reconstruction', in R. Sorabji (ed.), *Aristotle Transformed* (London), 141–71.
—— (1990*b*), 'Boethius as an Aristotelian Commentator', ibid. 373–92.
Edwards, M. J. (1990), 'Porphyry and the Intelligible Triad', *JHS* 110: 14–25.
—— (1991*a*), 'On the Platonic Schooling of Justin Martyr', *Journal of Theological Studies*, 42: 17–34.
—— (1991*b*), 'Middle Platonism on the Beautiful and the Good', *Mnemosyne*, 44: 161–6.
—— (1993), 'Ammonius, Teacher of Origen', *Journal of Ecclesiastical History*, 44: 169–81.
—— (2000), *Neoplatonic Saints: The Lives of Plotinus and Proclus by their Students* (Liverpool).
Elders, J. (1994), 'The Greek Christian Authors and Aristotle', in L. P. Schrenk, *Aristotle in Late Antiquity* (Washington, DC), 111–42.
Elferink, M. A. (1968), *La Descente de l'âme d'après Macrobe* (Leiden).
Ellis, J. (1990), 'The Trouble with Fragrance', *Phronesis*, 35: 290–302.
Elter, A. (1910), 'Zu Hierocles dem Neoplatoniker', *Rh. Mus.*, 65: 175–99.
Emilsson, E. (1988), *Plotinus on Sense-Perception: A Philosophical Study* (Cambridge).
—— (2005) 'Soul and *Merismos*' in R. Chiaradonna (ed.), *Plotino sull'anima* (Naples), 79–93.
Erler, M. (1991), '*ΕΠΙΤΗΔΕΥΕΙΝ ΑΣΑΦΕΙΑΝ*. Zu Philodem *Πρὸς τοὺς [ἑταίρους]* (*PHerc*. 1005, col. XVI Angeli)', *Cronache Ercolanesi*, 21: 83–8.
Evangeliou, Chr. (1988), *Aristotle's Categories and Porphyry* (Leiden).

Everson, S. (1997), *Aristotle on Perception* (Oxford).

Fine, G. (1986), 'Immanence', *OSAP* 4: 71–97.

Fladerer, L. (1996), *Antiochos von Ascalon: Hellenist und Humanist*, (Grazer Beiträge, 7: Horn and Vienna).

Fowden, G. (1977), 'The Platonist Philosopher and his Circle in Late Antiquity', *Φιλοσοφία*, 7: 360–83.

Frede, M. (1986), 'The Stoic Doctrine of the Affections of the Soul', in M. Schofield and G. Striker (eds.), *The Norms of Nature: Studies in Hellenistic Ethics* (Cambridge), 93–110.

—— (1987*a*), 'The Title, Unity, and Authenticity of the Aristotelian *Categories*', in *Essays in Ancient Philosophy* (Oxford), 11–28.

—— (1987*b*), 'Stoics and Skeptics on Clear and Distinct Impressions', in *Essays in Ancient Philosophy* (Oxford), 151–76.

—— (1987*c*), 'Numenius', in *ANRW* ii/36/2. 1034–75.

—— (1987*d*), 'The Original Notion of Cause', in *Essays in Ancient Philosophy* (Oxford), 129–50.

—— (1987*e*), 'The Skeptic's Two Kinds of Assent and the Question of the Possibility of Knowledge', in *Essays in Ancient Philosophy* (Oxford), 201–22.

—— (1990), 'La teoria de las Ideas en Longino', *Methexis*, 3: 85–98.

—— (1992), 'Plato's Arguments and the Dialogue Form', *OSAP* suppl. vol. 201–19.

—— (1994), 'Celsus Philosophus Platonicus', in *ANRW* ii/36/7. 5183–5213.

Gauthier, R. and Jolif, J. (1970), *L'Ethique à Nicomaque* (Louvain), i/1.

Gersh, S. (1992), 'Porphyry's Commentary on the *Harmonics* of Ptolemy and Neoplatonic Musical Theory', in S. Gersh and C. Kannengiesser (eds.), *Platonism in Late Antiquity* (Notre Dame), 141–55.

Gerson, L. (2004), 'Platonism in Aristotle's Ethics', *OSAP* 27: 217–98.

Gigante, M. (1999), *Kepos e Peripatos: Contributo alla Storia dell' aristotelismo antico* (Naples).

Gigon, O. (1959), 'Cicero und Aristoteles', *Hermes*, 87: 143–62.

Gioè, A. (1993), 'Severo, il medioplatonismo e le categorie', *Elenchos*, 14: 33–53.

—— (2002), *Filosofi medioplatonici del II secolo D.C. Testimonianze e Frammenti (Gaio, Albino, Lucio, Nicostrato, Tauro, Severo, Arpocrazione)*, (Naples).

Giusta, M. (1990), 'Antioco di Ascalona e Carneade nel libro V del *De finibus bonorum et malorum* di Cicerone', *Elenchos*, 11/1. 29–49.

Glucker, J. (1978), *Antiochus and the Late Academy* (Hypomnemata, 56; Göttingen.

—— (2004), 'The Philonian/Metrodorians: Problems of Method in Ancient Philosophy', *Elenchos*, 258, 99–153.

Göransson, T. (1995), *Albinus, Alcinous, Arius Didymus* (Götteborg).

Görler, W. (1990), 'Antiochos von Ascalon über die "Alten" und über die Stoa: Beobachtungen zu Cicero, *Academici posteriores*, 1, 24–43', in P. Steinmetz

(ed.), *Beiträge zur hellenistischen Literatur und ihrer Rezeption in Rom* (Palingenesia, 28; Stuttgart), 123–39.
—— (1994), 'Älterer Pyrrhonismus. Jüngere Akademie. Antiochos von Ascalon', in H. Flashar (ed.), *Ueberweg. Grundriss der Geschichte der Philosophie. Die Philosophie der Antike Bd. IV. Die Philosophie des Hellenismus* (Basle), 717–981.
Gottschalk, H. B. (1971), 'Soul as *Harmonia*', *Phronesis*, 16: 179–98.
—— (1980), *Heraclides of Pontus* (Oxford).
—— (1986), 'Boethus' Psychology and the Neoplatonists', *Phronesis*, 31: 243–57.
—— (1987), 'Aristotelian Philosophy in the Roman World from the Time of Cicero to the End of the Second Century AD', in *ANRW* ii/36/2. 1079–1174.
—— (1990), 'The Earliest Aristotelian Commentators', in R. Sorabji (ed.), *Aristotle Transformed* (London), 55–82.
Graeser, A. (1972), *Plotinus and the Stoics: A Preliminary Study* (Philosophia Antiqua, 22; Leiden).
Grant, R. M. (1956), 'Aristotle and the Conversion of Justin', *Journal of Theological Studies*, 7: 246–8.
Hadot, I. (1978), *Le Probléme du neoplatonisme alexandrin: Hieroclès et Simplicius* (Paris).
—— (1987*a*), 'Les Introductions aux commentaires exégetiques chez les auteurs neoplatoniciens', in M. Tardieu (ed.), *Les Regles de l'interpretation* (Paris), 98–122.
—— (1987*b*), 'La Division néoplatonicienne des écrits d'Aristote', in J. Wiesner (ed.), *Aristoteles: Werk und Wirkung*, ii (Berlin and New York), 249–89.
—— (1991), 'The Role of the Commentaries on Aristotle in the Teaching of Philosophy', *OSAP* suppl. vol, *Aristotle and the Later Tradition* (Oxford), 175–89.
Hadot, P. (1965), 'La Métaphysique de Porphyre', in *Porphyre* (Entretiens Fondation Hardt, 12; Geneva), 127–64.
—— (1968), *Porphyre et Victorinus* (Paris), i–ii.
—— (1986), 'Neoplatonist Spirituality', in A. H. Armstrong (ed.), *Classical Mediterranean Spirituality* (New York), 230–49.
—— (1990), 'The Harmony of Plotinus and Aristotle According to Porphyry', in R. Sorabji (ed.), *Aristotle Transformed* (London), 125–40.
Heinaman, R. (2002), 'The Improvability of *eudaimonia* in the *Nicomachean Ethics*', *OSAP* 23: 99–145.
Heinemann, E. (1926), 'Ammonius Saccas und der Ursprung des Neuplatonismus', *Hermes*, 61: 1–27.
Henry, P. (1937), 'Suidas, le Larousse et le Littré de l'Antiquité Grecque', *Les Études classiques*, 6: 154–62

—— (1973), 'Trois Apories orales de Plotin sur les *Categories* d'Aristote', in *Zetesis: Album amicorum door vrienden en collega's aangeboden aan Prof. Dr. E. de Strycker* (Antwerp and Utrecht), 234–65.

Hicks, R. (1907), *Aristotle De Anima* (Cambridge).

Hoffmann, P. (1987), 'Simplicius' Polemics', in R. Sorabji (ed.), *Philoponus and the Rejection of the Aristotelian Science* (London), 57–83.

Holford-Stevens, L. (1988), *Aulus Gellius* (London).

Holzhausen, J. (1992), 'Eine Anmerkung zum Verhältnis von Numenios und Plotin', *Hermes*, 120: 250–5.

Hunt, H. A. K. (1954), *The Humanism of Cicero* (Melbourne).

Igal, J. (1979), 'Aristoteles y la evolucion de la antropologia de Plotino', *Pensiamento*, 35: 315–46.

Immisch, O. (1906), 'Ein Gedicht des Aristoteles', *Philologus*, 65: 1–23.

Irwin, T. (1995), *Plato's Ethics* (Oxford).

Jaeger, W. (1948), *Aristotle: Fundamentals of the History of his Development*, tr. from the German by R. Robinson (Oxford, 2nd edn.).

Jones, R. M. (1916), *The Platonism of Plutarch* (Menasha; 2nd edn. New York, 1980).

Judson, J. (1983), 'Eternity and Necessity in *De Caelo* I. 12', *OSAP* 1: 217–55.

Kalligas, P. (1991), *Πορφυρίου, Περὶ τοῦ Πλωτίνου Βίου* (Athens).

—— (1994), *Πλωτίνου Ἐννεὰς Πρώτη* (Athens).

—— (1997), *Πλωτίνου Ἐννεὰς Δευτέρα* (Athens).

—— (2000), 'Living Body, Soul, and Virtue in the Philosophy of Plotinus', *Dionysius*, 18: 25–38.

—— (2004*a*), 'Platonism in Athens during the First Two Centuries AD', *Rhizai*, 2: 37–56.

—— (2004*b*), 'Plotinus on Evidence and Truth' in D. O'Meara and I. Schüssler (eds.), *La Vérité, Antiquité–Modernité* (Lausanne), 65–76.

Kappelmacher, A. (1928), 'Der schriftstellerische Plan des Boethius', *Wiener Studien*, 46: 215–25.

Karamanolis, G. (2004*a*), 'Transformations of Plato's Ethics: Platonist Interpretations of Plato's Ethics from Antiochus to Porphyry', *Rhizai*, 1: 73–105.

—— (2004*b*), 'Porphyry: the First Platonist Commentator on Aristotle', in P. Adamson, H. Baltussen, and M. Stone (eds.), *Science and Exegesis in Greek, Arabic and Latin* (London), 79–113 (supplement to *BICS* 83/1).

Kenney, J. P. (1991), *Mystical Monotheism: A Study in Ancient Platonic Theology* (Hanover and London).

Kobusch, T. (1976), *Studien zur Philosophie des Hierokles von Alexandrien. Untersuchungen zum christlichen Neuplatonismus* (Munich).

Kotzia, P. (1992), *Ο "σκοπός" των Κατηγοριών του Αριστοτέλη. Συμβολή στην ιστορία των αριστοτελικών σπουδών ως τον 6° αιώνα* (Thessaloniki).

Kraut, R. (1992), 'Introduction to the Study of Plato' in R. Kraut (ed.), *The Cambridge Companion to Plato* (Cambridge), 1–50.

Lakmann, M.-L. (1995), *Der Platoniker Tauros in der Darstellung des Aulus Gellius* (Philosophia Antiqua, 63 Leiden).

Langerbeck, H. (1957), 'The Philosophy of Ammonius Saccas and the Connection of Aristotelian and Christian Elements Therein', *JHS* 77: 67–74.

Larsen, B. D. (1974), 'La Place de Jamblique dans la philosophie antique tardive', in *De Jamblique à Proclus* (Entretiens Fondation Hardt, 21 Geneva), 1–34.

Ley, H. de (1972), *Macrobius and Numenius: A Study of Macrobins In Somn. I, 12* (Latomus, 125; Brussels).

Lilla, S. (1971), *Clement of Alexandria: A Study in Christian Platonism and Gnosticism* (Oxford).

—— (1990), 'Die Lehre von den Ideen als Gedanken Gottes im griechischen patristischen Denken', in *EPMHNEYMATA Festschrift für Hadwig Hörner zum sechzigen Geburtstag* (Heidelberg), 27–50.

—— (1991), *Introduzione al Platonismo Medio* (Rome).

Lloyd, A. C. (1955), 'Neoplatonic Logic and Aristotelian Logic', part I, *Phronesis*, 1: 58–79.

—— (1956), 'Neoplatonic and Aristotelian Logic', part II, *Phronesis*, 2: 146–60.

—— (1967), 'The Later Neoplatonists', in A. H. Armstrong (ed.), *The Cambridge History of Later Greek and Early Medieval Philosophy* (Cambridge).

—— (1990), *The Anatomy of Neoplatonism* (Oxford).

Loenen, J. H. (1956), 'Albinus' Metaphysics: An Attempt at Rehabilitation', part I, *Mnemosyne*, 4th ser 9: 296–319.

—— (1957), 'Albinus' Metaphysics: An Attempt at Rehabilitation', part II, *Mnemosyne*, 4th ser. 10: 35–56.

Long, A. (1986), *Hellenistic Philosophy* (London).

—— (1995), 'Cicero's Plato and Aristotle', in J. G. F. Powell (ed.), *Cicero the Philosopher* (Oxford), 37–61.

—— and Sedley, D. N. (eds.) (1987), *The Hellenistic Philosophers*, i–ii (Cambridge).

Luck, G. (1953), *Der Akademiker Antiochos* (Noctes Romanae, 7; Berne and Stuttgart).

Lueder, A. (1940), *Die philosophische Persönlichkeit des Antiochos von Askalon* (Göttingen).

Lynch, J. P. (1972), *Aristotle's School* (Berkeley, Calif.).

Mahdi, M. (1969), *Alfarabi's Philosophy of Plato and Aristotle* (Ithaca, NY).

Mallet, D. (1989), *Farabi Deux Traités Philosophiques: L'Harmonie entre les opinions des deux sages, Le divin Platon et Aristote et De la Religion* (Damascus).

Männlein-Robert, I. (2001), *Longin Philologe und Philosoph* (Beiträge zur Altertumskunde, 143; Leipzig).

Mansfeld, J. (1990), *Studies in the Historiography of Greek Philosophy* (Assen).

—— (1992), *Heresiography in Context: Hippolytus' Elenchos as a Source for Greek Philosophy* (Philosophia Antiqua, 56; Leiden).

Mariotti, I. (1966), *Aristone d'Alessandria* (Bologna).

Mazzarelli, C. (1985), 'Raccolta e interpretazione delle testimonianze e dei frammenti del medioplatonico Eudoro di Alessandria', *Rivista di Filosofia Neoscolastica,* 72: 197–209 (testimonianze e frammenti securi), 535–55 (testimonianze non sicure).

Mercken, H. P. F. (1990), 'The Greek Commentators on Aristotle's *Ethics*', in R. Sorabji (ed.), *Aristotle Transformed* (London), 407–43.

Merlan, P. (1934), Review of J. Baudry, *Atticos Fragments, Gnomon,* 10: 263–70.

—— (1960), *From Platonism to Neoplatonism* (The Hague).

—— (1967), 'Greek Philosophy from Plato to Plotinus', in A. H. Armstrong (ed.), *The Cambridge History of Later Greek and Early Medieval Philosophy* (Cambridge), 12–130.

—— (1969), 'Zwei Untersuchungen zu Alexander von Aphrodisias', *Philologus,* 113: 85–91.

Moraux, P. (1963), 'Quinta Essentia', in *RE* xxiv. 1171–1263.

—— (1973), *Der Aristotelismus bei den Griechen von Andronikos bis Alexander von Aphrodisias,* i. *Die Renaissance des Aristotelismus im 1 Jh. v Chr.* (Berlin).

—— (1984), *Der Aristotelismus bei den Griechen von Andronikos bis Alexander von Aphrodisias,* ii. *Der Aristotelismus im I. und II Jh. n. Chr.* (Berlin).

—— (1985), 'Porphyry, commentateur de la *Physique* d' Aristote', in *Aristotelica: Melanges offerts à Marcel de Corte* (Liège), 225–39.

Moreschini, C. (1987), 'Attico: Una figura singolare del medioplatonismo', *ANRW* ii/36/1. 477–91.

Mras, K. (1936), 'Zu Atticos, Porphyrius und Eusebius', *Glotta,* 25: 183–8.

Mueller, I. (1994), 'Hippolytus, Aristotle, Basilides', in L. Schrenk (ed.), *Aristotle in Late Antiquity* (Washington, DC), 143–57.

O'Meara, D. J. (1985), 'Plotinus on How the Soul Acts on Body', in O'Meara (ed.), *Platonic Investigations* (Washington, DC), 247–62.

—— (1989), *Pythagoras Revived: Mathematics and Philosophy in Late Antiquity* (Oxford).

—— (1993), *Plotinus: An Introduction to the Enneads* (Oxford).

Opsomer, J., (1994), 'L'Ame du monde et l'âme de l'homme chez Plutarque', in *Actas del III Simposio Espanol sobre Plutarco* (Madrid), 33–49.

—— (1999), *Searchers of the Truth* (Leuven).

Owen, G. E. L. (1986), 'The Platonism of Aristotle', in Owen, *Logic, Science and Dialectic* (London), 200–20.

Plezia, M. (1949), *De commentaries isagogicis* (Warsaw).

Praechter, K. (1909), 'Die griechischen Aristoteleskommentare', *Byzantinische Zeitschrift*, 18: 516–38 (cited from its translated version in R. Sorabji (ed.), *Aristotle Transformed* (London), 31–54).
—— (1910), 'Richtungen und Schulen im Neuplatonismus', in *Genethliakon Carl Robert*, Berlin (= *Kleine Schriften* (Hildesheim, 1973), 165–209).
—— (1913), 'Hierocles', in *RE* viii/2. 1479–87.
—— (1922), 'Nikostratos der Platoniker', *Hermes*, 57: 481–517 (= *Kleine Schriften* (Hildesheim, 1973), 101–37).
—— (1923), 'Severus', in *RE* 2/2. 2007–2010.
—— (1926) 'Das Schriftenverzeichnis des Neuplatonikers Syrianos bei Suidas', *Byzantinische Zeitschrift*, 26: 254–64.
—— (1934), 'Taurus', in *RE* xix/1. 58–68.
Prost, F. (2001), 'L'Éthique d'Antiochus d'Ascalon', *Philologus*, 145: 244–68.
Puglia, E. (1998), 'Senarco di Seleucia nella *Storia Dell'Academia* di Filodemo (*PHerc.* 1021 XXXV 2–18)', *Papyrologica Lupiensia*, 7: 143–51.
Rawson, E. (1985), *Intellectual Life in the Late Roman Republic* (London).
Reid, J. S. (1885), *M. Tullius Ciceronis Academica* (London).
Rich, A. (1954), 'The Platonic Ideas as the Thoughts of God', *Mnemosyne*, 4th ser. 7: 123–33.
Richard, M. (1950), 'Apo phônes', *Byzantion*, 20: 191–222.
Rist, J. M. (1965), 'Monism: Plotinus and Some Predecessors', *HSCPh* 69: 329–44.
Romano, F. (1979), *Porfirio di Tiro* (Catania).
—— (1985), *Porfirio e la fisica aristotelica* (Catania).
Ross, D. (1951), *Plato's Theory of Ideas* (Oxford).
—— (1961), *Aristotle De Anima* (Oxford).
Runia, D. T. (1989), 'Festugière Revisited: Aristotle in the Greek Patres', *Vigiliae Christianae*, 43: 1–34.
Saffrey, H. D. (1990), 'How did Syrianus Regard Aristotle?', in R. Sorabji (ed.), *Aristotle Transformed* (London), 173–80.
—— (1992), 'Pourquoi Porphyre a-t-il édité Plotin?', in Luc Brisson *et al.*, *Porphyre: La Vie de Plotin*, ii (Paris), 31–57.
Sandbach, F. H. (1982), 'Plutarch and Aristotle', *Illinois Classical Studies*, 7: 207–32.
Sandy, G. (1997), *The Greek World of Apuleius* (Leiden).
Santaniello, C. (1999), 'Traces of the Lost Aristotle in Plutarch', in *Plutarco, Platon y Aristôteles: Actas del V Congresso Internacional de la IPS* (Madrid), 628–41.
Sayre, K. (1983), *Plato's Late Ontology* (Princeton).
Schibli, H. S. (2002), *Hierocles of Alexandria* (Oxford).
Schoppe, C. (1994), *Plutarchs Interpretation der Ideenlehre Platons* (Münster).
Schrenk, L. P. (1993), 'The Middle Platonic Reception of Aristotelian Science', *Rh. M.* 136: 342–59.

—— (ed.) (1994), *Aristotle in Late Antiquity* (Washington, DC).

Schroeder, F. (1987), 'Ammonius Saccas', in *ANRW* ii/36/1. 493–526.

Schwyzer, H.-R. (1951), 'Plotinos', in *RE* i/21. 471–592.

—— (1974), 'Plotinisches und Unplotinisches in den *Aphormai* des Porphyrios', in *Plotino e il Neoplatonismo* (Rome), 221–52.

—— (1983), *Ammonius Saccas, der Lehrer Plotins* (Opladen).

Sedley, D. (1989), 'Philosophical Allegiance in the Graeco-Roman World', in M. Griffin and J. Barnes (eds.), *Philosophia Togata I* (Oxford), 97–119.

—— (1997*a*), 'Plato's Auctoritas and the Rebirth of the Commentary Tradition', in M. Griffin and J. Barnes (eds.), *Philosophia Togata II* (Oxford), 110–29.

—— (1997*b*), 'A New Reading in the Anonymus "Theaetetus" Commentary (PBerd. 9782 Fragment D)', in *Papiri Filosofici* (Florence), 139–44.

Sharples, R. W. (1987), 'Alexander of Aphrodisias, Scholasticism and Innovation' in *ANRW* ii/36/2. 1176–1243.

—— (1990), 'The School of Alexander', in R. Sorabji (ed.), *Aristotle Transformed* (London), 83–111.

Shiel, H. (1990), 'Boethius' Commentaries on Aristotle', in R. Sorabji (ed.), *Aristotle Transformed* (London), 349–72.

Sluiter, I. (1999), 'Commentaries and the Didactic Tradition', in G. Most (ed.), *Commentaries-Kommentare* (Göttingen), 173–205.

Smith, A. (1974), *Porphyry's Place in the Neoplatonic Tradition* (The Hague).

—— (1987), 'Porphyrian Studies since 1986', in *ANRW* ii/36/2.

—— (1992), 'A Porphyrian treatise against Aristotle?', in F. X. Martin and J. A. Richmond (eds.), *From Augustine to Eriugena* (Washington, DC), 183–6.

—— (1999), 'The Significance of Practical Ethics for Plotinus', in J. Cleary (ed.), *Traditions of Platonism: Essays in Honour of J. Dillon* (Aldershot), 227–36.

Sodano, A. R. (1993), *Vangelo di un Pagano* (Milan).

Solmsen, F. (1942), *Plato's Theology* (Ithaca, NY).

—— (1960), *Aristotle's System of the Physical World* (Ithaca, NY).

Sorabji, R. (1972), *Aristotle On Memory* (London).

—— (1983), *Time, Creation and the Continuum* (London).

—— (ed.) (1987), *Philoponus and the Rejection of Aristotelian Science* (London).

—— (1988), *Matter, Space and Motion: Theories in Antiquity and their Sequel* (London).

—— (ed.) (1990), *Aristotle Transformed: The Ancient Commentators and their Influence* (London).

—— (1993), *Animal Minds and Human Morals* (London).

—— (1996), 'Rationality', in M. Frede and G. Striker (eds.), *Rationality in Greek Thought* (Oxford), 311–34.

—— (2000), *Emotion and Peace of Mind* (Oxford).

Spanneut, M. (1994), 'Apatheia anclenne, apatheia chretienne', in *ANRW* ii/36/7. 4641–4717.

Staden, H. von (1982), '*Hairesis* and Heresy: The Case of the *haireseis iatrikai*', in B. F. Meyer and E. P. Sanders (eds.), *Jewish and Christian Self-Definition* (London), iii. 76–100.

Steel, C. (1978), *The Changing Self: A Study on the Soul in Later Neoplatonism. Iamblichus, Damascius, and Priscianus* (Brussels).

Strange, S. K. (1987), 'Plotinus, Porphyry, and the Neoplatonic Interpretation of the *Categories*', in *ANRW* ii/36/2. 955–74.

—— (1992), *Porphyry, On Aristotle's Categories* (London).

Striker, G. (1983), 'The Role of *Oikeiosis* in Stoic Ethics', *OSAP* 1: 145–67.

—— (1991), 'Following Nature: A Study in Stoic Ethics', *OSAP* 9: 1–73 (cited from her *Essays on Hellenistic Epistemology and Ethics* (Cambridge, 1996), 221–80).

—— (1997), 'Academics Fighting Academics', in B. Inwood and J. Mansfeld (eds.), *Assent and Argument: Studies in Cicero's Academic Books* (Utrecht), 257–76.

Szlezák, T. A. (1972), *Pseudo-Archytas über die Kategorien* (Peripatoi, 4; Berlin and New York).

—— (1979), *Platon und Aristoteles in der Nuslehre Plotins* (Basle and Stuttgart).

Taormina, D. (1989), *Plutarco di Atene* (Rome).

Taran, L. (1981), *Speusippus of Athens* (Philosophia Antiqua, 39; Leiden).

Tarrant, H. (1993), *Thrasyllan Platonism* (Ithaca, NY).

Taylor, A. E. (1928), *A Commentary on Plato's Timaeus* (Oxford).

Teodorsson, S.-T. (1999), 'Plutarch and Peripatetic Science', in *Plutarco, Platon y Aristôteles, Actas del V Congresso Internacional de la IPS* (Madrid), 665–74.

Theiler, W. (1964), *Die Vorbereitung des Neuplatonismus* (Berlin, 1st edn. 1930).

—— (1965), 'Ammonius und Porphyrios', in *Porphyre* (Entretiens Fondation Hardt, 12; Geneva), 88–123.

—— (1966*a*), 'Ammonius der Lehrer Origenes', in (Theiler 1966*b*): 1–45.

—— (1966*b*), *Forschungen zum Neuplatonismus* (Berlin).

—— (1970), 'Philo von Alexandria und der Beginn des kaiserzeitlichen Platonismus', in *Untersuchungen zur antiken Literatur* (Berlin) 484–501.

Tigerstedt, E. N. (1974), *The Decline and Fall of the Neoplatonic Interpretation of Plato* (Helsinki).

Torjesen, K. (1986), *Hermeneutical Procedure and Theological Method in Origen's Exegesis* (Berlin and New York).

Vander Waerdt, P. (1985*a*), 'The Peripatetic Interpretation of Plato's Tripartite Psychology', *GRBS* 26: 283–302.

—— (1985*b*), 'Peripatetic Soul-Division, Posidonius, and Middle Platonic Moral Psychology', *GRBS* 26: 373–94.

—— (1987), 'Aristotle's Criticism of Soul Division', *AJP* 108: 627–43.

Verbeke, G. (1960), 'Plutarch and the Development of Aristotle', in I. Düring and G. E. L. Owen (eds.), *Aristotle and Plato in Mid-Fourth Century* (Göteborg), 236–47.

Verrycken, K. (1988), 'Porphyry *In Timaeum* fr. XXXVII (Philoponus *De aeternitate mundi contra Proclum* 148. 9–23)', *L'Antiquité classique*, 57: 282–9.

—— (1990), 'The Development of Philoponus' Thought and its Chronology', in R. Sorabji (ed.), *Aristotle Transformed* (London), 233–74.

Vitelli, G. (1902), 'Due frammenti di Alessandro di Afrodisia', in *Festschrift Theodor Gomperz* (Vienna), 90–3.

Vlastos, G. (1975), *Plato's Universe* (Oxford).

Wagner, M. (1996), 'Plotinus on the Nature of Physical Reality', in L. Gerson (ed.), *The Cambridge Companion to Plotinus* (Cambridge), 130–70.

Wallis, R. T. (1972), *Neoplatonism* (London).

Walzer, R. (1965*a*), 'Porphyry and the Arabic Tradition', in *Porphyre* (Entretiens Fondation Hardt, 12; Geneva), 275–99.

—— (1965*b*), 'Furfuriyus' (= Porphyrios), *The Encyclopaedia of Islam* (Leiden and London), ii. 948–9.

Waszink, J. H. (1965), 'Porphyrios und Numenios', in *Porphyre* (Entretiens Fondation Hardt, 12; Geneva), 35–83.

Weber, K.-O. (1962), *Origenes der Neuplatoniker* (Zetemata, 27; Munich).

Wehrli, F. (1959), 'Der Peripatos in vorchristlicher Zeil' in *Wehrli, Die Schule des Aristoteles*, vol. X, Basel/Stuttgart, 95–188.

—— (1961), 'Aristoteles in der sicht seiner Schule' in *Aristote et les problems de Methode*, Louvain 381–331.

Westerink, L. G. (1990), 'The Development of Philoponus' Thought and its Chronology', in R. Sorabji (ed.), *Aristotle Transformed* (London), 233–74.

Westmann, R. (1955), *Plutarch gegen Kolotes–Seine Schrift 'Adversus Colotem' als philosophiegeschichtliche Quelle* (Acta Philosophica Fennica, 7; Helsinki).

Whittaker, J. (1969), ''Ἐπέκεινα νοῦ καὶ οὐσίας' *Vigiliae Christianae* 23, 91–104.

Whittaker, J. (1987), 'Platonic Philosophy in the Early Centuries of the Empire', *ANRW* ii/36/1. 81–123.

Zambon, M. (2002), *Porphyre et le moyen-Platonisme* (Paris).

Zeller, E. (1923), *Die Philosophie der Griechen in ihrer geschichtlichen Entwicklung dargestellt* (Tübingen and Leipzig).

General Index

Index of Passages